THE PAPERS OF WILL ROGERS

Wild West and Vaudeville

Volume Two

April 1904–September 1908

Will Rogers, ca. 1906. Photograph taken by the Otto Sarony Company, New York, and sent with an inscription by Rogers to his friend Tom P. Morgan. *(Tom P. Morgan Collection, RHM, neg. N008228)*

The Papers of Will Rogers

Wild West and Vaudeville

Volume Two

April 1904–September 1908

EDITED BY

Arthur Frank Wertheim

AND

Barbara Bair

UNIVERSITY OF OKLAHOMA PRESS : NORMAN

Library of Congress Cataloging-in-Publication Data
Rogers, Will, 1879–1935.
  The papers of Will Rogers / edited by Arthur Frank Wertheim and Barbara Bair.
  p.   cm.
  Contents: v.   2. Wild West and Vaudeville, April 1904–September 1908.
  ISBN 0-8061-3267-1
  1. Rogers, Will, 1879–1935—Archives.   2. Rogers, Will, 1879–1935—Corre-
spondence.   3. Performing arts—United States—History—20th century—Sources.
I. Wertheim, Arthur Frank, 1935–   .   II. Bair, Barbara, 1955–   .   III. Title.
PN2287.R74A25   1995, vol. 2
792.7'028'092—dc20   94-24165
                                                                          CIP

Book and series design by Bill Cason.

The paper in this book meets the guidelines for permanence and durability of the
Committee on Production Guidelines for Book Longevity of the Council on Library
Resources, Inc. ∞

THE WILL ROGERS PAPERS PROJECT IS A DOCUMENTARY HISTORY PROJECT OF THE WILL ROGERS MEMORIAL COMMISSION, CLAREMORE, OKLAHOMA. JOSEPH H. CARTER IS PROJECT DIRECTOR AND DIRECTOR OF THE MEMORIAL. FUNDING FOR THE PROJECT HAS COME FROM THE SARKEYS FOUNDATION, THE WILL ROGERS HERITAGE TRUST, INC., AND THE STATE OF OKLAHOMA.

Contents

Documents

1. THE WILD WEST

2. THE TRAINING GROUND

3. BERLIN'S WINTERGARTEN AND LONDON'S PALACE

4. CAUGHT IN THE VAUDEVILLE WARS

5. ON THE WESTERN VAUDEVILLE TRAIL

Illustrations

Acknowledgments

THE WILL ROGERS PAPERS PROJECT IS ESPECIALLY INDEBTED TO THE BOARD of Trustees and officers of the Sarkeys Foundation for funding that established crucial underwriting for the volumes. The start-up grant provided funds for staffing, equipment, travel, and other necessary expenses to carry out research and publication. We are very grateful to the trustees of the Foundation for supporting the legacy of Will Rogers: Richard D. Bell, Jane A. Jayroe, Joseph W. Morris, Robert T. Rennie, Robert S. Rizley, Paul F. Sharp, and Lee Anne Wilson. We also thank Cheri D. Cartwright, the director of grants for the Sarkeys Foundation.

State Senator Stratton Taylor and Representative Dwayne Steidley, with the backing of the Oklahoma legislature, helped provide public means to match private funds. We thank the citizens of Oklahoma for their support of our tribute to their native son.

This project would never have been possible without the endorsement of a number of other key individuals. We are especially thankful for the encouragement of Will Rogers, Jr., and Jim Rogers, both of whom strongly believed in the project's mission. Dean Robert H. Henry of the School of Law, Oklahoma City University, also deserves our gratitude for his support, which helped launch the project in its early phase.

We are also very grateful to the members of the Will Rogers Memorial Commission for their endorsement of the project: commissioners Patricia Crume, John Denbo, James L. Hartz, J. Kevin Hayes, Hunt Lowry, James B. Rogers, and Charles Ward.

We appreciate the time and effort the staff at the Will Rogers Memorial have devoted to the project. Joseph H. Carter, director of the Memorial and the Will Rogers Papers Project, first conceived of the project. Several dedicated staff members at the Memorial also contributed to the organization of documents and the ultimate success of the project, especially Patricia Lowe, Memorial librarian and archivist and the project's editorial assistant. She has lent her incomparable archival expertise, serving as an indispensable guide to the entire Will Rogers collection at the Memorial.

Jane Collings, an expert on the history of American film and the entertainment industry, was a key member of the editorial team preparing this and other volumes of the *Papers of Will Rogers*. When she joined the project as a part-time staff member, Collings was a Ph.D. candidate in the UCLA Department of Film. She worked as a research assistant under the direction of Arthur Wertheim in the project's Los Angeles office and made many important contributions to the scope and content of the project's archives, especially to the development of supporting materials used to supplement primary documents. She was instrumental in collecting documents during the early phases of research and in organizing and researching documents beyond the scope of Rogers's vaudeville years, in particular those dealing with Rogers's film career and the lives of his friends and colleagues who figured prominently in the development of the Hollywood film industry into the mid-Depression era. In working on the selected documents appearing in this volume, all pertaining to Rogers's vaudeville years, she ably ferreted out many an obscure reference, discovered information from historic newspapers and entertainment publications, and provided research that formed the basis of many of the annotations that appear in this volume. She also conducted research for and drafted selected biographical appendix entries, and participated in editorial discussions about the performers, audiences, and venues that made up the foundation of Rogers's vaudeville career. She contacted archives and archivists around the country and worked extensively on materials in Los Angeles archives that related to Rogers's early performances. Her many contributions proved very valuable to the success of the project.

Social historian Steven Leikin, who was a recent Ph.D. graduate in American History during the early phases of this project, served as a part-time editorial assistant for this volume. He maintained the database used to organize the project's documents, transcribed and proofread many documents selected by the editors, conducted background research, and visited archives in Wisconsin to research information and individuals involved in circus and Wild West performances that intersected with Rogers's career.

The Interlibrary Loan Office of the UCLA Libraries, headed by Ian Dacosta, ordered from other repositories many critical documents that were vital for research for the project. Librarians at the McHenry Library, University of California, Santa Cruz, also contributed to the project's research.

Extensive document collection and annotation research in primary materials were conducted by the editors, who traveled to university and public libraries, research centers, museum and theater archives, and special collections around the country and in London in pursuit of materials. Among the collections that were indispensable to our task of identifying information about the many individuals with whom Rogers performed in vaudeville were the Billy Rose Theatre Collection and Robinson Locke Collection of the New York Public Library for the Performing Arts, Lincoln Center, New York; the Theater Arts Collection of the Harry Ransom Humanities Research Center at the University of Texas at Austin; the Buck McKee Collection, California Section, California State Library, Sacramento; and the Theater Collection of the Philadelphia Free Library. We would like to offer very special thanks to Bob Taylor, curator of the Billy Rose Theatre Collection, and to the following librarians who serve on the staff of the New York Public Library for the Performing Arts: David Bartholomew, Roderick Bladel, Christopher Frith, Don Glenn, Christine Karatnytsky, Brian O'Connell, Daniel D. Patri, Louis Paul, Edward J. Sager, and Kevin Winkler. Melissa Miller, curator of the Theater Arts Collection at the Harry Ransom Humanities Research Center; Jeanette Rustan and John R. Gonzales, librarians, of the California State Library; and Geraldine Duclow, archivist, and Elaine Ebo, assistant archivist, of the Theater Collection at the Philadelphia Free Library, were all of special help in guiding our on-site research and arranging for the copying of photographs or primary materials.

We are also indebted to the following librarians, historians, and archivists who greatly helped with research or the location of photographs of the vaudeville and Wild West era: Annette Fern, reference and research librarian, Harvard Theatre Collection, Harvard College Library, Cambridge, Mass.; Kristen Tanaka, head librarian, San Francisco Performing Arts Library and Museum; Giuseppe Bisaccia, curator of manuscripts, Division of Rare Books and Manuscripts, Boston Public Library; Cathy Wright, director, Taylor Museum for Southwestern Studies of the Colorado Springs Fine Arts Center; Maryann Chach, archivist, and Mark Swartz, assistant archivist, Schubert Archive, New York; Fred Dahlinger, Jr., director, Robert L. Parkinson Library and Research Center, Circus World Museum, Baraboo, Wis.; Marty Jacobs, special consultant, Theatre Collection, and Marguerite Lavin, Museum of the City of New York; Marie Demeroukas, registrar, Rogers Historical Museum, Rogers, Ark.; Raymond Wemmlinger, curator and librarian, Hampden-Booth Theatre Library, New York; Mylon Houston, head librarian, and Paula Stewart, archivist, Amon Carter Museum Library, Fort Worth; Cathy Henderson, research librarian, Charles Bell, curator, and Andrea Inselmann, archivist, Film and Photograph Division, Harry Ransom Humanities Research Center, University of Texas, Austin; Nathan E. Bender, head, Special

Collections and Archives, Montana State University, Bozeman; Kathy Dickson, director of museums, Oklahoma Historical Society, Oklahoma City; Susan M. Kooyman, archivist, Glenbow Museum Library and Archives, Calgary, Alberta, Canada; Anne B. Wheeler, National Cowboy Hall of Fame, Oklahoma City; Virginia Artho, assistant director, National Cowgirl Hall of Fame and Western Heritage Center, Hereford, Tex.; Patricia Florence, assistant director and curator, ProRodeo Hall of Fame and Museum of the American Cowboy, Colorado Springs; Steve Gossard, curator of Circus Collections, Milner Library Special Collections, Illinois State University, Normal; Robert A. McCown, head, Special Collections and Manuscripts, University Libraries, University of Iowa, Iowa City; Bill Benedict, archive consultant, Theatre Historical Society of America, Elmhurst, Ill.; Eleanor J. Mish, registrar and manager, American Museum of the Moving Image, Astoria, N.Y.; Patricia Michaelis, Manuscripts Collection, Kansas State Historical Society, Topeka; Samuel Gill, archivist emeritus, Margaret Herrick Library, the Academy of Motion Picture Arts and Sciences, Beverly Hills, Calif.; Dace Taube, librarian, Regional History Collection, Special Collections, and Ned Comstock, archivist, Special Collections, University of Southern California, Los Angeles; Frances B. Clymer, associate librarian, Buffalo Bill Historical Center, Cody, Wyo.; Jerry Hatfield, librarian, Library of Congress, Washington, D.C.; William H. Richter, reference archivist, Center for American History, University of Texas, Austin; and Don Bell, of Byron, Wyo.

The editors are grateful for the assistance of the following archivists, librarians, curators, and scholars who provided information and material for the Rogers volumes: William D. Welge, director, Archives and Manuscript Division, Oklahoma Historical Society, Oklahoma City; Bradford Koplowitz, curator, Western History Collections, University of Oklahoma Libraries, Norman; Betty Bustes, Panhandle-Plains Historical Museum, Canyon, Tex.; Victoria Sheffler, university archivist, Northeastern State University, Tahlequah, Okla.; Annabell Southern, librarian, Vinita Public Library, Vinita, Okla.; Derrick Austin and Lance Vanzant, archival assistants, Southwest Collection, Texas Tech University, Lubbock; Richard Fusick, archivist, Civil Reference Branch, National Archives, Washington, D.C.; Joy Dodson, public services assistant, Central Methodist College, Fayette, Mo.; Robin Courtney, librarian, City County Library, Neosho, Mo.; Devon Mahesuah, professor, Department of History, Northern Arizona University, Flagstaff; Glenn Colliver, assistant archivist, Department of History, Presbyterian Church (USA), Philadelphia; Joan McCullough, librarian, Oklahoma United Methodist Archives, Dulaney-Browne Library, Oklahoma City University; Jim

Gatewood, director of public affairs, Kemper Military School, Boonville, Mo.; Marie Demeroukas, registrar, Rogers History Museum, Rogers, Ark.; Twila D. McClure, librarian, Chelsea Public Library, Chelsea, Okla.; Joan Singleton, public services librarian, Bartlesville Public Library and History Museum, Bartlesville, Okla.; Peter Stark, map librarian, University of Oregon, Eugene; Diane Boucher Ayotte, manuscript specialist, Western Historical Manuscript Collection, Ellis Library, University of Missouri, Columbia; and Heather Lloyd, head, Special Collections, Oklahoma State University, Stillwater; Valerie Helson, acting manuscript librarian, Australian Collections and Services, National Library of Australia, Canberra; Jo Peoples, curator, Performing Arts Collection of South Australia, Theatre Museum, Adelaide; Mark Valentine St. Leon, writer/researcher, Gleble, New South Wales, Australia; archivists of the Cape Archives Depot, Cape Town, the Free State Archives Depot, Bloemfontein, the Natal Archives Depot, Pietermaritzburg, and the Transvaal Archives Depot, Pretoria, South Africa; Rooksana Omar of the Local History Museum and Chantelle Wyley, history subject librarian, University of Natal Library, Durban, South Africa. Other individuals who answered inquiries and provided material were E. Paul Alworth, Jack D. Baker, Genny Mae Bard, Dr. Robert Henderson, Kathryn Jenkins, Harold Keith, Howard Meredith, Peter Rollins, Emil Sandmeier, and John and Faith Wylie.

Librarians, archivists, or curators at the following institutions have provided important help to the project in document collection and research: the Library of Congress, the National Archives, and the Smithsonian National Air and Space Museum Library, Washington, D.C.; the California Section, California State Library, Sacramento; the Oral History Project and the Rare Book and Manuscript Library, Columbia University, New York; the Missouri Historical Society, St. Louis; the Bancroft Library, University of California, Berkeley; the Hoover Institute, Stanford University, Palo Alto, Calif.; the American Film Institute, Charles Feldman Library, Los Angeles; the Keith-Albee Collection, University of Iowa, Iowa City; the Museum of Modern Art Film Center, New York; the Western History Collection, Denver Public Library; the Circus Collection, San Antonio Public Library; the Rodeo Historical Society and National Cowboy Hall of Fame's Rodeo Division, Oklahoma City; the Charles Lummis Collection, Southwest Museum, Pasadena, Calif.; the Montana Historical Society, Helena; the Tulsa Historical Society, Tulsa, Okla.; the Oologah Historical Society, Oologah, Okla.; the Newport Historical Society, Newport, R.I.; the New York Historical Society, New York; the Glenbow Museum and Archives, Calgary, Alberta, Canada; and the Victoria and Albert Theatre Museum, National Museum of the Performing Arts, Theatre Collection, Covent Garden, London, England. Special thanks go to Randy Young, Will Rogers State Park, Pacific Palisades, Calif.

A special note of thanks is due Carol Wertheim and Jason Wertheim, for their archival research and their support and encouragement. Personal thanks also go to Dana Frank, Jan and Stephen De Sal, Mari Jo and Paul Buhle, Sylvia Tidwell and William Brice, Heather Fischer and Kent Sandow, and Carol and Michael Wreszin, for their interest and aid during the production of the Rogers Papers volumes.

We are grateful to our many fine colleagues at the University of Oklahoma Press. Our thanks go to John Drayton, director and editor-in-chief, for his ongoing support of our project, and to associate editor Sarah Iselin and managing editor Alice Stanton, for their expert and friendly guidance of the Rogers volumes through the editorial process. Documentary editions, and Rogers's idiosyncratic habits of self-expression, pose special challenges for copy editors. This volume was adeptly copyedited and computer-coded for the press by Lys Ann Shore, of Shore Editorial Services, South Bend, Indiana, and we thank her for the high quality of her work.

Final acknowledgments are reserved for those who made valuable historical material available to us from private hands. We were very fortunate to come into contact with two women who were extremely generous to us in sharing their knowledge about family members who were friends and fellow performers with Will Rogers. Laurie Weltz of New York, the great-granddaughter of Louise Henry, graciously shared Louise Henry's written reminiscences of Will Rogers with us, as well as Henry's photographs and scrapbook. Martha Swanson Fisch of Guthrie, Okla., the daughter of Mildred Mulhall Carmichael Acton, granddaughter of Georgia Smith (Mulhall) Casey and Zack Mulhall, and niece of Lucille Mulhall, generously opened her home to our research, consented to participate in many hours of oral history interviews about the Mulhall family and their Wild West careers, and gave us free access to the scrapbooks, clippings, and photographs that her grandmother had saved from the days of the family's performances. Without the generosity of Weltz and Fisch, we would not have been able to rewrite the details of two important chapters in Rogers's life. Both Weltz and Fisch also allowed us to make copies of photographs in their family members' scrapbooks in order that they might appear for publication for the first time in this volume, and we are very grateful for their contributions, which have added to the quality and specificity of the content of this book.

THE PAPERS OF WILL ROGERS

Wild West and Vaudeville

Volume Two

April 1904–September 1908

Introduction

WILL ROGERS WAS AMONG THE MOST ACCLAIMED AND BEST-LIKED NATIONAL figures in the 1920s and early 1930s. His fame was garnered through both print and electronic media. His name appeared as a by-line on front-page newspaper columns and the magazine articles and books he authored. His voice and his wisecracks were favorite family fare, emanating from eagerly anticipated radio talks, and his face became known to audiences in towns large and small through his long string of popular films. The Will Rogers whom Americans adored was shaped by earlier experiences that determined the course of his later life and career. Knowledge of the roots of his personality and the evolution of his show-business life is critical to understanding the private and public Will Rogers.

Volume one (November 1879–April 1904) of *The Papers of Will Rogers* documents Rogers's early years, from his childhood in the Cherokee Nation in Indian Territory to his travels as a young man seeking fortune and adventure. It illuminates the impact on young Rogers of Cherokee culture, southern heritage, family relationships, schooling, ranch life, roping contests, boyhood friends, and a budding romance with Betty Blake, his future wife. The volume deals as well with Rogers's first professional experiences as a performer with Texas Jack's Wild West Show in South Africa and concludes with his appearance in the Wirth Brothers' Circus in Australia and New Zealand. When Rogers left Indian Territory in March 1902, he was a restless young man in search of himself and of a clear direction in his life. When he returned two years later, in April 1904, he was more assured and mature. Although still not completely committed to show business as a livelihood, Rogers had savored the excitement of performance art in Wild West shows and the circus, and he sought similar opportunities when he returned home.

The documents in volume two cover the period from mid-April 1904 to early September 1908, a pivotal time in Rogers's life and career. In this period, Rogers was transformed from an expert rider and roper in Wild West shows to a top-flight vaudeville entertainer. Appearances in rodeo-type events at the 1904 St. Louis World's Fair and the 1905 Madison Square Garden Horse Show set the stage for his entrance into big-time vaudeville.

Rogers's experience with the Wild West shows of Frederick Cummins, Jim Gabriel, and Zack Mulhall during the World's Fair in St. Louis was also part of his successful transformation into the entertainment medium of his real-life background as a working cowboy. As he performed rope tricks and participated in roping contests in the shows, and as he made his fledgling performances as a stage cowboy in the summer of 1904, Rogers was part of the larger mythologizing of the West that was sweeping American popular culture of the time. His appearance with the Wild West shows also marks a transition in the public perception of his ethnicity. Long proud of his strong family identity as leading citizens within the Cherokee Nation, Rogers had been billed as the Cherokee Kid in South Africa, Australia, and New Zealand. In St. Louis, in contrast to the Native American leaders who came to participate in the Cummins show from restricted lives on federal reservations, Rogers was identified not as a fellow Indian, but as a cowboy. The World's Fair was the beginning of his public "Angloization," from Cherokee Kid to Oklahoma Cowboy. Between 1905 and 1908 mention of Rogers's Native American heritage dwindled in reviews. Instead he came to encapsulate values associated with the Anglo-American experience of the West. His Wild West and stage image was linked not with his real past, but with new concepts of the West being shaped by mainstream popular culture. When Rogers and his friend Jim Minnick performed for President Theodore Roosevelt's children at the White House in 1905, they went as cowboys, the era's quintessential all-American figures. Shortly after the White House visit, Rogers made headlines in New York as a cowboy with wits and courage about him. He and Minnick were appearing with the Mulhall family at the Madison Square Garden Horse Show when a steer that Lucille Mulhall was roping broke away from the arena and thundered over the barriers up into the stands, scattering shrieking audience members left and right. Rogers helped rope in the beast, and the Garden returned to saner stability. The idea of Rogers as a gallant cowboy hero that was created by news coverage of this event stuck with him into his vaudeville days.

Appearing at the St. Louis World's Fair not only gave a nudge to Rogers's interest in show business, it also provided the backdrop for him to become reacquainted with Betty Blake, an old girlfriend whom he had first met when she came to visit her sister and brother-in-law who worked at the train depot in Rogers's hometown of Oologah. He and Blake had lost touch during Rogers's travels, but when she came to the World's Fair with her mother and sister from Arkansas in 1905, she overheard a woman in the Oklahoma Territory building mention that she had seen Will Rogers perform in the Wild West show at the Del Mar track outside the fairgrounds. She sent a note to

Rogers, and he replied. They had a romantic date that evening, enjoying the fantasy atmosphere of the Pike area of the Fair and hearing the young Irish tenor, John McCormack, sing beautifully at the Irish Village. It was the rekindling of a long courtship that would lead eventually to marriage. Theirs was not a smooth road to commitment. In between the meeting at the Fair and the marriage, Rogers would have other relationships with women whom he met in vaudeville. Blake, too, would prove for a long while to be a hesitant girlfriend. She wounded Rogers's feelings by rebuffing his overtures and was skeptical of his style of living and his chosen profession.

In addition to providing documentation of Rogers's Wild West performances in 1904–5 and his reacquaintance with Betty Blake, volume two charts the first three developmental years of Rogers's ten-year career on the variety stage. His first performances came in the summer of 1904 when, bored with his work at the Fair, he experimented with appearances on stage in St. Louis and Chicago. The vaudeville act he developed for 1905 was basically his Wild West show routine transferred to the vaudeville stage. Using the pony Teddy, which he purchased from the Mulhalls, and a cowboy assistant (for a brief time Jim Minnick, and then for many years Buck McKee), Rogers performed complicated lariat tricks, casting his rope in different configurations around a moving Teddy and rider. He also did other fantastic lasso stunts on his own, such as the Crinoline, a huge elongated loop that widened out and swept over the heads of the audience. There were other western lasso acts in vaudeville, but none that used a horse, and this was what made Rogers's stage routine unique.

Playbills in volume two reveal that Rogers started performing at the most prominent vaudeville theaters on the Keith Circuit and at other big-time venues—ranging from his first engagement at New York's historic Union Square Theatre to Oscar and Willie Hammerstein's renowned Victoria Theatre and its Paradise Roof Garden. That Rogers immediately played the big-time circuits rather than small-time theaters, as most newcomers did, was exceptional. Listings of vaudevillians who performed on the same playbill reveal that Rogers appeared with such well-known acts as the Three Keatons, Houdini, Pat Rooney and Marion Bent, Ernest Hogan, Josephine Cohan, George Fuller Golden, Fred Niblo, Bert Williams and George Walker, and Rose Stahl, among others.

Reviews and theater managers' reports reproduced in this volume illustrate the critical reception and success of Rogers's act. His sudden popularity with critics and the audience derived partly from the same trends he had benefited from as a Wild West performer: the vogue of the American West and the romanticization of the cowboy as hero. As he took his act on the stage, the fascination with the West was being manifested in many forms of popular culture, such as the Wild West show, best-selling books, dime novels, plays, and early silent films. Rogers was billed in his formative vaudeville years as the Lariat King, the Plainsman, and other western monikers. Instead of being associated with Indian Territory, he was identified with the new state of Oklahoma, which gained statehood in 1907 (his father, Cherokee Nation senator Clement Vann Rogers, was a delegate to the 1906 State Constitutional Convention). Publicity photos of Rogers in cowboy garb, as well as his stage wardrobe of chaps, bandanna, belt buckle, rustic-looking shirt, cowboy hat, and boots, bolstered his connection to the West. His southwestern drawl and use of slang expressions also reinforced the image.

It is clear that initially, Rogers had no intention of making show business his profession. He saw himself engaged on a kind of lark, but he was also proving to his father and family that he could support himself and make a go of things in his own way. Several articles describe Rogers as saying that he wanted to quit vaudeville, return to his birthplace, and become a rancher. Just as his public image was being Americanized and mythologized in the media and on stage, his private identity remained tied to home and heartland, and to the "real" jobs of ranching and farming.

Despite common belief that Rogers in his early years on stage performed his act silently, documents in this volume confirm that he used humorous chatter in his act almost from the start. After blowing planned catches on stage and getting a laugh out of the mishap, he prepared jokes about missing the horse with his rope and other comic material regarding his lasso stunts. Sometimes he made offhand comments about other performers on the playbill. Each year the amount of comic patter grew along with the need to broaden his act. Rogers's cowboy quips and expressions underscored his association with the West. As a result, Rogers began to create a type of crackerbarrel humor that differed sharply from that of the ethnic comedians who dominated vaudeville at the turn of the century. His heartland humor was greeted as more American than the routines of the ethnic comics, whose material was connected with European immigrants and their cultures and languages.

As the documents in volume two delineate, Rogers's career at this time was closely linked to developments in the vaudeville industry. His successful appearances at the Wintergarten in Berlin and the Palace Theatre in London showed that European audiences were likewise captivated by the American cowboy and the idea of the open spaces of the American West. There was considerable transatlantic interchange in European and American vaudeville.

Rogers's two European trips in 1906 and 1907 typified the experiences of many other big-time U.S. vaudevillians who crossed the Atlantic to entertain in British music halls, French theaters, and German venues. In turn, British music-hall stars often performed in prominent vaudeville theaters in large American cities.

Shifts in Rogers's vaudeville career from 1905 to 1908 mirror changes in the vaudeville industry. During the Progressive Era there was considerable consolidation in major industries and corporations, which led to the establishment of trusts, holding companies, and other types of mergers. These combinations created more organizational efficiency in production and distribution. The major vaudeville theater owners in the East applied the same organizational practices as large industries and businesses. Led by B. F. Keith and his partner Edward Albee, the theater managers consolidated bookings through the United Booking Offices (UBO), formed in 1907. Less powerful competitors and independent agents who did not book through the UBO were practically driven out of business. Through associations, the big-time eastern vaudeville managers were linked to the western vaudeville managers, primarily the Orpheum Circuit. These combinations essentially created an oligopoly—one controlling vaudeville east of Chicago, and the other, west of Chicago.

These developments affected Rogers's career at different times. In late 1905 he was forced to find a new agent who worked through the UBO; in 1907 he joined an opposition vaudeville circuit and was consequently black-balled by the Keith-Albee Circuit; and in the need to find employment he frequently performed in smaller theaters and sometimes in burlesque houses. Rogers's contracts reproduced in this volume illustrate that vaudevillians were governed by strict rules in numerous areas, including salary, censorship, commissions, scheduling, and behavior.

As a vaudevillian performing on the big-time circuits, Rogers was part of America's first nationwide mass entertainment system. By taking variety entertainment out of the saloon, where it was viewed primarily by working-class men, Tony Pastor, B. F. Keith, and F. F. Proctor became pioneers in the creation of a "wholesome" entertainment form that appealed to the entire family. Keith, in particular, established the continuous format, the neatly packaged program model, and the refined mass entertainment form with moralistic overtones that carried broad, middle-class appeal. Rogers's inoffensive, family-oriented, lariat-with-horse act fit squarely within the structure of mass vaudeville.

During this period Rogers performed in cities and towns across the country. A network of circuits and the expansion of the railroad, especially in the

West, permitted him to stop each week at a new locale. Documents regarding his western tour, from Butte, Montana, to San Francisco on the Sullivan and Considine Circuit illustrate the growth of vaudeville in the West. Population increases in cities created a need for new vaudeville theaters for the rising urban middle class. Rogers performed before large audiences of people who had more leisure time than ever before and who flocked to vaudeville theaters across the nation.

In his private life during this period, Rogers befriended numerous vaude-villians. Among them were Pat Rooney and Marion Bent, Houdini, and Joe Keaton, Buster's father. Rogers made the Putnam House (later Hotel Preston) near Madison Square Garden his home in New York. Here gathered a coterie of friends, many of whom were fellow Wild West show performers. Rogers's relationship with his father changed from 1904 to 1908. At first suspicious of a show business career, Clement Vann Rogers finally accepted Will's profession and proudly boasted about his son's achievements.

Rogers's letters to Betty Blake between 1904 and 1908 reveal considerable tensions in their on-again, off-again courtship. There are periodic disputes regarding jealousies over other relationships. As a single man on the vaudeville trail, Rogers cultivated a close friendship with Louise Henry, a vaudeville singer and comic impersonator, whom he met during his first vaudeville engagement in June 1905. In a letter to Betty Blake, he enclosed a note from Nina, a performer in the vaudeville act The Crickets, and wrote Blake that he had rejected Nina's affections. Betty Blake was reluctant to marry someone in show business, and she turned down Rogers's initial marriage proposal. Coming from a conservative background, she held traditional stereotyped views of actors as unprincipled, immoral, and irresponsible. Even Rogers had ambivalent feelings about continuing in vaudeville, a stance he possibly adopted to appease Betty Blake. As this volume closes, Rogers's letters to Betty Blake in 1908 reveal a renewed warmth between the two—recognition of a mutual love that would lead to their marriage in November of that year.

The period from April 1904 to September 1908 marked major transitions in Rogers's life and career. In Wild West shows in 1904 and 1905, Rogers solidified his skills as a first-rate rider and roper. He then transferred those skills successfully to the vaudeville stage. As Rogers later wrote, vaudeville was a training ground for him. He gained experience performing before a new audience night after night and in a new city week after week. The years on the vaudeville trail from 1905 to 1908 permitted Rogers to perfect his routine and to develop the public persona and characteristics that later endeared him to millions of Americans.

Chronology, April 1904–September 1908

1904

19 April	While visiting farms and ranches of friends in the Talala area, Rogers writes to inform his family that Zack Mulhall wants him to work as a cowboy in Wild West show performances at the Louisiana Purchase Exposition (St. Louis World's Fair) and that he will soon be going to St. Louis.
27 April	Writes home to say he has arrived in St. Louis and is staying with the Mulhalls, and will be appearing in Mulhall's cowboy contingent in connection with Frederic T. Cummins Indian Congress in performances outside the Pike at the fairgrounds.
30 April	St. Louis World's Fair opens; Rogers begins performances.
18 June	Zack Mulhall becomes involved in an angry altercation with employee Frank Reed after a performance. Mulhall is banned from the fairgrounds and the Cummins show continues without him.
24 June	Rogers remains loyal to Mulhall. He and friend Jim Hopkins work as cowboys for a smaller Wild West show on the Pike.
1 July	Rogers is working for Cummins again while waiting for Mulhall to open his own Wild West show.
22 July	Expresses boredom with the Wild West show life. Rogers and his cousin Theodore McSpadden are living with Mulhall and working in Mulhall's show, with just one performance each Sunday.

24 July	The owners of the Standard Theatre, St. Louis, part of the Empire Circuit, report in a letter of recommendation written for Rogers that Rogers has appeared at their theater as part of a burlesque show, doing a roping act with Theodore McSpadden. This appearance marks Rogers's debut in vaudeville and leads to a booking for an engagement in Chicago.
ca. 2 August	Rogers's sisters Sallie and Maud and their husbands Tom McSpadden and Cap Lane visit St. Louis to see the Fair.
ca. 16–30 August	Rogers goes home for a visit to Indian Territory. Makes plans to purchase Teddy, the pony he will train to use on the stage, from the Mulhalls.
1 September	Back in St. Louis, having traveled via Chelsea and Tahlequah, I.T.
ca. September	Breaks world's record in roping a steer in a contest at Delmar Race Track in St. Louis. Lucille Mulhall also participates in the contest. The Mulhalls put on a special show for an Elks excursion from Indian Territory, with Rogers billed as the "champion roper of the world."
ca. 25 September(?)	Betty Blake visits the Fair with her sister. Rogers invites her to come see him perform, and they spend the evening together on a date at the fairgrounds. They hear Irish tenor John McCormack sing on the Pike. The date rekindles their on-again, off-again relationship, and marks the beginning of a new phase of courtship.
ca. 26 September(?)	Rogers stands Betty Blake up for a morning meeting in St. Louis; writes her that he had to hurry home unexpectedly.
2 October	Consolidated Shows of the World's Fair extravaganza held at the Delmar Race Track. Performers from the Cummins, Mulhall, Hagenbeck, Boer War, and other shows that appeared at the Pike and the fairgrounds throughout the Fair participate in the joint performance.

ca. 10 October	Rogers is home in Claremore area for a visit. On the trip his train stops at the station at Jenny Lind, Ark., where he briefly visits Betty Blake, who works as a station clerk.
ca. 15 October	Leaves Claremore, I.T., after a brief visit home; heads for Chicago.
19 October	Reports from Chicago that his planned performance on stage at the Chicago Opera House, booked for the week of 17 October, has fallen through.
week of 23 October	Plays Cleveland's New Theatre in Chicago. Appears on stage with his rope but no horse.
26 October	Writes to Betty Blake from Chicago, beginning their long courtship correspondence.
4 November	Rogers's twenty-fifth birthday.
20 November	Appears in a special World's Fair Livestock Pavilion show for visiting cattlemen, and David Rowland Francis, president of the Fair, awards him a blue ribbon. Rogers invites Betty Blake to Claremore for a big Masque Ball on Thanksgiving.
26 November	Appears in second Consolidated show.
30 November	Writes Betty Blake from Claremore and reports on the fun he had, masked as a hobo, at the ball. Expresses hope that Blake will come for similar balls at Christmas or New Year's.
3 December	Goes to Mulhall, Oklahoma Territory, to fetch his horse Comanche.
25 December	Spends Christmas with his father and sisters in Chelsea.
29 December	Along with several old friends from Indian Territory, attends a New Year's dance in Chelsea

1905

7–10 January	Rogers makes the first of several trips to the Mulhall ranch in Oklahoma Territory, where he trains his horse Teddy and works with the Mulhalls in preparation for an appearance at Madison Square Garden in late Spring.
ca. 14 February	Travels to St. Louis.
21 February	Initiated into the Blue Lodge of the Masons in Claremore.
13–22 March	Joins a trainload of members of the Commercial Club of Tulsa on a ten-day civic boosterism tour through Indiana and other states.
21 March	Wild West show promoter William James Gabriel invites Rogers to perform with a show he is organizing to appear in New Jersey in May. Rogers is unable to accept because of a prior commitment to Mulhall.
1 April	Rogers is in Mulhall, O.T., practicing for the upcoming show.
6 April	Betty Blake quits clerk job at Jenny Lind, Ark., train station.
10 April	Rogers ships his horse Comanche east in preparation for appearance with the Mulhall troupe.
11 April	Leaves Claremore for St. Louis, then travels to New York with the Mulhalls.
22 April	Rogers and cowboy friend Jim Minnick perform in a roping exhibition for President Theodore Roosevelt's family at the White House.
23–29 April	Rogers participates in the Mulhall Rough Rider Congress at the Madison Square Garden Horse Fair Association show. Tom Mix is also part of the show.
28 April	Pandemonium breaks out in Madison Square Garden as a steer involved in a roping act escapes from the arena and races into the stands filled with people. Rogers has a role in roping the steer, making headlines in the newspapers.

29 April	Zack Mulhall gives Rogers a formal deed of sale for Teddy, the bay pony Rogers will use in his vaudeville act.
8 May	Rogers writes to his father that the Mulhalls have returned home but that he has remained behind in New York with plans to do some work on the stage with his horse. He is booked for one week at Proctor's Theatre, then at Hammerstein's Roof Garden for three weeks.
15–17 May	Appears at the Orange Horse Show in Newark, N.J., where he gives an exhibition of fancy rope throwing and bareback riding with his new pony Teddy. Jim Minnick helps him in the act.
24 March	The *Claremore Messenger* reports that Rogers was at the International Stockmen's Association at Fort Worth, Tex.
3 June	Rogers writes his sisters to say that he has sold Comanche. Betty Rogers later explains that Mulhall kidnapped the horse from Rogers over a disagreement regarding the length of time Rogers would be working for the Mulhall show. The incident causes a falling out between the two men.
9 June	Contract with B. F. Keith's Amusement Enterprises to perform in New York at $75 for one week, commencing on 12 June.
12–17 June	First New York vaudeville appearance at B. F. Keith's Union Square Theatre in horse-and-lariat act.
14 June	Contract to perform at Oscar Hammerstein's Victoria Theatre, commencing 19 June, at $140 for the week. Signs contract with B. F. Keith's Amusement Enterprises for two weeks at $140 per week for performances in Boston, beginning 26 June, and Philadelphia, beginning 3 July.
19–25 June	Performs matinees at Hammerstein's Victoria Theatre and in the evening appears upstairs at the theater's Paradise Roof Garden.

26 June–1 July	Entertains at Keith's Theatre, Philadelphia; signs contract with F. F. Proctor's Circuit to appear at Proctor's Twenty-third Street Theatre for one week, beginning 10 July.
3–9 July	Keith's New Theatre, Boston.
17 July–13 August	Appears at Hammerstein's Paradise Roof Garden, New York City, for four weeks.
18 July	Walter Scott, famous Death Valley miner, watches Rogers's act at the Paradise Roof Garden.
21 July	Rogers signs contract with Percy G. Williams to appear at his Manhattan Beach Theatre, New York City, for one week, commencing 21 August. He also signs contract to perform at Proctor's Newark Theatre for one week, beginning 28 August.
28 July	Signs contract with William Morris to appear at Patsy Morrison's Theater at Rockaway Beach, Long Island, N.Y., for one week beginning 14 August.
9 August	Signs contract with Samuel A. Scribner to play at burlesque/vaudeville theaters for five weeks at $250 per week.
14 August	Signs contract to play at the Chase Theatre in Washington, D.C., commencing the week of 30 October.
14–21 August	Performs at Morrison's Theatre at Rockaway Beach, Long Island, N.Y. Also on the program are humorist Fred Niblo and the team of Grace La Rue and Charles H. Burke.
18 August	Signs contract with William Morris for engagement at Toledo's Temple Theatre, week of 8 October.
21–27 August	Appears at Williams's Manhattan Beach Theatre, New York City. Also on the program is the team of Pat Rooney and Marion Bent.
28 August–2 September	Proctor's Theatre, Newark, N.J.

31 August	Signs contract with the Moore Circuit to play at Detroit's Temple Theatre, week of 16 October, and the Cook Opera House, Rochester, N.Y., week of 23 October.
3 September	Performs on a Sunday vaudeville bill at Proctor's Fifty-eighth Street Theatre, New York City. Boxer-actor James J. Corbett is also on the bill.
4–9 September	Star Theatre, Brooklyn.
11–16 September	Gaiety Theatre, Brooklyn.
18–23 September	Circle Theatre, New York City.
23 September	Signs contract to play at Hammerstein's Victoria Theatre, week of 6 November.
25–30 September	Empire Theatre, Cleveland.
2–7 October	Garden Theatre, Buffalo.
3 October	Signs contract to play at Harry Davis's Grand Opera House in Pittsburgh, week of 25 December; James L. Kiernan's Maryland Theatre, Baltimore, week of 1 January 1906. Contracts with B. F. Keith Theatres to perform in Boston (week of 20 November), Providence (week of 27 November), Philadelphia (week of 4 December), New York (week of 11 December), and Syracuse (week of 18 December).
8–14 October	Arcade Theatre, Toledo, Ohio. Rooney and Bent are also on the program.
10 October	Gives an exhibition of cattle roping for employees of the Toledo Union Stockyards. Contract with Hyde and Behman Amusement Co. to play at their Brooklyn theater, week of 8 January 1906.
11 October	Article published in *Toledo News-Bee* on Rogers's desire to leave vaudeville and return to his home ranch.
16–21 October	Temple Theatre, Detroit.
23–28 October	Cook Opera House, Rochester, N.Y.
23 October	Signs contract to appear at Keith's Park Theatre in Worcester, Mass., week of 13 November

30 October–4 November	Chase's Theatre, Washington, D.C. Performs on the same program with the comic monologuist George Fuller Golden.
5 November	Performs on a Sunday vaudeville program, probably at Proctor's Theatre, Newark, N.J.
6–11 November	Victoria Theatre, New York City. Bert Williams and George Walker are the headliners.
8 November	Contract to play at Brooklyn's Amphion Theatre, week of 15 January 1906.
13–18 November	Park Theatre, Worcester, Mass.
20–25 November	Keith's Theatre, Boston.
27 November–2 December	Keith's Theatre, Providence, R. I.
29 November	Contract to play at Keith's Theatre, Philadelphia, week of 22 January 1906.
3 December	Rogers is on a Sunday concert playbill at New York City's Casino Theatre, an engagement booked by Mort Shea, his new agent.
4–9 December	Grand Opera House, Lowell, Mass. Contract for performance is issued on 5 December.
11–16 December	Keith's Theatre, New York City.
16 December	Contract to play at the Hartford Opera House, week of 29 January 1906.
18–23 December	Grand Opera House, Syracuse, N.Y.
22 December	For Christmas, Rogers sends Betty Blake a lace handkerchief he obtained in South America, where he was told to give it to the woman he will marry.
25–30 December	Grand Opera House, Pittsburgh. Program includes The Three Keatons.

1906

1–6 January	Maryland Theatre, Baltimore.
5 January	Contract to play at Brooklyn's Imperial Theatre, week of 19 February 1906.
8–13 January	Hyde and Behman's Theatre, Brooklyn.

10 January	Contracts with the Casto Circuit to play at Fall River, Mass., week of 5 February 1906, and at Lawrence, Mass., week of 12 February 1906.
15–20 January	Amphion Theatre, Brooklyn.
22–27 January	Keith's Chestnut Street Theatre, Philadelphia; Houdini is also on the playbill.
29 January–3 February	Opera House, Hartford.
5–10 February	Savoy Theatre, Fall River, Mass.
12–17 February	Colonial Theatre, Lawrence, Mass.
19–24 February	Imperial Theatre, Brooklyn.
26 February	Applies for U.S. passport for travel to Europe.
26 February	Casino Theatre, Philadelphia.
3–6 March	Leaves by train for home, stopping for a day to see Betty Blake in Rogers, Ark.
7 March	Arrives home.
13 March	Leaves Claremore for New York City.
17 March	Departs from New York on S.S. *Philadelphia* bound for Europe.
24 March	Keith Circuit contract for sixteen weeks, commencing 3 September 1906.
25 March	Arrives at Cherbourg, France, and takes train to Paris.
28 March	Contract issued for Wintergarten engagement, Berlin.
1–30 April	Performs at the Wintergarten in Berlin.
7 May–9 June	Performs at the Palace Theatre, London. Also on the playbill are Rose Stahl and Julian Eltinge.
6 June	Performs at Ranelagh Club and receives silver club. King Edward VII present.
14 June	Visits Vienna, possibly sees or participates in Buffalo Bill's Wild West show.
17–19 June	Stays in Rome at the Grand Hôtel Continental.
19–22 June	Stays in Naples at the Grand Hôtel du Vésuve.
22 June	Sails first cabin class on S.S. *König Albert*, bound for New York City.

4 July	Arrives New York City.
9 July–29 August	Visits Claremore and Chelsea, and sees relatives and friends. Betty Blake visits his home and meets his relatives.
1 August	Best man at the marriage of Lorenzo Goodale to Ida Mae Collins in Claremore.
4 August	Rogers travels to Rogers, Ark., to see Betty Blake and proposes marriage to her, but she rejects his proposal.
29 August	Leaves Claremore and travels to Detroit.
3–8 September	Performs at Temple Theatre, Detroit.
10–15 September	Keith's Prospect Theatre, Cleveland.
17–22 September	Grand Opera House, Pittsburgh.
24–29 September	Shea's Theatre, Buffalo.
1–6 October	Shea's Theatre, Toronto, Ontario, Canada.
8–13 October	Cook Opera House, Rochester, N.Y.
15–20 October	Grand Theatre, Syracuse, N.Y.
22–28 October	Keith and Proctor's Twenty-third Street Theatre, New York City.
29 October–3 November	Keith's Theatre, Boston.
5–11 November	Keith and Proctor's Fifth Avenue Theatre, New York City.
6 November	Clement Vann Rogers elected delegate to the Oklahoma State Constitutional Convention.
12–17 November	Harlem Opera House, New York City.
19–24 November	Trent Theatre, Trenton, N.J.
26 November–1 December	Keith's Theatre, Philadelphia.
3–8 December	Maryland Theatre, Baltimore.
5 December	Rogers sends Betty Blake a letter from Nina, a friend and performer with the vaudeville act, The Crickets.
10–15 December	Lyric Theatre, Altoona, Pa.
16–23 December	Stays in New York City and sees Broadway shows.

23 December	Possible appearance at a New York City benefit called "A Night with the Vaudeville Comedy Club."
24–29 December	Victoria Theatre, New York City.
31 December–5 January	Star Theatre, Brooklyn.

1907

7–12 January	Gaiety Theatre, Brooklyn.
11 January	Oklahoma Constitutional Convention changes the name of Cooweescoowee County to Rogers County in honor of Clement Vann Rogers.
14–19 January	Gaiety Theatre, Baltimore.
21–26 January	Gaiety Theatre, Pittsburgh.
27 January–2 February	Rogers returns to New York City, no engagements.
3 February	Listed on Sunday playbill at New York's Murray Hill Theatre.
4–9 February	Orpheum Theatre, Brooklyn.
11–16 February	Colonial Theatre, New York City.
18–23 February	Orpheum Theatre, Boston.
25 February–2 March	Chase's Theatre, Washington D.C. Performances attended by Clement Vann Rogers.
4–9 March	Walderman's Theatre, Newark, N.J.
11–16 March	Alhambra Theatre, New York City.
18–23 March	Richmond Family Theatre, North Adams, Mass.
25–30 March	Family Theatre, Gloversville, N.Y.
1–17 April	In New York City, no engagements.
18 April	Sails on S.S. *Kaiserin Auguste Victoria* bound for England.
29 April–12 May	Palace Theatre, London.
20–25 May	Empire Theatre, Coventry.
27 May–2 June	Empire Theatre, Liverpool.
8 June	Sails for New York City on S.S. *Philadelphia*.
15 June	Arrives New York City.

24 June–6 July	Chestnut Street Opera House, Philadelphia. Performs in theaters associated with Klaw and Erlanger's Advanced Vaudeville.
8–20 July	Nixon Theatre, Pittsburgh.
5–10 August	Morrison's Theatre, Rockaway Beach, N.Y.
12 August	Travels to Chicago for appearances in *The Girl Rangers.*
19–31 August	Rehearsing *The Girl Rangers* in Chicago.
1–29 September	Appears in *The Girl Rangers* at the Chicago Auditorium.
7–20 October	With *The Girl Rangers* at the Walnut Street Theatre in Philadelphia.
28 October–2 November	New York Theatre, New York City.
4–9 November	Peoples Theatre, Philadelphia.
11–16 November	Grand Opera House, Brooklyn.
18–23 November	Shubert's Theatre, Newark, N.J.
25–30 November	Tremont Theatre, Boston.
2–7 December	Gaiety Theatre, Baltimore.
9–14 December	Gaiety Theatre, Washington, D.C.
16–21 December	Keith and Proctor's 125th Street Theatre, New York City.
23–28 December	Victoria Theatre, New York City.
30 December–4 January	Colonial Theatre, New York City.

1908

6–11 January	Cook Opera House, Rochester, N.Y.
13–18 January	Bennett's Theatre, Montreal, Quebec, Canada.
20–25 January	Bennett's Theatre, Hamilton, Ontario, Canada.
25 January–1 February	Gaiety Theatre, Toronto.
3–8 February	Poli's Theatre, Worcester, Mass.
10-15 February	Orpheum Theatre, Brooklyn.
17-22 February	Poli's Theatre, Springfield, Mass.
24–29 February	Poli's Theatre, Hartford.
2 March	Poli's Theatre, New Haven, Conn. Leaves show to return to Claremore because of his father's illness.

ca. 10 March	Arrives Claremore to visit his father.
ca. 16 April	Receives Scottish Rite Masonic Degree at McAlester, Okla.
18 April	Clement Vann Rogers is reported recovered.
ca. 20 April	Rogers leaves Claremore to visit Betty Blake in Rogers, Ark.
27 April–2 May	Returns to vaudeville at Poli's Theatre, Bridgeport, Conn.
ca. 11–22 May	No engagements. In New York City.
23 May	Begins Sullivan and Considine Circuit tour; writes his father from Chicago that he is on his way to Winnipeg, Manitoba, Canada.
25–30 May	Bijou Theatre, Winnipeg.
31 May	Travels by train from Winnipeg to Duluth, Minn.
1–7 June	Bijou Theatre, Duluth.
8–12 June	In transit to Butte, Mont. Visits Yellowstone National Park.
13–20 June	Grand Theatre, Butte.
17 June	Sends Betty Blake eight postcards illustrated by Charles M. Russell.
21–27 June	Washington Theatre, Spokane, Wash.
28 June	Travels to Seattle.
29 June–5 July	Star Theatre, Seattle.
6–12 July	Orpheum Theatre, Vancouver, B.C., Canada.
13–19 July	Grand Theatre, Tacoma, Wash.
20–26 July	Grand Theatre, Portland, Ore.
27 July–2 August	No engagement.
3–9 August	Grand Theatre, Sacramento, Calif.
10–15 August	National Theatre, San Francisco.
16–22 August	Bell Theatre, Oakland, Calif.
23–29 August	Wigwam Theatre, San Francisco.

Editorial Principles and Practices

DOCUMENT SELECTION FOR VOLUME TWO

VOLUME TWO OF *The Papers of Will Rogers* PRESENTS THE READER WITH printed transcriptions of documents of various types. These include handwritten personal correspondence; correspondence printed in newspapers; published newspaper articles, interviews, and reviews; typescript performance reviews by theater managers; theater and Wild West programs; vaudeville playbills and advertisements; and legal documents, including passports and a last will and testament. Emphasis is placed on personal correspondence, especially that of Will Rogers himself, and on documentation of Rogers's performance schedule. This collection includes about one out of ten noncorrespondence documents collected by the Will Rogers Papers Project for the 1904–8 period and about one out of four extant pieces of correspondence written by Rogers in those years, along with a sampling of letters written to Rogers by family members and friends. The personal correspondence, records, newspaper reports, performance reviews, and other documents have not been previously published in comprehensive form in a scholarly edition.

In the selection of documents for this volume, emphasis was placed on capturing both the facts and the flavor of Rogers's Wild West and vaudeville career. Correspondence was selected to elucidate his personal life and relationships. His own letters and postcards, and those written to him, help describe the nature of his act, his hopes and intentions. They display how he felt about his work, the places that he visited, and the people he met and those with whom he worked and socialized. They also make it possible to trace his travels from performance to performance, as he kept his loved ones informed of his next engagements. We are fortunate that, although Rogers destroyed some of his personal correspondence from this period, he maintained careful scrapbooks of his vaudeville engagements. These scrapbooks have been mined for both document and annotation materials. They include playbills and programs, clippings of reviews, photographs, and business cards. The vaudeville and Wild West materials drawn from the scrapbooks have been selected and combined with other types of documents—such as theater managers' reports, reviews and articles gathered from local newspapers in the towns and cities where Rogers appeared, and vaudeville contracts—so as to re-create for the reader Rogers's complete performance schedule, the details of his itinerary, the critical reactions to his act, and the ways in which he modified his performance as his career developed. Effort has been made to identify every location and venue where Rogers appeared in this time period, and to make available to the reader—either through the documents themselves or the annotations that link the documents—both the details of his personal experience and the larger cultural context. The volume is replete with coverage of both the performance and business ends of vaudeville. It provides capsule histories of theaters, managers, and agents. It profiles performers, acts, and union members; traces the history of the development of different circuits; and explains the conflicts that existed between the major booking agencies and circuit operators. It contains names and, when possible, profiles of those both famous and obscure who made vaudeville into the one of the primary forms of middle-class entertainment in the first two decades of the twentieth century. In many cases, information on performers and acts has been gathered from oral interviews with family members and from primary archival materials and has never before been published in book form. Attention has been given to the private as well as the public side of vaudevillians' lives. In particular, the personal correspondence of Rogers and the woman who would become his wife, Betty Blake, and between Rogers's vaudeville partner, Buck McKee, and his wife, actress Maud Florence, provides insight into the private aspects of life on the road and in front of the footlights. Photographs have been selected to show Rogers in the different phases of his vaudeville career, friends and actors and actresses with whom he shared the itinerant life, theaters in which he appeared, hotels in which he stayed, and his growing relationship with Betty Blake.

PLACEMENT OF DOCUMENTS

Documents are presented in chronological order, determined by date of authorship or period of performance. In cases where the date of creation is not known and a document appeared in published form, the date of publication is used to determine placement. Incompletely dated documents are placed at the end of a given time frame (e.g., a document dated August 1904, with no specific day given, would appear following all other documents for August 1904); similarly, a document dated with only a year or season (e.g., 1907 or summer 1905) is placed at the end of that year, or in context within the seasonal period of time. Dates construed by the editors are given in square brackets; these may have been construed either from the content of the document (e.g., mention within the document of a particular event or date or allusion to a stage in Rogers's itinerary) or from other material (e.g., a hotel letterhead that indicates context with other similar letters or a postmark on an envelope in which an original undated letter was received). The date designation of documents created on more than one day (e.g., a letter written over the course of several days or a composite document containing a series of reviews from a particular time period) indicates a time span (e.g., 15–27 May 1906), and the document is placed according to the first date in that span. Two or more documents of the same date are arranged according to historical sequence or in the best contextual relationship to documents that directly precede or follow.

Volume two has been broken into five thematic sections, each with its own introduction. Sections are based on discrete stages in Rogers's personal life or career. Part one, "The Wild West," brings Rogers back to the United States from his travels to Argentina, South Africa, New Zealand, and Australia chronicled in volume one. Upon his return to America, Rogers appeared as a cowboy rope artist in Wild West shows on the Pike at the St. Louis World's Fair. In the Spring of 1905 he traveled to New York City, where he appeared with the Mulhall family in a Wild West show at Madison Square Garden. At the end of the engagement he stayed on to begin his vaudeville stage career, which he had tried out the summer before while still working in St. Louis.

The remaining four sections trace the development of Rogers's vaudeville career. Part two, "The Training Ground," follows his training of his pony, Teddy, for the stage, and the beginnings of his partnership with Buck McKee. Part three, "Berlin's Wintergarten and London's Palace," takes him for his first performances in Europe; parts four and five, "Caught in the Vaudeville Wars" and "On the Western Vaudeville Trail," chronicle his return to the United States and his life on the circuits. Part introductions set the context and identify some of the major themes that appear in the documents that follow. Occasional headnotes introduce particular documents, further setting their context and supplying pertinent information.

PRESENTATION OF DOCUMENTS AND EDITORIAL ELEMENTS

All documents are presented with a caption or document heading, a place and date line, a descriptive source note, and, if appropriate, annotations.

Captions of correspondence assume that Will Rogers is either the author or the recipient of the letter and indicate only the other party in the correspondence (e.g., "To Betty Blake" or "From Clement Vann Rogers"). Noncorrespondence primary documents and published third-party documents are given descriptive titles (e.g., "Vaudeville Notes" or "Review from the *New York Dramatic Mirror*"). Document headings also include the date of the document and the place where it originated. The day-month-year dating style is used in the captions, and the abbreviation *ca.* (for *circa*) is used to prefix editorially construed dates. Documents that are printed as enclosures to other documents are labeled as enclosures, followed by a full descriptive heading in the same style as any other document.

Place and date lines are printed flush right at the beginning of the documentary text, regardless of where this information may have been presented in the original document. Lines breaks of the place and date information are structured in accordance with the original, unless they are of such length as to demand alteration. When no place or date appears on the original document, the place and date line is left blank.

For letters where a recipient's address is given on the original document, the address is set flush left above the salutation, regardless of where the information may have been given in the original. Salutations are similarly set flush left no matter how they appear in original correspondence. Headlines of printed documents taken from newspapers are centered and if abridged are so described in the descriptive source note.

Documents are presented with as little editorial intervention as possible. Texts are reproduced as written, with irregularities in grammar, punctuation, and spelling left intact. Paragraphs are indented. Rogers often wrote without punctuation and with irregular use of capitalization. In transcriptions of his handwritten letters, extra space has been added at the end of a sentence or phrase break where no period or other punctuation was supplied in the original, in order to make his correspondence easier to read. Italics are used to render single-underlined words in autograph texts and italicized text in printed documents. Double-underlined words in autograph texts are rendered in italics with underline. Documents such as letterheads with printed place and date lines or application forms that include blanks filled out by hand are presented with the filled-in words in roman type and the blanks indicated by underlining. Minor typographical errors in published documents have been silently corrected. Typescript manager's reports from Keith theaters have been regularized to paragraph format. Misspellings or abbreviations that occur in original documents are sometimes clarified in notes or with the use of square brackets. Illegible words or missing or mutilated text are indicated by an editorial message in italics and square brackets (e.g., [*word illegible*] or [*page torn*]). Interlineations are indicated by the use of a ▲ or ▼ symbol at the beginning and end of the superscript or subscript text. Marginal notes are quoted in annotations. Some documents that were not written by Rogers have been abridged. Abridgments are indicated by unbracketed ellipses. If ellipses occurred in the original documents, this is indicated either in the descriptive source note or by an annotation.

Closings of letters are set flush right or are run into the last paragraph of the letter, as they are in the original document. Signatures are set flush right, no matter how they were rendered in the original. Postscripts follow signatures, and mailing addresses, endorsements, or docketing are set flush left above the source note.

Descriptive source notes contain the following information: the type of document, given in abbreviated form (e.g., ALS for "autograph letter signed"); a brief indication of the nature of the document (e.g., rc for "recipient's copy"); the source of the document (repository, manuscript collection, or printed source), and any further information pertaining to the physical nature of the document or its content and presentation, including letterhead data. Facts printed, stamped, or written on an envelope are given if pertinent. All abbreviations used in the source notes are explained in the list of symbols and abbreviations that follows this section.

Annotations are used to clarify the text, to provide cross-references, or to identify people, places, and events. The full contents of playbills have been presented, whenever possible, with the acts listed in the order in which they appeared on stage. Descriptions of the acts have been repeated from the original bills or programs and presented in parentheses. Capitalization of these listings has been retained as it is in the original documents, but the descriptions are given in capital and lower-case letters, even if they appear in all capital letters or another form in the originals. Cross-references to other documents in the volume are given by description and date of the document, with a designation of whether the document is printed above or below (preceding or following) the cross-reference, rather than by page numbers. Cross-references to the Biographical Appendix are given by the name of the person profiled rather than by page numbers. Places, events, organizations, and institutions are identified when they are significant to Rogers's life and career or are not widely known. Annotations fully identify individuals who are referred to in the text by initials only or by first or last names (unless an individual appears frequently). Biographical annotations of individuals are presented at first appearance. Research has been conducted to identify individuals important to Will Rogers's life. In some cases, however, biographical searches either revealed no data or were limited by the obscurity of the individual and lack of public information.

Rogers's close friends or colleagues, and people of particular significance to his career or personal life, are profiled in the Biographical Appendix. The annotation at the first appearance of such an individual's name in the text is a cross-reference to the appropriate appendix entry. A comprehensive name index also appears at the beginning of the appendix as a guide to the reader. Additional information about individuals included in the appendix may also appear in annotations specific to documents in the volume. All other individuals named in the text whom we could identify are described in annotations, unless already annotated in a previous volume. An effort was made (through extensive archival research in Wild West, circus, theater, and film collections and through reviews of entertainment-trade periodicals and newspapers) to identify every individual or act with which Rogers performed that is named in the documents. Bibliographic source citations are given in annotations and in all Biographical Appendix entries in either abbreviated or short-title form. Complete listings of all sources appear either in Symbols and Abbreviations or in the Bibliography.

Symbols and Abbreviations

TEXTUAL DEVICES

[roman]	Editorial clarification or addition to text.
[roman?]	Conjectural reading for missing, mutilated, or illegible text.
[*italic*]	Editorial message regarding the nature of the original text (e.g., [*line missing*], [*page mutilated*], or [*word illegible*]).
. . .	Text editorially abridged.
~~canceled~~	Word deleted in original.
▲ ▲	Text that appears between markers is written above the line in original document.
▼ ▼	Text that appears between markers is written below the line in original document.

DESCRIPTIVE SYMBOLS

AD	Autograph Document
ADS	Autograph Document Signed
AL	Autograph Letter
ALS	Autograph Letter Signed
AMS	Autograph Manuscript
AN	Autograph Note
ANS	Autograph Note Signed
APC	Autograph Postcard
APCS	Autograph Postcard Signed
PD	Printed Document
TD	Typed Document
TG	Telegram
TL	Typed Letter
TLS	Typed Letter Signed
TMS	Typed Manuscript
cc	Carbon Copy
cy	Copy Other than Carbon (Correspondence)

dc	Draft Copy (of Printed Article)
rc	Recipient's Copy (Correspondence)

MANUSCRIPT COLLECTION AND REPOSITORY SYMBOLS

BBC-RHM	Betty Blake Rogers Collection, Rogers Historical Museum, Rogers, Ark.
BMc-C	Buck McKee Collection, California State Library, Sacramento
BMC-OkClaW	Buck McKee Collection, Will Rogers Memorial, Claremore, Okla.
CBevA	American Film Institute, Louis B. Mayer Library, Los Angeles
CL	Los Angeles Public Library
CLAc	Academy of Motion Picture Arts and Sciences, Margaret Herrick Library, Beverly Hills, Calif.
CLC-SWM	Charles Lummis Collection, Southwest Museum, Pasadena, Calif.
CLSU	University of Southern California, Los Angeles
CMR-MHS	Charles M. Russell research materials, microfilm reels, Montana Historical Society, Helena
CPpR	Will Rogers State Historic Park, Pacific Palisades, Calif.
CSf-PALM	San Francisco Performing Arts Library and Museum
GWP-GA	Guy Weadick Papers, Glenbow Archives, Calgary, Alberta, Canada
HCP-MoU	Homer Croy Papers, Western Historical Manuscript Collection, University of Missouri, Columbia
HTC-MH	Harvard Theatre Collection, Harvard College Library, Harvard University, Cambridge, Mass.
JLC-OkClaW	Joseph Levy, Jr., Collection, Will Rogers Memorial, Claremore, Okla.
KAC-IaU	Keith-Albee Collection, University of Iowa, University Libraries, Special Collections, Iowa City
LHM-LHP	Louise Henry Memoir, Louise Henry Papers, Laurie Weltz Private Collection, New York
LHS-LHP	"L. H. The Sal Skinner Gal Album," Louise Henry Scrapbook, Louise Henry Papers, Laurie Weltz Private Collection, New York
McK-CSL	Buck McKee Collection, California State Library, Sacramento

MFC	Mulhall Family Collection, Martha Fisch Private Collection, Guthrie, Okla.
MoSHi	Missouri Historical Society, St. Louis
NCHF	National Cowboy Hall of Fame and Western Heritage Center, Oklahoma City
NN	New York Public Library
NNC	Columbia University, Butler Library, New York
NNHi	New-York Historical Society
NN-L-BRTC	New York Public Library, Research Library for the Performing Arts at Lincoln Center, Billy Rose Theatre Collection
NN-L-RLC	New York Public Library, Research Library for the Performing Arts at Lincoln Center, Robinson-Locke Collection
NNMoMA-FC	Museum of Modern Art, Film Study Center, New York
NNMuS	Museum of the City of New York, Theatre Collection
NNSA	Shubert Archive, New York
OkClaW	Will Rogers Memorial, Claremore, Okla.
OkHi	Oklahoma Historical Society, Oklahoma City
OkTahN	John Vaughan Library, Northeastern State University, Tahlequah, Okla.
PP	Free Library of Philadelphia, Theatre Collection
PR-TxU	Pat Rooney Collection, Theatre Arts Collection, Harry Ransom Humanities Research Center, University of Texas, Austin
RHM	Rogers Historical Museum, Rogers, Ark.
THS	Theatre Historical Society of America, Elmurst, Ill.
TMC-RHM	Tom Morgan Collection, Rogers Historical Museum, Rogers, Ark.
TxFACM	Amon Carter Papers, Amon Carter Museum, Ft. Worth, Tex.
TxU-GL	General Libraries, University of Texas, Austin
TxU-HRHRC	Theatre Arts Collection, Hobilitzelle Theatre Arts Library, Harry Ransom Humanities Research Center, University of Texas, Austin
URL-CLU	Department of Special Collections, University Research Library, University of California, Los Angeles
VATM	Victoria and Albert Theatre Museum, National Museum of the Performing Arts, Theatre Collection (Study Room),

Covent Garden, London

WBaraC   Circus World Museum, Robert L. Parkinson Library and
                Research Center, Baraboo, Wis.
WRPP   Will Rogers Papers Project, Los Angeles

GUIDE TO ABBREVIATED CITATIONS FOR PUBLISHED SOURCES

NEWSPAPERS

CC   *Chelsea Commercial,* Chelsea, Okla.
CDP   *Claremore Daily Progress,* Claremore, Okla.
CM   *Claremore Messenger,* Claremore, Okla.
CP   *Claremore Progress,* Claremore, Okla.
CR   *Chelsea Reporter,* Chelsea, Okla.
CWP   *Claremore Weekly Progress,* Claremore, Okla.
IC   *Indian Chieftain,* Vinita, I.T.
LAHE   *Los Angeles Herald Express*
LAT   *Los Angeles Times*
ME   *Mulhall Enterprise,* Mulhall, Okla.
NYA   *New York American*
NYC   *New York Clipper*
NYDM   *New York Dramatic Mirror*
NYHT   *New York Herald Tribune*
NYT   *New York Times*
SFC   *San Francisco Chronicle*
StLGD   *St. Louis Globe-Democrat*
StLPD   *St. Louis Post-Dispatch*
StLR   *St. Louis Republic*
TDW   *Tulsa Daily World,* Tulsa, Okla.
WFB   *World's Fair Bulletin,* St. Louis, Mo.
WP   *Washington Post,* Washington, D.C.

REFERENCE WORKS

AAB   *American Authors and Books: 1640 to the Present Day.* Edited
                by W. J. Burlat and William D. Howe. 3d rev. ed. New York:
                Crown Publishers, 1972.
ABA   *American Biographical Archive.* Managing editor, Laureen
                Baillie. Edited by Gerry Easter. Microform ed. New York:
                K. G. Saur, 1986—90.
ABTB   *American and British Theatrical Biography.* Edited by J. P.
                Wearing. Metuchen, N.J.: Scarecrow Press, 1979.

BDAM	*Biographic Dictionary of American Mayors.* Edited by Melvin G. Holli and Peter Jones. Westport, Conn.: Greenwood Press, 1981.
BDGUS	*Biographical Directory of the Governors of the United States.* Edited by Robert Sobel and John Raimo. Westport, Conn.: Meckler Books, 1978.
BE	*The Baseball Encyclopedia.* Edited by Joseph L. Reichler. 6th ed. New York: Macmillan Publishing, 1985.
BEWHAT	*The Biographical Encyclopaedia and Who's Who of the American Theatre.* Edited by Walter Rigdon. New York: James H. Heineman, 1966.
CB	*Current Biography.* 53 vols. New York: H. W. Wilson, 1941–94.
CDAB	*Concise Dictionary of American Biography.* 3d ed. New York: Scribner, 1980.
CmpEnc	*Complete Encyclopedia of Popular Music and Jazz, 1900–1950.* Edited by Roger D. Kinkle. 4 vols. New Rochelle, N.Y.: Arlington House Publishers, 1974.
DAB	*Dictionary of American Biography.* Edited by Allen Johnson, Dumas Malone, et al. 22 vols. New York: Charles Scribner's Sons, 1928–80.
DE	*The Dance Encyclopedia.* Compiled and edited by Anatole Chujoy. New York: A. S. Barnes, 1949.
EAB	*Encyclopedia of American Biography.* Edited by Winfield Scott Downs. New York: American Historical, 1942.
EAM	*The Encyclopedia of American Music.* Edited by Edward Jablonski. Garden City, N.Y.: Doubleday, 1981.
EFB	*Encyclopedia of Frontier Biography.* Edited by Dan L. Thrapp. 3 vols. Spokane, Wash.: Arthur Clarke, 1990.
EncMuThe	*Encyclopedia of the Musical Theatre.* Edited by Kurt Gaenzl. 2 vols. New York: Schirmer Books, 1994.
ENYC	*The Encyclopedia of New York City.* Edited by Kenneth T. Jackson. New Haven, Conn.: Yale University Press, 1995.
FAP	*Facts About the Presidents.* Edited by Joseph Nathan Kane. 6th ed. New York: H. W. Wilson, 1993.
FYSC	*Forty Years of Screen Credits 1929–1969.* Edited by John T. Weaver. 2 vols. Metuchen, N.J.: Scarecrow Press, 1970.
GNAI	*Great North American Indians.* By Frederick Dockstader. New York: Van Nostrand, 1977

GRB	*The Green Room Book or Who's Who on the Stage.* Edited by John Parker. 3 vols. London: T. Sealey Clark, 1907–9.
NEB	*The New Encyclopaedia Britannica, Micropaedia.* 15th ed. 29 vols. Chicago: Encyclopaedia Britannica, 1994.
NotNat	*Notable Names in the American Theatre.* Clifton, N.J.: James T. White, 1976.
NYTheRe	*New York Times Theater Reviews.* 20 vols. New York: New York Times and Arno Press, 1975.
NYTheReI	*The New York Times Theater Reviews Index, 1870–1919.* New York: New York Times and Arno Press, 1975.
OCF	*Old Cherokee Families, Notes of Dr. Emmet Starr.* Vol. 1, *Letter Books A–F.* Vol. 2, *Letter Books G–L, Index to Letter Books.* Edited by Jack D. Baker and David Keith Hampton. Oklahoma City: Baker Publishing, 1988.
OF	*Obituaries on File.* Edited by Felice Levy. 2 vols. New York: Facts on File, 1979.
REAI	*Reference Encyclopedia of the American Indian.* 6th ed. Edited by Barry T. Klein. West Nyack, N.Y.: Todd Publications, 1993.
WhMuDr	*Who's Who in Music and Drama: An Encyclopaedia of Biography of Notable Men and Women in Music and the Drama.* Edited by Dixie Hines and Harry Prescott Hanaford. New York: H. P. Hanaford, 1914.
WhoHol	*Who's Who in Hollywood: The Largest Cast of International Personalities Ever Assembled.* Edited by David Ragan. 2 vols. New York: Facts on File, 1992.
WhoHolly	*Who's Who in Hollywood, 1900–1976.* Edited by David Ragan. New Rochelle, N.Y.: Arlington House Publishers, 1976.
WhoStg	*Who's Who on the Stage, 1908.* Edited by Walter Browne and E. De Roy Koch. New York: B. W. Dodge, 1908.
WhoThe	*Who's Who in the Theatre.* Edited by John Parker. London: Isaac Pitman and Sons, 1914, 1916.
WhScrn 1	*Who Was Who on the Screen.* Edited by Evelyn Mack Truitt. 3d ed. New York: R. R. Bowker, 1983.
WhScrn 2	*Who Was Who on the Screen.* Edited by Evelyn Mack Truitt. 2d ed. New York: R. R. Bowker Co., 1977.
WhThe	*Who Was Who in the Theatre: 1912–76: A Biographical Dictionary of Actors, Actresses, Directors, Playwrights, and*

Producers of the English-speaking Theatre. 4 vols. Gale Composite Biographical Dictionary Series 3. Detroit: Gale Research, 1978.

WNBD
Webster's New Biographical Dictionary. Springfield, Mass.: Merriam-Webster, 1988.

WNGD
Webster's New Geographical Dictionary. Springfield, Mass.: Merriam-Webster, 1988.

WWWA
Who Was Who in America. 27 vols. Chicago: A. N. Marquis, 1942.

WWWNAH
Who Was Who in Native American History: Indians and Non-Indians from Early Contacts through 1900. Edited by Carl Waldman. New York: Facts on File, 1990.

FREQUENTLY CITED SOURCES

AmSCAP
The ASCAP Biographical Dictionary of Composers, Authors and Publishers. Compiled and edited by the Lynn Farnol Group. New York: American Society of Composers, Authors and Publishers, 1966.

EV
The Encyclopedia of Vaudeville. Edited by Anthony Slide. Westport, Conn.: Greenwood Press, 1994.

FILM
Filmarama. Vol. 1, *The Formidable Years, 1893–1919.* Vol. 2, *The Flaming Years, 1920–1929.* Compiled by John Stewart. Metuchen, N.J.: Scarecrow Press, 1975, 1977.

FilmEnc
The Film Encyclopedia. By Ephraim Katz. 2d ed. New York: Harper Perennial, 1994.

GHNTD
Gus Hill's National Theatrical Directory. New York: Hill's National Theatrical Directory, 1914–15.

HRC
History of Rogers County, Oklahoma. Claremore, Okla.: Claremore College Foundation, 1979.

JCGHTG
The Julius Cahn—Gus Hill Theatrical Guide and Moving Picture Directory, Containing Authentic Information of Theatres in Cities, Towns, and Villages of the United States and Canada, also Details of All Moving Picture Theatres Giving the Name of the City, Population, Manager and Seating Capacity. Vol 20. New York: Longacre Building, 1921.

JCOTG
Julius Cahn's Official Theatrical Guide, 1906–1907, Containing Authentic Information of the Theatres and Attractions in the United States, Canada, Mexico and Cuba. New York: Empire Theatre Building, 1906.

OCAT	*The Oxford Companion to the American Theatre.* Edited by Gerald Bordman. 2d ed. New York and Oxford: Oxford University Press, 1992.
PWR	*The Papers of Will Rogers.* Edited by Arthur Frank Wertheim and Barbara Bair. Norman: University of Oklahoma Press.
VO	*Variety Obituaries.* 14 vols. New York: Garland Publishing, 1988.

1. THE WILD WEST
April 1904–May 1905

Will Rogers and Lucille Mulhall. Mulhall (1885–1940) was an early love interest of Rogers's. Though he had been a close friend of her family since his youth, their attraction to one another was discouraged by her father. The two shared a passion for riding and training horses. While she was a championship steer roper, he mastered the art of trick roping, for which he became famous. Rogers admiringly called Mulhall the "greatest Roper of any Girl before or since." *(OkClaW)*

WILL ROGERS RETURNED TO THE UNITED STATES IN THE SPRING OF 1904 after two years of living and working abroad. He had spent time unsuccessfully seeking jobs as a cowboy in Argentina, had tended cattle on a transatlantic voyage from Latin America to Africa, and had worked as a ranch hand in Natal, South Africa, before he earned a spot in an American-owned Wild West show by demonstrating his skill with a rope. The contrast between the harsh life of handling livestock or doing manual labor on a ranch and the rewards of performing on tour in popular tent shows convinced the young Rogers that entertainment was the profession he preferred. He learned a great deal about public performance by appearing as a trick roper and extra in Texas Jack's Wild West Show and Dramatic Company in South Africa and the Wirth Brothers' Circus in Australia and New Zealand.[1] When he made his way home, it was to follow up on this experience by seeking work at the upcoming Louisiana Purchase Exposition.

The exposition (most commonly known as the St. Louis World's Fair) was to be held in St. Louis, Missouri, beginning at the end of April 1904 and running on through the following Autumn. Rogers returned briefly to Indian Territory to visit with his family and childhood friends, all of whom were eager to see him after his long absence. He also contacted Zack Mulhall, a prominent Oklahoma Territory livestock agent who was going to be an administrator with the Wild West show that was being organized for the World's Fair.

Rogers knew Zack Mulhall well. They had met years before when Rogers competed in regional roping contests that Mulhall had helped to organize. In those earlier days Rogers had visited the Mulhall ranch and become good friends with the Mulhall family, including Zack's daughters Lucille, Agnes, and Mildred, his son, Charley, and his wife, Mary Agnes Locke Mulhall. While the teenage Rogers and Lucille Mulhall flirted and challenged each other to feats of horseback riding and steer roping, Rogers drew particularly close to "Mother" Mary Agnes Locke Mulhall during his times at the Mulhall home. Very much a matriarch of the Mulhall ranch, Mother Mulhall filled a maternal gap that had been left by the death of Rogers's own mother, Mary America Rogers, who had passed away when he was still a young boy. Lucille, meanwhile, was an early love interest and Rogers's pal in roping contests and Wild West performers' circles.[2] When Rogers returned to Indian Territory in 1904, Zack Mulhall was in charge of handling the horses and hiring and managing the cowboys to appear as a Rough Riders Congress with the Cummins North American Indians show billed at the exhibition grounds outside the Pike throughout the upcoming Fair.[3] Mulhall secured a job for Rogers, and Rogers headed for St. Louis, where he stayed much of the time at a second household Zack Mulhall had established there.

The St. Louis World's Fair took place from 30 April to 1 December 1904. Hosting the Fair was a coup for business promoters of the city of St. Louis, which at the time had the fourth-largest population of any urban area in the country. Civic boosters were eager to use the attraction of the Fair to further boost development. Although it came off a year later than planned, the Fair was organized to honor the centennial of the Louisiana Purchase, the 1803 land transaction negotiated between the United States and France that was a catalyst in the formation of the national policy of westward expansion, which shaped much of the course of nineteenth-century American history.

The economic planning and engineering that were necessary to create the fairgrounds were in themselves giant undertakings. Advance preparations included worldwide fundraising tours, solicitation of exhibits from foreign countries, intensive engineering work to rebuild and improve the quality of the city water supply, the construction of huge and elaborate temporary buildings, and the creation of beautiful gardens and a system of lakes, waterfalls, and lagoons over the fair's extensive acreage.

The fairgrounds were situated at the west end of Forest Park on more than a thousand acres of land, making the St. Louis event easily rival in size all the major international fairs that had preceded it, including the Columbian Exposition in Chicago in 1893 and the Pan-American Exposition that Will Rogers had attended in Buffalo, New York, in 1901. The grounds featured a huge Festival Hall auditorium and a Colonnade of States with pavilions representing the states and territories of the Louisiana Purchase (including Oklahoma and Indian Territories), as well as other states in the Union. Grand French-style palaces were devoted to exhibitions on such themes as the Liberal Arts, Mining and Metallurgy, Manufactures, Transportation (where the automobile exhibit was a sensation), Agriculture, Horticulture, and Electricity. The Arts Palace was one of the few permanent structures of the Fair; it now houses the St. Louis Art Museum. There was a large international presence. Foreign countries that contributed representative exhibits to the Fair included Argentina, Belgium, Brazil, Austria, China, Cuba, France, Great

Bird's Eye View of World's Fair, St. Louis, 1904

1. Grand Entrance   4. Liberal Arts   7. Manufacturers   10. Electricity   13 Varied Industries
2. Germany's Building 5. Cascades   8. Horticultural   11. Agricultural   14. Transportation
3. Mines & Metallurgy 6. Educational & Social Economy 9. Jerusalem   12. Machinery

Bird's-eye view of the St. Louis World's Fair, 1904. *(Historic postcard, anonymous)*

Britain, Ireland, Italy, Mexico, and Nicaragua. The exposition attracted over 19 million visitors, including Will Rogers's sisters Sallie McSpadden and Maud Lane and their husbands, and some of Rogers's close friends from the Claremore-Oologah area.

The theme chosen for the Fair was the march of civilizations. The content of its shows and exhibitions was planned to present a vision of Anglo-American society as the apex of human achievement and of scientific and technological development. Pseudo-scientific anthropological exhibits were prominent features of the Fair. These exhibits presented visitors with racial images that were born equally out of prevailing social science theory and out of familiar popular culture. Social scientists hired by the organizers to plan the ethnological aspects of the Fair used exhibits to instruct the public about concepts of human typology and evolutionary hierarchy.

W. J. McGee, the head of the Fair's Anthropology Department and the intellectual light behind its ethnological exhibits, showed representatives of the different peoples of the world "classed in terms of blood" and then further situated within one of four cultural levels. He labeled these gradations of biology and achievement as "savagery, barbarism, civilization, and enlighten-ment." The design of the Fair exhibits demonstrated McGee's belief in a model of evolutionary conquest, in which humankind was engaged in a march upward by means of the "extinction of the lower grades" and the subsequent dominance of Caucasian people, represented at the top by "Britain and [the] full-blown enlightenment of America."[4] Social scientists' participation in the planning of the Fair lent a veneer of academic credence to the kinds of white supremacist stereotypes of African Americans and Native Americans that infused the Fair's popular attractions—stereotypes that replicated those per-petuated by the ragtime and coon songs, dime novels, Wild West shows, and minstrel performances familiar to the audiences of the day. The line between side-show entertainment and politically laden didacticism thus was blurred in the various parts of the Fair, from the amusements of the Pike to the more staid presentations in the exhibition halls. All conveyed meaning and a partic-ular world view to the public. As McGee explained in the February 1904 edi-tion of the *World's Fair Bulletin,* "an exposition is the university of the masses."[5]

The Spencerian vision of the Fair was reflected in its physical planning, with exhibits conceptualized in topical groups arranged to represent various categories of human achievement. A great emphasis was placed on large anthropological compounds or "living" exhibits featuring nonwhite people of different nationalities. These were set apart from the "White City" section of the exposition, where "architecturally the main exhibition palaces were almost identical to those at Chicago and completely white."[6] The anthropological exhibit that had perhaps the greatest impact on visitors to the Fair was a forty-seven-acre compound occupied by over a thousand native people from the Philippines, an archipelago of Pacific islands whose residents had revolted against Spanish rule in 1896–99. U.S. troops had occupied the Philippines soon after the end of the Spanish-American War.

By presenting Filipinos to Fair visitors as primitives and offering a social-scientific interpretation of them as occupants of a lower rung of the evolu-tionary ladder, Fair promoters reinforced middle-class America's comfort with modern-day westward expansion, which by the turn of the century was taking the form of imperialism. The Indian Building, which was operated with federal funds allocated through the Interior Department, did much the same in reassuring those who attended the Fair that past repression and control of Indian tribes within U.S. borders, and prevailing federal Indian policies break-ing down tribal autonomy and imposing means of cultural assimilation, were justified in the name of progress. Related to these living exhibitions of Indians, Filipinos, and other nonwhites were dramatic reenactments of world conflicts in which Anglo-American or British forces had subdued or colonized white ethnic groups or peoples of color. Primary among these were battle scenes from the American Indian wars and the South African (Anglo-Boer) War, and a Wild West show starring cowboys representing the Rough Riders of the Spanish-American War.[7]

Seen in conjunction with the science and technology halls, these shows and anthropological exhibits underscored for those attending the Fair an ideological connection between economic advancement, imperial expansion, and the military subordination of nonwhite peoples. W. J. McGee summed up the message of the Department of Ethnology exhibits by stating that they demonstrated a range of humanity from the "darkest blacks to the dominant whites, and from the lowest known culture . . . to its highest culmination in that Age of Metal, which, as this Exposition shows, is now maturing in the Age of Power." He went on to speak of America "bearing 'the White Man's burden' . . . or performing the Strong Man's duty" in the world.[8]

The Pike was the amusement park and concession section of the St. Louis World's Fair. It stretched for a mile along the northern edge of the fairgrounds off Lindell Boulevard between the Administration entrance and the Plaza/Lindell entrance, with the Pike entrance supplying access in the middle. The Cummins performances were held in an open-air stadium outside the Pike on the exhibition grounds, and Cummins performers maintained a presence in costume on the Pike between show times.

The Pike featured international specialty food stands and restaurants. The ice cream cone was an innovation of one of the Pike food concessions. Visitors to the Pike (called "Pikers") could view the Hagenbeck Animal Paradise zoo, take tram rides through Siberia or Austria, or brave various water rides through the Galveston Flood, the Creation, or whirlpools and water chutes. They could linger at concerts and bandstands or eat at cafes; watch individual acts like that of Jim Key, the "educated horse"; or stroll through imaginative buildings representing different countries, including a fairytale Swiss village complete with mountains, and a Moorish palace. The international flavor of the Pike extended from the Tyrolean Alps and Irish Village (with its Blarney Castle and Carmac's Castle, and regular performances of Irish plays at the Dublin Theater) on one end through the Streets of Seville and Mysterious Asia (with a façade of the Taj Mahal, Persian rug weavers, and Burmese musicians), as well as villages representing Paris, Japan, China, and Turkey. A Battle Cyclorama was stationed on the western edge of the Pike, with representations of the battles of Gettysburg and Custer's Last Stand. Zuni Indians lived in a mock pueblo and demonstrated their crafts, and a

South African village associated with the Boer War show was home to Zulu people for the duration of the Fair. In the Old Plantation section, the "visitor finds a village inhabited by plantation darkies" who cultivated garden patches with cotton, tobacco, and watermelons; operated a cotton gin; and put on performances of "genuine plantation music and dancing" at the plantation theater.[9] The Pike was planned to present lighthearted versions of the same ethnological and imperial messages that were embedded in the exhibits of the Fair at large. As Norris B. Gregg, the director of admissions and concessions for the Fair, put it, a didactic comparison of the world's white and nonwhite peoples was offered on the Pike "through the guise of amusement."[10] For one fairgoer, even the monkey in the Pike's Cairo bazaar "suggested eloquently the correctness of the Darwinian theory."[11]

On Pike Day a parade of people and animals would gather from the separate exhibits on the Pike and wind their way through the avenues of the Fair. Rogers was inevitably among the "Rough riders of the world" who "crowded upon the heels" of Egyptians herding donkeys, along with "Bronchos . . . as numerous as the Indians of the Wild West Congress." "Flower girls and singers from Paris, merchants from Stanboul, gypsies from Spain . . . deep sea divers, Chinese silk weavers, fire worshippers from Persia, basket makers of the Zunis and scores of other groups had places in the polyglot parade."[12]

Rogers entered this milieu as a cowboy and rope artist with Frederick T. Cummins's North American Indians show (often simply called the Indian Congress). Rogers had undoubtedly seen the Cummins show perform before during his 1901 visit to the exposition in Buffalo. The show had originally had a strong ethnological emphasis. Under Cummins's direction, its early focus was on displaying the waning culture and rituals of various Native American peoples who had been brought under federal control in the late nineteenth century. It featured the starring presence of many of the actual Indian leaders who had led rebellions against white encroachment into traditionally Indian-occupied lands. Over time and in response to middle-class urban dwellers' fascination with the popular culture of the West, the Cummins show became steadily more commercialized. By the time Rogers joined it in St. Louis, the show still had ethnological elements—including demonstrations of Indian arts and crafts and ritual dances in living exhibits on the fairgrounds—but it had been largely reorganized to emphasize Wild West performance based on the better known model of Buffalo Bill's Wild West and other popular Wild West shows.[13] It featured casts of cowboys and Native Americans who thrilled arena audiences with trick and fancy riding and dramatic skits of stagecoach robberies and Indian battles, and included acts associated with the circus.

Frederick T. Cummins (1859–1932), Wild West show promoter. Rogers appeared in his show at the St. Louis World's Fair. *("The Creators of the Pike,"* World's Fair Bulletin *[April 1904])*

This popular presentation of the experience of western conquest was steeped in ironies. One small one was the fact that Will Rogers, a Cherokee Indian whose own people's collectively held lands had recently been subjected to allotment, played the role of a cowboy. Rogers's own experience as an Indian-cowboy highlights the class divisions that existed between privileged and integrated Native Americans like his own family and what he and Wild West advertisers referred to as "blanket Indians." Rogers's family had long been assimilated to American culture and had embraced Anglo-American ways, language, and styles of dress. Further, they had succeeded in the economy at large as ranchers and entrepreneurs. In contrast, the "blanket Indians" were primarily Plains Indians who had experienced the reservation system and/or the government's segregated Indian boarding schools. They had resisted relinquishing their traditional beliefs and ways or had done so under force of federal mandates, and had been excluded from the wealth that development of western lands had brought to Anglo-Americans. The divisions of culture, identity, and experience were so great that Rogers and other Cherokee friends of his from Indian Territory could appear in the show as quintessential cowboys, distinct from the aboriginal context in which other Indians were displayed. The distinction made in the arena seems to have been maintained offstage as well, for Rogers's friendships and social circles were formed among the Anglo-cowboys rather than the Indian contingent at the Fair.

Meanwhile, Rogers's presence in shows off the Pike involved another irony of history. Throughout the Fair African, Anglo, and Afrikaner participants in the South African War acted out mock Boer War battles in an area near the Fair's large Ferris wheel. In doing so they presented a fictionalized version of a war that had just come to a conclusion as Rogers arrived in South Africa on his travels some two years before. In the early summer of 1902 Rogers had gone to work for a livestock supplier in the war-torn province of Natal, where occupying British soldiers were still very much in evidence, and in 1904 his work brought him into close proximity with mythologized presentations of the real-life drama of the war. As the newspaper announcement of the opening of the Boer War performance put it, the "Boer War and National South African Exhibit" featured "300 Boer Troops, 300 British Troops, 100 Artillery, [and] 50 South African Savages, Cape Carts, Ox Wagons, Free State Bands, Etc." Subsequent ads simplified the description of the attraction as "Generals Cronje and Viljoen and 700 British and Boer Veterans, Reproducing Three Famous Battles."[14] The spectacle played on realities that Rogers had witnessed in faraway South Africa, transplanted as entertainment to showgrounds in America.

Rogers had formed a good working relationship with Texas Jack in his first Wild West show experience in South Africa, and he viewed Frederick Cummins as an honest and square-dealing employer at the Exposition. He found that the riding and roping work at the Fair felt like a comfortable cross between his old cattle-ranching and roping contest days, when he had worked and competed with friends from the Oklahoma and Indian Territories and Texas, and his experience doing a solo act and appearing in dramatic skits with the Texas Jack show and the Wirth Brothers' Circus.

The Cummins show was unofficially titled in its World's Fair program as "Cummins' Spectacular Indian Congress and Life on the Plains" and subtitled (in phrases redolent of both Buffalo Bill's more famous show and Theodore Roosevelt's corps of westerner soldiers in the Spanish-American War) the "Wild West Indian Congress and Rough Riders of the World." Described as a "Historic Aboriginal Educational Ethnological Industrial Exhibition," the show featured several hundred American Indians from dozens of tribes and a cavalcade of horses with cowgirls and cowboys. The Indians had been personally recruited by Cummins, who had grown up at a trading post in Council Bluffs, Iowa, and counted a large number of prominent Native American leaders among his personal acquaintances. The Indians lived in a village on the fairgrounds with their families, demonstrating dances and spiritual ceremonies, food preparation, and different styles of shelter. In

Native American performers with Frederick T. Cummins's Wild West Indian Congress and Rough Riders of the World, on the Pike, St. Louis World's Fair, 1904. Photograph of painting by C. D. Arnold. *(Thomas R. MacMechen, "The True and Complete Story of the Pike and Its Attractions," World's Fair Bulletin [April 1904])*

between Indian Congress shows many of them sat in booths in the official Indian Building, demonstrating such crafts as bead embroidery, leatherworking, the preparation of bows and arrows, and basket weaving. Fair promoters drew a strict line between the concept behind the exhibits and the purpose of the shows, announcing that in the exhibit hall it was the "purpose to avoid all objectionable features of wild west shows, and to demonstrate the progress of races and tribes."[15] Native American men participated in the Cummins show in traditional dress or, as the Fair program put it, "arrayed in all the picturesque and fearsome panoply pomp and paint of savage foray, chanting their strange battle ballads and executing thrillingly wild and expert equestrian evolutions."[16]

Cummins's headliners, Geronimo[17] and Chief Joseph,[18] had both been leaders of resistance to Anglo-American encroachment into and control of Native American lands in the 1870s and 1880s. As heroes of the Indian wars who had been vilified or glorified by the popular press, they had high name recognition among white audiences. Both were veterans of previous Cummins exposition shows. Geronimo, an Apache leader, had spent much of his early life in confrontation with U.S. and Mexican officials in the borderland areas of the Southwest. In 1885–86 (the year the equally famous Sitting Bull was performing on the east coast with the Buffalo Bill Wild West show) a kind of public hysteria built among whites in regard to Geronimo, who was personified in the media as the epitome of the villainous Indian. Thousands of U.S. soldiers were sent into Mexico to act in consort with the Mexican army to mount a campaign against the Apache resister, who surrendered in 1886 and became a prisoner of war.[19] Chief Joseph, a member of the Nez Perce peoples of the Northwest, was a leader in the Nez Perce war of 1877, during which allied bands resisted relocation to a reservation in western Idaho and led U.S. soldiers on a long-drawn-out chase over some 1,700 miles of terrain before being forced to surrender in October 1877.

Chief Joseph and Geronimo possessed physical traits and a type of personal history that Cummins looked for when he traveled around the United States in 1903 inviting Indian leaders to participate in the Fair. Both leaders were tall, impressive men of imposing physique. Both were excellent orators who were recognized by whites from among many other Indian leaders as spokesmen for their peoples. Both had reputations, at different parts of their careers, as shrewd warriors and as conciliators with federal authorities. The Louisiana Purchase Exposition played to both these sides of their personas. Fair promoters capitalized on the awe inspired by their reputation for violence and their impressive presence. At the same time, they secured yet another form of capitulation, as the former leaders collaborated with the commercial reduction of a former way of life to a series of exhibitions and entertainments for white tourists.

The Nez Perce and Apache leaders had long experience of encounters with white officials, from military officers to federal officials and, in their exposition careers, entrepreneurs. Like Cummins and Zack Mulhall, who were both friends and supporters of Theodore Roosevelt, Geronimo and Chief Joseph had personal ties with the president. Chief Joseph met with him in 1903 and Geronimo in 1905 (when he rode in Roosevelt's inaugural parade), and both used the encounters as opportunities to make (unsuccessful) pleas for greater freedoms.[20]

While mock cowboy confrontations were being staged among the Rough Riders in the showgrounds, real drama was brought to the sidelines of the Fair on the night of 18 June 1904, when Colonel Zack Mulhall got into an altercation with Frank Reed, the man in charge of the horses for the show, over Reed's treatment of one of the animals. Enraged by Reed's behavior, Mulhall drew his gun. In the struggle that ensued, Reed and two other men were shot. One of the injured men was the cowboy Johnny Murray (who was, like Will Rogers, an old friend of Mulhall's from earlier roping contest days, and who had stepped in to try to break up the fight). The other was an eighteen-year-old bystander who was a resident of St. Louis. As a result of the shooting incident and the scandal it created, Mulhall was banned from working with the Cummins show or appearing on the fairgrounds. As an alternative, he mounted Mulhall Rough Riders Congress shows in competition with the Fair. They were held out at the Delmar Race Track, where the Mulhall family had appeared in roping and riding acts many times in preceding years. The shooting caused factional divisions between the various performers in the Cummins and Mulhall shows. Will Rogers chose to maintain his old loyalties to Mulhall, observing in a letter home that he did not believe Reed to be a man of good character and thus implying that Mulhall had been understandably provoked to unintended levels of violence.[21]

After all the excitement with the Mulhall controversy quieted down, Rogers found himself a bit bored with the Fair. His work was concentrated on Sunday performances, and mid-week he had little to entertain him but the ongoing concessions at the Pike, which after many weeks had lost most of their novelty. He decided in his free time to try his hand doing his roping act in another venue. At the end of July he appeared on stage as part of a burlesque show at the Standard Theatre, an Empire Circuit establishment in St. Louis. This performance, marking the debut of his act on the American stage,

ZACH MULHALL SHOOTS THREE MEN ON THE PIKE; OKLAHOMAN IS ARRESTED; BYSTANDER FATALLY HURT

Live-Stock Agent of the Rock Island Railroad, Connected With Wild West Show, With a Six Shooter Wounds Frank Reed, a Stable Boss, in the Wrist; Ernest Morgan in the Abdomen and Cowboy John Murray Through the Chest.

DAUGHTER ACCOMPANIES FATHER.

INJURED BY BULLETS FROM MULHALL'S PISTOL.

Ernest Morgan, 16 years old, No. 3113 Sheridan avenue, shot in abdomen; probably will die.

John Murray, cowboy, Oklahoma, shot in left breast.

Frank Reed, 50 years old, cowboy, Oklahoma, shot in left arm; one ball grazed his neck.

"Zach" Mulhall, live stock agent of the Rock Island System, who is connected with Cummins's Wild West Indian Congress, an attraction on the Pike at the World's Fair, shot and wounded three men in an altercation which took place in front of the show last night.

John Murray, a cowboy, is in the Exposition Emergency Hospital, suffering from a serious, perhaps a fatal, wound in the stomach.

Frank Reed, a stableman, is wounded in the left wrist and neck. Ernest Morgan of No. 3113 Sheridan avenue, who was a bystander, received a bullet in the abdomen. Morgan is expected to die.

Mulhall is under arrest at the World's Fair Police Station.

The shooting is said to have been started by a quarrel which Mulhall and Reed had during the afternoon. According to Doctor Waddell, an attache of the Cummins's show, Mulhall threatened to kill Reed prior to the matinee.

Mulhall is said to have drawn a re-

ZACH MULHALL.

When the report of the pistol was heard, the crowd fled helter-skelter in an effort to get away from the range of the bullets.

At the police station he refused to discuss the matter. Lucille Mulhall, his daughter, comforted her father after the affray, and later upon his advice went home.

He did not seem a bit perturbed over the

Clipping, Zack Mulhall shooting incident, St. Louis World's Fair, June 1904. (Scrapbook 1902–4, CPpR)

impressed an influential viewer with connections to John J. Murdock,[22] vaude-ville theater owner and booking agent in Chicago. As a result Rogers was booked for a week's engagement at the Chicago Opera House in the fall.

In between his appearances on stage in St. Louis and Chicago, Rogers became reacquainted with his old girlfriend, Betty Blake, whom he had first met when she came to visit mutual friends in Oologah for a few months in 1899. Their on-again, off-again relationship had been off for some years and he had not contacted her during his entire time abroad in 1902–4. Blake came to St. Louis to see the Fair, and while strolling through the Oklahoma Territory exhibition hall with her sister Virginia, she overheard a young woman from Indian Territory say that she had seen Will Rogers perform with the Cummins Wild West show. Betty Blake sent Rogers a note; he replied; and that evening they had a date at the Fair. Betty came to his performance and was embarrassed by his garish outfit (which had been made for him with fond-ness by Margaret Wirth to wear in his performances with the Wirth Brothers' Circus, and which he had worn that night in St. Louis especially to impress Betty Blake), but she persevered despite the teasing of her sister and another girlfriend. After he got off work the two had dinner, enjoyed the concessions on the Pike, and heard the noted Irish tenor John McCormack sing.[23] The next day they were supposed to meet in the morning, but Rogers failed to keep the appointment, sending Blake a note explaining that he was off that day to Indian Territory. A letter of apology followed, and in the next months the two began to correspond.

After a second trip home in October, Rogers headed up to Chicago for his week's engagement at the Chicago Opera House, only to find on arrival that his failure to confirm the booking and provide publicity shots in advance had led to the act's cancellation. At the end of the month he found work for a week at Cleveland's New Theatre in Chicago, then traveled back down to St. Louis. After a grand finale performance with the Consolidated Wild West show at the St. Louis fairgrounds, he headed home to Claremore and Chelsea for the winter.

The next several months saw him training the pony Teddy (a new little horse, named for President Roosevelt, that he would purchase from the Mulhalls by the summer), for a roping act on the stage and making several visits to the Mulhall family ranch. There the Mulhalls—largely ignoring the ongoing legal case against Zack Mulhall stemming from the shooting at the Pike—were busy preparing to launch a new tour of the Mulhall Rough Riders Congress in 1905. Rogers joined them for the beginning of the tour, traveling east for a very successful engagement with the Horse Association Fair at

Madison Square Garden in New York City in April. Rogers and his friend Jim Minnick took an important side trip from their performances with the Mulhall show: They went to Washington, D.C., and did rope tricks to the delight of Theodore Roosevelt's family at the White House. The Horse Fair and the Mulhall family, including tiny ten-year-old Mildred, were a big hit in New York. Rogers earned his own stellar publicity during the show when he unexpectedly took on the role of the hero. He chased down a wayward steer that had broken loose from the arena during the act and had charged up into the aisles amid seats filled with people.

After the show closed at Madison Square Garden, Rogers and the Mulhall family parted ways. The Mulhalls continued on their tour, appearing with Geronimo at the Miller Brothers' 101 Ranch in June. Rogers went to the Orange Horse Fair in New Jersey and then left the regular circuit of the Wild West behind. He remained in New York and turned his spinning lariat toward vaudeville.

1. For documentation of this 1902–4 period of Will Rogers's life and his travels in Argentina, South Africa, Australia, and New Zealand see *PWR*, volume one.

2. Zack Mulhall (ca. 1847–1931) and his daughter Lucille Mulhall (1885–1940) are profiled in the Biographical Appendix of *PWR*, 1:516–18, 518–21. See also Biographical Appendix entries in this volume for Acton, Mildred Mulhall Carmichael; Casey, Georgia Smith (Mulhall); Mulhall, Charley;, and Mulhall, Mary Agnes Locke.

3. Frederick Cummins (1859–1932) was the president and general manager of Cummins' Wild West and Congress of North American Indians (see Biographical Appendix entry for Cummins, Frederick T.). The Cummins show had previously been featured at the Trans-Mississippi Exposition and Greater-America Exposition in Omaha in 1898 and 1899; at the Pan-American Exposition in Buffalo in 1901; and at Madison Square Garden, New York, in 1903 (Hill, *Great White Indian Chief;* MacMechen, "True and Complete Story of the Pike and its Attractions"; Russell, *Wild West: History of the Wild West Shows*).

4. W. J. McGee was an associate editor of *National Geographic* magazine, the former president of the American Anthropology Association, and the former ethnologist in charge of the Government Bureau of American Ethnology. He had already explained his racial classification system in two lectures given in 1899 (see Rydell, *All the World's a Fair*, 160–64; also Bennitt et al., eds., "Department of Anthropology and Ethnology," chap. 21 in *History of the Louisiana Purchase Exposition*, 673–85; Everett, "Study of Mankind," chap. 19 in *Book of the Fair*, 265–78; Hinsley, *Savages and Scientists;* and McGee, "Anthropology." The message of white supremacy carried over into the supposed "Olympic" events of the Fair, in which American Indians, African Pygmies, Patagonians, Japanese, and other participants in the living exhibits competed in "Anthropology Days" sports events (Bennitt et al., *History of the Louisiana Purchase Exposition*, 573).

5. McGee, "Anthropology," 4.

6. Allwood, *Great Exhibitions*, 112.

7. It is notable that Frederick Cummins's show chose to present Custer's massacre as its battle scene extravaganza, choosing one of the best known battles in which

Native American warriors, rather than U.S. troops, had achieved the upper hand. The choice may reflect both Cummins's sympathy with the Indian perspective and the concept of heroism and celebration of primitivism that exalted Indian bravery in the wars and the association of this noble-savage stereotype with the cult of masculinity and the West that infused popular culture during Theodore Roosevelt's years in office.

8. McGee, "Anthropology," 4, 6–7. See also McGee, "Anthropology Exhibit."

9. Wrenn, *Rand-McNally Economizer,* 183.

10. Rydell, *All the World's a Fair,* 179.

11. Everett, *Book of the Fair,* 106.

12. Francis, *Universal Exposition of 1904,* 1:601.

13. On Buffalo Bill's Wild West and the Wild West show as a cultural phenomenon of the turn of the century, see Russell, *Lives and Legends of Buffalo Bill* and *Wild West: A History of the Wild West Shows;* Sell and Weybright, *Buffalo Bill and the Wild West.* Biographical Appendix entries on William F. Cody (Buffalo Bill), Gordon William Lillie (Pawnee Bill), and Texas Jack appear in *PWR,* 1:487–88, 502–3, 559–61.

14. *StLGD,* 13 June and 8 September 1904.

15. *WFB* 4, no. 6 (April 1903): 17. The U.S. Congress allocated over $40,000 to the Department of the Interior to prepare an "exhibit showing aboriginal Indian culture and current educational methods" at the Louisiana Purchase Exposition (Debo, *Geronimo,* 409). The result was the U.S. Indian School Building and related exhibits.

16. Program of Cummins' Spectacular Indian Congress and Life on the Plains, St. Louis World's Fair, 1904, scrapbook A-1, OkClaW. On the imagery of American Indians in Wild West shows, see also Moses, *Wild West Shows.*

17. Geronimo (ca. 1829–1909) was born into the Bedonkohe clan of the Apache in southern Arizona or New Mexico. In his youth he fought with the Chiricahua Apaches, including Cochise, who were hostile to the encroachment of white prospectors, ranchers, and settlers into Indian lands and to the demands of acculturation that framed U.S. Indian policy. After a brief period of peace in the mid-1870s during which Apaches were granted homelands, federal officials—ostensibly reacting to Apache raids into Mexico—adopted a new concentration policy that called for the removal of Apaches from New Mexico and parts of Arizona and their consolidation at the San Carlos Reservation near Tucson. Geronimo was among those who participated in the resistance in a series of breakouts from San Carlos and in the Apache wars of 1881–86. The conflicts were interrupted temporarily in 1884 by an agreement struck between U.S. general George Crook and the Apaches in the Sierra Madre, in accordance with which Geronimo and other subchiefs observed the peace and farmed in the San Carlos area. Geronimo led another breakout in May 1885, and raids and skirmishes continued into 1886. After Geronimo's surrender in September 1886, many Apaches were relocated as prisoners of war by the War Department to Fort Marion, Fla., and later moved to Mount Vernon Barracks in Alabama, and finally to Fort Sill in Indian Territory.

Geronimo was seasoned to the exposition scene by the time he participated in the St. Louis World's Fair. He had appeared in the Trans-Mississippi and International Exposition in Omaha, Neb., in September–October 1898 and the Pan-American Exposition at Buffalo in the summer of 1901. Additional requests to the War Department by Pawnee Bill (Gordon W. Lillie) to have Geronimo appear with his Wild West Show on tour and at Madison Square Garden were denied (Debo, *Geronimo,* 407–8).

The year after the St. Louis World's Fair Geronimo dictated his memoirs, *Geronimo's Story of His People,* to Lawton School superintendent Stephen M. Barrett (the work was published by Duffield and Co. of New York in 1906) and rode in Theodore Roosevelt's inaugural parade in Washington, D.C. He took the latter opportunity to make a direct request to the president to be allowed to return to Arizona, but Roosevelt refused, citing fear of more violence. Not long after this encounter, in June 1905, Geronimo appeared for a day at the Miller Brothers' 101 Ranch in northern Oklahoma in a local exhibition that drew 65,000 spectators (and angered Roosevelt). Lucille Mulhall, whom Geronimo had admired in St. Louis as a woman of courage, was among the performers at the Miller ranch.

Geronimo died of pneumonia in February 1909 and was buried at Cache Creek, Okla. The surviving Chiricahua remained prisoners of war until 1913, when they were given the choice of remaining in Oklahoma or moving to a reservation in New Mexico. They were not allowed to return to Arizona (Davis, *Truth about Geronimo;* Debo, *Geronimo;* Geronimo, "Reasons for Leaving the Reservation"; MacMechen, "True and Complete Story of the Pike and Its Attractions"; Russell, *Wild West: A History of the Wild West Shows,* 73; *EFB,* 547–49; *GNAI,* 93–95; *WWWNAH,* 131–33).

18. Chief Joseph (ca. 1840–1904), a member of the Wallamwatkin band of the Nez Perce, was born in the Wallowa Valley in Oregon, the son of Chief Joseph (d. 1871, known as Old Joseph). With the Gold Rush of 1861 and white encroachment into eastern Oregon, the government took steps to consolidate the Nez Perce peoples into a 1,000-square-mile reservation in western Idaho. Old Joseph refused to comply with the settlement, and his band became part of the Nontreaty Nez Perce. After his death his sons Joseph and Ollikut led the band and practiced a policy of passive resistance to relocation as the white settler population continued to grow. The Nez Perce war, actually a series of eighteen battles, took place in Oregon and on into Idaho, Wyoming, and Montana, as Chief Joseph and other chiefs sought to lead their people into Canada to seek refuge with Sitting Bull and the Sioux. Chief Joseph surrendered after a final battle some thirty miles from the Canadian border and was taken as a prisoner of war to Bismarck, N.Dak., on to Fort Leavenworth, Kans., and finally on to Indian Territory. In 1884 he was relocated to the Colville Reservation at Nespelem, Wash. He met with President William McKinley in 1897 and with President Roosevelt in 1903 (*EFB,* 745–46; *GNAI,* 128–30; *WWWNAH,* 174).

19. Geronimo went to the Fair as part of the Fort Sill contingent of Apaches. During the Fair he lived in the Apache village exhibit near the Indian Building. While Will Rogers demonstrated roping tricks on the Pike for strolling tourists when he was not appearing in the organized shows, Geronimo had a booth in the Indian Building where he sat and made bows and arrows, which he offered for sale along with autographed photographs of himself. In his memoirs he reported that he left the Fair with more money then he had ever had in his life, and with an expanded knowledge of white people. The propaganda mills of the Exposition, meanwhile, presented Geronimo's presence in the Indian Village as evidence of a "mental transformation from savage to citizen" (Francis, *Universal Exposition of 1904,* 1:529; Barrett, *Geronimo's Story of His Life,* 197–206).

20. Chief Joseph's famous speech on the fate of the Nez Perce in 1879 (reprinted for white audiences in the *North American Review*) may elucidate some of the values that would lead him and the other Indian leaders to participate in the Fair many years later. The speech articulated his desire for equal liberties for Native Americans and also for conciliation between whites and Indians: "Let me be a free man—free to travel, free to stop, free to work, free to trade where I choose, free to choose my own teachers, free to follow the religion of my fathers, free to think and talk and act for myself. . . . Whenever the white man treats the Indian as they treat each other, then we will

have no more wars. We shall all be alike" (Chief Joseph, "Fate of the Nez Perces Tribe," 251). As Geronimo observed in his memoirs, people of a variety of ethnicities from other countries were treated as ethnographic exhibits at the Fair, much as were the different Indian peoples of the United States. At the same time that assimilation and the destruction of Indian ways of life were presented as progress in the Indian School section of the exhibits, other Fair activities, including traditional dances and the exhibition of Indian crafts, dress, living quarters, and songs, represented forms of cultural retention, self-assertion, and pride as well as commodification for white consumption. The appearances also afforded prisoners of war and their families—otherwise restricted in movement—freedom to travel and to reunite temporarily with people from their past from whom federal policy had made them estranged. Personal aggrandizement was another motive, and many of the Indians proved skilled at turning the commercialism of the expositions to their financial advantage. Events such as the St. Louis World's Fair also had potential political weight. They were forums for swaying white public opinion and in which there might be opportunity to encounter influential whites and use the occasions to lobby for a return to native homelands.

21. See Will Rogers to Clement Vann Rogers, 19 June 1904, below.

22. John J. Murdock (1865–1948) started his career managing the Masonic Temple Roof in Chicago. He became a leading executive in the Western Vaudeville Managers' Association and later assumed a prominent position with the B. F. Keith circuit (*EV*, 361–62; Laurie, *Vaudeville*, 348–53).

23. The McCormacks and the Rogerses later became friends. John McCormack (1884–1945) was at the beginning of his sterling career when he sang at the Irish Village at the St. Louis World's Fair. He had won the gold medal in a tenor competition at a music festival in Dublin in 1903, when he was not yet nineteen years old. His wife, Lily McCormack, was also a singer, who at age seventeen won a prize in the same 1903 competition that launched John McCormack's career. They both sang at the Irish Village at the Louisiana Purchase Exposition; like the Rogerses, the McCormacks dated at the Fair, and this marked the true beginning of their courtship leading to marriage. The friendship with Will Rogers blossomed when John McCormack made his one feature-length film, *Song of My Heart*, in 1929. He and Lily McCormack lived in Brentwood and used a cottage at Fox Studios during the filming. At the same time Rogers was also on the lot making another movie, and he often came by the McCormacks' cottage to socialize. Rogers later commented in one of his weekly columns that what made McCormack great was that "with all his God given voice he has never allowed himself to get High-Brow, and Artistic with the selection of his songs. A song don't get so common that John won't sing it" (*TDW*, 24 October 1926, reprinted in Smallwood and Gragert, eds., *Coolidge Years*, 257). McCormack's most popular number at the St. Louis World's Fair was "My Beautiful Irish Maid" (Brown and Knuth, *Tenor and the Vehicle*; Ledbetter, *Great Irish Tenor*; Lily McCormack, *I Hear You Calling Me*, 2–13, 152–53; StLGD, 14 August and 11 September 1904; Worth and Cartwright, *John McCormack*).

To Sisters
19 April 1904
Claremore, I.T.

In this letter Rogers writes to his sisters Sallie McSpadden and Maud Lane, who lived in Chelsea, I.T., to say that he has been visiting friends at local ranches and towns and has been out to the farm, part of the old Rogers ranch near Oologah.[1] He has received word from Colonel Zack Mulhall that the way is clear for him to go to work as a cowboy in Wild West show performances at the Louisiana Purchase Exposition. He will soon be off to Missouri with his father's blessing.

Claremore, I.T. Tuesday Night 1904

My Dear Sisters

Will write you to let you hear where I am   have been up to Talala   Mays Halls Ranch   the Farm   Lanes   Lipes[2] and all and will leave for Tahlequah in the a.m.   will only be there a bout two or three nights.   then back and by Chelsea for a day or so   then onto the Fair   I heard from Mulhall and he wants me   they will send old Comanche[3] in a day or so with a shipment that he is bringing from Sapulpa but I wont go for a few days   Papa says it is all right with him and he seems well pleased.   I will close

Love to all
Willie.

ALS, rc. OkClaW. On Lindel Hotel, E. H. Gibbs, Proprietor, letterhead.

1. For information on the history of the Rogers family ranch and Indian Territory and Oklahoma places important to Will Rogers's youth, see *PWR*, volume one.
2. The Lanes, including pioneer physician Andrew J. Lane and his wife Lucinda Journeycake Lane, lived at Oowala, I.T., north of Claremore. Rogers had been friends with the Lanes, including children Tom, Shasta, Scrap, Gordon, and Denny, most of his life. The Lipe family had long been close to Rogers's parents. Clement Vann Rogers was a friend and business partner of DeWitt Clinton Lipe in Tahlequah after the Civil War, and both men began cattle ranches in the Cooweescoowee District, the Lipes settling near Oowala. Like Clement Vann Rogers, who in his later life left the family ranch to live and conduct business in Claremore, D. W. Lipe became a civic leader in Claremore and a member of the Cherokee Nation Senate. Growing up, Will Rogers was a friend and schoolmate of the Lipe children, Nannie, Victoria, and Lola (see *PWR*, 1:104n.2, 497, 501–2, 504).
3. Comanche was Will Rogers's horse, an outstanding steer-roping pony (see *PWR*, 1:152–53, 296n.2).

To Sisters and All
27 April 1904
St. Louis, Mo.

4643 Washington Avenue
St. Louis[1]

Dear Sisters and all

got here all O.K.   it was cold but is warm now   only staying out at Mulhalls house[2]   living fine   till Saturday

Our Show is the biggest one at the fair   600 people   we are in connections with Cummins Indian Congress.   Mulhall only has the Cowboy part of it.   part of it is on the pike and part off of the Fair ground   but it is all the same   you see it all and are put back onto the pike.   Tell Theo[3] I promised to write to him but Mulhall said tonight he would   so tell him I am the only Territory boy here.   There is lots of good Cowboys from Buffalo Bills[4] and other wild west shows here so a man will do good to hold a job   I will write you soon.

Write soon.
Willie.

ALS, rc. OkClaW. On Cummins' Wild West Congress of North American Indians World's Fair letterhead.

1. An archival notation by Rogers's niece, Paula M. Love, who was for many years the curator of the Will Rogers Memorial, indicates that the date of this letter was 27 April 1904 (OkClaW; see also memorandum by Paula M. Love, "St. Louis World's Fair Letters," n.d., OkClaW).

2. Zack Mulhall maintained two residences, one at his ranch in Mulhall, O.T., and one in St. Louis, the city where he was raised. While his wife Mary Agnes Locke Mulhall stayed in Mulhall and maintained the ranch, he was on the road a good deal for his jobs as a railroad livestock agent and Wild West show promoter. His mistress, Georgia Smith Casey (who went by the name of Mulhall and was publicly presented in the Mulhall family show-business ventures as one of Zack Mulhall's daughters), lived at the residence at 4643 Washington Avenue in St. Louis and traveled with the Mulhalls on the Wild West show tours. For a good deal of his time at the Fair, Rogers lived at the Mulhall home in St. Louis (interview with Martha Fisch, Guthrie, Okla., January 1994, WRPP).

3. A reference to Theodore (Theo) Raymond McSpadden, the nephew of Will Rogers's sister, Sallie Rogers McSpadden, and a good friend of Will's since his youth (see Biographical Appendix entry, McSpadden, Theodore Raymond [Theo]). Theo, like Rogers, had ridden since he was a small child and was a veteran of the roping contest circuit. Rogers recommended him to Zack Mulhall as a good cowboy, and Mulhall agreed to hire him. Theo joined the cowboy contingent of the Cummins' Wild West Congress at the Fair at the end of May 1904. He stayed at the Mulhall home with Rogers and was Rogers's regular companion in St. Louis (*CR*, 20 May 1904; *HRC*, 300; see also *PWR*, 1:393n.5).

4. Buffalo Bill (William F. Cody, 1846—1917) was the promoter of the most successful Wild West show to emerge in the United States. Begun in 1884, the show attracted thousands of spectators in repeated tours of the United States and Europe. Annie Oakley and Sitting Bull were among its cast in 1885, and the show sold out at Madison Square Garden in 1886-87. It reached its height of popularity at the Columbian Exposition in Chicago in 1893, where Will Rogers saw the show with his father, and continued in performance into the early 1900s. The Buffalo Bill show later toured Europe at the same time that Rogers was working in vaudeville theaters abroad, and Rogers appeared at the show at Madison Square Garden in 1910.

St. Louis World's Fair organizers touted Zack Mulhall's cowboys as representatives of the "Real Wild West . . . an aggregation of real, genuine cowboys and Indians" in advance literature promoting the upcoming Fair. In an article graced by an illustration of an uncharacteristically demure Lucille Mulhall in genteel dress, the promoters claimed that "Col. Mulhall out-'Bills' and out 'Buffaloes' the famous Buffalo Bill show, inasmuch as it is not composed of professional show people; but, on the contrary, represents the best of the class of Western cowboy and ranchmen pursuing their daily vocations" (*WFB* 4, no. 7 [May 1903]: 1). The legitimacy of being an active ranchman lent prestige to Zack Mulhall in his role as the head of the cowboy contingent, and the Fair organizers' desire for real working cowboys apparently operated in Theo McSpadden's favor when it came time for Zack Mulhall to hire for the Fair.

To Clement Vann Rogers
27 April 1904
St. Louis, Mo.

June 27, 1904[1]

Dear Papa

I arrived here all O.K.   havent done anything yet only laying around until the Saturday   Our Show is in connection with the Cummins Indians   there is 4 or 5 hundred of them and quite a lot of Cowboys.   Mulhall is the head of the Cowboy outfit but its all the same show.   it is the biggest one at the Fair as there is 6 or 7 hundred people   We are just outside the grounds but the opening is in on the pike so you see it is just the same thing as being on the Pike   you go in off the pike then you are put back on the pike.   I dont know how I will like it but will work till I see it all.

I will write you again soon.   Pony is doing fine.   I wont trade you that horse of mine but you keep him on.   Love to all,

Willie.

(dont publish this)

ALS, rc. OkClaW. On Cummins' Wild West Congress of North American Indians letterhead.

1. Although Rogers wrote "June" he meant April. The envelope in which this letter was sent was postmarked St. Louis, 28 April 1904.

Looking down the Pike, St. Louis World's Fair, 1904. *(Collection 344, Box 6, Department of Special Collections, Charles E. Young Research Library, UCLA)*

Excerpt from Cummins Indian Congress Program
ca. April 1904
St. Louis, Mo.

Frederick Cummins built on his personal friendships with Native American leaders to assemble a remarkable group of notable Indian people to appear with the Cummins' Spectacular Indian Congress and Life on the Plains show at the St. Louis World's Fair and its related exhibits.[1] This illustrated program, the cover of which spelled out the "historical, aboriginal, ethnological" and "industrial" motives behind the Cummins show and exhibition, depicted or named many of the individuals who participated as arena performers and captured in summary the flavor of the show's acts.[2]

Program.

1. RECEPTION BY THE FAMOUS INDIAN CHIEFS OF 51 DIFFERENT TRIBES, Including:

CHIEF JOSEPH,	CHIEF GERONIMO,
" WOLF ROBE,	" RED SHIRT,
" CALICO	" TWO STRIKES,
" RED THUNDER	" LAST HORSE,
" HARD HEART,	" EAGLE HORSE,
" ROCKY BEAR,	" BLACK HEART,
" LONE WOLF,	" RED STAR,
" SEVEN RABITS,	" LONE STAR,
" BLACK HORSE,	" AFRAID OF BEAR,
" FLAT IRON,	" JACK RED CLOUD,
" BLACK BIRD,	" AMERICAN HORSE,
" CHIEF LONG BULL,	" NO NECK,
" PAINTED HORSE,	" WM. SITTING BULL
" HENRY STANDING BEAR,	" HOLLOW HORN BEAR,

With Braves, Squaws and Papooses, in the Red Men's Village—the first and only Aboriginal Home Encampment of the kind ever pitched in a Metropolis.

2. GRAND ENTRY—750 INDIANS, INCLUDING BUCKS, SQUAWS AND PAPOOSES. ABORIGINAL SAVAGE AMERICAN EQUESTRIAN REVIEW.

Ma[r]tially introducing the historically famous and most redoubtable War Chiefs and representative Braves of Fifty-one congregated Indian Tribes, arrayed in all the picturesque and fearsome panoply pomp and paint of savage foray, chanting their strange battle ballads and executing thrillingly wild and expert equestrian evolutions.

3. INTRODUCTION—
Indians, Cowboys, Miss Bossie Mulhall and Band of Lady Riders

4. INTRODUCTION—
COL. MULHALL

5. INTRODUCTION—
Miss Lucille Mulhall

6. INTRODUCTION—
Col. Cummins.

7. MAZE.

8. MISS NELLIE SMITH—
Champion Rifle Shot of the World.

9. "NEBRASKA BILL" and "BOUNDING FAWN"—
Impalement Act.

10. PONY EXPRESS—

11. RACE OF NATIONS, INDIAN LADY and COWBOY.

12. RIDING WILD CATTLE.

13. NEBRASKA BILL—
In Feats of Horsemanship.

14. JIM HOPKINS and BAND OF FANCY ROPERS IN FEATS NEVER BEFORE SEEN IN ANY ARENA.

In this act will be introduced Miss Lucile Mulhall, Champion Lady Rider and Roper of the World. . . .

PD. Scrapbook A-1, OkClaW.

1. Over 850 people, including Will Rogers and other members of the cowboy contingent, were hired in conjunction with the Cummins show (MacMechen, "True and Complete Story of the Pike and Its Attractions," 17).

2. Several of the Indian leaders who appeared together at the St. Louis World's Fair were part of a multi-generational network of friends and rivals who shared family ties and had in common many significant episodes in their pasts.

Jack Red Cloud was the son of the famed Red Cloud (ca. 1822–1909), principal chief of the Oglala Sioux and leader of the Battle of the Bozeman Trail of 1866–68 (also known as Red Cloud's War). Jack Red Cloud had fought at the Battle of Little Big Horn in 1876. His people, congregated at the Red Cloud Indian Agency, became part of what was eventually called the Pine Ridge Reservation. The elder Red Cloud, a respected statesman in the eyes of whites but the subject of considerable opposition among his own people, abdicated his leadership of the Oglalas to Jack Red Cloud in July 1903. Jack Red Cloud was a veteran of Buffalo Bill's Wild West show, as were Cummins participants Red Shirt and American Horse.

The genealogy of American Horse the Younger (1840–1908) is unclear. He may have been the son of Sitting Bull or Sitting Bear; he may also have been married to Jack Red Cloud's sister and/or may have been the nephew of the elder American Horse (ca. 1801–76), a leader of the Sioux wars of the 1860s and 1870s, who was himself a cousin of Red Cloud and a participant in the Battles of Bozeman Trail and Little Big Horn. The elder American Horse was part of Red Cloud's delegation to Washington, D.C., in 1870. American Horse the Younger, also an Oglala Sioux, fought with Crazy Horse in the Battle of the Bozeman Trail. He negotiated with General George Crook in the 1888–89 treaty in which the Sioux ceded large tracts of land in Dakota Territory to whites, and he earned a reputation among whites for his "oratorical elegance" (*WWWNAH*, 4). The Cummins publicity echoed this, stating that American Horse was the "Greatest Indian orator" (Hill, *Great White Indian Chief*, 8). He was a conciliator during the Ghost Dance Uprising of 1890 (during which the ailing Sitting Bull, who a few years before had been touring with the Buffalo Bill Wild West show, was shot and killed by federal gunmen), and in the following year he headed a delegation to Washington, D.C., to protest the violent events of Wounded Knee, which were the outgrowth of the repression of the revival of ghost dance ceremonies. American Horse toured with Buffalo Bill's Wild West and with Cummins's North American Indians shows. He participated in delegations to the nation's capital and made a pictorial history of the Oglalas. He sent his son Samuel to Carlisle Indian School. He died at the Pine Ridge Reservation in South Dakota.

Like American Horse, Hollow-Horn Bear (1850–1913), another performer in Cummins's Indian Congress, was a veteran of the Battle of the Bozeman Trail. A Brulé Sioux, he was the son of Iron Shell. He was born in Nebraska and as a teenager began fighting in raids against invading white settlers and miners in Montana, Wyoming, and the Dakotas. Like the others who participated in the show, he became a conciliator who was singled out as a negotiator by whites. He became a captain in the Indian police on the Rosebud Indian Reservation and met with General George Crook during the Ghost Dance Uprising of 1890. Like the others, he was noted as a "skilled orator" (*WWWNAH*, 155). Hollow-Horn Bear, Geronimo, and American Horse all rode in Theodore Roosevelt's March 1905 inaugural parade a few months after completing their stints at the St. Louis World's Fair. Frederick Cummins's biographer described Hollow-Horn Bear as "one of the handsomest men in his race. His profile . . . reminds one of Alexander the Great, so strong and chaste is its outline . . . a good type of the intellectual and progressive man" (Hill, *Great White Indian Chief*, 10). Chief Joseph was similarly described as "A Red Napoleon" (ibid., 12).

Calico (also known as Black Shield) was a judge of the Indian Court at the Pine Ridge Reservation. Two Strikes (Nomcapa, or He Who Strikes Two; ca. 1821–1914) was a Brulé compatriot of Spotted Tail and was part of Spotted Tail's 1872 delegation to Washington, D.C. Spotted Tail and Hollow-Horn Bear's father, Iron Shell, were political rivals. Hollow-Horn Bear was part of the opposition to Spotted Tail's leadership and was close to Crow Dog, who eventually murdered Spotted Tail. Red Shirt was the son of Red Dog. He appeared in the combined Young Buffalo Wild West and Colonel Fred Cummins Far East show in 1912–13, as did Chief Good Face, Painted Horse, and Flat Iron.

By some accounts Sioux Indians sometimes played the parts of other Indian peoples in the Cummins show, differentiating between supposed groups by riding different-colored horses (Debo, *Geronimo*, 419; *EFB*, 22, 1196–97; *GNAI*, 11–13; Hyde, *Red Cloud's Folk*; Hyde, *Spotted Tail's Folk*, 33, 39, 62, 63, 69, 101, 120n.2, 173, 197, 316–21, 332; Red Cloud, "Speech at Cooper Union, New York" and "Reasons for the Trouble between the Indians and the Government"; Russell, *Wild West: A History of the Wild West Shows*, 69; *WWWNAH*, 4, 293–95).

To Clement Van Rogers
2 May 1904
St. Louis, Mo.

St. Louis, Mo.
On the Pike
April 2   04[1]

Dear Papa.

I got your letter a few days ago but as we have started to work now I havent so much time.   We commenced to show last Saturday   we are only showing in the day time yet for our lights are not very good up yet but will be in a few days.   It is raining here every day and our grounds are a sight   I dont see any people from down there   I guess they havent started to come yet

Things are finishing up pretty fast but it will be a good month before they are all finished.

When are you coming up   let me know before you come but I guess you will come with Maud and Sallie

I know you get as much news from the papers about the fair as I could write.   you wouldent know old Comanche   he is slick and fat   I look after him myself.

I will sell you the *bay horse* and Buggy for $350.00 *cash*   I kinder want to buy me a horse or two up here   now if you want him this is your chance for he is cheap at that   I give $300.00 for him when he was a colt.

Say did you know that old *Comanche* had a knot on his leg just where a bone Spavin[2] comes   I dont know how long it has been there   it was there when he come up here   it may not be a bone Spavin   he hasent gone lame and if it was a spavin it would lame him   if it does turn out to be I will ship him home and turn him out on the farm for good for I wouldent sell him and I wouldent have him hurt by cutting it off.   but I dont think it amounts to anything.

Well I will close   write soon and say if you want that horse   Lots of love to all

your loving son
Willie.

ALS, rc. OkClaW.

1. May 1904.
2. A spavin is a bony enlargement of the hock of a horse, caused by strain.

To Clement Vann Rogers
19 June 1904
St. Louis, Mo.

Real-life drama struck the St. Louis show grounds on 18 June 1904, when an angry Colonel Zack Mulhall opened fire on one of his assistants and accidentally wounded innocent bystanders.[1] After the dust settled and the wounded men were hospitalized, a long legal battle ensued that would not be resolved until 1907.[2]

Sunday Morn.

Dear Papa,

I got your letter yesterday and was certainly sorry to hear about the granary burning down but it was lucky that the house did not go too.   Did you have any insurance.

Well I guess you will read in the paper about the big shooting scrape we had at our show.

Mulhall and the boss stable man got into the scrape and after the night show last night they met out at the front when all the people were coming out and got to shooting.   A Town boy that was standing near was Shot in the stomach and it is doubtful if he will get well   Johny Murray[3] from San Angelo Texas a cowboy was trying to stop them and he was shot through the side but he will get well and Reed the fellow Mulhall was shooting at was grazed twice. Mulhall done most of the shooting and if he had only hit the fellow and killed him it would have been all right.   The other fellow was no good.[4]   I think the show will go on just the same   Cummins is the whitest man I ever saw and will keep all of us on just the same.   I dont know how Mulhall will come out of it   he is still in jail   he was afful good to us boys   They can all say what they please about Mulhall but he has done more for us boys than any man on earth   last night we were even paid up in full all that they owed us. I got my expenses up there and all   we will get our pay every week.   The show will go on tomorrow just the same   none of the cowboys were mixed up in it   only the one that tried to stop it

I got the boots all O.K.   they were tight but if I cant wear them I will sell them to one of the boys and have him make me another pair   I dont think he made them to the measure I sent him   they are too little in the instep

All right I will sell you the horse[5]   I dont want all the money now   I will write to you in a day or so   I only want part of it when my saddle comes and you can keep the rest there with my other money   take out what those boots cost out of my money.   By the way how much does that leave beside the money for the horse.   I drew $50.00 when I come up here and $12.00 for boots   how much did I have there when I come home.

I will write to you in a day or so

Lots of love to all
Willie.

ALS, rc. OkClaW. On Greetings from World's Fair letterhead.

1. The altercation was between Frank Reed (b. 1854), who was the "boss hostler of the Wild West Show," and Zack Mulhall. Reed had formerly worked at the Hagan Opera House (Imperial Theater) and lived in St. Louis at Eleventh and Market Streets.

According to newspaper coverage of the shooting, Mulhall shot Reed "at the entrance of the show just at the conclusion of a performance while the Pike was crowded with people and great excitement was caused." Lucille and Charlie Mulhall had been walking alongside their father when the confrontation began, and many others from the Wild West show were crowded around the two arguing men. Will Rogers's acquaintance Johnny Murray "tried to stop Mulhall from shooting Reed and was shot" in the chest (*ME,* 24 June 1904). The bullet exited from his body below his arm on the left side. More shots were fired as the men struggled, and one of the stray bullets hit bystander Ernest Morgan (the "town boy" Rogers refers to in his letter) in the abdomen, perforating his bowels and lodging in one of his hips. Morgan was an eighteen-year-old who lived on Sheridan Avenue in St. Louis. He was wounded so badly that he was initially not expected to survive. Reed was grazed by bullets in the arm and the neck. Five cowboys from the show, including George Elser, were detained as witnesses to the fight; Will Rogers was not among them (*IC,* 18 June 1904; *ME,* 24 June 1904; *StLGD,* 19 June and 20 June 1904; *StLPD,* 19 June 1904).

2. Johnny Murray recovered from his wounds. Morgan was critically injured, and after a long convalescence was left permanently disabled.

Zack Mulhall left the scene of the shooting. He was apprehended by authorities at the opening to the Indian Village after he had cut through one of the concessions on the Pike. He was taken to the Emergency Hospital on the fairgrounds, where the wounded Murray and Reed identified him as the man who had shot them. He was then taken into custody and jailed, with a weeping Lucille Mulhall barred from entering the police station. Some 200 friends appeared the next day to visit Mulhall in his cell. Because of his very close association with the family, Rogers may have been among them. Others tried to win permission to post bail for him, but they were rebuffed pending news about the physical condition of the men who had been shot. On 20 June 1904 Mulhall's friend Ed Butler was allowed to post the $20,000 bond. From jail, Mulhall released a statement expressing his sorrow that an innocent boy had been hurt. He also gave an account of the incident, which he consistently repeated throughout the legal proceedings in the case. He implied that as Reed and he struggled, some members of the crowd had begun shooting at him, and that it could have been one of their bullets that wounded Morgan. He also said the situation with Reed had been one of self-defense, and that Reed—who had no weapon at the end of the incident—had been disarmed by George A. Fay, proprietor of the shooting gallery of the Wild West show and a friend of Mulhall's, before the authorities arrived at the scene. Reed refused to swear out a warrant against Mulhall, and Johnny Murray "disappeared" from the Fair hospital after receiving treatment (*StLPD,* 23 June 1904). Murray returned to the rodeo circuit a few months later and told a Texas friend that there had been a "hush up" after the shooting in St. Louis (letter of Bert Smith, Oceano, Calif., 4 July 1959, HCP-MoU).

A preliminary hearing was set in the Mulhall case for 29 July 1904, and on that date was continued until 25 August "to allow Morgan time to be able to recover enough to appear in court" (*ME,* 29 July 1904). In early August, when Morgan's condition had stabilized, Mulhall was formally charged with two motions of intent to kill in the attacks on Morgan and Reed. Morgan was not released from hospital care until the end of September 1904. The case came to full jury trial in January 1905, and Mulhall was found guilty. He was sentenced to three years in prison. Mulhall's attorney, Thomas J. Rowe, maintained that the jury was prejudiced against his client because they were from Texas (and thus were swayed by the rivalry between Oklahomans and Texans, aggravated by the fact that one of the victims was a Texan). Mulhall continued to claim that the bullet that hit Morgan had not come from his gun, and that he did not know Morgan had been hurt until he saw the critically wounded man when he was taken by authorities to the Emergency Hospital the night of the incident. Morgan testified that he was sure it was Mulhall who had shot him and that no other shots were fired than those from Mulhall's gun. After the criminal conviction, he filed civil charges against Mulhall claiming permanent injury. He won his civil case in December 1905 and was awarded $5,000 in damages. Meanwhile, Mulhall was denied appeal on the criminal conviction by the Circuit Court judge, sentenced again to three years, and again released on bond pending appeal to the Missouri Supreme Court. The case came to a close when he was acquitted on grounds of self-defense in 1907 (*CP,* 28 January 1905; *ME,* 29 July and 12 August 1904, 27 January, 3 February, 26 May, 22 September, and 29 September 1905; Koch, "Zack Mulhall," 41—42; *StLGD,* 20 June and 28 September 1904; *StLPD,* 20 June, 21 June, and 23 June 1904; see also *PWR,* 1:518–21).

3. Johnny Murray (b. ca. 1869) was raised in San Saba County in Texas on the Suggs ranch. He was an outstanding competitor on the roping contest circuit and earned a world championship title in steer roping. Unfortunately, he became involved in gambling on rodeo events and as a result became indebted to the Black Jack Ketchum gang of outlaws. He was eventually shot and killed by his brother-in-law in a dispute over funds. Murray had used his rodeo winnings to set up the brother-in-law in ranching. When he desperately needed money to pay back debts, he discovered that the steers from the ranch had been sold without his knowledge, and his brother-in-law was not able to show any evidence of profits from the transaction (letter of Bert Smith, Oceano, Calif., 4 July 1959, HCP-MoU; Hanes, *Bill Pickett,* 142, 149).

4. The seemingly matter-of-fact way that Rogers could evaluate the incident speaks to how often altercations of the time were settled with gunfire. Frank Reed had already been involved in at least two shooting incidents, in one of which a bullet meant for him struck and killed a woman with whom he had been living. The man who fired the shot was acquitted in the death when he testified that the bullet was meant for Reed rather than for Reed's girlfriend (*StLGD,* 20 June 1904; *StLPD,* 20 June 1904).

5. Both the boots and the horse had been a topic of discussion in previous correspondence between Rogers and his father. Rogers had asked his father to buy his horse because he needed the money and wanted to get a new saddle horse and saddle. Clement Vann Rogers seems to have responded immediately to his son's need for cash, as the next week Will wrote again and thanked him for the check (see Will Rogers to Clement Vann Rogers, 11 June, 28 June, and 2 July 1904, OkClaW).

To Clement Vann Rogers
24 June 1904
St. Louis, Mo.

Within a week after the shooting incident of 18 June 1904, Zack Mulhall was banned from the Pike and fairgrounds by Fair officials. Despite his pending prosecution, he soon regrouped and began offering his own show, Colonel Mulhall's Congress of Rough Riders and Ropers, at the Delmar Race Track outside the Fair boundaries. Will Rogers had appeared with the Mulhalls in a similar show at the same racetrack arena in 1899. Rogers soon was participating with his old friends in Sunday and Combined show performances at the old racetrack arena.

On the Pike
June 24. 04.

Dear Papa.

I will write you again to tell you the news   I just got a letter from Sallie saying Tom Lane was married[1]   tell me all about it

Well some of us boys that were working for Mulhall are not with the Cummins Show now   the show still goes on but Mulhall is out of it.[2]   I could of staid with them but they found out I was for Mulhall and so some of us left.[3] Hopkins and Me are working for another smaller Wild West on the Pike and are doing just the same.[4]   It cut a big hole in the show when Mulhalls crowd left he had all the best horses and furnished most of the show

address me in care of,

Old St. Louis Arena
on the Pike.

I dont know how he will come out   he says he wants to start a show of his own and if he does he will want me.[5]   I got all even with the show   everything they owed me.   I will write to you for some of that money in a few days when my saddle comes and I may get one of the Mulhall horses now.   Love to all   write often

Willie.

ALS, rc. OkClaW.

1. Will Rogers's childhood friend Tom Lane, who had been his roommate at Willie Halsell College in the early 1890s, married Nora Matheson on 1 June 1903. The couple made their home in Foyil, Okla., where Lane was employed as a cashier (*HRC*, 274–75; see also *PWR*, 1:501–2).

2. Almost immediately after the shooting incident of 18 June 1904, Norris Gregg, director of admissions and concessions for the Fair, notified Frederick Cummins that "Mulhall must not appear with the show as given on the Pike under Cummins management" (*ME*, 24 June 1904; see also *NYT*, 19 June 1904; *StLPD*, 22 June 1904; and *StLR*, 22 June 1904). The ban did not affect other members of the Mulhall family, and Lucille and Bossie Mulhall were permitted to continue with the Cummins show as usual; however, like Rogers, they soon left it. By 10 July 1904 they were performing with an alternative show directed by their father outside the fairgrounds.

3. Feelings against Zack Mulhall apparently ran quite strong among performers with the Cummins show, especially the Native Americans. Immediately following the shooting there was a severe factional split between the Indians appearing in the North American Indian Congress portion of the Cummins show and the cowboys who appeared in the contingent that had been managed by Mulhall. The action "taken by the exposition authorities" to ban Mulhall was reportedly "prompted by the fact that an indignation meeting was held by the 750 Indians at the Cummins show, presided over by Chief Geronimo and Chief Blue Horse" (*ME*, 24 June 1904). A few days after

the incident a representative of the Cummins show stated that "all the Mulhall cowboys had left the show on account of threats of the Indians." Doc Waddell, a Cummins spokesman, "said that the cowboys had snapped their revolvers in the faces of the redskins after the shooting, which resulted in a pow wow, followed by ominous signs which boded no good for the ropers, and they decided in order to prevent a conflict, to retire from the grounds" (*StLR*, 22 June 1904).

By the end of September 1904 relations seemed to have improved between Mulhall and Geronimo, because advertisements for the Mulhall Wild West show at the Delmar Race Track announced the appearance of "Chief Geronimo and his tribe of Apache Indians, Indian Dances, and Wild Horse Ride and Roping" as part of the show (*StLGD*, 25 September 1904; *StLPD*, 24 September and 25 September 1904; see also Reviews of Colonel Mulhall's Congress of Rough Riders and Ropers, ca. September 1904, below). Mulhall routinely invited acts from the other shows to appear as special guests, including Rogers and Jim Hopkins, who did double duty with the Mulhall and Charles Tompkins shows.

4. After leaving the Cummins show, Rogers and Hopkins worked for the Congress of Champion Ropers and Riders directed by Charles Tompkins. Tompkins later recalled running into Rogers and Hopkins by accident on a streetcar in St. Louis: "He and Hopkins were booked to be with the Mulhall Shows at The Fair, but on account of some trouble with the Fair Association, the Mulhall Shows did not last very long. So both Hopkins and Rogers joined my Show, which was inside the grounds. . . . I was very glad to have these two fine cowboys in my shows" (Tompkins, "My Association with Will Rogers," 10). The two roomed above the horse stalls during their stint with the Tompkins show, and Tompkins remembered that Rogers was constantly out in the empty arena at the off hours at the fairgrounds, practicing his rope tricks and developing new ones. "No one taught Will anything," he observed. "He got it the hard way by hard work" (ibid.).

Jim Hopkins, a Texan, had known Rogers from youthful days when they had worked together at the Rogers ranch and other ranches in Indian Territory, and at the Mulhall spread in Oklahoma Territory. They had also appeared together in roping contests, sometimes with Hopkins riding Rogers's horse. Hopkins had a long career in Wild West shows, and he and Rogers were lifelong friends. Hopkins later worked for Rogers, handling his polo ponies, when the Rogerses lived on Long Island and in California. As Charles Tompkins later put it, "Bill after he became great and famous took care of Hop" (Tompkins to Homer Croy, 16 October 1953, HCP-MoU; see also *PWR*, 1:494–95).

Charles Tompkins was an acquaintance from roping contest days who became a family friend after employing Rogers in 1904. When the two men first met in San Antonio in 1901, they found that they both knew Jim Hopkins, as well as Clay McGonigle and other Texan friends of Rogers who competed on the roping contest circuit. While Will Rogers was in Argentina in early 1902, Jim Hopkins worked for Tompkins supplying American-bred horses for use by the British in the South African War. Tompkins later ran one of the most respected small frontier shows in the business, Tompkins's Real Wild West.

Tompkins's 1904 show, Tompkins's Congress of Championship Ropers and Riders, was one of a handful that appeared in St. Louis during the Exposition. Unlike the others, it operated within the fairgrounds. Jim Gabriel also presented a Wild West show during the Fair. The Gabriel Brothers' Wild West show appeared at the Delmar Gardens, with continuing performances in July 1904. As was true for the other shows, there was considerable overlap between the personnel of Gabriel's show—which specialized in performers from the Cummins show who had previously appeared with Buffalo Bill's Wild West—and those of other Wild West productions (memorandum by Paula M. Love, "St. Louis World's Fair Letters," n.d., OkClaW; *StLPD*, 23 July 1904; see also Biographical Appendix entry, TOMPKINS, Charles and Mabel Hackney).

5. By 10 July 1904 Zack Mulhall was presenting a regular Congress of Rough Riders and Ropers show at the Delmar Race Track in competition with Cummins's show and the other Wild West entertainments going on in St. Louis. The Mulhall show continued on through the autumn, and the Mulhall performers often appeared in consolidated performances with riders from other shows and in fundraising benefits, including, somewhat surprisingly—or shrewdly, given Mulhall's legal difficulties— a Police Benefit on 13 November 1904 (St. Louis World's Fair newspaper ads file, 1903, 1904, WBaraC; *StLGD*, 9 July, 23 July, 30 July, and 13 November 1904; *StLPD*, 9 July, 30 July, and 13 November 1904; *StLR*, 10 July and 24 July 1904).

<h1 style="text-align:center">From Len Pedro
25 June 1904
Perth, Western Australia, Australia</h1>

Len Pedro was a circus performer who became Will Rogers's friend while Rogers was appearing with the Wirth Brothers' Circus in Australia and New Zealand in 1903–4.[1] Here he writes to Rogers to let him know how things are going with the people he knew in Australia, and to ask how Rogers has fared with the St. Louis World's Fair.

> Perth, *June 25th*—1904.
> Sunday.
> Perth Western Aus

Dear Kid,

Just a few lines to let you know that I have not forgotten you at all, I missed you very much when you left the show, & I think every body did, Johny [*last name illegible*] received your letter safely, & told us all the news about you, I suppose w this you will [be] working at the St. Louis Exhibition, & I'm surely hope [hoping] you will have success in everything you undertake, have you won any contests When you write let me know all the news available, & how things are with you, I hear that the St. Louis is not quite such a success as it ought to be, anyhow I am kicking myself for signing on with the show again, for I would have liked to have gone over with you, never mind. I will see you sooner or later I hope, all the boys send their hundred regards & remembrances to you as I & brother also do. We are doing a good aerial act now, Vic sits on the frame & Ernie stands upright on his shoulders, & turns a complete forward somersault into my hands & I dont mind telling you, it pulls the stuffing out of me, May does one & a half & I kick her a row of somersaults on my feet & then across to Victor, I fix my risley cradle up on my end of the frame, it looks fine,   Wirths are starring the act here, after the Howards (who by the way are a bit of a failure over here).   They play that old song of yours for the rings, "Creole Belle" it always brings a recollection up [of] you every time I hear it.   I hope you are all right & your people, & what do you think "Joe["], Duchie & C are back with the show, & doing acrobats, they are very quiet nobody has anything to do with them, we never let them gamble with us at all, too many arguments.   I would like to have seen that throwing act, which you saw in Frisco.   We have had our frame made over a foot longer, & we have put in a lot of practice since you went, every thing is our own now.   We finished our season here last night.   It has been raining ever since we have been here, & have done only medium business, we have two Hindu wrestlers with the show,   I will send you a programme of the show, which I want you to send to Sammy Bernard, if you ever get this address & drop him a line also, if you have time. I enclose my address, I will be on the look out for a reply shortly, by the way nobody has been practicing the crinoline, Sam's has forgotten all about it.   We play Fremantle three nights next week & then up to fields to Kulgoorlie & Coolgardie,[2] living (Hotels etc.) is very dear over here.   We play Adelaide a return season after we have done the West, we have several new animals added to the Zoo,   Is America any good for us?   Kid, you know what we can do, I have seen some of the shows & ought to have an Idea.   You might say when you write,   Now I think that I have told you all the news.   Pagel has finished up with us long ago, & is about in Germany eating Sauer Kraut by this time I suppose.   We have a man, who does a wonderful jumping act, he jumps out of a basket of eggs, without breaking any etc. & also over a hansom cab.   We played at Adelaide before coming here & Tasmania after N.Z.   We will be in Melbourne for [*word illegible*] Time I hear.   We have a new freak a live pony with long horns instead of hoofs on his feet.   "Bobs" that big [*word illegible*] we had died recently in Tasmania of consumption, he wasted away to a nere bag of bones,   Now I will say Au Revoir for the present, & hoping that you will get this letter safely,   I still have that card with your address on it, pasted in my scrap-book.   My brother & I send our kindred regards to you & wish you every success,   Dear old boy dont forget to drop us a line, as I am anxious to hear from you & how you are getting along.   So Good-bye & good-luck.

I remain your best Pal
Len Pedro

c/o Sydney [*word illegible*] Officer
Sydney
U.S.U. Australia

P.S. Did you meet Jack O'Donnell at St. Louis, he went over

ALS, rc. OkClaW.

1. On this period of Will Rogers's life, see part six, "Australia and New Zealand," in *PWR*, volume one. See also Biographical Appendix entry for George and Philip Wirth in *PWR*, 1:567–69.

2. Kalgoorlie is a municipality in south-central Western Australia, some 340 miles from Perth. It is a principal gold-mining center, situated in conjunction with the East Coolgardie Goldfield and mines that began operating in 1893. The town of Coolgardie is located 22 miles southwest of Kalgoorlie. Gold was discovered there in 1892 (*CLGW*, 445, 898).

To Sisters
1 July 1904
St. Louis, Mo.

Saturday
on the Pike

My Dear Sisters

I got Mauds letter yesterday   was sho glad to hear from her   but say Sis you spoke of a Hdkf [handkerchief]   I sent you.   You are mistaken   I dident send you any thing   it was some one else   if I did I was asleep   I havent seen any thing worth sending   it was some of your numerous friends.

Well I see the Girls from home   old Scrap dont get to have much fun she has to stay all the time with Ida and they dont come around very often but Rosan Harnage and Anna Sevier are the fast set   I see them often.   they were all in the show the other night and I had them Ride in the Stage Coach when the Indians held it up.   they seemed to of had a time   Jess B—was in last night   I see lots of people here now that is from home[1]

When are you coming up   you better hurry for I may go home in a month or so   but when you all come bring Papa and I will show you around.[2]

I am back with the Cummins Show now Mulhalls are not doing anything yet

The 4th will be a big day here   I guess we will show all day. Business is picking up now   more people are coming and it is all open now.

I hope Mays Baby is better by now[3]

Well I will stop   write soon   Love to all

Willie.

Indian Congress
On the Pike.

ALS, rc. OkClaW.

1. Rogers's cousin and Claremore schoolteacher Gazelle (Scrap) Lane was one of a group of good friends of Rogers from the Oologah-Claremore area, along with Ida Collins, Rosanna Harnage, and Anna Sevier. They were part of the social group that he spent his summers with as a teenager and young man. Jesse Bushyhead, a Claremore physician and close friend of the family, was also one of Rogers's cousins (see *PWR*, 1:485–86). The local Claremore paper reported that Ida Collins and Gazelle Lane went to the World's Fair with other Indian Territory teachers as part of an International Indian Teachers Association outing to St. Louis. The group gathered at Vinita on 23 June 1904 and returned to the area on 10 July 1904, having had a "fine time" (*CP,* 25 June and 16 July 1904).

2. Rogers wrote a similar letter to Clement Vann Rogers the next day and repeated his desire that his father come to visit. Rogers thanked him for the check and reported in connection with their recent financial transaction that "I may sell my Pony when I get ready to leave but I need him now" (Will Rogers to Clement Vann Rogers, 2 July 1904, OkClaW). In another letter mistakenly dated two days later but actually written a month later (on 4 August rather than on 4 July), he said he had not cashed the check his father had sent because he had decided not to keep the saddle he had ordered and was not sure he would be staying on in St. Louis much longer, and thus didn't think he needed all the money at the time ("I may need some of this money but not much as I think I will be there before long") (Will Rogers to Clement Vann Rogers, 4 July [misdated letter; actually 4 August] 1904, OkClaW).

3. In his 2 July 1904 letter to his father Rogers added, "I hope Mays baby is better by now for I certainly feel sorry for her   she works so hard" (Will Rogers to Clement Vann Rogers, 2 July 1904, OkClaW). Rogers's sister May and her second husband Frank Stine had two sons and three daughters. Two of the daughters died while still babies in the period ca. 1904–5. It is unclear which of the children was ill when Will Rogers was working in St. Louis. Mattie Lane Stine, known as Lanie, was about sixteen months old at the time. By different accounts, Gazelle (Zella) Mae Stine was born either in the spring or winter of 1904, and died in late 1904 or, according to the local newspaper, in mid-July 1905. The Stines also lost another baby girl, Vera, whose birth and death dates have not been documented. Both girls were buried at the Oak Hill Cemetery, as was Willie Yocum, May's son by her first marriage, who died not long after his second birthday in 1897. The local paper reported the illness of May's baby in the summer of 1904 but spoke only of the "infant child of Frank Stine and wife" and did not refer to the baby by name. The infant became ill at the end of May 1904 but seemed temporarily to be getting better. At the end of June Dr. Jesse Bushyhead was called to Oologah in the night to see to the child, and Will Rogers's sisters Sallie and Maud also went to Oologah to help out. The baby was still acutely ill at the beginning of July (*CP,* 4 June, 25 June, 2 July 1904; see also *WRFT,* 28; Will Rogers to Sister and Family, 26 July 1905, below).

To Clement Vann Rogers
22 July 1904
St. Louis, Mo.

Despite the seeming excitement of working in a Wild West show, by midsummer Rogers was expressing boredom and loneliness in his letters home. He repeatedly asked his relatives when they would be visiting and made statements that he had experienced what he wanted of the Fair and was planning to return soon to Indian Territory. In a letter to his sisters written the same day as this one to his father, he wrote, "I am living at Mulhalls and working for him.   Theo and I was only show on Sunday afternoons and have nothing to do during the week.   I fear I shall get lazy.   We show to big crowds every Sunday.   But as I only came here to see the fair and I have seen it I am about ready to go home and honest I will be there when Theo comes to start to school in a week or so."[1]

St. Louis. Mo.
July 22. 04.

My Dear Papa

I got your letter a day or so ago   glad to hear you was feeling better.

I may turn up at home any week now   I am with Mulhall and only show of a Sunday afternoon   I am staying at his home   McSpadden and I   How is your horse and what is the matter with him.

Oh but it is hot up here now . . .[2]

I dont see as many Territory folks up here as I did a while back.

I got that check you sent but as my Saddle has not come I have not had it cashed yet.

When are you and the Girls coming up.

Is there anything down there to do or that I could get into   I have seen the fair.

Well I will close

My Pony is looking fine

Love to all
Willie.

ALS, rc. OkClaW.

1. Theo McSpadden returned to Chelsea on 8 August 1904 after working at the St. Louis World's Fair for three months. Rogers's sisters Maud and Sallie and their husbands visited the Fair for a week at the beginning of August. Rogers acted as their tour guide. Tom and Sallie McSpadden returned home sooner than they had planned when their daughter May complained about problems she was having managing the household in their absence, but Maud and Cap Lane stayed through the week and

enjoyed the festivities (Will Rogers to Clement Vann Rogers, 4 July [4 August] 1904, OkClaW; *CR*, 5 August and 12 August 1904).

2. Rogers wrote his return address at the Mulhalls' at the top of the second page of his letter.

From Butler, Jacobs, and Lowry
24 July 1904
St. Louis, Mo.

As Rogers tired of the Wild West show scene, which left a lot of time with not much to do in mid-week when there were no performances, he tried his hand with a roping act in vaudeville. This letter of recommendation speaks to his debut performance on stage at the Standard Theater in St. Louis, which was part of the Empire Circuit.[1] Rogers appeared there as part of a burlesque show, doing a roping act with his cousin and fellow Wild West performer, Theodore McSpadden. The appearance at the Standard drew the attention of Colonel John D. Hopkins,[2] who recommended the act to John J. Murdock, owner of several vaudeville theaters, and this led to Rogers being offered an engagement at the Chicago Opera House Theatre in Chicago.[3]

St. Louis, *JULY. 24th. 1904.*

To Whom It May Concern.

I take great pleasure in recommending Mr. Will Rogers in his Specialty.   I played him at the Standard Theatre, and he proved a decided novelty.   He will make good on any bill and can follow any 'head liner.'

Butler, Jacobs & Lowry

TLS, rc. OkClaW. On The Empire Circuit Company, Standard Theatre, St. Louis, letterhead.

1. The Empire Circuit operated theaters in Baltimore, Birmingham, Buffalo, Cleveland, Cincinnati, Chicago, Detroit, Indianapolis, Kansas City, Louisville, Memphis, Milwaukee, Minneapolis, New Orleans, Pittsburgh, Philadelphia, St. Louis, St. Paul, Toledo, and Washington, D.C. The letterhead listed James J. Butler as president, Hubert Heuck as vice-president, James E. Fennessy as secretary, and John H. Whallen as treasurer. The directors were Edward Butler, James J. Butler, W. T. Campbell, James E. Fennessy, Hubert Heuck, James Kernan, George W. Rile, John Whallen, and Harry Williams.

2. John D. Hopkins (1846[?]–1909), a prominent theater owner, operated theaters in several cities, including the Hopkins Theatre in St. Louis (formerly the Grand Opera House), and other establishments in Chicago, Louisville, Memphis, and Providence. He also owned what was known in the trade as a combination roadshow (a traveling variety show, made up of various acts drawn from his theater venues), called the Hopkins Trans-Oceanic Company (*NYC*, 4 September 1897, 7 May 1898, 14 February 1914; *NYDM*, 27 July and 17 August 1895, 15 February and 6 June 1896, 11 September 1897; *Variety*, 6 October 1906, 30 October 1909).

3. Operated by George Castle and Charles Kohl, the Chicago Opera House was considered to be at the pinnacle of vaudeville venues (Laurie, *Vaudeville*, 348–49; Rogers, *Will Rogers*, 84–85).

To Clement Vann Rogers
1 September 1904
St. Louis, Mo.

St Louis   Mo
Sept   1st. 04

My Dear Papa

I got heare yesterday   I went by Tahlequah from Chelsea as they did not show here last Sunday   I was only in Tahlequah one night and left the next went on by Ark and strait on to here[1]   Went out and seen Aunt Martha[2] Christian is doing all right.

I dident know I could go by Tahlequah or I would of tended to that business for you but I dont think I would of had time anyway   well we are not going to K.C. at all but I guess we will show here   as soon as I get a chance to send my pony home I will be there for good.

I may be back in a week

Well goodbye   love to all

your son
Willie.

ALS, rc. OkClaW.

1. The *Claremore Progress* reported that Rogers was home visiting his friends in Oologah on 17 August 1904 and that he spent the rest of the week with his father in Claremore. He then went on to Chelsea to see his sisters Sallie and Maud and their families (*CP*, 20 August 1904; *CR*, 26 August 1904).
2. Martha Lucretia Schrimsher Gulager (1845–post-1907) was the youngest sister of Will Rogers's mother, Mary America Schrimsher Rogers. She married F. W. Gulager in January 1869 and lived in Eureka, I.T., where Will Rogers's mother was born and raised (*WRFT*, 112, 120).

Reviews of Colonel Mulhall's Congress of
Rough Riders and Ropers
ca. 11 September 1904
St. Louis, Mo.

Georgia Mulhall kept a careful scrapbook filled with clippings from the Mulhall family performances at St. Louis and Madison Square Garden in 1904 and 1905. Here are two clippings from the 1904 Delmar Race Track shows given on Sundays after Zack Mulhall was banned from the St. Louis World's Fair grounds. Several of the clippings mention Will Rogers, as well as his old friends from roping contests, Jim Hopkins and Johnny Murray. In addition to his cowboy performers, Mulhall also sometimes drew in other acts, which were appearing on the Pike or in the Indian Village and other parts of the Fair, for special performances and benefits. These included Geronimo, Hackenbeck's Elephants, and actors from the re-creation of the battles of the Boer War.[1]

BIG ROPING CONTEST
COLONEL MULHALL TO FURNISH SUNDAY ENTERTAINMENT

An international roping contest will take place when Colonel Mulhall's Rough Riders and Ropers give their usual Sunday afternoon exhibition at Delmar Race Track. American cowboys of Mulhall's troupe will compete with Indian riders, Patagonian plainsmen of South America, and Mexican vaqueros.

There will be a fight for supremacy in steer roping, and the competition will be sharp. Among the contestants will be Lucille Mulhall, the most famous horsewoman, Will Rogers of Oklahoma, Frank and Joe Murray of Colorado, and old Geronimo, the Apache chief, who though eighty-seven years old is yet a famous rider and expert with the lariat.

This contest of different nations is a new feature of the Mulhall show and will be entertaining, as well as of historic value.

ROPING CHAMPIONSHIP
CONTEST FOR WORLD SUPREMACY AT MULHALL'S SHOW SUNDAY

Out at Delmar Race Track Sunday afternoon at Colonel Zack Mulhall's Congress of Rough Riders and Ropers the big event of the afternoon will be the inauguration of the World's Fair championship roping contest at which event over a hundred expert plainsmen representing several nations will participate. The roping of wild Texas steers while dashing over the plains at breakneck speeds is one of the most thrilling sights ever witnessed, and to date has proven one of the main features of Mulhall's exhibition. Cowboys from Texas, Oklahoma, Indian Territory, Colorado, New Mexico, and several western states have entered. Chief among them are: Will Rogers, winner of three championship tournaments in Texas; the Murray brothers, noted rough riders and expert rope throwers; Chief Geronimo, the king of Indians and leader of the Apaches for many years, who is at present the prisoner of Uncle Sam and attending the fair in charge of two U.S. soldiers. Geronimo, though eighty-seven years old, can ride and rope with the youngest buck.

Lucille Mulhall, an expert rider and roper, was one of America's first acclaimed professional cowgirls. She achieved fame in roping contests and Wild West circles, and later as a vaudeville performer with her own western act. *(Mulhall Family Collection, Martha Fisch, Guthrie, Okla.)*

Colonel Mulhall announces that he has arranged one of the best and most interesting programs of the season. Miss Mulhall will appear with her champion saddle and trick horse, Governor, sending this beautiful animal through some of the most difficult feats ever witnessed. Will Rogers will give one of the thrilling exhibitions of dare devil rough riding and will also give his famous fancy lariat juggling act. There will be rides for life, quadrilles, dance on horseback just as the boys and gals do down Texas way.

The manner in which the western plainsmen handle horse and cattle thieves will also be vividly portrayed.

The performance will begin promptly at 3 o'clock.

PD. Clippings from Mulhall Scrapbook, MFC.

1. For Rogers, who had been in South Africa just after the end of the South African (Boer) War and had become acquainted with real British and Afrikaner soldiers, the latter act (especially in conjunction with cowboy and Indian performances in which cowboys demonstrated skills previously used to practical purpose on the range and Indians displayed traditional dances of spiritual importance) must have seemed like a somewhat odd situation of art imitating life (see *PWR*, volume one). A benefit given at the Delmar Race Track on 13 November 1904 featured Mulhall's cowboys along with Hackenbeck's Elephants, the "Entire Boer War," and several other acts ("Police Benefit, Delmar Race Track," advertisement, Mulhall scrapbook, MFC). On other occasions there were "combination performances of the Boer War and Mulhall shows" in which Zack Mulhall arranged for squads from the Boer War act to demonstrate various cavalry maneuvers, including lance exercises and various races ("British Lancers from Boer War will Join with Mulhall's Men Today," clipping, Mulhall scrapbook, MFC; *StLGD*, 7 August 1904; *StLPD*, 6 August 1904). When Theodore Roosevelt, Jr., and Kermit Roosevelt attended the Fair, Colonel Mulhall arranged a special exhibition for their enjoyment, including Lucille Mulhall roping a steer, Boer War actors doing a drill, and "Filipinos under the management of Dr. Hunt" appearing from the Philippines village. "Dr. McGee, who is in charge of the Indian exhibit at the World's Fair, has consented to allow two hundred of his charges to appear in the arena and give exhibitions of riding and dancing" ("President's Son to Attend Performance This Afternoon," clipping, Mullhall scrapbook, MFC; see also *StLGD*, 18 September, 25 September, and 13 November 1904; *StLPD*, 13 November 1904).

Scrapbook Clipping
ca. 19 September 1904
St. Louis, Mo.

WILL RODGERS BROKE WORLD'S RECORD IN ROPING A STEER
Miss Lucille Mulhall Roped a Texas Long-Horn in
Forty Seconds at Delmar Race Track Sunday Afternoon.

The record of roping a steer was broken at the performance of Col. Mulhall's Congress of Rough Riders and Ropers of the World at the Delmar Race track yesterday afternoon. Will Rodgers of Indian Territory roped a brute in thirty seconds, lowering the world's record by a quarter of a second.

John Murray of Oklahoma tied the record, and Miss Lucille Mulhall, the talented daughter of Col. Zach Mulhall, roped the animal she chased in forty seconds. The day was ideal for fast work with the lariat. The wind was calm and the infield was in great condition.

The crowd of 20,000 persons cheered wildly when it was announced by Announcer Frank Frost that Rodgers had broken the record. The steer that was selected for Rodgers was a fine one. Both rider and animal got away from the pen with a running start. Rodgers was on the animal at once and quickly had the lariat around his neck and the steer down on the ground and fled.

Miss Mulhall would have probably beaten the time she made yeterday afternoon. In the second trial her Lariat broke and she was unable to tie the animal.[1]

The show given yesterday afternoon was made more agreeable by the plainness of Announcer Frank Frost. Frost is the man who made Pawnee Bill's show famous by his announcing. He is a former newspaper man and has circled the globe three or four times in the interest of Pawnee Bill and other showmen of the West.

PD. Unidentified news clipping. Scrapbook A-1, OkClaW.

1. Not long after this event, "three trainloads of Texans and Oklahomans" arrived at the Fair at Zack Mulhall's invitation. Members, like Mulhall, of the Elks Club, the "western visitors" knew Mulhall by reputation. Lucille Mulhall was billed as the "big attraction" for the Elks show, but Will Rogers was presented as the "champion roper of the world" because "at last Sunday's performance Rogers roped a steer in thirty seconds." Filipinos and Native Americans from the village exhibits in the Fair also appeared in the show for the Elks ("Texans, Oklahomans, Coming to Mulhall's: They Will Visit the Congress of Rough Riders," clipping, Mulhall scrapbook, MFC). Indian Territory Day at the Fair, during which many visitors from the Cherokee Nation traveled to St. Louis, occurred 1 October 1904 (*CR*, 29 July 1904).

To Betty Blake
ca. 25 September 1904
St. Louis, Mo.

Betty Blake first met Will Rogers in 1899 when she went to visit her sister, whose husband was the station agent for the Missouri Pacific Railway in Oologah, I. T., the depot nearest the Rogers ranch and farm. She became a part of his circle of close hometown friends. A few occasional meetings followed that happy period of her stay in Indian Territory—the two met at a roping contest in Springfield, Mo., and at a street fair at Fort Smith in Betty's home state of Arkansas—but Betty Blake and Will Rogers did not communicate during his years of travel. They did not see each other again until she came to St. Louis with her sisters in 1904 to see the World's Fair. Touring the Oklahoma Territory exhibition hall, Blake by chance overheard a young Cherokee woman who was visiting from Indian Territory say that she had seen Will Rogers perform in the Cummins Wild West show off the Pike. Blake immediately sent Rogers a note. This is his reply.

4643 Washington Av.
St Louis. Mo.

Miss Betty Blake
3435 Vista Ave.
St. Louis. Mo.

Dear old Pal

I sho was glad to hear from you.   and it is only a *Rumor* that I dont want to see [you] right now.

Come to Delmar Track this eve if you can for it is all the combined shows of the fair in one   I am working there   send for me when you get to the front and I will come out and take you in   if you cant[,] come meet me in front of the other wild west show at Delmar *Garden* at 8 oclock tonight

I just got your letter 5 minutes ago   this is about 12:30 oclock *Sunday*

Come this eve *sho* and we will have a time tonight[1]

your Cowboy friend.

Will Rogers

ALS, rc. OkClaW.

1. It is not known exactly when Betty Blake visited the Fair. It is possible that this note was written, and Rogers and Betty Blake's date took place, on Sunday, 25 September 1904. Blake's hometown newspaper, the *Rogers Democrat,* reported on 28 September 1904 that Betty, her sister Zuleki, and her mother Amelia Blake "have been recent Fair visitors." Indeed, thousands of visitors from Arkansas crowded the Fair the week of 22 September, which was Arkansas Day, with open house in the Arkansas

Building, a big parade celebrating Arkansas, and a speech by the governor ("Arkansas Plans to Celebrate at Fair," *StLGD*, 22 September 1904). Their date occurred also just before Rogers departed for a trip home. Rogers went home to Claremore for approximately the last two weeks in August, and again in October, placing their date in either mid-August or late September/early October. He refers in this note to "all the combined shows of the fair in one." The main consolidated show of the Fair took place on Sunday, 2 October 1904; however, there were many combinations of the various Wild West and circus acts performing at different times throughout the exposition, so this could refer to an earlier combined show. The dating of this note and the encounter between Rogers and Blake becomes more complicated when the issue of John McCormack is considered. In her memoirs Betty Rogers recalled hearing John McCormack sing at the Fair the night she and Rogers went out together; however, McCormack's wife, Lily McCormack, recalled in her own memoirs that McCormack left the Fair to return to Ireland on 8 July 1904 (McCormack, *I Hear You Calling Me*, 10). The important fact is that during the Fair, Rogers and Blake renewed their acquaintance—the beginning of a sporadic courtship that would eventually lead to marriage.

Rogers tried to put on his best performance for Betty Blake, who attended the Wild West show with her sisters Zuleki Blake and Virginia Quisenberry. During his roping act Rogers wore a special scarlet velvet suit with gold braid that had been handmade for him during his time with the Wirth Brothers' Circus in Australia and New Zealand. Blake found the garish costume embarrassing, and her companions teased her about it during the performance. Rogers also made her wait after the show was over, finally appearing "breathless and apologetic" after the rest of the audience and performers had departed, explaining that he had been "chasing the manager all over the grounds, trying to get his back salary" (Rogers, *Will Rogers*, 83; see also 20, 21, 82). This confusion aside, Betty Blake and Will Rogers had a good time that evening. He took her to dinner, and they toured the Midway, enjoying its carnival atmosphere.

To Betty Blake
ca. 26 September 1904
St. Louis, Mo.

Rogers had told Betty Blake the night of their date that she had caught him on his last day of working as a cowboy with the Wild West acts in St. Louis, and that he was leaving in the morning for Indian Territory. Apparently the two had made plans to get together again before his departure, but he either needed or decided to cancel those arrangements, leaving Blake feeling somewhat jilted and surprised.[1]

Dear Betty

Say do you know that it is going to be impossible for me to be with you this morning but it cant be helped and I am certainly *some* of the sorry.

but the old man told me this a.m.   he had my pass home for me and I will have to go[2]   I think at 2:30 today   also my horse   I think I will get away today also   I do hate so much to dissapoint you and I would of enjoyed it immensly myself or I never would of asked you to go.

Betty Blake (1879–1944) *(lower right)* with three of her sisters, aboard a locomotive at the Frisco railroad station, Jenny Lind, Ark., where she worked as a billing clerk, 1904. *(OkClaW)*

But say will you drop me a line to Claremore in the next few days and tell me where your address is please for I want to write to you *see*

I am sorry I wont get to see you but will have to go out for my pony

My best to all the folks

yours

Will.

ALS, rc. OkClaW.

1. Rogers, *Will Rogers,* 83.

2. Rogers later explained that he had no choice but to make an abrupt departure the morning he and Betty Blake had planned to get together because his father had wired him to come home on some business (see Will Rogers to Betty Blake, 26 October 1904, OkClaW). It is possible that he fudged the timing of his trip home as an excuse to Betty Blake, perhaps because at the time of the Fair he had been seeing Lucille Mulhall. Not meeting Blake on Monday might have helped him avert some ire from the Mulhall quarter.

Program from Will Rogers's Scrapbook
2 October 1904
St. Louis, Mo.

CONSOLIDATED SHOWS OF THE WORLD'S FAIR

DELMAR RACE TRACK

SUNDAY, OCT. 2, 1904.

PROGRAMME

UNDER DIRECTION OF

MR. FRANK E. FILLIS,[1]

MANAGING DIRECTOR OF THE "BOER WAR."

Introduction by the Lecturer, Captain Peter J. Visser (Boer War Exhibit). Opening Concert by the Philippine Constabulary Band of 85 pieces, under direction of LIEUTENANT LOVING.

Grand parade of participants.

Item 1—Entertainment by representatives of Mysterious Asia, comprising acrobatic feats, jugglery, etc. Silori Stick Dancers, etc.

Item 2—Entertainment by representatives of Fair Japan, specialties by six Jiu Jtsi tumblers and jugglers. Richards, hoop manipulator and juggler.

Item 3—Entertainment by representatives of the Chinese Village, wrestling contests by six Chinese; grand introduction of the world-famous Chinese Dragon, 129 feet long. Fifteen Chinese musicians.

Item 4—Spear throwing contest by the Igorrotes, in charge of Governor Hunt, introducing Chief Antonio and the most talked of people in the world. Bow and arrow contests by the Negritos, famous representatives of the Philippine natives. Highly entertaining dances by the Visayans (the elite of Philippine society), led by Visayan Orchestra and Chorus.[2]

Item 5—Sun dances by the Moki Indians and Cliff Dwellers. Snake dance by the same quaint people.

Item 6—Sham battle between the Indians from Col. Cummins' Wild West, Blackfeet and allies versus Sioux and their allies.

Item 7—Grand drill by the world-famous Marion Zouaves. Fancy Bag Punching, Miss Belle Gordon.

Item 8—Naval drill by sailors from the Naval Exhibit. Naval Band under the direction of Professor H. Lempke.

Item 9—Exhibition of High school and trick riding by Miss Lucille Mulhall on her famous horse, Colonel. Roping and tying three wild steers by Miss Mulhall in record time. These steers were never roped or tied before. Rogers, fancy rope twirler. Broncho riding by Jackson brothers, of Montana; Charles Mulhall, of Mulhall, Oklahoma; Jack Joyce, of Colorado. George Elser,[3] fancy trick rider.

Item 10—Scenes of exciting races—

(1) Camel race driven by native drivers.
(2) Ostrich versus horse. The trained ostrich is ridden by Mr. Frank Wiggins of the Ostrich Farm on the Pike.
(3) Elephant races, ridden by native Mahouts.
(4) Sled and dog race, driven by Esquimaux from the Esquimaux Village.
(5) Horse race between Boers and Britons for the championship of the Boer War Camp. Pony race for championship of the Boer War Camp.

Item 11—Entertainment from Hagenbeck's,[4] including trained elephant act and zebu race—concluding with January and Joey, the highly amusing mule and clown act.

Item 12—Fire drill and hose coupling contest, by Hale's Fire Fighters. Comedy Bicycle act by Rube Shields.

Item 13—Five-mile automobile race, gentlemen drivers, 12 H. P. St. Louis Cars, for silver cup presented by Mernod & Jaccard.

Item 14—Entertainment by Boers and British from the Boer War Camp, concluding with the famous battle of Colenso.

Item 15—Grand Display of Fireworks by "Pain." (A guarantee of success.)

EDITOR'S NOTE—The public will appreciate the fact that in a general program of this nature it is almost impossible to carry same through in its entirety without some slight alterations. For these we crave pardon, but assure the public that the announcements are well taken care of in the hands of Captain Visser.

SPECIAL NOTE.

During the afternoon a newsboys' race, in which 2,000 newsboys will participate, will be given under the auspices of the St. Louis Star, which has also donated the prizes.

PD. Scrapbook A-1, OkClaW.

1. Frank Fillis (1858–1921) was a prominent showman in England and the British colonies, and a former animal trainer for the Barnum and Bailey Circus. He came from a famous circus family and followed in the footsteps of his uncle, James Fillis, who developed a unique and highly admired technique for breaking and training horses. Like Will Rogers, Fillis had previous experience with circuses in South Africa, Australia, and the United States. He was known for hiring the "best circus acts from England" for his shows (*Billboard,* 25 February 1922). A circus historian has described him as the "greatest showman South Africa has ever seen" (Birkby, *Pagel Story,* 91).

Fillis began his career as a jockey and horse trainer. He went to work for Bell's Circus in South Africa in 1880, and when the circus's owner died a few years later, he purchased the show, renamed it Fillis's Circus, and ran it in permanent buildings in Kimberley, Cape Town, and Johannesburg, South Africa. The circus also toured overland by wagon and rail, playing mining camps and towns. Fillis specialized in spectacular tableaux, including large numbers of circus animals. He worked with the Barnum and Bailey Circus in a high-school horse act and also as a trainer, and he was a performer in and proprietor of Fillis's Circus until his death. By different accounts, he was born either in London, England, or in Australia.

In 1899 Fillis brought a show called "Savage South Africa" to England. The precursor to his St. Louis World's Fair show, it was a "spectacular entertainment," including "five hundred Zulus, ten families of Boers, four hundred Basuto ponies, eighty buck, lions, tigers, and elephants" (Birkby, *Pagel Story,* 93). The show ran in England for six months. In response to the war in South Africa, Fillis hired hundreds of ex-soldiers and refashioned the show as a re-creation of the battles of the South African War. Fillis lost his investment and profits when the huge show went on tour in the provinces. He returned to South Africa, and in 1904 he traveled to St. Louis, where he directed the Boer War exhibition at the 1904 Exposition.

The show, starring generals Cronje and Viljoen reproducing famous battles, played three times daily at 1:00, 3:30, and 7:30 P.M. in a special station not far from the Ferris wheel and east of the livestock and agricultural buildings. Admission cost 50 cents for grandstand seats and a dollar for box seats. The show was a success at the

Fair (grossing over $535,000), but it went bankrupt when Fillis tried to tour with it after the Fair's end. He remained in the United States in 1905 and worked at the Brighton Beach, N.Y., Arena. In the latter years of his life, Fillis's Circus performed in residence in Johannesburg and Cape Town, South Africa, and toured in South Africa, Australia, South America, the Netherlands, Japan, China, and India. Fillis was described as "a splendid man" who "was known all over the Cape country, Australia, and up through the Straits settlement" (*Billboard*, 25 February 1922). Fillis died in Bangkok on 18 or 21 November 1921. His widow (d. 1947) (whose first name is not mentioned in news accounts, but who later remarried and became Mrs. Clarke), carried on Fillis's Circus after his death, including tours from Bangkok to Saigon. She had previously managed the circus in residence in South Africa when Fillis was on tour abroad, and after Fillis's death she opened a resort on the Rand frequented by people in vaudeville theater and the circus professions.

There was an overlap in performers between Texas Jack's Wild West Show, in which Rogers participated in 1902, and Fillis's Circus acts in South Africa. For example, Raymond Staines, who was an animal trainer with Texas Jack's show when Rogers was doing his lariat act with that show in South Africa, later worked with the Fillis show (miscellaneous clippings, WBaraC; *Billboard*, 30 March 1912, 28 January 1922, 18 February 1922; Birkby, *Pagel Story*, 91—96; Parkinson, "Horse King of the World," 18; *Rand-McNally Economizer*, 189; StLGD, 19 June, 8 September, 26 September, and 2 December 1904; StLR, 26 September 1904; WFB [March 1904], 39). A photograph of Frank Fillis and his trained horse appears in Bennitt et al., eds., *History of the Louisiana Purchase Exposition*, 711.

2. All the villages of the Philippines exhibition included a combination of music and demonstration of daily life and ceremonial rituals. The regular program for the Negritos village, for example, included the celebration of mock marriages and of memorials for deceased relatives, a public meeting for the election of village leaders, singing and dancing, bow-and-arrow hunting, rice planting, weaving, the making of combs and bracelets, and various food preparation tasks (Francis, *Universal Exposition of 1904*, 572; see also "Visayan Girls Discuss Conditions in America," StLGD, 25 July 1904).

3. George Elser came from San Antonio. He was a trick rider who, like many performers, began as a professional cowboy, working on cattle drives and as a ranch hand in his youth before becoming an entertainer. Over a long career he worked with several different circuses, carnivals, and Wild West shows, including Pawnee Bill's Wild West and the Buffalo Bill Wild West show in the 1890s and the Cummins Indian Congress and Rough Riders show in 1904. He had previously appeared with Lucille and Charley Mulhall and Jim Hopkins, doing fancy trick roping and riding, at the fairgrounds in St. Louis, Oklahoma City, and other venues in 1903. He was described as "one of the best broncho riders known in the West" and a "genial, open-hearted and thorough horseman" in Pawnee Bill show literature in 1895 (Pawnee Bill's Historical Wild West program, 1895, WBaraC). He toured Canada with the Miller Brothers' 101 Ranch Real Wild West in 1908, appeared as "Horsehair George" with the Parker Carnival Co. in 1912, and starred with Dickey's Circle-D Ranch Wild West in 1916. He died following surgery in Kansas City, Mo., on 25 January 1954, and was buried in the Heart of America Showmen's Club cemetery (miscellaneous clippings, WBaraC; *Billboard*, 25 July 1908, 13 January 1912, and 6 February 1954; Hanes, *Bill Pickett*, 73).

4. In his Fair presentations, Carl Hagenbeck combined elements of the circus, the side show, and the petting zoo with new ideas about environmental zoological display.

Some of Hagenbeck's trained circus animals appeared as acts in the arena shows at the Fair. Hagenbeck also produced a huge zoological exhibit, called the Hagenbeck Animal Paradise, located on the Pike. Eight hundred animals were on display in scenic areas representing several different ecological zones—savanna, jungle, pine forest and meadow, even an Arctic zone—all designed in panoramic form. Trained animals, including several polar bears and seals, a lion, a tiger, and a zebra, were on display in shows that were run continuously from morning to night in a three-thousand-seat theater on the Pike. Children were allowed to ride giant tortoises, zebras, camels, llamas, and ostriches (*WFB* [April 1904]: 8, 13). In 1910 the Hagenbeck-Wallace Circus collaborated with the Miller Brothers' 101 Ranch Wild West show in creating an amalgam show similar to that mounted at the St. Louis Fair.

To Clement Vann Rogers
19 October 1904
Chicago, Ill.

Rogers went home to Indian Territory for a brief visit after he finished his work with the Consolidated Wild West Show in St. Louis in early October. Local papers reported that he was about to set out to seek work as a vaudeville artist and mentioned that his friends wished him good luck in the endeavor. Meanwhile, his name appeared on the bill of coming attractions for the Chicago Opera House for the week of 17 October 1904. Unfamiliar with the standard procedures of the vaudeville circuit, Rogers failed to send advance publicity material to the theater to back up his engagement, and thus arrived in Chicago to find that his booking had been canceled by the management. He had lost what would have been an excellent opportunity to debut at a truly bigtime theater. He performed at Cleveland's New Theatre in Chicago at the end of the month.[1]

Chicago.
Wednesday

My Dear Papa

I will write you a short letter and let you know that I am doing all O.K.   I dont know yet about using my horse   I am doing all right this way or will after I get started good.   I may go back to St Louis for a week as these people have a theatre there if I do I think I will train my pony and bring him away with me.   He is out about 6 miles in the country from St Louis and doing fine being fed all the time.   I may come home soon but if I dont I will be there Christmas sure

I will write you again soon.

Love to all
Willie

ALS, rc. JLC-OkClaW.

1. Rogers was listed in the bill of coming attractions for the Chicago Opera House ("High-Class Continuous Vaudeville") for the week of 17 October 1904 (scrapbook A-1, OkClaW). The coming attractions included comedians Charles Hawtrey and Carlin and Otto, the Messenger Boy's Trio, and Will "Rodgers" as the tenth act. Newspaper advertisements for the Chicago Opera House for the weeks in the latter part of October do not mention Rogers's name, and Betty Blake Rogers explained that he failed to send in his publicity materials and thus arrived to find he had no engagement (Ketchum, *Will Rogers,* 93; Rogers, *Will Rogers,* 85).

Program, Cleveland's New Theatre
23 October 1904
Chicago, Ill.

Disappointed by the mix-up with the Chicago Opera House, Rogers looked for other venues of employment in Chicago. One afternoon while buying a ticket at Cleveland's New Theatre,[1] he overheard the manager seeking an act and volunteered his own. He started that day and played the theater for a week. Betty Blake Rogers related that Rogers said a trained dog from another act came running onto the stage during his performance at the Cleveland and he roped it, winning a big audience reaction. The experience reinforced his desire to include a horse in his act, and he made plans to go to Oklahoma Territory to train a pony at the Mulhall ranch for use on the stage.

PROGRAM

Week Commencing Oct. 23, 1904.

1   WM. RODGERS
                                              World's Champion Roper.

2   JOE BELMONT
                                                  The Human Bird.

3   UNITA & PAUL
                                              Marvelous Gymnasts.

4   ARTHUR HAHN
                                              The Australian Basso.

10 Minutes Intermission

5   World's Champion Banjoists
             The Charming
           CARMEN SISTERS

6   Second Week of Musical Success
             SCHILZONYI'S
           HUNGARIAN BOYS BAND

7   THE MOLASSOS
           French Whirlwind Dancers.

             7 Minutes Intermission

8   Musical Farce Comedy and Musical Star
             BURT HAVERLY

9   PROF. WOLFINGS BOXING STALLIONS

The Best and Most Beautiful Trained Horses in the World Performed by "Mlle de Montmorency" the Charming French Equestriene—Famous Lady-Trainer in a Splendid Exhibition of Horsewomanship Showing Prof I. S. Wolfing's Handsome and Wonderfully Trained, Imported, Arabian Stallions, Emperors of Waltzing Horses.

P. S. The only lady in the world exhibiting at the same time two stallions during an entire act.

Program SUBJECT TO CHANGE

PD. Program, Cleveland's New Theatre, week of 23 October 1904. Scrapbook A-1, OkClaW.

1. Cleveland's New Theatre, which operated under the motto "Devoted to High Class Vaudeville," was managed by W. S. Cleveland. The theater was located at the southwest corner of Wabash Avenue and Hubbard Court in Chicago.

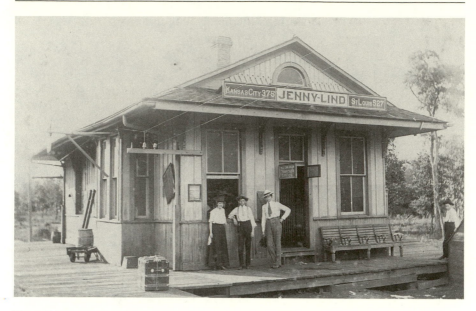

Betty Blake *(far left)* at the Jenny Lind railroad station, 1904. *(OkClaW)*

To Betty Blake
26 October 1904
Chicago, Ill.

Rogers traveled east via Tahlequah, I.T., and on through Arkansas on his way back to St. Louis after his trip home to the Cherokee Nation in August 1904. He apparently had a chance to see Betty Blake for a few minutes en route. She was working at the railway station at Jenny Lind, Ark., and this letter implies that he visited with her briefly while his train stopped at her depot.[1]

Chicago
Wednesday.

My Dear *old* Pal
    Say I just got your little letter that had come up from home after I left   I went back to St. Louis for a day or so then up here   I don't like it much up here   I am doing all O.K.   I dont know how long I will be here   I think I will be back in St. Louis soon at the Columbia as that is one of these people places   I hope so then I will get my horse and take him along and make a big act out of it.

Say Betty I was affuly sorry I could not keep my promise that day ~~but~~ But papa wired me to come on some business and I went that day at 2:30. We would of had some fun that day "and not got *Loaded* either."

Oh but things are on the Bum down home.   I dident do a thing down there this trip only see the folks   I will be there Christmas and I would like to see you some old time there.

But say I am Goatinskying here just as though I knew all about you and had things all fixed.   And I only seen you a minute and then only found out you were not married   That is about all   Lord knows how near it you may be for I know about how you would stand with all those Railroad Gisables and you know according to form we both should have matrimonied long ago   it wouldent do for this young gang to look at our *teeth* you know.

Now what I want to *shake* to you is this: if you are contracted for or have a steady fellow why please put me down and out in the 1st round.   But if not then please file my application.

Out of paper kindly take a back track.

Do you know I havent had a girl since I left on that trip or Kate was my last.   on the tour I had all I could do to live much less sport a damsel and when I come back I felt so out of place and behind the times I was ashamed and they will tell you at home now that I am a girl hater.   Shows what they know about it   I could just love—

a girl about your caliber see   you know I was always kinder headstrong about you anyway   But I always thought that a cowboy dident quite come up to your Ideal   But I am plum Blue up here and kneed consolation and havent a soul that I can confide in.   Now for Good luck, hard luck and no luck at all Experiences I am the limit.

And then I am about froze   is it any warmer down at Jenny Wren than it is here?   If so I am only awaiting transportation.   and at odd times when you are not *Kidding* Conductors, brakemen and such, I will teacheth thou the manly art of Lasso Manipulating   then you are *doomed*

Now I must reluctantly draw this long distance interview to a close Hoping some of these broad minded views of mine (especially the one pretaining to said application) have met with your kind *approbation* I am yours

Any old time
Bill. thats all.

By the way

Subject this penmanship to rigid treatment of *guessing,* then serve

I cant give you an address   But this will reach me   please write soon and a long letter

c/o Pike Hotel
    St. Louis
    Mo.
Pike Entrance

ALS, rc. OkClaW.

1. Will Rogers to Clement Vann Rogers, 1 September 1904, OkClaW.

To Betty Blake
5 November 1904
St. Louis, Mo.

Back to the Pike
Saturday Night

Well Bravo Betty,

I knew you couldent shake an old pal when he was down and out of mail for yours is the only news since I left home and I am deeply grieved to think that I was so unthoughtful as to refer to something that you could in the least get offended at but it was all a joke meaning we both should of married *each other* or somebody by now *sabe*

Say that old Spending a day down home strikes me just fine and dandy and it makes me want to go home all the more for Xmas.

I could of went East from Chicago but dident care to till after Xmas   I made good in C—— and may return to play two other Theatres there   dont know for sure yet about using the horse   But as usual I never know anything one day in advance   I am here for a big combined show to be held inside the Worlds fair grounds one day next week *Range Day*   My Pony is still here   all the Mulhalls people and stock went to oklahoma but I hear will be back to show here a week from Sunday and want me here then.   I will be here for those fairs show but dont think I will for the Mulhall show   I know my letters are of great interest with nothing but work and shows and all that stuff that is of no interest to no one   I am getting homesick and want to go home and stay not for a day or so but a month or two   I am tired of all this Hurrah for awhile

Now write to me soon Kid. (Excuse my familarity) but that is my star expression   I always enjoyed your letters so much for I know you have a head of your own.   Well I know a few more than when I last knew you if my actions dont show it but Betty Honestly how can I change and do different   I havent been a bad fellow and never did anything bad only just foolish and a spendthrift and blew in a little fortune all my own not a cent of my Fathers as people might think only mine   But at that I have done some good   I spent it on other people   I have done lots for other boys there and given my people lots   now I am making my own way and dont feel like staying at home for people would say I was living off my Father who of course is pretty well fixed and would do anything for me   I still own the old home place and farm and am even with the world and am as happy as can be but thats why I dont stay at home

Now Dear I will expect to hear from you soon and a nice long letter   your dearest friend

Will

Best to Sandy[1] and the Folks.

Pike Hotel
Pike Entrance   St. Louis

ALS, rc. OkClaW.

1. Betty Blake's brother, J. R. (Sandy) Blake.

To Betty Blake
20 November 1904
Claremore, I.T.

CLAREMORE, IND. TER., <u>Nov 20th</u> 1904

My Dearest Pal

Well Betty I put off writing to you for a day or so till I knew where I was going   well I am back at home and think I will be here till after Xmas any way I just lobbed in from the Pike today   We had a great show there in the World Fair Live stock Pavalian for the benefit of the visiting cattlemen and oh there was a crowd there   President Francis[1] of the fair and a bunch of officials and he presented me with a First Prize Blue Ribbon of the worlds fair. when I finished my act and I am kinder foolish about my little Ribbon.

Then on sunday they had another one of those combined shows (I guess you have heard of those) at Delmar   well we done our part and the finish was to of been a head on collision   well they set one old enjine at one end and then they tried to run the other into it   well there was a little up hill to start and the old enjine couldent get up and the Cow boys all hooked on and pulled the enjine up the grade and me *four flushing* as usual I roped the head light and jerked it off and run all over the place dragging it and caused the biggest laugh of all "it was a shame to take their money"

You railway people should of seen it   it was a gorgeous Spectacle.

Say how about that Nowata trip   I am here and will show you a time any old time.

My Pony went through here and was not unloaded and went on to Mulhall Oklahoma with their horses   now I will have to go out and ride him back.[2]

There is a big Ball Masque on tap here for Thanksgiving   I dont know if I will attend   cant you come up and I will guarantee you a good time   I will sho go then

Well Kid I was a bit creepy when I wrote you before but then even the gayest of us have our serious spells and then I kinder wanted to tell you anyway for I dont like to "sail under false colors" in any ones estimation and not for the world would I do so with you for you are my style through and through

See here Betty Blake a longer letter from you next time and take care it is not one that I will have to take my overcoat to read for the other was on the chilly order

Write me right away will you please

your
Bill.

Claremore
Ind Ter.

ALS, rc. OkClaW. On C. V. Rogers Bank Building letterhead.

1. David Rowland Francis (1850–1927), a prominent St. Louis merchant and business leader, was a former mayor of the city (1885–89) and governor of Missouri (1889–93). He was appointed secretary of the interior by President Grover Cleveland (and served from 1896 to 1897). He was president of the Madison Ferry Company and the Missouri Historical Society; vice president of the Merchants' National Bank; owner of the Mississippi Life Insurance Co. and the Democratic newspaper, the St. Louis *Republic*; and director of the St. Louis Art Museum.

Francis was elected president of the Louisiana Purchase Exposition Co. after the passage (in March 1901) of the congressional act that added federal funds to the money raised by the city of St. Louis to put on the Fair. Francis was a tireless fundraiser who wooed many national and international exhibitions to the fairgrounds and oversaw the construction boom that preparations for the Fair brought to the city's West End. He gave an account of his trip to Europe to encourage participation by other countries in *A Tour in Nineteen Days* (1903) (see also Francis, *Universal Exposition of 1904*).

After the Fair's end Francis made another bid for political office. He was defeated as a candidate for the U.S. Senate from Missouri in 1910. President Woodrow Wilson nominated him as ambassador to Russia in 1916, and Francis subsequently became the U.S. representative during the Russian Revolution. He supported anti-Bolshevik leaders and spent the rest of his years advocating a strong anticommunist and militaristic foreign policy position. His memoirs of his time in Russia were published as *Russia from the American Embassy* (1921). (See *BDAM*, 123–24; *BDGUS*, 2:855–56; Bennitt et al., eds., *History of the Louisiana Purchase Exposition*, xii; Cockfield, ed., *Dollars and Diplomacy*; De Young, "David Rowland Francis"; Hawes, "David Rowland Francis"; *DAB*, 577–78; *StLGD*, 2 December 1904 and 16 January 1927.)

2. Rogers went to Mulhall, O.T., to retrieve Comanche at the beginning of December. Lucille Mulhall had been caring for the horse (*CP*, 10 December 1904).

To Betty Blake
30 November 1904
Claremore, I.T.

CLAREMORE, IND. TER., <u>Nov 30.</u> 190<u>4</u>

Miss Betsy:

My Dearest friend

Well I sho did get your letter and with all that big envelope Mo. P. paper I thought the Railway was notifying me of a law suit   not that I was expecting one but you never know   Well Thanksgiving is a dead one   and, oh, that Ball it was the kind we used to make long ago   oh there was a lot of the old gang there and on the square I had more good old fun than I have had for some distance

I was masked as a kind of a Simple Simon or a Hobo or something and had them all fooled to death   some got next when I had acted a fool so long and said yes that's Bill for he is acting so natural.   I just turned myself loose and, oh, I sho did enjoy myself.

We will have some kind of a Ball Xmas and New Years and I am plotting very deeply for your presence.

Well kid I am here I guess for the winter as my Father is in very bad health and I am the only one who can stay with him all the time and he dont want me to go east after Xmas   so I am having a time as usual so will remain.

Now you come up here and stay a long time and I will show you a time. My best old Boy Pal lives in Nowata[1] and I will see him when you are up there, *see.*

I know you had some fun at home

I saw some one you know here the other day Joe Reavis from Van Buren He lives here   do you know him

I am keeping up my Rope practice pretty good and I have a nice little rope for you to start in with when you come up so beware

Now look here Betty Blake you had better write me a fine long letter at once or —

Now you come on up here see   I want to see you bad

Your admirer
Bill

Claremore.
I.T.

ALS, rc. OkClaW. On C. V. Rogers Bank Building letterhead.

1. A probable reference to Theo McSpadden, who settled in Nowata.

To Betty Blake
16 December 1904
Claremore, I.T.

CLAREMORE, IND. TER.   <u>Dec 16</u> 1904

My Dearest Friend

Well Betty I just got in here from up to the farm and around last night and found your letter here   of course its only a rumor that I am glad to hear from you for the way you "jolly me along" is mearily kidding me about what a jollier I am   why Lady you have on the dead thieving square got me beat a thousand ways from the centre as a laugh distributer.

Say *podner* that extensive trip you are contemplating Xmas   are you not afraid you will get homesick staying away so long   come and stay a month anyway and we might scare up something but I will try my best and get a birdseye view of you somewhere on the trip but you see I have to spend Xmas with my folks at Chelsea   that is not on this road and I am plotting densly to try and strike a plan.[1]

I am thinking of going to the city in a day or so   either K.C. or St.L.   I dont know which

Now when you write tell me once more just when you will be up here and go back and I sho do want to see you   Well it is train time so   Goodbye

all the time
Bill

ALS, rc. OkClaW. On C. V. Rogers Bank Building letterhead.

1. Rogers spent Christmastime with his father and sisters and their families in Chelsea. The *Claremore Progress* reported that Will Rogers attended a dance in Chelsea the Thursday after Christmas, along with his Claremore-area friends Ida Mae Collins,

Gazelle Lane, Clem Musgrove (who had appeared with him in the Wild West shows in St. Louis) and Ada and Vic Foreman (*CP*, 31 December 1904). There is no evidence that Rogers went out of the Cherokee Nation until early in January 1905, when he went to Oklahoma Territory to visit the Mulhalls (*CM*, 12 January 1905).

Article from the *Claremore Messenger*
10 March 1905
Claremore, I.T.

In the first weeks of 1905 Rogers made several visits to the Mulhalls in Oklahoma Territory and to his sisters in Chelsea and Oologah. In February he was invited to join the members of the Commercial Club of Tulsa[1] on a civic boosterism trip through Indiana and other states. Rogers joined the boosters in Tulsa on 13 March 1905. The train, with Rogers aboard, passed through Chelsea the next day on the first leg of its interstate journey.[2]

Tulsa, I.T. March 6.—(Special.)

TULSA'S SPECIAL BOOM TRAIN.

What to do with 100,000,000 cubic feet of natural gas, hundreds of acres of undeveloped coal field, five railroads and other resources has been a problem for Tulsa to solve.

At a meeting recently held, 100 men volunteered to make an advertising trip through several states in the east and assist in the colonization of this rapidly developing country, and for that purpose, have chartered a special train and in a few days will invade the crowded districts of the United States.

An entire train of sleepers and parlor cars, at an expense of several thousand dollars, has been secured. This train will carry the party through Illinois, Indiana, Ohio, Iowa and Missouri.

A baggage car has been fitted up as a newspaper office, a daily paper will be issued on the train. Each town or city visited will get an edition of the Daily Record, which will be filled with information of the country it represents, besides furnishing information as to the cause of the trip. A brass band of fifty pieces, the crack musical organization of the Southwest, will be with the train; and in a day coach with the seats removed will be an exhibit of the natural resources of the country surrounding Tulsa.

PD. Printed in *CM*, 10 March 1905.

1. Tulsa, which is located on the Arkansas River southwest of the Oologah-Claremore area where Rogers grew up, was settled in the 1830s by the Creek Indians. The modern town was founded in 1882 and officially incorporated in 1898. Already a transportation and commercial center, the city boomed in the early twentieth century because of the oil development of the region, which began in force in July 1903, when the Department of the Interior opened up oil leasing under department supervision.

The Commercial Club of Tulsa was founded in 1902 to take advantage of the financial changes oil was bringing to the area. G. W. Mowbray was the club's first president. The first priority of the club was to convince railroads to build links with Tulsa. Club members raised bonus funds and lobbied landowners to donate right-of-way in order to induce the Katy railroad to construct a branch through their city. They were successful, and the railroad went through in 1903, linking Tulsa with Cleveland. What followed was a "frenzy of townsite promotion," as Commercial Club members promoted real estate sales and more extensive railroad access, and worked to attract oil companies to establish their headquarters in Tulsa (Debo, *Tulsa*, 86). By 1905 Tulsa had four railroads, and about twenty trains passed through the city junctions per day. The city was thus poised to take advantage of the first huge oil strike made in Indian Territory, when on 22 November 1905 wildcat drillers struck the Glenn Pool, an extraordinarily rich small field: "Since the opening of the Glenn Pool, every major oil development in Oklahoma has been operated wholly or partly by Tulsa men and capital" (ibid., 88). Early skyscrapers and large hotels that were planned or begun in 1904 were finished during the boom of 1905. The Frisco railroad added a special train that enabled oil field workers to live in Tulsa and commute to the outskirts for their jobs. Commercial Club members also worked to bring refineries to Tulsa, and by 1906 the club was dominated by oil men. The boom that overtook the city in the first years of the twentieth century is reflected in its growth: the population of Tulsa increased by 425 percent from 1900 to the time of statehood in 1907. Under the combined impact of the allotment of Indian land, the discovery of oil, and the political dissolution of Indian Territory with Oklahoma statehood, the old "Indian regime was swept away" and the "whole country stood open to the white man's enterprise" (ibid., 90). While "fullbloods" (Native Americans who had not intermarried with whites and who maintained and protected traditional cultural practices and world views) decried the commercial transformation of the landscape and mourned the loss of old collective ways, the Rogers family were among the "mixed bloods" (elite families who had intermarried and assimilated to "white" ways, acquiring wealth and elevated class status in the process) who "entered actively into the striving and the achievements of the new competitive order" (ibid., 90).

Clement Vann Rogers's businesses in Claremore benefited from the development of the area, and the Lane and McSpadden families invested in the oil fields outside Chelsea.

2. *CC*, 17 March 1905; *CM*, 17 March 1905; *CP*, 18 March 1905. As part of his entrée into middle-class civic proprieties, Rogers was also initiated into the Masons, as his businessman father had been before him (*CM*, 24 February 1905; *State Herald*, 22 February 1905).

The Tulsa advertising train was sponsored by the Tulsa Commercial Club. The club representatives toured for ten days through Missouri, Iowa, Illinois, and Indiana, visiting various cities and parading up and down the city streets, staying as the guests of other commercial clubs and being greeted by public dignitaries. The press coverage offered several variations on the truth regarding Will Rogers. When the group of one hundred reached Indianapolis, Rogers's name was given in the local account as "Tom

Rogers," but he was described as a champion rope artist who amazed spectators and was "cheered to the echo." In "Tulsa Boosters as Transient Guests" he was hailed as a champion of many roping contests and as "a Cherokee, being wealthy. He owns much land and his cattle number by the thousand head. His father is president of the First National bank at Claremore" (clippings, scrapbook A-1, OkClaW; *CM,* 24 February 1905).

Article from the Marion *News-Tribune*
19 March 1905
Marion, Ind.

This account of Rogers's participation in the Tulsa Manufacturing Association's promotional tour is evidence of the spin that journalists sometimes put on his Indian heritage. Here, as in some other news accounts of the period, he is described as a "chief" because he is an Indian, and his identity is confused with that of W. C. Rogers, the principal chief of the Cherokee Nation, who had the same first and last names but was no relation. Rogers later wrote of the Tulsa Commercial Club trip as a turning point in his growing conviction that he wanted to make a lasting career in entertainment. He recalled doing rope tricks in the lobby of the Claypool hotel in Indianapolis as part of the expedition, and the applause he received "right then and there sort of inclined me to the idea that maybe I could make my living that way." [1]

MARION VISITED BY THE TULSA SPECIAL

The Tulsa special has come and gone. The train, consisting of four cars, arrived over the Big Four from the south at 2 o'clock yesterday afternoon, and was switched on the siding just south of the depot. The party consists of one hundred citizens of Tulsa, and were accompanied by a band of sixteen pieces. Upon their arrival the party made a parade of the city, having as a feature two sons of the west who have risen to affluence in the bounds of the state which they were representing. These two men, both of whom are known as chiefs in their western city, garbed in the dress of the western plainsman gave an exhibition of the skill of the daring riders of the west. Chief Bill Rogers gave an excellent exhibition of rope throwing and juggling in front of the Spencer house that won him the admiration and plaudits of the crowd. The other rider was a full-blooded Creek, and an expert horseman. While the parade was passing down Adams street they halted in front of the News-Tribune office and the band rendered several splendid selections.

During the afternoon many people visited the train and were shown through the exhibit cars. Large photographs of the city, its industries and of the surrounding country were shown and the different members of the party took great pleasure in answering all questions as to their little city. In the baggage car is a small printing plant from which is issued a daily paper, with an edition for each town they visit. Several thousand of these papers were distributed among our people. The entire party was composed largely of Hoosiers, many of whom had not visited their native state for years, and thus this trip is doubly of interest to them.

Between the first and second periods Bill Rodgers, who is with the Tulsa, Indian Territory, delegation, gave an exhibition of rope throwing and juggling with [which] was indeed clever. Rodgers was with the Cummins wild west show at the world's fair at St. Louis, and while stationed there became acquainted with the Marion Zouaves. Rogers is styled the champion rope thrower of the world, and his work last night certainly demonstrated his right to the title.

PD. Printed in Marion *News-Tribune*, 19 March 1905.

1. *Indianapolis News* clipping, scrapbook 1914, CPpR.

From William James Gabriel
21 March 1905
New York, N.Y.

While Rogers was on the train trip promoting the city of Tulsa, William James Gabriel,[1] a prominent Wild West show promoter and performer, wrote to invite him to join his show in New Jersey. Rogers was already committed to appear with the Mulhall Rough Riders Congress at the Madison Square Garden Horse Fair Association show at the end of April.[2] He performed at the Orange Horse Show in New Jersey in May.

NEW YORK, N.Y.   Mar. 21, 1905.

Mr. Will Rogers,
Claremore, I.T.

Dear Sir,—

We will open up our Wild West Show in Newark, N.J., on May 20th. If you are not engaged for this coming season, would like to have you join us.

I am going on to St. Louis the early part of next month to buy horses, and will arrange to ship your pony. If satisfactory to you, you can ship up and meet me there and we will come on to Newark together. Let me know by return post the lowest salary per month.

Trusting this will find you well, I remain

Yours truly,
William James Gabriel

TLS, rc. OkClaW. On Gabriel and Langan's Wild West and Indian Congress letterhead.

1. William James (Jim) Gabriel, a self-proclaimed veteran of the federal campaign against the Sioux and a performer with Buffalo Bill's Wild West show, was the acting manager of Gabriel and Langan's Wild West and Indian Congress. The Gabriel show had appeared in special exhibition at the St. Louis World's Fair and as the Gabriel Brothers Wild West at the Delmar Gardens. The show had over seventy performers, including Indians, cowboys, and cowgirls. Among them were the champion roper Johnny Blocker, Jack Joyce, and Mabel Dodge. Rogers may have worked with the show in July 1904 after the Mulhall shooting incident, when he also appeared with the Charles Tompkins Wild West and with the Mulhall Rough Riders Congress at the Delmar Race Track on Sundays. Gabriel Brothers performers were also probably part of the Consolidated Wild West shows in which Rogers rode and roped.

Jim Gabriel (who sometimes used the stage name Cheyenne Bill) claimed to have been a dispatch bearer for General Nelson Miles during the campaign against the Sioux Ghost Dance resurgence in 1890–91, and to have been the head of the Cheyenne scouts stationed at Fort Keogh in Montana. Gabriel was a horse wrangler, ranger, and roper in the Dakotas and Texas. Both he and his brother H. D. (Kid) Gabriel were born in New York and worked as cowboys in Wyoming as young men. They joined Buffalo Bill's Wild West show in 1893 and appeared with it as cowboys in its 1893–96 and 1898–1902 seasons. They produced the Gabriel Brothers Champion Long Distance Riders Wild West show at the Delmar Gardens during the St. Louis World's Fair. Jim Gabriel became an independent promoter, directing special Wild West exhibitions and drawing on his experiences appearing at the Chicago World's Fair and at expositions in Buffalo, St. Louis, Atlanta, Nashville, Charleston, and Omaha. He also toured in Europe.

Gabriel was a friend of Zack Mulhall and knew Will Rogers's friend, the cowboy artist Charles Russell. He probably knew Rogers personally when they were both in St. Louis. Like Mulhall, Gabriel was a charismatic man known for his somewhat overbearing personality. He was also respected in some circles as a superb bronco rider and rodeo entrepreneur.

William Langan performed with the Buffalo Bill show for seventeen years (1883–1900) before joining with Gabriel to mount the Gabriel and Langan shows. He was the business manager for Gabriel and Langan in 1905; Clark Ball was the director, and George W. Armstrong was the secretary treasurer.

Gabriel produced Blanche McKenney's Wild West Indian Congress with L. M. Hunter in performances in New York in 1907, Illinois in 1909, and elsewhere. He also took his own show, Cheyenne Bill's Wild West, to the Alaska-Yukon-Pacific Exposition in Seattle in 1909. In the following year he was the arena director for Mulhall's Wild West show, which revived for another tour in 1910. Rogers appeared with the show when it played in Madison Square Garden (see Article in *Variety*, 30 April 1910, below). Jim Gabriel's daughter Helen Gabriel was often billed as one of the Mulhall sisters during the tour. During the same period when Gabriel was doing arena directing for Cody, Mulhall, and others, he wrote a "Frontier Celebration Events" column for *Billboard* and reported on Wild West shows for the magazine. He helped produce Lucille Mulhall's vaudeville western act and appeared on stage in it as one of the "ranch boys" with Martin Van Bergen in late 1910, but by the end of February 1911 Mulhall and Van Bergen announced that they had severed all ties with Gabriel and had gone with a different producer. Gabriel's riding career ended in 1908 when he was thrown backward from a bucking bronco in the Buffalo Bill show and the horse fell on him. In 1909 he was presenting tableaus of cowboy life on the vaudeville stage (*Billboard*, 5 June 1909, 10 July 1909, 10 September 1910, 25 February 1911; letterhead, Gabriel and Langan's Wild West and Indian Congress, 1905, OkClaW; Mulhall scrapbook, MCF; route book, Buffalo Bill's Wild West, season 1900, WBaraC; Charles Russell to Jim Gabriel, March–April 1910, in Dippie, *Charles M. Russell*; *New York Clipper*, 28 May 1904; *New York Dramatic Mirror*, 24 July 1909; Tompkins, "Gabriel Brothers Wild West").

2. The show ran from 23 to 29 April 1904. Rogers's plans to participate had already been well announced in Claremore (*CM*, 17 March 1905; *CP*, 11 March 1905).

To Clement Vann Rogers
1 April 1905
Mulhall, Okla.

Mulhall. O.

April fool (1905)

My Dear papa

I will write you a short letter   I am out here helping get things ready to go to N.Y. and practicing   I will be home about Monday or tuesday[1]

Love to all

Willie

ALS, rc. OkClaW.

1. Rogers shipped Comanche east on 10 April 1904 and left from Claremore himself the next day. He went up to St. Louis, where he met the Mulhalls and other members of the show, and traveled with them to New York (*CP*, 15 April 1904).

Article from the *New York Times*
2 April 1905
New York City, N. Y.

COW PUNCHING IN GARDEN.
HORSE FAIR ASSOCIATION PROMISES THIS AS PART OF EXHIBITION.

Real Wild West cow punching will be one of the features of the Horse Fair Association's exhibition in Madison Square Garden[1] April 24 to 29. A number of steers, fresh from the Western ranches, and several typical cowboys who have spent years in rounding up great droves of cattle, will be brought to the city to give the performance.

Madison Square Garden, 1924, northeast corner of Madison Square, Madison Avenue and Twenty-sixth Street. Building designed by McKim, Mead, and White, 1890. *(Underhill Collection, NNMus)*

Cow punching contests are frequently held in Indian Territory and other cattle districts of the Southwest, and prizes are awarded to the cowboy who brings a certain number of steers down in the shortest time. In Madison Square Garden there will not be so much room for running, and the steer will have less opportunity of escaping, but the publicity promoter promises plenty of excitement. The cowboys will ride their Western bronchos. Horses and riders have been secured from Texas, the Indian Territory, and Oklahoma Territory.

PD. Printed in *NYT*, 2 April 1905.

1. The Madison Square Garden in which the horse show and Mulhall Rough Riders Congress performance took place was a Renaissance-style building located at the northeast corner of Madison Square at Madison Avenue and 26th Street. Designed by McKim, Mead, and White, it was erected in 1890 at a cost of $3 million. It epitomized the new trend in the entertainment industry to appeal to middle-class patrons. The Garden was directed by promoters P. T. Barnum, J. P. Morgan, Darius Mills, and "other prominent men conspicuous in the horse shows" ("Madison Square Garden," 513). At the time Rogers performed there, it was the "largest building in America devoted entirely to amusements" (Birkmire, *Planning and Construction*, 2). It included a large restaurant, theater, "concert hall, ballroom, executive rooms, roof garden and apartments in the main tower" ("Madison Square Garden," 513). The arena where Rogers and the Mulhalls performed was 125 by 265 feet with three balconies of seating for some five thousand people. Stable facilities that could accommodate four hundred horses were located in the basement. The building's tall Moorish tower, graced by a statue of Diana, was a city landmark and the Garden halls and arena hosted a cavalcade of famous speakers, performers, concerts, and events. When the facility was built, it was "at the Northern rim of the amusement center of New York. The rialto was along Fourth Avenue and West from that point was the real congested amusement center of the city" ("Madison Square Garden," 513). Over time the entertainment district moved northward. In response the old Garden was demolished in 1925, and a new Madison Square Garden was built on the block between Eighth and Ninth Avenues and 50th and 51st Streets (Birkmire, *Planning and Construction*, 1–4; Stern, Gilmartin, and Massergale, *New York 1900*, 10, 203–4).

Article from the *Washington Times*
23 April 1905
Washington, D.C.

*Rogers wrote to his sister Sallie to tell her that on 22 April 1904 he had given a rop-
ing exhibition on the White House grounds for Theodore Roosevelt's family[1] and a
few invited guests. After he and his friend Jim Minnick[2] performed, they were given
a personal tour of the White House by first lady Edith Roosevelt, who warmly invited them to visit again when the president was in Washington. Rogers reported "having a great time on the trip."[3]*

TWO COWBOYS WILL TRY TO TAKE BIG PRIZE
MINNICK AND ROGERS ON WAY TO NEW YORK
TO ENTER BRONCHO RIDING CONTEST.

J. H. Minnick, of Seymour, Tex., and Will Rogers, of Claremore, I.T., two
of the most celebrated cowboys of the Southwest, passed through Washington
yesterday on their way to New York, where they will enter the $1,000 prize
broncho riding contest in Madison Square Garden on Monday night.

Mr. Minnick was here during the inauguration, and is remembered as the
cowboy in the red shirt who did such wonderful tricks with his pony and rope
on the Avenue as the parade passed by. His friend and comrade, Will Rogers,
is perhaps the finest ropeman in the world, doing a number of fancy tricks
with a rope which few cowboys ever attempted.

This morning the two Westerners, attired in their cowboy boots and hats,
went to the White House, and did some of their choice tricks for the entertainment of the children of the President. Rogers showed the children how a
cowboy jumps the rope.

Rogers is one of the few cowboys who can use two lassoes at once, and he
has attained more success at this feat than any man living. He can catch a rider
with one rope and the horse with the other.

The two companions will try to capture the $1,000 prize in New York
Monday. They will come back through Washington, and say that they will be
here when President Roosevelt arrives. [It] is their intention to give a spe[cial]
performance for his benef[it.]

PD. Printed in *Washington Times*, 23 April 1905, Jim Minnick file, OkClaW.

1. Progressive Republican Theodore Roosevelt (1858–1919), author of *The
Wilderness Hunter* (1893), *The Winning of the West* (1894–96), and *The Rough Riders*
(1899), was a central figure in the cult of manhood and the West that seized the east-

ern establishment from the 1880s through his terms in political office. A former governor of New York, Roosevelt was president of the United States from 14 September 1901 to 3 March 1909. He succeeded to the presidency in mid-term upon the death of William McKinley and won the presidential election of 1904 for the 1905–9 term.

Roosevelt's first wife, Alice Lee Roosevelt (1861–84), died two days after giving birth to their only child, Alice Lee Roosevelt (1884–1980). Roosevelt married his second wife, Edith Kermit Carow Roosevelt, in December 1886. They had a daughter, Ethel (1891–1977), who married Richard Derby in 1913, and four sons: Theodore (1887–1910), Kermit (1889–1943), Archibald (1894–1979), and Quentin (1897–1918).

Kermit was the dreamy and quiet one among the president's children; he was tutored at home in the summers and attended the Groton School during the period of Rogers's visit to the White House. His brother Ted entered Harvard the following fall (1905), and Alice Roosevelt married congressional leader Nicholas Longworth at the White House in February 1906. Quentin and Archie would have been home with Edith Roosevelt in April 1905.

Roosevelt was a "passionately devoted" father, who, even as president of the United States, read to his children at night, played games with them in the White House (including hide-and-seek and regular bouts of pillow fights down the White House corridors), took them horseback riding, and, when he was traveling or they were away at school, wrote them copious letters (McCullough, *Mornings on Horseback,* 366). When Rogers and Minnick came to entertain the children at the White House in April 1905, Roosevelt had just been to Texas and Oklahoma to attend the Rough Riders' reunion at San Antonio and to go wolf hunting in Oklahoma. He wrote about the experiences in letters to Kermit (14 April 1905) and Ted (20 April 1905). Wild West stars and cowboys were frequent visitors to the White House. Buffalo Bill (William Cody) had been to lunch in February 1904, and cowpuncher Jim White, who had worked on a roundup that Theodore Roosevelt had ridden with twenty years before, visited in December 1904. The president and his wife would typically have guests to lunch and reserve dinner as a time for family.

It is unknown how the invitation was extended to Rogers and Minnick to come to the White House, but Roosevelt was very much a presence in the western circles in which Rogers moved. Some of the cowboys Rogers performed with were veterans of Roosevelt's Rough Riders unit in the Spanish-American War, and some, like Minnick, had ridden in the president's inaugural parade and the Rough Riders Reunion rodeos. Theodore Roosevelt was also a friend of the Mulhall family and had visited the Mulhall ranch in Oklahoma for hunting expeditions. He is credited with having encouraged Zack Mulhall to put his riding-and-roping daughters into show business. To mark the opening of the St. Louis World's Fair on 30 April 1904, President Roosevelt gave an address in Washington, D.C., which was a tribute to America's westward expansionism and the idea of the course of empire. He was represented by Secretary of War William H. Taft at the actual opening ceremonies in St. Louis. Roosevelt visited the Fair in November 1904 (Bennitt et al., eds. *History of the Louisiana Purchase Exposition,* 127; Bishop, *Theodore Roosevelt's Letters to His Children,* 4, 91–92, 95, 108, 109–110, 119–21, 121–24; *DAB,* suppl. 3 [1941–45]: 667–69; *FAP,* 157–58; Irwin, *Letters to Kermit,* 58, 87; McCullough, *Mornings on Horseback,* 282–85, 316–50; *StLGD,* 1 May 1904; *StLPD,* 27 November and 28 November 1904; see also *PWR,* 1:194, 194n.1, 197n.1, 197n.3, 198n.8, 222n.2, 519–20).

2. It was Minnick's second trip to the White House. He had been there earlier in the year as part of a reception for Colonel Seth Bullock's Cowboy Troupe after riding

in Roosevelt's inaugural parade (Jim Minnick clippings file, TxU-GL; see also Biographical Appendix entry, MINNICK, J. H.).

3. *CP*, 29 April 1905. The *Claremore Messenger* and *Chelsea Commercial* also reported the story. The *Messenger* editorialized that the trip to the White House was "an honor of which he may well be proud, as it is accorded to but few men" (28 April 1905).

Clipping from Will Rogers's Scrapbook
ca. 23 April 1905
New York, N.Y.

The appearance of Zack Mulhall's Rough Riders Congress at the Horse Association Fair was billed as an education for New Yorkers in the ways of the West. One New York article from the period explained that "President Roosevelt's friend Zack Mulhall, with his clever daughters and wealthy fellow ranchmen will portray real life on the range. . . . They are bringing with them a small trainload of horses and frontier paraphernalia with which to illustrate to Eastern people the real, real life of the cow country and the plains."[1] The article printed below made the same point in a more satirical manner.

COWGIRLS JOIN IN FASHION'S THRONG
COL. ZACH MULHALL'S PRETTY DAUGHTERS RIDE UP
FIFTH AVENUE IN FULL RANCH COSTUME.

BIG RETINUE OF COWBOYS

TRICK HORSE GOVERNOR RUNS LOOSE IN THE PARK AND
GIVES AN EXHIBITION.

Cowgirls riding astride in Fifth avenue! Did you ever?

Through a long lane of raised lorgnettes, behind which fluttered society's leaders, they cantered in wonder. Colonel Zach Mulhall's lively daughters, attired in ranch clothing, with an escort of broncho-busting cowboys yesterday afternoon ran the gauntlet of Fashion's icy stares.

"How dreadful!" gasped one jewel-bedecked woman as the cowgirls and cowboys swept past a lumbering stage, from the cushioned seat in her victoria.

"Positively shocking," replied her monocled escort, stroking his drooping mustache.

Little care the band of cowgirls for the comments of the ladies weighted down in Easter hats and dresses with mighty trains. Chattering like magpies, they in turn criticized the women of the East, and had a real jolly time all the way up the great avenue.

The Mulhalls posing on the street near Madison Square Garden, New York City, April 1905. Zack Mulhall (ca. 1847–1931) *(standing)* with *(left to right)* daughters Mildred (1895–1957), Agnes (Bossie) (1877–1916), Georgia Smith (1872–1955) (who was booked in the Mulhall acts as one of the Mulhall daughters), and Lucille. *(Photograph by Haas; Mulhall Family Collection, Martha Fisch, Guthrie, Okla.)*

It was a meeting of the extremes—the open-air flowers of the West arrayed against the hot-house plants of the East.

THE WEST SIZES UP THE EAST.

Rough Riders in divided skirts; the female conquerors of beef and horns; the girl broncho busters; the lassooer in lingerie—-clear-eyed, sunburned, fearless and yet very curious. What cared they for the upturned noses, the pitying smiles, and the mgawkish laughter?[2]

"Did you ever see such complexions?" remarked Cowgirl Lucile Mulhall, a handsome blonde, to Cowboy Bill Rogers as the cavalcade turned into Central Park at Fifty-ninth street.

"Umph!" replied the favorite son of the chief of the Cherokee Nation, a white man, "these New York gals need a bit of God's sunshine."[3]

"What strange perfumes float from the carriages," commented Miss Bossy Mulhall, the brunette member of the family, as several open landaus were left in the stretch.[4]

"Reminds me of a Texas funeral," replied Jim Minnick. "Same sort of smell from the funeral flowers, only a heap sight deader."

"Do many of the New York women ride?" questioned Miss Georgia Mulhall of a mounted policeman, who joined the Western party. Georgia is the domestic member of the famous Oklahoma family.

"Not many, miss," responded the mounted officer. "They h'ain't got time between shopping and calls and theatres."

It Was Charley's Birthday.

Little 10-year-old Deputy Sheriff Mulhall,[5] a pretty, blonde girl, who rides like a cavalry officer, was the life of the party. She and her brother Charley soon outstripped the rest. Yesterday was Charley's seventeenth birthday, and the outing of the cowgirls and cowboys was in his honor.

Miss Lucile took along her trick horse Governor, which ran loose in the crowded avenue and drives and obeyed her every command. This young woman is the bright star of the Mulhall aggregation, and her horse yesterday gave a public exhibition of his skill.

Governor is probably the best trained horse in the world, and he has never felt the stroke of a whip.[6] His exhibition this week at the Madison Square Garden demands the special services of Leader Charley Seymour, of Mulhall's Cowboy Band,[7] who will then swing the baton for the Seventh Regiment Band. Governor is the only horse known that walks upon his knees.

Now, Col. Zach Mulhall's daughters are educated and convent-bred.[8] Miss Bossy possesses a sweet contralto voice. Two weeks ago she was kicked in the head by a wild horse, but what of that? Miss Lucile wears four medals which she received at cowboy contests at roping in the Southwest,[9] and her father has brought here two savage steers which she will rope in the New York arena.

After a ride as far north as 125th street the picturesque cavalcade returned to the Garden, the Mulhall girls going over to the Fifth Avenue Hotel, where they slipped into their society clothes and, appearing in the dining-hall, were noticeable only for their healthier color and athletic stride. Their mother has remained at Mulhall, Okla., but a woman long in the family accompanied the girls to New York.[10]

THIRTY-EIGHT HORSES WITH THEM.

Colonel Mulhall has a ranch "six miles long," and he has brought thirty-eight horses East with his party. Twelve of the horses are wild "outlaws."

His band of riders and ropers are the winners of many cowboy contests. They are the cream of the horse-handling talent of the West—the men who teach the circus people how to ride.

Bill Rogers is worth $100,000 in his own right, and he rides over an engraved leather saddle that cost $250 and which he won last year at El Paso. Tom Mixco[11] hails from Mexico, while the two Jackson boys, Otis and Charles, are from Montana. Jack Joyce[12] is the fastest roper and one of the best riders Texas ever produced, and in the Oklahoma delegation is George Elser, a trick rider.[13]

The judging of the cowboy contests will be in the hands of T. Harry Shanton and Col. Charles Toups.

PD. Unidentified clipping, ca. 23 April 1905. Scrapbook A-1, OkClaW.

1. "Western Cattle King to Ride at Horse Fair," unidentified clipping, New York, April 1905, Mulhall scrapbook, MFC.

2. The reporter's use of "mgawkish" was apparently a play on words, combining *mawkish* and *gawkish*.

The Mulhall parade of "steer ropes, bronco busters and rough riders" wended its way up Fifth Avenue, north through Central Park, and up "toward the Bronx" to 125th Street, galloping down the bridle path in Central Park on the return route and arriving back at Madison Square Garden after dark (*NYT*, 24 April 1905).

3. Rogers is again incorrectly identified here as the son of the principal chief of the Cherokee Nation, William Charles (W. C.) Rogers.

4. See Biographical Appendix entry, WOLFE, Agnes (Bossie) Mulhall.

5. A reference to Mildred Mulhall. The nickname of Deputy Sheriff stuck with Mildred and continued to be used through the years in show publicity literature, including during the 1910 revival tour of the Mulhall Rough Riders Congress (Mulhall scrapbook, MFC).

6. During performances Governor, who was trained in Spanish high-school (dressage-like) maneuvers, also did audience-pleasing tricks at Lucille's direction.

7. Zack Mulhall made his entrée in roping contests and riding expositions and the Mulhall Cowboy Band. The band played for Theodore Roosevelt at the Rough Riders Reunion in Oklahoma City, 4 July 1900, when Roosevelt was a vice-presidential candidate on William McKinley's ticket. The band was subsequently invited to play at McKinley's inauguration in 1901. The band came to be known as the Frisco Cowboy Band and was used for promotional purposes by the Frisco railroad. Mulhall, who was a livestock agent for the railroad, managed the group and organized its bookings, and

the Frisco railroad company provided travel expenses and uniforms. The band appeared under the direction of Charles Seymour at the Fourth International Fair in San Antonio in 1902. Bossie Mulhall sang when the band performed at the Grand Opera House, and Will Rogers's friend Jim Hopkins did rope tricks on stage. The band played mainly classical music, along with some military marches and popular songs. It toured livestock fairs and cattle rancher conventions and paraded at fairgrounds before roping contests, including those held in St. Louis in 1903. It also played concerts in local opera houses.

8. Agnes, Lucille, and Mildred Mulhall received a sporadic education at St. Joseph's convent school in Guthrie, Okla. Their father often removed them from school for months at a time to travel for performances. Lucille's early start in show business meant that much of her schooling was received at home or on the road. Agnes, the eldest, was educated in St. Louis as well as in Guthrie and excelled in music. Most of Mildred's convent school years followed her appearance in New York, and Mulhall publicists often drew on the juxtaposition of her school and show lives, presenting her as a daintily trained and sequestered young girl, who knew how to tat and crochet, but then could mount a powerful horse and gallop and trick-ride along with the men. One such source reported that she graduated at the age of sixteen with honors from a convent school in Nashville, Tenn. (see "Convent Girl the Star of Wild West Show," unidentified clipping, 15 May 1910, and "Convent Girl Can Ride Like a Man," *New York Morning World,* 29 April 1905, both in Mulhall scrapbook, MFC).

9. In 1907 Lucille Mulhall proudly explained two of her valued medals to an interviewer: "I have two medals that I value very highly. This one has the name at the top and the date, 1902. It is a Lone Star state emblem, with the raised head of a steer in the center, and is of solid gold. I won it at San Antonio, Texas. This is another medal that I value highly. The top piece has my name and the date, 1903; the pendant is of heavy gold with a raised star containing a diamond and a center of blue enamel contains a reproduction of a scene in which I roped a steer at Dennison, Texas, in thirty seconds" (interview with Lucille Mulhall by Hildebrand Fitzgerald, *Philadelphia Evening Item,* 6 September 1907).

10. References to Mary Agnes Locke Mulhall (see Biographical Appendix entry, MULHALL, Mary Agnes Locke) and Georgia Mulhall.

11. Rogers's friend Tom Mix, called "Tom Mixco" and publicized as a "cow runner from Old Mexico" for the purposes of the show, had worked with Rogers at the Mulhall ranch in Oklahoma and was destined, like Rogers, to stardom in Hollywood. Rogers also knew the artist Olive Stokes, who became Mix's wife and who, like Rogers, was of mixed Cherokee and Scotch-Irish ancestry and had grown up on a ranch in Indian Territory. Rogers introduced Olive Stokes to Tom Mix at the St. Louis World's Fair, when he and Mix were both appearing with the Mulhall show at the Delmar Race Track. The morning after the introduction Mix waylaid Stokes in the lobby of the hotel where Stokes was staying, and they began their courtship with a day at the Fair. Like Betty Blake and Will Rogers, Stokes and Mix spent much of the next four years apart but maintained the connection that had been established during their dates at the

Fair. Stokes and Mix married in January 1909, just weeks after Rogers and Betty Blake.

The *New York Times* claimed that Tom Mix was a drum major with the Mulhall Oklahoma Territory Cowboy Band when it played at the inaugural parade of President McKinley. Like Rogers, Mix played a role in the Mulhall Rough Riders Congress shows of 1910. Olive Stokes Mix became a good friend of Georgia Smith Mulhall (Mix, *Life and Legend of Tom Mix*; Mix and Heath, *Fabulous Tom Mix*, 4—13; *NYT*, 29 April 1905; Biographical Appendix entry, MIX, Tom).

Will Rogers later recalled the Horse Fair in one of his weekly articles (*TDW*, 19 April 1925). He wrote that his friend Tom Mix had recently stopped by to see him perform (Mix, Rogers explained, was "on his way to Europe taking Tony the horse, over to show him the Country. Tom said he had read 'somewhere in history that some fellow over there had offered, A Kingdom, A Kingdom, for a Horse, and he was going over to try and make a deal with him'") and that "it seemed sort of a co-incident that just exactly 20 years ago this week Tom Mix and I arrived in New York with Col. Zack Mulhall's Wild West Outfit to show in Madison Square Garden as part of the Horse Show. . . . That was Tom Mix's first start on his Wild West career. We didn't get much money; in fact our salary was supposed to be $20 a week. I told Tom in the Theater the other night, that was the only time we were ever paid just about what we were worth. That was one time we were not overpaid Actors, because we didn't even get the twenty" (reprinted in Smallwood and Gragert, eds., *Coolidge Years*, 18–19).

12. Horse trainer and rider Jack Joyce, like his colleagues, was a seasoned cowboy who had a varied career in Wild West shows and circuses in the United States and abroad. He was both an accomplished roper and rough rider and a trick rider who rode high-schooled horses performing complicated dressage routines to music. He was a regular in Busch Circus tours in Germany and other European countries. In 1911 he performed in Sweden with Scandanavian-produced Wild West acts, did a stage act at the Victoria Palace in London, and lived for a while in Russia, where he appeared with the Busch Circus. In the following year he teamed up, as he often did, with his good friend Joe Lynch in a Wild West act at the Coliseum in London. In the 1920s Joyce developed an act with nine highly trained thoroughbred horses and traveled with it between London, the Continent, and the United States. In 1925 he opened with the act at the Hippodrome in New York, where he performed on a bill with Houdini, Eddie Leonard, and others, and then toured on the Keith-Albee vaudeville circuit. In some cities the roping act of Will Ahern and Gladys joined the show Jack Joyce and His Wonder Horses (*Billboard*, 8 April 1911, 13 May 1911, and 9 December 1911, 20 January 1912, 24 January 1925, 31 January 1925, 7 February 1925, 28 March 1925; Jack Joyce files, WBaraC).

13. The other performers who participated in the Mulhall show at the Horse Fair, along with George Elser, Tom Mix, and Jack Joyce, were Charley Seymour, a horse wrangler from Mulhall; Otis Jackson, a bronco buster from the Yellowstone River region of Montana; Curtis Jackson, a rough rider from Chadron, Neb.; William Craver, a lariat expert and bronco buster from Laramie Plains, Wyo.; Joe Lynch, a rough rider from Magdalena, New Mexico; Colonel C. H. Toups, a rough rider from Fort Worth, Tex.; Zack Miller, a prominent rancher and Wild West show promoter and one of the brothers of the Miller Brothers' 101 Ranch near Bliss, O.T.; and the members of the Mulhall family. Will Rogers was listed in the program as a lariat expert from Indian Territory.

When he described his experience at the Horse Fair twenty years later, Rogers recalled that the troupe that went to Madison Square Garden "was not a regular Wild

The Mulhall family of Wild West performers. Promotional program including son Charley (1888–1958), a regular performer in the family troupe, but not including daughter Agnes. *(Mulhall Family Collection, Martha Fisch, Guthrie, Okla.)*

West Show; it was a bunch of boys he [Zack Mulhall] had gathered together out on his ranch in Oklahoma, with his daughter Lucille Mulhall, who was the greatest Roper of any Girl before or since." Zack Mulhall, he observed, "was a great old fellow . . . a typical old time westerner. We would touch him so much at odd times we never had anything coming. He was a very liberal fellow and in those days of Bar Rooms would always order drinks for everybody in the place and hand the Bar Tender a Bill or perhaps $20 to pay for what was [a] $5 or 6 Dollars check and my great habit was to edge in next to him when the man put the change back in front of him, and I would grab it and duck with it." Mulhall thought this was very funny, and so did Rogers. "In fact," he observed, "I think it was one of the best jokes I ever pulled" (*TDW*, 19 April 1925; reprinted in Smallwood and Gragert, eds., *Coolidge Years*, 19).

Article from the *Morning Telegraph*
25 April 1905
New York, N. Y.

QUEENS OF SADDLE, ONE ONLY TEN, MAKE HIT OF SEASON AT HORSE FAIR

THE MISSES MULHALL SHOW A NERVE AND DARING THAT SETS GARDEN CROWD WILD.

OPENING NIGHT PROVES SUCCESS FOR UNIQUE ENTERTAINMENT THAT SAVORS OF THE WEST

The Horse Fair—tried successfully for two days last year—which combines the regular Horse Show with indoor trotting races and exhibitions of broncho busting and roping, formally opened last night at Madison Square Garden. In addition there were real Indians and a lively concert by the Seventh Regiment Band.

The layer of dirt left in the Garden by the circus has been increased to a depth of four feet at the turns, and eighteen inches in the center of the arena.

Upon this firmly packed foundation trotters sped under the saddle—the old-fashioned way of showing an animal—cowboys and cowgirls cavorted, danced a-horseback, roped wild "outlaw" horses and Texas steers, rode bucking bronchos and threw the lariat in competition, while the Indians danced a war dance.

The opening of the programme at 8.30 o'clock was a congress of rough riders of both sexes. The cowboys included George Elser and Col. C. H. Toups, Jim Minnick, broncho buster from Texas; Tom Mixco, cow runner from Old Mexico; Otis and Curtis Jackson, broncho busters from Montana; William Craver, lariat expert from Wyoming; Joe Lynch, rough rider from New Mexico; Will Rogers, lariat expert from Indian Territory; Jack Joyce, Charley Seymour and Zack Miller, rough riders, and the famous Mulhall Family—father, son and four daughters—from Oklahoma.

A Virginia Reel by the Mulhall girls with cowboys for partners was an attractive feature.

COWBOY AND COWGIRL COMPETE.

This was followed by the riding of wild horses by the cowboys, and Miss Lucille Mulhall for the championship and a gold medal, which will not be awarded to the winner until the close of the Horse Fair by T. H. Stanton, the judge in this event.

Miss Lucille Mulhall, "Queen of the Range," assisted by her 10-year-old sister Mildred and her trick horse Governor, gave a splendid exhibition. Both girl and child made their initial bow, and then, as the special music played began their act, which is without doubt the finest equestrienne turn of its kind New York has witnessed in years.

Governor is a chestnut-colored animal with a white forehead and three white feet.

Going down upon one knee, the animal permitted the child to dismount and her elder sister to leap into the saddle. After cake-walking, then a quick-step and then a sidestep, the horse with a foreward paw bored a hole in the turf and swung around the imaginary Maypole as gracefully as a grand dame.

But the horse does so much that the half is lost. He picks up a hand-kerchief, rings a bell, takes off his mistress' hat, goes lame, plays dead, walks on his front knees (the only horse in the world to do this), picks up a whip, and sits on his haunches and crosses his forelegs. Before Miss Mulhall and her mite of a sister had gone half through their act the Garden was wild-ly cheering.

THE PROUD FATHER.

Col. Zach Mulhall, their proud father, owner of an 80,000 acre ranch in Oklahoma, kissed both of his children as they backed their horses out of the arena. He said to a Morning Telegraph reporter: "This is the proudest moment of my life. She is a true Western girl, and she has been to school, too, graduated out of a convent, same as the rest of my girls. I would not swap her for twenty ranches and 10,000 head of horses thrown in."

Then came the Indian war dance and some cowboy sports. Here again Miss Lucille got the house by picking up a pin from the ground while her horse was running. The trotting horses followed.

Among the boxholders were J. Campbell Thompson, M. C. Byers, J. D. Carroll, Mrs. J. B. Grosvenor, S. L. and S. Frank, George Watson, David Welsh, Allen MacNaughton, Mrs. Stephen Ralli, S. N. Hexter, Mrs. L. Strauss and W. L. Watt.

ROUGH RIDING MADE TROTTING SEEM TAME

A reproduction of Rosa Bonheur's picture was presented as the opening attraction of the second annual Horse Fair in Madison Square Garden last night. Eighty-four lordly Percherons and horses of other draft breeds were led into the ring. The cavalcade was headed by a sprightly little Welsh pony, whose sixty inches looked small beside some of his eighteen-hand brothers.

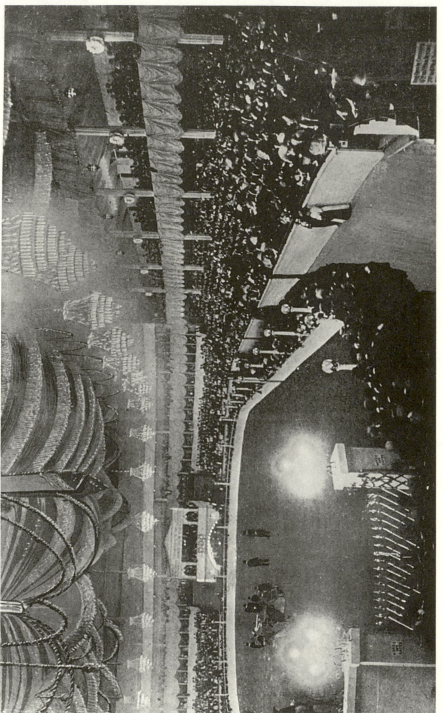

Madison Square Garden (interior) during the National Horse Show, New York City, 1910. *(NNMuS)*

The scene was quickly changed, and the cowboys' carnival was in progress.

After the ring was cleared a demonstration of the pony express was given, the rider changing horses so quickly he could hardly be seen to touch the ground.

The box holders will long remember the riding of the "outlaws." Several of them tried to climb into the boxes, and only the shrieks and flutter of feminine finery drove them back to the center of the ring. An "outlaw," so an accommodating announcer explained, was a horse that was halter broken and would lead quietly, but was inclined to be unrestful when the rider had mounted. All the announcer said was true, and more. Monkey Wrench refused to be saddled, and it took the combined forces of three men and two lariats to get on the instrument of torture.

Will Rogers, a full blood Cherokee Indian and Carlisle graduate, proved a right to his title of lariat expert.[1] He threw it in every conceivable shape, and thought nothing of balancing a rolled lariat on his toe and throwing it over a horse's head. His final feat took the audience by storm. He threw two lariats at an oncoming rider, lassooing both horse and rider. George Elser followed with feats of rough riding.

Miss Lucille Mulhall, after exhibiting her trained horse "Governor," joined the cowboys in their sports. Miss Mulhall had a very narrow escape from a curious accident. While she was leaning far from her horse to pick up a handkerchief her mount stumbled and she was thrown to the ground.

In the steer roping contest only a cowboy's warning, "Look out, Lucille," saved her horse from becoming entangled in the ropes around an infuriated steer.

PD. Printed in *Morning Telegraph*, 25 April 1905. Scrapbook A-1, OkClaW.

1. Will Rogers did not attend Carlisle Indian School. On his education, see part two, "School Days," in *PWR*, 1:69–144.

Clipping from Will Rogers's Scrapbook
ca. 28 April 1905
New York City, N.Y.

Reports of the details of this incident vary, but all agree that pandemonium broke out briefly in Madison Square Garden when a steer broke away from a roping act in the arena and hurtled into the audience. The New York Herald *reported that "Will Rogers, a Cherokee Indian, and three other cowboys" gave chase after another cowboy missed his throw at the animal in the stands. "Rogers got a rope over the steer's horns just as he turned to run down into the arena. Rogers clung to the rope, but was dragged over seats and down the stairs. He was seriously bruised." Five thousand spectators were in their seats at the time. The* Herald *reporter concluded that the steer was by all odds the "worst behaved animal on the American continent, and yesterday was one of his bad days."[1] After they had retired from active Wild West work, Lucille and Charley Mulhall loved to laugh over this incident of the steer that went astray.*

STEER RAN AMUCK IN BIG GARDEN.

Leaped Rails at the Horse Fair and Climbed Three Flights of Stairs into Balcony, Cowboys Pursuing.

Wild Stampede Of Band And Scared Spectators.

Indian Cowpuncher's Quickness Prevents Harm—Two of the Riders Have Falls.

A Texas steer running among the spectators at the Horse Fair in Madison Square Garden yesterday afternoon caused great excitement for five minutes. That no one was hurt was due to the skill of the cowboys, who roped it and guided it back to the arena.

The steer came from Col. Mulhall's Oklahoma ranch, a dun-colored animal, weighing 800 pounds with horns that spread five feet. It is a restive beast and resents its part in the roping exhibition given by Miss Lucille, the Colonel's daughter.

Yesterday the brute had been admitted from the pen at the corner of Fourth avenue and Twenty-sixth street, and was urged to its highest speed by six shouting cowboys. It ran into the centre of the ring and down toward the entrance at Madison avenue. As Miss Mulhall followed at top speed and the cowboys drew off, the steer leaped the bars protecting the steps on the Twenty-sixth street side.

Usher Tried to Throw Him.

There was a wild scamper of spectators to get out of its path, but it kept up the stairs without a misstep. At the top of the first flight Claude Lanigan, an usher, seized its horns and was thrown across several tiers of seats. Lanigan scrambled to his feet and grabbed the animal's tail just as several lassoes ensnared him and several chairs.

The steer went up the second and third flights into the balcony and disappeared in the corridor back of the Madison avenue boxes.

The six cowboys, lariats in hand, were following. The Indian Will Rogers ran up the Twenty-seventh street side and headed the steer off. As it passed from the corridor again into view of the spectators he roped the steer's horns. Alone and afoot, he was no match for the brute's strength, but he swerved it down the steps on the Twenty-seventh street side, where it jumped again into the ring. Immediately the ropes of a dozen cowpunchers fell over it from all sides, and it was brought down with a quick turn and led from the track. The regular exhibition was abandoned.[2]

MUSIC TO THE WINDS.

During the excitement the Seventh Regiment Band, in the Madison avenue balcony, abandoned horns of all sizes and fled. Occupants of seats along the Twenty-seventh street side made a stampede for cover. Women screamed and men shouted.

While all this was going on Col. Mulhall shouted to his daughter in his excitement asking her why she didn't "follow that baby up the stairs and bring him back or else stay there" herself.

The rails at the stairways will be raised six feet to prevent a repetition of the incident.

Will Craven, a cowboy, was thrown while making his entree and broke his collar-bone. A few minutes later Charles Mulhall was thrown from the bucking broncho Texas Pete. He escaped with a few bruises.[3]

PD. Unidentified clipping, ca. 28 April 1905. Scrapbook A-1, OkClaW.

1. *New York Herald,* 28 April 1905; see also "Bull at Garden Show Leaps into the Boxes: Spectators Alarmed, Musicians Put to Flight: Cowgirl's Act Cut Short," *NYT,* 28 April 1905; "Texas Steer in the Balcony," unidentified clipping, scrapbook A-1, OkClaW; and oral history sessions with Martha Fisch, WRPP. The *Times* estimated the attendance at six thousand.
2. The "Texas Steer in the Balcony" version of the story had the steer breaking back into the arena where it was "roped by Will Rogers, a Cherokee, who belongs to the show, and Cowboy Tom Mixco. They threw him, instead of the cowgirl, and he was dragged out of the arena." The *New York Herald* version of the incident said the steer escaped from Rogers near the bottom of the stairs and leaped, with his rope trailing behind it, back into the arena, where Lucille Mulhall continued on with "her act and roped him with apparent ease." Rogers's friend Jim Minnick, who was a witness to the steer incident, said that "that story about Rogers roping a steer after it had jumped out of the arena and leading it back after he had roped it is all hooey. It was Lucille's steer, and it had jumped the fence. The audience scattered. The steer went up in the balcony. A policeman went after it. Rogers asked him, 'What are you going to do with it, when you catch it?' Rogers knew the steer would come around to the back side, and it did. HE DID NOT ROPE IT" (Jim Minnick interview with Homer Croy, HCP-MoU). According to Mildred Mulhall Carmichael Acton, who was ten

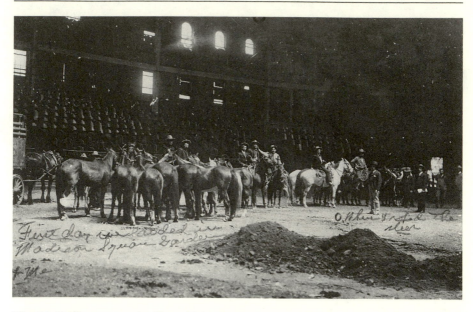

The Mulhall troupe at the Horse Fair, Madison Square Garden, New York City, April 1905. Rogers, who is in the center of the photograph with his hand on another rider's shoulder, wrote an *X* to identify his location. The letter *O* marks the spot where he roped the steer. "First day we landed in Madison Square Garden," wrote Rogers. *(OkClaW)*

years old at the time, it was indeed Lucille Mulhall's steer that escaped. "Jimmy Minnick, Tom Mix, and Will run the steer back into the arena," whereupon Lucille promptly "roped and tied him" (Mildred Acton to Homer Croy, 30 September 1952, HCP-MoU).

3. The author of the "Texas Steer in the Balcony" story reported that Charley Mulhall was brought to Bellevue Hospital for treatment after his mishap with the bucking bronco.

From Zack Mulhall
ca. 29 April 1905
New York, N.Y.

New York
N.Y.

To whom it may Concern

I have this day sold transferred and delivered to Will Rogers one bay Poney named (Teddy) for sum of one Hundred and no/100s—[1]

Zack Mulhall

Witness

ALS, rc. OkClaW. On Gilsey House letterhead, Broadway and 29th Street, New York.

1. After appearing at the Cleveland Theatre in Chicago, Rogers was determined to develop an act with a small horse that he could rope on stage. In the fall and winter of 1904—5 he trained a little bay pony named Teddy that was owned by Mary Agnes Locke Mulhall. The Mulhalls asked $100 for the horse, and Rogers had to earn the sum over time through his performances with the Mulhalls. The payments were apparently completed by the end of the Horse Fair in New York, and Zack Mulhall gave Rogers this bill of sale to verify the transaction. The two men would soon have a serious falling out over Rogers's other horse, Comanche, which he had shipped separately from Claremore for use in the Madison Square Garden show.

Teddy proved an ideal choice for the stage. He responded well to training, to performing indoors in cramped spaces, and to the constant travel and odd accommodations the vaudeville circuit entailed. Several vaudeville performers who worked on the same bill with Rogers had fond memories of standing in the wings to push Teddy, who wore soft felt shoes, back into the view of the audience when he slid off the stage into the curtains during Rogers's act (Croy, *Our Will Rogers,* 96–97; Rogers, *Will Rogers,* 85–86; autobiography of Pat Rooney, ms., PR-TxU; BMc-C).

To Clement Vann Rogers
8 May 1905
New York, N.Y.

New York, <u>May 8</u> *1905*

My Dear Papa

Well I guess you think that I am not going to write but I will at last   Well we had a great week here   done fine   all the folks have went back but me   I will stay a week or so yet and do some work on the stage as I made a great success the week I worked here but I might be there anytime

your loving son
Willie

(over)[1]

ALS, rc. OkClaW. On Putnam House, Fourth Avenue and 26th Street (Opposite Madison Square Garden), New York, letterhead.

    1. Rogers included a postscript to A. L. Kates. See enclosure, following.

Enclosure
To Albert Linwood Kates
8 May 1905
New York, N.Y.

To *Kates*[1]

I never did get to write you but here is a clipping or two[2]   I made the biggest hit here I ever dreamed of in my roping act and finished my good luck by catching the wild steer that went clear up into the dress circles of the garden among the people   I will stay here to do some theatre work for a while.[3]

yours
Will Rogers.

ALS, Clement Vann Rogers copy. OkClaW. Postscript on verso of letter to Clement Vann Rogers, 8 May 1905. On Putnam House letterhead.

    1. This note was written on the back of a letter to Rogers's father. It is written to Albert Linwood Kates, the editor and publisher of the *Claremore Progress* newspaper. Rogers knew Kates well, and Kates had published many of Rogers's letters home from abroad in 1902–4. Rogers also wrote his first published pieces for Kates, accounts of his travels. Rogers evidently had told Kates that he would try to send him some material about the Mulhall show, but instead of writing his own account of events, he enclosed clippings from newspapers about his visit to Washington and the incident

with the steer (see, for example, Will Rogers to the *Claremore Progress, PWR,* 1:269–73, 354–57; see also *PWR,* 1:495–96).

2. Rogers enclosed "Two Cowboys Will Try to Take Big Prize" from the 23 April 1905 *Washington Times,* about his trip to the White House with Jim Minnick, and "Texas Steer Ran Amuck in Big Garden," the clipping from the New York newspaper about the Mulhall cowboys chasing the wayward steer. Kates printed a story combining the news from the two articles in "Work with His Rope," *CP,* 13 May 1905.

3. Rogers wrote to his sisters the same day that he wrote these notes to his father and A. L. Kates. "I dont think I ever done better work or made a bigger hit than I did there," he wrote about his Madison Square Garden work. He told Sallie and Maud that he was going to "fix up some stage work for this winter as you have to book way ahead." "Oh Ive had a royal time here," he concluded (Will Rogers to Folks, 8 May 1905, OkClaW).

To Betty Blake
10 May 1905
New York, N.Y.

The White House and Madison Square Garden appearances had obviously been good for Rogers's self-confidence and his belief in the possibility of his own success as a performer. Here—in a note written on the sole of a shoe and sent through the mail to Rogers, Ark.—he shares his happiness with Betty Blake and at the same time chides her for her doubts about his hopes for making a career in show business.

Hello Old Pal:

I am still in N.Y. dont know what I will do yet.   I was quite a hit in Madison Sq. Garden and I am letting my head return to its normal size before going home.   Kid, you done me wrong.

Pon my SOLE you [*cartoon drawing of a monkey in an automobile*] Be With Me in N.Y.

Address Putnam House, N.Y.

AN, rc. OkClaW. Written on the sole of a shoe. Postmarked New York, 10 May 1905.

Clipping from Will Rogers's Scrapbook
18 May 1905
Newark, N.J.

Rogers had evidently learned a thing or two at Madison Square Garden about adding spontaneity to an act and earning publicity for so doing. He also used a trick he had already put to good use on stage—roping an unsuspecting dog that had the misfortune to wander into the range of his lariat. Rogers was at the Orange Horse

Show on 15, 16, and 17 May to give an exhibition of fancy rope throwing and bare-back riding with his new pony Teddy. His big hit was with his two-rope trick, simul-taneously lassoing Teddy with one rope and the rider—in this case, his friend Jim Minnick—with the other. He would repeat this trick in performance after perform-ance in his regular stage act with Teddy and Buck McKee.

HORSES CUT UP LIVELY CAPERS

SOME EVENTS AT ORANGE SHOW
WHICH WERE NOT DOWN ON THE PROGRAM.

JUDGE LASSOED BY AN INDIAN.

Some lively incidents occurred last night at the closing performance of the Orange Horse Show. For one thing the judges stand in the middle of the ring was smashed and the judges scurried to shelter. Then there was a mixup in the four-in-hand class and some extra stunts in the lasso throwing.

The stand was broken by Master Claude and Miss Earle, the pair owned by Miss Luella Day, which, with Saint and Sinner, owned by Mrs. A. O. Van Heusen, were the only competitors in the class for harness tandems. C. F. Lawton was driving Miss Day's pair, and in bringing the horses around turned them into the judges' stand. There was a crash of the railing as the animals stepped into it, and grooms rushed out to seize the horses, which were unin-jured. They continued around the ring and won the first prize of $50. . . .

William Rogers, the Cherokee Indian, whose performances with the lariat have been features of the show, added a few new tricks last night. He was gal-loping wildly around on the fiery little pony, waving the lariat, when sudden-ly he swerved along close to the judges' stand. In an instant he had one of the judges in the rope. The horse stopped almost instantly, but there was great laughter at the trick.

DOGS CAUGHT BY LASSO.

At the matinee there was another unexpected lassoing. A dog which had been put out of the building several times during the day managed to slip in and ran inside the ring. Rogers threw the lariat and caught the animal by its hind legs.

PD. Scrapbook A-1, OkClaW.

———

2. THE TRAINING GROUND
June 1905–March 1906

B. F. Keith's Union Square Theatre (constructed 1870, rebuilt 1888), Fourteenth Street between Broadway and Fourth Avenue, New York City, where Rogers made his first appearance in vaudeville in June 1905. *(Byron Collection, NNMuS)*

WHILE IN NEW YORK AT THE MADISON SQUARE GARDEN HORSE FAIR, ROGERS SAW the large number of vaudeville theaters that lined the streets. In 1905 vaudeville was the nation's most popular form of entertainment, attracting a mass audience in thousands of theaters nationwide. At that time vaudeville had not yet reached the height of its popularity, and was growing every year. New theaters were being built, and well-organized circuits were efficiently marketing an amusement form that appealed to millions.

As vaudeville's center, New York had approximately forty variety theaters in 1905. Here were located big-time vaudeville offices with bookers, agents, and theater managers and owners. From his room in the Putnam House on Fourth Avenue and Twenty-sixth Street, Rogers could walk down Broadway from Madison Square to Union Square, where vaudeville thrived from West Twenty-third Street to Fourteenth Street, New York's Rialto. The area between Thirty-fourth and Thirty-eighth Streets also contained vaudeville theaters.

Farther uptown was Oscar Hammerstein's Victoria Theatre, located on the corner of Seventh Avenue and Forty-second Street in recently named Times Square. Formerly called Longacre Square, the plot of land was renamed in 1904 when the *New York Times* tower was completed. Opening in 1899, the Victoria was initially a legitimate theater but changed to vaudeville in 1904. The Victoria began the boom of theater building in the Times Square area, a trend that created the "Great White Way," so called for its bright lights.[1]

Vaudeville was an exciting world of show business, which attracted a host of aspirants, such as Rogers. Looking back in 1933, Rogers called his ten-year vaudeville career a "training ground" to learn the art of entertaining. He lamented the demise of vaudeville. "You see now with no vaudeville, I mean real vaudeville, high class houses, playing to the very best people, well now there is none, and there was your training ground for talent," he wrote in his weekly article. "There is where every comedian was trained. Every vaudeville bill was full of clever comedians that on a moments notice could step into a musical comedy. No sir, the loss of old vaudeville was more than just the loss of seeing the show. Taking away vaudeville was just like taking the high school away, and wanting the pupil to jump from grammar school to college."[2] For

Rogers, vaudeville was an invaluable education in the art of performance between his Wild West show experience and his career in the *Ziegfeld Follies* and in film.

The publicity Rogers received from the steer-roping story that ran in New York newspapers helped create the opportunity for him to try vaudeville. He wrote his father that he had decided to "do some work on the stage as I made a great success the week I worked here."[3] There were other cowboy-and-lasso acts in vaudeville but none with a horse. The adventurous Rogers decided to develop a roping act and asked Jim Minnick to remain in New York temporarily as his assistant. Needing a small horse for the stage, he trained Teddy, the pony he had bought from the Mulhalls.

Rogers made the rounds of vaudeville booking agents in an attempt to sell his act. Initially, he was told that there was no call for a roping and horse act. Finally, Daniel F. Hennessy,[4] a booking agent for Benjamin F. Keith's circuit of vaudeville theaters, arranged a tryout at Keith's Union Square Theatre on Fourteenth Street. With his pony Teddy and the help of Jim Minnick, Rogers performed at the supper show, a time of day known for its poor attendance. He appeared around 6:30 P.M. on a hot day, when there were only ten or twelve people in the theater. Rogers jokingly recalled that initially the audience was not even watching and that it was Teddy who saved his act: "But that's such a nice little pony and seems to be the only one that knows what he is doing, and if we dont help him out he will get rode plain back to Oklahoma. So for the ponys sake, they laid their papers down."[5]

His tryout a success, Rogers received a contract dated 8 June 1905 to appear at Keith's Union Square Theatre for one week beginning 12 June 1905, at a weekly salary of $75. This first contract was the starting point of ten years on the vaudeville trail, traveling from one engagement to another each week with only rare time off. The schedule was grueling, but it was a learning experience that shaped his entire stage career and persona as the Oklahoma cowboy.

Rogers wrote to Betty Blake that the Union Square Theatre was "the swellest Vaudeville house in N.Y." and to his sisters that the Keith Circuit was "the swellest in the east."[6] The Union Square was a prominent theater in the Keith Circuit, which was the largest and most powerful vaudeville chain in the East. Most first-year vaudevillians usually began in small-time, modest theaters, where low salaries and four to six shows a day from noon to midnight were the rule. Rogers was exceptional in starting his vaudeville career in big-time vaudeville, with its higher salaries, glamorous theaters, and only two to three performances daily.

Benjamin Franklin Keith (1846–1914) operated the largest vaudeville circuit in the East. *(The Harvard Theatre Collection, The Houghton Library, Fredric Woodbridge Wilson, Curator.)*

Vaudeville was a form of entertainment that had evolved from multiple sources. The word itself derived from the French term *vaux-de-Vire,* a combination of light pastoral plays and satirical songs performed in the fifteenth century in the valleys *(vaux)* near Vire, a town in the province of Normandy. Vaudeville could be traced back to the traveling troupes of European acrobats, jugglers, magicians, singers, musicians, and sketch actors who entertained in royal courts and town squares in the Middle Ages and the Renaissance.

Vaudeville's more recent roots were varied: nineteenth-century variety theater, the rowdy urban concert saloon, the olio (second act) of the minstrel show, small variety shows in dime museums, and the potpourri of acts in the circus. Earlier forms of variety amusement were unruly and boisterous, and catered to the white, working-class men and European immigrants. The concert saloon, a combination of alcohol consumption and risqué entertainment, was extremely popular in cities in the mid-nineteenth century. There men were entertained by scantily clothed dancing girls, comics telling dirty jokes, noisy singing, circus-type acts, and the "finale afterpiece," a saucy sketch involving all the performers. While watching the entertainment, patrons indulged in food and liquor (served by flirtatious "waiter girls"), cigar smoking, and gambling, and made after-hours assignations with prostitutes.[7] During the summer variety entertainment also flourished in beer gardens.[8]

Still another source of vaudeville was the olio or second act of the three-part minstrel show. The olio was essentially a variety program performed before a dropped curtain, with each performer doing his or her specialty. Depending on the special talent of the minstrels, the audience might enjoy singing, dancing, acrobatics, comic monologues, or other acts. Many vaude-villians, both black and white, got their start in the minstrel show: Al Jolson, Fred Stone and his partner David Montgomery, and the team of Bert Williams and George Walker, among others.[9]

In the mid-nineteenth century some theaters offered "wholesome" variety entertainment for the family.[10] But it was not until 1875–85 that variety theater broadened its audience to include the middle class. The key figure in this development was the singer and impresario Tony Pastor (1832–1908), who took variety entertainment out of the concert saloons and into first-class theaters. In 1875 he managed New York's Metropolitan Theatre at 585 Broadway, where he introduced what he termed "vaudeville" programs with acts that appealed to family members and special matinees for women and children. When the policy proved successful, he initiated similar programs at his Bowery Opera House and Broadway Theatre. Pastor's biggest success was the New Fourteenth Street Theatre where, beginning in 1881, he offered variety programs that featured the best talents from across the United States and abroad. By avoiding vulgarity and prohibiting alcoholic beverages, Pastor created a format that appealed to a broader, middle-class audience of mixed generations and sexes, while wielding social control over lower- and working-class patrons.[11]

Pastor set the stage for Benjamin F. Keith, who created the type of "refined," continuous programming with a standardized format that dominated vaudeville during Rogers's time. As head of the nation's largest circuit, comprising theaters in the East, Keith transformed the big-time vaudeville business into an efficient, highly organized structure that mass-produced and distributed entertainment nationwide.

Keith's career demonstrates the influence of the circus and the dime museum on vaudeville's development. Like several other major vaudeville theater owners, Keith first gained show-business experience with various traveling circuses. In the late 1870s he arrived in New York City and worked at Bunnell's dime museum, which displayed exhibits of dead and live curiosities and also offered a variety stage show as an extra attraction to lure customers. In 1883 Keith opened his own dime museum in Boston, called the New York Dime Museum (it later became Keith and Batcheller's Mammoth Museum [1884] and the Gaiety Hall and Museum [1885]). Here Keith presented displays of unusual objects, caged animals, human oddities (such as midgets and tattooed men), optical illusions, and other curiosities. In a second-floor Theatre Room, which contained 123 seats and a standing area, he presented a variety show. But the show was not continuous, and Keith thought an ongoing program that allowed people to arrive at any time might increase his customers. On 6 July 1885, working with a new partner, the showman George H. Batcheller (1829–1913), Keith began to stage continuous variety shows from 10 A.M. to 10 P.M. He found that this format did indeed modify his audience, simultaneously shifting the appeal from working-class men to middle-class families. Inspired by their success, Keith and Batcheller leased Boston's Bijou Theatre, which opened on 1 August 1887 with a policy of continuous variety entertainment.

With his chief executive, Edward F. Albee, who would eventually become the dominant executive in vaudeville, Keith created a big-time circuit by building and leasing theaters on the East Coast. In 1905, the year Rogers began vaudeville, the Keith Circuit comprised twenty theaters. By 1907 there were over eighty theaters affiliated with Keith through his United Booking Office.[12] As head of the circuit, Keith possessed a strong talent for entrepreneurship and organizational management. He chose able managers such as Albee and promoted skilled administrators in his organization. A shrewd, sometimes ruthless, show-business magnate, Keith resisted actors' unions, blacklisted performers who played in opposition theaters, and fought independent agents and theater owners. He threatened to build theaters in a competitor's area if they refused to affiliate with his chain. A 1906 alliance with the Orpheum Circuit allowed Keith to control vaudeville east of Chicago, while Martin Beck, head of the Orpheum Circuit, kept control west of the Windy City. As a result an oligopoly reigned over big-time vaudeville from coast to coast. By adopting the consolidation practices of large corporations that prevailed in the Progressive Era, Keith brought order to what had been a chaotic mishmash of separate circuits. Overall, he revolutionized the business of popular theater by applying the principles of organizational consolidation to an amusement enterprise.[13]

Keith also presented a tightly structured program, packaged for the average customer. A standard playbill consisted of eight to ten acts, each running from ten to twenty minutes. The program was arranged so that there would be

Edward Franklin Albee (1857–1930) began as Keith's assistant, headed the circuit after Keith's death, and became the most powerful figure in the vaudeville business. *(Gift of Harold Friedlander, NNMuS)*

no duplication in the type of act. Each act's nature and degree of popularity dictated its position on the playbill; a well-known name always appeared in the slot before intermission, and the headliner performed next to last. The opening, nontalking acts, called "dumb" acts, began the program as the audience arrived and settled in their seats. These might be acrobats or animal acts—performances that did not need to be heard in the commotion. The opening bills were followed by various acts ranging from a song-and-dance routine to a melodramatic playlet. The result was a well-organized program with a fast pace, precision timing, and controlled uniformity. It was a formula designed to appeal to middle-class audiences, including women and children, and one that expressed family values.[14]

Vaudeville thus had a mass-produced quality, the distribution of a sure-fire commodity for the average consumer. The downside of uniform programming was mediocrity with little creativity. Consequently, big-time vaudeville was regularly criticized for dullness and lack of innovation. What saved it were exceptional talents such as Will Rogers, top-flight acts that were the best in their specialty, and the presence of the finest English music-hall performers. Keith also featured stars from the legitimate stage in his programs. Dramatic actors and actresses performed playlets–either scenes from a longer play or short pieces especially written for vaudeville. Keith was among the first vaudeville managers to use films as an added attraction on the playbill (introduced in 1896 at the Union Square Theatre), and they were not always positioned as so-called "chasers" to signal the end of the show. Both one-act plays and motion-picture photoplays were regularly included in the Keith playbills by the late 1890s.

To attract a broad audience, Keith offered high-class family vaudeville for low prices ranging from 25 cents to a dollar. A strict code of manners and conduct was enforced in the Keith theaters. Vaudevillians called the Keith chain the "Sunday School Circuit." Well-dressed ushers in immaculate uniforms distributed instructions asking ladies to remove their hats and men not to smoke, talk, or stamp their feet. Cleanliness was vigorously enforced from the lobbies to the restrooms. Every Keith theater had stringent censorship rules. A Keith contract stipulated strict adherence to the rules or a performer would be canceled. For example, comedians were not permitted to tell dirty jokes.[15] To make his audiences feel that they were in elegant surroundings, Keith built luxurious vaudeville palaces to equal the grandeur of Europe's finest theaters. Albee was charged with overseeing the design and decorations of the theaters, and his taste leaned toward the opulent. As a result, gilded mirrors, red carpets, marble lobbies, exquisite paintings, and other elegant accoutrements embellished the interior of Keith theaters.

Rogers traveled the Keith Circuit for most of a year, from the time he entered vaudeville in June 1905 to March 1906. Rogers appeared at Keith's flagship theater in Boston, the venerable Union Square Theatre in New York, and Keith's first-class house in Philadelphia. He performed at Oscar Hammerstein's famous Victoria Theatre and at its Paradise Roof Garden. He appeared on the same playbill with stars such as Houdini, the Three Keatons, Josephine Cohan, Fred Niblo, and Ernest Hogan. That a newcomer to vaudeville could perform in theaters that most acts aspired to only after years on the road was remarkable. Rogers's act was exactly the type of wholesome entertainment the Keith organization liked. Often advertised as the Lariat King, Rogers dressed in a red shirt and buckskin pants to accentuate the cowboy image. As the orchestra played western theme music, he began doing a few lariat tricks. Buck McKee, the assistant who replaced Jim Minnick, would ride Teddy onto the stage, and Rogers would rope the pony around its feet. Teddy wore rubber or felt shoes to prevent him from slipping on or damaging the stage. After more lariat stunts, Rogers took two lassos and simultaneously roped McKee with one rope and Teddy with the other. Sometimes Rogers rode Teddy as he did his lasso tricks. As a climax, Rogers took an eighty-foot-long rope, formed it into a huge crinoline, and spun it over the heads of the audience. His novel lasso act with horse and assistant drew good reviews practically everywhere he went.

Contrary to popular belief and most accounts of Rogers's life, he would talk and joke throughout his vaudeville performances. In fact, Rogers made comments almost from the start of his vaudeville career. He explained his stunts, joked when he missed a trick, teased other performers on the bill, and made other off-the-cuff comments. His patter drew laughs, and fellow performers encouraged him to tell more gags. To gain more laughs, he would rope people in the theater wings and drag them out on stage. As his first year in vaudeville went on, he talked and joked more regularly. He began to whoop and holler. Although he was not yet called a humorist, reporters frequently mentioned his wry wit as much as his roping skills. Reviewers found his southwestern drawl humorous–what they called "plainsman talk." The talk would evolve into the wisecracking topical humor that gained Rogers fame in the *Ziegfeld Follies,* radio, and films.

Rogers's droll comments and witticisms at this time differed greatly from the humor of the urban ethnic comics (Irish, German, and Jewish) who dominated early vaudeville. In their portrayals of immigrant stereotypes, the dialect comics employed staccato punch lines, eccentric sight gags, slapstick, malapropisms, insults, and double entendres. Whether a monologuist or two-man act, the ethnic comics engaged in self-deprecating humor and mocked newly arrived immigrants. Others made fun of types such as the conceited politician, the dandy, the erudite college professor, the braggart, and the prudish society woman, among others.[16]

By contrast, Rogers's stage persona was that of a heartland cowboy rather than an urban immigrant or city slicker.[17] He personified the homespun country boy fresh from the Plains with an innocent grin and a disarming manner. Rogers's act perfectly expressed the goals of Keith vaudeville—family entertainment, fun for the children, and innocuous humor. The cowboy attire, horse, and lasso reminded urban audiences of traditional values associated with the frontier. When Rogers later performed in the West, his lasso stunts appealed greatly to theatergoers familiar with ranch life and the skills of the cowboy.

Rogers's vaudeville career commenced at a time when Americans were captivated by the myth of the West. The cowboy vogue was evident in both fine

Louise Henry (ca. 1887–1941), cover of *New York Morning Telegraph*, 23 February 1908. Henry and Rogers met in vaudeville and had a love affair. *(Laurie Weltz Private Collection, New York City)*

arts and popular culture, from the sculpture and paintings of Frederic Remington and Charles Russell (who became a good friend of Rogers) to dime novels and silent films, such as Edwin Porter's *Great Train Robbery* (1903). The New York stage featured western melodramas, such as the 1905 hit *The Girl of the Golden West.* A proponent of the West and all it stood for was President Theodore Roosevelt, a Rough Rider, Dakota rancher, big-game hunter, environmentalist, and rugged individualist.

In this cultural environment Rogers was portrayed as the lariat expert "direct from the ranches of Indian Territory" and "loyal to the life of the ranger and cattle-raiser."[18] The publicity stories played up Rogers's cowboy image. Several times he told reporters that he was going to give up vaudeville, return home, and become a cattleman on his ranch. Despite the good reviews Rogers received, he was hesitant about a career in show business. He found the routine monotonous and the travel tiring. Often lonely, he missed his family and friends back home.

As a single man on the vaudeville trail, he had opportunities to meet many female performers. He developed a close, and probably romantic, relationship with the singer and comedienne Louise Henry.[19] She performed on the same bill with Rogers at Keith's Union Square Theatre, the week of 12 June 1905. They shared a love of horses and nature, and on stage Henry played a comic country bumpkin—a role Rogers could identify with. While staying at the Putnam House, his home in New York City, Rogers spent considerable time with her. But it was a difficult relationship to sustain, since both were often on the road performing in different cities. Moreover, Henry was already married.

At the same time as he was seeing Henry, Rogers resumed his correspondence with Betty Blake in letters that confessed his love for her and his goal of marriage. For Christmas, he sent her a handkerchief he had bought in South America–a gift he said he had saved for the woman he would marry. Although Betty continued to reject his overtures, he visited her in early March 1906. In Claremore and Chelsea, Rogers was warmly greeted by his father and sisters, who were proud of his success in vaudeville.

Before leaving, Rogers conveyed to his family the biggest news yet: He had procured a four-week engagement at the world-famous Wintergarten Theatre in Berlin, beginning 1 April. In just nine months, Rogers managed to transfer the skills of the range and his Wild West show routine to the vaudeville stage. During this period he went from being an obscure Wild West show rider to a successful performer in big-time vaudeville. He would soon gain even wider recognition in Germany and England.

Louise Henry portraying The Sal Skinner Gal on stage. Henry and Rogers were part of a close circle of performing artists whose social life revolved around the Putnam Hotel in Manhattan. *(Laurie Weltz Private Collection, New York City)*

1. Stern et al., *New York 1900,* 203; Van Hoogstraten, *Lost Broadway Theatres,* 41.
2. *TDW,* 21 May 1933.
3. Will Rogers to Clement Vann Rogers, 8 May 1905, above.
4. Daniel F. Hennessy (ca. 1855–1937) was a long-time employee of the Keith organization. During his early career he managed legitimate theater shows. Around 1900 he became an executive with the Vaudeville Managers' Association, which had offices in New York's St. James Building. Known for his shrewdness, he was responsible for bringing small-time managers into the association. Many years later, Hennessy managed small-time vaudeville for the UBO. On 20 November 1937 he died in New York at the age of eighty-two. "He could have made a fortune," wrote Joe Laurie, Jr., "but died a poor man–because he was honest" (*Vaudeville,* 241; see also *VO,* 2:24 November 1937).
5. Yagoda, *Will Rogers,* 87; quoted from Rogers's unpublished autobiographical manuscript, which he wrote by hand for Sime Silverman, the founder and publisher of *Variety.* Yagoda, who transcribed the document as part of his research at the home of Will Rogers, Jr., calls it the Sime manuscript (pp. 342, 355; see also Excerpts from Unpublished Autobiography, ca. Late 1910, *PWR,* vol. 3).

6. Will Rogers to Betty Blake, 3 June 1905, and Will Rogers to Sisters, 3 June 1905, below.

7. Stein, ed., *American Vaudeville As Seen by Its Contemporaries,* xi, 3–4; Wilmeth, *Variety Entertainment and Outdoor Amusements,* 130–32; Zellers, "Cradle of Variety."

8. *EV,* 373; *OCAT,* 81–82, 506; Toll, *On with the Show!* 173–76.

9. Toll, *On with the Show!* 89.

10. Early variety theaters included New York's Lafayette Theatre (1827) and Franklin Theatre (1842), and in the 1860s Butler's American Theatre and the Great New York Aquarium (Nye, *Unembarrassed Muse,* 167–78).

11. Zellers, *Tony Pastor,* 54. The Metropolitan's opening bill on 4 October 1875 featured a smorgasbord of acts much like vaudeville: "Gus Williams . . . Dutch dialect comic . . . Sanford and Wilson, comic musicians on a variety of instruments; . . . grotesque song and dance performers; Jennie Morgan, Vocalist; William Carlton, Irish vocalist and comic; the Lenton Brothers, acrobats; Venus and Adonis, young veloci-pede riders; and a number of others" (Zellers, *Tony Pastor,* 52).

12. *Variety,* 15 July 1905; B. F. Keith's International Circuit Theatrical Enterprises listing, Columbus, Ohio, 4 November 1907, THS.

13. On Keith and Albee see Allen, "B. F. Keith and the Origins of American Vaudeville," 105–15; Allen, *Horrible Prettiness,* 180–93; Connors, "American Vaudeville Managers," 24–27; *DAB,* 5:289; Gilbert, *American Vaudeville,* 197–207; Grau, *Stage in the Twentieth Century,* 142-45; *GRB,* 247; King, "Keith-Albee et al. . . .," 3–10; Laurie, *Vaudeville,* 337–41; McLean, "Genesis of Vaudeville," 82–95; *OCAT,* 395–96; *EV,* 278–85; Snyder, *Voice of the City,* 3–25, 64–81; *VO,* 1:3 April 1914; see also Biographical Appendix entry, ALBEE, Edward Franklin.

14. Snyder, "American Vaudeville—Theatre in a Package," 35–46.

15. Allen, *Horrible Prettiness,* 183; Gilbert, *American Vaudeville,* 202; Laurie, *Vaudeville,* 337–41.

16. Distler, "Rise and Fall of the Racial Comics"; McLean, "U.S. Vaudeville and the Urban Comics," 47–52.

17. It is interesting to note that Rogers sometimes joked about immigrants, espe-cially Jews, in his vaudeville routine. His imitation of what he called a "Yiddisher cow-boy" is an example.

18. Article from the *Worcester Sunday Telegram,* 19 November 1905, below. See also Nye, *Unembarrassed Muse,* 288–90; Toll, *Entertainment Machine,* 75–78; Yagoda, *Will Rogers,* 96–97.

19. Louise Henry (ca. 1888–1941) was a comedienne, singer, and actress who gained popularity with her imitation of a country girl, Sal Skinner (see Biographical Appendix entry, HENRY, Louise).

———

To Sister
3 June 1905
New York, N.Y.

New York, June 3 1905

My Dear Sister

Well I know you all have forgotten how to write   it is generally me but not this time   here I am waiting to hear from you.

Well I am still in our big city and will be for some time yet.   I am getting my act in good shape to do some good and make some Money.   I have had it on the stage using a horse and all.

Here is a little Clipping from a paper at a swell horse show I worked at in the Swell Subur[b]s where seats the cheapest were $20.00[1]   I got $25 a show worked three shows.   only engaged just for a little novelty for the big bugs.

All the Mulhall outfit have gone back   but one boy and I   he is selling his horses here.

It takes time to get my act started but I start the 12 of June over the Keith Vaudeville Circuit the swellest in the east.[2]   I will take a spin down home as soon as I get a little money and time which wont be later that [than] August not sure

I sold old Comanche to a man in N.Y. and Mulhall sneakingly bought him from him and he owns him now for little Mildred[3]   he bought him when he found out I was going to stay east he thought I would follow him as he was mad because I quit them.

But here is good news for you all   it is either stage and make a good living or no show business at all for me   never to the Wild West ▲ show ▲ any more.

I have the finest little pony that is really better than old Comanche for he is sound   younger and he works fine on the stage[4]   he suits me better for my present work than Comanche   I bought him from Mulhall.   I will send you some pictures in a few days as I have to have some made to use in my act.

Well I will close   write when you can

Lots of Love to all

Yours
Willie

Putnam House, northeast corner of Fourth Avenue and Twenty-sixth Street, where Rogers resided when in New York City. *(Byron Collection, NNMuS)*

  send this down to Papa

  None of this is for publication only to let my *own* folks know how I am doing

always

  see address

  Putnam House[5]

  New York City.

TLS, rc. OkClaW. On Putnam House letterhead.

  1. The Orange Horse Show in Newark, N.J.

  2. At this time Keith's Union Square Theatre was one of twenty in the Keith Circuit. In July 1905 the chain included theaters in New England states, Pennsylvania, upstate New York, and Ohio, and in the cities of Detroit, Baltimore, and Toronto. Keith's empire virtually controlled big-time vaudeville theaters and bookings from the

East Coast to Chicago (*EV*, 278–85; Keith Circuit advertisement, *NYDM*, 15 July 1905; see also B. F. Keith's Amusement Enterprises contract, 8 June 1905, below).

3. A reference to Mildred Mulhall. Another story is that Mulhall wanted Rogers to remain with his show and not enter vaudeville, so Mulhall kidnapped the horse (Marquis, "Will Rogers and His Horses," 30; see also *PWR*, 1:516–21).

4. A reference to Teddy.

5. Located at 367 Fourth Avenue at the corner of Twenty-sixth Street, the Putnam House (later called Hotel Preston) was Will Rogers's home during his early years in vaudeville. It was a small, modest theatrical hotel where single rooms cost 50 cents a night and double rooms started at a dollar. It was opposite Madison Square Garden and convenient to other theaters in the Union Square, Chelsea, and Times Square areas. Consequently, it attracted performers who played in Manhattan's showplaces. The hotel was constantly sold out when the circus and Buffalo Bill's Wild West performed at the Garden. Vaudevillians, theater managers, and agents met frequently at its cafe and bar.

The hotel's first owner was Lawrence B. Kerr (ca. 1810–88). As a youngster, Kerr began by selling milk in the Madison Square area. Eventually he established a stand at the corner of Fourth Avenue and Twenty-sixth Street where he sold milk, pies, and cakes. Probably around 1870, he used his earnings to open a small family hotel, which he named the Putnam House, in a four-story building at the corner. Its street-level restaurant is believed to have been the first establishment to serve doughnuts and coffee. By the time he died at the Putnam House at the age of seventy-eight, Kerr had amassed considerable wealth. His son, Lawrence R. Kerr, inherited the Putnam and took over its management. In 1891 he leased it to the Foster brothers; however, they lost money and after two years were dispossessed. Threatened by foreclosure proceedings on a mortgage on the site for $211,000, the Putnam Holding Co. sold the hotel for $300,000 in 1909. In 1955 the building was still standing and was called the Elton Hotel. Renovated inside and out, it then had a fifth story; Ming's bar and restaurant occupied the street level (Quinn Hotel Collection, NNHi, Hotel Mail, 15 December 1888, in env. B, 1888; Hotel Mail, 10 June 1893, in env. A, 1898; Hotel "P" File, NNMus).

Rogers stayed at the Putnam House when he was performing in New York vaudeville theaters or between vaudeville dates during 1905 and 1906, and perhaps for a time thereafter. Quite possibly, Rogers had a permanent room or apartment there even when he was on the road. He was very fond of the hotel and called it his "Dobe House" or "Shack." Rogers's friend Louise Henry wrote: "This is where Will Rogers made his New York home on this occasion and for a long time later. He loved this little hotel. It was an old four story building with its main entrance going in from the side street, marked 'Ladies Entrance' through a narrow hall-way which led to the grill with its bar-room leading in from Fourth Avenue" (LHM-LHP).

Rogers and his intimate circle of cowboy friends congregated at the hotel. Among those who visited Rogers at the hotel were Jack Joyce, Jim Gabriel, Charles Russell, Ed Borein, and Leo Carillo. The Putnam's restaurant had popular prices, and its chef, Charlie, whom Rogers had met in Argentina, prepared beans, Rogers's favorite dish. Louise Henry wrote that "long after Bill moved uptown, his love never died for the Putnam. Many times afterwards, when we go for a walk below Forty-second Street, Will would say 'let's drop by the Putnam, maybe some of the old gang are there'" (LHM-LHP; letterhead information; see also *Summer Days and Nights in New York*, 1898, pamphlet, NN).

To Betty Blake
3 June 1905
New York, N.Y.

In the last week of May or early June 1905, Rogers had a successful tryout at Keith's Union Square Theatre and was contracted to perform there during the week of 12 June. According to Rogers, the tryout was at a supper show on a warm day and there were only ten or twelve people in the audience. The supper show attracted a smaller crowd than the matinee or the evening performance. "I remember they put me on first and, knowing might little about theaters, I thought it was a position of honor. I made good, and the following week was billed regularly for three shows a day." In the following letter Rogers shares with Betty Blake the news that he is going to perform at the Union Square Theatre.[1]

New York, June 3 *1905*

My Dear old Pal

Say you are the extremity, you are one Kid that puts me on the guess list for fair.   its me to the dopey gang when I unfold one of your packages   you can make me feel better and worse than any one I know.

Look here Bettie dont think I am Kidding you   on the level you are my best old pal and I like you for it and again I hate you for not allowing me to be more.

you always kept me at a distance allright   you know Bettie thats why I dident write to you after the Nowata affair.[2]

I just sized you up that night and I thought No she dont give a d___ only to be a good old pal and honest it hurt me and I said I wont even write to her for your letters are no encouragement to me   I wish to G___ that I could look at it as you do but I cant.   I know you might laugh and say old Bill is just handing out this line as he always does but It aint so I swear   You know I have had some experience and have been some to the flirt talk with lots of them but this has been maturing for years   I got to love someone and it dont take me many guesses to tell who it is.

What would be my object in telling you all this and you there and me here if it wasent so and so whatever you do believe me even if you wont do anything else

I know you will say this is a foolish letter and that you dont like me in this new role but thats why I am taking chances on losing a friend simply because you got to know some time

Here is a couple of clippings from a swell horse show I worked at in the swell suburb of N.Y.   I have worked on the stage using my horse and I open

June 12 at the swellest Vaudeville house in N.Y.   I think I can make good   I am on a fair road to success in my line   am having a swell time.   I am acquainted with some pretty big men here and stand pat with them.   But there [is] a little lacking some old place.   See if you cant offer some remedy for it in the way of honestly good encouragement   only truthfully tell me that you could some time learn to love me just a little and I bet there will be a cowboy doing 100% better act and feeling fine.

Now Sister Bettie I am as honest in this and if you dont like me a little bit Bettie dont even write to me for it would make me all the worse.

But I hope to ___ you will be able to write to this *Nutty foolish Cowboy* you will then get pictures in bunches.

Yours

Bill.

TLS, rc. On Putnam House letterhead.

1. Unidentified clipping, scrapbook A-3, OkClaW. Keith's Union Square Theatre was located on Fourteenth Street, near Broadway and Fourth Avenue, on the southeast side of Union Square in the Rialto, New York's main theatrical center at this time. Designed by H. M. Simons, the theater was built in 1870 by Sheridan Shook. Located on the ground floor of a five-story hotel, the theater's auditorium was horseshoe-shaped. It accommodated 12,000 people in its orchestra ground floor, a dress circle, and a gallery or family circle. In the family circle spectators sat on wooden pew benches, for which they paid 10 cents (in the boxes the price was 75 cents). The theater was recognized as one of the most beautiful in the city. Embellishments included boxes decorated in an ornate Byzantine style, a proscenium arch painted maroon with gold trim, and a sculptured, domed ceiling.

Performances over the years mirrored the transformation of popular amusement and included variety, drama, burlesque, vaudeville, and films. The Union Square Theatre opened on 11 September 1871, and under the management of Albert M. Palmer its stock company gained considerable fame. A fire on 28 February 1888 destroyed the auditorium, but it was rebuilt and reopened on 27 March 1889.

On 4 April 1893 it was announced that B. F. Keith and his partner Edward Albee had leased the theater from the Courtlandt Palmer estate. The Union Square was Keith's first theater in New York. Beginning on 18 September 1893, Keith presented continuous "polite" vaudeville, with the show usually starting at midday. Admission to the theater in June 1905 ranged from 25 cents for an unreserved seat to a dollar for a reserved seat. The Union Square was a financial success, and one time grossed $104,000 in a single year. When F. F. Proctor merged his theaters with the Keith organization in May 1906, the name was changed to Keith and Proctor's Union Square Theatre.

The growth of the motion-picture industry eventually ended Union Square's heyday as a leading vaudeville venue. In 1908 Keith eliminated vaudeville in favor of a potpourri of silent films, and changed the name of the theater to the Bijou Dream. In 1911 the Union Square adopted a mixed bill of vaudeville and movies. Rogers was featured on the bill that closed the theater as a vaudeville house, when he appeared there during the week of 23 June 1914. Later, as the Acme (1922–32), the theater showed first-run movies, and from 1932 to 1936 it featured films from the Soviet Union. In 1936 the theater was closed, its lobby was razed, and a large portion of its interior was walled up to make way for small shops. For years the exterior shell of the theater remained, and its roof was visible from the street. A journalist in 1989 reported that behind the brick wall the horseshoe balcony and the ceiling were still intact. In 1992 New York's oldest surviving theater was demolished when the entire block on which it stood was razed for a development (Brown, *History of the New York Stage,* 3:145–90; "City Strikes Its Oldest Set," *New York Daily News,* 1992, clipping, THS; clippings, Union Square Theatre file, NNMus; Frick, *New York's First Theatrical Center,* 32–41; Frick and Ward, eds., *Directory of Historic American Theatres,* 190; Grau, *Forty Years Observation of Music and Drama,* 3–8; Gray, "The Ghost behind a Huge Sign," *NYT,* 29 January 1989; Henderson, *City and the Theatre,* 134, 140, 143, 145; King, "New York's Oldest Existing Theatre–The Union Square," 48; Marston and Feller, *F. F. Proctor,* 97–106; Musser, *Before the Nickelodeon,* 372–74; Robinson, "Fourteenth Street, Cradle of American Vaudeville," 19–20; Yagoda, *Will Rogers,* 87; Zellers, *Tony Pastor,* 67–86, 96, 108–9).

2. There is no specific information on this incident. James (Sandy) Blake was a railroad agent stationed at Nowata, I.T., located north of Oologah on the Iron Mountain Railroad line (Shirk, *Oklahoma Place Names,* 152).

Keith Circuit Contract
8 June 1905
Boston, Mass.

Rogers's first vaudeville contract to play at New York City's Union Square Theatre reflected the power and stringent policies of the B. F. Keith vaudeville circuit and its emphasis on genteel respectability. The contract prohibited the performer from play-ing at opposition theaters, subjected him or her to strict rules of decorum, and insist-ed on an act's uniqueness and excellence. The artist had little protection should a vio-lation of contractual rules occur.

B. F. KEITH'S AMUSEMENT ENTERPRISES.[1]

EDWARD F. ALBEE, GENERAL MANAGER.[2]

ARTIST'S CONTRACT.

Agreement entered into this <u>8th</u> day of <u>June</u> A.D. 1905<u>–</u> between B. F. KEITH, of the City of Boston, Mass., party of the first part, and <u>WILL ROGERS</u> party of the second part.

Witnesseth That in consideration of the sum hereinafter mentioned, the said party of the second part hereby agrees to render services to the party of the first part at such theatres and in such cities as said Keith shall designate herein, for a term of <u>one</u> week _ commencing on the date and as per route below mentioned, viz.:

New York, June 12th–1905–

and said party of the second part agrees to render _ best skill and services in presenting _ specialties at —3— performances each day (except as hereinafter provided) in such part of the programme as may be selected by the party of the first part, for which services, so to be rendered by the said party of the second part, the said party of the first part agrees to pay the party of the second part the sum of Seventy-five dollars ($75.00) weekly,[3] payable upon the conclusion of the final performance of the party of the second part at the end of each and every week during the period of _ service under this contract.

1. The party of the first part reserves the right to cancel before its date or terminate within its time the engagement of any artist who is incompetent, or who has (in making terms) grossly exaggerated the value of his act; or, whose act is improper, offensive or other than first-class.

2. It is further distinctly agreed and understood, in the event of cancellation or termination, for any of the causes aforesaid, that no claim or right of action shall exist in favor of the party of the second part as against the said party of the first part by reason of such cancellation or termination. And the said party of the second part hereby agrees to abide by the rules and regulations of the party of the first part now in force in any of his said theatres.

3. The said party of the second part agrees that after the signing of this contract and during the continuance of the engagement herein provided for, the said party of the second part will not, in any of the cities in which said party of the first part is operating or booking for a theatre, render or present, either privately or publicly, specialty, act or performance, in any other theatre, music hall or place of amusement of any kind for any person whomsoever, without the written consent of the said party of the first part first had and obtained.

4. And the parties hereto further stipulate and agree that the several theatres under the direction of the party of the first part are conducted upon a high plane of respectability and moral cleanliness, and that in so doing he makes such rules and gives such informal directions as he thinks proper for the government of all employees and performers in the conduct of his business; that the several theatres under the direction of the party of the first part open at noon and close at 10.45 P.M.,[4] and that no Sunday performances are given; that all performers must report for rehearsal at 9 A.M. on Mondays.[5]

5. The party of the second part further agrees that whether engaged for two or three performances daily, _ will, when required, give extra performances on holidays and special occasions, while performing in any theatre or under the direction of the party of the first part; and, in Boston, extra performances on Saturdays.

6. The party of the first part further stipulates that for each act engaged under this contract, the party of the second part must provide billing, scene and property plots, and a complete set of photographs sufficient for a large frame, to be sent to each theatre of the party of the first part at least ten days in advance of the beginning of each engagement; that for each act under engagement to the party of the first part the party of the second part must furnish the General Manager of party of the first part with the route upon which _ are scheduled for three weeks previous to the opening date under this contract.

7. The party of the first part reserves the right to advertise, bill, programme and schedule acts and assign dressing rooms as he deems best in the interests of the management. It is further agreed by the parties hereto, that any arrangement of routes as herein stipulated is subject to change by the party of the first part.

8. It is further stipulated by and between the parties hereto that failure to comply with any of the above conditions will be deemed a violation of the contract and sufficient cause for cancellation.

9. And the said party of the second part hereby agrees that the services which _ contracts under this agreement to render to the said party of the first part, in any or all of his theatres, as aforesaid, are of the highest standard of excellence, and are special, unique and extraordinary, and that no other artist can be obtained to render similar services, and the said party of the second part hereby agrees in case of a violation of this contract by _ that an injunction may issue to restrain the rendition of services or unauthorized performances of said party of the second part, in any of the cities in which said party of the second part is to appear under this contract, at any time after the signing and before the completion by the party of the second part of the services herein contracted for, and that in such an action the said party of the second part will consent to the issuance of such injunction, and that in such action the party of the second part will not offer or seek to establish in defense that _____ services are not special, unique and extraordinary, or that such services can be or could have been supplied by any other artist; but will admit in such an action that irreparable damage will ensue to said party of the first part in case of such violation; and hereby waives any defense that the said services are not special, unique and extraordinary, or that irreparable damage will not ensue to the party of the first part, or that some other artist could render the services herein contracted for by the party of the second part, the said party of the second part intending by this clause to waive the right to be heard upon the question of the issuing of an injunction as herein provided.

10. The party of the second part agrees to furnish complete orchestrations of all _ music for the following instruments: first violin, piano, flute, clarinet, 'cello, bass violin, cornet, trombone and drums, with all cues marked plainly on the conductor's sheet. Violation of this clause will subject the act to being worked with piano only.

11. All the foregoing provisions are, and are hereby agreed to be fully binding in this contract, as in every contract for the engagement of artists at any of the theatres of the party of the first part.

In WITNESS whereof the parties hereto have hereunto set their hands and seals the day and year first above written.

In presence of—

It is distinctly understood
that 5% commission on this salary
will be deducted weekly during
this engagement on account
of Office—[6]

_____

_____

Performers will please remember that full orchestrations
of all their music will be required.

PD. OkClaW.

1. Benjamin Franklin Keith (1846–1914) is a major figure in the history of vaudeville. Born at Hillsboro Bridge, N.H., he left home in 1868–69 and obtained a job as a messboy on a coastal freight steamer. During the 1870s he traveled with various circuses, and in New York he worked at Bunnell's Museum, a dime museum that offered a stage show and curiosities. An attempt to form his own traveling museum show failed, and in 1880 he went to Providence, R.I., where he manufactured and sold brooms. Returning to Boston, Keith opened a dime museum with Colonel William F. Austin on 8 January 1883. (See introduction to Part Two, above.) Inspired by his success, Keith and his partner George H. Batcheller leased the 900-seat Bijou Theatre in Boston. It opened on 1 August 1887 and soon became a leading vaudeville house offering continuous "refined" variety entertainment. With a new partner and general manager, Edward F. Albee, Keith expanded his operation along the East Coast, opening the Gaiety in Providence (1888), the Bijou in Philadelphia (1889), the Union Square Theatre in New York (1893), and Keith's New Theatre in Boston (1894). Keith was a pioneer in combining his theaters into a circuit, which allowed vaudevillians to travel from one engagement to another.

Keith possessed a strong talent for entrepreneurship and organizational management. He chose able managers, such as Albee, and promoted skilled administrators in his organization. In 1909, as a result of illness, Keith reduced his involvement in the organization and retired to Palm Beach, Fla. When he died on 26 March 1914, his wealth was estimated at between $8 million and $10 million, and several hundred theaters carried his name. On the day of his funeral all Keith theaters were closed in his honor until the evening performance (Allen, "B. F. Keith and the Origins of American Vaudeville," 105–15; Allen, *Horrible Prettiness*, 180–93; *OCAT*, 395–96; Connors, "American Vaudeville Managers," 24–27; *DAB*, 5:289; *EV*, 278–85; Gilbert, *American Vaudeville*, 197–207; Grau, *Stage in the Twentieth Century*, 142–45; *GRB*, 247; King, "Keith-Albee et al. . . .," 3–10; Laurie, *Vaudeville*, 337–41; McLean, "Genesis of Vaudeville," 82–95; Snyder, *Voice of the City*, 64–81; *VO*, 1:3 April 1914).

2. As general manager of the Keith Circuit and the UBO, Edward Franklin Albee (1857–1930) played a primary role in the circuit's operations by supervising the construction of Keith theaters in a lavish palatial style, and by merging booking and theatrical management into a streamlined central organization. Over the years Rogers got to know Albee personally. Albee admired his homespun vaudeville act–exactly the type of entertainment that met the ideals of the Keith organization (see Biographical Appendix entry, Albee, Edward Franklin).

3. Considering that he had to pay an assistant's salary and upkeep expenses for his horse, Rogers's initial salary was at the low end of the scale for big-time vaudevillians. Six days after his opening at the Union Square Theatre, Rogers signed a contract with Keith at $140 per week for his engagements in Boston (week of 26 June) and Philadelphia (week of 3 July). A few months later he would receive $250 a week from Samuel Scribner and the Keith operation. In February 1919 big-time acts at Keith's theaters in New York averaged $427 a week. During his vaudeville career Rogers's weekly salary was mostly around $300. If one considers that in December 1910 Pat Rooney and Marion Bent, Joe Welch, and Fred Niblo were earning $500 a week; Julius Steger, $1,000; Julian Eltinge, $1,500; Annette Kellerman, $2,000; and Eva Tanguay, $2,500, Roger's salary was in the middle range among the hundreds of acts that received less than $500 (B. F. Keith's Amusement Enterprises contract, 14 June 1906, OkClaW; Davis, "Business Side of Vaudeville," 527–37; Robert Grau, "Growth of Vaudeville," *NYDM*, 6 August 1913; "Some Vaudeville Salaries," *Variety*, 10 December 1910; Snyder, *Voice of the City*, 47).

4. An example of Keith's continuous vaudeville, which ran from midday to late evening. Within this time span, each act generally performed three times.

5. Vaudevillians relied on Sunday as their day of travel between dates. If a performer missed train connections and as a consequence the Monday rehearsal, he or she was subject to cancellation for that week.

6. This was the notorious 5 percent commission fee that the Keith enterprise charged performers for the privilege of playing on the circuit. It was vigorously attacked by the White Rats, the vaudevillians' independent union. (See Review from the *Washington Times*, 31 October 1905, n. 1, below.)

Manager's Report, Union Square Theatre
12 June 1905
New York, N.Y.

Unique insights into Rogers's career and vaudeville acts in general can be obtained from the weekly manager's reports from the Keith theaters. Usually these critiques were written by the theater manager on Monday afternoon after the matinee performance. The evaluation of each act generally reflected the manager's opinions.[1] If an act received consistently bad reviews or made use of profanity, it was unlikely to be booked again on the Keith Circuit. On the following playbill with Rogers was the actress Louise Henry. The two quickly became close friends and spent time together in New York.

CRITICISM

New York June 12th, 1905.

ST. JOHN & LEVEVRE[2]   Man and woman, singing, dancing and a few imitations   The same act as presented here before, always goes well here and an excellent three show act.[3] Fourteen minutes in one.[4]

NIBLO & RILEY   Two men, white and black-face. Singing dancing and talking comedy. Singing and talking don't amount too much. Received a big lot of applause for their eccentric dancing. Good act for the three a day class. Thirteen minutes, full stage,[5] close in one.

STONE & LYNN   Two young men, club juggling, with a little bag punching. Club juggling very ordinary, received some applause for the bag punching. Good opening act. Twelve minutes full stage.

WILLIE GARDNER[6]   There is a little bit of novelty to this young man's act. Dancing on roller and ice skates. Greatly appreciated throughout. Nine minutes in one, three shows.

NORMAN D. STELL   Under the impression this young man's voice was rather phenomenal, to the contrary, it is unnatural, weak and sounds more like an imitation. Received very little applause. Eleven minutes in one, two shows.[7]

MITCHELL & CAIN   Two men, talking comedy. Some new material. Plenty of laughs, always goes well here. Received the biggest lot of applause up to this time, took three bows on their finish. Twenty minutes in one, three shows.

WILL ROGERS   Lasso manipulator. This man gi[v]es us a genuine novelty. The act is on the style of the Chamberlains, but far superior. Lassos a horse and rider, while going at good speed across the stage. Big applause all through the act. Full stage, can close in one, three shows, ten minutes.[8]

VAN ALSTYNE[9] & HENRY   Singing comedy. Received a big lot of advance applause. Van Alstyne scored big with his piano playing   Louise Henry is only a fair singer, looks attractive and being the "Sal Skinner Gal" lets her out. They received quite a number of laughs in spots, but closed very weak. Twenty-three minutes in two, two shows.

EMMA FRANCIS[10] with her Arabian Whirlwinds. Singing, dancing and a little acrobatic work. The boys are clever and received big applause all through their acrobatic work. Miss Francis dancing went big. They all work fast, full of ginger. Received a lot of applause on the finish. Nine minutes full stage, two shows.

SEARL & VIOLET ALLEN[11] In their talking comedy skit "The Sign Painter" The material in this act is about the same as when last presented. They scored fully as strong as before and held this place down in good shape. Fifteen minutes in one, two shows.

HENRY V. DONNELLY[12] Assisted by a woman, in the farce "Mr. & Mrs. Nagg"[13] First appearance, received a big lot of advance applause. The idea is that of a nagging married couple. Donnelly is a clever comedian. The business in the act don't amount too much, the success depends solely on the lines, some of which are funny and laughable in spots. This being the first presentation I believe the act will improve daily. Twenty-three minutes, full stage, two shows.

HOEY & LEE[14] Two men, hebrew comedians, and two of the best we have had here for some time. All new and good material. Sang four parodies on their opening and they wanted more. Big hit. Seventeen minutes in one, two shows.

ZAZELL-VERNON CO[15] In an acrobatic pantomime "The Elopement" One of the best acts they have ever given us, one continual laugh from start to finish, elegant closing act. Fifteen minutes, close in one about three minutes. Two shows.

BIOGRAPH[16]

The Life of a miner[17]	Rather serious, but interesting, for a fake picture it is very good.
The Insolvent Guest	Comedy good.

TD. KAC-IaU.

1. The singer Sophie Tucker (1884–1966) recalled that the Monday matinee was a time when the manager could censor material in an act: "During the Monday matinee we all knew he was watching and making notes; not on what the audience liked or didn't, but on what he liked or—more frequently—disliked" (Tucker, *Some of These Days*, 148–49).

2. Johnnie LeFevre (ca. 1873–1952) was a long-time vaudeville performer. He also

acted in legitimate theater, including John Golden's 1908 production of *Lightnin'* (*VO,* 4:5 November 1952). Frankie St. John was likewise on the stage, and appeared in *Ten Nights in a Barroom* (1892) and starred in *On the Sahara* (1893) (Odell, *Annals of the New York Stage,* 15:243, 822).

3. Three shows meant the matinee, the supper or late afternoon performance, and the evening performance.

4. The vaudeville stage was divided into four parts. The front part, which was the section before the curtain, was called "one." Brett Page, in *Writing for Vaudeville* (1915), described this area: "The space lying between the tormentors [the stage's first wings] and a line drawn between the bases of the proscenium arch is called 'One'. It is in One that monologues, most 'single acts'–that is, acts presented by one person— and many 'two-acts'—acts requiring but two people—are played. Behind the tormentors is a curtain called the 'olio', which fulfills the triple purpose of hiding the rest of the stage, serving as scenery for acts in One and often as a curtain to raise and lower on acts playing in the space back of One" (28).

5. The term *full stage* meant that performers were using the entire four areas of the stage for their act. In *Writing for Vaudeville* Page defined the area: "Behind the wings that bound Three are another pair of wings, set an equal number of feet back, which serve as the boundaries of 'Four'. But, as there are rarely more than four entrances on any stage, Four is usually called 'Full Stage'. In Full Stage are presented all acts such as acrobatic acts, animal turns, musical comedies, playlets and other pretentious acts that require deep sets and a wide playing space" (29).

6. Possibly William Gardner (ca. 1874–1930), who was a vaudevillian and a musical director and arranger (*VO,* 2:27 August 1930).

7. Two shows usually meant the matinee and the evening performance.

8. Rogers also received a favorable newspaper review in the *New York Clipper:* "Will Rogers made his debut at his house, being billed as the 'World's Champion Lasso Manipulator'. To even the layman it was apparent that he had some right to his claim, and the audience marveled at his skill" (*NYC,* 17 June 1905; also clipping, scrapbook A-1, OkClaW). On 12 June, the day Rogers opened at the Union Square Theatre, the Otto Sarony Co. wrote him that "we would like to have a new Photograph of you to add to our collection of people in whom the public are interested" (Otto Sarony Co. to Will Rogers, 12 June 1905, OkClaW). The Sarony Co. was the best-known theatrical photographers in New York (Frick, *New York's First Theatrical Center,* 112–14). As a useful form of publicity for his new vaudeville career, Rogers did have his photograph taken by the Sarony Co. (see frontispiece to this volume).

9. Henry's vaudeville partner and husband was the songwriter Egbert Anson Van Alstyne (1882–1951), who provided piano accompaniment for Henry's singing. A popular composer, Van Alstyne was first employed as a pianist and as a music director for touring variety stage shows. About 1900 he teamed up with the lyricist Harry H. Williams to write songs. They went to New York, where Van Alstyne worked as a company pianist and song plugger for Remick, a Tin Pan Alley music publisher. Williams and Van Alstyne wrote a series of hits and also composed music for the Broadway musicals *A Broken Doll* (1909) and *Girlies* (1910). In addition, Van Alstyne also wrote "Good Night, Ladies" (1911) and "That Old Girl of Mine" (1912), as well as the music for many other Broadway musicals (*AmSCAP,* 747; Craig, *Sweet and Lowdown,* 79–81; Ewen, ed., *American Popular Composers,* 169–70; Gammond, *Oxford Companion to Popular Music,* 355; Hitchcock and Sadie, eds., *New Grove Dictionary of American Music,* 4:444; Lax and Smith, *Great Song Thesaurus,* 329; Laurie Weltz to the WRPP, 12 May 1994; LHM-LHP).

10. Emma Francis (b. ca. 1880) specialized in acrobatic wooden shoe dancing and was considered among the best in her profession. Her vaudeville act reflected the popularity of clogging, which had become a craze among the public at this time. She was born in Leadville, Colo., and at age ten began her show-business career. From 1893 to 1899 she played engagements with several variety companies, including Gus Hill's New York Stars. During the season of 1899–1900 she was in *A Hot Old Time*. The following season she was engaged with the Rogers Brothers Co. and remained with it for three years, doing specialties with Pat Rooney. In 1914 she was back in vaudeville with a trio of Arabian dancers, called Emma Francis and her Arabs. In 1920 she teamed up with Harold Kennedy, an eccentric dancer. In 1938 she was featured at Billy Rose's Diamond Horseshoe nightclub in New York, in a lavish cabaret show. Seven years later, at age sixty-five, she was still performing handsprings, cartwheels, tap dances, and a soft-shoe routine at the Diamond Horseshoe (Emma Francis clippings file, NN-L-BRTC and series 3, 497:16-43, NN-L-RLC; Laurie, *Vaudeville*, 42–43, 234; Mantle and Sherwood, eds., *Best Plays of 1899–1909*, 371, 393; *NYDM*, 5 August 1914; see also Review from the *Philadelphia Item*, 27 June 1905, below).

11. Searl Allen and Violet Allen performed comedy sketches in vaudeville for many years either as a team or as part of a troupe called Searl Allen and Co. Searl Allen wrote the dialogue and music for many of his company's sketches. In 1908 he formed a partnership with the author Jack Burnett to produce and write vaudeville acts and musicals. In 1916 he teamed up with Eddie Howard in a two-man vaudeville comedy skit act (Searl Allen and Co. clippings file, NN-L-BRTC).

12. A successful and versatile stage actor, Henry V. Donnelly (ca. 1862–1910) appeared in vaudeville and many theatrical productions, including both musical comedy and drama. He was best known as a talented comic actor. With his partner Eddie Girard, Donnelly acted in many shows in the early 1890s, including two farces, *Natural Gas* (1892) and *The Rainmakers* (1894), which played in New York theaters and toured the country. For six seasons Donnelly had his own stock company at New York's Murray Hill Theatre, where he presented a repertoire of classical and new plays that was noted for the quality of production. Donnelly's other stage appearances included a revival of the musical comedy *Floradora* (1905) and the musical comedy *The Vanderbilt Cup* (1906). With the growing popularity of playlets in vaudeville performed by stars from the legitimate theater, Donnelly was the headline act on the bill at the Union Square Theatre. One reviewer wrote that his "quaint humor is well known to both vaudeville and dramatic audiences, and in the few moments he is before the footlights he shows an infectious, unctuous humor, which keeps everyone happy" (clipping, scrapbook A-1, OkClaW). Toward the end of his career he appeared in Oscar Strauss's operetta, *A Waltz Drama* (1908) and was a member of Henry Miller's company. On 15 November 1909 the *New York Times* reported that he was afflicted with Bright's disease at his home on West 145th Street. He died the following year on 15 February 1910 (Brown, *History of the New York Stage* 3:616-19; Chapman and Sherwood, eds., *Best Plays of 1894–1899*, 233–36; Mantle and Sherwood, eds., *Best Plays of 1899–1909*, 379, 507, 559; Mantle and Sherwood, eds., *Best Plays of 1909–1919*, 427; *NYDM*, 26 February 1910; *NYT*, 15 November 1909; Odell, *Annals of the New York Stage*, 13:442, facing p. 444, and 15:68, 74, 240, 329, 473, 495, 496, 524, 526, 625, 638, 785, 821; *VO*, 1:19 February 1910).

13. The playlet *Mr. and Mrs. Nagg* was written by Edgar Selwyn (1875–1944), a prolific actor and playwright. Born in Cincinnati, Selwyn first appeared in William Gilette's *Secret Service* (1896) and then played in stock companies. With his brother Archibald Selwyn (ca. 1877–1959) he formed Selwyn and Co., play brokers, produc-

ers, and theater builders. With his wife Margaret Mayo, Selwyn wrote *The Wall Street Girl* (1912). Will Rogers had a role in this production. Later he produced *Gentlemen Prefer Blondes* (1926) and *Strike Up the Band* (1930) (Mantle and Sherwood, eds., *Best Plays of 1899–1909*, 521, 570–71; Mantle and Sherwood, eds., *Best Plays of 1909–1919*, 451–52; *OCAT*, 607; *WhoStg*, 391–92; *WhMuDr*, 278; see also Review from the *New York Times*, 16 April 1912, below).

14. Charles Hoey (ca. 1872–1922) and William Henry (Harry) Lee (1872–1932) were one of many ethnic comedy teams that were popular in early vaudeville. Rogers also played on the same playbill with them two weeks later in Philadelphia (see Review from the *Philadelphia Item*, 27 June 1905, below). Hoey and Lee had a well-known "Hebrew" comedy act that specialized in parodies featuring comic altercations over pronunciations, manners, and misunderstandings. Hoey grew up on New York's Lower East Side, and around 1900 he began his partnership with Lee. Although they broke up several times, they played together for approximately fifteen years. Hoey was also a comic parody writer who wrote many vaudeville acts. Born in Richmond, Va., Lee appeared in silent action pictures and in Paramount sound films, after he moved to Hollywood in 1928. On 8 December 1932 Lee fell to his death from a fire escape at the Roosevelt Hotel; he had made several previous attempts to kill himself. Hoey died in New York City on 7 March 1922 from a cerebral hemorrhage (Gilbert, *American Vaudeville*, 290; Laurie, *Vaudeville*, 83, 322; *VO*, 1:10 March 1922 and 2:13 December 1932; *WhoHol* 1:953; *WhScrn*, 1:427).

15. M. H. Zazell and B. S. Vernon were a two-man act, playing together in Europe and the United States, beginning in 1895. They specialized in comic pantomime stories with scenery. By 1906 they had expanded their act to include Katherine Hefferman (ca. 1872–1922), who used the stage name Miss Zazell. A *Billboard* reviewer in the 31 March 1906 issue wrote: "For the past twelve years Messr ZaZell and Vernon have proven themselves master fun-makers in this country and in Europe. Mr. Vernon entered the profession some twenty years ago as aerial artist and has since played with all the leading circuses. Mr. Zazell made his debut as a song and dance artist, and during his long career he has acquired an acrobatic ability which he has used to advantage in many dramatic productions. Readily recognizing the fact that the public wants to laugh, his troupe prepares its stunts with a view to this end, and it may be said to their credit that they throw their audience into convulsions of laughter at every performance. Miss ZaZell and Miss Hefferman are the young ladies. . . . The troupe sails for Europe next month for a short tour of the Continent, returning in September to play the leading vaudeville houses in America." In 1909 the troupe played in Hamburg, Germany, and in January 1910 made its first appearance in Berlin. That year it also signed for a tour of South America. In her later years Katherine Hefferman was a wardrobe attendant in the theater. She was stricken blind a few weeks before her death on 26 August 1922 (Locke env. 2683, NN-L-RLC; *VO*, 1:1 September 1922).

16. In 1897 the Biograph Co. was organized by Henry Marvin, a manufacturer, and William Laurie Dickson, the former chief engineer at the Edison studios in West Orange, N.J. The company was first called the American Mutoscope, after its mutoscope camera and mutoscope flip-card viewing device. In 1899 the name was changed to the American Mutoscope and Biograph Co., to reflect the development of a new projection device, the biograph. In 1909 the company's name was officially changed to Biograph Co.; it had been popularly known by this shorter name for some time. The mutoscope camera used by the company was developed in large part by Dickson and was similar to, but significantly different from, the kinetograph camera in use by Thomas Edison. By 1896 the biograph projector was making several appearances on

the vaudeville circuit. On 12 October 1896 the biograph appeared at Hammerstein's Olympia Theatre, where a film of President McKinley at a parade and at his home in Canton, Ohio, was shown with great success. Other successes earned Biograph a place on the Keith Circuit, which it held on and off for eight and a half years. Biograph offered a complete service to Keith theaters, supplying projector, film, and operator.

In 1897 Biograph's films of local actualities—scenes of fires, parades, neighbors, and towns that were actually shot on site—gave audiences a chance to view familiar scenes and proved popular at several vaudeville houses. Keith began showing Biograph films on the Spanish-American War in 1898. The Biograph film showing Admiral Dewey's triumphant return from the Philippines was given feature billing at the Union Square Theatre in 1899. Due to the competitive nature of the fledgling motion-picture business and litigation over patent and copyright suits, Keith's relationship with Biograph became strained. In April 1903 Keith switched to Vitagraph, but by early 1905 he was again showing Biograph films. Angry over an incident involving exclusive rights to show the film *Personal* (1904) in his Cleveland theater, Keith deserted Biograph for Percival Waters's Kinetograph Co. in July 1905.

By 1902 40 percent of Biograph's films were fictional, and by 1904 the company was producing 653 films a year. Biograph's most famous director was David Wark Griffith, better known as D. W. Griffith, who made 350 films for the company between 1908 and 1913. Biograph was dissolved in 1915 after the U.S. government filed antitrust action against it (*FilmEnc*, 128; Musser, *Emergence of Cinema*, 150–57, 250–52, 308, 337–45, 375, 452; Niver, *Biograph Bulletins*, 21; Niver, *D. W. Griffith, His Biograph Films in Perspective*, i–ii; Sklar, *Movie-made America*, 33, 50–55).

17. As part of early cinema's reliance on informative human-interest stories, *The Life of a Miner* was one of several occupation-related films that were favorites with audiences. Others included *Life of a Fireman* (1900), *Life of an American Fireman* (1902–3), *Life of an American Policeman* (1905), and *Life of a Cowboy* (1906) (Musser, *Before the Nickelodeon*, 10). Another film shown at Union Square Theatre this week was a scene from the Russo-Japanese War (1904–5) entitled *Russia's Forlorn Hope* (Musser, *Beyond the Nickelodeon*, 273–74, 322–23).

To Sister and Family
18 June 1905
New York, N.Y.

New York, June 18, 1905

My Dear Sis *and gang.*

I got your letter and was glad to hear from you.   Well I am doing all O.K. got started last Monday at Keiths Theatre and finished last night   my first actual week using the pony and all.   the act was a *hit* from the start   I am being offered lots of work   I go this week tomorrow night to Hammersteins Roof Garden for a week   that is the swellest Vaudeville place in America and it is a great thing to be able to work there[1]   they sent for me too   I dident ask them for the work   if I go good there I am alright and every one says I will be a hit there.   oh it is a grand place on top of one of the big buildings just like a garden   covered over with a sliding glass roof   Keiths was a fine

Oscar Hammerstein's Victoria Theatre and Paradise Roof Garden (1899), northeast corner of Seventh Avenue and Forty-second Street, New York City, designed by architect John B. McElfatrick. Rogers's second engagement in vaudeville was at the Victoria in June 1905, and he appeared there numerous times during his stage career. (*Byron Collection, NNMuS*)

indoor theatre but this has them all beat for the *summer.*   My pony is a peach.
send this to papa   tell him I got the letter and papers and I see he is quite a
big thing down there   making so much money   I will be down to help him
spend some of it.

I go to Philadelphia week after next to play Keiths place *there*

Write all letters to the Putnam House

N.Y. City

Here is a Programme of last week and Bill from this mornings paper of the
people that will play at Hammersteins Next week.   I take my pony up on the
Roof on the elevator about 10 or 15 stories.   hope I dont fall off.

did you and papa get the *photos*

ALS, rc. OkClaW. On Putnam House letterhead.

1. Rogers signed a contract on 14 June to appear at Oscar Hammerstein's (1847–
1919) Victoria Theatre of Varieties beginning the week of Monday, 19 June 1905, at
a salary of $140 (Office of Oscar Hammerstein Contract, 14 June 1905, OkClaW).
William Morris, Rogers's first agent, received a 5 percent commission. The contract
was signed by Hammerstein's son Willie, who managed the theater for his father.
Known as the "Corner," the theater was situated on the northwest corner of Seventh
Avenue and Forty-second Street. In the evening Rogers performed at the Paradise
Roof Garden, atop the Victoria Theatre. For the afternoon matinee Rogers and the
other artists appeared downstairs in the large indoor theater. By this time the Victoria
was a famous vaudeville showplace, and its Paradise Roof Garden was a popular
attraction during the summer months. From the 1880s onward roof-garden theaters
were extremely popular in New York. By 1905 they served as important venues for
both legitimate theater and vaudeville, showcasing established entertainers and introducing new acts before they went on tour. Considered the city's leading roof-garden
theater, the Paradise Roof Garden drew large crowds of New Yorkers and tourists.
The Victoria's location in the heart of Longacre Square (renamed Times Square in
1904) marked the start of Broadway's era as the Great White Way. The Victoria was
Hammerstein's replacement for his Olympia Theatre (1895), a box-office failure.
Bankrupt in 1898, Hammerstein sold the Olympia at auction. The indefatigable
impresario nonetheless quickly seized the opportunity to build another theater. Using
secondhand materials, workers built the Victoria in nine months. Its name was chosen
to symbolize Hammerstein's victory over what he called his enemies at the New York
Life Insurance Co., which had foreclosed on his Olympia mortgage. The Victoria
opened on 3 March 1899 as a legitimate theater. The partially enclosed roof-garden,
open-air theater opened on 26 June 1899. Its promenade and al-fresco area, attached
to the roof garden of Hammerstein's Theatre Republic (1900; renamed the Belasco in
1902), offered patrons an opportunity to escape the heat and imagine themselves in
the country. At first Hammerstein's roof (initially called the Venetian Terrace Garden)
was designed as an intimate outdoor theater with electric lights and a center stage surrounded by tables for patrons. In 1901 Hammerstein enlarged the theater, and it
reopened in May as the Paradise Roof Garden. When Rogers performed there in 1905,
it resembled a formal theater, seating a thousand spectators under a glass roof open on
one side to catch cooling breezes. Patrons sat on fixed seats in rows facing the east-end
stage, in the balcony that surrounded the sides, or on tables and chairs behind the

orchestra section. The forty-foot-wide stage could accommodate large production numbers and full-stage sets.

The Victoria flourished under the able management of Willie Hammerstein, who had a flair for doing promotion and booking box-office draws (see Biographical Appendix entry, HAMMERSTEIN, William). Oscar Hammerstein, devoted to grand opera, much preferred his Manhattan Opera House (1906). The opera house was supported by the Victoria's earnings, which averaged $200,000 annually at its peak of popularity. In February 1904 Willie Hammerstein shrewdly changed the Victoria's policy of offering variety acts, plays, and flashy song-and-dance musical productions. Instead, he began to stage vaudeville shows both in the indoor theater and on the roof; these became extremely popular because of the potpourri of acts. The bawdy Victoria show differed markedly from Keith's refined vaudeville, and the audience was often boisterous. The Victoria offered an eclectic bill of stars, newcomers (such as Rogers), novelties, animal acts, acrobats, celebrities of all sorts (from sports figures, such as the boxer Jack Johnson, to accused murderers, notorious divorcees, or bridge jumpers), physical curiosities, freak acts, contortionists, illusionists, technological marvels, and exotic dancers. The theater's circus and side-show style of entertainment often verged on the zany, the ridiculous, the fraudulent, the sensational, and the risqué. Hammerstein kept his prices low; admission was 25 cents or 50 cents to see Rogers perform at the matinee. When Willie Hammerstein died in 1914, his brother Arthur (1872—1955) assumed the management, but the Victoria never recovered. Its last week in April 1915 featured an all-star bill of Willie Hammerstein's favorites. Among the performers was Will Rogers. The popularity of the movies and competition from other nearby theaters such as the Palace, as well as other financial problems, forced its closing. The Hammersteins sold the building in 1915 to a syndicate operated by S. L. (Roxy) Rothafel, who demolished the interior the next year to build his lavish movie palace, the Rialto. The Rialto in turn was torn down in 1935 and replaced by a new theater building and shopping complex (Blumenthal, *My Sixty Years in Show Business,* 111–29; Brown, *History of the New York Stage,* 3:620–21; *EV,* 226–28, 528–29; Gilbert, *American Vaudeville,* 245–50; *DAB,* 4:199–200; Johnson, *Roof Gardens of Broadway Theatres,* 77–95; Knapp, "Historical Study of the Legitimate Playhouses on West Forty-second Street between Seventh and Eighth Avenues," 46–57, 79–82, 117–24, 155–64, 177–79, 194, 200–203, 235–36, 247–51; Laurie, *American Vaudeville,* 380–96; Morrison, "Oscar Hammerstein I," 10–11, 14; *NYT,* 11 June 1914; *OCAT,* 318; Shean, *Oscar Hammerstein I,* 110–17; Snyder, *Voice of the City,* 74, 85–90; van Hoogstraten, *Lost Broadway Theatres,* 37–49; Victoria Theatre file, NNMus; "William Hammerstein," *Variety,* 25 December 1914; *VO,* 1:12 June 1914, and 1:8 August 1919).

Review, Hammerstein's Paradise Roof Garden
20 June 1905
New York, N.Y.

Although Hammerstein's Paradise Roof Garden engaged new acts, it was remarkable that Rogers played there so early in his career. "Direct from Hammerstein's" was the best billing a vaudevillian could have, and Rogers's appearance undoubtedly helped him obtain bookings on the Keith Circuit. The orchestra played a western song as Rogers entered wearing chaps, a cowboy hat, and colored shirt. The various per-

William Hammerstein (1874–1914), who managed the Victoria for his father, Oscar, was a great fan of Rogers. *(Locke Collection, Billy Rose Theatre Collection, The New York Public Library for the Performing Arts, Astor, Lenox, and Tilden Foundations.)*

formers on the playbill reflected the eclectic nature of a Hammerstein bill, which offered patrons a smorgasbord of acts.

FINE BILL FOR PARADISE PATRONS

GRAND OPERA TRIO WITH MYSTERIOUS WOMAN SINGER MAKES ENORMOUS HIT. "DIDA" WITH NEW FEATURES[1]

Last night ushered in the third week of the Paradise Gardens with an entirely new bill and one which is, if possible, better than anything Mr. Hammerstein has yet offered the public this season.[2] The chief attraction was the singing of the Grand Opera Trio, that made such an enormous success at this house some weeks ago. The members of the little company are doing what

Paradise Roof Garden (interior). In the rear was an outdoor farm complete with animals for summer enjoyment. *(Byron Collection, NNMuS)*

is indisputably the best singing in vaudeville to-day and is of a class so far superior to anything seen on this stage that it is entitled to be ranked as the headline feature par excellence.

Miss Decker, who was the original Marguerite of the sketch, has retired, and in her place is a young woman whose name is not given on the programme, but who has a voice that is wonderfully sweet and convincing one. Her range is startling at times and in the finale, when she gives it full scope, the audience rises to a burst of enthusiasm that is remarkable. The prison scene from "Faust" lends itself wonderfully well to the vocal efforts of the trio, and the act is, in addition to its excellence, quite a spectacular bit of work.

Bedini & Arthur, doing their familiar turn of the juggling variety, have added a new feature for this week, which is a scream of the first water. They have put on a burlesque of "Dida," which is sufficiently ridiculous to obtain bursts of laughter from the audience. In place of the glass tank they make use of a pine box and over this is drawn a sheet, quite in the "Dida" manner. Arthur is, of course, the subject who climbs into the tank, while Dehan Bedini takes off the near-German demonstrator in charge. In addition to this, their excellent juggling turn is well appreciated.[3]

GOOD WORK WITH THE LARIAT

Will H. Rogers has an expert lariat throwing turn that is novel and effective in every way and makes for the interest that is so necessary in this style of act. He is remarkably expert with his rope and does some seemingly impossible feats with it.[4]

Hickey & Nelson,[5] with their old act, "Twisted and Tangled," are as big a scream as ever. There are no adequate words to describe this turn, for it is as different from anything that was ever attempted as could be imagined, but it is a go from the start and winds up in a perfect cyclone of applause.

Mills & Moore[6] have a singing and dancing turn that is good and well worth watching. They have brought forward some new dancing steps and that in itself is a novelty of the first water.

Another big act that is being presented for the first time in vaudeville is Ernest Hogan's "Memphis Students."[7] There are twenty-five of these and they are appropriately costumed and cleverly drilled. The scenery carried with the act is splendid, and the "songs of the black folk" are so well rendered that the audience becomes more than ordinarily enthusiastic. In itself the act is a distinct novelty and should create a sensation in vaudeville wherever it appears. The Rappo Sisters are still doing their Siberian dances with good effect, and the Mysterious To-To[8] is as much of a mystery as ever.[9]
By Robert Speare

PD. Scrapbook A-1, OkClaW.

1. Dida was a classic illusion act in which a large, water-filled glass box was covered with a cloth; when the cloth was removed, a woman would appear in the water. Magician Howard Thurston popularized this act, in which assistants were hidden in a dry secret compartment behind the box (Waters, *Encyclopedia of Magic and Magicians,* 104).

2. A reference probably to Oscar Hammerstein's second eldest son, William or Willie.

3. Dehan Bedini and Roy Arthur were a popular two-man comic juggling act. Arthur (in blackface) and Bedini performed skits and parodies of famous stars and dancers, such as Ruth St. Denis and Gertrude Hoffman. For their finish they did a comic burlesque skit, with one of them doing a female impersonation. About 1910 the young Eddie Cantor (1892–1964), who was just breaking into show business, joined them. In blackface, Cantor did impromptu nonsense stunts and impersonated an African American who spoke Oxford English. The partners renamed the act "Bedini and Arthur assisted by Eddie Cantor," and Cantor traveled with the team for two years, learning much about comic delivery (Cantor, *My Life Is in Your Hands,* 116–26;

Cantor, *Take My Life,* 65–67; *NYT,* Sunday magazine section, 18 June 1905; Laurie, *Vaudeville,* 25–26, 90).

4. Rogers was billed erroneously as Will R. Rogers. Perhaps Hammerstein wanted to distinguish him from the Rogers Brothers (Gus and Mack Rogers), a two-man ethnic comedy team who regularly performed at the Victoria. Several other reviews and articles on Rogers's Victoria debut are also in his scrapbook. One recounts that his horse, named Jimpsy in the article, had a difficult time ascending the roof via the elevator on opening night: "Mr. Hammerstein had a long conversation with him," and Jimpsy "walked into the elevator with the best grace in the world." The article went on to report that "Rogers made a great hit with his lariat throwing. Secretary of War Taft being an interested spectator. There was a delegation of cowpunchers in the audience, for the act was greeted with the 'Yip! Yip! Yip!' of the cowboy at the end" ("Jimpsy Makes Debut in Paradise Gardens," clipping, scrapbook A-1, OkClaW). The *New York Clipper* printed a composite drawing by P. Richards of the show's feature acts. In the righthand corner Rogers was depicted riding a horse with a twirled lasso in his right hand and titled "Will R. Rogers. From the 'Wild West'" (P. Richards, "Features of the Weekly Show," scrapbook A-1, OkClaW). Rogers appeared at the Victoria Theatre and its Paradise Roof Garden from Monday 19 June through Sunday 25 June when he did a matinee (see *NYT,* Sunday magazine section, 18 and 25 June 1905).

5. Bill Hickey and Sadie Nelson, a noted husband-and-wife team, performed a bone-cruncher act, a burlesque of strongmen and acrobats. Hickey wore an oversized coat and pants and enormous shoes. Nelson, a Danish woman, was huge, and was nicknamed the Great Dane by her husband. The pair started with a romantic song and dance that quickly descended into knockabout comedy. Hickey would overturn chairs and tables, and kick a hat, while his wife played tricks on him. As a finale the hat would explode, and Hickey would be thrown into the air performing a headspin. A cartoon of Hickey shows him tumbling off a chair backward, doing the split, and standing on top of a table (Hickey and Nelson clippings file, NN-L-BRTC). Hickey hailed from Seattle and before teaming up with his wife had performed as a single in mining towns, saloons, and cow camps. Together, he and Nelson came to New York, where they were a big hit on the roof of the New York Theatre. For many years they toured the vaudeville circuits. After Nelson's death, Hickey performed with another partner. He spent his retirement years on a farm in upstate New York (Gilbert, *American Vaudeville,* 263–66).

6. Lillian Mills (ca. 1870–1949) was born in Detroit and was a legitimate actress for many years. She lived in Los Angeles for twenty-six years and was married to Edgar Norton. Mills died in Los Angeles on 24 March 1949 (*LAT,* 25 March 1949; *VO,* 4:30 March 1949).

7. Ernest Hogan (ca. 1859–1909) was a leading African American actor and songwriter. He was born in Bowling Green, Ky., and his real name was Ernest Reuben Crowders. He began his show-business career in minstrel shows and joined Richard and Pringle's Georgia Minstrels. With Harry S. Eaton he organized Eaton and Hogan's Colored Minstrels in 1891. As part of the ragtime craze, Hogan wrote the popular song "All Coons Look Alike to Me" in 1896. The song perpetuated negative racial stereotypes, and some sources suggest that Hogan later regretted the composition. The success of the tune led to a job in 1897 with Black Patti's Troubadours (a popular black musical group starring Sissieretta Jones, who was called Black Patti after Adelina Patti [1843–1919], the celebrated Italian soprano [Rosenthal and Warrack, *Concise Oxford Dictionary of Opera,* 377]). On this show he was billed as the "Unbleached American," an appellation that remained with him all his life. In 1898

Hogan was featured in Will Marion Cook and Paul Laurence Dunbar's all-black rag-time musical, *Clorindy, the Origin of the Cake Walk,* at New York's Casino Theatre Roof Garden. Hogan received long ovations for his singing of "Who Dat Say Chicken in Dis Crowd," another stereotype-laden song. Sometime around 1902 or 1903 Hogan entered vaudeville, appearing in the one-act play *The Military Man,* in the production *Uncle Eph's Christmas,* and in the one-act farce *Missionary Man.* Hogan viewed vaudeville as an excellent opportunity for black performers, but he urged his fellow actors to be more original in their work. He also performed on the stage of many roof gardens, and once appeared for forty-four weeks at the New York Theatre Roof Garden, a record for a black vaudevillian. Hogan and the Memphis Students were a big hit at the Paradise Roof Garden during the week Rogers was there. A reviewer reported that "the roof garden fairly reeked with melody. . . . The audience could not get enough of the specialty" (*New York World,* 20 June 1905, quoted in Sampson, *Ghost Walks,* 345). Appearing with Hogan at the Victoria was another black musical star, Abbie Mitchell (1884–1960). Among Hogan's biggest hits was his star role in *Rufus Rastus* (1905), for which he also composed the music. Two years later he assisted in writing and composing *The Oyster Man* (1907). The strain of staging the production, however, ruined his health, and he had to leave the show in June 1908. Upon his death in 1909, Hogan left an important legacy to the black musical theater and to American popular song (Charters, *Nobody,* 49–50; Ernest Hogan, "Negro in Vaudeville," *Variety,* 15 December 1906; DiMeglio, *Vaudeville USA,* 35, 115, 117; *EV,* 242–43; Laurie, *Vaudeville,* 201; Sampson, *Blacks in Blackface,* 375–76; Sampson, *Ghost Walks,* 344–45, 347–48, 351, 352; Toll, *On With the Show!* 121, 125, 130; Woll, *Dictionary of the Black Theatre,* 216; and Woll, *Black Musical Theatre,* 4–11).

8. To-to exemplified Willie Hammerstein's penchant for booking unique novelty acts to draw customers. *Theatre* magazine described To-to's performance as "an automaton musical 'mystery'. It is a figure dressed as a clown, and everyone imagines it to be a living boy until the woman who accompanies it suddenly removes its head, the fingers, meantime, playing expertly on an instrument. The key to the mystery probably is that the hands belong to a man who is hidden behind a mirror" ("Roof Gardens Open the Summer Season," 158).

9. Also on the playbill was Irene Bentley (ca. 1870–1940), a well-known actress, singer, and musical comedy performer. Born in Baltimore, she made her New York stage debut in *Little Christopher* (1895). After performing in several parts, she achieved stardom as the lead in *The Wild Rose* (1902), singing "My Little Gypsy Maid," written by the African American poet Paul Dunbar. She retired from the stage in 1910. Bentley died at her home in Allenhurst, N.J., on 3 June 1940 (Mantle and Sherwood, eds., *Best Plays of 1899–1909,* 409, 448, 528, 564; *NYT,* 4 June 1940; *VO,* 3:5 June 1940; *WhoStg,* 35–36; Ziegfeld and Ziegfeld, *Ziegfeld Touch,* 312).

Also on the playbill with Rogers was John Chevalier De Loris, an expert marksman. Born in Greece, De Loris developed an early talent for sharpshooting. On the vaudeville stage he captivated audiences with stunts such as partly disrobing his assistant by shooting away the fastenings of her garments; firing point blank at another rifle, the discharge of which sent a bullet through his hat; and with a pistol hitting two domino-shaped pieces of sugar on a dummy's head. He appeared at Hammerstein's Victoria several times, as well as at New York's famous Hippodrome, and at the Seattle Fair in 1909 (J. Chevalier De Loris clippings file, NN-L-BRTC).

Review from the *Philadelphia Item* 27 June 1905 Philadelphia, Pa.

INTERESTING NOVELTY AT KEITH'S THEATRE[1]

WILL ROGERS,[2] WESTERN COWBOY, DOES SOME REMARKABLE WORK WITH THE LASSO—HERBERT LLOYD'S[3] FAREWELL ENGAGEMENT—CHAS. GUYER AND NELLIE O'NEIL[4] HAVE A TERRIFIC FINISH TO THEIR SKETCH—CLOSING WEEK AT FOREPAUGH'S AND YE PARK.[5]

Edited by Hildebrand Fitzgerald
Keith's Chestnut St. Theatre.

There were four features at Keith's, yesterday, that aroused the audience. The first was Will Rogers, a Western cowboy, who did some wonderful work with the lasso; the second was Miss May Vokes,[6] whose impersonation of a slavey was capital; the third was Herbert Lloyd, whose multiplicity of shirt-bosoms "brought down the house," while the fourth was the Bowery-girl dance of Charles Guyer and Nellie O'Neil, during which everything on the stage was more or less wrecked!

Will Rogers is a typical man of the Far West. He is a character who has lots of character, and as an expert with the lasso he is remarkable. His exhibition opened with whirling the lasso, in which he was both skillful and graceful, and received well-deserved applause. Lassoing a man on horseback followed, and then came a difficult feat—whirling the lasso completely over the man and horse, so as to catch the horse by all four feet. "I'll do it," observed Rogers, "ef I hev luck!" He didn't succeed the first time, but on the second try he accomplished the feat in fine style, and was enthusiastically applauded.

Then he did another clever bit of throwing, by making a noose on the throw. (Applause.)

The most difficult feat followed—throwing two lassos, catching the man on the horse with one lasso, and the horse with the other lasso, using a lasso in each hand. Rogers declared that this was a new trick which he had kept from the "boys" on the plains. His first try was a miss, when he observed, in his characteristic manner: "I'm handicapped up h'yar, as the manager won't let me swa'ar when I miss!"

This remark caused a great deal of laughter, as it's truth was appreciated.

Rogers made ready again, and this time he caught both man and horse as they dashed across the stage. Appreciation was enthusiastic. Then he showed the audience how a cowboy dances, in skipping-rope style with the lasso, whirling it from side to side, and jumping in and out of the loop made.

He closed by mounting the Western pony, and keeping an 80-foot lasso in motion. He was recalled three times, and made an unmistakable hit.

Herbert Lloyd, "Jack of All Trades and Master of None," is a capital entertainer, and his burlesque impersonations, imitations and juggling caused continuous laughter. His shedding of an unlimited number of shirt-bosoms was uproariously funny. His work throughout is so rapid and amusing, that one laugh crowds on another, from beginning to conclusion. The pretty girl who assists him so cleverly, got a share of attention and admiration.

When called before the curtain, Mr. Lloyd told a good story, which he located at West Chester, Pa. While he was walking on the long station platform there, an old lady, accompanied by a lovely young girl, came up to him and asked: "Is there a train going South, sir?" He hastened to the station office, and was informed that there was no train going South, so he hastened back to tell the old lady and her lovely companion. Then she asked if there was a train going North, and the same thing was repeated, Mr. Lloyd illustrating his story by crossing from one side of the stage to the other; the same thing was repeated for an East and West train, when the old lady, after expressing her thanks, turned to the lovely young lady, and said: "Come, Alice! We can cross now—it's [sa]fe!"

Miss May Vokes, the clever comedienne, was seen to advantage in a sketch by Charles A. Byrne,[7] entitled "The Model Maid." As a slavey, Miss Vokes danced the quadrille alone in very amusing style, while her drunken scene was capital, and not overdone; the climax—falling down a dumb waiter shaft, and having a huge piece of ice pitched down after her, caused unlimited laughter.

Charles Guyer and Nellie O'Neil, who were identified for two years with "Babes in Toyland," gave a sensational finish to their sketch, which aroused the audience. After a lot of good comedy work, singing, and dancing, "the real thing" in the shape [of] a tough Bowery dance, was given. Chairs were upset, sofas overturned, tables crashed into, and the entire room made a wreck, before the dance was concluded, when both artists, by an acrobatic movement, went over backward, and raised from the stage high enough to show their backs to the audience! Such a wrecking of properties has never been seen on the stage, while the dance was of the wild, terrific, catch-as-catch-can, throw-me-around style, which baffles description.

Tom Moore proved to be a coon shouter of unusual merit, and a capital imitator of the real Southern negro.[8]

The Three Hickman Brothers gave a comedy act that contained a great deal of amusement, the comedian's work being a feature.

Emma Francis and her Arabian assistants, proved interesting. Miss Francis dances as well as ever.

The horizontal bar and casting act of McPhee and Hill, deserved the enthusiastic applause it received. Among the difficult feats were a backward catch with the legs, combined with giant's swing and double somersault at finish. The second part of the act included a change in the bars, one bar being elevated to almost twice the height of the other, thus affording opportunity for many novel casting feats. The closing feat was daring and brilliant, consisting of a cast and complete circle around the highest bar. The audience held its breath, and then the applause was tremendous.

Probably the best xylophone playing ever heard is that done by the Musical Avolos Quartette—two men and two women. They received hearty applause, and were twice recalled.

The programme also included J. Warren Keane,[9] whose manipulation of the cards was a feature of his good work; George N. Barry and Maude Wolford,[10] two bright entertainers, whose dialogue was excellent; Hoey and Lee, Hebrew impersonators, whose rapid-fire conversation aroused lots of laughter.[11]

PD. Scrapbook A-1, OkClaW.

1. Keith's Theatre at 1116 Chestnut Street in Philadelphia was built in 1902. Keith had opened his first Philadelphia theater, the Bijou on Eighth Street, in 1889. For his second theater, Keith purchased land on Chestnut Street that was the former site of the residence of Matthias Baldwin, owner of the Baldwin Locomotive Works. Opening on 10 November 1902, Keith's Chestnut Street Theatre was among the first elaborately decorated theaters in his circuit. At the time it was considered perhaps the most lavish theater in the country, constructed at a cost of $1 million. Built from marble, limestone, and terra cotta, the theater was designed by the architect Albert E. Westover in the French Renaissance style. It was located on the bottom floor of a five-story office building. The façade was decorated with filigree ironwork over the arch and an abundance of carved figures, festoons, and garlands. Its Grand Entrance Hall featured a mahogany ticket booth, murals, and a domed ceiling from which hung a crystal chandelier. A patron entering the Crystal Lobby through french doors encountered a large marble staircase leading to the mezzanine, two crystal chandeliers, and a ceiling mural with a mythological subject. Downstairs were several rooms, including a music room, a gray room where hung an oil portrait of Keith, and a green room. The auditorium with cerise silk plush seats contained an abundance of plaster figures and configurations, columns of Italian marble, and a proscenium decorated with sculptures of dancing cupids. According to a 1921 guide, the theater had seats for 2,300 spectators with a 30-row orchestra, 2 balconies, and 4 levels of box seats. Its huge stage, designed for large productions, measured 40 feet deep and more than 100 feet wide. A large contingent of uniformed usherettes, matrons, check-room boys, messengers,

and doormen catered to the audience. In 1928 it became a legitimate theater operated by the Shubert Brothers organization. Two years later it was turned into a movie theater. Harvard College was willed the property at the death in 1918 of A. Paul Keith, B. F. Keith's son. In 1943 the theater was sold by Harvard to William Goldman for $250,000, and in 1949 the new owner ordered the interior gutted and renovated. The refurbished theater was renamed the Randolph, and it continued to show films, including Cinerama productions. The theater was demolished after it closed on 3 January 1971 (Keith Chestnut Street Theatre file, PP; Gilbert, *American Vaudeville,* 204–5; Glazer, *Philadelphia Theatres, A–Z,* 142–45; Glazer, *Philadelphia Theaters,* 3; *JCGHTG,* 61; King, "Keith-Albee et al. . . ," 5; PA #46 and #47, postcard file, THS).

2. The report, written by the theater's manager, Harry T. Jordan, stated that Rogers made amusing remarks when he missed a trick. He wrote: "Lasso manipulator. This fellow is a crack-a-jack and gives a better act than the Chamberlains [a lasso and whip act]. Uses a cow-pony and a cow-boy assistant. He's a typical westerner, and his remarks when he misses a trick are very funny. All his tricks were applauded and he closed very strong. Very good act. 13 mins. Water landscape in 4" (manager's report, Keith's Philadelphia, 26 June 1905, KAC-IaU; see Laurie, *Vaudeville,* 36).

3. Known as "The Diamond King" in vaudeville, Herbert Lloyd (ca. 1873–1936) was a comic juggler. He often danced when he was juggling and said, "No good, Napoleon," when he missed a trick. The manager's report mentioned that his act resembled W. C. Fields (then a comic juggler) but was not as good. He was apparently from Philadelphia and well known among vaudeville patrons in the city. In 1919 Lloyd wrote *Vaudeville Trails thru the West,* a guide to theaters, hotels, railroads, towns, and many other necessary pieces of information for vaudevillians primarily on the western Orpheum Circuit and the Sullivan and Considine Circuit. He died on 24 May 1936 of a heart attack (Gilbert, *American Vaudeville,* 404; Laurie, *Vaudeville,* 25; *VO,* 2:27 May 1936).

4. Charles Guyer and Nellie O'Neill were considered the first roughhouse dancers. They appeared in Victor Herbert's musical extravaganza *Babes in Toyland* in 1903 and 1905. Nellie O'Neill, whose real name was Nellie Daly, played Jill in the show. Earlier, she performed in the musical comedy *A Female Drummer,* which opened at the Star Theatre on 26 December 1898. For several years she teamed with Guyer, and they did an acrobatic act with singing and dancing. During their knockabout act tables, sofas, and chairs were overturned. Guyer also performed a special dance number playing a drunkard. On 3 October 1908 *Variety* reported that Guyer and Crispi had broken up. By late 1909 Guyer had a new partner, a young Frenchwoman, Mona Valle, whom he married. Early in her career O'Neill was married to the comedian Billy B. Van (1878–1950) (Chapman and Sherwood, eds., *Best Plays of 1894–1899,* 248; Charles Guyer clippings, Locke env. 554, NN-L-RLC; Laurie, *Vaudeville,* 321; Mantle and Sherwood, eds., *Best Plays of 1899–1909,* 440; Nellie O'Neill clippings file, NN-L-BRTC; Odell, *Annals of the New York Stage,* 15:130, 530, 531, 706, 707).

5. The Forepaugh and Park theaters were two popular vaudeville houses in Philadelphia (*JCOTG,* 119, 129, 133).

6. May Vokes (d. 1957) was a well-known comedienne in vaudeville and the Broadway theater in the 1920s and 1930s. Her appearance in June 1905 was her vaudeville debut in Philadelphia. During her act she was supported by Neil McCay, who sang and played piano. Known for playing foolish servant girls, she made her professional debut on Broadway in 1896 playing Tillie in *My Friend from India.* She is best remembered for portraying the silly maid, Lizzie Allen, in the 1920 Broadway play *The Bat* by Mary Roberts Rinehart. Over the years she appeared in musicals and dramatic

plays. Vokes was in the film *Janice Meredith* (1924) and played Marion Davies's maid, Susie. The wife of Robert Lester, Vokes died at Stamford, Conn., on 13 September 1957. She was in her seventies (Bird, "May Vokes," 241; *FILM,* 2:543; *NYT,* 14 September 1957, 19; *NYTheReI,* 390; *VO,* 6:18 September 1957; *WhoHol,* 2:1743).

7. The dramatist Charles Alfred Byrne (1848–1909) was born in London. He founded the *Dramatic News* (1875) and *Truth* (1879), and worked as a journalist for several London newspapers. During his career he wrote the plays and comic operas *Venus* (1893) and *Le Voyage de Suzette* (1893), and co-authored the libretto of the musical *The Princess Nicotine* (1893) and *The Isle of Champagne* (1892). He also published *Dreamland: A Book of Modern Fairy-Tales* (2d ed., 1888). He died in Jersey City, N.J., on 23 August 1909 ("Le Voyage de Suzette," *NYTheRe,* 5:24 December 1893; *NYTheReI,* 55; Odell, *Annals of the New York Stage,* 15:347, 606, 618; "Venus," *NYTheRe,* 5:12 September 1893; *WWWA,* 1:180).

8. Possibly the Tom Moore (1885–1955) who later worked in films. Born in Ireland, he grew up in Toledo, Ohio, where he had his first stage appearance. He next gained experience touring with stock companies. He started his silent-film career in 1912 with an appearance in *A Daughter's Sacrifice* and *A Race with Time.* In 1917 he went to Hollywood and starred in numerous silents for Goldwyn as well as sound films. He retired in the mid-1930s, but appeared in several movies from 1946 to 1950, as well as television. He died in Santa Monica (*FilmEnc,* 967–68; Fox, *Famous Film Folk,* 46; *VO,* 4:16 February 1955).

9. The magician J. Warren Keane (ca. 1885–1945) was born in San Francisco and joined the Keith vaudeville circuit at an early age. During his thirty years in vaudeville he entertained in Europe, Australia, and Canada. Regarded as a talented magician, Keane was a charter member of the Society of American Magicians and, like Harry Houdini, a member of the elite Academy of Magic, which had only twelve members. Keane was married to the musician Grace C. White. He retired around 1915 and died on 30 March 1945 in Brockton, Mass. (*VO,* 3:4 April 1945).

10. Barry and Wolford were a well-known comedy team in which Wolford played the straight while George Barry delivered the punch lines. Barry (1873–1930) lived for many years in Freeport, Long Island, where many other performers resided. Later he moved to Hollywood, where he wrote dialogue and special material for sound movies. He died in Los Angeles (Laurie, *Vaudeville,* 230; *VO,* 2:10 December 1930).

11. Also on the bill were the opening act, a piano overture by Frank J. Kelly; the Three Delton Brothers, hand balancers; and the final act, two Biograph films, *The Miners' Lot,* called a "story of everyday life of the miners," and *The Insolvent Guest,* "a fair comedy picture" (manager's report, Keith's Philadelphia, 26 June 1905, KAC-IaU). Arminta and Burke, advertised in the playbill as "The Lady Gymnast and the Aerial Comedian," apparently did not perform (B. F. Keith's Philadelphia playbill, week commencing Monday, 26 June 1905, scrapbook A-1, OkClaW).

B. F. Keith's New Theatre (interior), Boston (1894), designed by architect John B. McElfatrick. The New Theatre was considered one of early vaudeville's most elegant theaters. Rogers first appeared there in July 1905. *(The Harvard Theatre Collection, The Houghton Library, Fredric Woodbridge Wilson, Curator.)*

Manager's Report, Keith's Theatre
3 July 1905
Boston, Mass.

Early in his vaudeville career Rogers performed at Keith's Theatre in Boston.[1] Located in the city where Keith began continuous vaudeville, the palatial playhouse was the flagship theater in his circuit.

Boston Show, Week of July 3, 1905

Fadettes,[2] 2 shows, 55 min. full stage—Usual weekly change of selections. No dimunition [diminution] in interest: every number encored, in fact, they were looking for more on the conclusion.

Dave Nowlin, 3 shows, 15 min. in 1—Mimetic comedian and vocalist.[3] He imitates a few domestic animals and then sings a couple of songs, both bass and soprano. He filled in this spot most acceptably.

Norton and Nicholson,[4] 2 shows, 19 min. full stage—Man and woman, in the comedy skit, "The Lady's Tailor." The sketch is without plot, but serves the purpose to introduce several clever imitations including one of Dan Daly,[5] which scored the biggest hit. Won considerable applause at the finish.

Hickman Brothers, 2 shows, 17 min. open full stage, close in 1—Three men, acrobatic comedians, vocalists and dancers. Well-known on the circuit. Secured quite a number of laughs and they will do very well for the early 2-show section.

Nina Morris[6] and Company, 2 shows, 18 min. full stage—Quite a nice appearing woman, assisted by Arthur Hoops[7] and Sumner Gard,[8] in the somewhat melodramatic sketch, "A Friend's Advice." It tells the tale of a jealous husband and wife. While Miss Morris's work is quite clever her support is nothing to speak of. There is good comedy in the piece with considerable laughs, but it fell flat at the finish, securing scanty applause.

Cheridah Simpson,[9] 2 shows, 12 min. opens in 1, goes to 3 and closes in 1—Received a big advance reception when the card announcing her was put on. She is quite a pretty woman, handsomely gowned; sings a couple of songs and then gives a few imitations on the piano. All her work was generously applauded. Applause hit of the show up to this point.

John Donahue and Mattie Nichols,[10] 2 shows, 12 min. open full stage, close in 1—Man and woman in acrobatic and eccentric dancing with a little vocalism. They are clever dancers and good workers. It is time they inject something new in to their act. Just about held their spot in the bill.

Will Rogers, 3 shows, 13 min. full stage—Typical Western Plainsman, assisted by a man and a broncho in wonderful exhibition with the lasso. Mr. Rogers performs feats with the lasso such as I have never seen before and his western talk is really excellent comedy. Of course the introduction of the broncho into the act adds greatly to its value. There is no doubt but what he will create considerable talk about town, in fact, one newspaper man has already offered to write him up.[11]

Biograph, 3 shows, 20 min. in 1—Showing the following list of pictures:
1. The Flower Harvest. Quite an interesting picture.
2. The Burglar's Slide for Life. Good comedy picture.[12]
3. A suit of Armor. Fair.
4. A London Suburbanite's Unlucky Day. Fair comedy picture.
This week's list is not up to last weeks' by any means.

Sid Baxter, 3 shows, 10 min. full stage—Quite a neat looking man, assisted by Beatrice Southwick. A slack wire artist and juggler[.] Does some clever riding on bicycle and unicycle on the wire and also juggles small articles. Excellent "sight" act for the 3-show section. Received a big amount of applause for this spot in the bill and is entitled to a much better position than we can give him.

Barry and Wolford, 3 shows, 15 min. in 1—Conversational comedians, vocalists and dancers. Their "talk" and vocalism is very bright and they got laughs all through. Good act from the 3-a-day standpoint.

Wilbur Amos, 3 shows, 15 min. full stage—Juggler of small articles. Quite a clever chap in his way and would do very well for the early 3-show section.

Tom Moore, 2 shows, 11 min. in 1—Greatest of all "coon" shouters and strenuousity is certainly the feature of his act. Although there were only a few in the house when he was on, he made good with them and can be considered a good act from the 3-show viewpoint.

Comment: The show is a good one from top to bottom. If there is a weak place, it is Nina Morris who did not come up to expectations, although it did not hurt the show. I was laboring under the impression that Norton and Nicholson did only 12 minutes but they did 19.

The audience was unusually large and enthusiastic for a pleasant Monday afternoon,[13] owing to the fact that many of the business houses are shut down, and a good report of the show will no doubt be passed along and felt in the business for the balance of the week

(P. J. O'Connor)

TD. KAC-IaU.

1. On 24 March 1894 B. F. Keith's Theatre (also known as the Gaiety Theatre) opened with great fanfare when over two thousand guests attended its first programs. Guests arrived by special train from New York and Washington, including Senator Chauncey M. Depew, Robert Ingersoll, and opera star Edouard de Reszke. Anxious to construct a spacious and luxurious theater, Keith and his partner, Edward Albee, had bought property on Washington Street behind their Bijou Theatre. The site they chose was on the city's main street and in a busy shopping area, adjacent to the Adams House hotel and the Boston Theatre, which Keith and Albee had acquired in 1892.

Designed and built by the architect John B. McElfatrick (d. 1906), Keith's Theatre was the first of the magnificent houses erected by the Keith organization. Because of its luxurious accoutrements Keith's Theatre in Boston drew wealthy patrons, even the city's social set. The Boston theater featured a cornucopia of imported marble, ornamental plaster, stained glass, gargoyles, antiques, and paintings. Behind the façade's entry arch, which was decorated with stained glass, was a loggia featuring an inlaid mosaic floor and wainscoting in Siena marble. Lining the entrance were two circular box offices of marble and plate-glass, topped with gold domes decorated in gold and ivory. The opulent grand foyer was decorated with rose-colored walls, marble floors, ornamental mirrors, and panel paintings by Eduardo Tojetti (1851–1930). It was lighted by over three hundred incandescent lamps with brass fixtures.

The spacious auditorium seated 2,700 spectators in the orchestra (in 1906 a front orchestra seat cost 75 cents and a rear orchestra seat, 50 cents). Less expensive seats were located in two balconies reached by a marble staircase (admission to the first balcony cost 35 cents, and to the second, 25 cents). The auditorium walls, with cherry woodwork, were painted in green and rose to resemble brocaded silk. An expensive English Melton carpet covered the floor. Three tiers of two private boxes on each side of the proscenium were upholstered in plush green. The passageway from the foyer to the engine room was highlighted by a white marble staircase. The generator room contained a marble floor, white walls, nickel-plated railings, and brass light fixtures; the engineer attendants wore spotless white uniforms. In the boiler room area Albee ordered the installation of a red velvet carpet.

After Albee completed the nearby B. F. Keith Memorial Theatre in 1928 as a tribute to his deceased colleague, the theater was sold to the Shubert brothers. It reopened in 1929 as the Apollo Theatre (later called the Shubert Lyric Theatre). Eventually it became a movie theater (the Normandie and later the Laffmovie theater). Neglected and in a state of disrepair in the 1950s, the structure was demolished to make way for a parking lot (Allen, *Horrible Prettiness,* 184–85; "B. F. Keith's Memorial Theatre," 8–11; Birkmire, *Planning and Construction,* 48–56; Gilbert, *American Vaudeville,* 206; *JCOTG,* 111; King, "From Museum to Multi-Cinema," 17–18).

2. The Fadettes Women's Orchestra from Boston was directed by Caroline B. Nichols. It was one of several women's orchestras in vaudeville. The Fadettes gave renditions of popular and classical music, including a piece called "Roosevelt's Rough Riders" by Laurendeau. Estelle Churchill was a prominent member of the Fadettes, played the drums with the group, and was an accomplished pianist (Keith's Theatre Program, week of 3 July 1905, scrapbook A-1, OkClaW; series 2, 64:149–51, NN-L-RLC).

3. Dave Nowlin later teamed with Gertrude St. Clair to form a musical comedy act. A concert singer, St. Clair joined the American Musical Comedy company and made a trip through the Orient. It was in this organization that she first became associated with David Nowlin. They traveled through Japan, China, the Philippine Islands, and Australia. A specialty of the act was performing animal imitations as they sang a farm song. In a parody of opera they mimicked chorus entertainers, a soprano, and a tenor. Nowlin and St. Clair were a hit at the Loew's Orpheum Theatre in November 1914 and at McVicker's in February 1915 (Locke env. 1624, NN-L-RLC).

4. A graduate of Smith College, Angelina Norton began as a newspaper writer who did satire. She started in show business as a member of the Richard Mansfield Co. In vaudeville she performed a comic monologue single act called The Talkative Miss Norton. Her first partner was Sidney Grant, and together they introduced the drawing-room style of variety entertainment, which consisted of skits about domestic life. In 1901 she left Grant. One night Paul Nicholson saw her perform and sent her flowers. This led to a partnership on the stage. In vaudeville they performed comic sketches, some written by Norton. Their one-act comic sketches or dramatic cartoons, as they were called, were often about married life. One, entitled *Ella's All Right,* was about poor newlyweds who live on love. During their performance they also did single specialty numbers. Nicholson imitated the boxer James J. Corbett, and Norton sang comic songs. They appeared occasionally on the legitimate stage and in Broadway musicals, including the *Cohan Revue of 1918* (Locke env. 1635, NN-L-RLC).

5. The performer Dan Daly (1858–1904) started as a circus acrobat and in variety shows in which he played castanets while standing on his head. He became a comic actor in the theater, where he gained fame for his unique characterizations. Daly appeared frequently on the New York stage in such plays as *A Society Fad* (1893), *The Golden Wedding* (1893), and *About Town* (1894). His most popular role was Ichabod in the 1897 musical comedy *The Belle of New York*. At the Herald Square Theatre in 1900–1901 he starred in musical comedies, and in 1903 he was in the farce *John Henry* (*BEWHAT*, 1019; Brown, *History of the New York Stage*, 3:294, 500; Mantle and Sherwood, eds., *Best Plays of 1899–1909*, 368, 385, 397, 433; *OCAT*, 69–70, 183).

6. Nina Morris played in vaudeville playlets as well as full productions in New York. She also organized her own company to present vaudeville playlets. Critics generally viewed her as an extremely talented actress who mostly performed in mediocre plays. A person who followed her career commented that she was a "bright, volatile woman, quick at repartee, guarded in thrust and with that supreme courage in endeavor for which the theatrical profession is noteworthy" (*Minneapolis Journal*, 21 December 1913, clipping, Nina Morris file, NN-L-RLC).

During their courtship Rogers enclosed in a letter to Betty Blake an undated letter from an actress named Nina (see Will Rogers to Betty Blake, 5 December 1906, and enclosure: Will Rogers from Nina, below). He sent the letter to Betty to prove his faithfulness to her. In his biography, Ben Yagoda states that Nina could possibly be Nina Morris (*Will Rogers*, 107). But in his letter to Betty, Rogers states that the actress was on the same bill with him for three weeks and was with a girl act. Shortly thereafter, they also performed in the same week at different vaudeville theaters in New York. There is no evidence that Morris performed in New York around November 1906 when Rogers was performing there. Nor did Morris ever play three weeks on the same playbill with him. It was a girl act called The Crickets that played three consecutive weeks with Rogers (Pittsburgh's Grand Opera House, the week of 17 September 1906; Shea's Theatre, Buffalo, the week of 24 October 1906; and Shea's Theater, Toronto, the week of 1 October). During the week of 12 November 1906 Rogers performed at Keith and Proctor's Harlem Opera House and The Crickets were at Keith and Proctor's Twenty-third Street Theatre in New York. In Nina's letter she states, "We are changed to Harlem next week." The Crickets performed at the Harlem Opera House the week of 26 November 1906 (see "This Week's Attractions," *NYDM*, 1 December 1906; and "Last Week's Bills, Keith and Proctor's Harlem Opera House," *NYDM*, 8 December 1906). Thus more than likely it was a woman named Nina in the act The Crickets who wrote to Rogers.

Nina Morris was first a member of the Castle Square Stock company in Boston; in her second season she joined Frank Mayo's traveling company. First published notice of her work came in 1897 when she played Mrs. Sabiston in Arthur W. Pinero's *The Princess and the Butterfly*, a comedy of English life. In the early 1900s she turned to performing playlets on the vaudeville stage. During the spring of 1904 she was a leading lady with the Harry Glazier Stock Co. Next, she formed her own vaudeville company to present the sketch *A Friend's Advice*, which was tried out in New York in November 1904 to mixed reviews. During the summer of 1908 Morris appeared at the Wintergarten in Berlin as an actress with James K. Hackett's company. On 9 August 1909 Morris opened in a three-act farce called *The Florist Shop*, by Oliver Hereford, at New York's Liberty Theatre, which ran for forty performances. She received excellent reviews for her portrayal of Claudine Benoit, a French shopkeeper. Two years later, in February 1911, Morris was back in vaudeville. Her company appeared at Hammerstein's Victoria Theatre in a dramatic sketch entitled *Who Shall Condemn?* and in

September 1912 they presented another sketch at Keith's Union Square Theatre and Hammerstein's Victoria, called *The Yellow Peril*. As late as 1918 Morris appeared on stage, playing Mrs. Gresham in Harry James Smith's comedy-drama *The Little Teacher*, which opened on 4 February at New York's Playhouse Theatre and ran for 128 performances (*Leslie's Animated Weekly*, 19 August 1909, 175, 2 September 1909, 223; Louise Drew scrapbook, NN-RLC; Mantle and Sherwood, eds., *Best Plays of 1899–1909*, 568; Mantle and Sherwood, eds., *Best Plays of 1909–1919*, 396, 621; Nina Morris file, Locke env. 1543, NN-L-RLC; *NYTThRe*, vol. 1896–1903, 24 November 1897; *NYTThRr*, vol. 1904–11, 22 September 1908, 10 August 1909, 28 February 1911; *NYTThRe*, vol. 1912–19, 5 February 1918; *OCAT*, 313; *Theatre*, October 1909, 119).

7. The actor Arthur Hoops (1870–1916) appeared in many dramas and silent films. He performed roles in *In Mizzoura* (1893) and *The Gilded Fool* (1895) with the actor Nat Goodwin (1857–1919). For several years Hoops belonged to a stage company headed by the well-known actor/producer James K. Hackett (1869–1926). During his silent-movie career Hoops worked with the Famous Players Co. and subsequently with Metro. Hoops died on 17 September 1916 while riding in a newly purchased automobile (*BEWHAT*, 1034, 1036–37; *FILM*, 1:133; Mantle and Sherwood, eds., *Best Plays of 1899–1909*, 400, 568; *NYTheReI*, 194; Odell, *Annals of the New York Stage*, 15: 590; *VO*, 1:22 September 1916; *WhScrn*, 1:348).

8. A dramatic actor, Sumner Gard played character parts on the New York stage. He was in the cast of *The Light That Lies in Woman's Eyes* (1904) and *The Love Route* (1906). He played Philip Clandon in George Bernard Shaw's *You Never Can Tell* (1904) starring Arnold Daly, which ran for 129 performances at New York's Garrick Theatre (*Boston Post* clipping, ca. 4 July 1905, scrapbook A-1, OkClaW; Mantle and Sherwood, eds., *Best Plays of 1899–1909*, 481, 495; *NYTheReI*, 148, 453, 524).

9. The singer and actress Cheridah Simpson (ca. 1865–1923) began her show-business career during her teens and was for many years on the vaudeville and musical comedy stage. She played the lead in musicals from 1890 to 1900 and after that time was a featured performer in vaudeville. She was one of the first women entertainers to do a vaudeville "pianolog," singing tunes to her own piano accompaniment. A review of her performance at Keith's called her a "handsome and beautifully gowned person [who] was tendered quite a reception on her appearance, and sang a couple of songs superbly and gave several pleasing imitations on the piano" (*Boston Post* clipping, ca. 4 July 1905, scrapbook A-1, OkClaW; see also Mantle and Sherwood, eds., *Best Plays of 1899–1909*, 474; Odell, *Annals of the New York Stage*, 15:348; *VO*, 1:19 January 1923).

10. John Donahue and possibly Mattie Nichols appeared in the musical play *Woodland*, which opened at the New York Theatre on 21 November 1904 (Mantle and Sherwood, eds., *Best Plays of 1899–1909*, 274–75; Mattie Nichols clippings file, NN-L-BRTC).

11. Rogers was given considerable space in the *Boston Herald* (see review, 4 July 1905, below), as well as other Boston newspapers. The playbill described Rogers as "a typical western Plainsman, in a wonderful exhibition with the lasso. First time here" (Keith's Theatre Program, week of 3 July 1905, scrapbook A-1, OkClaW).

12. *The Burglar's Slide for Life* (March 1905) was a film made by Edwin S. Porter for the Edison Co. A comment on society and its outcasts, the film deals with a tramp who enters an apartment seeking food. When the tramp is discovered, he escapes out a window and down a clothesline, but once on the ground he is assaulted by neighbors and bitten by the family dog (Keith's Theatre Program, week of 3 July 1905, scrapbook A-1, OkClaW; Musser, *Before the Nickelodeon*, 311, 312, 317, 324).

13. The doors opened at 1:30 P.M., and the program was offered continuously until 10:30 P.M. (Keith's Theatre Program, week of 3 July 1905, scrapbook A-1, OkClaW).

Review from the *Boston Herald*
4 July 1905
Boston, Mass.

KEITH'S NEW BILL PROVES WINNER

"A FRIEND'S ADVICE," WITH NINA MORRIS
AS STAR, A NEAT SKETCH—
CHERIDAH SIMPSON, WILL ROGERS
AND OTHERS WIN GREAT FAVOR.

Yesterday, at Keith's an unusually large audience for this season of the year was assembled, and to judge by the pleased expression on their faces as they passed out, they thoroughly enjoyed the excellent programme provided.

Nina Morris made her first appearance in vaudeville in this city in a somewhat melodramatic sketch, entitled "A Friend's Advice," which is a usual enough story of the troubles of husband and wife. Miss Morris takes the role of the wife who has not been making due outward show of affection for her husband. The star is assisted by Arthur Hoops and Sumner Gard, two young actors who are well-known to the "legitimate." Cheridah Simpson, who last appeared in Boston in "Woodland," was tendered quite a reception on her first appearance. She was handsomely costumed, and every one of her songs and imitations were enthusiastically encored.

Will Rogers, another newcomer to Boston, was the applause hit of the entire bill. Mr. Rogers is a typical western plainsman and gave the best exhibition of lasso manipulation that has ever been seen at Keith's. He enters on a broncho, and his first bit of work is the lassoing of the horse so as to catch the animal by all four feet. His greatest feat is the lassoing of a man[1] on horseback and the horse at the same time, with two different lassos—that is, by throwing a lasso with each hand.[2] Sid Baxter gave one of the best exhibitions on the slack wire seen here for many a day. Wilbur Amos, who was seen here last fall, did some clever juggling of small articles.

There was a host of good entertainment in the comedy department, including Norton and Nicholson,[3] in the skit "The Lady's Tailor," with imitations of well known celebrities; the Hickman brothers, a trio of grotesque comedians, musicians and dancers; Dave Nowlin, mimetic comedian and vocalist; Tom Moore, the greatest of all "coon" shouters; Donahue and Nichols, comedians, acrobats and singers, and Barry and Wolford, in bright dialogue and dances.

The Fadettes women's orchestra made its usual weekly change of selections, prominent numbers in the programme being the overture "Fra Diavolo," by Auber, and the "American Fantasie," by Herbert.[4] The biograph exhibited a complete change of motion pictures.

PD. Scrapbook A-1, OkClaW.

1. By this performance, Buck McKee had replaced Jim Minnick as Rogers's assistant and would continue in this role until 1911.

2. Two other reviews specifically noted Rogers's humorous talk and his dancing. The *Boston Post* reported that Rogers "gave a really remarkable exhibition of rope juggling and lasso throwing. His cowboy talk captured the audience at the start, and when he threw two lassoes at one time, looping horse and rider, the patrons were aroused to enthusiastic applause. Mr. Rogers also gave an exhibition of real cowboy dancing" (clipping, ca. 4 July 1905, scrapbook A-1, OkClaW). The *Boston Globe* reviewer wrote that "his plainsman 'talk' is real comedy of the sort that is seldom heard on the stage" (clipping, ca. 4 July 1905, scrapbook A-1, OkClaW).

3. The *Boston Post* reported that Norton gave "satires on society, sang clever little songs and told good stories. Mr. Nicholson has quite a pleasing baritone voice, and his imitation of [the boxer and vaudevillian] Jim Corbett is really marvellous" (clipping, ca. 4 July 1905, scrapbook A-1, OkClaW).

4. Daniel-François-Esprit Auber (1782–1871) was a well-known French composer. Born in Ireland, Victor Herbert (1859–1924) became one of America's most celebrated composers and was especially noted for his operettas. His most popular shows included *Babes in Toyland* (1903), *It Happened in Nordland* (1904), *Mlle. Modiste* (1905), *The Red Mill* (1906), and *Naughty Marietta* (1910). His songs, including his 1910 classic "Ah, Sweet Mystery of Life," belonged to the pre–World War I era of the waltz. His music lost its appeal in the 1920s with the rage of jazz (Ewen, *American Popular Composers*, 87–91; *OCAT*, 338–39).

To Sisters
5 July 1905
Boston, Mass.

In this letter to his sisters Rogers comments on the success of his act. He was already aware of the significance of humorous patter in his act. Audiences like the "few funny things I say," he wrote to his sisters.

Boston, Mass.
July 5th   05.

My Dear Sisters

Well here I am in Boston and doing all O.K.   will play here till Saturday night then back to N.Y. and play there for 4 weeks   1 week at Proctors Theatre[1]   then ▲ back ▲ to Hammersteins Roof Garden for 3 straight weeks[2]

I like to work in N.Y. I have my pony here shipped him up on the boat the act went fine every place so far I want to get home for a few weeks in August or September Here is Clipping from the Boston Papers you see it is the way I do my work is what takes with them and a few funny things I say

Write to me at the Putnam House write often

I will close did you get last weeks clipping from Philadelphia I sent you

Love to all

Willie

ALS, rc. OkClaW.

1. Rogers appeared at Proctor's Twenty-third Street Theatre from 10 July to 16 July. He signed a contract with F. F. Proctor's Circuit on 1 July 1905 at $150 per week for two performances daily to do his specialty. William Morris, his agent, received a 5 percent commission deducted from his salary (F. F. Proctor's Circuit contract, OkClaW). The theater's slogan was "All-Star Vaudeville," and its seating capacity was 1,551. It offered two performances daily, with an afternoon matinee for shoppers at a reduced price of 25 cents. Heading the playbill the week Rogers performed at the Twenty-third Street Theatre was the singer and comedienne Edna Wallace Hopper. Another star attraction was the actor Charles Grapewin in the farcical sketch, *The Awakening of Pip,* with Anna Chance. Others mentioned were the Elinore Sisters (Character Comediennes); To-To (The Mysterious Musician); the Esmeralda Sisters and the Four Flower Girls (A Novel and Singing Act); Harding and Ah Sid (Comic Acrobats in *Fun in a Chinese Laundry*); James H. Cullen (The Man from the West); and Mlle. Olive (Novelty Juggling) (*JCOTG*, 67; Proctor's Twenty-third Street playbill, week beginning Monday, 10 July 1905, clipping, scrapbook A-1, OkClaW).

Frederick Freeman Proctor (1851–1929) was a leading big-time vaudeville magnate and theater owner/manager who initiated important changes in variety entertainment. A shrewd and frugal businessman, Proctor possessed an innate talent for profit making and built or leased theaters in growing neighborhoods. In 1889 he opened his Twenty-third Street Theatre, at 141 West Twenty-third Street, near Sixth Avenue, at the site of a former church and the Temple Theatre (1883). Initially Proctor's Twenty-third Street Theatre was the home of Charles Frohman's dramatic stock company. It was one of several theaters on Twenty-third Street, including Koster and Bial's Music Hall, which made New York's Chelsea district a center of theatrical life.

With Keith, Proctor is recognized as a pioneer in continuous vaudeville. On 9 January 1893 Proctor adopted a policy of continuous vaudeville running from 11 A.M. to 11 P.M. (later he introduced an early-bird matinee at 10 A.M. at reduced prices). Proctor's Twenty-third Street Theatre was the first venue in New York to offer a continuous format, with the slogan "After Breakfast Go to Proctor's, After Proctor's Go to Bed." Like Keith, he advertised refined, high-class vaudeville "kept scrupulously free from any gross or objectionable features" and at prices the public could afford (in 1902, 25–50 cents for unreserved seats, 75 cents for reserved seats, and a dollar for box seats). For these prices he featured American headliners as well as leading acts from European music halls, and he was among the first producers to book stars from the legitimate stage in vaudeville. On Labor Day, 2 September 1895, he opened the lavish and spacious Pleasure Palace on Fifty-eighth Street between Third and Lexington Avenues. Proctor subsequently opened additional theaters in New York City (the 125th Street and the Fifth Avenue, both in 1900), as well as New Jersey houses. By 1912 he was operating twenty-four playhouses in the city and its environs devoted to "high-class vaudeville and modern photo plays" (Leavitt, *Fifty Years in Theatrical Management,* n.p.). Proctor also owned or managed theaters in upstate New York (Albany, Schenectady, and Troy). In 1906 he merged his New York theaters with the Keith Circuit to form the Keith and Proctor Amusement Co. The alliance was a precarious partnership that lasted until 1911. Proctor continued to operate and build more theaters in the New York suburbs, and in 1928 he opened his Eighty-Sixth Street Theatre in Manhattan. In 1929 he sold his theaters to Radio-Keith-Orpheum (RKO), properties estimated to be worth $16 million to $18 million. Proctor died on 4 September 1929 from lung congestion, and his passing was mourned by both performers and producers. At the time of his death Edward F. Albee called him "one of the great showmen of the country" (Marston and Feller, *F. F. Proctor,* 179; see also Allen, *Horrible Prettiness,* 316–17; Connors, "American Vaudeville Managers," 38–42; Grau, *Business Man in the Amusement World,* 301–306; Henderson, *City and the Theatre,* 147–48; Leavitt, *Fifty Years in Theatrical Management,* 195–96; *NYT,* 5 September 1929; *VO,* 2:11 September 1929; *WhoStg,* 352; Zellers, *Tony Pastor,* 88, 95–96).

2. Rogers actually performed at Hammerstein's Paradise Roof Garden for four weeks from 17 July to 13 August. The playbill for the week of 17 July listed the acts in the following order: Lutz Brothers (European Novelty Act); The Doherty Sisters (Singers and Dancers); Mme. Adelaide Hermann (The Queen of Magic); Flossie Crane (The Girl from Coney Island); Reno and Richards (Comedy Acrobats); The Juggling MacBans (Sensational Club Swinging Exhibition); Ford and Guthrie and their Rollicking Girls; Will R. Rogers (Sensational Lariat Thrower); Three Musical Johnsons (Xylophone Experts); Rossi (The Musical Horse—the Only Act of Its Kind); Rice and Prevost (Bumpty Bumps); Ernest Hogan (The Unbleached American) and his 25 Memphis Students with Abbie Mitchell (The Little Song Bird) in *Songs of the Black Folks;* and Capt. Bloom's Demonstration of Marconi's Wireless Telegraphy (Hammerstein's Paradise Roof Garden playbill, week commencing Monday matinee, 17 July 1905, scrapbook A-1, OkClaW). (For the acts Rogers played with beginning the week of 24 July 1905, see Will Rogers to Sisters, 26 July 1905, below. For the playbill during the week of 31 July, see Review from the *New York Dramatic Mirror,* 12 August 1905, below, and for the playbill during the week of 7 August, see Will Rogers to Betty Blake, 10 August 1905, below).

To Clement Vann Rogers
16 July 1905
New York, N.Y.

New York, July 16 *1905*

My Dear Papa

I have been waiting to write to you till after pay day so I could send you the money that I borrowed from Godbey[1] $100   I dont know where it is due and I had $30. in the bank to my credit so you can pay the interest and it should leave me about $25 there[2]   I am working in N.Y. and will be here till August 14th[3]   I play 4 weeks in one theatre.[4]

I want to come home perhaps after that.

It is sure hot here[5]

I sent Gordon Lane $20 for wintering my old pony

Write me all the news when you can

I will close

Love to all

Willie.

ALS, rc. OkClaW. On Putnam House letterhead.

1. A banker, C. F. Godbey was a director and cashier of Claremore's First National Bank, founded in 1895. Godbey also helped establish the Claremore Federal Building and Loan Association in 1921 (DuPriest et al., *Cherokee Recollections*, 30, 155, 219; *PWR*, 1:171n.2, 246).

2. In a subsequent letter to his father Rogers sent him $50, writing, "I am going to save up a little money" (Will Rogers to Clement Vann Rogers, 24 July 1905, OkClaW).

3. A reference to his four-week engagement at Hammerstein's Paradise Roof Garden. In his letter of 24 July Rogers sent his father a review from a New York paper of his performance at the Paradise Roof, entitled "Rogers Has Made a Hit." It was published in the *Claremore Progress* on 29 July 1905 and cited incorrectly as a *New York World* article. The clipping appears in Rogers's scrapbook A-1 under a *New York Morning Telegraph* heading dated 18 July 1905.

4. New York City inhabitants experienced a week-long, record-breaking hot spell. On 17 July the temperature reached ninety-five degrees, and the *New York Times* reported the next day that eight people had died from the heat and thirty-seven had suffered heat prostration. On 18 July the temperature reached a record-breaking ninety-six degrees; 23 people died and 207 experienced heat prostration. Another record was broken on 19 July when the temperature registered ninety-four, and the *Times* reported that sixty-three people had died. The temperature began to drop on 20 July, and two days later New York experienced a cool spell (*NYT*, 16–23 July 1905). In his letter of 24 July to his father Rogers wrote that "thousands of people died here from heat during the hot spell" (24 July 1905, OkClaW).

5. A boyhood friend of Rogers, Gordon Lane was the second son of Dr. Andrew Lane and Lucinda Elliott Journeycake. He lived for many years at his father's place in the Oowala area near Oologah and later moved to Claremore. On 24 December 1912 he married Mary Katherine Cushenberry, and they had five children (*As I Recollect*, 19–24; DuPriest et al., *Cherokee Recollections*, 57, 231, 282; *HRC*, 34, 274–75; *PWR*, 1:117, 175n.3, 176n.1, 189n.2, 497–98).

To Sister and Family
26 July 1905
New York, N.Y.

New York, July 26 19[05]

My Dear Sis and gang

just got Sallies letter and one from papa telling me of Mays Baby dying[1] which was too bad.   but it was never strong was it

How is Mays health and how are they getting on   I dont hear from her

I want to get down there in September   about the 5 for a few weeks   any way if I can I am only now booked to sept 3.   and if I accept any more I will make them in October   I will be at work for the next 6 weeks steady   havent lost a day since I started in   but I am homesick now

Papa is blowing about Claremore all the time   dont hear much of Chelsea I am still at Hammersteins Roof garden   in my 3rd week and have two more yet[2]   as they gave me another the other day   then I go for a week to Rockaway Beach on Long Island   a swell summer resort

I will get plenty of baths (which I need)   the Theatre is out over the water.[3]   then the week of Aug 21 I go a short piece from there to Manhattan Beach[4]   Another resort   for a week   then Aug 28 to Newark N.J. for a week[5]   that is right near here   then I will try and come home

Well I will close

Write often

Lots of love to all

Willie

ALS, rc. OkClaW.

1. Gazelle (Zella) Mae Stine, who was nine months old, died on 16 July 1905. She was the daughter of May Rogers Yocum Stine, Will Rogers's sister, and Jake Stine, her second husband (*CP,* 22 July 1905; *PWR,* 1:553, 554–58, 569; *WRFT,* 28).

2. Rogers was actually in his second week at the Paradise Roof Garden. During the week commencing 24 July he performed with the following acts, in order of play-bill appearance: Ia Page (The Great Sensational High Jumper); The Girl from Coney Island (Flossie Crane); Rice and Prevost (Continuous Success of Bumpty Bumps); The Peskopff Troupe (Russian Dancers); The Four Musical Avalos (Xylophone Experts); Col. Gaston Bordervery (The Piano Marksman); Rossi (The Musical Horse); Bard Brothers (Sensational Acrobats); Ernest Hogan and His 25 Memphis Students with Abbie Mitchell (Entirely New Repertoire of Songs); and Pewitt (The Mysterious Face). Rogers was listed as "Will R. Rogers (Second Week of Lariat Thrower)" and was act number twelve on the bill. The *New York Morning Telegraph* reviewer called Rogers a "hit" and wrote that "in the auditorium proper every seat was occupied and all of the boxes were filled" ("Music A-Plenty in Paradise

William Morris, Sr. *(right)*, with Al Jolson. Morris, who was Rogers's first agent, founded the well-known agency that still bears his name. *(Gift of Ruth Morris White and William Morris, Jr., NNMuS)*

Gardens," 24 July 1905, scrapbook A-1, OkClaW; see also Hammerstein's Paradise Roof Garden playbill, week commencing Monday matinee, 24 July 1905, scrapbook A-1, OkClaW).

3. On 28 July 1905 Rogers signed a contract with his agent William Morris to play at Patsy H. Morrison's Theatre at Rockaway, Long Island, for one week commencing 14 August. The contract stipulated a weekly salary of $150 for two performances daily. Rogers played a matinee at 3:00 P.M. and an evening performance at 8:30 P.M. Rockaway was a popular New York City seaside resort. A *New York Times* advertisement on 19 July 1905 referred to it as "Nature's Own Pleasure Ground." The ad went on to describe its accessibility by regular train service via the Long Island Railroad with connections from Manhattan and Brooklyn. Several hotels were featured in the advertisement. Rockaway Beach lots were for sale at prices ranging from $1,000 to $3,000. One of the resort's feature attractions was Morrison's Theatre, located at Seaside Station. Patrick Henry (Patsy) Morrison (ca. 1875–1930) first operated a beer garden and restaurant where he offered his customers an inexpensive variety show. The agent William Morris convinced Morrison to switch the theater's format to presenting headliners. He assured Morrison that he could get leading vaudevillians at half price, and subsequently the beach theater became a popular summer showplace. Many top vaudevillians played Morrison's, and he proudly published his Hall of Fame list of stars that included Marie Dressler, Nat Wills, Weber and Fields, Sam Bernard, and Rose Stahl. Morrison operated his Rockaway theater for thirty years and retired in 1918. On 5 October 1930 he died of heart trouble at his home in Lynbrook, Long Island (Gilbert, *American Vaudeville*, 227; *VO*, 2:8 October 1930; William Morris Vaudeville Engagement Contract, 28 July 1905, OkClaW).

Of special significance on the Morrison playbill was Grace La Rue (1882–1956). A dancer and singer, La Rue would become a well-known vaudeville headliner. In a memoir of her vaudeville years La Rue recalled seeing Rogers at Morrison's Theatre: "On the Monday we opened at Rockaway, there were two small horses, saddled, standing near the stage door. After rehearsal I went out to admire them, and had my arms around the neck of one when the owner came up. He told me I could ride the pony up and down the side street by the theater if I wished. He was on the same bill— a wild-west riding and rope-throwing act. His name was Will Rogers" (LaRue, "My Vaudeville Years," in Slide, ed., *Selected Vaudeville Criticism*, 276).

The Morrison playbill listed the following acts in order: Morrison's Theatre Orchestra (Fred E. Brooks conducting a medley overture by Haviland); Taylor Twin Sisters (Skatorial Artists); Hines and Remington (Miss Patter of Patterson); Charles Wayne and His "Incubator Girls"; Charles J. Ross and Mabel Fenon (Presenting an Original Domestic Comedy *Just Like a Woman*); Overture (Sel. Lady Teazle by Sloane); Fred Niblo (The American Humorist); Charles H. Burke and Grace La Rue (and the Inkey Boys, The Silver Moon); and Will Rogers (Direct from Hammerstein's, "Putty Tolerable Clever Cowboy") (Morrison's Theatre playbill, week commencing 14 August 1905, scrapbook A-1, OkClaW).

4. On 21 July 1905 Rogers signed a contract to play at Percy Granville Williams's Manhattan Beach Theatre in Coney Island, New York, commencing the week of 21 August. For daily matinee and evening performances he was paid $150 with a 5 percent commission deducted from his salary and paid to his agent, William Morris. A major vaudeville theater manager and builder, Percy Williams began to acquire theaters in Brooklyn, and by July 1905 he was operating six houses in the New York area. A place to escape the summer heat, Manhattan Beach was, as Rogers wrote his father, "a fine Summer resort where all the swell people go" (Will Rogers to Clement Vann

Rogers, 22 August 1905, OkClaW). In addition to the Manhattan Beach venue, Williams operated two theaters in midtown Manhattan (Circle and Colonial), one in Harlem (Alhambra), four in Brooklyn (Orpheum, Crescent, Bushwick, and Greenpoint), one in Williamsburg (Gotham), one in the Bronx (New York), and one in East New York (Gotham). With four theaters in Brooklyn, Williams was a key figure, along with Hyde and Behman, behind Brooklyn's importance as an area of popular entertainment. In 1912 he sold his theaters to Keith (Connors, "American Vaudeville Managers," 45–48; *EV,* 559-60; *NYT,* 22 July 1923; Laurie, *Vaudeville,* 353–59; Percy G. Williams, "Headliner and the Box Office," *Variety,* 14 December 1908; Percy G. Williams Greater New York Circuit Contract, 21 July 1905, OkClaW; "Williams Goes with Keith," *Variety,* 16 February 1907; Williams, "Vaudeville and Vaudevillians," 45–47).

The following acts played with Rogers at the Manhattan Beach Theatre: Louis C. A. Reinhard's Orpheum Orchestra; The Larsen Sisters (European Lady Horizontal Bar Performers); Polk and Collins (Banjoists); Coin's Pantomimic Dogs (An Animal Novelty); Theresa Dorgeval (Prima Donna Soprano, Late of La Scala, Milan); The Mysterious De Bièrre (Introducing a Few New Feats in Magic and Illusion); Flossie Crane (The Girl from Coney Island . . . Discovered by Mr. Hammerstein Singing in Smith's cafe"); Pat Rooney and Marion Bent (In *Making Yourself at Home*); and Carolatta (In her Death Defying Plunge). Rogers was listed as Will R. Rogers, "Lariat Thrower, Direct from Hammerstein's Roof Garden," and appeared seventh on the bill (Manhattan Beach Theatre playbill, week commencing Monday, 21 August 1905, scrapbook A-1, OkClaW; see also "Vaudeville in Brooklyn," *NYDM,* 26 August 1905). Rogers would play with Rooney and Bent several times in his vaudeville career, and they would become good friends (see Biographical Appendix entry, ROONEY, Pat and Marion Bent).

5. On 21 July Rogers signed a contract with F. F. Proctor's Circuit to play at his Newark Theatre for one week, commencing 28 August 1905. For two performances daily, at 2 p.m. and 8 P.M., he received a weekly salary of $150 with 5 percent going to his agent, William Morris. The theater, which had opened in 1898, became very successful. It was located at the junction of Broad Street and Park Place, facing Military Park, and its façade featured an iron grill canopy entrance and classic pillars with a scroll-designed roof (Marston and Feller, *F. F. Proctor,* 52–53, 159–60; F. F. Proctor's Circuit artists' contract, 21 July 1905, OkClaW; Proctor's Theatre, postcard file no. NJ-31, THS).

On the playbill with Rogers at Proctor's Newark were the following artists, as listed in the program: Deltorelli and Clissando (European Musical Comiques); May Yohe and Putnam Bradlee Strong (Presenting *The Actress and the Detective*); Nat Clifford (Eccentric Dancing Comedian); Six Heidelberg Girls (European Singing, Dancing and Acrobatic Novelty); Orpheus Comedy Four (Fifteen Minutes of Fun and Riot); Valerie Bergere and Co. (Presenting Their One-act Comedy by Miss Grace Griswold, entitled, *His Japanese Wife*); Cooper and Robinson (The Clever Colored Entertainers); Motion Pictures (A Stunning Creation, *Raffles the Dog*); Orchestra Selections; and an extra number. Rogers, listed as Will R. Rogers, appeared eighth on the bill and was described as a "Cowboy on Horseback, from the Plains, Giving Exhibitions of Lariat Throwing" (Proctor's Newark Theatre program, week commencing Monday afternoon, 28 August 1905, scrapbook A-1, OkClaW).

From Sam A. Scribner
9 August 1905
New York City, N.Y.

Rogers signed a contract with Sam A. Scribner[1] to perform in so-called refined burlesque theaters in September and October. The contract stipulated $250 per week, which would be his average salary for the rest of the year. Burlesque producers such as Scribner were eliminating lewd and striptease acts in order to attract larger audiences. A cross between vaudeville and musical comedy, these cleaned-up popular theaters featured vaudeville multi-act programs with farces, comedians, variety acts, and skits.

New York, August 9th *1905.*

Mr. Will Rogers,

We have booked you the following five weeks, commencing Sept. 11th, Gaiety Theatre, Brooklyn,[2] Sept. 4th Star,[3] Brooklyn,[4] Sept. 16th ~~Gaiety Theatre Pittsburg~~ ▲ Circle New York ▲,[5] Sept. ~~25th Empire Theatre~~ ▲ Garden Theatre Buffalo ▲,[6] Cleveland, Oct 2nd,[7] ~~Garden Theatre, Buffalo.~~ ▲ Gaiety Theatre Pittsburg ▲[8] Salary to be Two Hundred and Fifty Dollars weekly, less five percent. Mr. Rogers to do the usual performance in the above theatres.

Mr. Rogers agrees not to play in the above Cities before the dates mentioned above.

ACCEPTED. Sam A Scribner

TLS, rc, with autograph deletions and insertions.[9] OkClaW. On Sam A. Scribner, 1358 Broadway, New York, letterhead.

1. Samuel Alexander Scribner (1859–1941) was an influential manager in American burlesque and was involved in practically every form of popular entertainment. Born in Bookville, Pa., Scribner as a young man joined medicine shows, minstrel companies, Wild West shows, and circuses. After several years he turned to burlesque management with his partner Sam H. Harris. At first Scribner produced stock burlesque shows, a mixture of rowdy variety entertainment, dirty jokes, and strippers. A skilled manager, Scribner recognized that the burlesque booking operation was in disarray, with numerous little companies competing with one another. To end the chaos, he formed in 1900 the Travelling Variety Manager's Association and the Columbia Amusement Co. (Eastern or Columbia Wheel). In the early 1900s burlesque was divided into two major circuits, the Eastern or Columbia Wheel and the Western or Empire Wheel. Scribner became a dominant figure in the Columbia Wheel, which, much like a vaudeville circuit, assured long-term booking of performers (up to forty-five weeks) and touring shows that moved from city to city (the shows were thus like revolving spokes on a wheel). Sensing that there was a middle-class audience for burlesque that included women and children, and acting in response to growing censorship, Scribner cleaned up the Eastern Wheel shows by offering performances without smut and spice—essentially variety shows that resembled vaudeville. In so doing he enlarged the audience for burlesque. In 1913 Scribner and I. H. Herk

consolidated both the Eastern and Western burlesque wheels under the Columbia Amusement Co. banner. Much like the Keith Circuit exerting organizational control in vaudeville, Scribner's company absorbed burlesque houses from New York to Omaha. At one time he operated more than forty theaters. In the New York area alone he had nine theaters under his management. After his retirement, Scribner remained active in show-business philanthropy as treasurer of the Actors Fund of America, president of Theatre Authority, Inc., and treasurer of the Percy Williams Home at East Islip, Long Island. He died of heart disease on 8 July 1941 at his home in Bronxville, N.Y. (Allen, *Horrible Prettiness*, 248–49; Leavitt, *Fifty Years in Theatrical Management*, 325–28; *NYT*, 9 July 1941; Sam A. Scribner, "Some Dates and Experiences," *Variety*, 14 December 1908; Sobel, *Pictorial History*, 81–84, 101, 106; Toll, *On with the Show!* 231; *VO*, 3:16 July 1941; Zeidman, *American Burlesque Show*, 52–54, 62–66, 73–82).

2. Under the management of the Hyde and Behman Amusement Co., the Gaiety (or the Gayety according to the playbill) Theatre was one of five burlesque house in Brooklyn that offered entertainment to a large immigrant and working-class population. Located on Broadway and Throop Avenue, the theater had a seating capacity of 1,800 in 1906, and ticket prices were 15 cents in the gallery, 25 cents to a dollar in the orchestra, and a dollar for box seats. It had a varied history, offering clean burlesque and vaudeville in 1905, then by the 1920s reverting to old-time raucous shows under the management of Sam Raymond. It eventually became a Mutual Wheel theater and the target of New York's license commissioner for its suggestive and lusty shows. It was forced to close its doors in the late 1930s (*JCGHTG*, 33, 37; *JCOTG*, 77, 91; Zeidman, *American Burlesque Show*, 176–77, 188, 223). Rogers played at the Gaiety from 11 to 17 September, performing a matinee and evening show each day. He was advertised as a special feature, and the *Brooklyn Times* called him "a cow puncher from the western plains . . . the chief attraction" (clipping dated 12 September 1905, scrapbook A-1, OkClaW). The playbill (similar to that of Rogers's appearance at Brooklyn's Star Theatre the week of 4 September) listed the following acts, in order: the New York Stars under the direction of M. M. Theise performing the one-act farce comedy *Society Swells* by J. E. Cooper and Thomas Haverly; Campbell and Caulfield (Irish Comedians); Faust Trio (Comedy Acrobatic Act); Raymond and Clark (Rapid Fire Conversationalists); Majestic Musical Four (Comedy Musical Act); Will Rogers (the Sensation of the Season, Expert Lassoist); Catherine Taylor (Late of Bostonians, Novelty Singing); and the New York Stars in the one-act farce comedy *Easy Does It* (Gayety Theatre playbill, week commencing Monday matinee, 11 September 1905, scrapbook A-1, OkClaW).

3. In this sentence the date for the Gaiety Theatre was typed as the fourth and changed by hand to the eleventh; the date for the Star Theatre was originally typed as September eleventh and changed by hand to the fourth.

4. Brooklyn's Star Theatre was under the management of Hyde and Behman's Amusement Co. and later the Columbia Amusement Co. It seated 1,670 people at prices ranging from 15 cents to a dollar. Its history was similar to the Gaiety, offering a mixture of burlesque and vaudeville, and eventually it became a standard burlesque house. The Star closed temporarily in 1933, but reopened in 1934 as a burlesque house featuring four-a-day routines and an unruly audience who shouted obscenities at the strippers. A popular Brooklyn showplace, it was a training ground for up-and-coming comics, such as Red Buttons and Gus Schilling. The theater's management was constantly under attack by the church and the license commissioner for its lewd shows. By the end of the 1930s it had been transformed into a *Follies* theater, but after

a few years it closed (*JCGHTG*, 41; *JCOTG*, 87; Zeidman, *American Burlesque Show*, 176–79, 229; for Rogers's performance here, see Review from Will Rogers's Scrapbook, 4 September 1905, below).

5. Opening in 1901 and located at 1825 Broadway and Sixtieth Street, the Circle Theatre was the first theater in New York City's Columbus Circle area. After a battle with the elders of the nearby church of the Paulist Fathers, the Circle Music Hall opened with programs of orchestra concerts, but after financial losses it switched to legitimate theater and subsequently vaudeville. In 1905 it became a burlesque house operated by the Columbia Amusement Co. and managed by Lew Parker. The theater featured an orchestra surrounded by boxes and an upper tier of boxes. In 1906 the Circle was redesigned by the architect Thomas Lamb who increased its height and installed a second balcony. After its refurbishing the theater offered a series of musical shows produced by Gus Edwards, including *The Merry-Go-Round* (1908) and *School Days* (1908), and Klaw and Erlanger's blackface musical, *In Hayti* (1909). It then entered a long period of presenting vaudeville and burlesque, and eventually became a Loew's film theater for twenty-one years. In 1935 the theater was damaged in a bombing stemming from a labor dispute. In 1939 it was rebuilt and became the Columbus Circle Roller Rink. It was demolished in 1954 to make way for the New York Convention Center (van Hoogstraten, *Lost Broadway Theatres*, 53–55).

Rogers performed at the Circle from 18 to 23 September with some top-notch vaudevillians. Among them was the comedian James C. Morton (1884–1942), who later became a well-known screen actor playing comic parts. His partner at this time was his wife Mamie Diamond (née Huls; ca. 1874–1927), formerly with the Diamond Sisters, who played straight to her husband's comedy. Later he did a family vaudeville act with his wife and two children, Alfred and Edna (Laurie, *Vaudeville*, 147, 182–83, 336; *WhMuDr*, 232; *WhoHol*, 2:1196; *WhScrn*, 1:526; *VO*, 1:28 September 1927 and 3:4 November 1942). Also on the program were the Blue Ribbon Girls, a popular comedy ensemble that staged one-act farces with musical medleys in vaudeville and burlesque houses (Blue Ribbon Girls program file, NN-L-BRTC). Appearing with Morton and the Blue Ribbon Girls was Ezza Matthews (ca. 1884–1922), of the vaudeville team Matthews and Miller, and Stella Gilmore (d. 1950), who played in burlesque and musical comedy for many years (*VO*, 1:7 April 1922 and 4:27 September 1950; Circle Theatre playbill, commencing Monday matinee, 18 September 1905, OkClaW).

6. Rogers played Buffalo's Garden Theatre from 2 to 7 October (see Review from the *Buffalo Evening News*, 3 October 1905, below). Formerly Mike Shea's Theater, it offered popularly priced matinees with all seats reserved at 10 cents and 25 cents and evening performances at 15, 25, and 50 cents. Smoking was allowed throughout the theater, which seated 1,374 spectators in 1921 (Garden Theatre advertisement, scrapbook A-1, OkClaW; *JCGHTG*, 61A; *JCOTG*, 157; Review from the *Buffalo Evening News*, 3 October 1905, below).

7. Rogers performed at Cleveland's Empire Theatre from 25 to 30 September. The Empire was called "the New Home of the Best Burlesque." It offered daily matinees at 2:15 P.M. and evening performances at 8:15 P.M. In 1906 the theatre was owned by P. F. Shea. The orchestra seated 1,205 customers and the box seats held 160 patrons (*JCGHTG*, 69; *JCOTG*, 184, 187).

8. Rogers did not perform at Pittsburgh's Gaiety. Instead, he appeared at Toledo's Arcade Theatre during the week of 9 October. He did, however, perform at Pittsburgh's Grand Opera House during the week of 25 December 1905 (*JCGHTG*, 68; *JCOTG*, 178–79).

9. Autograph changes and notes were made on this typed letter in two different hands. Changes in theater engagements were made in one hand by crossing out the originally scheduled theaters and writing in the alternate places above the deleted portion of the lines. Another person annotated these changes with notes. Above "Gaiety Theatre," and next to "Circle New York," this person wrote the word "right," verifying the engagement. There is an arrow pointing at the deleted Garden Theatre entry with the note "(program)." These notes made in a second hand may have been added to the document by a researcher at some later date. They may also be notes verifying the correct engagements for Rogers that reflected changes in his schedule by the Scribner management in September. In his letter to his father on 11 September, Rogers commented, "I am playing in Brooklyn this week [Gaiety] and was to have gone to Pittsburg, Pa. next but they changed it to a Theatre in N.Y. City [Circle]" (OkClaW). On 18 September he wrote his father regarding his appearance at Cleveland's Empire on 25 September rather than 2 October (see Will Rogers to Clement Vann Rogers, 18 September 1905, below).

To Betty Blake
10 August 1905
New York, N.Y.

New York, Aug 10 *1905*

My Dearest Bettie

Well I landed your letter a day or so ago.   Why dont you write often for if you knew how anxious I always am to get a letter from you

Well its the same old thing   out twice a day and do a little bum Roping hear them holler and applaud   smile   bow and then do it again the next day I am still on the Roof.[1]

Finish Sunday Night then to the beach and I will take a few *long needed* baths

But here's what breaks my heart   I wont get to see you in September   I had planned to, and a manager wanted me for 5 weeks about then   I told him I was going home but of course if he would pay me so much (I wont tell you) I would take it and I dident think he'd kinder do it but yesterday he sent me the contract and I had to take it[2]   I will finish Oct. 9, and then Willie for Rogers and the old I.T. for a few Weeks[3]   and say I can get engaged for Europe so go to piling up your doll rags and prepare to see the world as the *wife* of Rogers the Lariet Expert.   this might sound like a joke but its certainly so   I go to [Europe] about Nov 1st if I take it   play several weeks in Paris then London and Berlin   back to the Ark. and I.T. hills for the Summer of 1906.   Now, what better than that, can you beat that.   get to thinking and we will pull it off if you are willing[4]

Now you know what I think of you or should by now and when I make up my mind I at least want to do all I can to accomplish   now I suppose if I cryed and begged and acted nutty then you'd believe me.   Now you better give me an outline of my prospects in the next letter and it must come pretty soon.

With all my love I am yours

Bill.

ALS, rc. OkClaW.

1. As in his previous weeks at Hammerstein's, Rogers did a matinee performance downstairs on the Victoria Theatre stage. Many of the same acts from the previous week appeared on the Paradise Roof Garden playbill during Rogers's fourth and last week from 7 to 13 August. Listed in playbill order were Sailor and Barberetto (Singing Act); Martini and Maxmillian (Burlesque Magic); Hill and Sylviany (Bicycle Sensationalists); Abdul Kader (Artist to His Majesty, The Sultan of Turkey) and His Three Wives ("In a Unique and Extraordinary Feat of Painting in Oil, with Perfect and Beautiful Color Effects, with Lightning Rapidity"); Rice and Prevost (Bumpty Bumps); The Cuttys (Remarkable Family of Instrumentalists); Carmencita (The Famous Spanish Dancer); Will Rogers (Last Week, Lariat Thrower); Ernest Hogan (The Unbleached American) and his 25 Memphis Students; Three Joscarys (Comedy Acrobats); The Zanzigs (Those Who Remain to the Conclusion of the Programme Will Be Astounded by the Marvelous Inexplainable Features of this Act) (Hammerstein's Paradise Roof Garden playbill, week commencing Monday matinee, 7 August 1905, scrapbook A-1, OkClaW; see also the performers' list in the "The Roof Gardens," *NYT,* 6 August 1905, pt. 3, magazine section; and the review "Hammerstein's Paradise Gardens," *NYDM,* 19 August 1905).

2. See From Sam A. Scribner, 9 August 1905, above. Rogers received $250 per week, considerably more than the $150 he earned at Hammerstein's.

3. Rogers's plans changed due to receiving other engagements. On 14 August 1905 he signed a contract with P. B. Chase to perform at Chase's Theatre in Washington, D.C., the week commencing 30 October. On 18 August he signed a contract with his agent William Morris to appear at Toledo's Arcade Theatre the week commencing 8 October. On 31 August he contracted with the Moore Circuit to perform at Detroit's Temple Theatre the week of 16 October and at the Cook Opera House in Rochester, N.Y., the week beginning 23 October (Chase's Theatre Vaudeville Contract, 14 August 1905, below; William Morris Vaudeville Engagement Contract, 18 August 1905, OkClaW; Moore Circuit Artists' Contracts, 31 August 1905, OkClaW).

4. Rogers would not travel to Europe until March 1906. He did begin negotiations with the international agents Richard Pitrot and Robert D. Girard regarding a European tour, but apparently the salary they offered was too low (see Pitrot and Girard to Will Rogers, 6 October 1905, below).

Review from the *New York Dramatic Mirror*
12 August 1905
New York, N.Y.

HAMMERSTEIN'S PARADISE GARDENS.—Carmencita,[1] who created a furore at Koster and Bial's[2] old place on Twenty-third Street a dozen years ago, returned to New York last week, and was warmly greeted by large audiences. For those who are fond of Spanish dancing her turn proved as attractive as ever, and she seems to have lost none of the suppleness and grace that characterized her performances in the old days. She was assisted by Mlle. Aurora. Holdovers who continued to win applause were Ernest Hogan and his Memphis Students,[3] Rice and Prevost,[4] the quaint comedy acrobats; Four Bard Brothers,[5] fine gymnasts, and Will R. Rogers, lasso expert. Barney Fagan and Henrietta Byron[6] scored heavily in their splendidly costumed act, and Alliene's monkey, Hayes and Healey, the Great Valmont and the Taylor Sisters[7] rounded out a splendid programme.[8]

PD. Printed in *NYDM,* 12 August 1905.

1. There is considerable debate regarding the appearance of Carmencita. According to Joe Laurie, Jr., this was not the original Carmencita, who had died around 1899, but a stunt concocted by the publicity-hungry Willie Hammerstein. The bogus Carmencita was a chorus girl Hammerstein had seen perform a Spanish dance in *The Rose of the Rancho.* He signed her to a contract, and she received rave reviews for her performances at the roof garden. If it was a hoax, it apparently was not discovered until later. In the early 1890s the real Carmencita, whose name was Carmen Dausset, was the rage of New York and given considerable publicity by the city's newspapers. Born in 1868 in Almería, Spain, she gave her first performance in Málaga, followed by appearances in other Spanish cities and Paris. Her American debut was at Niblo's Garden on 7 August 1889, and she danced in a production of *Antiope.* After a tour in the West, she performed at Koster and Bial's Music Hall on 10 February 1890 in *The Pearl of Seville.* Here she captivated audiences with the fandango and castanets, and was acclaimed in reviews that compared her to a freedom-loving child of nature. She was very much responsible for the Spanish dancing craze that swept the United States in the 1890s. During the 1891–92 theater season she appeared at Koster and Bial's Music Hall again and at Brooklyn's Grand Opera House with the Spanish Students. She became the darling of high society, and wealthy patrons flocked to her exhibitions and received dancing lessons from her. Two portraits of Carmencita were done in 1890, one by John Singer Sargent (Musée d'Orsay, Paris), the other by William Merritt Chase (Metropolitan Museum of Art, New York). She was honored at a "Carmencita Ball" in Madison Square Garden on 30 January 1891. Carmencita entered the arena on a green-and-gold dragon chariot before a sold-out crowd estimated at ten to twelve thousand people. In August 1893 she danced at the premiere of Koster and Bial's New Music Hall. In March 1894 she performed a dance before the kinetograph motion-picture camera at Thomas Edison's Black Maria studio at

West Orange, N.J. Shortly thereafter she left the United States and eventually faded from popularity (Boone, "Torpedo in Dance Shoes?"; Brown, *History of the New York Stage*, 3:369, 411, 574; *EV*, 87; Hardy, "Flashes of Flamenco"; Laurie, *Vaudeville*, 40, 393–94; McCabe, "Carmencita and Her Painters"; Musser, *Before the Nickelodeon*, 40, 42; Odell, *Annals of the New York Stage*, 15:127–28, 192, 210, 316, 622, 680).

2. Koster and Bial's first Music Hall, formerly Dan Bryant's Opera House (1870; a popular minstrel hall), was a famous concert saloon and variety theater located on Twenty-third Street and Sixth Avenue. In 1879 the theater was leased to John Koster (d. 1895) and Adam Bial, who were in the brewery business. Opening on 5 May 1879, it featured the best variety stars from Europe and America. In the orchestra customers sat at tables drinking as they enjoyed presentations of singing, dancing, and burlesques of classics on a platform stage where a large parted fan was used as a curtain. On 28 August 1893 the partners opened a new music hall at Oscar Hammerstein's former Manhattan Opera House on Thirty-fourth Street, between Sixth Avenue and Broadway. It was at Koster and Bial's New Music Hall on 23 April 1896 that the first public exhibition of Thomas Alva Edison's vitascope took place with the showing of five films by the Edison Co. The old Music Hall (renamed the Bon Ton in 1896) continued as a vaudeville house until 1924, when it was razed. Never a popular success, the New Music Hall was destroyed in 1901 and became the site of Macy's Department Store (Brown, *History of the New York Stage*, 3:367–71, 574–77; *EV*, 291; Gilbert, *American Vaudeville*, 186–94; Henderson, *City and the Theater*, 123, 147, 149, 161, 163–64; Musser, *Beyond the Nickelodeon*, 60–64; *OCAT*, 409).

3. For information on Ernest Hogan and his Memphis Students, see Review, Hammerstein's Paradise Roof Garden, 20 June 1905, above.

4. Rice and Prevost were popular comedy acrobats noted for performing a "rough" or "sight" act in which Eddie Prevost would fall in the orchestra pit. Rice had a tragic death. Unemployed, he became mentally ill and wandered around New York, where one day he was killed by a truck on Eighth Avenue (Gilbert, *American Vaudeville*, 263, 267–68; Laurie, *Vaudeville*, 29).

5. The Four Bards were a gymnastic act of brothers. The *Louisville Record* of 31 December 1907 said that "among the best acrobatic feats ever seen on the American stage are performed by The Four Bards, as the star special this week at the Mary Anderson. They perform their difficult feats with an ease that is remarkable, and instead of leaning up against the scenery after doing a difficult stunt, they tackle a harder one. They introduce a phenomenal outline of inimitable balancing, which is the feature of the turn, and they have rightly earned the title 'The Greatest of All American Gymnasts.'" The Four Bards continued to perfect their act over the years, headlining programs from 1909 to 1916. Based in New York, they completed tours of the West and Europe. The *Variety* critic Epes W. Sargent (Chicot) wrote that "no words can be found for . . . the grace and finish of the Four Bards in their more stylized acrobatic act" (Laurie, *Vaudeville*, 419). Rogers performed with them again at Keith's Chestnut Street Theatre in Philadelphia the week of 9 February 1914 (See Manager's Report, Keith's Chestnut Street Theatre, 9 February 1914, *PWR*, vol. 3; see also Four Bards clippings file, NN-L-BRTC; *Toledo Blade*, 28 January 1913; *Variety*, 14 August and 4 December 1909, 14 January 1911).

6. Barney Fagan (1850–1937) and his wife Henrietta Byron (d. 1924) did a novelty, singing and dancing vaudeville act together for nearly twenty-five years. Fagan was a soft-shoe and clog dancer in variety and performed at Tony Pastor's. At one time he teamed up with another partner named Fenton in the hit act Fagan and Fenton's

Minstrels. In 1884 Fagan performed in Gus Hill's touring show World of Novelties. During the 1880s he wrote and produced several minstrel shows, including the Phantom Guards, and Sweatnam, Rice and Fagan's Minstrels. A composer, Fagan wrote the songs "My Gal's a High-Born Lady" and "Riding in a Heavenly Rowboat," the latter a hit in *The Passing Show* (1894). In 1889 he teamed up with Henrietta Byron, and they performed extensively on the Keith Circuit and in music halls abroad. On 1 June 1924 Byron died of cancer while on the road with the show *Sally, Irene and Mary*. At the height of his vaudeville career Fagan was earning $1,000 a week. During his long career he also appeared in several films. But as he grew older he could not find work and became impoverished. Fagan lived the last six years of his life at Percy Williams's retirement home for performers at Islip, Long Island, where he died on 12 January 1937 at the age of eighty-seven (Laurie, *Vaudeville*, 47; Leavitt, *Fifty Years in Theatrical Management*, 48, 173; *NYT*, 13 January 1937; *OCAT*, 242; Odell, *Annals of the New York Stage*, 15:55–56; *VO*, 2:13 January 1937 and 1:4 June 1924).

    7. The Taylors were twin sisters noted for their novel skating act and excellent skating stunts. Later they added a red umbrella song-and-dance skit to their act that dealt with their flirtations with two young men (Gilbert, *American Vaudeville*, 165).

    8. Also listed on the playbill were Julius and Agnes Zanzig, a mind-reading act that became very popular in America and England. In 1906 they traveled with Houdini's road show in the United States, offering a demonstration of telepathy. They gained fame for their act in which Julius would ask his blindfolded wife on the stage to identify objects belonging to the audience. In their reading routine Agnes Zanzig identified and read from the pages of a book her husband held. Their act depended on their clever use of vocal cues, gestures, signals, and other secret messages. After the death of his wife, Julius Zanzig worked with other partners, but he never achieved the same success. He sold the secrets of his mind-reading act to Houdini and retired to California, where he became a noted astrologer before his death on 29 July 1929 (Busby, *British Music Hall*, 190–91; Gilbert, *American Vaudeville*, 317–19).

Chase's Theatre Vaudeville Contract
14 August 1905
Washington, D.C.

CHASE'S THEATRE[1]
POLITE VAUDEVILLE
WASHINGTON, D.C.

P. B. CHASE[2]   H. WINNIFRED DE WITT
PROPRIETOR   MANAGER
C. J. STEVENSON,[3] N.Y. REPRESENTATIVE,
823 ST. JAMES BUILDING, N.Y. CITY.

    This Agreement, made and entered into this <u>14th</u> day of <u>August</u> A.D. 190<u>5</u>, by and between P. B. Chase, of Washington, D.C., party of the first part, and <u>Will R. Rogers</u> party of the second part.

WITNESSETH, that the party of the second part has hereby contracted and does hereby agree to perform, act, or exhibit for party of the first part at CHASE'S THEATRE, Washington, D.C., as said first party may require for a period of one week, commencing <u>Oct. 30th</u> 190<u>5</u>, and does hereby relinquish all claim to compensation or salary if said services or exhibition shall not be satisfactorily rendered the first party by the party of the second part.

And it is further contracted and agreed by and between said parties that said second party shall play two performances daily, except Sunday, during the term of this engagement.

It is further understood that the second parties shall not perform or exhibit at any other theatre, hall, or club in Washington, D.C., during the season of 1905 or 1906.

On three weeks' written notice by either party this contract may be canceled without any liability thereunder.

Our aim is to elevate and refine, while amusing our patrons, and nothing that appeals to a morbid or depraved nature will be permitted, and in the presentation of an act nothing shall be spoken or acted that will offend the sensitive ear of the most refined lady.

The management positively reserves the right to annul and terminate an engagement with forfeiture of all claims for services at any time before or after a single performance of an incompetent person or one whose representations are grossly excessive, or performer using profane or vulgar language or appearing upon the stage intoxicated, and when an act is not suited to the house the management reserves the right to cancel the said party of the second part by paying them pro rata for the time of actual services at any time during said engagement.

The management will terminate an engagement after a single appearance without any allowance for services of an incompetent or one presenting an act unsuited to the house, or cut down the figures of one excessive in making terms.

All persons engaged must send their Photos, Billing, Program Matter, Press Matter, Time of Act, Scene and Property Plots to Chase's Theatre, *Washington, D.C., so that they be received not less than ten days in advance of opening, and also one half sheet, a one sheet and a three sheet litho, if they have any.*

Deviation from this rule will give the house the option to cancel the date without further notice from the management.

All artists engaged must be in the theatre for rehearsal on day of opening by 10 o'clock A.M., and if not there by that hour the management may engage some one in their place.

It is further contracted and agreed by and between said parties that if second party should at any time miss a performance said party of the second part is to forfeit pro rata of the salary to party of the first part or a discharge at the option of the management.

Said P. B. CHASE shall pay second party for such services for the week when the same shall have been satisfactorily rendered as above mentioned the sum of <u>Two Hundred Fifty ($250)</u> Dollars, less a commission of 5 per cent to C. J. STEVENSON.

Cheerful obedience to the will of the management is at all times necessary, and its requirement is made a part of this contract.

IN WITNESS WHEREOF said parties have hereunto set their hands this _ day of _ A.D. 190_

<u>P B Chase</u>

<u>Will Rogers. By C J Stevenson</u>

IMPORTANT—SPECIAL NOTICE.—There must be no neglect in sending in Lithos, Billing, Program, and Press Matter, Time of Act, Photos, Scene and Property Plots, so as to be delivered not less than ten days in advance of the time of opening the engagement, and if not received by ten days in advance then the management has the option of canceling such engagement. Bring baggage checks to theatre. Don't put music in trunks but bring it with hand baggage.

Bill me as _____

Time of Act _____ Minutes. If necessary can do encore in one ____Minutes.

Scene required _____

Properties _____

Printing at _____

Permanent address _____

Will you send in Photos two weeks in advance? _____

PDS. OkClaW.

1. Chase's Theatre was the major vaudeville theater in the nation's capital. It was formerly the Grand Opera House, built in 1884, and situated atop the Washington Light Infantry armory. The theater was located on Pennsylvania Avenue at the corner of Fifteenth and E Streets, N.W. Chase and his partner, J. K. Burke, began to present vaudeville at the theater beginning 16 January 1899. In charge of the management, Chase called his attractions "polite" vaudeville. Much like Keith, he offered clean and continuous entertainment. A Chase Theatre advertisement read: "Polite vaudeville is a clean and wholesome pleasure for the refined men, women, and children. It is wholly American, and attracts to its theatre only the best element in the community." A mother exclaimed: "The Polite Vaudeville theatre is the only one where I should feel absolutely safe in taking a young girl without making preliminary inquiries" (Mudd,

"History of Polite Vaudeville in Washington, D.C."). In May 1900 the theater offered a ten-hour continuous program from two o'clock until midnight. The theater had a seating capacity of 2,083. When Rogers played there in 1905, it had an orchestra (50 cents), balcony (25 cents), and gallery (15 cents). Matinee tickets were 25 cents. Chase's final program was presented in April 1912. The following year Sylvester Poli purchased the lease, and Chase and his new partners, Lee and Jacob Shubert, operated a new theater one block away (Chase's advertisement, *Washington Times*, 30 October 1905; *JCOTG*, 155; King, "Sylvester Z. Poli Story," 14).

2. Born in Mt. Gilead, Ohio, Plimpton B. Chase was a prominent theater owner and manager. Before he operated Chase's Theatre in Washington, D.C., he established the Hiawatha amusement park at Mount Vernon, Ohio. His daughter Mabel became the second wife of B. F. Keith. He died on 4 April 1938 at his winter home in St. Petersburg, Fla. (Mudd, "History of Polite Vaudeville in Washington, D.C."; *VO*, 2:20 April 1938).

3. Charles J. Stevenson was a theatrical manager for forty years. He began his career in Cleveland and later went to New York, where he was associated with Keith's booking office. Afterward he managed theaters in Denver, where he died in 1944 (*VO*, 3:29 March 1944).

To Clement Vann Rogers
29 August 1905
Newark, N.J.

New York, Aug 29 *1905*[1]

My Dear Papa

I got your letter all O.K. and glad to hear all the news.   I would like to see Claremore since it has got to be a City   I am still at work near N.Y.   I am this week at Newark, New Jersey, about 15 miles out of the city[2]   next week I go to Brooklyn for two weeks then I go away out to Pittsburg, Pa.   Here is $50.00[3]   I will send you for me.   Did Maud pay my insurance   When you write tell me what I have there now for I have forgot what I sent home   tell me just what it is.   I am going to try and get home in Oct[4]

Well I will close

ans soon

Your son

Willie.

ALS, rc. OkClaW. On Putnam House letterhead.

1. Rogers wrote this letter in Newark, using the Putnam House letterhead from New York.

2. Rogers played at F. F. Proctor's Newark Theatre from 28 August to 2 September. On 3 September Rogers performed at a special Sunday vaudeville program at Proctor's Fifty-eighth Street Theatre, located on the southwest corner of Third Avenue in midtown Manhattan. Also known as Proctor's Pleasure Palace, the massive theater was built in 1895 by J. B. McElfatrick and Son in a Romanesque and Renaissance style. Inside were a German cafe and stage, library, writing room, and

F. F. Proctor's luxurious Pleasure Palace (1895), Lexington Avenue and Fifty-eighth Street, New York City, where Rogers performed in September 1905. *(Byron Collection, NNMuS)*

other amenities, while outside was a lush palm garden and roof garden (Birkmire, *Planning and Construction*, 32–40; Miller, "Proctor's Fifty-Eighth Street Theatre," 8). The special Sunday performance was in the 2,100-seat auditorium. Joining Rogers on the playbill was the former heavyweight boxing champion James J. Corbett (1866–1933), now a successful actor and vaudevillian (*WhoStg*, 97–98). The acts were listed as follows: Views of Travel; Malvene and Wilde; Henry Frey; Lizzie Evans and Harry Mills; Adamini and Taylor; Will R. Rogers; Fanny Rice; Wheelock's U. S. Indian Band; Caron and Farnum; and motion pictures (Proctor's Fifty-eighth Street Theatre playbill, Sunday, 3 September 1905, scrapbook A-1, OkClaW).

3. Rogers had sent his father $40 in his letter of 22 August 1905 (OkClaW).

4. Two days later, on 31 August 1905, Rogers signed two contracts with the Moore Circuit to play at Detroit's Temple Theatre (week of 16 October) and the Cook Opera House in Rochester, N.Y. (week of October 23), making it impossible for him to return home that month (Moore Circuit Artists' Contracts, 31 August 1905, OkClaW). Around this time Rogers's agent, William Morris, sent him a tentative schedule of theater bookings from 4 September 1905 to 19 February 1906. Many of them were on the Poli Circuit in New England and the Proctor Circuit in New Jersey and New York (William Morris vaudeville schedule, 4 September 1905–19 February 1906, OkClaW; see also Biographical Appendix entry, MORRIS, William).

Vaudeville Routine
ca. Summer or Fall 1905
New York and Elsewhere

During his first year in vaudeville Rogers wrote some notes for his routine. They reveal that he was already talking on the stage and was making humorous comments about his roping and about missing the horse with his lasso, and making other jokes about his routine.

THE OLD ACT–

Now folks I want to call your sho nuff attention to this next little stunt its a pretty tolerable good one if I happen to get it.   I'll throw about two of these things at once I'll throw one of them at the horse and the other one at that other thing and they will both go exactly at the same time.   I don't have any idea they will catch but I'll throw them anyway.

Got em all on but one.   if that old Pony had of been trained properly he would of stuck his head in there.

---

after missing both man and horse.

Well I better learn to throw one of these before I try two.

Well I am at least improving after throwing and catching one of them.

---

if that old Pony had of had horns I would of got him.

To Man it wouldent of been much trouble to you to stuck your hands or head in there would it you are the worst I ever roped at.

If I dont get this pretty soon I will give out rain checks
if i dont run the horse down I may get this.

Who ever put this trick into my head any way.

Im a bit handicapped up here the boss of this Ranch dont even allow a fellow to *swear* or *cuss a* little even ▲ when ▲ if he ▲ the ▲ misses out loud.[1]

---

yes you dont hope so anymore than me.   [L]ets us hope as old Dr [Murry?] once said.

---

any body that thinks I am doing this thing on purpose they got another guess coming
tie a bad man up if you are afraid to go close to him like I am this one.

Poke out your *Lunch Hooks.*

It wouldent been much trouble to put your hands in.

Now Ha you *Seldom Fed Hard Luck.*   I want to get one over you too.

Now I show you how to put a halter on a horse standing away from him.

His nose wasent in right place.

If he had had a Jew (Roman[)] nose I would of got him
He dont know a thing about this trick does he

---

if I am lucky I generally get this about the 20 throw

Put a little Rosin on his nose and that would stay on.

He *NOSE* more about this trick than I do.

_____

Then hand him the rope and he goes off with it on him and pony

_____

First trick over horse man and horse by all 4 feet.

_____

Then for long time at first throw Rope with foot and catch horse

_____

Then jump through catch four feet

_____

Then tie up with Half hitches
then all trick Roping.

_____

Then ▲ Then tied the knots in Rope. ▲ double throw

_____

Then cowboy jumping Rope.
finish big loop on horse.

_____

Later on tail catch in there

_____

He run out on pony and jumped off.   I say look out dont get to[o]
Western there we want to finish the week out here

_____

I did the little jump up and catch the foot in the stirrup and on easy.

_____

The[n] on clear over and back up on the horse.

_____

I'll try and make the Crinoline with this little short piece clothes line.
Well Rope sometimes stretched it out in audience
Boy comes down the aisle I pitch him Rope and he drops it and I hand it
too him easy.   Rehersal at 10 tomorrow.   Then I say to him dont get out of
town with the thing.   then get on horse and Spin it out ▲ give pony piece of
Sugar out of mouth ▲

_____

Here's a little style of Crinoline I'll bet the Ladies dont wear for some
time.

_____

At Hammersteins first Summer did Gun Spinning in both hands for an
Encore and showed how to turn it over and shoot when you go to hand it _to

anyone_ A fellow in the audience says talk Louder.   I was missing a trick at the time and I says you dont mean talk louder you mean Rope better.

———

I try and show you how to tie a knot in Rope and not use the hands.   first an ordinary hard knot like this showing them then tieing it then a bow knot show them and then tie it.   ▲ thats *not* it. ▲

———

Thats a young one but its in there.   Bear bat and *Wampus.*

———

The Tail catch—if he had had a tail as long as the comet I might of got it. His tail not in right place
Trained properly would stick his tail in.

———

you know I dont like to knock anyone or anything but I think he is wise to this tail thing and he duckes it just as I throw.

———

That was getting down towards the tail end of my act.

———

That would be a good trick to do if it was done on one of these cob tail city horses.

———

You know I got to stay up here so long as I dont collect.   I dont collect much any way but I'd like to get what little is coming to me.

———

The Pretzel–you Germans ought to know what that is thats a natural born pretzel.   In Hoboken that trick went better than any one.   One fellow said it looked natural enough to eat.   But I needed the rope and wouldnt let him have it.   *"Joke"* see I needed the Rope that I made the pretzel with and the Baker that makes the pretzels he needed the one that he made the pretzels with.   silly Joke.   no sense to it.[2]

AMS, OkClaW.

1. Rogers refers to the censorship in vaudeville.
2. This last line ("that he made the pretzels . . . sense to it.") was written sideways in the margin.

Review from Will Rogers's Scrapbook
4 September 1905
Brooklyn, N.Y.

NEW YORK STARS AT THE STAR THEATER.

Typical holiday crowds packed the Star Theater at both performances yesterday and witnessed a first-class entertainment of burlesque and vaudeville by Theise's[1] New York Star Company. "Society Swells" and "Easy Doesit" are the two burlettas in which able comedians and a charming lot of show girls entertain most pleasingly. The costuming [is] most elaborate, and the numerous musical numbers are rendered in good voice by the chorus, particularly so was this noticeable in the two numbers lead by Cath[e]rine Taylor.[2]

The olio[3] begins with a good Irish comedy talking act, by Campbell and Caulfield. The Faust Trio[4] are clever comedy acrobats, and their antics through "The Haunted Castle" brought much applause. Raymond and Clark, rapid fire talkers and parodists, have a good act and work hard to please their auditors. The Majestic Musical Four[5] in an excellent musical specialty in which they introduce good comedy into their act, were well received. Will Rogers, an expert lassoist, made the hit of the show with his truly marvelous feats of all sorts of rope throwing while seated astride a horse in realistic Western style. Miss Catherine Taylor, vocalist, and late of the Bostonians, sings several operatic numbers in a clear sweet voice and was liberally applauded.

Next week the Golden Crook Company will be the attraction.[6]

PD. Scrapbook A-1, OkClaW.

1. Mortimer M. Theise, theater manager and burlesque producer, was born in Putney, Vt., on 1 August 1866. At an early age Theise was a lecturer with the Engul Clock traveling company and a salon entertainer with the Allegheny Bell Ringers and Vocalists. Next he held a series of jobs with the Batchelor and Doris Circus, Whitmore and Clark's Minstrel Troupe, and a light opera repertoire company. After a four-and-a-half year stint in the diamond business, he built the Metropolis Theatre in New York, which was finished in August 1898. In March 1899 he sold his interest and opened a vaudeville theater in Syracuse, N.Y. The same year he produced a burlesque show called *Wine, Woman and Song*, which traveled the burlesque wheels for six seasons. Beginning 26 October 1906, the show had a long run at New York's Circle Theatre. During the theater season of 1907–8 Theise produced *Across the Pond* and *The Two Islands* (*WhoStg*, 427; Zeidman, *American Burlesque Show*, 56).

2. *Society Swells* was a one-act farce by J. E. Cooper and Thomas Haverly that opened the program at the Star Theatre. The farce was staged by a large number of players including a Society Swells Opera Co. Stars of the production were Herbert Simon, Will F. Collins, and Catherine Taylor. The latter was identified in the program

as the leading lady of the Society Swells Burlesque Co. She also did a single act of novelty singing as a separate item on the program. Five musical numbers were introduced during the performance. The program concluded with *Easy Doesit,* another one-act farce with musical numbers performed by the same cast (Gayety Theatre playbill, week commencing Monday matinee, 11 September 1905, OkClaW; Society Swells program file, NN-L-BRTC).

3. In refined burlesque the olio was the vaudeville or variety part of the show with a mixture of acts, which appeared after the opening travesty or spoof by a company such as The New York Swells. Another farce concluded the program. Burlesque derived some of its structure (songs, gags, and chorus) from the minstrel show, in which the olio was the section when the performers did their specialties (Zeidman, *American Burlesque Show,* 20).

4. The members of the Faust Trio were Victor Jerome, Lottie Freemont, and John Russ (Star Theatre playbill, week commencing Monday matinee, 4 September 1905, scrapbook A-1, OkClaW).

5. The Majestic Musical Four were listed as Collins, Terrill Brothers, and Simon (Star Theatre playbill, week commencing Monday matinee, 4 September 1905, scrapbook A-1, OkClaW).

6. *The Golden Crook* was a successful burlesque and variety show at this time starring Billy Arlington. Its title was borrowed from *The Black Crook* (1866). It was a mixture of drama, farce, and spicy variety acts that included a dance of scantily clad women. It played to capacity audiences at Niblo's Garden for 474 performances. The show is considered to be a forerunner of modern burlesque and the musical comedy (Sobel, *Burlesque,* 108; Toll, *On with the Show!* 173–77; Zeidman, *American Burlesque Show,* 21, 203). The bill at the Star Theatre was repeated in its entirety during the week of 11 September 1905 at Brooklyn's Gayety Theatre.

To Clement Vann Rogers
18 September 1905
New York, N.Y.

New York, Sept. 18 *1905*

My Dear Papa

Just got your letter   will write and send you some Money as *I know you are in* need *of some*   Here's $110.00   One hundred and ten[1]   This is my last week in N.Y.   I go to the Empire Theatre, Cleveland. Ohio   Next week they have changed me from my original route   Write me there and I will get it.   I am there from Sept. 25 to Oct 1st.   Then to the Garden Theatre Buffalo N.Y.   from Oct 1st to 7th.

Lots of love to all

from your son
Willie

ALS, rc. OkClaW.

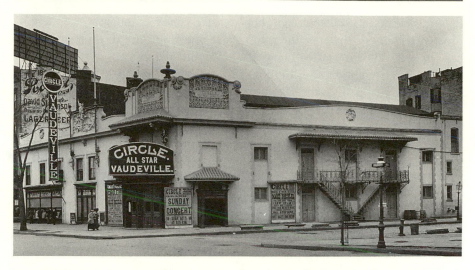

Percy Williams's Circle Theatre (1901), Broadway and Sixtieth Street, New York City, the first theater in the Columbus Circle area. Rogers played the Circle in September 1905. *(Byron Collection, NNMuS)*

1. Rogers also sent his father $60 from his salary in his letter to him on 5 September 1905, and in his 11 September 1905 letter he sent him $166. "I sent this will make $450 wont it," he wrote (to Clement Vann Rogers, 5 September 1905 and 11 September 1905, OkClaW).

To Clement Vann Rogers
27 September 1905
Cleveland, Ohio

Cleveland, O.
Sept 27. 05

My Dear Papa.

I arrived here from N.Y. all O.K. and am at the Empire Theatre and have been quite a success[1]   finish here Saturday night and go to Buffalo next week then out to Toledo, O.

I will send you $115.00 which will make me $675 there wont it   did you get the $110 I sent last week

I am going to put in a part of the winter and save up my money and when I come home I am going to get me a little bunch of cows and back up on the farm I am going[2]

Did you get the pictures I sent you by express from New York.[3]   Papa send me about 35 ft of small light hard twisted rope like the boys use there to rope with   any of them would know   get one from one of them that they have used if you can as it will be better.   Light hard twist.   to throw not to twirl.[4]   also two good red or big check flannel shirts size 15 1/2.   and one of those pretty stripped Osage Blankets that you buy at Ruckers[5] for a saddle blanket   Gordon or Clem or Bright or some of those boys will have the kind of rope[6]   send them so I will get them ~~Monda~~ Sunday Week Oct 8th in Toledo.   By express and I will pay you what it is

% Arcade Theatre[7]

Toledo, Ohio

Love to all

Willie

ALS, rc. OkClaW.

1. The *Cleveland Leader* reviewer commented that "there is the lasso throwing act of Will Rogers, who does some astounding things and puts the experts with Buffalo Bill and Pawnee Bill in the shade" (clipping, 26 September 1905, scrapbook A-1, OkClaW). Listed in the Cleveland Empire playbill that week was The Gay Masqueraders company in *The Adviser*, a musical by James E. Cooper; Edith Murray (the Jolly and Winsome Singer of Coon Songs That Have Been the True Essence of the Sunny South); Haverly and M'Rae (Punsters and Discussers of Modern Topics); Berry and Berry (Whose Mastery of Music and Comedy Shows Plainly in the Rendition of their Various Selections); James and Lucia Cooper (Dispellers of Care in an Interchange of Tangletalk); Will Rogers (Extra–Expert Lassoist in Wonderful Act); the Gayoscope (Presenting the Principal Rounds of the Nelson-Britt Fight, also the latest hit, *The Moon's Lover*); the Gay Masqueraders in *Way Up Yeast*, a satire by John J. Black (Empire playbill, week commencing Monday, 25 September, scrapbook A-1, OkClaW). Burlesque shows often traveled intact from town to town, so it is not surprising that the same program was repeated the following week at Buffalo's Garden Theatre (see Review from the *Buffalo Evening News*, 3 October 1905, below).

2. At this time Rogers begins to have doubts about a show-business career and thinks of returning to Indian Territory. His desire to return home will be repeated in many publicity stories in the coming months (see, for example, Review from the *Toledo Times*, 11 October 1905, below).

3. In his letter to his father dated 22 September 1905, Rogers wrote that he had sent four pictures, one for his father and three for his sisters, May, Maud, and Sallie (OkClaW).

4. In his act Rogers used tightly twisted half-inch hemp ropes and took special pride in the fact that they were from his hometown (Will Rogers to Clement Vann Rogers, 12 October 1905, OkClaW; and Article from the *Rochester Union and Advertiser*, 26 October 1905, below).

5. Frank Marshall Rucker (1866–1953), a rancher, and his brother, Dr. John G. Rucker, owned a large general store in Claremore (*HRC*, 381; *PWR*, 1:214, 215n.6, 216 and n.1).

6. References possibly to Fortner Gordon Lane; Clement Mayes (Clem) McSpadden (1886–1912), son of Rogers's sister Sallie and her husband Tom

McSpadden; and Bright Drake (1876–1959), a boyhood friend who drove cattle and roped coyotes with Rogers in the Oologah/Chelsea area (*HRC,* 176, 274, 301; *PWR,* 1:75, 290n.12).

7. Toledo's Arcade Theatre belonged to the Keith Circuit. It was listed in 1914–15 as having a seating capacity of 1,563 and as being part of the Gus Sun Circuit. H. H. Lamkin represented the theater in the signing of Rogers's contract (*GHNTD,* 544; William Morris Vaudeville Engagement Contract, 18 August 1905, OkClaW; see also Article from the *Toledo Times,* 11 October 1905, below).

Review from the *Buffalo Evening News*
3 October 1905
Buffalo, N.Y.

GOOD BURLESQUE AT THE GARDEN

The Gay Masqueraders,[1] a sprightly bunch of burlesquers, hold forth at the Garden Theater this week. Yesterday the show opened with two performances both of which taxed the seating capacity of the new home of burlesque.

The show is one of the best played at the Garden this season and its success is assured. "The Adviser," the opening burlesque, is clever and full of ginger. A prettier or sweeter-voiced chorus of girls than those with the company would be hard to find. The olio is made up of high class vaudeville artists such as Edith Murray in coon songs; Haverly and McRae, funmakers; Berry and Berry, refined musical artists; and James and Lucia Cooper.[2] James Cooper, with his funny sayings keeps the audience in an uproar.

Special extra attractions are Will Rogers, lassoist, who considering the small space to work in, gives a wonderful demonstration of his ability as a cow puncher. His act is new and he was roundly applauded.[3] The Britt-Nelson[4] fight pictures pleased the sporting element. The closing piece "Way Up Yeast" is well produced. The comedians are good and the musical numbers catchy. Foster and Kienan, who sang "The Reporters" were well received. A matinee will be given daily.

PD. Scrapbook A-1, OkClaW.

1. The Gay Masqueraders was a burlesque company operated by the producers Gus Hill (ca. 1860–1937) and Bob Manchester. The star of the company was Harry Emerson, a dialect comedian. Early in her career, the singer Sophie Tucker was with this company for one season and received $50 a week for an eight-month tour. She did a blackface act in the olio portion (*EV,* 239; Tucker, *Some of These Days,* 53–59; Zeidman, *American Burlesque Show,* 69).

2. The married comic entertainers Lucia Cooper and James E. (Blutch) Cooper were featured performers with The Gay Masqueraders. They toured with this burlesque show for several years until 1907. In 1908 they were performing in vaudeville on the Sullivan-Considine Circuit. Between 1909 and 1914 James Cooper owned and

starred in his own show called The Jersey Lilies. Cooper, who also wrote the show's material, was known for portraying the character Gus Grouch, a crank. Cooper also played this part in the 1909 farce *Twisted Mixups*. By 1913 the pair was acting in the musical comedy show *Beauty, Youth and Folly*. They also did olios for The Jersey Lilies between 1909 and 1912. As late as 1920 James Cooper was staging and writing shows for the American Burlesque Circuit. Etta Cooper, their daughter, was also an actress, who made her stage debut in 1917 (series 3, 346:231–46, NN-L-RLC).

3. The playbill described Rogers as an "Expert Lassoist in his Marvelous Casting Act Roperina" (Buffalo Garden Theatre playbill, week of 2 October 1905, scrapbook A-1, OkClaW).

4. The match between Battling Nelson (1882–1954) and Jimmy Britt (1879–1940) on 9 September 1905 in Colma, Calif., was a rematch of their twenty-round fight in 1904, which Britt won. In the rematch Britt won by a knockout in the eighteenth round. In another rematch in 1907 Nelson defeated Britt. Battling Nelson, whose real name was Oscar Nielson, was born in Copenhagen, Denmark, and became known as the "Durable Dane." Known for his untiring, raging style, which appealed to many fans, he was a box-office draw. He won the world lightweight championship on 4 July 1908 when he knocked out Joe Gans in the seventeenth round in San Francisco. He lost the title to Ad Wolgast on 22 February 1910 at Port Richmond, Calif., when the referee stopped the match in the fortieth round. During his long career Nelson fought 132 fights, of which he won 78 (38 by knockout) and lost 19; 35 had no decision.

Jimmie Britt (James Edward Britt) fought 23 fights, of which he won 14 (3 by knockout) and lost 7; 2 had no decision. On 31 October 1904 Britt lost a title fight with Joe Gans by a foul in the fifth round, but authorities claimed Britt had won the title because Gans was overweight. Britt was one of many famed boxers who entered vaudeville (among them, John L. Sullivan, Bob Fitzsimmons, Jim Jeffries, Tom Sharkey, Jim Corbett, Jack Dempsey, and Jack Johnson). Known as the "handsomest fighter in tights," Britt performed a monologue act in San Francisco, his hometown, in 1911 (Laurie, *Vaudeville*, 122, also 118–24; and Burrill, *Who's Who in Boxing*, 30, 143–44; Lardner, *White Hopes and Other Tigers*, 26–27, 59–60).

Boxing films were a popular genre in early cinema history. One of the first was the Edison Manufacturing Co.'s *Leonard-Cushing Fight* (1894), a six-round match between Michael Leonard and Jack Cushing. It was quickly followed by *The Corbett-Courtney Fight* (1894), another Edison kinetograph, in which Jim Corbett knocked out Peter Courtney in the sixth round (Musser, *Before the Nickelodeon,* 47–49). In addition, the playbill advertised the showing of the hit film *The Moon's Lover.*

From Richard Pitrot and Robert D. Girard
6 October 1905
New York, N.Y.

As this letter indicates, Rogers was exploring the possibility of performing in Europe and corresponded with the international agents Richard Pitrot and Robert D. Girard.[1]

NEW YORK CITY ___ 6th 1905

Mr. Will Rogers,
    Garden Theatre,
    Buffalo, N.Y.
My Dear Sir:—

Yours of the 4th received.

Am sorry you could not see your way clear to accept our offer of three thousand marks: you did not figure same correctly, as three thousand marks a month, is equal to $187.50 a week.

However, since you say you are receiving $250.00 here, it would not pay you to go to the other side for less.

Yours truly,
Pitrot & Girard

TLS, rc. OkClaW. On Pitrot & Girard, Agents for American and Foreign Vaudeville Novelties, Room 607, 1265 Broadway, New York City, letterhead.

1. Born in Europe, Richard Pitrot (ca. 1851–1929) was a leading theatrical international agent who booked American acts for engagements abroad and European acts for appearances on the Keith Circuit and other chains. Before entering the agency business, Pitrot was himself a vaudevillian who performed imitations. Known as "The Monarch of Mimicry," he was best known for his impersonations of George Washington and Abraham Lincoln. Around 1889 he came to the United States and that year performed his impersonations at Koster and Bial's Music Hall. Pitrot gave up his stage career for the agency business. He was nicknamed The Globe Trotter because of his travels abroad in search of talent to bring to America. He was also known as The International Amusement Explorer. He was the European representative of the Pantages Circuit in 1911. That year he signed 125 European acts for both the Pantages and William Morris circuits. Pitrot was greatly respected by his colleagues for knowing the value of an act and by performers for his integrity in obtaining fair salaries. He was the exclusive manager of well-known European vaudevillians, such as Paul Cinquevalli, a juggler, and The Rappo Sisters, a singing and dancing act. In addition, he was the foreign representative for the booking office of the vaudeville actors' union, the White Rats of America. He served as the American representative of many international circuses. Pitrot organized The American Globe Trotter's Co., which performed in South Africa, and produced a show called *The Dark Secret* in Europe. Pitrot also contributed to the *New York Clipper* theater newspaper and had an office on the top floor of the newspaper's building. A familiar figure at Union Square, he was remembered for his idiosyncrasy of walking with a silver cane. He married Mme. Ancion, a circus trapeze artist, and they had one son. In his later years Pitrot was practically penniless and was supported by William Morris and the National Vaudeville Association. He died in a New York hospital of diabetes on 21 March 1929 (Gilbert, *American Vaudeville*, 18, 225; Grau, *Business Man in the Amusement World*, 96; Leavitt, *Fifty Years in Theatrical Management*, 202–3; *VO*, 2:27 March 1929; Richard Pitrot scrapbooks and clippings, NN-L-BRTC).

Robert D. Girard was the New York representative for the Orpheum Circuit for eight years. Always on the lookout for new artists, he used to attend regularly a theater in New Rochelle, N.Y., that was known for its tryouts of unknown artists. He became a partner of Pitrot in February 1905. The agents had offices at 1265 Broadway, near Thirty-second Street. They dissolved their partnership in August 1906 (Grau, *Business Man in the Amusement World,* 102–3; *New York Clipper,* 4 March 1905, 38; *Vaudeville Review of Vaudeville Favorites,* February 1905, 21; *Variety,* 1 September 1906, 38).

To Sisters
ca. 7 October 1905
Buffalo, N.Y.

What do you think of these   just got them.   give them to the Kids.

I leave here Buffalo tonight for Toledo.   will be at Arcade Theatre Toledo untill Oct 15 then Detroit Temple Theatre[1] for week.[2]

write soon

Love
Willie

APCS, rc. On The Greatest Catch in Vaudeville photographic postcard.

1. Detroit's Temple Theatre was owned and managed by James H. Moore, who also operated the Cook Opera House in Rochester, N.Y. The two theaters earned him a considerable fortune (see Will Rogers to Sisters and All, 11 October 1905, below). He had an interlocking business relationship with B. F. Keith; the Temple was listed as a Keith theater in 1905. The Temple Theatre had a seating capacity of 1,750. In 1895 Moore initiated four shows a day, but by 1905 this policy was evidently no longer in effect, for Rogers made only two appearances in his theater (Grau, *Business Man in the Amusement World,* 316–17; Leavitt, *Fifty Years in Theatrical Management,* 161, 203; *JCGHTG,* 79; *JCOTG,* 219).
2. Rogers's itinerary was receiving press coverage back home. On 6 October 1905 the *Claremore Messenger* reported that Rogers "who has been in New York for some time past, doing fancy roping, is now in Cleveland: goes from there to Detroit, and will be in Washington, D.C., the last of the month. His skill and experience with the rope is attracting popular attention and proving a winner for him."

Article in the *Toledo Times*
11 October 1905
Toledo, Ohio

COWBOY CAUSED FLURRY ON LAGRANGE STREET

WILL ROGERS, INDIAN LARIAT THROWER,
VISITED TOLEDO STOCK YARDS.

That portion of Toledo's population residing along Lagrange street yesterday morning were astonished at the sight of a real Indian cowboy, garbed in fringed leather breeches, fiery red flannel shirt, wide sombrero hat, and mounted on a wiry mustang pony, galloping along their thoroughfare. Visions of train hold-ups, express robberies and other wild western pranks fitted through their minds, and it is even hinted that some of the more timid took to the cellar for a brief period.

The cause of all the speculation and "rubbering" was Will Rogers, the lariat manipulator, whose wonderful skill is this week making Arcade audiences "sit up and take notice."[1]

Rogers was on his way out to the Toledo Union stockyards to give an exhibition of expert cattle roping for the benefit of the stockmen employed out there, who are often called upon to deal with unruly bovines. For a couple hours Rogers showed them a line of horsemanship and lasso-throwing stunts that served to give them many a valuable pointer for their line of work.

His visit to the yards was due to an invitation from Manager F. E. Humphrey, who saw his exhibition at the arcade the night before, and who was so impressed with it that he asked Manager Lamkin's[2] permission to invite Rogers out. Rogers is nearly a full-blooded Cherokee Indian, born and raised on a ranch in the Indian Territory.

His father is the Hon. C. V. Rogers, president of the First National bank at Claremore, I.T. Besides this the elder Rogers is a member of the Cherokee nation's senate, and one of the foremost men in all tribal affairs of this civilized and wealthy tribe of Indians.[3]

PD. Printed in the *Toledo Times*, 11 October 1905.[4] Scrapbook A-1, OkClaW.

1. Rogers appeared at the Toledo Arcade from 8 to 14 October. He was the last live act on the playbill, which also included Pat Rooney and Marion Bent. The playbill was as follows: Overture (E. R. Schremsher and Orchestra); 3 De Greaus (Singing and Dancing); Santoro and Marlow (The Tramp and the Piquant); Werden and Gladdish (Ballads with Semi-Oil Painting); Pat Rooney and Marion Bent (In Make Yourself at Home with Neat and Eccentric Dances); James Richmond Glenroy (The Man with the Green Gloves); Edward LaVine, Lillian Waltone and Co. (In a Spectacular Comedy entitled *The Explorer's Dream*); Harper, Desmond and Bailey ("Hot Stuff from Coontown"); and Will Rogers (King of the Lariat in an Exhibition of Marvelous Skill and Dexterity). An American Vitagraph film called *The Servant Girl* was also shown (Toledo Arcade playbill and advertisement, week commencing Sunday, 8 October, scrapbook A-1, OkClaW).

2. H. H. Lamkin was the manager of Toledo's Arcade and joint proprietor with a man named Newton. Rogers's contract with William Morris was signed by Lamkin, as the theater's representative (William Morris Vaudeville Engagement Contract, 18 August 1905, OkClaW). A clipping in Rogers's scrapbook reads: "Last summer while booking attractions in New York Manager Lamkin saw an act that he says is a real novelty, which will be seen on this week's bill. It is Will Rogers, known as 'The King of the Lariat'" (clipping, scrapbook A-1, OkClaW).

3. On Clement Vann Rogers's business and political affairs see *PWR*, 1:71, 83n.21, 104n.1, 123n.2, 170, 171n.1, 171n.2, 171n.4, 282–83n.3, 283–84, 289n.10, 291n.16, 327, 536–43, 542. While in Toledo Rogers continued to question the notion of a show-business career. On 11 October 1905 the *Toledo News-Bee* printed an article entitled "King of the Lariat Longs for Plains and Round-up." In it Rogers expressed his hope to return to Indian Territory and the ranch life. "It's back to the teppe and the tall grass with William Rogers," he told the reporter. "Not saying . . . that we aint getting a square deal or that these eastern folks aint all right, bit it aint our way, that's all. When a man's system gets inoculated with the life o' the plains he's like a sailor ashore when he's off the prairie" (clipping, scrapbook A-1, OkClaW).

4. Rogers enclosed this clipping in one of the two letters he sent to his father from Toledo (Will Rogers to Clement Vann Rogers, 12 October 1905 and 13 October 1905, OkClaW) or to his sisters (Will Rogers to Sisters and All, 11 October 1905, below).

To Sisters and All
11 October 1905
Toledo, Ohio

Toledo, Ohio.
Oct 11th.   05.

My Dear Sisters and all.

Well I am about as far out your way as I will get this trip for after next week in Detroit   all my work up to Xmas is in the East   I am the *Headliner* or the main squeege here this week[1]   I finish Saturday night and my man[2] and pony will go up by boat Sunday to Detroit.   but not any boat for me if I can go on land   we open there Monday afternoon.   *Here's* a lot of Newspaper stuff that has appeared this week   the picture was in Sundays [paper][3]   It is getting a bit cold up around these lakes.   Say I wrote to papa for some things did he ever send them   he dont even write and I dont know if he gets all the money I send him   did Maud get the package of summer clothes I sent and did you all get the 4 large pictures   please tell me when you write.

Now here is my route   if you will just notice when you write yo cant miss it   I am in each town from the beginning of a week till the end   just allow two or three days for it to come   and it will get me.

Week of Oct 16th.
          Temple Theatre
          Detroit. Mich.
Week of Oct 23rd
          Cooks Opera House[4]
          Rochester N.Y.
Week of Oct 30th
          Chases Opera House
          Washington

from Nov 6th for the next two weeks I will be in N.Y.   address Putnam House untill Nov 20.   I play one week at *Hammersteins* and one in Brooklyn then Nov 20 I go to Boston. Mass. for a week.   Nov 27.   Providence. R.I. a week.

Week of Dec 3rd   Philadelphia.
" " " 11th   New york. City[5]

Heres some paper clippings for you[6] or Sallie   she wanted some.

AL, rc. On St. Clair Hotel, American & European, Toledo, O., letterhead.[7]

1. Although Rogers received considerable publicity in the Toledo newspapers, he was only one of several featured acts. "The Arcade bill is full of headline vaudeville features this week," wrote one reporter. "Will Rogers is one of the most popular" ("Headliners at Arcade," clipping, scrapbook A-1, OkClaW). The *New York Dramatic Mirror* reviewer reported "business good" and wrote that Rogers "could do almost anything with a lariat" (21 October 1905, 22).

2. Buck McKee, who handled Teddy from engagement to engagement and also rode him on stage during Rogers's act.

3. The picture, published in the *Toledo Times-Bee* on Sunday morning, 8 October 1905, depicted Rogers in cowboy garb, leaning on his horse ridden by Buck McKee. It was captioned "Lariat Thrower and Assistant–Arcade" (scrapbook A-1, OkClaW).

4. Cook's Opera House in Rochester was leased by James H. Moore. Rogers had signed a contract to appear at the theater on 31 August 1905 with a salary of $250 a week for two performances each day (Moore Circuit Artists' Contract, 31 August 1905, OkClaW). Moore had earlier presented a variety bill at Rochester's Musee (later called the Wonderland) in 1894. The Cook Opera House, which had been rebuilt after a fire in 1892, was a showcase for variety, melodrama, plays, and light opera. With the growing popularity of vaudeville, Moore needed larger quarters, so he leased the Opera House in 1898. It had a seating capacity of 750 in the orchestra, 423 in the balcony, 800 in the gallery, and 104 in the boxes. Admission prices were 30 cents and 50 cents in the orchestra, 20 cents and 30 cents in the balcony, and 10 cents in the gallery. In 1906 the Cook Opera House was one of five theaters in Rochester, which then had a population of approximately 200,000. During the first decade of the twentieth century Rochester's civic boosters took pride in their city's cultural enrichment. By 1911 it had eight vaudeville, variety, and legitimate theaters that drew top stars in each medium. Vaudeville troupes and stock companies would commence their Rochester appearance with colorful street parades (*JCOTG*, 163, 167; McKelvey, *Rochester*, 14, 29, 215–17, 220).

5. Rogers signed a contract on 23 September to perform at Hammerstein's Victoria Theatre the week of 6 November (OkClaW). On 3 October he signed three contracts with B. F. Keith to appear in Boston, Providence, Philadelphia, and New York on the dates Rogers stipulated in his letter (OkClaW). After his engagement at Hammerstein's Victoria he did not perform in Brooklyn but at the Park Theatre in Worcester, Mass. (calendar and date book, OkClaW).

6. Although addressed to the family, this letter was directed particularly to Maud Lane, the sister with whom Rogers had the closest relationship.

7. The letterhead provided the following information regarding the St. Clair Hotel: American and European plans, refurbished and redecorated rooms, steam heat, elec-

tric elevator and light. The hotel was owned by the St. Clair Hotel Co., and B. H. Burt was the manager.

To Clement Vann Rogers
12 October 1905
Toledo, Ohio

Toledo, Ohio

Oct 12   05

My Dear Papa

I just got your letter.   Why papa when you write you must always put the name of the Theatre or I wont get it for these are big cities and I always tell you where I am at.

I got a rope from Lee Barrett[1] but it is no good to me   I aint roping steers on the stage   its big enough for a well rope.   No those [there?] are cotton ropes at Chelsea   I remember them   I want little hard twist throwing rope I will write to Jim Rider or Johny Lipe for it[2]   I dident get anything else   did you send anything   Now next week   I am at Detroit at the

Temple Theatre

Detroit   Mich

Did you get the $125 I sent you last week[3]

Love to all

Willie.

ALS, rc. OkClaW.

1. Around 1894 Lee Barrett (b. 1866) and his brother John Crutchfield Barrett (b. 1872) came to Claremore, where they established a saddle and harness business. Together they developed oil properties in Nowata, Alluwe, Bartlesville, and Inona, Okla. Lee Barrett married Elizabeth Narcissa Clark (b. 1871) on 11 September 1895 (*HRC*, 102–3; *OCF*, 1:176, 234).

2. On Jim Rider, see *PWR*, 1:529–30; on Johnny Lipe, see *PWR*, 1:395n.3.

3. The next day Rogers wrote his father again, reminding him to "see about the rope" and asking for two red shirts in his trunk (Will Rogers to Clement Vann Rogers, 13 October 1905, OkClaW).

To Betty Blake
17 October 1905
Detroit, Mich.

While playing at Detroit's Temple Theatre, Rogers wrote Betty Blake expressing concern about their tenuous relationship. The letter suggests mutual disagreements over other relationships. Despite his success on the vaudeville stage, Rogers once again stated his desire to give up vaudeville.

Detroit, Mich.
Oct. 17. 05

My Dear old pal

Betty I got your *plum* good letter yesterday and I dident know what to make of it   you are away past the limit   I know it is foolish for me to write to you but I just cant help it and some time when you dont ever hear from old Bill it wont be because he is mad or is fascinated with some other but only because he is at last able to abide by his own judgement

you know Betty old pal I have always had about what I wanted and it breaks my heart when I think I'll never get it.   I am ordinarily a good loser but I guess my nerve is fooling me this trip

I dont know how long I will stay at this   I might leave it any day and go back to the ranch   I have made a success and thats all I wanted to do.

I want home afful bad and I am going to stay there too.

Here's another bunch of stuff you can glanse over if you care too

I am going big *here*[1]   a swell stage   high class people and lots of them this is a beautiful city almost as good as Washington.   Say give Jim Hinton my best regards   he's a good fellow.

Well Goodbye

just
Bill

next Week   following week
Cooks Opera House   Chases Theatre
Rochester, N. Y.   Washington D.C.
No picture yet

ALS, rc. OkClaW. On The Griswold, Detroit, Mich., letterhead. Postal and Moret, proprietors.[2]

1. Rogers received rave reviews in the Detroit newspapers. "There seems to be nothing that he cannot do with the rope," wrote a reviewer in the *Detroit Free Press.* The *Detroit News* called him a "wonder" with the lariat; the *Detroit Journal* deemed his act "a hit" (clippings, scrapbook A-1, OkClaW). The Great Lafayette (1872–1911), a

star magician, illusionist, mimic, and travesty actor, was the playbill's headliner and appeared in his famous pantomime *The Lion's Bride,* an allegory about a prince who wins the love of a beautiful princess by killing her tormentor. Lafayette performed all over the world until his death in a fire at an English theater (*EV,* 331; Gilbert, *American Vaudeville,* 52, 313; Laurie, *Vaudeville,* 103, 107). The performers were listed as follows in the playbill: Overture ("Orpheus" by Offenbach); Charles Serra (Unique Gymnastic Act, "On the White Column"); Will Rogers (Lariat Expert); Helen Reimer (In a Character Monologue, "Mrs. Hulla Baloo and a Friend or Two"); The Great Lafayette (In Remarkable Protean Changes and with His Travesty Band, Presenting Humorous Impersonations of the World's Noted Musical Directors); Fay and Clark (In a New Act, "The Modern Jonah"); Hoey and Lee (Creators of Hebrew Parodies); The Great Lafayette (Presents the Gorgeous Pantomimical Spectacle, "The Lion's Bride") (Temple Arcade playbill, week of 16 October 1905, scrapbook A-1, OkClaW).

2. Griswold House offered both an American plan ($2–$3 daily) and a European plan ($1–$2 daily). It was owned by Fred Postal and Austin E. Morey. They also owned the Oriental Griswold Annex, which offered a European plan as well as Turkish and Russian baths.

Article from the *Rochester Union and Advertiser* 26 October 1905 Rochester, N.Y.

The following article illustrates the type of publicity Rogers received during his first year in vaudeville. A mixture of fact and hyperbole, the piece views Rogers as a natural-born roper from the Plains. The plainsman image, which set him off from other performers and reflected the vogue of the West, would remain with Rogers throughout his career from stage to films.

THROWS TWO LARIATS AT SAME TIME

AND WILL ROGERS IS ONLY MAN PERFORMING THE FEAT.
ROPING EXPERT FROM INDIAN TERRITORY EXPLAINS SOME OF
THE POINTS OF HIS PECULIAR ART.
CAPTURE OF A WILD ZEBRA FEAT THAT GAVE HIM MOST
SATISFACTION—TRICKS DON'T COUNT ON RANCH.

"How long have I been at it? Well, I can remember when I was two years old chasing and roping my mother's turkeys out on the ranch and I could catch 'em too. Reckon that makes it pretty close to twenty-three years I've been using a rope." The speaker was a slender built chap, square shouldered and with the keen eyes, alert look and clear complexion that mark the man accustomed to outdoor life, and the accent, practically impossible of reproduction, stamped the speaker as a native of the southwestern section of the country where the cowpuncher still flourishes and where the peculiar dexterity which has amazed audiences at the Cook Opera House this week is one of the requisites in securing a position.

Will Rogers is the young man's name, and on the programme he is billed as "The Great Lariat Expert."[1] A native of Indian Territory he has spent the greater part of his life in that section of the country, his family being among the most influential in the Cherokee nation, for there is Indian blood in the Rogers family, the lasso expert's father being a senator of the Cherokee nation, while his father's first cousin, after whom the young man appearing at the Cook Opera House is named, is the present head of the nation.[2]

Three years ago young Rogers left his home to see the world. He did. Before he returned he had visited almost every country in the civilized world, Australia, South America, England and even Africa he spent some time in. Thirteen months was the duration of his stay in Africa at the time of the Boer war.[3]

"Fighting?" he repeated the query. "Not me. I was horse breaking for the British government, and it was while I was up near Bulawayo that I did a trick that had never been accomplished before and to date hasn't been since. That was the lassoing of a zebra, not one that had been caught in a trap, but a wild one. And it certainly was a wild one," and Rogers smiled at the recollection.[4]

"Like this theater work? Not much. There's too much sameness about the game. You know just what you're going to do this week, next week, the week after that and every week right through the season. Out on the ranch when you get up in the morning you can never tell what will happen before night. And the tricks with the rope on the stage, most of them, are as different from actual roping as can be."

"Why," and his tone was almost contemptuous, "if I did just a lot of that rope spinning the boys would say, 'Well, can you catch anything?' You've got to do that to score home. When I was competing down at Fort Worth this spring at a cattlemen's convention I started off with a lot of those tricks and the crowd was as quiet as a funeral.[5] Made me a little anxious to show 'em I could do the real work, and I just had 'em send a horse down past me and jumped through my rope before I noosed him. Then they woke up, and any little trick I did they thought was all right. But you've got to make a catch to win home there," and he emphasized his declaration with a nod.

"Roping means lots of practice," he continued, "and you'll find as a general rule that the boys from the south are better ropers while the boys from up north are the better riders. Mexicans are good men with the rope on foot, but not so good on horseback. That big chap you've seen with Buffalo Bill, though, is the daddy of us all. He's a middle-aged man, but he can do more things with a rope than anybody else."[6]

In his stage performance Rogers uses the same sort of ropes that the cow-puncher uses in his daily work. In fact, the ropes he has been using were sent to him from his home town, Claremore, I.T. They are half-inch hemp, very tightly wound so that ravelling is practically impossible. In length the ropes range from twenty-eight to fifty feet, much depending upon the speed of the mount owned by the cowboy. Occasionally a man is found who uses a rawhide lariat, but they are inferior to the rope.

One rope that Rogers uses in the feat which brings his act to a close is of braided cotton. This is about ninety feet long and the loop through which the rope runs is fitted with what he calls a "hondu," a sort of iron eyelet that adds a trifle to the weight of the noose and causes the rope to run more smoothly. Such a rope, however, is used solely for exhibition work, as it would part under the strain resulting from the plunge of a frightened horse or steer. Rogers uses it as he sits upon horseback, gradually paying it out into a circle until the entire ninety feet forms what he terms "crinoline," a sort of big revolving frame about the operator and his horse.

There has been a change in the style of roping, according to Rogers. Where formerly the lariat expert was wont to keep the rope circling about his head he now imparts a side motion to it, altogether with the wrist and releases it with a snap when making the cast. As a result the noose often strikes sideways but it is bound to go over the object at which it is thrown because of the twist imparted to it.

Description of Rogers' various feats would occupy columns of space, but brief mention may be made of a few. Other lasso performers have been seen here who manipulate the rope in the circles, but one variation that takes immensely as Rogers performs it is his method of skipping the rope. The rope is run out into a loop some seven or eight feet in diameter which he sets going at parallel to his body and then skips back and forth through it as nimbly as a little girl doing "peppers" with the ordinary skipping rope. Half hitches he throws without effort and he also shows a number of ways of forming nooses in a rope by snapping it through the air.

Probably his most difficult feat is the throwing of two lassos at the same time, one with either hand. They are thrown at a horse and rider, one encircling the neck of the man while the other finds a resting place about the horse's neck.

He claims to be the only man performing this feat and Buck M'Kee, who works with him, backs up the claim.

"That's one trick I never miss on purpose" he says. "When they get away from me on that, it's because I can't get 'em. The horse may start a little slow or not come just straight and of course I can only see 'em when they get right out in front on the stage, but I won't miss 'em in the open" and Rogers busies himself with the cow pony he uses in his act and which was brought east with Mulhall rough riders, who exhibited at Madison Square Garden early in the year. It was Rogers who distinguished himself at that time by lassoing a steer which had broken out of the arena and made its way to the third balcony of the garden before it was thrown.

Rogers has been busy all the time he is recalling this incident in looking to the trappings of his pony and the last glimpse gained of him he is just making his entrance and announcing to the audience the double throw, remarking that "This one will be a plumb good one, if I can do it."

PD. Printed in Rochester *Union and Advertiser,* 26 October 1905. Scrapbook A-1, OkClaW.

1. The playbill listed the following performers: Musical Program (Prof. Jos. Monk, Musical Director); The Military Octette and the Girl with the Baton (Lasky and Rolfe's Spectacular Production. Presenting England's foremost cornetist, John S. Leick); Nick Long and Idalene Cotton (Presenting Their New and Original Comedietta, Managerial Troubles); Will Rogers (The Great Lariat Expert); Rice and Cady (Only Successors to Weber and Fields); A. O. Duncan (Vaudeville's Cleverest Ventriloquist); and Helen Reimer (Cook Opera House Program, week of 23 October 1905, scrapbook A-1, OkClaW).

Of special note on the program was Jessy L. Lasky (1880–1958) and Ben A. Rolfe's The Military Octette and the Girl with the Baton. Lasky would later produce *The Squaw Man* (1913), the first feature film shot in Hollywood, and would become the head of Paramount studios. He and his sister Blanche performed in the act playing cornets. It was one of many musical comedy vaudeville acts that Lasky produced with his partner Rolfe. The act also featured quick costume changes, imitating Russian Hussars and American soldiers, among others. Lasky recalled: "I added a Girl with a Baton, who blew a bugle in the back of the theatre, then marched up the aisle in a spotlight to lead the pit orchestra" (Lasky, *I Blow My Own Horn,* 65; see also *EV,* 299–300).

Clippings from Rochester newspapers in Rogers's scrapbook reveal that he continued to receive good reviews. Besides praising his lariat tricks, reviewers commented on his "droll, drawling dialect" and use of southwestern expressions: "It is not the words so much as the way he says them," wrote one critic. For instance: "'The one I'll spring aon yuhall naou is a plum good one'" (clippings, scrapbook A-1, OkClaW).

2. William C. Rogers, who served as principal chief of the Cherokee Nation from 1903 to 1917, was not related to Will Rogers. Rogers was named after William Penn Adair, Cherokee public official and friend of Clement Vann Rogers (see *PWR,* 1:61, 482–85); Wardell, *Political History of the Cherokee Nation,* 348).

3. Rogers visited England, Argentina, South Africa, Australia, and New Zealand during the period from March 1902 to April 1904. The South African or Boer War ended on 31 May 1902. Rogers did not arrive in South Africa until August 1902 and left the following August (see *PWR,* 1:12, 321–434).

4. "I got a job trying to break horses at the British Remount Station," Rogers recalled in his autobiographical notes. "You know the American and Australian horses killed and crippled more soldiers than the Boars [Boers]." Rogers wrote that the

British had trouble controlling their horses: "When a company of 70 or 80 would get a new string of horses and the commander holler–Company Mount!, after ten seconds you would see nothing but loose horses and tommies wondering what had hit them. If one of them kept his seat and stayed on it would be a big average" (transcription of autobiographical notes, OkClaW).

5. On 24 March 1905 the *Claremore Messenger* reported that F. M. Rucker and William P. Rogers represented Claremore at the International Stockmen's Association, at Fort Worth, Tex., this week.

6. A reference to Vincente Oropeza who was with Buffalo Bill's show for many years. Rogers had seen him perform with the show at the Chicago World's Fair in 1893. In 1899 he competed against Oropeza in a steer-roping contest at the St. Louis annual fair (*PWR*, 1:181–85, 522–23).

To Maud Lane
26 October 1905
Rochester, N.Y.

Rochester. N.Y.

Oct 26. 05

My Dear Sis

Well I am back in N.Y. State doing fine   here this week   finish Saturday Night and jump to Washington Sunday   open Monday   it is pretty cold up around these lakes   I go from Washington back to N.Y. at Hammersteins again.   I certainly would like to see you all but cant for a couple or three months I guess.   Will Sallies folks be gone Xmas if she is not there I think I will put off my trip till Spring for I can get steady engagements all winter   I think and then I can stay when I come home.   I want to get back a little money and then go back and restock the farm and stay there.   This is nice work but I am not in love with it   only for the money   Ask papa if he is going to give me the rent off of the farm this fall as[1] I am trying to get ahold of a little money and he might help it along.

Say you all are *dandy*   I dident want that old cheap thing of a shawl   I wanted the Mexican one I got in San Antonio like I give you all one   and if it is not nice and pretty dont send it for I want to give it to a married couple I know for a cozy cover   if its nice send it to me at Washington next week please and tell me for the Lords sake did you get my clothes I sent you 5 weeks ago   I cant fine out   I will *wire* and ask you

Well Goodby

Lots of love to all

Willie

Oct 30 to Nov 4th.
Chases Theatre
Washington D.C.

Nov 5th to 12th
Putnam House
N.Y. City.
I will be playing at Hammersteins.

Nov 13 to 20
Keiths Theatre
Worcester
Mass.[2]

Nov 20 to 26
Keiths Theatre
Boston   Mass[3]

ALS, rc. OkClaW.

1. The third page of Rogers's handwritten letter began "so I am trying. . . ." He inserted the following note in the top margin of the page: "Heres a clipping from this eve paper   tell Sallie I will send her one to if she wants one."
2. On 23 October Rogers had signed a contract to play at Keith's Park Theatre in Worcester, Mass., the week of 13 November, at a salary of $225. The proprietor of the Park Theatre was John H. Meagher. The theater was part of the Keith Circuit. Samuel K. Hodgdon, long-time Keith executive, signed the contract for Meagher (Park Theatre, Worcester, Mass., Artist's Contract, 23 October 1905, OkClaW).
3. Rogers's ended his letter with his itinerary, dividing the different stops in his performance schedule by drawing wavy lines above and below each entry.

To Maud Lane
30 October 1905
Washington, D.C.

Washington, D.C. <u>Oct 30</u> 190<u>5</u>

My Dear Sis.

I just got Cap's[1] letter telling me you were not so well   Say Sis I ought to be whipped for not writing you oftener and paying more attention to how you was   but say I just today realized how sick you had been and how little I had thought of it   for you know none of us are ever sick much[2]   and when I would get letters I would think it was just sick for a day or so   and I dident take it seriously at all   Now I see how heartless I was and I feel ashamed of myself.   But I am certainly uneasy for you now   and just for a little I would come home and see you   if you dont get better soon I will certainly be there. It might not do you much good but I know it would do me a lot of good to see *you* and I could make you forget you were so sick

I hope May is still there   Tell her I said *to stay there* till you *are all well* for I know how lonesome it will be without Sallie.

I dont think they will stay long out there   I give them to Xmas at the longest[3]

Well I am going to send you a lot of Clippings and things to lay there and read.   I got in here (Washington) last night at 8 o'clock from Rochester N.Y. was all sunday on train   it was through Pennsylvania and the poorest country I ever saw

It is nice and warm here.

I opened up at Matinee today   I was anxious to make good in Washington and from the way I was received this evening and tonight I have certainly made a hit.[4]

I think I went bigger than any place yet and thats saying some   Oh it is a swell theatre   all high class people come here   a big stage and I like it   they have me billed and advertised like a circus   I finish saturday Night and go to Newark N J. right across the river from N.Y.   and I play Sunday there[5]   and over and open at Hammersteins Theatre   N.Y. City   Monday   you see I had this open Sunday as they dont show in Washington Sunday   so I contracted or booked as we call it to play Newark   I get $50.00 fifty for that day alone   you see outside of my weeks salary which is the same even if you dont play Sunday   Still I have quite a bit of transportation to pay   sometimes two people and a horse   I ship the pony by *excess* baggage and it dont cost much generally just about what it would be for one person   making it cost me 3 peoples fares in all.[6]   You see in Vaudeville you are working for different people almost every week   some you might have to work for cheaper than others and you are with different acts as you are not in a company   you are by yourself and book your act wherever you can[7]   *see.*

I am booked up till after Xmas   My Route is.

Washington–	Oct	30	to	Nov	5.
New York. *Hammerstein*	Nov	6	to	"	13th
Worcester, Mass.	"	13	"	"	20
Boston "	"	20	"	"	27
Providence R.I.	"	27	"	Dec	2.

Philadelphia.	Dec	3	"	"	10
New York. Keiths	"	11	"		16[8]
Syracuse. N.Y.	"	17	"		23[9]
Pittsburg, Penn	"	25	"		30[10]
Baltimore	Jan	1	"		7[11]
New York	"	8	"		15[12]
New York	"	15	"		22.[13]

Thats all.

You see the good part about it is that I havent lost a single week since I started   now some acts think they do well to work one week and lay of one for you know you cant always find people to play you at their houses   but that will make me 32 straight even if I shouldent get any more

All other performers think I have the greatest act in the business and I stand well with all of them I play for a week with.

Dont know if I will make the white house this trip as old Teddy aint here and young Teddy is away at school[14]   I dont much care to as I did it once and they might think I wanted to use it for advertising purposes   but I dont know what will show up before the week is over

Say did you get my clothes a long time ago   I am going to send you some more summer clothes from N.Y.   Where is my friend Ada[15]   she wont write any more   is she married   I met a boy in Rochester who has a brother   a lawyer in Chelsea   dont remember his *name*

Well sis I will close Now   I sho hope you are better by now   for you dont deserve to be sick   Maude if papa says anything to you about that money you dont pay any attention for we know how he is and I dont want it for a long time and dont need it.

Well Goodby all   lots of love to Cap and kids   and all I have got for you.

Your brother

Willie

next week
　Putnam House
　　N.Y. City.

ALS, rc. OkClaW. On National Hotel, Washington, D.C., letterhead. O. G. Staples, proprietor, and G. F. Shutt, manager.[16]

　1. Captain (Cap) Lane, Maude Rogers Lane's husband (see *PWR*, 1:498).

　2. Maude Lane had typhoid fever. On 20 October 1905 the *Chelsea Reporter* announced that "Mrs. C. L. Lane suffered a serious relapse Tuesday but has again commenced to improve." A week later the newspaper reported that her condition was "much improved and speedy recovery is hoped for." She must have suffered another relapse, however, because on 17 November the paper declared that she "was able to

breakfast with the family last Tuesday for the first time in fifty one days." By the end of November she was able to see friends (*CR*, 24 November 1905; see also *CP*, 4 November 1905).

3. In late October Sallie McSpadden and her children went to Los Angeles to escape the winter and to visit Sallie's son Clem, who was employed as a surveyor in California. Sallie's husband, John Thomas McSpadden, and their son Herbert had left earlier that month (*CR*, 13 October and 27 October 1905). On 7 November 1905 the *Chelsea Reporter* printed a letter from John McSpadden describing Los Angeles in glowing terms: "We are all delighted with this country, with its flowers, mild climate, sunshine and beautiful scenery. . . . It has a fine street car system, all the near-by towns being connected by electric lines and the fare is low. It has sixty-three public schools . . . the city is well supplied with parks, most of them have a lake in the center and is surrounded by a great variety of beautiful trees and flowers." The family returned in March 1906. McSpadden purchased property in Los Angeles, and there were rumors that the family would move there permanently, but they never did (*CP*, 24 February 1906).

4. The *Washington Post* reported that Rogers's "performance created lively interest and evoked marks of hearty appreciation." The *Evening Star* called his act "a marvelous exhibition of dexterity" (clippings, scrapbook A-1, OkClaW; see also Review from the *Washington Times*, 31 October 1905, below). Rogers also sent his father a postcard with a picture of the Washington Monument and wrote that he had climbed the stairs to the top. He told his father: "I am certainly a big hit in Washington" (1 November 1905, OkClaW).

5. Rogers probably played at F. F. Proctor's Sunday concert at his Newark Theatre. The staging of Sunday theatrical presentations was still banned in many cities. In the New York area theater managers such as Proctor circumvented the law by advertising the programs as concerts. The following was printed in a 1902 Proctor promotion booklet: "Sunday concerts are given at the four Proctor theatres in New York, beginning at 2 o'clock P.M. and running continuously afternoon and evening. Vaudeville specialists whose offerings are in keeping with the character of the day are specially engaged to augment the variety numbers which claim attention on week days at the various theatres. For the Sunday concerts there is no increase in the popular scale of prices, and yet the entertainments are admittedly the best to be seen anywhere in the city. Dainty souvenirs are given to the ladies in attendance upon the daily matinees at the One Hundred and Twenty-fifth St., Fifty-eighth St. and Proctor's Newark Theatres" (quoted from Marston and Feller, *F. F. Proctor*, 75).

6. The cost of shipping his horse and paying his assistant, Buck McKee, plus the cost of their room and board, must have added considerably to his expenses. This could be a major reason why Rogers dealt increasingly with the question of money in his letters.

7. Rogers was solidly booked on the Keith Circuit until early January. There are no agents listed on his contracts at this time. The booking was probably done by the Keith organization itself, which would have charged Rogers a 5 percent booking fee. The contracts were stamped and initialed by Keith executive Samuel K. Hodgdon.

8. Rogers played at Keith's Theatre in New York from 11 to 16 December 1905. He was engaged at the Grand Opera House in Lowell, Mass., from 4 to 9 December (calendar and date book, OkClaW).

9. On 3 October Rogers signed a contract to appear at Harry Davis's Grand Opera House (Keith Circuit) in Syracuse the week of 18 December. He played there through the twenty-third. His salary was $200 for the week, lower than the average $250 he had

been receiving (Grand Opera House, Pittsburgh, Artist's Contract, 3 October 1905, OkClaW).

10. On 3 October Rogers signed a contract to appear at James L. Kernan's Grand Opera House (Keith Circuit) in Pittsburgh the week of December 25 (salary $250). He played there until 30 December (Grand Opera House, Syracuse, Artist's Contract, 3 October 1905, OkClaW).

11. Rogers first wrote a "6" and then a "7" on his listing. On 3 October 1905 Rogers signed a contract to play at the Maryland Theatre in Baltimore the week of 1 January 1906 (salary $250). The engagement lasted until 6 January (Maryland Theatre, Baltimore, Artist's Contract, 3 October 1905, OkClaW).

12. On 10 October 1905 Rogers signed a contract to appear at Hyde and Behman's Brooklyn Theatre the week of 8 January 1906 (salary $250). He played there until 14 January (Hyde and Behman Amusement Co. Artists' Engagement Contract, 10 October 1905, OkClaW).

13. Rogers played at Brooklyn's Amphion Theatre from 15 to 21 January (calendar and datebook, OkClaW).

14. Roosevelt had left for a tour of the South on 18 October. It was a goodwill journey with the purpose of gaining support for his policies. On 26 October he left on the ship *Magnolia* from New Orleans, and on 30 October he was on the cruiser *West Virginia,* encountering heavy seas. Roosevelt arrived at the nation's capital on 31 October via the dispatch-boat *Dolphin.* The *Washington Post* editorialized: "The President returns to Washington much stronger with the masses of people than he was when he started from the Capital" ("Presidential Journey," 31 October 1905; see also "President Is Home," *WP,* 1 November 1905; "President Near Home," *WP,* 31 October 1905; "President on Sea," *WP,* 27 October 1905; "Starts for Dixie," *WP,* 18 October 1905). Theodore Roosevelt, Jr., was at that time a first-year student at Harvard University ("Roosevelt, Theodore," *DAB* supp. 3:668; see also Performance Review from the *Lowell Daily Courier,* 4 December 1905, below).

15. Either Ada Gray or Ada Foreman. They were two people whom Rogers liked very much during his youth in the Indian Territory (see *PWR,* 1:175n.2, 176n.1, 177, 177n.2, 397, 401, 402n.5, 402n.6, 414).

16. The Washington Hotel, opposite the Pennsylvania Railroad depot, advertised itself as the "largest hotel in Washington," with 350 rooms.

Review from the *Washington Times*
31 October 1905
Washington, D.C.

The headliner at Chase's Theatre was George Fuller Golden, a well-known comic monologuist and founder of the White Rats of America, an independent union for vaudevillians.[1]

CHASE'S
VAUDEVILLE HOUSE HAS A STRONG BILL OF CLEVER SPECIALTIES

Whatever may be the shortcomings of some features of the entertainment this week at Chase's,[2] the latter part of the bill is strong.

George Fuller Golden returns with a monologue over which he need have no worry. Mr. and Mrs. Truesdale and company appear in a little playlet, "Aunt Louisa's Advice," fairly brimming over with humorous situations.[3]

The audience was most liberal in its greetings of Will Rogers, a cowboy who gives a clever exhibition of the use of the lasso.[4] Dan Harrington presents his ventriloquial turn; Dorsch and Russell please in a musical novelty, and Josephine Gassman struggles through fifteen minutes of work with three pickaninnies.[5]

The three Zoellers conclude with some excellent trapeze work.[6]

PD. Printed in *Washington Times*, 31 October 1905.

1. Known for his witty monologues, George Fuller Golden (1868–1912) was a popular satirist and humorist in vaudeville. Born in Alabaster, Mich., Golden was initially a prize fighter and then part of a two-man, song-and-clog act with his partner, James (Gypsy) Dolan. Together they did a sketch called "The High-toned Burglar." When the pair broke up, Golden started performing a monologue. Golden became famous for his rhapsodic oratories and his humorous recitations of poetry and biblical passages. At Chase's Theatre Golden concluded his program with his musical recitation "That Was the Way in Grandfather's Day." Golden also wrote many vaudeville sketches for other performers, including Al Jolson. Known for his unselfish concern for his fellow performers, Golden fought for actors' rights. He was the founder and first Big Chief (head) of the White Rats. ("Rats" was "star" spelled backward.) It was modeled on the Grand Order of Water Rats, an English union that in 1900 had helped a financially strapped Golden in London after he failed in British music halls. Although seven other actors (including Fred Stone, Rogers's close friend) were involved with its establishment, Golden is credited as the main inspiration behind the founding of the White Rats on 1 June 1900. He wrote a book about the organization called *My Lady Vaudeville and Her White Rats* (1909). Golden and his colleagues attacked the growing collusion among vaudeville managers, particularly the Keith-Albee forces and their agency, the United Booking Offices, which were controlling salaries, bookings, and commissions, and could arbitrarily destroy the career of a vaudevillian. Tuberculosis forced Golden to retire from the theater in 1907, and he spent his last two years in Los Angeles, where he died of consumption on 17 February 1912. At Golden's funeral *Variety* called him "the best known and most beloved actor who ever appeared in vaudeville" (*VO*, 1:24 February 1912; see also *EV*, 208, 554–55; Gilbert, *American Vaudeville*, 231–35; Golden, *My Lady Vaudeville and Her White Rats*; *Player*, Official Organ of the White Rats of America, 1909–11, NN-L-RLC; Laurie, *Vaudeville*, 173–74, 310–16; *NYT*, 18 February 1912).

2. On Chase's Theatre see Chase's Theatre Vaudeville Contract, 14 August 1905, above.

3. Howard Truesdell was a legitimate stage actor. He played the role of Croton in the play *Quo Vadis*, which opened on 9 April 1900 at New York's Herald Square Theatre. He was also in the cast of the four-act comedy *Cordelia Blossom*, which premiered at the Cort Theatre on 26 August 1914 (Mantle and Sherwood, eds., *Best Plays of 1899–1909*, 366; Mantle and Sherwood, eds., *Best Plays of 1909–1919*, 529; *NYTheReI*, 383). Truesdell's wife was a member of the company for many years (*VO*, 1:1 October 1910). At Chase's Theatre they performed the one-act comedy, *Aunt*

Louisa's Advice, which was advertised as having been written for the actress Blanche Bates (1873–1941), who for many years was a star in David Belasco's theater productions. (Mantle and Sherwood, eds., *Best Plays of 1899–1909,* 500; *NYT,* 26 December 1941; *VO,* 3:31 December 1941; *WhMuDr,* 34; *WhoStg,* 30–31; *WhScrn,* 1:42; *WhThe* 1:151–52).

4. The Washington newspapers gave Rogers considerable publicity. One article mentioned that he was the second attraction after Golden and an act that "is said to be the most complete and perfect replica of Western life ever presented on the stage in such a limited space of time as this feature consumes" ("Chase's—George Fuller Golden," *Washington Times,* 29 October 1905). Another dwelt again on his youthful experience with lariat roping and his desire to return home ("Will Abandon the Stage," clipping, scrapbook A-1, OkClaW).

5. Josephine Gassman (ca. 1882–1962) played on the major vaudeville circuits with her act called Josephine Gassman and Her Pickaninnies (earlier, Phina and Her Picks). In her performance at Chase's Theatre she was "assisted by Three Clever Picks in her New Act, 'A Chinese Idyl'" (Chase's Program, week of 30 October 1905, scrapbook A-1, OkClaW). Acts with female singers and dancers accompanied by African American child performers were common in vaudeville (others were Grace La Rue and Her Inky-Dinks, Louise Dresser and Her Picks, and Mayme Remington and Her Black Buster Brownie Ethiopian Prodigés). The talented youngsters would often appear in a rousing finale. The use of the term *pickaninnies* or its abbreviation *picks* was part of the negative stereotyping of blacks on stage and was similar to the derogatory term *coon songs.* Several white women singers who performed with African American children were known as "coon" shouters. A vaudeville regular, Gassman performed on the same bill with Will Rogers at San Francisco's Orpheum Theatre during August 1913 (see Review from the *San Francisco Bulletin,* 11 August 1913, *PWR,* vol. 3). Gassman, whose married name was Josephine Sullivan, died in Youngstown, Ohio, on 24 January 1962 (*EV,* 114–16; Laurie, *Vaudeville,* 56; Sampson, *Ghost Walks,* 354; *VO,* 5:31 January 1962).

6. Included on the bill was the American Vitagraph film *The Adventures of Sherlock Holmes.* The main acts for the following week were advertised as follows: Hermann the Great (World Renowned Prestidigitator, New Mysticisms, Notable Illusions); Emmet Devoy and Co. (In *The Saintly Mr. Billings,* a Screamingly Funny Farce); the Village Choir (A "Way Down East" Quartette); and Kern's Mimic Dog (The Only Canine Character Impersonator in the World). On Election Day, 7 November 1904, voting returns from the presidential election were read between the acts. The Republican Theodore Roosevelt defeated the Democrat candidate, Judge Alton B. Parker.

To Maud Lane
4 November 1905
Washington, D.C.

Roger celebrated his twenty-sixth birthday in Washington and wrote the following letter to his sister Maud.

> Washington D.C.
> My Birthday.
> (Say How old am I).

I got your letter sure enough on my birthday and it was the most acceptable thing you could of sent for it makes me feel good to know you are able to
write.   And I got a letter from Sallie at the same time too.   I am feeling fine
it is the prettiest warm day here.   I go to N.Y. tonight at 12.[1]   it is 7 hours
run   Mrs Dick Adams was at the Theatre the other day and afterwords invited me out and I took dinner with them and I go out there for dinner tonight
also Judge Thomas was in last night and sent his card back and I was out to a
feed with him last night   he was pleased great with the show.[2]

I kinder feel like going home to get back to N.Y.   I know it so well
Write next week to
      Putnam House
      N.Y. City.

Nov 13 to 19.   Keiths Theatre Worcester *Mass.*
" 20 to 26   Keiths " Boston Mass.

ALS, rc. OkClaW.

1. An example of Rogers's grueling schedule was having to leave at midnight
Saturday so he could be in Newark to perform on a Sunday playbill.
2. In a letter to his father sent from New York, Rogers also wrote that he had had
dinner twice with Dick Adams and once with Judge Thomas in Washington (6
November 1905, OkClaW).

Review from the *New York Dramatic Mirror*
18 November 1905
New York, N.Y.

*During Rogers's engagement at Hammerstein's Victoria Theatre from 6 to 11
November, the headliners were the famous singing and comedy team of Bert Williams
and George Walker.[1] Williams and Walker had the eighth spot on the playbill. Rogers
appeared on stage right after their performance. Rogers and Bert Williams starred in
the* Ziegfeld *Follies of 1916 and 1917.*

HAMMERSTEIN'S VICTORIA.—Williams and Walker continued to make
successful appearances during the second week of their special engagement.[2] Anna Laughlin, dainty and attractive as ever, scored with some very
well chosen songs.[3] Ward and Curran were very amusing in The Terrible
Judge.[4] Searl and Violet Allen and company were well received in their latest
offering, which is the best thing they have done.[5] Will R. Rogers, the lariat
expert; Hickey and Nelson in Twisted and Tangled; the Peschkoff Troupe,

Russian dancers; Willie Gardner, skater, and the vitagraph rounded out the list.[6]

PD. Printed in *NYDM,* 18 November 1905.

1. Bert Williams and George Walker were one of musical comedy's most famous teams, and they performed together in big-time vaudeville (see Biographical Appendix entry, WILLIAMS, Egbert Austin [Bert], and George Walker).

2. At the Victoria, Williams and Walker performed *The Detective Story* from their hit in the all-black musical *In Dahomey.* In the humorous sketch Walker told stories about Nick Carter and the Old Sleuth. Williams sang his well-known song "Nobody" and "Pretty Desdamone" (Hammerstein's Victoria playbill, week commencing Monday matinee, 6 November 1906, scrapbook A-1, OkClaW; Smith, *Bert Williams,* 75–78). "Nobody" (music by Williams, words by Alex Rogers) is about a downtrodden and lonely person longing for friendship and respect. Williams introduced it on the vaudeville stage in the summer of 1905. It was copyrighted that year by the black-owned Attucks Music Publishing Co., and a Columbia cylinder recording was made the following year (Charters, *Nobody,* 9, 107, 135–37, 149, 150; Smith, *Bert Williams,* 81–82).

Williams and Walker continued to perform at the Victoria the following week, beginning 13 November 1905. During that time a racial incident occurred. The comic monologuist Walter C. Kelly (who grew up in Virginia and performed a skit called *The Virginia Judge*) was on the bill, and he refused to appear with Williams and Walker. Willie Hammerstein was so upset with Kelly that he replaced him with the team of Toledo and Price. Walker responded angrily to Kelly's remarks: "The man is foolish. . . . The day is past for that sort of thing. . . . But if vaudeville performers are going to draw the color line, either they will have to give up their work, for there is hardly a vaudeville show in which colored performers do not appear" (quoted from *Indianapolis Freeman,* 9 December 1905, in Sampson, *Ghost Walks,* 353–54; see also *EV,* 287–89; Laurie, *Vaudeville,* 193–94; Smith, *Bert Williams,* 85–86). African American artists had a difficult time breaking into big-time vaudeville and had to form small-time circuits of their own. Only gradually were vaudeville playbills in the North integrated, and there was an unwritten rule allowing only one black act on the bill. The many African Americans in vaudeville (estimated at 1,400) faced institutional racism and discrimination as well as social ostracism by white performers. For example, the White Rats of America was formed as an all-white male actors' union, and the Friars, an actors' social organization, likewise did not admit African Americans. They consequently had to form their own clubs and protective associations, such as the Frogs (a theatrical organization based in Harlem and founded by Williams and Walker as well as others in 1908) and the Colored Vaudeville Benefit Association (1909). Moreover, black vaudevillians faced a color barrier in the South. Williams was the only black performer Keith could book in Washington, D.C. (Charters, *Nobody,* 93–94; *EV,* 49–52; Smith, *Bert Williams,* 105–7).

In December 1905 rumors circulated that Williams and Walker were breaking up, but although the two had their differences, the story proved false. One reason that Williams and Walker were performing at the Victoria was that their scheduled appearance in the musical comedy *Abyssinia* (music by Will Marion Cook and Williams) had been delayed due to lack of financial backing. It opened on 20 February 1906 at the Majestic Theatre (Mantle and Sherwood, eds., *Best Plays of 1899–1909,* 509; Sampson, *Ghost Walks,* 350, 352; Smith, *Bert Williams,* 85–86).

3. The playbill advertised the comedienne Anna Laughlin (1885–1937) as making her first appearance in vaudeville, but she might have been in variety earlier. Born in Sacramento, Calif., Laughlin began her career in 1892 playing child parts in San Francisco theaters. A year later she played Little Eva in *Uncle Tom's Cabin* at New York's Park Theatre. Her biggest theatrical success was as Dorothy in the popular musical comedy *The Wizard of Oz* (1903). After her engagement at the Victoria, she was in the musical *His Majesty* (1906). In 1914 and 1915 she performed in early silent-film dramas, including *What Happened to Father, Crooky Scruggs,* and *The Crown Prince's Double* (Hammerstein's Victoria playbill, week commencing Monday matinee, 6 November 1906, scrapbook A-1, OkClaW; *FILM*, 1:151; Laurie, *Vaudeville,* 59; Mantle and Sherwood, eds., *Best Plays of 1899–1909,* 372, 397, 427, 511; Odell, *Annals of the New York Stage,* 15:624; *WhoHol,* 2:938–39; *WhoStg,* 276–77).

4. Ward and Curran were known for their long-running courtroom sketch act, which they performed at the Victoria Theatre (Laurie, *Vaudeville,* 52).

5. Searl and Violet Allen performed on the program at Rogers's vaudeville debut in June (see Manager's Report, Union Square Theatre, 12 June 1905, above).

6. Rogers performed on the same bill with Bill Hickey and Sadie Nelson at Hammerstein's Roof Garden in June (see Review, Hammerstein's Paradise Roof Garden, 20 June 1905, above). He performed with Willie Gardner also in June (see Manager's Report, Union Square Theatre, 12 June 1905, above). Listed last on the playbill were films, New Vitagraph Views.

Article from the *Worcester Sunday Telegram*
19 November 1905
Worcester, Mass.

COWBOY LIFE IN INDIAN TERRITORY.

WILL ROGERS, PURE CHEROKEE, IS AN EXPERT WITH LARIAT.

IS TOURING THE WORLD WITH BUCK MCKEE AS STAGE PARTNER.

SAYS HE WILL SOON DROP THEATRICAL LIFE AND
BUY A CATTLE RANCH.

Direct from the ranches of Indian Territory, expert as cowboys and proficient in the other pursuits of the western cowboy, Will Rogers and Buck McKee, whose lariat throwing turn at the Park theater[1] all last week amazed their audiences, chatted with a Telegram man in their dressing room one afternoon last week.

While at home upon the bucking broncho, rounding up cattle in the spring, branding them, and, perhaps, chasing out many miles in quest of "strays," they are both educated and refined—in no sense cowboys as the word is generally understood—and to The Telegram man they talked entertainingly of Indian Territory and its prospects, of the chance of success that that section of the United States holds out to the young man of today. Both are still loyal to the life of the ranger and the cattle-raiser, and declared that after they have seen the United States—and they have already seen a

Good Portion of the World—

they will return to Indian Territory, acquire ranches of their own, and live in ease and comfort for the rest of their lives.

"How long have you been at this game of rope-throwing?" asked The Telegram man.

"Well, I can remember when I was two years old, of chasing and roping my mother's turkeys out on the ranch, and I could catch 'em, too. Reckon that makes it pretty close to 23 years that I have been using a rope." The speaker was a slender built chap, square-shouldered and with the keen eyes, alert look and clear complexion that mark the men accustomed to outdoor life, and his accent, impossible of reproduction, stamped the speaker as a native of the southwestern section of the United States, where the cowpuncher still flourishes and where their peculiar dexterity, such as the speaker exhibited in his act upon the stage is one of the requisites in securing a position. He was Will Rogers, the lariat-throwing end of the combination.

A native of Indian Territory, he has spent the greater portion of his life in that section of the United States, and after his stage career is over he proposes going back again. His family is among the foremost

in the Cherokee Nation

and of nothing is young Rogers more proud than of the fact that he is a Cherokee. His father is a senator of the Cherokee nation.[2] Had Will Rogers followed his father's desires after finding that his son was inclined to give more attention to his rope than to the cattle upon the range, he would have been today a Methodist clergyman, for Rogers was sent to a Missouri seminary with that end in view.[3] But somehow the ministerial life didn't appeal to the young man, and he went back again to the range.

Three years ago young Rogers started out to see the world, and he did. Before he returned he had visited almost every country in the civilized world. Australia, South Africa, England and Central America were all traversed by him. Thirteen months was the duration of his stay in Africa at the time of the Boer war. "Fighting?" He repeated the inquiry. "Not me. I was breaking horses for the British government and it was while I was up near Bulawayo that I did a trick that had never been accomplished before and to date hasn't been since. That was the lassooing of a zebra. Not one of the kind that has been caught in a trap, but a real wild one. And it certainly was a wild one," and Rogers smiled at the recollection.

"Do you like this theater work?" The Telegram man asked.

"Not much," was the reply. "There's

Too Much Sameness to It

all. You know just what you are going to do this week, next week, the week after that and every week through the season. Out on the ranch when you get up in the morning you can never tell what is going to happen before night. And the tricks with the rope on the stage are as different from actual roping as can be."

"Why," and his tone was almost contemptuous, "if I did just a lot of that rope spinning, the boys down my way would say 'Ever catch anything?' You've got to do that to win out down in the country where I come from. When I was competing at Fort Worth, this spring, in a cattlemen's convention, I started off with a lot of those tricks and the crowd was as quiet as at a funeral. It made me a little anxious to show them that I could do the real work and I just had 'em send a horse down past me and I jumped through my rope before I noosed him. Then they woke up and any little trick I did after that they thought was all right."

Rogers, by the way, showed that he could deliver the goods in Madison square garden, last spring, when at the horse fair there, a wild Texan steer with horns that spread five feet apart, ran amuck, jumping the bars of the ring and started for the second and third balconies,

While Spectators Scrambled

to places of safety in all directions. Rogers followed up the infuriated animal, succeeded in getting his lariat over the beast's horns and with others who came to his assistance, finally got the animal into submission.

Rogers and his partner, Hugh McKee, who was for four years sheriff of Pawnee, had a lot of interesting observations to make regarding the Indian Territory country and its prospects.

"There isn't a better country in the world to live in today, and we have been almost everywhere," said Rogers, "than down home in Indian Territory. Down near my father's ranch they have struck oil six miles to the east of us and four miles to the west of us. We burn natural gas and have plenty of coal mines.[4] All of the natural resources of the world are right at our very door and we have the best sort of a climate."

"The people that are today getting a better living out of Indian Territory than they could get in any other place in the union, have come there from almost everywhere. They are engaged, very largely, in agricultural pursuits and, of course, in cattle raising, although the cattle raising industry is not being conducted on quite as extensive a basis as formerly. But there is

MORE MONEY IN IT,

and certainly there is no occupation that is more fascinating. The cattle business is more cut up than it was, and for that reason cowboys are not so numerous. Take a ranch that formerly had 10,000 of cattle, on the same ranch there will not be today more than 3000 head. But they will be better animals individually, and where a steer of the old style commanded $20 or $30 in the market at Kansas City or Chicago, today a steer brings $40 or $50. This is because the type of the breed is being improved. Some of the ranches there have bulls that have cost from $2000 to $4000 to stand at the head of their herds. It is a mistake to believe that the cattle of Indian Territory today are a mongrel lot.

"I said that the cowboys were not so numerous as formerly. That is because the herds are not so large and the country is fenced in better. But, of course, we have many cowboys out there today, but the more adventuresome, those who prefer the open country, are going into New Mexico. Many of the cowboys, especially the best ones, come to us from the eastern states. They are usually fellows who were originally venturesome and have gone into the West expecting to make a fortune in a minute. They have finally

DRIFTED INTO RIDING

and in that way have taken up the cowboy's life.

"Cowboys, like everybody else, differ greatly. They divide themselves into two classes, those who have no higher aspirations than of being cowboys all their lives and those who hope ultimately to have a ranch of their own and a herd of cattle and are saving up their money with that end in view. A cowboy gets good pay in dollars and cents. Their wages run all the way from $40 to $50 a month and their board. The proprietor of the range sends out provisions to the camps once or twice a week, as the case may be, and the cowboy's only expense is for tobacco. Many of the cowpunchers will not draw a cent of their salary through the entire season, preferring to get it in a lump at the end. Then you can tell to which class they belong. Those who are satisfied with the life of cowpunching that they are leading will go into the nearest city or town and spend a week in dissipation and will spend their entire earnings before they go back again. The other class will deposit their money in the bank; and I tell you, some of those cowboys are better fixed financially than you would imagine."

"I don't know as I have any desire to be a cowboy again," said Rogers in conclusion, "but I can tell you one thing: You won't see me in this business very much longer. I'll take a cattle ranch for mine every time."[5]

PD. Printed in the Worcester *Sunday Telegram,* 19 November 1905. Scrapbook A-1, OkClaW.

1. The Park Theatre at Worcester, Mass., was owned by John H. Meagher and was part of the Keith Circuit. The theater was known as Worcester's Home of Refined Vaudeville. On 23 October 1905 Rogers signed a contract to play there at a salary of $225 for the week of 13 November. The contract was stamped and initialed by Samuel K. Hodgdon, Keith executive, acting for Meagher (Park Theatre, Worcester, Mass., Artist's Contract, 23 October 1905, OkClaW).

On the playbill were the following: John C. Rice and Sally Cohen (The Laughing Stars of Vaudeville in "Our Honeymoon"); Will Rogers (King of the Lariat on Plains and Cattle Trail, Assisted by "Buck" McKee, Ex-Sheriff of Pawnee Co., Oklahoma, and Favorite Broncho, "Arcade." in a Marvelous Exhibition of Skill and Dexterity); Harry Le Clair (The Popular Character Comedian, "The Bernhardt of the Vaudevilles"); Lew Sully (The Well Known Monologist); Borani and Nevarro (European Comedy Grotesques); Mitchell and Marron (Originator of 2 Man Minstrel Co.); and the Three Zoellers (Sensational Novelty Gymnasts) (Park Theatre playbill, scrapbook A-1, OkClaW). A review entitled "Dizzy Rope Thrower" pointed out that both Rogers and McKee were dressed in red shirts and buckskin trousers. Another article, in the *Worcester Evening Gazette* for 14 November 1905, described the lariat tricks Rogers was now doing: "With the horse and rider traveling across the stage Rogers caught the animal by throwing the lasso with his foot. One of the most interesting feats was shown when the horse and rider were on one end of the stage, and Rogers, standing at the other, twirled the rope in such a way that he put a double noose about the man's wrists to the saddle and pinioning his arms. Then he bound the wrists to the saddle and put nooses about the horse's neck and nose without approaching it. Then he tried catching the man and horse with a lasso in either hand. His last feat was letting out a lasso 82 feet long and swinging it about his head while on horseback" (Worcester clippings, scrapbook A-1, OkClaW).

2. Clement Vann Rogers was elected a fifth time to the Cherokee Nation Senate in 1903 (see *PWR,* 1:536–43).

3. Rogers attended the Scarritt Collegiate Institute at Neosho, Mo., in 1895 and 1896. It was affiliated with the Methodist Episcopal Church South and was first called the Neosho Seminary. Although his mother wanted him to become a Methodist clergyman, he was really sent to the school because of its good reputation (see *PWR,* 1:127–31).

4. Coal had been discovered in the Oologah, I.T., area by the early 1890s. One of the people who was in the coal business was Ed Sunday, a Rogers family friend, who owned the Sunday Coal Works. With his son, William E. Sunday, he leased land from the Cherokee Nation. His son recalled, "We hauled coal three miles by wagon team; we loaded eight to ten carloads a day. This hauling was over dirt roads. We paid the men in those days by script. Times were hard and they worked teams at $1.75 to $2.25 a day for ten hours and men, $1.25 a day. At one time we had out as much as

$10,000.00 over the town in script, which was at first just paper money" (Sunday et al., *Gah Dah Gwa Stee*, 67). In the 1890s and early 1900s Oologah became a coal-mining boom town. A strip pit coal mine, operated by L. J. Snarr, was known to have fifty teams of miners to extract the coal. Coal was shipped from Oologah on the Iron Mountain Railroad line.

Production of oil had begun in the Indian Territory in 1891, but it was not until the early 1900s that drilling yielded major results. In 1900 the combined production in Indian and Oklahoma Territories was 7,500 barrels; it reached 50 million barrels in 1910. Nearby Tulsa with its Red Fork reserve began to experience an oil boom in 1901. On 10 July 1903 the Interior Department issued regulations that allowed leasing under its supervision, an action that motivated oil executives from the East to go to Indian Territory to obtain leases and to begin test drilling. Soon oil was discovered in the Chelsea–Coody's Bluff district, near where Sallie McSpadden, Will Rogers's sister, lived. (Earlier, in August 1889, oil had been found in the Spencer Creek area of Foyil, a town just south of Chelsea.) John T. McSpadden (Will Rogers's brother-in-law) offered to lease his son Clem's land for oil- and gas-mining purposes to the highest bidder (*CM*, 22 September 1905). On 22 November 1905 oil was discovered on the Glenn Pool reserve, twelve miles south of Tulsa. By mid-1907 the reserve had 516 wells that yielded 117,440 barrels daily. The first well in the Claremore area began to produce oil on 3 April 1906. It was called Taylor Well No. 1 and was situated four miles west of the town (Dale and Wardell, *History of Oklahoma*, 421–22; Debo, *Tulsa*, 88; *HRC*, 29; Wyche, "History of Chelsea," 9, 12). Natural gas was also plentiful in the area by the early 1900s. In 1905 the Claremore city council granted franchises for natural gas distribution rights to Harry Jennings, and for natural gas plant rights to Joseph Martin LaHay (Debo, *Tulsa*, 85–88; *HRC*, 29; *History of Oologah*, 9–10).

5. In a letter to his sister Maud Lane, Rogers wrote, "Heres another clipping from yesterdays Rochester [Worcester] paper they ask you a few questions and then put it down to suit themselves" (20 November 1905, OkClaW). Similar stories regarding Rogers, his background, and lariat skills were repeated regularly in newspapers during the following months as part of Keith Circuit publicity about his act (see "Throws Two Lariats at Same Time," *Keith Theatre News*, 8 January 1906, OkClaW).

To Clement Vann Rogers
20 November 1905
Boston, Mass.

Boston. Mass.
Nov 20. 05

Dear Papa

got here this morning from Worcester   only a short distance and will be here this week.   I played here before last summer   it is the finest Theatre in the east.[1]

Now here is $200.00 for you to put in the bank   that will be $1450.00 in all   it is cold here.   I think I will be home *sure* about Feb 1st but am engaged for Xmas[2]   Write when you can   what rent will we get from the farm this fall.

Write to me at
    Keiths Theatre
    Providence
    Rhode Island
I play there next week[3]

your son
Willie

ALS, rc. OkClaW.

1. Rogers played at Keith's Theatre in Boston from 3 to 8 July 1905. On the the-
ater see Manager's Report, Keith's Theatre, 3 July 1905, above. The playbill list for
the week commencing 20 November 1905 at Keith's Theatre was as follows:
Stereopticon Views (Of Tokyo; Mexico; and Miscellaneous Subjects); Thomas and
Paine ("Real Coon" Comedians, Singers and Dancers. First Time Here); Cherry and
Bates (Comedy and Trick Bicyclists. First Time in 2 Years); Lillian LeRoy ("The
Little Girl with the Big Voice." First Time in a Year); Louis Granat (Clever Whistling
Soloist. First Time in 2 Years); Cabaret's Dogs (One of the Prettiest Canine Acts Ever
Seen in America. Specially Imported for the Keith Circuit. First Time Here); Cartmell
and Harris (Pleasing Singers and Clever Dancers. First Timer Here); Mr. and Mrs.
Howard Truesdell (In the Comedy Sketch, *Aunt Louisa's Advice*); William Delmore
and Millie Oneida (In a Wonderful Japanese Perch Specialty. First Time in 17
Months); O. K. Sato (Skillful Juggler and Comedian. First Time in 2 years); The Four
Welsons (Quartet of Famous Rope Performers. Specially Imported for the Keith
Circuit. Direct from the Wintergarten, Berlin. First Time in 2 Years); Quartet Basque
(Noted Organization of Vocalists, in High-Class Selections. First Time in a Year);
Louis Simon and Grace Gardner (And Company, in the Screamingly Funny Farce,
"The New Coachman"); Elmer Tenley (One of the Cleverest Monologue Comedians
in the Varieties. First Time This Season); Will Rogers (A Typical Western Plainsman,
in a Wonderful Exhibition with the Lasso. First Time This Season); The Kinetograph
(Showing the Following Interesting and Humorous Pictures, The Vanderbilt Cup
Races, The Children's Quarrel, Black and White, The Joys of Marriage) (Keith's
Theatre Program, week of 20 November 1905, OkClaW). The program announced
that the theater would open at 1:00 P.M. and that performances would be continuous
until 10:30 P.M. The program also stipulated that the order of performers in the program was subject to change and that their position in the program did not indicate the
value of the acts.
    Review clippings in Rogers's scrapbook about his Boston performance praised his
dexterity with handling eighty feet of rope. One reviewer wrote that he "is not only a
clever roper and lasso expert, but a good comedian in his typical Western dialect"
(*Boston Post,* 21 November 1905, scrapbook A-1, OkClaW). According to the manager's report, written by F. J. O'Connor after the Monday matinee on 20 November,
Rogers performed in two shows, each thirteen minutes long, and used the full stage
(the first five acts on the playbill did three shows). O'Connor commented: "Lasso
expert and rope manipulator, assisted by another cowboy and broncho. Mr. Rogers is
by far the best rope manipulator we have had. His work is not only excellent, but his
talk is real comedy of the best kind for our patrons. Went big this afternoon." The
manager, however, was disappointed with the show as a whole: "This week's show is
quite a drop from those of the previous weeks. The early 2-show section from 2:00 to

3:00 o'clock is of the kind that you only care to have one act of the sort on the bill. When we get to the Welsons, it is all right. Will struggle along and do what we can with the material on hand, but it can never be a good show for this house" (Manager's Report, Boston, week of 20 November 1905, KAC–IaU).

2. Rogers appeared at the Grand Opera House in Pittsburgh beginning the week of 25 December. He came home in early March before leaving on his European tour.

3. Keith's Theatre in Providence was among the circuit's chief venues. Keith's first theatre in Providence was the Gaiety, which opened in 1888, but after a time he found it too small and searched for a new place. He secured Lowe's Opera House, then the largest theater in Providence. The theater was renamed B. F. Keith's Opera House and opened in 1894.

In 1900 Keith gave the theater to his general manager Albee in gratitude for his dedication and hard work. Through 1918 it had several name changes: Keith's New Theatre, Keith's, and Keith's Theatre. In 1906 the theater had a seating capacity of 1,801 (orchestra, 750; gallery, 500; balcony, 551). Prices for the orchestra were 50 cents. The balcony was 25 and 35 cents, and the gallery was 15 cents. The theater was devoted to vaudeville in the fall and winter, while the Edward Albee Stock Co. performed in the spring and summer. High-class vaudeville was presented continuously from 1:30 to 10:30 P.M. (*JCOTG*, 117; "Keith-Albee Collection MsC 356 Inventory," 6–7, KAC–IaU; *WhoStg*, 10).

As a prelude to his Providence performance, Rogers received considerable publicity by appearing in a front-page story in the *Keith News* for 20 November 1905 (the four-page paper was a publication of the Keith Theatre in Providence). Entitled "Will Rogers, 'The Lariat King,'" the story featured a photograph of Rogers on horseback and holding in his right hand a lasso, which was looped in a large circle around the horse. The article described Rogers's Cherokee heritage, the prominence of his father, and the steer incident at Madison Square Garden, and related several other anecdotes that had appeared in earlier publicity stories (how he had roped turkeys as a child, how his parents had wanted him to be a preacher, and his plans to quit vaudeville—"this theatre work is like a funeral compared with life on a ranch" [OkClaW]).

Excerpt from Review from the *Providence News*
28 November 1905
Providence, R.I.

KEITH'S THEATRE.

Proprietor Albee's coffers are likely to over-run this week, for Providence theatregoers, however cold they may be, are quick to realize when they are getting full measure. The bill at Keith's this week just brims over with enjoyable and interesting features, the kind of program that brings a look of surprise to every face when the time for the motion pictures arrive, so quickly does the time pass when one is being entertained so completely.[1] The big novelty of the bill and one of the most unique attractions of the vaudeville season is Will Rogers, who is known as "The Lariat King." Much has been heard here, and all over the country for that matter, of Rogers' skill with the lasso and he surely lives up to the fame that has preceded him. There is no gainsaying the fact that Rogers is a typical western cowboy. His mannerisms and accent are essentially those of the plains. He is a slight youth, seeming hardly to have the amazing muscle that he must have to perform his difficult feats. He throws a lasso with his feet as well as with his hands, and throws one with both hands at the same time.

Another remarkable "stunt," as he called it, in his quaintly witty side remarks which were so thoroughly enjoyed by the audience, was what he called "the crinoline," consisting of the wielding of a long rope which reached to the very rear of the orchestra floor. He uses a bronco pony, which has evidently been excellently trained, and an assistant, "Buck" McKee, said to be a former sheriff of Oklahoma Territory, who is almost as much of an Indian as Rogers himself. The pair enjoy their work, it is evident, and so does the audience, and by the end of the week all the youngsters in town will be flocking to see Rogers and themselves trying to throw ropes. . . .[2]

PD. Printed in *Providence News,* 28 November 1905. KC-IaU.

1. Rogers was listed first in the playbill, and one review suggested that he had the "honor place" in the program (*Providence Journal* clipping, scrapbook A-1, OkClaW). He was described as "The Lariat King. Assisted by Buck McKee, former Sheriff of Oklahoma, and a genuine prairie pony from Indian Territory." Other performers were Toozoonin Whirlwind Arabs (Tumblers); Clay Clement and Co. (in *The Baron's Love Story*); 4 Piccolo Midgets (Comedians and Acrobats); Harry Le Clair ("The Bernhardt of Vaudeville." In His Original Satirical Impersonations of Stage Celebrities); 4 Welsons (European Rope Performers); Cartmell and Harris (European Dancing Duo); Elmer Tenley (Comedian); Musical Simpsons (Instrumentalists); Norcross Minstrels (A miniature old-fashioned minstrel entertainment); Savoy Quartette (Comedians and Vocalists); Billy Kin Kaid (Eccentric Juggler); Heeney and Steele (Singers and Dancers); Travel Views; Keith Motion Pictures (Keith Theatre playbill, Providence, R.I., week of 27 November 1905, scrapbook A-1, OkClaW).
2. Rogers received other, very positive reviews from the Providence press that pointed to the novelty of his act and its western cowboy origins (Providence, R.I., clippings, 28 November–2 December 1905, scrapbook A-1, OkClaW).

From Mort A. Shea
1 December 1905
New York, N.Y.

In November Will Rogers found another agent, Mort Shea.[1] His first agent, William Morris, was losing many of his performers due to his continued opposition to the Keith Circuit. An independent agent, Morris opposed the growing consolidation of circuits in vaudeville. The Keith office was making agreements with the major vaudeville theater managers in an effort to control bookings (developments that led in 1906 to the formation of the United Booking Offices under the control of Keith forces). Morris unsuccessfully opposed the formation of these interlocking arrangements. Consequently the Keith organization prevented him from booking his clients in Keith theaters and blacklisted Morris performers who played opposition houses. These factors probably led Rogers to find a new agent.

New York, Dec. 1, 1905.

Will Rogers,
   Keith's Theatre,
      Providence, R.I.

You play Casino[2] Sunday night salary one hundred   answer.[3]

M. A. Shea.

TG, rc. OkClaW. Postal Telegraph Commercial Cables telegram, received at Banigan Building, Providence, R.I.

   1. See Biographical Appendix entry, SHEA, Maurice [Mort] A.
   2. Located on the southeast corner of Broadway and Thirty-ninth Street, the Casino Theatre was designed by the architects Francis Kimball and Thomas Wisedell in a Moorish style. Its terra cotta exterior was marked by a seven-story round tower. Inside was an ornate 1,300-seat auditorium that continued the Moorish motif. It vaunted a velvet curtain laced with jewels, orchestra boxes embellished with carved arabesque patterns, and walls painted in rich, metallic colors. The Casino boasted New York's first summer roof garden for outdoor entertainment. At the time of its construction in 1882, it was the farthest uptown legitimate theater. The Casino had a long and distinguished history in the American musical theater. Well-known writers and composers of light operas and musical comedy revues were associated with the Casino. It opened on 21 October 1882 as the home of a resident light opera company headed by the producer Rudolph Aronson. He had convinced many financiers and businessmen (J. P. Morgan, Jay Gould, Louis Tiffany, and Cornelius Vanderbilt) to finance the Casino's construction. In November 1900 the Casino offered the popular, long-running (505 performances) English musical *Floradora*, featuring the "Floradora Girls." This production started the fad for chorus-girl revues. When Rogers was performing at the Casino, the theater was operated by the Shubert organization. Early in 1905 much of the Casino's interior was destroyed by fire. The damage was repaired, and the theater reopened in December 1905. Over the next twenty-five years the Shuberts staged many successful musicals here. The Casino was demolished in 1930 to make way for a thirty-story structure for the garment industry. By this time over eighty legitimate theaters were situated in the midtown area that extended to Columbus Circle (Henderson, *City and the Theatre*, 168, 219; McNamara, *Shuberts of Broadway*, 16–18, 34, 38; Mantle and Sherwood, eds., *Best Plays of 1899–1909*, 379, 499–500; van Hoogstraten, *Lost Broadway Theatres*, 14–18).
   3. Rogers was listed on the Sunday evening concert program on 3 December 1905 at the Casino Theatre. The order of acts was as follows: Murphy and Francis; Ireland's Own Band; Press Eldridge; Ojee; Three Sisters Constantine; Miss Edna Aug; Will Rogers; Grand Opera Trio; Seymour and Hills; and Kinetograph (Casino Theatre program, Sunday concert, 3 December 1905, OkClaW). The *New York Times* also

advertised Rogers's appearance in its Sunday magazine section, 3 December 1905 (pp. 4–5). Rogers's engagement exemplified the tight time schedule vaudevillians had to meet. He finished at Keith's Theatre in Providence the night of 2 December, performed in New York the following evening, and traveled to Lowell, Mass., on 4 December 1905 for a Monday matinee.

<h2 style="text-align:center">Article from the Lowell Daily Courier
4 December 1905
Lowell, Mass.</h2>

In the early 1900s the romanticization of the cowboy and the West became increasingly the subject of silent films, fiction, and art.[1] As cities grew through immigration from Europe and migration from rural areas, urban audiences increasingly craved those values associated with the West. Rogers's sudden popularity in vaudeville reflected the vogue and idealization of the cowboy. Rogers's stage persona (his casual mannerisms and drawl, his horse, lasso, chaps, and cowboy outfit) served to reinforce this image. In the following article the author compares Rogers with the hero of the best-selling novel, The Virginian *(1902), which set the tone for the modern Western.*

<h3 style="text-align:center">LARIAT KING</h3>

Famous Cowboy Tells Courier Man About Himself.

Dislikes Vaudeville.

Will Leave the Stage After Contract
Runs Out to Return to the Plains
and Former Life.

The passionate press agent never does full credit to a vaudeville performer like Will Rogers, the lariat thrower who is at the opera house, this week, demonstrating how rope throwing is done on the plains.

To meet Rogers and talk with him is as good as reading a half dozen chapters of Owen Wister's "Virginian."[2] Somehow Rogers doesn't talk readily. He knows the English language as she is spoken in Indian Territory, but he simply doesn't care much about being interviewed.

It was hard work yesterday for a Courier-Citizen man to get this rare man to talk and for once the credit is going to be given the reporter. He got Rogers into a reminiscent vein and held him there for three-quarters of an hour and until his act was ready to be put on.

"I don't care for this vaudeville life," said the cow puncher, "I don't have to do it and I'm not going to do it much after Christmas. My father is a senator of the Cherokee tribe of Indians and I'm a quarter breed Cherokee myself. Father has a big ranch down near Claremore, Indian Territory. I was raised there and 'Buck' McKee, my mate here, came not very far from the same place.

"You see I'd tried and tried to get this act onto the stage, but every one of the managers said it wouldn't go. I begun to think myself it wouldn't. I've known Col. Mulhall a long time. When he was going out to give a performance anywhere I'd settle into the saddle and go off with him. Last June I went to Washington with him and we roped steers and mustangs for the president of the United States. Then we went on to Madison Square Garden and played a week there.

"I met the Keith people and signed 40 weeks with them and over 30 of those weeks have gone by and I'm not going to renew a contract.[3]

"No, sir: This stage business was never built for me. A feller will have an off day and there ain't no reason for it and it shouldn't be. But it is. Out on the plains, among fellers of your own kind, if you miss why you can try it over again and there's nothing said. But plumb up in front of an audience when you miss they think you're no good and it rattles the best feller the Lord ever allowed to rope a steer.

"You see there are some pretty good chaps on the plains. Your president liked them mighty well and when I was in Boston last week young Theodore Roosevelt[4] come over from Harvard college to see me and got turned down because the stage rules were too strict. That's what galls me: Those stage rules. I was never bound to them and it simply cuts into my bones when I've got to stand for it.

"In Oklahoma city I've roped for the president and 'Buck' McKee has done the same thing.[5] Downeasters, like you, look upon us as something like freaks. Well, we are, I suppose. But we're not a bad kind when we're dug out enough.

"I've seen a whole lot of roping for a feller of my age. I'm only 24. When the British and the Boers were having their set-to, I went out for the British government and broke horses for 'em. Then I went to Australia and after that I was down in South America. In South America I got so I could throw the bolos pretty well, but the old hard hemp rope is still my strong point. Some people, you see, think that a man isn't a real cow boy unless he uses raw hide. I carry a raw hide lariat with me all of the time, just to satisfy those stickers for the real thing. Out in Australia I tried to use the boomerang the way the natives do. Well, I never got the blooming thing to come back to me unless I hired a nigger to get it and then I didn't always get it."

Since Mr. Rogers has been in the East he has had many adventures, and one of the most notable took place in Buffalo when he was playing there last summer. He had just come into the city after a long horse-back ride in the country when, in one of the public squares there, he saw a large crowd in commotion, and upon drawing nearer he saw that a spirited horse was running wild with a physician's carriage.

The horse was likely at any moment to run down some of the women or children who were about, and when Mr. Rogers saw the situation he turned his horse's head and began to race along just ahead of the runaway animal. As everybody knows, a cowboy never goes away from home without a lasso attached to his saddle, and Mr. Rogers rapidly unshipped his rope and as he raced along just ahead of the runaway horse, he began to hurl the lasso in the air. He allowed the runaway horse to overtake him, and just as he was pushing alongside his mustang he threw the lasso.

Not wishing to injure the horse by roping it about the legs and throwing it, he let the lasso settle down over its neck pulling it taut. This did not seem to check the animal to any extent, but seemed to frighten it more, so the cowboy, with a twist of the rope, such as he shows on the stage at every performance, made another running leap through the air and in a moment there was a knot tied around the horse's nose. This, in addition to the circle around his neck, and with the added purchase which he secured on the horse rapidly brought him to a halt, amid the cheers of admiration from the crowd who witnessed the feat by the cowboy.

Mr. Rogers is now giving one of the greatest acts in vaudeville, with his cowboy companion and his mustang. He will appear every afternoon and evening this week at the opera house along with the rest of the great performers who make up what is undoubtedly the finest and highest class vaudeville show ever seen in this section of the country.[6]

PD. Printed in the *Lowell Daily Courier*, 4 December 1905. Scrapbook A-1, OkClaW.

1. See, for example, Edwin S. Porter's film *The Great Train Robbery* (1903) for the Edison Co. With its subject of outlaws who hold up a train and are eventually captured (crime, pursuit, and retribution), it helped set the course of the Western film as a genre. Another Porter film was *The Life of a Cowboy* (1906), which featured trick roping and cowboy heroes saving a young girl who had been abducted by Indians. David Belasco's *Girl of the Golden West* was an enormously popular play that opened on 14 November 1905 at the New York Theatre, running for 224 performances. In the field

of art Frederic Remington and Charles M. Russell were establishing careers as painters of the American West with portrayals of cowboy life, Native Americans, wild horses, buffalo hunts, and other scenes. Russell would become a good friend of Rogers (Mantle and Sherwood, eds., *Best Plays of 1899–1909*, 500–501; Musser, *Before the Nickelodeon*, 253–59, 359–63; *OCAT*, 295; see also Biographical Appendix entry, RUSSELL, Charles M.).

2. The American novelist Owen Wister (1860–1938) gained fame with the publication of *The Virginian* in 1902. His summers in the mid-1880s, spent on a Wyoming ranch for his health, kindled his infatuation with the West and the cowboy. Between 1891 and 1893 he began to write short stories of western adventures in popular magazines. Considered a landmark in the development of the Western, *The Virginian* romanticized the West and the cowboy. The popular novel was printed six time in six weeks and sold 300,000 copies in two years. Its noble hero, the Virginian, epitomized the old American virtues identified with the West—courage, individualism, honor, and integrity. The novel contained many of the elements that would become standard in the Western: the virtuous ranchers versus the evil rustlers, the good and gallant woman, and the showdown between two gunmen on an empty street. Wister portrayed the cowboy as an American hero, the standard bearer of traditional rural values in a new century that would increasingly be marked by urbanism and technology (Nye, *Unembarrassed Muse*, 288–91; White, *Eastern Establishment and the Western Experience*, 122–44). The comparison of Rogers to the protagonist of *The Virginian* was repeated in other publicity stories. A reviewer in the *Brooklyn Times* commented on Rogers's performance at the Amphion Theatre: "The lariat throwing of Rogers, who, by the way, has the fascinating drawl in speech of that creation of Owen Wister's, 'The Virginian,' is strikingly interesting and accurate" (clipping, Scrapbook A-1, OkClaW).

3. Although Rogers appeared in many Keith theaters during his first year in vaudeville, he did not have a long-term contract with the Keith organization. Individual contracts for each Keith Circuit theater were issued. He also played at non-Keith houses during his first forty weeks on tour.

4. Theodore Roosevelt, Jr. (1887–1944), had a distinguished career as a politician, author, soldier, and explorer. The president's oldest son had entered Harvard in 1905. After graduation he became a businessman and banker. A supporter of military preparedness, he served in both world wars and in 1919 helped organize the American Legion. After a stint as a Republican New York assemblyman, he was appointed assistant secretary of the navy (1921–24), governor of Puerto Rico (1929–32), and governor general of the Philippines (1932–33). An explorer like his father, the young Roosevelt led zoological expeditions to central and southeast Asia (1925, 1928–29). His literary career included an editorial position at Doubleday Doran and Co., and he was also the author of several books. On 12 July 1944 Roosevelt died from a heart attack while serving as military governor at Cherbourg, France, during World War II (*DAB* supp. 3:668–69; *WNBD*, 862).

5. Rogers had met Roosevelt in Oklahoma City while he was participating in a steer-roping contest during a national reunion of Roosevelt's Rough Riders from 1 to 4 July 1905. Rogers was then with Zack Mulhall's Wild West show. Roosevelt had attended the show on 3 July 1905 (see *PWR*, 1:193–98).

6. The Lowell Opera House was associated with the Keith Circuit. Owned and managed by Fay Brothers and Hosford, it had a seating capacity of 1,200. Noted for its textile industry, Lowell supported several vaudeville and legitimate theaters. Rogers's contract was arranged on 5 December 1905, the day after his first appearance. It was signed "Will Rogers" by his agent Mort Shea, who initialed the contract

"MAS." The Fay Brothers and Hosford were represented by Samuel K. Hodgdon, Keith executive, who stamped and initialed the contract. Rogers's salary was $250 for the week for two daily performances (Lowell Opera House, Lowell, Mass., Artist's Contract, 5 December 1905, OkClaW; *JCGHTG,* 150A).

Rogers was advertised as a "special added attraction." His schedule had called for him to be in Philadelphia. "They changed me from Philadelphia this week and sent me to Lowell Mass. and I will play Philadelphia in a few weeks," Rogers wrote his father (to Clement Vann Rogers, 4 December 1905, OkClaW). Rogers wrote this letter on stationery bearing a picture of George Washington and the letterhead of the old-Washington-Tavern, which was near the Opera House. He used the same stationery when he wrote his sister Maud on 8 December 1905. The article from the *Lowell Daily Courier* might have been enclosed in this letter. He wrote "Here [is] another of those fishy writeups from here" (to Maud Lane, mistakenly dated by Rogers, 8 November 1905, OkClaW).

The following were listed in order of appearance on the playbill: Les Auberts (European Novelty. Acrobatic Dancing); C. W. Littlefield (Master Mimic and Impersonator); DeWitt, Burns and Torrance (In Frank DeWitt's Mirthful Creation "The Awakening of Toys"); The Three Roses (Refined Musical Act); The Famous Four Londons (European Sensational Aerial Marvels); Hines and Remington (Unique Character Creators); Gallagher and Barrett (Two Funny Comedians in "Stocks and Bonds"); Will Rogers, Cowboy (King of the Lariat); and New Moving Pictures (Special: "The Train Wreckers," Better Than "The Train Robbery").

In another review Rogers made an interesting joke about the censorship rules on the Keith Circuit: "He said he was handicapped because the management would not allow him to cuss a little when he failed to succeed in his stunts" (*Lowell Daily Mail,* clipping, scrapbook A-1, OkClaW).

Manager's Report, Union Square Theatre
11 December 1905
New York, N.Y.

Rogers returned to New York for his second engagement at Keith's Union Square Theatre. "I just got back in N.Y. yesterday and play here this week in the same theater I first started in 27 weeks ago," Rogers wrote his father.[1] Six months on the vaudeville stage had brought Rogers unexpected success.

New York Criticism—Dec. 11th, 1905.

TOTO:[2] Musical Mystery. Second week. No applause on the finish of the act. They would not have it. 9 min. in two—2 shows

THREE MADCAPS: 3 women. Acrobatic Dancers. Well known. Some little scattered applause throughout. A pleasing three show act. 11 min.—full stage—3 shows

HARRY PILCER:[3] Character Vocalist. Young man. Pleasing personality with a very peculiar voice although acceptable. Gives an imitation of Geo. M.

Cohan which is fairly good and with his dancing, which is excellent, makes the act alright for an early place on the bill. 10 min. in one—3 shows

IMPERIAL JAP. TROUPE: Not as strong as some of the other Japanese acts we play. They secured some scattered applause for the work. Act is alright at the price on account of the time and the three shows. 21 min.—full stage—3

MCKISSICK & SHADNEY:[4] Colored Man and woman. Singing and dancing. Singing does not amount to much. Dancing is alright which just about lets them out as an opening act. 10 min. in one—3 shows

MULLEN & CORELLI: 2 men. Acrobatic comedy. First time here. One works straight while the other is eccentric. First act on the bill which made the audience sit up and take notice. All their acrobatic work is new and good and was greatly appreciated. Their comedy is excellent. Act is quick and full of life. They close the act tumbling through a trick-piano which they carry, making a strong finish. 11 min.—full stage—2

EDWARD MOLLENHAUER:[5] Violinist. Received some advance applause. All of his numbers were appreciated and strongly applauded, and I presume a little bit of the enthusiasm was through sympathy. A mighty clever musician. 17 min. in two—can close in one—2 shows

PAUL BARNES:[6] Monologue and Songs. This man has a big lot of new material. With the cream spot on the bill, he couldn't go otherwise, but make a hit. His parodies went exceptionally strong. 16 min. in one—2 shows

WILL ROGERS:[7] Lasso Manipulator. One of the best on the stage. His lasso work got very little applause, although he closed strong, showing that they appreciated his work. 11 min.—full stage—2 shows

FRED NIBLO:[8] The American Humorist. Has a big lot of new material. Had them with him on the start-off and carried them all through his act. Closed very strong. Cut out:—"Dam sight." "Don't take a married woman, take a single one; you will keep out of trouble." And when audience laughs:— "Naughty audience, I don't mean what you mean." Also make no reference to Adam and Eve.[9] 17 Min. in one—2 shows

JOSEPHINE COHAN & CO:[10] Company includes Josephine Cohan, Morgan Wallace[11] and Edward Powers in a musical farce:—"Friday, the 13th." Miss Cohan received a reception on her entrance. The sketch tells a little story with a good vein of comedy running through it; and with the singing and dancing makes it a very acceptable musical farce. They scored quite a number of laughs. Company is excellent. She was compelled to take two bows on her finish. 23 min.—full stage

MAYME REMINGTON & HER PICKANINNIES:[12] I think this woman gave us the best act we ever had. She carries two drops to represent Japanese and

Indian Village scenes. The "picks" make four changes. The singing is excellent and they close with a good lively dance, making a very strong finish. Was applauded throughout. 12 min. in one—2 shows

PARROS BROTHERS: Eccentric Hand-to-hand Acrobats and Equilibrists: Acrobatic work is excellent. Balancing is very good and recognized the equal of any that we ever had. Finished very strong. A good closing act. 14 min. full stage

KINTEOGRAPH:[13] "A Christmas Miracle." Good

"The Train Wreckers."[14] Intensely interesting throughout. Excellent subject.

TD. KAP-IaU.

1. Will Rogers to Clement Vann Rogers, 11 December 1905, OkClaW.

2. Rogers had performed with To-to in June (see Review, Hammerstein's Paradise Roof Garden, 20 June 1905, above).

3. The dancer and screen and stage actor Harry Pilcer (1885–1961) had a long and colorful career. Born in New York, the son of Samuel Pilcer, he made his stage debut at age fourteen. Beginning around 1912, Pilcer gained considerable notoriety when he teamed up with the French dancer Gaby Deslys (1881–1920), who had a sensational love affair with King Manuel of Portugal that caused considerable scandal and led in part to his downfall. Pilcer and Deslys performed together for several years, and it was Pilcer who created the dance named The Gaby Glide. In 1920 Desly died from consumption in Pilcer's arms. In the 1920s Pilcer had a new partner, Mistinguette, known as the dancer with "the million dollar legs." Pilcer worked with Mistinguette for ten years. At one time Pilcer was reputed to have been a male prostitute early in his life. In the late 1920s and 1930s he performed in Parisian cafes, European music halls, and Berlin cabarets. In his later years he became an entertainer and master of ceremonies for French gambling casinos at Cannes and LaBaule. He died in Cannes from a heart attack shortly after his performance as a master of ceremonies at the Ambassador Casino. He was seventy-five (Burns and Mantle, eds., *Best Plays of 1909–1919*, 447–48, 494–95; *EV*, 127–28; Goldman, *Fanny Brice*, 104; *NYT*, 16 January 1961; *VO*, 5:18 January 1961; *WhScrn*, 2:582; *WhThe*, 3:1917).

4. In 1903 McKissick and Shadney, blackface minstrel performers, were members of The Hottest Coon in Dixie Co. McKissick had another partner named Jones in the touring company. Probably they decided to do a vaudeville act after being with the company (Simpson, *Ghost Walks*, 293).

5. The violinist and composer Edward Mollenhauer (1827–1914) was born in Erfurt, Germany. After becoming a professional violinist in Germany, Mollenhauer went to the United States on tour with Jullien's orchestra. Mollenhauer appeared as soloist with several orchestras, including the New York Philharmonic. Later, he was conductor of the orchestra at Augustin Daly's Theatre, where he also arranged the scores of musical shows. Among his compositions are symphonies, concertos, and works for the violin. According to the playbill he was the founder of the first conservatory of music in America. Mollenhauer died on 7 May 1914 in Owatoma, Minn. (Claghorn, *Biographical Dictionary of American Music*, 314; *Grove Dictionary of American Music*, 3:255).

6. Comic and song writer Paul Barnes (ca. 1864–1922) began his vaudeville career around 1902 as a blackface single act. For a time he teamed with his wife on the vaudeville stage. He was one of many variety tramp comics, then in vogue in vaudeville. On stage Barnes would dress in ragged clothes and crushed derby, his face highlighted by a red nose and shabby beard. His monologue often used local material, and he relied on rambling comic patter. Blind as a consequence of a stroke, he died at the Manhattan State Hospital on Ward's Island, N.Y., where he was confined for two years due to mental illness (Gilbert, *American Vaudeville*, 269, 271; Musser, *Beyond the Nickelodeon*, 173–74, 311–12; *VO*, 1:5 May 1922).

7. Rogers's performance was mentioned in a review in the first edition of *Variety*, which was published on 16 December 1905. Sime Silverman, *Variety*'s founder and editor, wrote (p. 9) that "Will Rogers placed the large end of a lasso wherever he liked."

8. Fred Niblo (1874–1948; born Frederico Nobile) had a long and successful career as vaudeville monologuist, stage actor, and film director. Born in York, Neb., Niblo began his career as a lyceum entertainer in New York City. In 1897 he appeared on the stage in juvenile parts in New York stock companies. He performed in minstrel shows and graduated to the vaudeville stage, where he performed as a blackface monologuist. Playbills regularly identified him as "The American Humorist." Considered one of vaudeville's best monologuists, Niblo had a routine of funny talk and gags. He was known to have invented one of the stage's longest running jokes: "I asked my girl to marry me. And she told me to go to Father. Now she knew that I knew her father was dead, and she knew that I knew the life he had led, and she knew what she meant when she said, 'Go to Father!'. Well, we weren't married!" (Laurie, *Vaudeville*, 177). Niblo believed that the comic monologuist in vaudeville must know his audience. He wrote: "The monologuist who walks out on the stage, forlorn and alone, talking to those who like him and those who don't, comes pretty nearly anticipating every thought and impression that runs through the minds of his auditors. It is his business to do so. It is dangerous if he doesn't" (Fred Niblo, "English and American Audiences," *Variety*, 15 December 1906).

A turning point in his career began when he became associated with the Four Cohans. In 1903 he produced their show *Running for Office* at the Fourteenth Street Theatre. A year later he married Josephine Cohan. For the next twelve years Niblo was associated with the Cohans as manager of George M. Cohan and as an actor with the Cohan and Harris company. His association with Cohan ended abruptly in 1916 when his wife died and an unresolved feud developed with his brother-in-law.

Later Niblo was involved in the film industry. Using a special moving-picture camera manufactured by the Pathé Brothers, Niblo filmed a series of travelogues in Africa and in late 1908 and 1909 presented his films in lectures in legitimate theaters. In 1918 he went to Hollywood, where he became a director for the producer Thomas H. Ince. That same year he married Enid Bennett, and the couple had three children. Niblo became a prominent director in the 1920s and was associated with some of the most popular films and stars of the period. He had a flair for swashbucklers, spectacles, and romances. Niblo directed many pictures for Metro-Goldwyn-Mayer, and his last pictures were with RKO-Pathé. In 1938 he retired to live on a ranch, but he remained prominent in civic and cultural affairs and served as a speechmaker at Hollywood functions. He returned to acting in 1940 and 1941, playing character parts in films. While on a Caribbean cruise with his wife, he was afflicted with pneumonia and died two weeks later, on 11 November 1948, in a New Orleans sanitarium (*EV*, 372; Fred Niblo biographical file, CLAc; *NYT*, 12 November 1948; Laurie, *Vaudeville*, 177;

Mantle and Sherwood, eds., *Best Plays of 1909–1919*, 464, 557–58; *Variety*, 4 July 1908; *VO*, 4:17 November 1948; *WhMuDr*, 236; *WhoHol*, 2:1231).

9. As part of Keith's refined vaudeville for the family, the theater managers used the Monday matinee performances to censor any lewd jokes or skits. Swearing, off-color comments, and biblical references were prohibited.

10. Josephine Cohan (1876–1916), dancer and stage star, had a distinguished career in the theater. Born in Providence, R.I., she was the daughter of Jerry J. and Helen F. Cohan and the sister of George M. Cohan (1878–1942). She began her stage career at age seven playing juvenile parts in her parents' stock company in Providence. With her parents and brother, she appeared on the stage in 1889 in a family act called The Cohan Mirth Makers, "The Celebrated Family of Singers, Dancers, and Comedians with Their Silver Plated Band and Symphony Orchestra." They soon changed their name to the Four Cohans, which became the most popular family act in vaudeville, featuring a combination of singing, dancing, comedy, and playlet acting. The Four Cohans turned to the Broadway stage, where they appeared in George M. Cohan's musical comedies *The Governor's Son* (1901) and *Running for Office* (1903). Next Josephine formed her own company to perform playlets on the vaudeville stage. Rogers was on the same playbill. Later, she appeared in many of her brother's Broadway productions, including *The Honeymooners* (1907) and *The Yankee Prince* (1908). In 1909 she began to suffer from heart trouble brought on by overexertion from dancing. In hopes of recovering her health, she and her husband, Fred Niblo, went to Australia in 1912, where they remained three years. While there they performed a repertoire of George M. Cohan's musicals and were a big hit. After several months in critical condition, Josephine Cohan died from heart failure on 12 July 1916 at the Hotel Belleclaire in New York City (*EV*, 105–7, 372; Gilbert, *American Vaudeville*, 183–85; Laurie, *Vaudeville*, 177; Mantle and Sherwood, eds., *Best Plays of 1899–1909*, 388, 432, 464, 562; *NYT*, 13 July 1916; *VO*, 1:14 July 1916).

11. Born in California, the actor and playwright Morgan Wallace (ca. 1881–1953) attended the University of California and the American Academy of Dramatic Arts in New York. He began his career with New York stock companies and in 1903 founded his own stock company in Bangor, Me., but shortly thereafter a fire destroyed the theater. He was a member of a traveling Shakespeare repertory company, starring Julia Marlowe and E. H. Sothern. Beginning in 1913, he was associated with several local stock companies as an actor-manager in the Midwest. Broadway appearances over the years included *Women Go On Forever* (1927), *Ballyhoo* (1927), and *Loco* (1946). Wallace also acted in many films. He retired from acting in 1948 and died at his home in Tarzana, Calif., on 12 December 1953 (*FILM*, 2:549; *FYSC*, 2:1380; Mantle and Sherwood, eds., *Best Plays of 1899–1909*, 469; *NYT*, 15 December 1953; *NYTheRel*, 395; *VO*, 4:16 December 1953).

12. Mayme Remington was accompanied by young, talented African American youngsters (derogatorily named "pickaninnies") who would sing and dance. At one time she called her act Mayme Remington and Her Black Buster Brownie Ethiopian Prodigies. A member of her troupe was Eddie Rector (ca. 1890s–1962), who joined her act at the age of fifteen and became one of the nation's best soft-shoe and tap dancers. Another dancer who performed with the Remington troupe was Dewey Weinglass (Laurie, *Vaudeville*, 56; Sampson, *Blacks in Blackface*, 415–17, 447).

13. In 1900 the Thomas Edison film company formed a film rental and exhibition service called the Kinetograph Co. This service provided films to vaudeville managers, who were always looking for a new film to place in the scheduled motion-picture slot on their bill. In 1888 Edison was working on a kinetoscope, a peephole viewing device

(the name is derived from the Greek *scopos,* "to watch"), as well as on a kinetograph, a camera (the name is derived from the Greek *kineto,* referring to "movement"). One of the innovations of the Edison kinetoscope was its use of perforations to keep the film running smoothly past the gate. It wasn't until 1894 that the kinetoscope could be introduced to the public. In 1912 Edison's kinetoscope became available to the home market. Sales were not good, and the project was abandoned in 1914 (Ceram, *Archaeology of the Cinema,* 84–85; Hendricks, "History of the Kinetoscope," 47, 48; Musser, *Emergence of Cinema,* 62–96, 110–16, 365–66; Singer, "Early Home Cinema and the Edison Home Projecting Kinetoscope," 45.)

14. Edwin S. Porter's *Train Wreckers* (released in November 1905) for the Edison Manufacturing Co. illustrated several motifs prevalent in early cinema: the chase, the outcast, and the need for social order. It also helped make the train a dominant icon in early film. The story concerns outlaws who attempt to wreck a train but are prevented by the courage of the passengers and trainmen. The outlaws kidnap the switchman's daughter, but her beau, the engineer, kills her captors. The theme of good prevailing over evil and the defeat of the outlaws reassured audiences of stability in society. A popular film (157 prints were sold between 1905 and 1906), its story was reworked in 1912 as the basis for D. W. Griffith's Biograph film, *The Girl and Her Trust* (Musser, *Beyond the Nickelodeon,* 316–17).

To Family
20 December 1905
Syracuse, N.Y.

SYRACUSE, N.Y. <u>Dec 20.</u> 1905[1]

Dear Maud. May. Papa and all the others

I will write you all this letter togeather as I guess you few straglers that are left in the Nation will surely spend Xmas togeather at your house.   sorry *the health-seeker and actors* cant be present but will sho see you soon.

Well I just this eve forwarded you all a little satchel of stuff by United States Express   did you land it   It aint much but lord I dident know what to get. sent Sallies a few days ago.   Papa did you get the overcoat I sent and will you wear it   I dident send you any money last week and lord knows when I can send any more

It is as hot as summer up here.   I will be traveling most of Xmas.   so Xmas eve (Sunday Night) you can think of me boarding a train after the show and leaving for Pittsburg, Pa.   I get there Xmas day at 11.30 and show that day so it will be a moving Xmas with me.

My Route.

Next Week. Dec 25 to 30
    Grand Opera House[2]
        Pittsburg. Pa.
New Years Week.   Jan 1st to 6.
    Maryland Theatre[3]
        Baltimore. Md.
Next *two* Weeks.   Jan 8 to 22.
    Putnam House. N.Y.
as I will be playing in Brooklyn.[4]
Week of Jan 22 to 28.
    Keiths Theatre
        Philadelphia. Pa.[5]

A great Xmas to all of you with lots of love

                                        from Bro Willie

ALS, rc. OkClaW. On Hotel St. Cloud letterhead. Reeve and Wilcox, proprietors.[6]

    1. At the time Rogers wrote, he was performing at the Grand Opera House in Syracuse, then a Keith Circuit theater, managed by the Shubert organization. It had a seating capacity of 656 in the orchestra, 439 in the balcony, and 800 in the gallery. Admission ranged from 50 cents and 35 cents in the orchestra to 15 cents in the gallery. It was one of three major theaters in Syracuse, which then had a population of 130,000 (*JCOTG*, 175, 177). On the playbill were the following acts: LeClair and Hardt (The Comedy Novelty, The Two Strong Men); Azra (Europe's Greatest Billiard Table Manipulator in Original Juggling Feats); Eddie Girard and Jesse Gardner (In their Character Comedy "Dooley and the Diamond"); Reiff Brothers (The Best of All Dancers); Miss Maud White and Stephen Grattan (Presenting the Unique Playlet *Locked Out at 3 A.M.*); La Basque Quartette (Grand Opera Selections); Will Rogers (The Lasso King and Rope Wizard. In a Marvelous Exhibition of Lasso Throwing and Rope Juggling as Practiced by the Cowboys on the Plains). Rogers performed two shows daily, a matinee at 2:15 P.M. and an evening performance at 8:15 P.M. (Grand Opera House playbill, week commencing Monday, 18 December, scrapbook A-1, OkClaW). The *Syracuse Herald* reported that "the whoop of the show is that of Will Rogers, the lasso thrower. Every time he makes a hoop out of his rope he whoops" (clipping, scrapbook A-1, OkClaW).
    2. The Grand Opera House in Pittsburgh was owned and managed by Harry Davis. Its seating capacity was 860 in the orchestra, 152 in box seats, 686 in the balcony, and 1,100 in the gallery. Prices ranged from 15 cents to a dollar. In 1906 Pittsburgh, which had a population of 130,000, had nine theaters. Davis is recognized as the first manager to open a nickelodeon (June 1905). By 1907 Davis was operating fifteen nickelodeons in different cities. Later he entered the film distribution business (*JCOTG*, 179, 181; Robinson, *From Peep Show to Palace*, 89–90, 96).

3. The Maryland Theatre was owned and managed by the James L. Kernan Co. It had a seating capacity of 1,972, and prices ranged from 15 cents to 75 cents. With a population of 500,000 in 1906, Baltimore had ten legitimate and vaudeville theaters (*JCOTG*, 139, 143).

4. Rogers performed at Hyde and Behman's Theatre in Brooklyn from 8 to 13 January 1906 (see Review from *Variety*, 13 January 1906, above). From 15 to 20 January 1906 he played at Brooklyn's Amphion Theatre. On the Amphion Theatre playbill were the following: Les Ortaneys (European Comedy Acrobats and Their Acrobatic Dogs); Ford and Wilson (Eccentric Black Face Comedians); The Three Roses (A Dainty Musical Offering); Zazell and Vernon Pantomime Troupe ("The Tourist and the Valet" in "The Elopement"); Intermission (Song—"Don't Be Angry" by Harry Rogers); Althea Twins (Singing and Acrobatic Dancing); Frederick Hallen and Mollie Fuller (In a One-Act Musical Comedy *A Morning Plunge*); Gus Williams ("Our German Senator" in Songs, Stories and Recitations); Will Rogers (Lariat Thrower); and the Kinetograph (Amphion Theatre playbill, week commencing Monday, 15 January 1906, scrapbook A-1, OkClaW; see also "Amphion," *Variety*, 20 January 1906).

5. On Keith's Theatre in Philadelphia, see Review from the *Philadelphia Item*, 27 June 1905, above.

6. The Hotel St. Cloud advertised rates for the American plan at $1.50, $1.75, and $2.00 daily, as well as special rates for the theatrical profession (*JCOTG*, 175).

To Betty Blake
22 December 1905
Syracuse, N.Y.

Despite Rogers's busy life in vaudeville, he found time to write to Betty Blake. In this letter Rogers gives her a Christmas present that had a very special meaning for him.

Dec 22nd ___1905[1]

Dearest Betty

As it is Xmas and you are "one best fellow" I want to send you a little token that I have carried with me and which I prize very highly (although not of much financial value) for I do believe you will receive it and apreciate it accordingly.

Now Betty I got this *Hdkf.* in South America   it is supposed to be very fine work done by the *Paraguay* Indians who are noted for their needlework.

I landed there quite *flush*   and I bought my sisters some two hundred dollars worth of this and sent them by my partner who was coming home and he smuggled them in this country as there is a large duty.[2]

The old Indian Lady I bought from then gave me *this* asking me if I was married   I said No.   she said then give it to the wife when you do marry.   I have kept it   carried it all through Africa at times when I dident have a cent

and was actually hungry.   then to Australia   most of the time in an envelope
in my pocket   then back home and on all all my travels   I did intend always
to do as the old woman said but I guess theres nothing doing for me   I will
just give it to you as I kinder pride it and you might do the same.

Hoping you a grand Xmas and a Happy year

I am always the same

to you Betty

yours Will.

ALS, rc. OkClaW. On Hotel St. Cloud, Syracuse, letterhead.

1. Rogers crossed out all the printed letterhead information, including the place
line and the return address on the envelope, when he wrote this letter to Blake. He was
nearing the end of his week in Syracuse and was headed to Pittsburgh next.
2. Rogers had given his friend Richard Parris lace collars to bring home for his sisters (see *PWR*, 1:275–78).

Manager's Report, Grand Opera House
25 December 1905
Pittsburgh, Pa.

*At Pittsburgh's Grand Opera House Rogers performed on the same playbill as the
Three Keatons (Joe and Myra Keaton and their son Buster). During his vaudeville
years Rogers appeared with the popular knockabout acrobatic comedy team several
times. Joe Keaton, who had roots in the Oklahoma Territory, befriended Rogers at
this time. Vaudeville was a training ground for Buster Keaton, the great silent-com-
edy film star, as it was for Rogers.[1]*

GRAND OPERA HOUSE

PITTSBURGH, PA.
DECEMBER 25TH, 1905.

YANKEE & DIXIE—3 shows. Time of act 18 minutes. Doc act. This is an
exceptionally good act for the three a day section.

LARSEN SISTERS—10 minutes, wood. This act is going very well with us,
their work being much more difficult than that attempted by other lady acrobats. We consider this a good act.

O. K. SATO—Juggler.[2] 15 minutes, 10 minutes full stage, interior—5 minutes in one. This man does very little juggling but gets a lot of comedy out of
his attempts and is pleasing very much.

CHARLOTTE GUYER GEORGE—Mezzo soprano.[3] 3 shows. 11 minutes in one. Olio. This is the best three a day singing act we have ever played. She is on at 8:10 with us and going very well.

PICCOLO MIDGETS[4]—15 minutes, opening in one 3 minutes, closing full stage, wood. This is undoubtedly the best midget act in the business, introducing wrestling at the matinees, boxing at the night performances, heavy weight lifting, trapeze performance and travesty on the Salvation Army. The act is an enormous hi[t] with the patrons, especially this week since we are playing to so many children.

BASQUE QUARTETTE—15 minutes in one. This is a very good singing act. It is their fourth appear[a]nce with us and while they are not going as strong as they did on their first appearance, they are going very well.

HUGH J. WARD & JESSIE IZETT[5]—23 minutes, interior.

These two people were formerly favorites of our stock company and, of course, are doing very well for us. I consider their sketch a very good one and feel sure that after a couple of performances it will be good enough for any bill.

CLIFFORD & BURKE[6]—Black face singing, dancing and talking act. 22 minutes in one-street. This is a good act, going very, very big, which may be due to the fact that they were residents of Pittsburgh and have a number of their friends in to see them. However, I consider the act one of the best of its kind in the business.

WILL ROGERS—"The Lariat King" 15 minutes, full stage.

This is a very novel act; two men and a horse being used. There is quite a little comedy in this act which helps it considerable. The act is going very well and I feel sure that it will make the people talk.

THREE KEATONS—27 minutes, closing in one 10 minutes.

This act is too well known to need any extended comment. They are repeating their old success here and when they introduce the fourth member of the family—Jingles—it causes a howl to go up from every one in the house. We could not have made a better selection for this week as Buster is a big hit with the children.

BROTHERS DURANT—3 shows. Monologue while in balloon, followed by trapeze act. This is a very good act for the three a day section.

John P. Harris.

TD. KAP-IaU.

1. An immensely popular comic act, The Three Keatons included Joseph Hollie (Joe) Keaton (1867–1946), his wife Myra Keaton (1877–1955), and their son Joseph Francis Keaton, better known as Buster (1895–1966). Buster's parents, veterans of the traveling medicine show, first had a husband-and-wife vaudeville act called the Two Keatons, in which Joe Keaton performed eccentric acrobatics on a kitchen table while

The Three Keatons, Joe (1876–1946), Myra (1877–1955), and Buster (1895–1966) in their vaudeville knockabout act. Joe Keaton was an acquaintance of Rogers and once recommended to him a theatrical boardinghouse in New York City. *(Billy Rose Theatre Collection, The New York Public Library for the Performing Arts, Astor, Lenox, and Tilden Foundations.)*

Myra danced and played the cornet. Buster began to perform with his parents in 1899 or 1900. In the roughhouse act Buster did his own slapstick acrobatics and was tossed playfully about the stage by his father. Soon the Keatons were headliners on the Keith and Proctor Circuits. Joining the act around this time was Jingles, Harry Stanley Keaton (ca. 1904–66), Buster's younger brother, who later became a theater manager and also played in two-reel film comedies. Myra Keaton kept a scrapbook in which there is a review of their performance at the Grand Opera House. The Keatons are called "a hysteria of acrobatic fun" (Myra Keaton Scrapbook, CBevA; see also Blesh, *Keaton,* 16–42; Buster Keaton, interview, November 1958, oral history collection, NNC; *EV,* 498–500; "'Jingles' Keaton Kidnapped," *NYDM,* 31 March 1906; Keaton, *My Wonderful World of Slapstick,* 15–21; *WhoHol,* 1:862; see also Biographical Appendix entry, THE THREE KEATONS).

2. O. K. Sato (ca. 1866–1921), whose real name was Frederick L. Steinbrucker, was born in Trenton, N.J. Sato made his first professional performance as an eccentric comedy juggler in Coney Island. According to Joe Laurie, Jr., he was also one of the first successful American vaudeville acts in Europe (*Vaudeville,* 137). Sato was a frequent performer at Tony Pastor's and Hyde and Behman's, and he regularly toured the Orpheum Circuit. After retiring from the stage, Sato entered the realty development business in Irvington, N.J. He died from a sudden heart attack on 22 March 1921 (*NYT,* 25 March 1921; *VO,* 1:1 April 1921).

3. The playbill advertised George as formerly the solo flower girl in *Parsifal* (Grand Opera House playbill, week of 25 December 1905, scrapbook A-1, OkClaW).

4. The Four Piccolos, from Germany, were a popular "midget" act on the vaudeville stage, a type of entertainment that was a holdover from the circus and museum shows. They were managed by a tall person who always appears in their photographs, probably Mike Piccolo. The four performers had different birth names. A review listed them as Otto Thiome, twenty-nine years old and weighing fifty pounds; Alex Ebert, thirty years old and weighing fifty-five pounds; Adolf Schemmel, thirty-four years old and weighing fifty pounds; and Otto Schemmel, twenty-seven years old and weighing forty-two pounds. After performing in Europe, they came to the United States around 1904. Their act might be connected with Jean Piccolo, or may have been named after this well-known German midget, who was a star at Berlin's Wilhelmstadtische Theater between 1848 and 1859 (Günter, *Geschichte des Variétés,* 129). The playbill from the Pittsburgh Grand Opera House advertised The Four Piccolos as "Delightfully Clever Little Entertainers from the Lilliput in a Versatile Diversion Comedy, Singing, Acrobatics" (scrapbook A-1, OkClaW). They appeared in a spoof of the Salvation Army band during their performance. Each Piccolo had a different stage personality. A reviewer commented: "There is a comedy Piccolo, but funny though this one was the big laugh was the serious manner of a tiny, venerable Piccolo, who seemed to boss the act" ("What Is Doing at the 125th St.," *New York Telegraph,* Piccolo Midgets clippings file, NN-L-BRTC). Publicity stories regarding the Piccolos reported that all four were married and had children who were normal size. In 1911 they became American citizens. They owned a large farm in the Catskill Mountains, near Phoenicia, N.Y. (Piccolo Midgets clippings file, NN-L-BRTC). Rogers befriended the Piccolos at this time. They sent him a photograph of themselves with the following note: "To our friend, Will Rogers from The four Piccolo Midgets. Buffalo, January 3, 1906." They also sent him a postcard dated 1 April 1906 from Los Angeles with a picture of a local tourist attraction, the Ostrich Farm. It read: "With Best Regards from The four Piccolo Midgets and Mike." It was addressed to Rogers at the Wintergarten Theatre in Berlin where he was playing at the time (JLC-OkClaW).

5. Hugh J. Ward (1871–1941) had a successful career as a dancer, actor, and manager. Born in Philadelphia, Ward first appeared on stage as a dancer with a minstrel company. He then turned to playing juvenile parts in the theater. He worked for twelve years in stock companies, including four years with Harry Davis's Stock Companies and Players in Pittsburgh. During the latter part of his life Ward became a successful actor and theater producer in Australia. He died of heart failure in Sydney in April 1941 (Odell, *Annals of the New York Stage*, 15:626; *NotNat*, 479; *WhThe*, 4:2497; *VO*, 3:23 April 1941).

Ward's partner, Jessie Izett, was a talented actress who played with stock companies and on the Broadway stage. She came from Denver, Colo., and began her theater career in the late 1890s. In 1898 Izett was with the Davis Stock Co. in Pittsburgh and afterward joined the James A. Hearne Co. In 1901 she played Alice Adams in *Nathan Hale* and was praised for her portrayal. She appeared as the lead in *The Suburban* (1903). In 1907 she performed in Los Angeles in *Salomy Jane,* a western melodrama set in the California redwood and gold-mining area, Eugene W. Presbrey's adaptation of Jerome K. Jerome's comedy *Susan in Search of a Husband.* This was followed by appearances in *The Regeneration* (1908) at the Wallack Theatre and in Edwin Milton Royal's *These Are My People* (1909), a sequel to *The Squaw Man,* about a married English man who falls in love with a Native American woman. *Variety* considered Ward and Izett one of the headliners on the bill at Pittsburgh's Grand Opera House (30 December 1905). The reviewer wrote: "Ward is the same unctuous comedian, with a little more of the finish and less of the flourish than of yore. Miss Izett has some good opportunities, and shows marked improvement since her stock company days" (Mantle and Sherwood, eds., *Best Plays of 1899–1909,* 342, 567; *NYTheReI*, 203; series 2, 258:85–103, NN-L-RLC).

6. Clifford and Burke (1905) were a comical singing, dancing, and talking blackface act. Their comedy consisted of funny dance steps, a take-off on the word *soup,* and singing "You Ain't Talking to Me." Apparently they came from Pittsburgh, since one reviewer wrote: "Clifford and Burke, the black face comedians in vaudeville, still have a tender spot for old Pittsburgh. They recall with something of the thrill of boyhood days the stone fights between the Bluff boys and the Hardscrabble legins in the valley below. Those were the halycon days in Pittsburgh when the young idea was taught the use of the sling shot rather than how to shoot. When Clifford and Burke come to the Grand the week of April 11, several large theater parties made of their boyhood friends will greet them" (unidentified clipping, 3 April 1910, series 3, 334:1, NN-L-RLC).

To Clement Vann Rogers
2 January 1906
Baltimore, Md.

Baltimore   Md.
Jan 2nd. 06.

Dear Papa.

Here is $100 I will send[1]   you this is a very good place here[2]   I was glad to get out of Pittsburg   it is the dirtiest place I ever saw   I am going down

to Washington some night after the show and see Scrap Lane[3]   she is there
it is only 40 miles   I am in N.Y. next week and the week after.

Love to all

Willie

address

Putnam House

4 ave. 26th st. N.Y.

ALS, rc. OkClaW.

1. The money Rogers sent was deposited in Claremore's First National Bank, the slip signed by C. F. Godbey, the cashier (duplicate deposit slip, 5 January 1906, OkClaW). Rogers also sent his father $100 in his next letter from New York City's Putnam House. He wrote that "this will make about $2050" (to Clement Vann Rogers, 8 January 1906, OkClaW).
2. Rogers was performing at Baltimore's Maryland Theatre. The playbill was as follows: Brazil and Brazil (In their Clever Specialty, Introducing Singing, Dancing and Acrobatic Comedy); Dora Pelletier (In Mimicry and Impersonations); Eckhoff and Gordon (Comedy Musical Act); Josephine Cohan and Co. (Presenting a One-Act Musical Farce *Friday, the 13th*); Will Rogers ("The King of the Lariat"); Fred Niblo ("The American Humorist"); Paul Conchas (Europe's Greatest Novelty Act. Kaiser Wilhelm's Military Hercules in his Military Act, Introducing German Krupp Shells and an Assortment of the Principle Weapons of Modern Warfare); and the Kinetograph (New Series of Motion Pictures. Raffles, De Cracksman) (Maryland Theatre playbill, scrapbook A-1, OkClaW). One reviewer wrote that Rogers "slipped nooses around whatever he took a fancy to aim at, so misled the spectators that when they saw the rope stretched out the entire length of the aisle and still some more remained their amazement at its length was almost comical" (*Baltimore Evening Herald*, 2 January 1906, clipping, scrapbook A-1, OkClaW). *Variety* reported that the "splendid bill for New Year's week drew crowded houses" (6 January 1906).
3. In his letter to his father of 8 January 1906, Rogers wrote that he had seen Scrap Lane in Baltimore (OkClaW).

To Clement Vann Rogers
13 January 1906
New York, N.Y.

As the following letter suggests, Rogers's feelings were hurt when his father returned the Christmas present he had sent him.

New York, Jan 13   1906

Dear Papa

I got the coat allright and cant imagine why it did not suit you   I am keeping it to wear myself and I gave mine to a friend   it was not as fine as some for   lots of them cost 3 and 4 hundred dollars and I could not afford a fine one but I thought it would do.

Write when you can

Love to all

                                                                                    Willie

Next Week.

Putnam House.

following week

Keiths Theatre

Philadelphia. Pa.

ALS, rc. OkClaW. On Putnam House letterhead.

Review from *Variety*
13 January 1906
New York, N.Y.

The following review of Rogers's performance at Hyde and Behman's Theatre[1] in Brooklyn was written by Epes Winthrop Sargent, who used the pen name Chicot. He was one of the most talented vaudeville critics, and one who did not hesitate to criticize a poor performance.[2]

HYDE AND BEHMAN'S
BY CHICOT

Will Rogers has his lariat throwing to close in just before the pictures. The use of a horse in this act improves the old idea immensely, and the horse is quite the best trained stage animal shown in vaudeville.[3] Most acts using horses scare the audience by the occasional factiousness of the beasts; this recruit from the plains is as cool and collected as any of the humans with whom he is associated.[4] There is a gaudy reel of pictures this week showing the rise of a foundling to the proud position of judge. We see the policeman take him from the street to the station and from that time on his rise is as rapid as the most ambitious might desire. It is rather humorous when you come to think it over.[5]

PD. Printed in *Variety,* 13 January 1906.

1. The theater managers Richard Hyde (1856–1912) and Louis C. Behman (1855–1902) operated four vaudeville and burlesque theaters in Brooklyn in 1906, including the Star Theatre, the Grand Opera House, and the Folly Theatre (Brooklyn, with a population of 1.2 million, then supported nineteen theaters), as well as Hyde and Behman's, their flagship house. According to Epes Sargent, Hyde and Behman's

"was a temple of variety second only to Tony Pastor's latest house in the old Tammany Hall" (Laurie, *Vaudeville*, 417). It had a seating capacity of 1,800. The two partners were schoolmates in their native Brooklyn and became pioneers in variety and burlesque. After establishing theaters in Philadelphia (1876) and Baltimore (1877), they operated theaters in their hometown. They also established a traveling show called Hyde and Behman's Combination. In 1899 they consolidated their holdings into the Hyde and Behman Amusement Co. After Behman's death in 1902, Hyde became a prominent theater manager in the Eastern Wheel burlesque circuit (*JCOTG*, 77, 85; Leavitt, *Fifty Years in Theatrical Management*, 323, 573; *OCAT*, 364; Zeidman, *American Burlesque Show*, 36, 176).

2. Epes Winthrop Sargent (1872–1938) was born in Nassau, Bahamas, where his father was a pineapple trader. In 1878 he emigrated to the United States with his parents. Early in his life he was hired as an usher at Pat Harris's Bijou Theatre in Washington, D.C. He began as a reviewer covering concerts for the *Musical Courier*. Afterward, he worked for Leander Richardson's *Dramatic News* until it failed. Next he was a critic with Blakely Hall's *Daily Mercury* and its subsidiary the *Metropolitan Magazine*. After leaving Hall he was associated with the *Germanic News,* and then with Hall's *New York Morning Telegraph,* a racing and theatrical newspaper. It was here that he began using the nom-de-plume Chicot, after a character from an Alexandre Dumas novel. A turning point in his career occurred when Sime Silverman hired him for his new trade paper *Variety* in 1905. The critic's lively style added much to the success of the publication. Known for his honesty, Sargent criticized sentimental melodrama, and he was unafraid to pan headliners. He also exposed the corruption among actors' agents and publicity agents (one practice he exposed was a newspaper printing favorable reviews of an act if it bought advertising space in the paper). According to Joe Laurie, Jr., he once refused a $100 bribe from B. F. Keith. As Laurie wrote, Sargent's "knowledge of vaudeville was encyclopedic" (*Vaudeville*, 417; Sargent wrote an introduction to Laurie's book). When a quarrel caused Sargent's departure from *Variety,* he started his own paper, *Chicot's Weekly*. After its demise he became a press agent for William Morris and F. F. Proctor. Sargent was also a scenario writer and editor with Stuart Blackton's Vitagraph Co. In 1928 he was rehired by Silverman and spent his remaining years on the *Variety* staff. Sargent died on 6 April 1938 in his Brooklyn home (*EV*, 453; Gilbert, *American Vaudeville*, 152–56; Laurie, *Vaudeville*, 340; *VO*, 2:14 December 1938). For a sample of Sargent's critiques see his reviews of Yvette Guilbert and Vesta Tilley in Slide, *Selected Vaudeville Criticism*, 90–91, 183–85).

3. There were many animal acts in vaudeville. Most were used to open the show, like Les Ortaneys and Their Acrobatic Dogs, listed first on the Hyde and Behman's playbill. Animal acts likewise often closed the show. Other circus-type animal acts included big cats (an assortment of lions, leopards, and tigers), bears, monkeys (among the most popular was Richard the Great, "The Monkey Who Made a Man of Himself"), and dancing elephants. There were also trained birds (especially pigeons, cockatoos, and canaries), roosters, goats, kangaroos, alligators, pigs, sea lions, and cats (*EV*, 13–15, 130–31, 335, 404, 486; Laurie, *Vaudeville*, 155–70; Gilbert, *American Vaudeville*, 322–24).

4. There were numerous equestrian acts in vaudeville that emphasized horsemanship and horse tricks. According to Joe Laurie, Jr., there were two types of horse acts. One, called Liberty, featured riderless horses jumping, posing, and strutting at the command of a trainer. The other, called High School, featured saddled horses with riders. Well-known vaudeville horse acts were Lucille Mulhall and Co., May Wirth and Family, Professor Buckley's Curriculum, Mme. Etoile's Society Horses, the

Davenports (bareback riders who put rosin on their horses' back), Ella Bradna and Fred Derrick, the Duttons, the Five Lloyds (in Indian garb), the George St. Leon Troupe with Boston's Riding School with Lillian St. Leon, Rossi's Musical Horse, The Sheik (a white horse), and Poodles Hanneford (a clown bareback rider). In addition, there were roping and whip acts. Lasso acts included Clinton and Beatrice, Chuck Haas, the Chamberlains (who also used whips), Shield and Rogers (a Native American and cowboy, no relation to Will Rogers), and Guy Weadick and Florence LaDue (a husband-and-wife team who did a rodeo-type act). Weadick and LaDue were friends of Rogers; see Biographical Appendix entries, LaDUE, Florence, and WEADICK, Guy, *PWR,* vol. 3). Acts specializing in whips were Fred Lindsay, the Shephards, and Jack and Violet Kelly (*EV,* 13–14, 185, 228; Laurie, *Vaudeville,* 22, 36, 160, 165; on Lucille Mulhall see *PWR,* 1:516–18).

5. The films were listed last on the playbill and titled The Kinetograph, In Laughing Pictures. Other acts were as follows: Les Ortaneys (European Comedy Acrobats, Introducing Marvelous Acrobatic Dogs); J. Aldrich Libby and Katherine Trayer (In their Musical Melange, "Buffalo Bill and the Lady"); May Duryea and W. A. Mortimer (In a playlet by Edmund Day, *The Imposter*); Harrigan (The Tramp Juggler); Klein-Ott Bros. and Nicholson (America's Leading Musical Artists); John T. Kelly (The Favorite Irish Comedian in his Latest Original Howling Skit, "Finnegan's Finish"); Miss Edna Aug (The Rage of Two Hemispheres, Comedienne, In Her Justly Celebrated Impersonations); Will Rogers (The Lariat Thrower) (Hyde and Behman's Theatre playbill, week commencing Monday matinee, 8 January 1906, scrapbook A-1, OkClaW).

Excerpt from Manager's Report, Keith's Chestnut Street Theatre 22 January 1906 Philadelphia, Pa.

Among the stars Rogers played with during his first year in vaudeville was Harry Houdini. By this time Houdini was already known as a masterful magician and great escape artist.[1] The New York Dramatic Mirror *reported that people were "turned away at every performance."[2]*

HOUDINI.—All that has been said of Houdini may be repeated with emphasis. He is proving himself the greatest winner in vaudeville. Elsewhere I do not bank on, but here he has the town going. He came in at a very opportune time of the year, and made friends with the City authorities, the press and the public at once by reason of his sincere and straightforward work. This is his third week and he has the house jammed. Cheers and curtain-calls every performance. Will make good the rest of this third week without a shadow of a doubt. Opened doors half an hour earlier than usual this afternoon because of crowd that jammed lobby and blocked street, and standing-room only is the invariable rule. Balconies shut off this afternoon. Breaks out of straightjacket every performance this week, with some surprises up his sleeve if there is seen any falling-off in interest. 27 min in full stage.

WILL ROGERS.—Badly placed on bill, owing to a three-minute wait between two full-stage features.[3] Rogers works with horse and extra man, and is certainly the leader of ropers in the vaudeville stage. Every feat won applause, Can hold any place on the bill. Rocky Mountain set adds greatly to the act. Big hand at close. . . . 12 min. F.S.[4]

TD. KAP-IaU.

1. See Biographical appendix entry, HOUDINI, Harry.
2. *NYDM,* 27 January 1906.
3. According to the listing in the manager's report, Rogers performed between Houdini and a sketch presented by Annie Yeamans and her daughter Jennie. In the published playbill the performers were listed in a different order: Davey and Phillips (Comedy Entertainers); The Gillette Sisters (A Study in Black); Mr. and Mrs. Cal Stewart (Presenting "Uncle Josh on the Bowery"); Eddie Mack (Novelty Dancer); Keith's Orchestra (Charles Schrader, Director); Mrs. Annie Yeamans and Daughter Jennie ("December and May"); Sig. Luigi Dell'Oro (Virtuoso Musicale, on his own invention, "The Armonipede"); Edmund Day (Assisted by Patrice Winston and Robert Watson in Mr. Day's Latest Comedy Success *The Sheriff*); Violet Dale (The Charming Mimic. Late Prima Donna of "A Chinese Honeymoon" Co.); Gallagher and Barrett (The Polite Comedians in a Modern Travesty *The Stock Brokers*); Houdini ("The Jail-breaker and Handcuff King"); The Great Wotpert Trio (Wonderful Acrobatic Performance); Messenger Boys Trio (Harmony Singers and Comedians); Will Rogers (The Lariat King); Kinetograph (The Bicycle Robber. A Thrilling Rescue. A Country Courtship.); Burton and Brookes (The Favorite Comedians and Singers in a New Act, Entitled *Always in the Way*) (Keith's Chestnut Street Theatre playbill, week commencing Monday, 22 January 1906, scrapbook A-1, OkClaW).
4. As part of the publicity for his performance, a long article on Rogers, entitled "Throws Two Lariats at Same Time," was published in *Keith's Theatre News,* Philadelphia, week of 8 January 1906 (OkClaW). *Variety* reviewed the playbill on 27 January 1906 and commented that Rogers was a "decided novelty, and besides his clever handling of a lasso he has a sense of humor and style which aided in making his act a success, not to mention his bronco." The report was written by C. Barbs, who concluded: "Show rather top heavy in two-a-day stuff, while falling short in the three-a-day. Houdini for a third week probably accounts for this in a measure. By rearrangement this will not be obvious and the entire list of features will run smoother."

To Maud Lane
26 January 1906
Philadelphia, Pa.

Philadelphia. Pa.
Jan 26. 06.

My Dear Sis

I just got your letter yesterday and am mighty glad to hear from you   you
are about the only one that writes often.   And Mary[1] is there   I wish I was
there now   we would have a great time   she must stay till spring.

Well I am working as usual and I cant tell just where I will go or when I
will get home   but it will either be in March or April   I kinder want to wait
till it is warm   I am mighty homesick for I have been doing the same old *stunt*
for 35 weeks.   I am a bigger hit here than I was last summer.[2]   I go up
toward New England for 3 weeks now then back to Brooklyn[3]

It is as warm as summer here all the time

I got a letter from *Theo* Mc[Spadden] and wrote him but have not got an
answer

Say Cap can you invest 5 or 6 hundred dollars in a little piece of land there
or lots or anything so it will make me anything or more if it takes more[4]   I
havent any use for it in the Bank for I dont think they pay anything on it   only
what papa uses   I want to get a few cattle when I come home and back up
home for me.

Write soon and often and tell *old Mary* to write me all the Tahlequah news
My Route
Next Week.   Jan 29.–Feb 4.
Hartford Opera House Hartford. Con.[5]
Week Feb 5–11–
Al. Haynes Theatre Fall River, Mass[6]

Lots of love to all
Willie

ALS, rc. OkClaW.

1. Mary Elizabeth Gulager (b. 1880) was the first cousin of Will Rogers. Her
mother, Martha Lucretia Schrimsher (b. 1845), was the sister of Rogers's mother,
Mary America Schrimsher (1839–90). Martha Schrimsher had married Frederick
William Gulager (b. 1844) on 27 January 1869. They were the parents of five children.
Mary Gulager often visited the Lanes in Chelsea. On 20 January 1906 the *Claremore
Progress* reported that "Miss Mary Gulager, of Tahlequah, who has been the guest of
Mr. and Mrs. Dyke Robinson for some time, went to Chelsea Sunday for a visit with

friends before returning home." The next week the paper published another notice: "Miss Mary Gulager stopped off for a few days visit with friends here while on her way from Chelsea to her home in Tahlequah" (*CP*, 27 January 1906). On 16 February 1906 another local paper reported that "Miss Mary Gulager, of Oolagah, visited Mrs. C. L. Lane the first of the week, leaving for Claremore Wednesday to attend the masquerade ball at that place" (*CR*, 16 February 1906). Mary Gulager graduated from the Cherokee National Female Seminary in Tahlequah on 25 May 1900 (*OCF*, 1:56; Starr, *History of the Cherokee Indians*, 638, 657; *WRFT*, 120, 125; see also *PWR*, 1:200 and n.2).

2. See Review from the *Philadelphia Item*, 27 June 1905, above.

3. Rogers's schedule included stops at the Opera House in Hartford, Conn., the week of 29 January; the Savoy Theatre in Fall River, Mass., the week of 5 February; the Colonial Theatre, Lawrence, Mass., the week of 12 February; and the Imperial Theatre, Brooklyn, the week of 19 February 1906.

4. Cap Lane, who was married to Rogers's sister Maud Lane. The Lanes lived in Chelsea, I.T., where oil was being discovered. The local newspaper reported that "Mr. and Mrs. C. L. Lane drove to the oil fields Tuesday to witness the shooting of a well" (*CR*, 24 November 1905). Possibly Rogers was interested in buying property that could yield oil.

5. On 16 December 1905 Rogers received a contract to play at the Hartford Opera House the week of 29 January 1906. The contract originated from the offices of B. A. Myers at 31 W. Thirty-first Street, New York City. Barney A. Myers was a theatrical manager and booking agent who became an independent agent. H. H. Jennings represented the Hartford theater and signed his name to the contract. Rogers was represented by his agent Mort Shea, who signed Rogers's name and underneath wrote "By MAS." Rogers received $250 for the week (Agreement, Offices of B. A. Meyers, 16 December 1905, OkClaW). The playbill that week at the Hartford Opera House was as follows: Ford and Wilson (America's Foremost Black Face Comedians); The Zazell-Vernon Pantomime Troupe (The European Sensation in "The Elopement"); Bertha Allison (Singing and Dancing Comedienne); Flo Irwin and Walter Hawley (In Their Comedy Sketch "Caught With The Goods"); Will Rogers (Champion Lasso Thrower and Lariat Expert Direct from Keith's New York theatre); Hal Merritt (And His Poster Girls); The Musical Cuttys (America's Greatest Musical Act); John Calvin Pratt (And His Wonderful Performing Dogs) (program, Hartford Opera House, week commencing 29 January 1906, scrapbook A-1, OkClaW). Reviews from the Hartford newspapers continued to compare Rogers's skills with the feats of the cowpuncher (clippings from the *Hartford Daily Courant, Telegram,* and *Evening Post,* scrapbook A-1, OkClaW). Rogers wrote his father from Hartford stating that the weather was warm and sent him $250 in savings (29 January 1906, OkClaW).

6. On 10 January 1906 Rogers had signed a contract to appear at the Savoy Theatre in Fall River, Mass., the week beginning 5 February 1906 and at the Colonial Theatre in Lawrence, Mass., the week commencing 12 February 1906. Both theaters were part of the Casto Circuit, and Al Haynes was the general manager of the Casto Theatre Co. (*BEWHAT*, 1040; Grau, *Business Man in the Amusement World,* 69). The contract was stamped "Al. Haynes by S. K. Hodgdon." Mort Shea signed Rogers's name and inserted underneath his signature "By MAS." Rogers received $225 a week for both engagements and performed twice daily (Casto Circuit Artist's Contract, 10 January 1906, OkClaW). The Savoy Theatre had a seating capacity of 1,200 (*JCGHTG*, 119A). On Rogers's appearance at the Savoy Theatre in Lowell, Mass., see Review from the *Fall River Daily Courant*, 6 February 1906, below.

Excerpt from Review from the *Fall River Daily Courant*
6 February 1906
Fall River, Mass.

Will Rogers, the "Lariat King," has set all the town talking about his wonderfully clever exhibition of rope-throwing and men, women and children will flock to the Savoy to see him. Rogers is a product of the Western plains, and seems hardly to have the strength necessary for the work he does in his slight frame. He keeps up a running comment of talk that hands the audience many laughs. With Buck McKee, another Westerner, and a broncho, Rogers has built a novel and entertaining act. . . .[1]

PD. Printed in the *Fall River Daily Courant,* 6 February 1906. Scrapbook A-1, OkClaW.

1. The playbill described Rogers as "The Western Plainsman and Lariat Thrower." Joining Rogers on the program were the following: Mabel McKinley (The American Soprano); Mr. and Mrs. Mark Murphy (In their Latest Comedy "The Coal Strike"); Sydney Crant (Stories, Songs, and Mimicry); Bessie Valdare Troupe (The Great Bicycling Sextette); Brooks Brothers (Comedy Singers and Talkers); Zay Holland (The Girl With the Violin); and The Kinetograph (Latest in Animated Pictures) (program, Savoy Theatre, week of 5 February 1906, scrapbook A-1, OkClaW). The *New York Dramatic Mirror* called it "one of the best bills of the season" ("Fall River, Mass.," 17 February 1906, 19).

To Clement Vann Rogers
13 February 1906
Lawrence, Mass.

Lawrence Mass.[1]

Feb. 13. 06

Dear Papa.

Did you get that $250.00 I sent you from Hartford, Conn. 2 weeks ago.[2] I have never heard from you   write at once

address Putnam House   N.Y.   as I will be playing in N.Y. next week.

Love to all

Willie

ALS, rc. OkClaW.

1. Rogers was performing at the Colonial Theatre in Lawrence. The following acts were listed on the bill: Bessie Valdare Troupe (The Great Bicycling Sextette); Zae Holland (The Girl With the Violin); Harry Edson and "Doc" (The Dog With the Human Brains and Gold Teeth); Brooks Brothers (Comedy Singers and Talkers); Mr. and Mrs. Mark Murphy (In Their Latest Comedy "The Coal Strike"); Coakley and McBride (Singing, Talking and Dancing Comedians); Will Rogers and his Bronco

(The Western Plainsman and Lariat Thrower); The Kinetograph (Colonial Theatre playbill and advertisement, week of 12 February 1906, scrapbook A-1, OkClaW). Performances at the Colonial were given every afternoon at 2:30 and every evening at 8:15. *Variety* called Rogers and his horse "an interesting pair," while the *New York Dramatic Mirror* reported "packed houses" ("Lawrence, Mass. Colonial," *Variety,* 17 February 1906; "Lawrence, Mass.," *NYDM,* 24 February 1906).

2. Rogers had sent the money in a letter to his father on 29 January 1906 (OkClaW).

To Maud Lane
ca. 20 February 1906
New York, N.Y.

Rogers sent his sister a note on a postcard that had been designed to publicize his act. The card had two photographs of Rogers on the front performing lasso tricks and one picture of him standing rope in hand. Imprinted on the front was "The Greatest Catch in Vaudeville. Compliments of Will Rogers the Larie[a]t Expert."[1] In his note he relates the news that he has been booked for a one-month engagement in Germany.[2]

Dear Sis.

Will be home about Mar 2. or 3rd. for 2 weeks[3]   go to Germany to work a Month.   Sail Mar 21[4]   will see you all   Sallie is coming too.   Sho am *glad*

Love
Willie

APC, rc.

1. In the two roping photographs Rogers is spinning a large loop overhead; the other depicts him on horseback with a huge wedding-ring loop spinning around himself and the horse. A caption explains that Rogers was "Manipulating 90 ft of Rope."

2. On 17 February 1906 *Variety* reported that "Will Rogers, the lariat thrower, has been booked through M. Shea for the Wintergarten in Berlin, opening about April 1. Alex. Steiner completed the arrangements" (p. 4). According to Rogers's friend Louise Henry, Steiner was the "premiere theatrical European booking agent" and had seen Rogers perform at Percy Williams's Orpheum Theatre in Brooklyn (LHM-LHP, 10). She might have meant Hyde and Behman's in Brooklyn or the Imperial, since Rogers did not perform at the Orpheum in 1906. Rogers was appearing at Brooklyn's Imperial Theatre when he wrote the postcard.

On the playbill at Brooklyn's Imperial (formerly the Montauk) Theatre were The Six Peri Sisters (In Novel Japanese and Hungarian Songs and Dances); Chas. Kenna (Presenting His Original One-Man Sketch, "The Street Fakir"); Prelle's Wonderful Dogs (The Most Original Act of Its Kind in the World. Presenting a Miniature Hippodrome Circus); Mlle. Verera (Operatic Prima Donna); Will Rogers (Greatest Lariat and Rope Thrower in Vaudeville); Byers and Herman (In a Sensational Spectacular Pantomime); Harrigan (The Tramp Juggler); Katie Barry and Co. (In a

Musical Comedy by Porter Emerson Browne, Entitled *Just a Joke*); "The Little Black Man" (Shaum Sing Hpoo, the Smallest Man in the World. Height 34 Inches; Weight, 20 Pounds. Presenting an Original Athletic Competition) (Imperial Theatre playbill, week beginning Monday matinee, 19 February 1906, scrapbook A-1, OkClaW).

3. Rogers returned home early on the morning of 7 March (*CP*, 10 March 1906). His engagement at Philadelphia's Casino Theatre ended on 3 March.

4. Rogers would sail on the S.S. *Philadelphia* on 17 March.

Passport Application of Buck McKee
24 February 1906
New York, N.Y.

With their engagement in Germany assured, Rogers and Buck McKee applied for passports.

No. <u>67</u>   Issued <u>7472</u>

UNITED STATES OF AMERICA.

STATE of <u>New York</u>

        } *ss:*

COUNTY of <u>New York</u>

I, <u>Buck Mc Kee,</u> a NATIVE AND LOYAL CITIZEN OF THE UNITED STATES, do hereby apply to the Department of State at Washington for a passport for myself and wife, and my minor children as follows: _____ born at _____ on the ___ day of _____, 1_____, and

_____

In support of the above application, I do solemnly swear that I was born at <u>Oskage Mission,</u> in the State of <u>Kansas,</u> on or about the <u>21st</u> day of <u>April, 1871</u>; that my father is a <u>native</u> citizen of the United States; that I am domiciled in the United States, my permanent residence being at <u>Pawnee,</u> in the State of <u>Oklahoma,</u> where I follow the occupation of <u>actor</u>; that I am about to go abroad temporarily; and that I intend to return to the United States <u>about one year</u> with the purpose of residing and performing the duties of citizenship therein.

OATH OF ALLEGIANCE.

Further, I do solemnly swear that I will support and defend the Constitution of the United States against all enemies, foreign and domestic; that I will bear true faith and allegiance to the same; and that I take this obligation freely, without any mental reservation or purpose of evasion; SO HELP

ME GOD.

Sworn to before me, this 24th day

                      }   Buck McKee

of February 1906
Paul Tausig[1]
    Notary Public.

DESCRIPTION OF APPLICANT.

Age: 35 years.

Stature: 5 feet/8 1/2 inches, Eng.

Forehead: high

Eyes: black

Nose: long

Mouth: smal

Chin: round

Hair: dark brown

Complexion: fair

Face: long

IDENTIFICATION.

New York, February 24th 1906

I hereby certify that I know the above named Buck McKee personally, and know him to be a native born citizen of the United States, and that the facts stated in his affidavit are true to the best of my knowledge and belief.

Will Rogers

[ADDRESS OF WITNESS.] Putnam House
4 ave. 26 st N.Y.

Applicant desires passport sent to following address:

Paul Tausig
104 East 14 St.
New York

PDS, with autograph insertions. OkClaW.

1. Paul Tausig (ca. 1857–1931) was the best known theatrical steamship agent in international show business. His firm, called Paul Tausig and Son, was organized in 1901 and was the oldest agency of its kind. Tausig first had offices at 104 East Fourteenth Street in the heart of New York City's Rialto. Over the years many performers, including Joe Keaton, faithfully used his services, and Tausig was considered to know every important figure in European and American show business. When the center of New York's theatrical life shifted to Times Square, Tausig formed a business partnership with the Times Square Trust Co. and moved his office to its bank building on Seventh Avenue. Tausig died unexpectedly from pneumonia on 1 February 1931. His son and partner, Karl Tausig, subsequently continued the business ("Paul Tausig," *VO*, 2:11 February 1931).

Passport Application of Will Rogers
26 February 1906
New York, N.Y.

On 27 February 1906 Rogers was issued passport no. 7479 from the Department of State signed by Elihu Root, then secretary of state in the Theodore Roosevelt administration. The passport repeated Rogers's physical descriptions as described in this application. It was mailed on 27 February 1906 from Washington, D.C., to Paul Tausig, Esq., at 104 East Fourteenth St., New York, New York.

No. <u>68</u>   Issued <u>7479</u>

UNITED STATES OF AMERICA.

STATE of <u>New York</u>
        } *ss:*
COUNTY of <u>New York</u>

I, <u>Will Rogers,</u> a NATIVE AND LOYAL CITIZEN OF THE UNITED STATES, do hereby apply to the Department of State at Washington for a passport for myself and wife, and my minor children as follows: children as follows:____ born at _____ on the ___ day of _____, 1_____, and _____

In support of the above application, I do solemnly swear that I was born at <u>Claremore,</u> in the State of <u>Indian Territory,</u> on or about the <u>4th</u> day of <u>November, 1879;</u> that my father is a <u>native</u> citizen of the United States; that I am domiciled in the United States, my permanent residence being at <u>Claremore,</u> in the State of <u>Indian Territory,</u> where I follow the occupation of <u>artist;</u> that I am about to go abroad temporarily; and that I intend to return to the United States <u>in about one year</u> with the purpose of residing and performing the duties of citizenship therein.

OATH OF ALLEGIANCE.

Further, I do solemnly swear that I will support and defend the Constitution of the United States against all enemies, foreign and domestic; that I will bear true faith and allegiance to the same; and that I take this obligation freely, without any mental reservation or purpose of evasion; So HELP ME GOD.

Sworn to before me, this 24th day

} <u>Will Rogers</u>

of February 1906
<u>Paul Tausig</u>
       Notary Public.

DESCRIPTION OF APPLICANT.

Age: <u>26</u> years.
Stature: <u>5</u> feet/<u>11</u> inches, Eng.
Forehead: <u>high</u>
Eyes: <u>blue</u>
Nose: <u>flat</u>

Mouth: <u>large</u>
Chin: <u>round</u>
Hair: <u>dark brown</u>
Complexion: <u>fair</u>
Face: <u>long</u>

IDENTIFICATION.

<u>New York, February 26th 1906</u>

I hereby certify that I know the above named <u>Will Rogers</u> personally, and know him to be a native born citizen of the United States, and that the facts stated in his affidavit are true to the best of my knowledge and belief.

<u>William Kasl</u>
[ADDRESS OF WITNESS.] <u>238 East 58 St N.Y.</u>

Applicant desires passport sent to following address:

<u>PAUL TAUSIG</u>
<u>104 EAST 14TH STREET</u>
<u>New York</u>

PDS, with autograph insertions. OkClaW.

Vaudeville Notes
ca. 1 March 1906
Philadelphia, Pa.

Rogers sometimes made notes for his vaudeville act.[1] Compared to his gags about missing his horse with the lasso, these humorous comments are more topical.[2] His one-liners included ethnic jokes based on stereotypes that were common in vaudeville.

Philadelphia, _____ 190

Where you been
down to the old steel works ▲ (City Hall.▲

———

To a Foot Ball Game 3 dislocations and 3 fractures.

———

Bad fix has a knot hole breaking out on his wooden leg.

———

Street Car run over his leg and he give Motorman $100, had rheumatism ▲ in it.▲

———

Cant go to work nothing to do am a Sailor on an airship.

———

You belong to Union no [men?] the Union deport and pulled out. She—I have Union labels on all my clothe   got one on your corset...Im from *Missouri*

———

Brother has new job he is Cond[uc]t[or] on Street-Car.   Well the change will do him good.

———

I'm a Ball player.—Why you ~~cant~~ _are not a_ play ball. Dont have to be to play with u—

———

Put filters on Sprinkling wagons to keep street clean.

———

Walks in his sleep.   aught to be a policeman then.
Policeman have ball team Oh we cant catch anything now.

———

John D.[3] has dollar for every hair in your head.   Yes and we for him ▲ too ▲.

———

Must of been Man and wife dident speak all evening.

———

Right in front of us sat a Man and Woman talking they were Married but not to each other.

———

Sweep dust up in piles wind blows it in your eyes and you go home and wash it out

———

Pay twelve $ for sticking.   dont care which way the wind blows

———

She—Im sorry since I seen you that I married.   He—so am I for your husband   My husband married me for my money   well he earned it.   He was crazy to marry me.—he must of been.

———

Leading lady been to South Dakota 6 times

———

~~He~~ A Man [said?] all the Men was to be cut up.   Well I d like to have your gall.

———

Irish only people who can start a fight without cause

———

Irish make the Money and Jews ~~spend~~ take it from ▲ them ▲

———

When a dutchman dies he's dead but when an Irishman dies you have to sit up and watch him ▲ 3 nights ▲

———

Wherever you go you will find an Irishman if you are lookin for a fighter

———

Have an outside business could live on.   only short time.

AMS, OkClaW. On Marquito Apartments, 118 South 12th St., Philadelphia, letterhead.

1. Rogers composed these notes on the same letterhead stationery (Marquito Apartments in Philadelphia) he used to write Betty Blake on 1 March 1906 (see Will Rogers to Betty Blake, 1 March 1906, below). Thus this document has been dated according to the time he wrote Betty Blake. It is also probable that Rogers might have saved the stationery and written these notes at a later date.

2. See Vaudeville Routine, ca. Summer or Fall 1905, above, and Vaudeville Notes, ca. 19 September 1907, below.

3. John D. Rockefeller.

To Betty Blake
1 March 1906
Philadelphia, Pa.

In the following letter to Betty Blake, Rogers writes about his intention to see her
briefly on his way home. He also discusses his plans to go to Europe.

118 South 12th St.

Philadelphia, <u>Thursday Night</u>

Well I just come back from the show shop and found your letter there and
am afful sorry you are not feeling so well   hope it wont last long

Well I am kicking in my last week in this country for a while   have only 4
more shows to do but I am very uneasy about my foreign *opening* as you never
know how things will go any place[1]   while they all predict a great big hit   *I*
dont   and I do so hate the voyage although it is a little jump to some I have
taken.

Well I finish here Sat night and do you know I cant get a train west until 1
oclock Sunday that will take me clear to St Louis   but it is a fast one and I
will get there at 1 30 Monday eve   then out of there and as you predicted
(How did you know) should get to your place about 7 Tuesday A.M.   it does
seem that trains and boats go *backward.*   There is none going near the time
I want them   Now I have to sail from N.Y. Mar 17.[2]   now if I could get a
boat it might as well be Mar 20. or 21 see   and to go   then I go to England
and *tranship.*   now that will only give me 6 days at home and I wont be able
to stay in your town only for a short time   I did intend to be there Tuesday
and then up to Monett Wednesday A.M.   but that train wont get me there in
time to catch the West bound and I really must be home *Chelsea* at my sisters
Wednesday on the Noon train[3]   so all I see is get that 9.20 to Monett[4]
Tuesday Night   But I think you will get an ample sufficiency of me in that
time   Oh I have studied time tables and steam ship sheets till I am black in
the face

Now if I can catch a freight, Local, or something later so I can get to
Monett by 9.35 Wednesday A.M. it will be the *Candy Kid*

My horse and Man go back to N.Y. and sail on Mar 10.   direct to
Hamburg then by train to Berlin   he will land in time to give the pony a rest
as it is hard on a horse   they have to stand up all the way over.

I should get there about 3 or 4 days before I open[5]

And say   oh my   there is more rough weather than you ever heard of just
now ships all late   having rough passages (Now I am not saying this to scare

anyone) for I believe a rough sea voyage is considered the thing for coughs, colds, noises in the head and *overwork*

Say never mind meeting that early train for if I do make it why at that hour when I emerge I dont think I should be ~~in a~~ very presentable   for they wont get me out of bed till the train stops and then me off with about half of the old rags on and the other half in course of construction, but I will be raisin a disturbance at your door as soon as I displace a portion of soil gathered from many states,   full of a small feed   interview a barber (and say that town aint prohibition is it)   Well I should arrive somewhere around the 9 hour   That is if I have a whole lot of good luck.

Now that big *9* might be a little *premature* for your convenience for thats a milk mans date   but look out about then and you'll see a dark Man coming with a bundle (of Music)   Nothing worse I hope (or have you all got that song there   if not this requires a dictionary   Now I have you several pieces of music here   some late others not so late   still they may be there   but they are ones I have heard and like and think you would too   Anyway I will bring you a *supply.*

if I knew just what you all had there I would know better what to bring

Now see here Betty   Nothing doing on the old entertaining thing.   I am just coming down to spend *a good old day with you* and require no entertaining and meeting folks and all that.   Pull through in your same way and dont you *dare* put yourself out one bit.

Well I *must stop*   hope all plans turn out O.K.   and I see you as expected

My best regards

Will.

ALS, rc. OkClaW. On Marquito Apartments, 118 South 12th St., Philadelphia, letterhead.

1. Rogers was finishing his engagement at Philadelphia's Casino Theatre, which had begun on Monday, 26 February, and concluded on Saturday, 3 March 1906. The Casino was a burlesque theater on the Eastern Wheel Circuit and had a seating capacity of 2,295 (*JCGHTG*, 59). Rogers was an added attraction in the program and was booked to "strengthen" the New York Stars Burlesque Co. show (*Variety*, 3 March 1906). To publicize Rogers's engagement, the theater manager and advance man staged a parade with a "basket carriage drawn through the city by four 'prop' horses and followed by ten men with banners announcing the engagement of Mr. Rogers, who followed behind on his bronco" (*Variety* clipping, scrapbook A-1, OkClaW). Three hours after the parade, the theater was sold out for the entire week. Rogers played with the same artists he had performed with at Brooklyn's Star Theatre, the week of 4 September 1905, and Brooklyn's Gayety Theatre, the week of 11 September 1905. The playbill was as follows: New York Stars (In the One-Act Farce Comedy, *Society Swells*); Campbell and Caulfield (Irish Comedians); Faust Trio (Vic. Jerome,

Lottie Freemont, John Russ); Raymond and Clark (Rapid Fire Conversationalists); Majestic Musical Four (Collins, Terrill Brothers and Simon); Will Rogers (The Sensation of the Season, Expert Lassoist); Catharine Taylor (Late of Bostonians. Novelty Singing); *Easy Doesit* (Funny One-Act Comedy) (Casino Theatre playbill, scrapbook A-1, OkClaW).

2. On 17 March 1906 Rogers left on the S.S. *Philadelphia,* the same ship he had taken to England in March 1902. It was listed as an outgoing ship set to sail at midnight (*NYT,* 17 March 1906).

3. Rogers arrived in Chelsea around 10 A.M. on Wednesday, 7 March (*CP,* 10 March 1906). One reason Rogers wanted to be in Chelsea was that his sister Sallie McSpadden and her family had returned from California on Monday, 5 March. They lived on the outskirts of Chelsea, and Clement Vann Rogers went to see his daughter and family that day. A family reunion was thus expected. Rogers wrote Betty Blake: "Well I got to Chelsea the next day at 10. and all the folks were at one of my sisters and we did the big reunion act for 6 days" (to Betty Blake, 26 March 1906, below; see also *CM,* 9 March 1906; *CP,* 10 March 1906; *CR,* 9 March 1906).

4. Monett is located in southwest Missouri, thirty-five miles southeast of Joplin (*WNGD,* 780). It is about forty miles north of Rogers, Ark., where Betty Blake lived, and ninety miles east of Claremore. Betty Blake would make the same trip in the summer of 1906 and wrote: "Chelsea was hardly a hundred miles from my home in Arkansas, but I had to take a roundabout way to get there. Leaving on a slow train at four-thirty in the morning and changing to another slow train at Monett, Missouri" (Rogers, *Will Rogers,* 94).

5. Rogers opened at Berlin's Wintergarten Theatre on 1 April. A contract dated 28 March 1900 was issued for his performances from 1 April to 30 April. Mort Shea signed for Rogers and received a 10 percent commission from Rogers's monthly salary of 3,700 marks (Wintergarten Contract, 28 March 1906, OkClaW).

Article from the *Claremore Progress*
17 March 1906
Claremore, I.T.

Will Rogers spent several days in Claremore this week with his father, C. V. Rogers. He left Tuesday night for Germany for a three months stay, after which he will return to continue his work on the stage in the east. His horse was shipped last week. Will's many friends here wish him a pleasant voyage and much success.[1]

PD. Printed in *CP,* 17 March 1906. Scrapbook A-1, OkClaW.

1. On 16 March 1906 the *Claremore Messenger* also announced Rogers's departure and his plans to travel to Berlin. On 17 March 1906 the *New York Dramatic Mirror* listed Rogers's engagement dates at the Wintergarten in Berlin as 1–30 April 1906 (p. 21).

3. BERLIN'S WINTERGARTEN AND LONDON'S PALACE

March 1906–July 1906

Program cover, London's Palace Theatre of Varieties, where Rogers performed in 1906 and 1907. *(OkClaW)*

EXCITED BY THE OPPORTUNITY TO PERFORM IN EUROPE, ROGERS BOARDED THE S.S. *Philadelphia* on 17 March 1906 and embarked for France. Four years earlier, he had sailed to England with Dick Parris on the same steamer, a trip that took him to Argentina, South Africa, Australia, and New Zealand. In South Africa he joined Texas Jack's Wild West Show and in Australia the Wirth Brothers' Circus. When he went to Europe for a second time, he was a first-year vaudevillian on his way to perform in two of Europe's most famous theaters, London's Palace and Berlin's Wintergarten.

Rogers's lariat tricks with a horse on stage promised to appeal to European audiences who, like many Americans, were captivated by the current cowboy vogue and shared in the romanticization of the West. William Cody's Buffalo Bill's Wild West and other shows were extremely popular in Europe. By coincidence, Cody's extravaganza of the western experience was touring Europe during the time Rogers was abroad. He may have either seen or participated in the show in Vienna around 14 June.

It was not unusual for top American vaudevillians to perform in Europe. Indeed, there was considerable transatlantic activity, with European variety artists touring the major U.S. circuits and American artists appearing in British music halls and variety theaters on the Continent. English variety stars would typically play in New York, Chicago, and San Francisco, and then continue their tour in Australia. In New York and European capitals international talent agents organized the crisscrossing paths of American and European vaudeville performers. Also, American theater owners had either offices or representatives in the principal cities of Europe. Rogers's contract for the Wintergarten involved his agent Mort Shea as well as Alex Steiner, the Berlin theater's foreign representative.[1] American theatrical agents made frequent trips abroad in search of talent. William Morris, for example, arranged for the Scottish star Harry Lauder to perform in New York to sold-out audiences. Willie Hammerstein frequently engaged European acts for the Victoria Theatre; indeed, sometimes they made up half the program.

H. B. Marinelli, a former vaudeville contortionist, was a top international agent who had offices in New York, Paris, London, and Berlin. His World Agency claimed that it booked artists in Europe, the United States, South

America, Africa, and Australia, and guaranteed them a global tour of three to four years.[2] Marinelli brought to the United States British music-hall head-liners such as Vesta Tilley, Marie Lloyd, Lillie Langtry, and Vesta Victoria. He obtained European engagements for the dancer Ruth St. Denis and the for-mer chorine Evelyn Nesbit Thaw.

Prone to seasickness, Rogers wrote Betty Blake that after five days of rough seas he thought he would "die." "But I stuck it out. . . . and that Ocean was certainly having a revolution most all the way."[3] Rogers arrived at the French port of Cherbourg on 25 March and proceeded by train to Paris. He stayed at the elegant Grand Hôtel where "*Champagne* flows like water" and attended what he called "the swellest variety show." Rogers was enthralled with the French capital, its night life, crowded boulevards, and delicious food—"the best cooked stuff I ever eat." Paris, he wrote, was a "wide open place" with "no laws and especially of morality." The women he found "very well groomed," but the men, with curled mustaches, dressed disgracefully. "Why any Mut in America has them skinned a mile."[4]

Rogers reached Berlin in time for the opening of his act at the Wintergarten Theatre on 1 April. There he met up with Buck McKee (who, along with the horse Teddy, had taken a different steamer to Hamburg). The Wintergarten was the most famous vaudeville theater in Germany, perhaps, as Rogers wrote, "the best class variety theatre in Europe."[5] Vaudeville was an extremely popular form of entertainment in Germany, and its capital Berlin was an exciting center of culture. The grand boulevard, Unter den Linden, was the focal point of the city and led to the Arch of Triumph at the Brandenburg Gate, beyond which was the well-known Siegessäule in the cen-ter of the large Tiergarten park. The headquarters of banks and companies and elegant department stores lined the Leipzigerstrasse and the Friedrichstrasse. Rogers was enthralled by the city's flourishing night life: "It seems that it is a fact here that people dont sleep. . . . everything is wide open all night."[6] Rogers confessed to Betty Blake that he never went to bed before eight or ten in the morning.

Like Keith and Albee's theaters, the Wintergarten was elegantly furnished and catered to the middle and upper classes. Here the best international vaudeville stars performed. During his one-month engagement Rogers received excellent reviews from Berlin critics.

In the afternoon Rogers exercised his horse in the Tiergarten, where he encountered Kaiser Wilhelm II on horseback. "Oh he is a dandy good fellow," Rogers wrote Betty Blake.[7]

While in Berlin, Rogers received the news that he had a second European

Autograph photograph of Rogers *(center)* and friends sent to Louise Henry, probably from London, May–June 1906. Inscribed: "We are *laughing* but we aint happy–there's somebody Missing The 'Hard Luck Gang.' All join me in sending *Love* and all want you to join." *(Laurie Weltz Private Collection, New York City)*

engagement at London's Palace Theatre, beginning 7 May. Like the Wintergarten, the Palace Theatre of Varieties was considered one of Europe's leading theaters that offered acts from all over the world. It catered to what Rogers called "the very swellest London society people."[8] Rogers's lariat act with his horse Teddy and Buck McKee received rave reviews, and he was held over for extra weeks until 9 June. One critic commented that it was "easily the best novelty act that has been in London in a long time, and it is going some when a Palace audience can be made to shout bravo, and more than once too."[9]

This was Rogers's second visit to England, and compared to Berlin he found it "slow." A highlight of his stay was his special performance on the polo grounds at the Ranelagh Club, with King Edward VII supposedly in the audience. After his performance Rogers was presented with a silver cup.

When he finished his engagement at the Palace, Rogers went on to Italy by way of Vienna and spent several days in Rome. Reaching Naples, he sailed for home on 22 June 1906 aboard the S.S. *König Albert*. Rogers arrived in New York City on the Fourth of July and from there traveled home to Claremore and Chelsea. Rogers's visit and his European tour made news in the local papers. "Mr. Rogers is of international fame," proclaimed the *Chelsea Reporter.* The *Claremore Messenger* referred to him as the "World's Champion Lassoer."[10] With the knowledge that he was now a hometown celebrity and a name known to audiences in London and Berlin, Rogers prepared for a long vaudeville tour on the Keith Circuit.

1. In his book *Vaudeville,* Joe Laurie, Jr., wrote: "One of the famous characters on Broadway in those days was Doc Steiner, a vaude agent with a thick German accent that matched his thick eyeglasses" (p. 386).

2. Rogers's vaudeville journal was published by Marinelli's agency. On Marinelli see *EV,* 335, 494–95; *GHNTD,* 561; Gilbert, *American Vaudeville,* 230, 247; Grau, *Business Man in the Amusement World,* 94; Laurie, *Vaudeville,* 37, 133; Leavitt, *Fifty Years in Theatrical Management,* 269–70; *NYT,* 8 January 1924.

3. Will Rogers to Betty Blake, 26 March 1906, below.

4. Will Rogers to Betty Blake, 26 March 1906, below.

5. Will Rogers to Betty Blake, ca. 8 April 1906, below.

6. Will Rogers to Betty Blake, 17 April 1906, below. For a description of Berlin and its culture, see Tuchman, *Proud Tower,* 353–55.

7. Will Rogers to Betty Blake, 17 April 1906, below.

8. Will Rogers to Betty Blake, 10 May 1906, below.

9. Unidentified clipping from Will Rogers's Scrapbook, 12 May 1906, below.

10. *CR,* 20 July 1906; *CM,* 20 July 1906, below.

To Betty Blake
26 March 1906
Paris, France

Before the engagement at the Wintergarten Theatre in Berlin,[1] Rogers stopped in Paris, where he wrote the following letter to Betty Blake.

Le <u>Mar 26</u> 190<u>6</u>

Polly vue Francaise.

Wee Wee   yah, yah.   I dont know a *damn* word anybodys saying.   But *Pal of Mine* I sho do know that I am in *Paree*   and old hand   *she* is certainly the Goods   All I regret is you are not here if we wouldent go the pace *that kills*

From present indications I dont think the old Hamlet has been at all *over-ated* as to her speed for they do sho travel on 2 nothing.

Its got N.Y. whipped to a whisper for continuous performances and never stopping and all the other joints I ever saw *shun* 40 ways from the jack and take in the lookout.

I did when last I saw you intend going by London but on the boat I got up against a good bunch and decided to come by France instead and up to now havent had *time* to regret

Well now to start in where I left you last which do seem a long time ago *Kid* (and thats no Paris booze you hear speaking either)

Say that was a lonely two hours I did put in walking up and fro on that *lousy* Rogers platform that Night and you knew all about railroading[2]   why you are the Kandy Kid *stawler* to put me on a dead one or else you are the rottenest railroad guide in all the Ozarks.   I hated you like a bull dog does a tramp.

Well I got to Chelsea the next day at 10.   and all the folks were at one of my sisters and we did the big reunion act for 6 days   only went to Claremore once and that was to lodge to get initiated into the Masons[3]   oh I am one of the hands now   Well we did have a good old time   just the family for the whole week and I kinder hated to put forth on this ramble but then back to old N.Y. town and bid all the young gang so long (and found a *mighty* nice little letter there from a Pal) which kinder done my old heart good till I got over here and I might have a bit more news   That little letter was mighty consoling for you know *dear* its kinder lonesome when you shove out on the old blue and leave all behind   and not with a soul you know and it made me feel good to know that I at least had one good old Pal that wished me a safe return and I am more thankful for it than you will ever imagine

Well we put out and sick   oh louie louie   I thought die I should   but I stuck it out   but it lasted till Wednesday afternoon (sailed Saturday)   then I got a bite to eat down that by some miracle that couldent find its way up again and I done pretty fair the rest of the way   and oh that Ocean was certainly having a revolution most all the way   Well we got to Cherburg France Sunday Morning early and went ashore and took a special train for Paris   about 7 hours and   oh the pretty sights en route would pay on[e] for the trip   oh it was grand   got to Paris Sunday afternoon and Sunday is the day of days   oh I never seen such a mass of people as are out on the Boulevards on a Sunday. I have been about some bit   you got to hand it to Paris   for a wide open place there seems to be no laws and especially of morality   when the kinder jar me they are going some   but I must advise they kinder did   but then its all to be expected here   thats Paris.   Stage Women aint one two one. with these for paint and make up   oh how they do *strut*   you see some very well groomed women and offul pretty dresses but the Men   they just seem to be a disgrace to appear in their get ups with the women   why they havent the 1st idea of dress   there is absolutely no fashions   they just curl their mustache and put on all they have got   why any Mut in America has them skinned a mile.

And how they do sit and drink at Cafe's with the tables right out on the sidewalk   they seem to have nothing else to do.

Well I am certainly going some   in with a good gang   we are at one of the swellest Hotels[4] here and *Champagne* flows like water   we took in the swellest variety show[5] last night   where I will probably play if I take an engagement there later on.

But say the *Grub* it might be because I pay for it that it is so good   but on the dead   it is the best cooked stuff I ever eat   when you can find a guy that can savee enough to know what you want   oh it has made an offul hit with me   they do know how to *cook*.

I wired to Berlin yesterday to see if my pony had got there but they say *no* he is now two or three days overdue and I am a bit uneasy and will leave here tomorrow direct for Berlin   still all the boats have had rough passages and are more or less late.

If they had landed and anything had happened to the pony why the Man would have wired the Garden   I know they are at sea yet

They tell me Berlin is as swift as this and then some   but I will quiet down up there   Wont know a thing about how long I will be over here will after a week or so more[6]

I want to put in 3 or 4 weeks when I am not working traveling and seeing several different places

Heres a post card picture of the ship which by the way is the same one I and Dick Parris come over on 4 years ago.

Well I will close   please dont think hard of me for not writing sooner but I was only waiting till I landed   did you get that Bill Bailey song I sent you[7]

I will write you after I open and tell you all.   Now listen Kid write to me often for its mighty good to get your letters.   Be good and dont hand out too much of that *Con* of yours to all those guys.

My very best to all the folks.   All yours.   Bill

Wintergarten
Berlin

ALS, rc. OkClaW. On Grand Hotel, 12 Boulevard des Capucines, Paris, letterhead.

1. The Wintergarten was one of the most famous theaters in the world, and its history is intimately connected to the popularity of the metropolitan and international variety show. The origins of the Wintergarten can be traced back to the popular Promenaden Park at the center of Berlin, an attractive area for families to relax and enjoy themselves in a restaurant and to hear music. Here in 1880 the Hotel Central, the biggest hotel in Berlin, was built, attracting guests from all over the world. It was noted for its exquisite service and lavish Wintergarten, a gigantic hall covered with a glass dome that featured a pleasant garden where the hotel guests could enjoy tropical and exotic plants, springs, and waterworks.

In 1884 a concert podium was erected, and regular live entertainment was offered. Increasingly, the Wintergarten attracted audiences through performances of extravagant soirees, balls, and exhibitions. In 1886 the Hungarian impresario Julius Baron organized nightly variety performances with the goal of establishing the Wintergarten as the premier theater in Europe. Baron was the first person to forge a link between vaudeville artistry and bourgeois society. He and his partner, the actor Franz Dorn, rented the hall and added a small stage frame. The Wintergarten soon became the most elegant theater in Berlin; its fame extended well beyond Germany. International variety stars, including dancers, singers, acrobats, and clowns, performed there. The Wintergarten was a prime variety theater attraction through the early twentieth century.

In 1928 a new phase began when the Wintergarten was completely modernized and equipped with the largest and most technically sophisticated stage in Europe. Critics, however, began complaining that eroticism was replacing the high artistic acts. The Nazi era brought enforced politicization and censorship, causing the shows to lose their luster. The rapid demise of the Wintergarten and other German variety theaters had begun. By 1933 the Wintergarten had declined in popular appeal and was losing money; its existence was dependent on a large subsidy. On 21 June 1944 the Wintergarten was destroyed in a bomb attack (*50 Jahre Wintergarten*; Günter, *Geschichte des Variétés*, 144–48; Jelavich, *Berlin Cabaret*, 249–50).

2. The town of Rogers was located on the St. Louis and San Francisco (Frisco) railway line; it was named after Captain C. W. Rogers, vice president and general manager of the railroad. Several of Betty Blake's relatives worked for the railroad, including her brothers John and Sandy. Betty Blake herself once worked as a billing clerk at the Frisco station in Jenny Lind, Ark. (see *PWR*, 1:531–33).

3. At a meeting of the Masons on 13 March, the night he left Claremore, Rogers "was initiated into the mysteries of the 3rd degree" (*CP*, 17 March 1906). According to a report in the *Claremore Progress*, Rogers first became a Mason around 7 February 1905 (*HRC*, 28). Freemasonry began in Indian Territory on 9 November 1853, when a charter was granted to the Flint Lodge by the Grand Lodge of Arkansas. Other early lodges were formed at the old Creek Agency and Doaksville. The Grand Lodge of Indian Territory was organized in 1873. The Grand Lodge granted dispensation to the Oologah Lodge on 8 November 1906 and a charter on 14 August 1907. The Masons in Claremore operated a school (Dale and Wardell, *History of Oklahoma*, 533; *History of Oologah*, 41–42). Rogers was very proud of belonging to the Masons. He sent a post-card to Betty Blake on 16 April 1908 with a picture of the Scottish Rite Masonic Temple in McAlester, Okla. In a letter to her the next day he wrote, "Well I am a *Mason   Are you   *and I tell you it is great and it should make me a lot better boy" (Will Rogers to Betty Blake, 17 April 1908, below).

4. The Grand Hôtel where Rogers resided was among the city's largest and most luxurious establishments, with 800 rooms. Baedeker's 1907 guide to the city listed it among "hotels of the highest class." It was located at the point where the Boulevard des Capucines crosses the Place de l'Opéra. The hotel was adjacent to the magnificent Opéra, France's renowned theater, designed by Charles Gaunier and built between 1861 and 1874. On the ground floor of the hotel was the famous Café de la Paix (Baedeker, *Paris and Environs*, 3, 78–79).

5. There were two variety theaters near his hotel, the Théâtre du Vaudeville and the Olympia. But he might also have attended a show at the Palace Theatre or the Folies-Bergère (Baedeker, *Paris and Environs*, 32, 34, 77).

6. A contract for Rogers's engagement at the Wintergarten for the entire month of April was not issued until 28 March 1906.

7. The popular song "Bill Bailey, Won't You Please Come Home" was written in 1902 with words and music by Hughie Cannon. The song was first popularized in vaudeville by the African American singer Harry Brown. Later, such artists as Pearl Bailey, Sarah Vaughn, and Louis Armstrong revived the song (Cohen-Stratyner, ed., *Popular Music, 1900–1919*, 34).

Wintergarten Program and Excerpts from Reviews
ca. 6 April 1906
Berlin, Germany

PROGRAMM.
Freitag, 6. April 1906

Anfang der Vorstellung 8 Uhr.
Ouverture[1]

2

5 BELLATZER-SISTERS
Gymnastischer Act[2]

[3]
ROBERTUS UND WILFREDO
Balljongleure[3]

[4]
PROFESSOR THERESES
Komisch-Hypnotischer Act[4]

[5]
MARGUERITE BROADFOOTE
Englische Sängerin[5]

[6]
DE BIÈRE
Zauberkünstler[6]

7
DIE BAGGESEN'S
Komische Jongleure[7]

[8]
ALEXIA
Pariser Tänzerin[8]

9
WILL ROGERS
Lassowerfer
Assistirt von Mr. Buck McKee
Herr Rogers wird u. a. durch einen Wurf gleidizeitig Pferd
und Reiter mit je einem Lasso fesseln.[9]

[10]
TORTAJADA
Spanische Tänzerin und Sängerin.[10]

[11]
"KÖNIG DOLLAR"
Balletszene, ausgeführt von der
John Tiller—Gesellschaft. London[11]

[12]
DIE 2 SANDWINAS
Handstandkünstler[12]

[13]
DE DIO
Phantasietänzerin[13]

Der Biograph[14]

From. ▲ different.▲ Berlin Papers.[15]

Very unique is the performance of the lasso thrower Will Rogers who catches his companion Mr. Buck McKee with complete confidence whether he simply walks on foot or sits high on a horse—childhood days when the mind was filled with romanticism about Indians are revived with this show.

DeBiere, the fabulously skilled Will Rogers, Therefes with his comic act.

The highlight of the program is definitely the lasso thrower Will Rogers who with his lasso fetters his partner and his galloping horse with the most graceful knots. So that dance in the Wintergarten is not given short shrift. . . .

. . . fantasies before the eye, however the climax of the evening constituted Parisian whirl dancer Alexia and the lasso thrower Will Rogers, assisted by Mr. Buck McKee. We definitely do not want to describe the shows of these two numbers in too much detail lest the curiosity of the audience should be stilled even before it has seen the April program. The biograph as always ended the exceedingly abundant program with an interesting presentation.

. . . in the truest sense of the word dancing in the air, while Will Rogers and McKee offered amazing things as lasso throwers. The ballet dances "King [Dollar"] performed by the Londoner John Tiller company. . . .

. . . always welcome guests in Berlin are greeted with the greatest friendliness with their present debut. New for Berlin and very interesting was the American cowboy Will Rogers who, assisted by Mr. Buck McKee, introduced himself as a lasso thrower with unfailing certainty and executed a series of original tricks with his lasso. A very pretty, brilliantly costumed ballet was performed by the John Tiller company. . . .

. . . fantasy dancer Mademoiselle De Dio enchanted with various delightful and resplendent dances. We also mention the lasso thrower Bill Rogers and Buck McKee who presented true to life a piece of authentic "western life" or rather "life in the Plains," in which of course the typical "bucking horse" wasn't missing, further the comic-hypnotic act of the professor. . . .

Of particular appeal is the performance of the lasso thrower Will Rogers who catches horse and horseman with his inextricable nooses. The gorgeous ballet "King Dollar" of the. . . .

PD. Wintergarten Program and unidentified clippings, ca. 6 April 1906. Scrapbook A-1, OkClaW. Translated from the German by Sylvia Kratzer.

1. (Friday, 6 April 1906 Beginning of the Show 8 P.M. Overture).
2. (5 Bellatzer-Sisters Gymnastic Act).
3. (Robertus and Wilfredo Ball Jugglers). These jugglers were well known for returning balls by reverse english (Laurie, *Vaudeville*, 26).
4. (Professor Thereses Comic-hypnotic Act).
5. (Marguerite Broadfoote English Singer). Broadfoote first performed as an actress and in musical comedy, and in the late 1890s became a pantomime artist. She turned to music-hall entertainment while on tour in South Africa. Back in London she became a successful singer of popular songs in British music halls. She appeared at the Royal Command Performance at London's Palace Theatre on 1 July 1912 (Mander and Mitchenson, *British Music Hall*, picture caption nos. 163, 230).
6. (De Bière Magician). Born in Germany, Arnold De Bière (1878–1934) was a prominent illusionist. He came to the United States as a youngster and at an early age started in small-time variety theaters. De Bière was well known in England, Europe, and Australia, where he toured extensively. At one time he had his own show with lavish scenery. He was best known for several tricks, The Egg Bag, The Clock Dial, and The Ten-Ichi Thumb Tie. A spectator once described the climax of his act, called The Sculptor's Dream or Leda and the Swan, during a 1912 performance at the Tivoli Theatre in Melbourne: "De Bière in sculptor's beret and smock, and showing great weariness, stretched himself on a couch close to the wings. Soon he slumbered. When a white clad female, presumably a dream form, approached the couch, he seized her. She melted away leaving only her robe in his hands. Awake now, and apparently greatly refreshed by his exceedingly brief sleep, De Bière moved to the bench, and back to the audience, commenced modelling with big lumps of white clay. He was a quick worker—in almost no time he had evolved Leda, the Swan and the chariot. Immediately following our realization of the fact that the girl was alive, the long bench, operating like a pantomime transformation, converted itself into a beautiful illuminated lake scene" (Waller, *Magical Nights at the Theatre*, 183). De Bière made his home in England, where he died on 5 August 1934.
7. (The Baggesens Comical Jugglers). Joe Laurie, Jr., wrote: "The Baggesens were a swell comedy act, juggled and broke plates, and were the first ones we ever saw do the flypaper bit (while holding an armful of plates which his wife throws to him, his other hand gets stuck on flypaper, and he tries to get rid of it while holding about 100 dishes; well, just imagine)!" (*Vaudeville*, 26).
8. (Alexia Parisian Dancer). Born in France, Alexia was raised in Russia and thus was often described as a French-Russian dancer. Alexia was a Wintergarten regular known for her pantomime La Dance Tornado. She was a success in Europe for fifteen years before she made her American debut at Hammerstein's Paradise Roof Garden in 1908. She was an immediate hit, and audiences especially enjoyed her creation called The She Devil and the Demon, a diabolical scene with dance and transformation.

Sime Silverman praised her performance in *Variety*: "Alexia may be an acrobat, whirl-wind or contortional dancer, whichever term one is pleased to apply, or she may be called all, which she is. A brunette, with much personality, all the little tricks of the acrobatic, whirlwind or contortional dancer are brought into play, and the effect produced brings the applause" (Alexia clippings file, NN-L-BRTC).

9. (Will Rogers Lasso Thrower Assisted by Mr. Buck McKee. Mr. Rogers will catch a galloping horse and rider through a throw with a lasso.)

10. (Tortajada. Spanish Dancer and Singer). La Tortajada, whose real name was Consuelo T. Hernandez, was a famous flamenco dancer. She was a regular headliner at the Wintergarten and other major European variety theaters. She and her band of Spanish Troubadours were on the opening bill of Koster and Bial's New Music Hall on 28 August 1893. She retired in 1911 and died at the age of ninety on 7 February 1957 in Granada, Spain (Brown, *History of the New York Stage*, 3:574; *VO*, 5:27 February 1957).

11. ("King Dollar" Ballet scenes, direct from the John Tiller Co. London). John Tiller, who came from Manchester, England, was a noted choreographer and dancing master who founded a school of dance that became an important training ground for dancers. Tiller specialized in teaching teams of women to dance in unison with a high-kicking, long-legged precision style. The Tiller Girls were popular in England and often performed at London's Palace Theatre, including a Royal Command Performance at the theater in 1912. They were also well known on the Continent, and the Tiller troupe became a regular attraction at the Folies Bergère in Paris. In the United States they performed in several editions of the *Ziegfeld Follies*. Rogers appeared with The Tiller Girls in the *Follies* of 1922 and 1924 and the spring edition of the 1925 *Follies*. Tiller died on 22 October 1922, but The Tiller Girls continued for many years thereafter. Tiller's company influenced the style of the Radio City Music Hall Rockettes (Busby, *British Music Hall*, 169; *EV*, 98; Short, *Fifty Years of Vaudeville*, 131; Ziegfeld and Ziegfeld, *Ziegfeld Touch*, 102, 117, 252–53, 257, 258).

12. (The 2 Sandwinas Handstand Artists). The two Sandwinas were Kati Sandwina Heymann (1884–1952), billed as the "world's strongest woman," and her husband, Max Heymann (b. ca. 1881). According to her husband, Kati Sandwina was born in a Gypsy wagon in Essen, Germany. Her father was a circus strong man, and her mother Johanna was apparently also a circus performer. She began her professional career at the age of two doing handstands on her father's arm. She soon became a child acrobat and trapeze artist with her family's Sandwina Circus in Germany. At age fourteen she started performing feats of strength. As part of Sandwina's circus act, her father offered 100 marks to any person who could pin her shoulders to the mat in a wrestling match. Her future husband, then an unemployed acrobat, volunteered and was whirled over her head and tossed flat on his back. Lying on the mat in pain, Heymann recalled: "I knew that I had never before been in the presence of such love-liness. Before I realized what I was saying, the words were out: 'I love you'. . . . Then she lifted me in her arms as though I was a toy doll and carried me inside her dressing tent. . . . Before the day was out, we decided to get married" ("I Married the World's Strongest Woman," clipping, Kati Sandwina file, NN-L-BRTC). The pair toured with leading circuses all over the world and gave command performances before many presidents and royalty. Besides her vaudeville appearances with the Keith and Orpheum Circuits, she was a regular with the Ringling Brothers and Barnum and Bailey Circuses. The 6-foot, 210-pound strongwoman with 14-inch biceps became well known for her spectacular feats of strength. These included tossing her 160-pound husband into the air and holding him in one hand; balancing a 1,200-pound cannon

on her shoulders; holding a merry-go-round on her chest while 6 adults rode around; balancing an iron bar with 40 men in the air; supporting a wooden bridge while 40 men and 4 horses rode across it, followed by an automobile with 6 passengers; and lying on 500 sharp nails while a 220-pound anvil on her stomach was pounded with a series of blows from 10-pound hammers. "I watch for each blow and make hard the back muscles," she once explained ("Kate Sandwina, 58, Still Harder Than Nails, Bounces on a Bed of Them to Prove It," clipping, Kati Sandwina file, NN-L-BRTC). Kati Sandwina also held several weightlifting records for women. When she retired in 1941, she and her husband operated a bar and grill in Queens, N.Y., and frequently they would perform for customers. Ill since 1949, she died on 21 January 1952. "They all said she had the strength of 10 men," recalled her husband shortly after her death. "None of them knew—as I did—that she also had the warmth and loveliness of 100 women" (Sandwina clipping file, NN-L-BRTC; Locke env. 2007, NN-L-RLC).

13. (De Dio Fantasy Dancer). Marietta de Dio was an Austrian singer and dancer who made her American debut on 10 September 1894 at Koster and Bial's New Music Hall. Her appearance caused a rift between Adam Bial, the theater's owner, and Oscar Hammerstein, who was his partner. Hammerstein felt she really did not have much talent and one night hissed while she performed. His behavior accentuated a rift between him and Bial, and soon thereafter Hammerstein severed his relationship with Bial (Brown, *History of the New York Stage*, 3:575; *EV*, 291; Gilbert, *American Vaudeville*, 191–92).

14. Two Biograph films were presented, *Der Treue Hund* ("The Loyal Dog") and *Eine Heirathsannounce* ("Marriage Announcement") (Wintergarten programs, 19 and 28 April 1906, OkClaW). The Wintergarten claimed to have presented the first official public film showing in Europe on 1 November 1895—*Das Bioskop*, invented by Max Skladanowsky (1863–1939). But this fact is disputed, as the public had already seen the Edison kinetoscope and the Anscutz tachyscope (Ceram, *Archaeology of the Cinema*, 146–48; *50 Jahre Wintergarten*, 77–79; Musser, *Emergence of Cinema*, 168, 345–49).

15. Rogers wrote in these words in pen as an introduction to the clippings in his scrapbook.

To Betty Blake
ca. 8 April 1906
Berlin, Germany

Hello Pal

Say just landed   quite a cute *card* from down your way   Say this is a photo of the *joint*   Now you see all that front on that stage out there is where I work   Things are going all O.K. but I dont like it here at all and am booking no more work.   Will see you soon   Write   yours

Bill[1]

Keep these and I will send you a lot.[2]

This is considered the best class variety theatre in Europe.[3]

APC, rc. Picture postcard.[4] OkClaW.

1. Written in the right margin of the card and underneath the picture.
2. Written in the left margin of the card.
3. Written in the top margin of the card.
4. The postcard pictured the interior of the Wintergarten Theatre, Berlin (captioned "Gruss aus dem Wintergarten, Berlin"), with autograph text written around the margins of the picture. Postmarked received, Rogers, Ark., 19 April 1906.

To Betty Blake
17 April 1906
Berlin, Germany

Berlin.
April. 17.

My Dear Dear Betty

Good old Pal   your letter of April 1st landed this morning and say old hand I could just love you to death for writing it for I hadent got anything from out west since I come

Well things are going on nicely   half of the month has passed and it wont be long till I am done here   I am still the hit of the Bill and have been offered several engagements but I got a letter from my N.Y. agent and he says No, to come straight back and then we can book the work for future time at a big salary.

My agent is coming over himself in a few weeks and he will fix it all up   he already has   me booked in America for 36 weeks all in the East   as you see Im all fixed but I am coming home July and August and start work in September[1]

I am going by London on my way home and may put my act on there just to show it for a week at one of the best theatres[2]

Well this is the fastest 2 weeks I ever went in my life and thats saying something   It seems that it is a fact here that people dont sleep   why I never get in till 8 or 9 or 10 in the morning   everything is wide open all night and we just go from one Cafe to another and all over town then in a Cab   and drive awhile and then out and drink and its that day and night.

There is quite a bunch of English girls[3] and a few of us boys and I dident think it was possible to go such a clip   oh we do have some great old times but I will be glad when it is all up and I get back to America again   They talk of Gay N.Y.   why N.Y sleeps more in one night than Berlin in a week. Honest I havent had my eyes closed here while it was dark   what sleeping I have done has been in the day.   Oh I have met the *Kaiser* when I was out exercising my pony in the park and he rides every day   he always *salutes* as he gallops past   oh he is a dandy good fellow[4]

Well I guess you have got the letter I wrote you from Paris and the other one from here by now

I think I will go direct to London on May 1st   I will write you on a card where to address my mail   as a letter here would not get me   now I wont be in London longer than two weeks   I dont think

Well I will close   I hope you are having a good time and dont forget your old Cowboy   I will see you before long

I have wrote to my Music publisher friend in N.Y. to send you some Music[5]

Solong regards to all and lots of love to you

Old Bill

ALS, rc. OkClaW.

1. On 24 March Rogers's agent, Mort Shea, had obtained a sixteen-week contract at $250 weekly for the Keith Circuit, commencing 3 September 1906 (B. F. Keith's Amusement Enterprises Artist's Contract, 24 March 1906, OkClaW). Shea took out a large advertisement in *Variety* on 28 April 1906 featuring three photographs of Rogers and headlined "Will Rogers Opened at Wintergarten, Berlin, April 1st Created a Sensation."

2. Rogers performed at London's Palace Theatre from 7 May to 9 June 1906.

3. Presumably a reference to the John Tiller dancers from England. Rogers apparently made several friends from the theater during his stay. Shortly after he left, he received two postcards addressed to the Province Hotel in London. Each postcard was signed by several friends, who wrote short messages such as "I wonder what you doeth in the big London"; "Hope you have three weeks of bliss"; "I am very sorry to tell you they have taken the candy machine away since the big Rogers is no longer a customer"; and "I hope you are fortunate enough to find the big swell dame" (postcards, postmarked 3 May 1905, Berlin, OkClaW).

4. A reference to Kaiser Wilhelm II riding his horse in the Tiergarten. Friedrich Wilhelm Viktor Albert (1859–1941) was emperor of Germany and king of Prussia from 1888 to 1918. Possessed of a strong antipathy toward England, Kaiser Wilhelm II helped precipitate many of the events that led to the outbreak of World War I in 1914. He supported Austria-Hungary in the conflict over Serbia, the event that started World War I, and approved the war plans of his foreign minister. As Germany began to lose the war, his authority was diminished and he opposed peace plans. Between 1916 and 1918 he was very much a figurehead, as party leaders in the Reichstag took control. He fled to the Netherlands, where he abdicated on 28 November 1918. He established residency in Doorn, near Utrecht, and died in exile on 4 June 1941 (*WNBD*, 1059).

In 1919 Rogers interpreted the incident differently when he talked to a reporter: "I used to go riding in the Tier Garten on my pony every afternoon, as there was no matinee, and I always met alot of officers. One day I met a guy riding ahead of the others. He nodded, and turned and looked at my Western outfit, but I never paid him any attention. A little farther on, some man stopped me and said, 'You didn't salute him.' I said, 'Salute who?' 'Why the Kaiser; didn't you know that was him you just met on the bridle path?' I said, 'I'm sorry, but if he's so great why don't he have his own path and stay off mine?' I met him lots of days after that, and he always seemed pretty good and would nod at me. I guess he was kinder sorry for me 'cause I wasn't a German. I never did salute him. I just nodded back. I didn't know anything about saluting. I might have used the wrong hand or something'" (Martin, "Wit of Will Rogers," 109).

Years later, Buck McKee, Rogers's partner on his tour, recalled the incident: "We played four weeks in Berlin and the Kaiser Wilhelm came to see our act. Will was exercising Teddy one morning on the Friedrichstrasse and whom should he meet galloping down the bridle path but the kaiser and his entourage. 'Hi there,' shouted Will at the kaiser, 'that's a pretty good looking horse you are riding.' The kaiser's guards closed in protectively and people on the streets alongside the drive stood with mouth agape, but the kaiser merely smiled and replied, 'You also are riding a very fine horse, a little small perhaps, but fine looking.' 'You should never do a thing like that,' said an indignant bystander. 'Did you not recognize the kaiser?' 'Goodness,' or words to that effect, said Will, whose awe and reverence for personages in high places was notoriously negligible, 'that does not mean a thing to me'" (Bagley, "Riding, Roping and Trouping with Will Rogers," 3; see also Buck McKee notes, BMC-OkClaW).

McKee recollected two other events in Berlin. While watching a parade of German soldiers doing the "goose step," Rogers commented: "These German soldiers must be a lazy bunch of loafers—every one of them has to kick the man in front of him in the pants every step to keep them all going" (Buck McKee notes, BMC-OkClaW). McKee also recalled that during a performance at the Wintergarten Rogers roped a fireman standing in the wings and dragged him sprawling onto the stage. Although the audience thought it was amusing, the fireman was indignant, and it took considerable explanation to prevent civil authorities from arresting Rogers (Bagley, "Riding, Roping and Trouping with Will Rogers," 3).

5. Possibly a reference to the songwriter Egbert Van Alstyne, who worked as a song plugger for the Remick Music Corp. Rogers was on the same bill with Van Alstyne at Keith's Union Square Theatre the week of 12 June 1905 and at Keith's Prospect Theatre in Cleveland in September 1906 (*New Grove Dictionary of American Music,* 4:444; see Manager's Report, Union Square Theatre, 12 June 1905, above).

Review from Will Rogers's Scrapbook
ca. 9 May 1906
London, England

From Berlin Rogers traveled to London, where he performed at the Palace Theatre of Varieties.[1] London theatergoers were amazed by Rogers's lasso tricks.

Whether Mr. Will Rogers, who is now appearing at the Palace, is the first of Mr. Butt's[2] discoveries during his recent visit to America, I do not know, but he is a very remarkable performer. He is a lassoist of amazing dexterity, and his little performance is one of the most striking and picturesque turns I have seen for some time. No small part of the charm of it lies in the novelty of the show. Mr. Rogers wears long leather leggings and a red shirt, and he shows off his skill by lassoing his assistant, who rides an excitable little nag backwards and forwards across the stage. There is nothing seemingly that he cannot do with a long length of rope. He can trail it along the stage, and then, with a sudden wrist movement, jerk it into the air, and behold there is a knot tied in the middle. He can keep a length of rope as long as the depth of the whole parterre of the house circling round his head in a wonderful loop, while with a smaller rope he keeps a snake-like circle in constant rotation, increasing and diminishing its size, jumping through it, skipping with it, and making it perform gyrations. Lassoing a horse or its rider is the merest child's play to him. On plunge horse and rider, a snake of rope flies through the air, and the man could be jerked out of the saddle in a minute. Or, if horse, not man, is aimed at, the rope flies lower, and the animal stops with a stagger its two forefeet held grimly.

Another "Stunt."

Mr. Rogers, I imagine, hails from America, or, if he does not, he ought to. There is a nice Mayne Reid suggestion about him, and though his performance is a little too large in scope for the Palace stage, the trio (horse and two men) make a very effective stage picture. The lassoist has an accent and a manner of speaking which I believe it is correct to describe as "redolent of the plains." The odd thing, too, is that they sound natural, and not like the acquired intonations of the young women who figure as American heiresses in modern comedies. He does not show you a new trick, but puts up another "stunt." This is a new word to me, but I like Mr. Rogers's "stunts." The one I like most is when he shows you how to catch and tie up a "bad man" who happens to be riding by while you are lounging round with a rope. In a flash you have a tightening coil round his neck or shoulders (you or I wouldn't, but Mr. Rogers would), and there you have him hooked. You notice then that his arms are free. In tones which brook no denial you accordingly tell him to "put up those flappers," and two arms are held out in token of surrender. Standing twenty or thirty feet away ("it don't do you no good to get too near a bad man," Mr. Rogers will tell you), you give your rope a couple of quick jerks, and the man's arms are caught and bound together; another rapid motion runs along the cord, and the arms are lashed securely to the saddle. You can complete the picture, if you like, by binding the poor wretch to the horse, and then, without ever having gone near your victim, you can drag him off to the police station. It pre-supposes a blind quiescence on the part of the quarry, but I daresay a bad man knows when he is "downed." Any way, it is a capital "stunt." I like also the way of catching horse and man at the same time. As the rider goes past you in a real hurry—he doesn't slouch—you fling two coils, one with each hand. One settles on the man, the other hobbles his mount, and both are helpless. Mr. Rogers is modest about this feat, and approaches it in the you-never-can-tell spirit ("I may do it; I don't know"); but it was done with perfect precision, and "I guess you're not half so pleased as I am," he said, as, acknowledging our applause, he vanished, after giving one or two ear-piercing prairie yells. We train our police in ju-jitsu now. Why not train them also as lassoists?

PD. Unidentified review, ca. 9 May 1906. Scrapbook A-1, OkClaW.

1. At this time the Palace Theatre of Varieties was considered among the foremost variety theaters in the world. Located at Cambridge Circus on Shaftesbury Avenue, the building was designed by G. H. Holloway and decorated by T. E. Colcutt. The theater was initially built for Richard D'Oyly Carte to produce Gilbert and Sullivan operas. Initially named the Royal English Opera House, it opened on 31 January 1891 with Sullivan's *Ivanhoe*. After a few more productions D'Oyly Carte sold the building to Sir Augustus Harris in 1892. Its name was subsequently changed to the Palace Theatre of Varieties, and it became a music hall in 1892. Just about every British and American variety star played the Palace. The Palace's heyday as a variety music hall ended around 1914 when it began a policy of presenting revues. Over the years it has continued as a prime venue for musical comedy, ranging from Vincent Youmans's *No, No, Nanette* (1925) and Cole Porter's *Anything Goes* (1935) to Andrew Lloyd Webber's *Jesus Christ Superstar* (1972) and the musical *Les Misérables* (1985) (Bergan, *Great Theatres of London*, 115–18; *GRB* [1907], 544–45; Howard, *London Theatres and Music Halls*, 169; Mander and Mitchenson, *British Music Halls*, picture caption nos. 73, 230; Short, *Fifty Years of Vaudeville*, 135–39).

2. Sir Alfred Butt (1878–1962), a well-known figure in the English theater, was managing director of the Palace Theatre. After a short career as an accountant, Butt became associated with the Palace in 1898 as a secretary. He eventually became assistant manager and in 1904 succeeded Charles Morton as manager. Daring to take chances, Butt was responsible for making the Palace one of the world's leading variety theaters. He chose for his programs the best talent as well as newcomers. To obtain top stars outside England, he made periodic visits to European capitals as well as New York and Chicago. At one time Butt headed a circuit of eleven provincial music halls. He left the Palace in 1920 to become managing director of London's Gaiety, Empire, and Adelphi theaters. He also managed London's Drury Lane Theatre when it staged many successful musicals. Butt was knighted in 1918 and was a Unionist member of Parliament from 1922 to 1936. His involvement in leaking confidential material regarding the budget led to his resignation from the House of Commons. Butt died on 9 December 1962 and left an estate worth £250,000 (Alfred Butt Biographical File, VATM; Blathwayt, "Control of a Great Music-Hall"; *GRB* [1908], 67; Leavitt, *Fifty Years in Theatrical Management*, 215; *WhoThe* [1916], 10–11; *VO*, 5:19 December 1962).

To Betty Blake
10 May 1906
London, England

London
May 10. 06

My Dearest Girl

Say I am here and have been for over a week and not a line has come from you or any one in America and I know I wrote all of you and gave you my London address   but perhaps the letter went astray

Well I come right here and put on my act for a trial just to show them and I am working at the smart select vaudeville theatre here at more money than I ever got before any place and my act has not only made good but it is said to be a sensation and they want me for 3 or 4 more weeks[1]   oh it simply knocked them a twister and its all the very swellest London society people that come here but I think I will sail for home in a week   but I have wired my N.Y. agent for I see I can get all kinds of coin out of these people to stay on longer but at any rate I will be out there about the 10th of July   even if I go home now I have 5 weeks work down south before I could come home and if I stay here I will cancel that   oh this is a great show place   but very slow   otherwise I was kinder glad to get away from there   it was to swift   oh Kid I am *dying* to get home and I sho do want to see you

Well I have a lot of stuff to tend to and I will write you more[2]   now Goodbye dear

Yours   Will

Province Hotel
Leicester Square[3]
London England

ALS, rc. OkClaW.

1. Rogers began his engagement the week of 7 May 1906. In the program for 9 May, he is listed as number fourteen on the bill. The following acts were listed in the program with the times given for their performance: March ("Guards to the Front" by Trotére 7.55); Fred Frampton (Burlesque Entertainer 8.0); Jennie Johns (Comedienne 8.10); Carola Jordan (Trapeze Artiste 8.22); The Palace Girls 8.32); Nina Gordon (Mimic 8.45); Grant and Grant (The Coon Duettists 8.55); Daisy Jerome (Comedienne 9.5); Toch and Tard (Eccentric Acrobats); Millie Lindon (Will Sing "Mary Kept a Diary" and "In Barcelona" assisted by the Palace Girls 9.34); Robert Cole and J. Rosemond Johnson (The Great American Colored Entertainers in A Repertoire of Their Own Compositions "I'll Keep a Warm Spot in My Heart For You," "The Darktown Elopement," "Lazy Moon" 9.51); Intermezzo (Entr'acte from "L'Amico Fritz," Tarrantelle from "The Gypsy Suite" 10.11); De Gracia's Elephants

(10.21); Will Rogers (Lassoist 10:39); Les Trombetta (Eccentric Duettists 10.49); The Bioscope (Arrival of the Prince and Princess of Wales, 8th May; The Olympic Games; Eruption of Mount Vesuvius; Humorous Phases of Funny Faces; Italian Cavalry Manoeuvres 11.7) (Palace Theatre program, 9 May 1906, OkClaW).

2. Rogers penned another letter on 14 May 1906, in which he thanked Betty Blake for her letter and the photo she sent to Berlin. He wrote, "Oh Kid I am homesick and I sho do want to see you" (OkClaW).

3. Leicester Square, located north of Charing Cross and near the theater district, had many hotels and rooming houses. The Province Hotel was not listed in the Baedeker guide, but the book warned: "The stranger is cautioned against going to any unrecommended house near Leicester Square, as there are several houses of doubtful reputation in the locality" (Baedeker, *London and Its Environs* [1906], 5).

Clipping from Will Rogers's Scrapbook
12 May 1906
London, England

OUR LONDON LETTER.
FROM OUR OWN CORRESPONDENT.

Clipper Bureau,
48 Cranbourne Street,
Leicester Square,
London, W.C.
May 12.

During his recent trip to America, Manager Butt, of the Palace, is said to have booked the following acts for his house, in addition to Rose Stahl[1] and company and Eltinge,[2] who open Monday: Walter Kelley,[3] Fred Niblo, Clarice Vance,[4] Charles Lamon, and Toledo and Price.[5] Will Rogers, the lariat throw-er, who is homeward bound from a successful month's stay at the Wintergarden, Berlin, opened last Monday, for a week, at the Palace. His act made such an instantaneous hit on the opening night that he was immediate-ly moved down to a star place on the bill (10.30), and Mr. Butt tried to sign the wonderful man with the rope for a month or five weeks. Rogers will remain another week at the Palace, but is undecided about a longer period, as he is booked in the States, and will not know until his agent, Mr. Shea,[6] arrives from New York early next week, if the American time can be set back. The act is eas-ily the best novelty that has been seen in London in a long time, and it is going some when a Palace audience can be made to shout bravo, and more than once, too. Rogers' patter is most amusing, especially to an English audience.

PD. Unidentified clipping, 12 May 1906. Scrapbook A-1, OkClaW.

1. Rogers played on the same Palace program with the well-known actress Rose Stahl (1870–1955) from 14 May to 9 June. Born in Montreal, Canada, she began her stage career at the age of seventeen with a repertoire stock company at the Girard Avenue Theatre in Philadelphia. Then she joined a series of traveling stock companies. Stahl gained fame when she played Patricia O'Brien in a one-act comedy about stage life called *The Chorus Girl,* by James Forbes (1871–1938), which premiered at Proctor's Music Hall on 13 June 1904. She performed this playlet at the Palace Theatre, which was her London debut. Rogers sent a postcard to Betty Blake depicting posters and billboards outside the Palace Theatre (Rose Stahl was listed first, and Rogers's name was in the middle but in slighter larger type). Rogers wrote on the card: "This was taken for Rose Stahl but you see who had the big type on the bill" (postcard to Betty Blake, postmarked 15 June 1906, Vienna, OkClaW). Stahl's playlet was subsequently made into a four-act play, which was a big hit. She played in the production for five years, including a popular engagement in London in 1909. Stahl's thin face, hazel eyes, and tousled blonde hair became well known to theatergoers. Afterward she assumed other stage roles but never regained the fame of her earlier parts. She died on 16 July 1955 at the age of seventy-four (Mantle and Sherwood, eds., *The Best Plays of 1899–1909,* 518; *FILM,* 2:235; "How Rose Stahl Became a Metropolitan Star," *Theatre,* January 1907, 21–22; *OCAT,* 266, 639; "Rose Stahl Closed in London," *Billboard,* 7 August 1909, 6; *WhMuDr,* 289–90; *WhoThe* (1914), 530; *WhoStg,* 410; *WhThe,* 4:2237).

2. Julian Eltinge (1883–1941) was considered the best known and most talented female impersonator of his era. Some critics, such as *Variety's* Sime Silverman, believed he was the most talented performer in vaudeville. Rogers was on the same London Palace playbill with him from 14 May through 9 June 1906. Eltinge, whose real name was William Dalton, was born in Newtonville, Mass. He was first introduced to show business in Boston. He was inspired by a Mrs. Wyman who operated a Boston dancing school and encouraged his mimicking. Other versions hold that he first appeared in an annual revue staged by Boston's First Corps Cadets or that he worked as a bank clerk and played in a show staged by clerks. In Boston he appeared on stage dressed as a young woman, mimicked a ballerina, and was the hit of the show. Legend has it that Lillian Russell saw him perform and encouraged him to pursue a theater career. Eltinge toured the major vaudeville circuits for five years. To make his female impersonation acceptable, his act was described as "clean-cut, legitimate and artistic without any suggestion of burlesque," and he was said to be "engaged in entertaining the most select circles of society in New York, Boston, Newport, and Bar Harbor" (*NYDM,* 29 July 1905, 16). In vaudeville, Eltinge did several impersonations, including a takeoff of the Gibson Girl called The Simpson Girl, an impression of a young party girl, and his finale, a little-girl impression that led to many encores. Clothed in elaborate dresses and imitating a female singing voice, Eltinge could deceive his audiences until the finale, when he intentionally removed his wig. He spent nearly two hours preparing for his act by painstakingly applying makeup, powder, greasepaint, and lip rouge to his face, as well as a special formula to make his arms soft and white. Eltinge was known for his elaborate stage costumes and devoted considerable time to matching colors, textures, and patterns. A heavy-set person, he wore a corset that reduced his forty-six-inch waist to twenty-four inches, an undergarment that he called "Old Ironsides." In addition, he wore tiny satin slippers that pinched his large feet. He studied the behavior and movement of many women, especially their hands and arms, to create what he called a composite creation. "I had to modulate my natural stride, to change the abrupt manual gestures of a man to the softer, more graceful postures of a

woman, and to learn the proper manoeuvering of skirts, both short and long," he wrote (Eltinge, "How I Portray a Woman on the Stage," ix). The *Julian Eltinge Magazine,* which was sold at his performances, offered beauty and cosmetic tips. Eltinge had many Broadway stage successes and starred in silent films. He took pains to create a personal image that stressed his masculinity. "I'm mighty glad at the end of the day's work to be a man again," he wrote (Eltinge, "How I Portray a Woman on the Stage," ix). (Offstage he engaged in various barroom brawls and fights with stagehands, and participated in outdoor sports.) Eltinge's success led to a proliferation of female impersonators in vaudeville in the 1910s and early 1920s. He was a headliner on vaudeville circuits until the mid-1920s and performed at New York's famed Palace Theatre several times. In the early 1930s Eltinge toured with his own company, performed in *The Nine O'Clock Revue* (1932) at the Music Box Theatre in Hollywood, and starred in the film *Maid to Order* (1932). Around 1933 Eltinge retired and lived in a hillside home in the San Fernando Valley as well as a large ranch east of San Diego, Calif. The 1930s was a time when female impersonation became unpopular due to its association with homosexuality and social prejudice against gay people. He had trouble finding movie parts because, as he said, "producers won't imagine me without a gown" (Louis Banks, "The Man Who's Tired of Wearing Skirts," 12 September 1937, clipping, Dobson file, CL). Needing money, Eltinge attempted a comeback in 1940. That year he played a part in the Universal film *If I Had My Way.* He performed at the White Horse, a seedy Los Angeles cabaret, and in New York at Billy Rose's Diamond Horseshoe Jubilee revue. While appearing at Rose's Diamond Horseshoe night club, he was suddenly stricken with a kidney ailment. This precipitated his death a week later from a cerebral hemorrhage, on 7 March 1941 at his apartment in New York City ("A Dressing Room Marvel," *Variety,* 11 December 1909, 28; Eltinge, "How I Portray a Woman on the Stage," ix, 56, 58; *EV,* 158–61, 172–75; *LAT,* 8 March 1941; Louis Banks, "The Man Who's Tired of Wearing Skirts," 12 September 1937, clipping, Dobson file, CL; *NYHT,* 8 March 1941; *NYT,* 8 March 1941; Toll, *On With the Show!* 246–56; van Hoogstraten, *Lost Broadway Theatres,* 146–49; *VO,* 3:12 March 1941; *WhoHol,* 1:491; *WhThe,* 2:758).

3. Walter C. Kelly (1873–1939) was a comic dialect monologuist in vaudeville, best known for his act The Virginia Judge. Born in Mineville, N.Y., Kelly was raised in Newport News, Va., where he found a job as a shipyard machinist. Here he encountered Judge Dudley Brown, who oversaw the police court, and the character of the homespun judge became the inspiration for his act. Kelly began entertaining shipyard workers at a local restaurant and pool room and from there gradually moved into big-time vaudeville, playing London's Palace Theatre and other theaters in Europe and Australia. In his portrayal of a small-town Virginia judge, Kelly wore a baggy black alpaca coat, carried a gavel, and tried cases standing behind a pedestal. Kelly would play all the characters and perform dialect impersonations of the plaintiffs and the defendants, including a southern gentleman, Irish laborer, and an African American. His act contained considerable racist stereotyping, especially when he portrayed a lazy and illiterate black person accused of a crime. Kelly played his favorite stage character in the Paramount film *The Virginia Judge* (1935) and also appeared in other movies. Kelly died from head injuries as a result of being hit by a truck in Hollywood (*EV,* 287–89; Gilbert, *American Vaudeville,* 284–85, 305; Laurie, *Vaudeville,* 194–95, 202; *OCAT,* 397–98).

4. Clarice Vance was a vaudeville headliner who did a single singing and dancing act. She was known as the first entertainer to wear a mirror dress. For a time she was married to Mose Gumble, who was in the music business. Vance played the character

Nahoma in the film *Down to the Sea in Ships*. She died of cancer at Napa, Calif., on 24 August 1961 (*FILM*, 2:537; Laurie, *Vaudeville*, 59, 324; *VO*, 5:30 August 1961).

5. Toledo and Price played on the same playbill with Rogers at the Palace during the weeks of 21 May, 28 May, and 4 June. They were advertised as novelty gymnasts and contortionists (Palace Theatre of Varieties playbills and programs, OkClaW).

6. Shea was Rogers's agent at this time; see Biographical Appendix entry, SHEA, Maurice (Mort) A.

Palace Theatre Reviews
ca. 15–27 May 1906
London, England

THE EXTRAACTE.

The Palace audience is like a child with a new toy when Will Rogers, the cowboy lassoist, comes on.[1] He shakes all the apathy out of them with his amazing tricks, and the conversation he indulges in is just the sort to wake up such a blasé assembly.

DAILY ▲ ~~TRIBUNE~~ ▲ NEWS
PALACE THEATRE.

One of the most entertaining items in the Palace programme is the performance of Will Rogers as a "cowboy lassoist." He is a genuine Yankee with a quaint method of expression, which is hardly less interesting than his clever manipulation of the lasso. Assisted by a well-trained cob and rider he demonstrates the practice adopted in pulling up the animal at a gallop and pinning the rider to the saddle with a series of deftly thrown loops. One of his cleverest tricks is throwing two ropes at the same time, one encircling the horse and the other fixing the rider securely round his neck.

THE ERA.

Will Rogers, the cowboy lassoist, brings something of the wild, breezy life of the prairies across the footlights in his act, which is quite unique in its way. He loops his mounted quarry—another Texan, apparently—quite easily, and then leashes both horse and rider with a double throw. He whirls the cord round himself with such wonderful regularity that it has the appearance of the framework of a crinoline. It is a remarkable show, and is not likely to have imitators.

MORNING POST.
PALACE THEATRE.

Among the turns that Mr. Butt has brought with him from America—
many more are to come later when engagements permit—is a display of lasso
work by Will Rogers, a cowboy. The lasso is not wholly unfamiliar in the variety theatres; a couple of years since a gentleman and lady, Chamberlain[2] by
name, were delighting Hippodrome audiences with their rope work. But one
sees very little of it, and the present performance is as novel, as wonderful, and
as fascinating as anything to be seen in London. After some simple feats, such
as making a 30ft. rope tie knots and loops in itself, Mr. Rogers sets to work on
another cowboy on horseback. With successive casts he adds knot to knot till
at last the man has his hands bound together and his arms lashed to his sides,
is tied to the pommel of his saddle, and has a noose round his neck, while his
horse is no less strictly pinioned and is unable to move. Having released them,
Mr. Rogers proceeds to lasso man and horse simultaneously, using one rope
for each. He does many other extraordinary feats, in which the rope seems
endowed with intelligence and grace. He appears to send messages by it; you
see the message run along the line, and at the other end the thing is done. It
is a surprising and very beautiful performance, and the audience rose at it. It
made one feel that it is a mistake when tying up a refractory parcel to stand
over one's work. One should retire to the other end of the room and make
casts at it.

SPORTING LIFE.

Another of Mr. Butt's discoveries is Will Rogers, the Texan Cowboy, called
"The Cherokee Kid." His specialty is lasso-throwing, and in that art he is said
to be unbeaten. Besides his skill with the rope, his quaint American expressions will render him a great favourite in London.

DAILY CHRONICLE.

At the other end of the scale, but not less entertaining, are the feats of Will
Rogers, the cowboy lassoist. There have been lassoists before, but never, perhaps, such a master of the art as Will Rogers, who seems capable of doing
everything with a rope except of hanging himself.

DAILY EXPRESS.

One of the cleverest and most effective "turns" which the Palace has yet given us is that of Mr. Will Rogers. Mr. Rogers appears as a cowboy, and, aided by another cowboy on horseback, he gives us an exhibition of lassooing and tricks in rope-twirling. The business at the Palace has gone up splendidly lately, and Will Rogers is just now the feature of the programme.

★ ★ ★

He catches the rider with a throw of the rope, then the horse, and in no longer time than the average man takes in tying his bootlace Will Rogers has bound horse and rider helplessly to his side. Then taking a piece of rope as long as the building—it is passed up the whole length of the stalls—he makes a hoop of it, and keeps it flying in mid-air. It is an amazing exhibition.

★ ★ ★

"Very few people could do this," he says in his merry way, adding, "and very few would be crazy enough to try."

AD and PD. Scrapbook A-1, OkClaW.

1. During the week of 21 May 1906 Rogers was listed as number sixteen on the playbill, just before the films. The playbill was as follows Ethel Negretti (Comedienne); Frank Lynne (Comedian); Nina Gordon (Mimic); Robert Michaelis (Vocalist); Daisy Jerome (Comedienne); the Gems (Entertainers); De Gracia's Elephants; Louis Bradfield; Julian Eltinge (In Feminine Characterizations); Hansl Schon (Vocalist); Rose Stahl; Intermezzo; Toledo and Price (Novelty Gymnasts and Contortionists; Les Trombetta (Grandes Originalites); Will Rogers (Cowboy Lassoist); The Bioscope (Palace Programme, 21 May 1907, scrapbook A-1, OkClaW). During the week of 28 May Rogers was again next to last on the playbill, and most of the same acts from the previous week appeared (Palace Programme, 28 May 1905, scrapbook A-1, OkClaW). The bill during Rogers's last week at the Palace, beginning 4 June, was as follows: Frank Lynne (comedian); Ethel Negretti (comedienne); Nina Gordon (mimic); Brothers Miller (comedians on the horizontal bar); Woodward and Walton (singing and dancing specialty act); Alice Russon (comedienne); Toledo and Price (novelty gymnasts and contortionists); Julian Eltinge; Alice Hollander (Australian Contralto); Rose Stahl; Intermezzo; Les Trombetta; Rosario Guerrero; Will Rogers (Cowboy Lassoist); the Bioscope (Palace Programme, 9 June 1906, scrapbook A-1, OkClaW).

In addition to Julian Eltinge and Rose Stahl, Rogers performed with several other well-known vaudevillians at the Palace Theatre. Louis Bradfield (1866–1919) was an English actor and singer who had starred in the hit musical *The Gaiety Girl* (1893) and was a member of George Edwardes's Gaiety Co. (*GRB* [1909], 60; Short, *Fifty Years of Vaudeville*, 43). Daisy Jerome was a successful music-hall performer and variety actress whose biggest success was singing "Click Went the Kodak" in *The Medal and the Maid*. She was well known in London and provincial music halls for her singing and mimicry. Jerome performed on the vaudeville stage in the United States in 1913 and 1917. Critics were impressed by the gowns she wore, her vivacious style, and her song "Press, Pulpit and Petticoat" (Locke env. 838, NN-L-RLC; *GRB* [1909], 270; Felstead, *Stars Who Made the Halls*, 173).

2. The Chamberlains performed a lasso-and-whip act (Laurie, *Vaudeville*, 36).

Clipping from Will Rogers's Scrapbook
6 June 1906
London, England

The spectators at Ranelagh Club[1] on Wednesday were treated to a pleasant surprise. After the polo match, between the Moonlighters and the 1st Life Guards, Will Rogers, the Texas cow-boy, who is one of the "stars" at the Palace Theatre, appeared with his pony and assistant, and gave a remarkable exhib tion of lassooing, trick-riding, and other forms of cow-boy maneuvers. He wɛ received with much enthusiasm, and at the conclusion of his performance he was presented by the club with a silver cup as a souvenir of the occasion.[2]

PD. Unidentified clipping, 6 June 1906. Scrapbook A-1, OkClaW.

1. The Ranelagh Club was located in Putney in the environs of London. On the grounds of the club were polo fields, a golf course, lawn tennis courts, and a historic manor called Barn Elms. The manor house first belonged to the Canons of St. Paul in the tenth century. In the thirteenth century the property was transferred to Thomas Thwayte, chancellor of the exchequer and of the duchy of Lancaster. Next to the manor was a house that was owned by Jacob Tonson, a bookseller and publisher. He started a club devoted to the fine arts and literature that soon developed a political orientation. Club membership was restricted to men of distinguished learning, many serving the government or the army. In 1708 its name was changed to the Kit Kat Club. In 1883 Barn Elms and the adjoining house became the Ranelagh Club (Barret, *History of Barn Elms and the Kit Cat Club Now the Ranelagh Club*).

2. According to the program the polo match was on the Old Ground at 3 P.M., while Rogers's appearance was on the Show Ground at 4 P.M. The program stated that "Mr. W. Rogers" was appearing "by kind permission of the Management of the Palace Theatre" and "will give an Exhibition of Throwing." That afternoon three other polo matches were given on the Barnes Ground, two of them including teams from the Ranelagh Club. Many military officers and members of the nobility were on the teams (Ranelagh Club Program, scrapbook A-1, OkClaW).

Article from the *Claremore Messenger*
20 July 1906
Claremore, I.T.

After a long voyage to New York, Rogers went to Claremore and Chelsea to visit his sisters and their families.

WORLD'S CHAMPION LASSOER.

W. P. Rogers, son of our fellow townsman, C. V. Rogers, returned home the 9th of this month for a short visit at home. He has been giving exhibitions over the European continent, and returned here direct from Rome, where he finished up his European career. It was our pleasure the first of the week to see him juggle a rope some, and he can certainly do things a tender foot would never dream of. He will begin a twenty-three week tour the first of September, starting from Detroit, Michigan.[1] During the summer months he will continue to practice with the rope as it requires constant practice for a man of his calibre to do the difficult trials and keep in shape all the time. Claremore people who have never seen him will doubtless have chances during the summer.[2]

PD. Printed in the *CM*, 20 July 1906.

1. Rogers began his tour at Detroit's Temple Theatre on 3 September 1908. His agent, Mort Shea, had obtained a sixteen-week contract from B. F. Keith's Amusement Enterprises on 24 March 1906. The contract stipulated a salary of $250 a week for two performances each day (B. F. Keith's Amusement Enterprises Artist's Contract, 24 March 1906, OkClaW).
2. Rogers's sudden vaudeville fame was also publicized in Chelsea, the hometown of his sisters, Maud and Sallie. The *Chelsea Reporter* stated that "Mr. Rogers is of international fame, and its a mighty sorry little kingdom or republic in the globe that can't boast of having seen the greatest manipulator of a 33 foot rope that ever followed a chuck wagon on a round-up" (20 July 1906).

———

4. CAUGHT IN THE VAUDEVILLE WARS
July 1906–June 1908

Rogers sent this photograph, taken by the Otto Sarony Co., to his friend Tom P. Morgan, probably in 1906. *(Tom Morgan Collection, RHM, Neg. N008229)*

WHEN ROGERS ARRIVED IN NEW YORK ON THE FOURTH OF JULY, 1906, ABOARD the steamship S.S. *König Albert,* he found the vaudeville business in turmoil. Big-time circuit operators were battling each other for control of vaudeville. In June the Keith-Albee Circuit had begun to consolidate vaudeville through an arrangement with the Western Vaudeville Association that gave the chain power to book acts at theaters from the East Coast to Cleveland. During the next seven months the circuit forced the leading vaudeville theater owners in the East to join a new organization, the United Booking Offices of America (UBO), which the Keith organization controlled. These vaudeville wars would affect Rogers's career.[1]

For the moment, however, Roger had the opportunity to take a much-needed rest from travel. With no engagements scheduled until early September, Rogers decided to go on home. Since beginning in vaudeville in June 1905, Rogers had been on a grueling schedule, working almost every week for over a year. He left New York on 9 July and arrived in Claremore five days later, where he stayed until 29 August. The time he spent in Claremore and Chelsea was the longest period he had been at home since leaving in 1902.

During his stay Rogers visited his relatives and renewed his ties with friends from his youth. On 1 August he attended the wedding of Ida Mae Collins and Lorenzo Clinton Goodale. Rogers was Goodale's best man and gave the couple a cut-glass fruit bowl as a wedding present. Earlier in the summer Betty Blake had visited the area. She was invited by the Lanes to a welcome-home party in Rogers's honor in Chelsea. Although the two went horseback riding and attended parties, Blake later recalled that Rogers "never looked in my direction or singled me out."[2]

Around 4 August 1906 Rogers traveled to Rogers, Ark., to visit Betty Blake. With his vaudeville career on the upswing and feeling that this might be an opportune time, Rogers proposed marriage but was turned down. She was not prepared to assume the role of a vaudevillian's wife. "I simply could not see a life of trouping the country in vaudeville," she wrote. "Our parting was a sad one, but we promised to write."[3]

Betty Blake shared the common belief that show business was not a respectable career and that many stage performers lived scandalous lives. Her suspicions reflected traditional animosities toward actors that can be traced back to Puritanism in the Massachusetts Bay colony and its emphasis on the work ethic rather than recreation. The more conservative religious groups viewed actors as the devil's advocates. The low pay of the average performer, frequent unemployment, and a reputation as alcoholics and philanderers only served to intensify the stereotype.[4]

Blake's and Rogers's relationship was still shadowed by the disturbing question of rival beaux. Their long separations while Rogers was on the road led to jealousy over other relationships. Courtship via mail failed to heal the wounds.

Often lonely on the vaudeville trail, Rogers sought the friendship of other women, especially fellow performers. His fondness for Louise Henry continued during this period. He befriended a woman named Nina who was a performer with The Crickets, an act that appeared on the same program with Rogers three times in September and October 1906. Nina developed a crush on Rogers, but he did not want to become seriously involved. When she learned about his intentions, Nina wrote him a friendly letter stating her acceptance of his feelings. She thought highly of Rogers and wrote: "The girl that wins your love may consider herself fortunate, only wish the average man were more like you."[5] Naively, Rogers enclosed Nina's note in a letter he wrote to Betty Blake.

In other letters Rogers claimed that these affairs were not serious. Once Blake penned a cold response that mentioned her hometown beau, Tom Harvey. Hurt by the tone of her letter, Rogers replied that she was the only woman in his life. He kept chiding Betty about another beau, this one a lawyer. A short time later he was asking forgiveness for his indiscretions. "I told you I had always been a *bad boy* and guess I will continue to be one till you are with me and then its all over I will put all of this old life behind and I think I am man enough to do it too."[6]

Rogers's visit home convinced him that the vaudeville trail was more exciting than the cattle trail. Certainly, the contrast between Claremore and the cosmopolitan cities of New York, Paris, London, and Berlin must have been striking. Although he loved the more exciting aspects of ranch life (cattle drives, horse breaking, the roundup), he disliked its day-to-day drudgery. Rogers was now captivated by show business. During his sixteen-week engagement on the Keith Circuit, which commenced 3 September at Detroit's Temple Theatre, he rarely spoke to reporters about leaving vaudeville to become a cattleman.[7]

When Rogers joined the Keith Circuit in September 1906, the powerful chain had increased its holdings. With only one major vaudeville location (the

Union Square Theatre) in New York, Keith wanted to extend his operations in the city. He decided to threaten F. F. Proctor, who owned a prestigious vaudeville chain in New York, that he would build or lease theaters in his area and drive him out of business. To avoid an all-out battle with Keith and fearing competition, Proctor merged his popular New York theaters with Keith's New York operations in May 1906. A new corporation was formed, called the Keith and Proctor Amusement Co. Henceforth, Proctor's properties would be called Keith and Proctor theaters. Albee was appointed general manager of the corporation. Proctor agreed to book acts through Keith's agency, while Keith pledged not to build any theaters in Proctor's area. Including Proctor's theaters, Keith now had thirty-five theaters affiliated with his growing empire.[8]

For some time Keith and Sylvester Z. Poli, owner of a large chain of New England variety theaters, had been at loggerheads. Keith knew Poli was a roadblock to building theaters in New England. He also wanted Poli to book acts through his agency. During their quarrel both showmen threatened to build opposition theaters in each other's territory. To force Poli to the table, Keith tried blackmail. He threatened to build theaters in those cities where Poli houses existed. Taking Keith at his word, bankers refused to loan Poli any money. Further, Keith banned from his affiliated theaters vaudevillians who played Poli houses, thus pressuring performers not to sign on with Poli. Realizing he had no other option, Poli reached an agreement with Keith. Both pledged to keep out of each other's territory, while Poli agreed to book his acts through Keith despite the higher costs.[9]

Another rival in New York was the impresario Oscar Hammerstein, a theater magnate as ambitious and voracious as Keith. Keith feared that the Hammerstein would merge his New York holdings with other opposition theater owners, thereby creating a circuit as extensive as his. When Hammerstein considered operating another high-class vaudeville theater in New York, Keith struck a deal. He granted Hammerstein a territorial franchise that gave him exclusive rights to vaudeville theaters in mid-Manhattan. In exchange, Hammerstein agreed not to extend his vaudeville operations and to book acts at his Victoria Theatre through Keith's agency. The agreement lasted until 1913, when Keith bought Hammerstein's rights in order to assume management of the Palace Theatre.[10]

The last holdout was Percy Williams, who operated houses in Harlem, Manhattan, and Brooklyn. Like Proctor, Williams was a leading figure in New York vaudeville and a potential threat to Keith. Using similar tactics, Keith persuaded Williams to affiliate his theaters with the Keith and Proctor Circuit by agreeing to book performers only through the UBO.[11]

The creation of the UBO in 1907 was a major turning point in the vaudeville business. It was essentially a Keith-run organization, although Proctor, Williams, Poli, and Hammerstein also profited from its huge assets. The UBO controlled all bookings east of Chicago and charged commissions for its services. A performer paid commissions both to the UBO and his or her agent. The split-commission assessment cost vaudevillians twice as much, and they understandably disliked the policy. Performers, agents, and theater managers had little choice unless they wanted to remain independent, but in that case they risked being blackballed. Performers who did not book through the UBO could not perform at a Keith-affiliated theater. By agreement with the UBO, the Orpheum Circuit controlled bookings west of Chicago. Over the next few years consolidation in the big-time vaudeville business continued. Adopting the combination practices of large corporations and trusts, the eastern and western big-time vaudeville associations created an oligopoly by absorbing small competitors, streamlining operations, and combining the functions of production, booking, and exhibition.

. Rogers's stage career was dramatically affected by these changes. First, if he wanted to play Keith theaters, he had to find a new agent. William Morris was an independent agent who opposed Keith's stranglehold on vaudeville. When Williams, Poli, and Hammerstein defected to Keith, Morris was left with very few first-class theaters where he could book his acts. Morris consequently lost most of his clients, including Rogers, who found a new agent, Mort Shea, allied to Keith. From 1906 to 1908 Shea obtained engagements for Rogers at Keith theaters and at houses operated by Proctor, Poli, Williams, and Hammerstein. Rogers performed at several newly named Keith and Proctor houses in New York, including the Fifth Avenue Theatre, the Twenty-third Street Theatre, and the Harlem Opera House. He also appeared at Hammerstein's Victoria Theatre and three Poli theaters in New England. In addition, he played at theaters in Buffalo and Toronto operated by Mike Shea, another manager affiliated with the UBO. He also had engagements at Percy Williams's Colonial Theatre in Manhattan, the Orpheum Theatre in Brooklyn, and the Alhambra Theatre in Harlem.

At this time the Harlem community supported several big-time vaudeville theaters. Besides the popular Alhambra, the area had the Harlem Opera House, Keith and Proctor's 125th Street Theatre (where Rogers performed during the week of 16 December 1907), and Hurtig and Seamon's theater. In the mid-nineteenth century Harlem had been a rural village of modest cottage residences in open fields. By century's end transportation improvements, such as the elevated railway and subway, had begun to draw people to the area and

Ben Hurtig and Harry J. Seamon's Music Hall (1894) on 125th Street between Seventh and Eighth Avenues in Harlem was a popular vaudeville venue seating 1,400. It is pictured here in 1902. *(Byron Collection, NNMuS)*

had generated a middle-class housing boom. Brownstones, tenements, and large apartment buildings with elevators lined the streets. By 1906 Harlem had become a fashionable middle- and upper-middle-class area of first- or second-generation Jews from Eastern Europe and Germany. In its northern part there was a community of African Americans, who increasingly populated Harlem through the 1920s. In 1917 Harlem had a Jewish population of 170,000, second only to the Lower East Side.[12] This provided a large audience for vaudeville houses, legitimate theater, and nickelodeons. In 1889 Oscar Hammerstein built the Harlem Opera House specifically to draw middle-class families into the area. Harlem also had several fine legitimate theaters—for example, J. B. McElfatrick's Harlem Auditorium (1904) on 126th Street and Seventh Avenue. Considered the area's social and cultural center, the large building contained a theater, restaurant, cafe, rathskellers, and a roof garden used for summer vaudeville.[13]

During this period Rogers also performed in Brooklyn, another thriving locale of theater and the arts. Its growth as a middle-class residential suburb of frame houses was spurred by improved mass transportation, chiefly the Brooklyn Bridge (1883); the expansion of the Brooklyn, Bath, and West End Railroad in the 1880s and 1890s; electric street railways; and the subway (1908). In 1870 Brooklyn's population was 396,099; by 1890 it had more than doubled, to 806,343; and by 1900 it had reached more than 1 million.[14] In 1898 Brooklyn became a borough of New York City. Jobs in industry, manufacturing, and shipping also stimulated Brooklyn's growth. Simultaneously, cultural resources, both in the popular theater and the fine arts, were built in the area. By the first decade of the twentieth century Brooklyn provided vaudeville, burlesque, and legitimate theaters for its residents.[15]

Between 1906 and 1908 Rogers performed in several Brooklyn variety theaters, including Hyde and Behman's theater and the Grand Opera House. Hyde and Behman also managed the Star, Gayety, and Olympic theaters. Percy Williams operated the popular Orpheum as well as Brooklyn's Novelty and Gotham theaters.

During this period Rogers also returned to London, where he made a second appearance at the Palace Theatre of Varieties. On 18 April 1907 he sailed first-class to England on board the S.S. *Kaiserin Auguste Victoria,* a Hamburg-American ocean liner bound for Hamburg via Plymouth, England, and Cherbourg, France. Disembarking at Plymouth, Rogers traveled to London in time for his opening at the Palace on 29 April. During his engagement Rogers again made a hit with British audiences. He also performed at theaters in Coventry and Liverpool. Liverpool's Empire Theatre belonged to Moss' Empires, Ltd., a chain much like Keith's Circuit that operated many music-hall and variety theaters in England. On 8 June 1907 he left on the S.S. *Philadelphia* and arrived in New York on 15 June.

Back home, Rogers's career was once again affected by changes in the vaudeville business. The battle between the UBO and opposing independent theater managers had intensified. To challenge Keith, a new vaudeville chain was established in April 1907—the United States Amusement Co., commonly called Advanced Vaudeville. It was organized by two powerful rivals in the legitimate theater business, Marc Klaw and Abraham Erlanger of the Theatrical Syndicate and the Shubert brothers. To manage their operation, they selected William Morris, who arranged a contract for Rogers. On 20 June 1907 Rogers signed a vaudeville contract with Klaw and Erlanger for twenty-five consecutive weeks of engagements, commencing on 2 September, at a weekly salary of $300. By signing with Klaw and Erlanger, Rogers could not perform at Keith- and UB0-affiliated theaters and was essentially blackballed, just like other artists who joined Advanced Vaudeville.

Rogers began his Advance Vaudeville tour on 24 June 1907, when he appeared for two weeks at Klaw and Erlanger's Chestnut Street Opera House in Philadelphia. From there he went to Pittsburgh for a two-week engagement at Klaw and Erlanger's Nixon Theatre. Then suddenly in mid-August Rogers's career took a new turn. He obtained a role in *The Girl Rangers,* a western musical starring Reine Davies (sister of Marion Davies), which opened on 2 September at the Chicago Auditorium for a four-week engagement. This was Rogers's first appearance in a large-scale musical comedy production. On stage Rogers performed lariat tricks in a mining-town scene and received good reviews.

When *The Girl Rangers* closed, Rogers returned to playing in Advanced Vaudeville theaters. By this time the new vaudeville organization was in financial trouble due to poor attendance and management. In early November 1907 the company was sold to the Keith Circuit for a large sum. Klaw and Erlanger and the Shubert organization agreed to stay out of vaudeville for ten years. With the demise of Advance Vaudeville, Rogers returned to the Keith Circuit. In December he performed at Keith and Proctor's 125th Street Theatre and made a Christmas-week appearance at Hammerstein's Victoria Theatre. In February 1908 he began a tour of the Poli Circuit in New England.

During his performance at Poli's Theatre in New Haven on 2 March 1908, Rogers was called home because his father was ill. He went home at once, and stayed in the Claremore area until his father had recovered. Returning to the vaudeville trail, Rogers traveled to Bridgeport, Conn., where he performed at Poli's Theatre the week of 27 April. On his way east he visited Betty Blake. Apparently, the short visit temporarily reconciled their differences. "My Own Sweetheart," he wrote after he left, ". . . I just love you more all the time."[16] In total, the period from July 1906 to April 1908 was a whirlwind for Rogers, with ups and downs in his romantic relationship with Betty Blake and volatile changes in the vaudeville field at large.

1. The earlier corporation was called the United Booking Agency of America (*Variety,* 23 June 1906, 2). It should not be confused with the United Booking Offices of America, formed in February 1907, which replaced the agency.

2. Rogers, *Will Rogers,* 96. This was the first time she met Rogers's family. Betty Blake's visit could have been around the time Rogers was visiting his sisters in Chelsea, 15 and 16 July. Clement Vann Rogers held a large dinner at the Hotel Sequoyah in Claremore on 26 July 1906. Rogers's sisters and thirteen other guests were present, and it is quite possible that Betty Blake was there (*CP,* 28 July 1906; Rogers, *Will Rogers,* 94–96).

3. Rogers, *Will Rogers,* 97.

4. McArthur, *Actors and American Culture,* 123–26.

5. See Will Rogers to Betty Blake, 5 December 1906, with Enclosure: Nina to Will Rogers, Week of 26 November 1906, below.

6. Will Rogers to Betty Blake, ca. 2 March 1908, below.

7. Mort Shea, Rogers's agent, had signed a contract on Rogers's behalf with B. F. Keith's Amusement Enterprises on 24 March for a sixteen-week period beginning 3 September. At the time Rogers was in Europe. The contract stipulated that he would receive $250 weekly for two performances daily (B. F. Keith's Amusement Enterprises Artist's Contract, 24 March 1906, OkClaW).

8. Marston and Feller, *F. F. Proctor,* 96–106. The corporation was dissolved in 1911.

9. King, "Sylvester Z. Poli Story," 13; Laurie, *Vaudeville,* 397–400; "Poli in the News," *Variety,* 13 January 1906.

10. Morrison, "Oscar Hammerstein I," 14; Sheean, *Oscar Hammerstein I,* 117. These sources claim the area covered by the agreement was between Thirtieth Street and Ninety-sixth Street.

11. "Williams Goes with Keith," *Variety,* 16 February 1907.

12. *ENYC,* 523.

13. Ibid., 523–25; Gurock, *When Harlem Was Jewish,* 6–57; Lockwood, *Manhattan Moves Uptown,* 305–10; Peiss, *Cheap Amusements,* 146; Stern et. al., *New York 1900,* 208.

14. *ENYC,* 149, 152.

15. Ibid., 148–53; Stern et. al., *New York 1900,* 15, 87–98, 212, 421–25; Zeidman, *American Burlesque Show,* 176–83.

16. Will Rogers to Betty Blake, ca. 1 May 1908, below.

In the summer of 1906 Betty Blake was invited by Rogers's sister, Maud Lane, to a party in his honor in Chelsea, Okla. During her visit she posed with his many friends on a wagon. Betty is seated in the front row, hand on chin, wearing gloves. Next to her is Ida Mae Collins. Standing in the rear, smoking a cigar, is Richard (Dick) Parris, who went to South America with Rogers in 1902. Next to him *(left to right)* are Thomas Lipe (Tom) Lane; Taylor Foreman, brother of Ada Foreman; and Andrew Denny Lane, brother of Tom Lane. Seated in the front row *(left to right)* are Rogers's cousin Elizabeth Belle (Bess) Schrimsher, daughter of John Gunter Schrimsher and Juliette Schrimsher; Nancy Shasta Lane and Gazelle (Scrap) Lane, daughters of Dr. Lane and Lucinda Elliott Lane; unidentified man; Ada Foreman, daughter of Stephen Taylor Foreman and Ada Carter McClellan Foreman; and Rogers. During Betty Blake's stay Rogers was apparently more interested in Ada Foreman than in Betty, who later remembered that Rogers "never looked in my direction or singled me out." *(OkClaW)*

Article from the *Claremore Progress*
4 August 1906
Claremore, I.T.

Goodale—Collins.

One of the largest and prettiest weddings that has ever taken place in the Cherokee Nation occurred Wednesday last at the country residence of Mrs. Lucinda Lane,[1] when her daughter, Miss Ida Mae Collins,[2] was united in marriage to Mr. Lorenzo Clinton Goodale, of Collinsville. Rev. J. R. Finley pastor of the Presbyterian church, of our city, officiating.

It was a little after 12 o'clock when the wedding march started and the bridal party proceeded to the front porch, where the ceremony took place. The bride came in on the arm of Mr. Thomas Lane,[3] who gave her away. The groom was accompanied by Mr. Will Rogers. The rest of the bridal party consisted of Misses Gazelle Lane[4] and Martha Goodale,[5] and Mr. Gordon F. Lane,[6] and Master Lane Johnston,[7] who acted as ring bearer.

At the close of the ceremony the happy couple received the congratulations of the assembled guests, after which all repaired to an harbor [*arbor?*], where a course dinner was served.

The bride is one of the most accomplished ladies in the Cherokee Nation and enjoys a large circle of friends, who extend to her their heartiest wishes.

The groom is one of the rising young men of this section, being cashier of the bank of Collinsville, where the couple will make their future home.

Close to two hundred were present at the wedding and the afternoon was given up to social intercourse, which all seemed to enjoy.

We were unable to get the full list of all the presents of which the couple were recipients. . . .[8]

PD. Printed in *CP*, 4 August 1906.

1. Lucinda Elliott Lane, the daughter of James and Nancy Elliott, was born on 15 April 1850 in the Delaware Indian settlement at Leavenworth, Kans., where her father operated a trading post. She attended a missionary boarding school. She married George O. Collins, a Civil War veteran. They had two sons and one daughter, Ida Mae Collins, who was born in Kansas on 10 April 1867. After the death of her husband in 1871, Lucinda married Elijah Journeycake (d. 1875), and they had one daughter, Lenora Aurora (Dolly), born 25 February 1873. On 25 December 1877 Lucinda married Dr. Andrew Jackson Lane (ca. 1851–96), a pioneer physician in the Oowala and Claremore area, and they had five children. Dr. Lane was a friend of the Rogers family and their family doctor. Lucinda Elliott Lane died on 20 October 1923 (*As I Recollect*, 19–24; *HRC*, 274–75; Starr, *History of the Cherokee Indians*, 568; see *PWR*, 1:213n.5, 497–98.

2. Ida Mae Collins (b. 1867) was the eldest daughter of Lucinda Elliott Lane and the stepdaughter of Dr. Andrew Jackson Lane. She was of Delaware and Cherokee Indian descent. Collins attended several schools in the Indian Territory, including the Worcester Academy at Vinita and the Cherokee National Female Seminary. In 1899 she and her friends founded the local Pocahontas Club, a social organization devoted to perpetuating the members' Cherokee heritage. As the club's first president from 1899 to 1900, she supported the honorary membership of Will Rogers and several of his friends. Ida Mae Collins taught school in Bartlesville (DuPriest et al., *Cherokee Recollections*, 53–54; *PWR*, 1:176n.1, 177, 211, 213n.5).

3. Thomas Lipe Lane (ca. 1879–1924), the son of Andrew Jackson Lane and Lucinda Elliott Lane, was a boyhood friend and schoolmate of Will Rogers (see *PWR*, 1:104n.5, 501–2).

4. Rosa Gazelle (Scrap) Lane Luckett, the maid of honor at the wedding, was the youngest daughter of Andrew Jackson Lane and Lucinda Elliott Lane. She attended the Oowala School and the Willie Halsell School in Vinita for two years and the Cherokee National Female Seminary, where she graduated on 10 June 1903. She also studied at schools in Lexington, Mo., and Petersburg, Va. She was a teacher and was elected city clerk of Claremore in 1921. A charter member of the Pocahontas Club, she was involved in her local Presbyterian church and in the Eastern Star organization. Scrap Lane lived to be ninety-one (*As I Recollect*, 19–24; *HRC*, 274–75; *PWR*, 1:506; Starr, *History of the Cherokee Indians*, 568).

5. Martha Goodale, the bridesmaid, was the sister of the groom. Ada Foreman was the other bridesmaid (*CM*, 3 August 1906).

6. Fortner Gordon Lane, the son of Andrew Jackson Lane and Lucinda Elliott Lane, married Katherine Cushenberry on 24 December 1912. They had five children. They lived on the Lane property in Oowala and later in Claremore (*As I Recollect*, 23; DuPriest et al., *Cherokee Recollections*, 231; *PWR*, 1:117, 154, 175n.3, 176n.1, 189n.2).

7. William Lane Johnston (b. 1902) was the only son of William Percival Johnston of Tahlequah and Nancy Shasta Lane (d. 1923), the daughter of Dr. Andrew Jackson Lane and Lucinda Elliott Lane. William Johnston, who owned a business in Claremore, married Nancy Lane on 14 June 1899. After attending schools in Claremore, Lane Johnston went to the University of Oklahoma. He married Inza Alexander, and they had one daughter, Shasta Ruth. He was employed by a radio company in Tulsa (*As I Recollect*, 22–23; *HRC*, 331–32; *OCF*, 2:168).

8. The article concluded with a list of wedding presents.

To Clement Vann Rogers
6 September 1906
Detroit, Mich.

Detroit.   Sept 6. 07 ['06][1]

Dear Papa

I got your letter with the two letters in it.   good   send me any mail that comes for me

Well I got here and started to work and my act was a bigger success than last year and I am doing fine[2]   finish here Sunday and go to Cleveland Ohio. They are having the Michigan State Fair here and the City is full of people Bryan spoke here Monday.[3]   it is getting cool up here on the lakes   we go from here to Cleveland by boat Sunday Night

Say what did you do about those Johnny Lipe[4] lots and also about that Nigger boys land   please see to them   buy anything you see there that looks cheap and borrow the money for me to pay for it[5]

Papa settle that business up with Spi.[6]

Well I will stop

where is Parris.

Lots of Love Willie

Next Week
  Keiths Theatre
    Cleveland
      Ohio[7]

ALS, rc. OkClaW. On Griswold House, Detroit, Mich., letterhead.

1. This letter was apparently mistakenly dated 1907. The postmark on the envelope in which it was mailed reads, "DETROIT, MICH., SEP 7 1906, 2:30 P.M.," and the vaudeville itinerary for Rogers's performances in Detroit fits 1906 and not 1907.

2. Rogers had performed at Detroit's Temple Theatre in October 1905 and received good reviews (see Will Rogers to Sisters, ca. 7 October 1905, and Will Rogers to Betty Blake, 17 October 1905, above). The reviews in Rogers's scrapbook for this appearance were equally complimentary. Although he was not the headliner on the bill, one review called him the "best entertainer" at the Temple Theatre. Typical of the review was the following: "There is a hearty reception every time he shambles before an audience in his loose-jointed cow-boy style. He and his horse and 'that other thing,' as he refers to his unnamed partner on the stage, always make a hit. His tricks are quite wonderful; his language is droll and his movements depict a sort of awkward grace which is an amusing entertainment in itself" (scrapbook A-1, OkClaW). The manager's report also praised Rogers: "This comedian lasso-thrower repeated the big hit he made here on his first appearance. He had all other acts of this kind completely overshadowed" (Manager's Report, Temple Theatre, Detroit, 3 September 1906, KAC-IaU). The playbill listed the following acts in order: Al Green's Orchestra (Overture—"Orpheus" Offenbach); Count DeButz and Brother (Parisian Comedy Cyclists); The Two Pucks (America's Foremost Juvenile Artists); The 3 Donals (Marvelous Herculean Acrobats); John Hyams and Leila McIntyre (In Herbert Hall Winslow's Comedy Sketch Entitled "Two Hundred Wives"); Will Rogers (The Lasso Thrower); Polk, Kollins and Carmen Sisters (A Pleasing Combination of Banjoists); Alliene's Acrobatic Monk (Peter the Great—On Trapeze) (Temple Theatre playbill, week of 3 September 1906, scrapbook A-1, OkClaW). The manager also reported that the film *The 100 to One Shot* was shown. Also titled *A Run of Luck,* the Vitagraph film (1906), produced by J. Stuart Blackton and Albert E. Smith, concerns a young man who wins enough money at a racetrack in a city to save his family's house from foreclosure. In its interpretation of luck in the city, the film takes a favorable view of urban life (Musser, *Before the Nickelodeon,* 310).

3. William Jennings Bryan (1860–1925) was born in Salem, Ill. In 1896 Bryan won the Democratic nomination for president, and at the convention he delivered his famous oration on the subject of the free coinage of silver. Although he lost the election in a landslide, he was henceforth identified as a voice of the people. He ran for president again in 1900 and was defeated even more soundly than the previous time. On Monday, 3 September 1906, Bryan spoke at the Michigan State Fair. It was a point of pride for fair organizers that "no laboring man is going to be made to pay extra for the sake of hearing him" ("Bryan Today," *Detroit Free Press,* 3 September 1906). On the day of the visit, fair attendance broke records as 115,000 visitors came to the grounds. In the evening Bryan spoke to a Democratic rally of 5,000. The rights of working people, he said, must be upheld at the expense of corporate wealth. He defended the rights of workers to arbitrate their grievances against companies and opposed the formation of large industrial monopolies. Bryan denied that these were socialist positions, saying:

"How are you going to answer the socialist when he asks you to explain why a few people should have the benefit instead of all? I deny the economic advantage of the trust" ("Five Thousand at Armory," *Detroit Free Press*, 4 September 1906).

In another address at the fair, Bryan focused his remarks on the nation's workforce and said that the "solution of all problems of society and government is human sympathy, and . . . that human sympathy cannot be . . . [unless] all people know something of the condition and experience of those who toil" ("Twenty Thousand Hear State Fair Addresses," *Detroit Free Press*, 4 September 1906). His speech called for an eight-hour work day and universal education for the workers ("Bryan's Down for Two Speeches," *Detroit News*, 3 September 1906; "Bryan is Greeted by 115,000 at State Fair," *Detroit Free Press*, 4 September 1906; *DAB*, 2:191–92, 194–96; "Five Thousand at Armory," *Detroit Free Press*, 4 September 1906; "Flays Trusts, Senate and Railroads," *Detroit Free Press*, 4 September 1906; *WNBD*, 147).

4. Probably John Gunter Lipe (1864–1913), the son of Major DeWitt Clinton Lipe (1840–1916) and Victoria Susan Hicks Lipe (d. 1867). John Lipe was educated at the University of Arkansas at Fayettevile. In 1892 he purchased a ranch at Talala, I.T., and entered the cattle business. He married Sarah Lulu Foreman on 4 January 1899, and they had five children (*HRC*, 280–81; see also *PWR*, 1:178n.3).

5. Rogers's lifelong practice of investing in real estate began early in his life and was influenced by his father, who was a large landowner. On 18 August 1906 the *Claremore Progress* reported that "Will Rogers was the recipient this week of the handsome present from his father of the home place on Fifth Street. Will announces his intention of erecting some rent house on the rear of the lots."

6. In 1903 Spi Trent received acreage from the Rogers ranch when it was divided in the allotment process in the Cherokee Nation. A distant cousin, Trent was undoubtedly someone the family could trust to either give back the land or sell it at a reasonable price. Clement Vann Rogers repurchased Trent's allotment, but not without considerable conflict (see Will Rogers to Clement Vann Rogers, 27 September 1906, below; and *PWR*, 1:562–64).

7. Keith's Prospect Theatre in Cleveland was then managed by Edward F. Albee. It had a seating capacity of 1,725 (orchestra, 600; balcony, 525; gallery, 600). It featured two shows a day, a matinee at 2:15 P.M. (admission, 15–50 cents) and an evening performance at 8:15 (admission, 25–75 cents). In 1923 a larger and more elegant showplace, the Keith Palace Theatre, was opened in Cleveland. In addition, the Keith Circuit operated the Hippodrome in the city for many years (*Cleveland Plain Dealer*, 9 September 1906; *JCOTG*, 185; "Keith Palace Theatre, Cleveland, Ohio," 110–11).

Clipping from Will Rogers's Scrapbook
12 September 1906
Cleveland, Ohio

The following article is typical of the many publicity stories on Rogers at this time. The details in this interview were used frequently in local newspapers where Rogers performed.

BY W. E. SAGE

This will be a dismal failure of an interview with Will Rogers, the cowboy, who does such wonderful work with the lasso at Keith's this week. I went to it shy too many things for anything like success.

In the first place, I should have had a moving picture machine to give the grace of his movements and particularly to catch that smile of his. Then there should have been a photograph [*phonograph?*] of the very best make to get the mellowness of his tones and the picturesqueness of his vocabulary, its aptness and its spontaneity. The words he used seem to belong to him as if he coined them some place in his throat and stamped his own sign manual on them as they were passing out.

Last and most important, I would have had to invent a machine to get his most fascinating quality. If I had a Boyoscope to register his frankness, his good nature, his irrepressible boyishness, I would have got you nearer to Rogers when you read the markings on it than in any other way.

I see many delightful people in my walks and talks and many who are just the reverse. Human nature makes a funny parade before the newspaper man who questions and records. But it has been a month of the bluest kind of blue moons since I have struck hands with a fellow who has won the heart out of me so completely as this boy from the Indian Territory.

Is he an Indian?

Sure! And he steps high over it.

"I'm a quarter-breed," he said to me, "and its the thing above all others that I'm proud of. I'm a Cherokee and they're the finest Indians in the world. No 'blanket Indians' about them. We are civilized and educated. Why, the government don't allow the Cherokees to go to Carlisle and the other big schools for Indians. They're for the ignorant kind. We have our own schools, and the boys' and girls' seminaries in the Territory are just as fine as any in the country. And if the boys want a better education their folks send them away to schools in the East and pay their expenses themselves.

"My father is president of the bank in our town and he wanted to make something of me in the way of education, but I just nacherally was a ranch-man. He sent me to a military school in Missouri and I used to run away from it regularly.[1] I'd get back to one of the far-away camps on our ranch and stay there for ten days or so, and then when the boys would ride back to the main camp I'd come projecting along with them. And then father'd say, 'What in hell are you doin' here?' and send me back to the school. I did this a dozen times, I guess.

"Here's another thing that strikes me as plumb ridiculous. You read in books that such a puncher was a great rider and a great roper. You never find that. A man that rides well don't rope well. And if he is great with the rope he is no shakes of a rider. You see he just goes in and devotes himself to one thing and makes a success of it. The men from the North are the best riders and the men from the South are the best ropers. They get more practice.

"How did I get to do all these things with the rope. Oh, just by being at it all the time. That's the way of the kids down home. I taught some of them tricks when I was there last year, and, hell, they'd surprise you by the way they do 'em. In two or three years some of 'em will be great.

"Why, I could rope better when I was eight than I can now. Was surer at it. I could rope a horse passing me in any way. And I was boss of the ranch when I was fifteen. Forty thousand acres and ten thousand head of cattle. Why, I never wore skirts like the kids about here. I just went from long baby clothes into pants. That's the way they do with us.

"All this fancy work with the rope is new. Ten years ago you never saw any of it. That fellow with Buffalo Bill was the first to do it and he taught me my first trick, too. He was a Mexican and that's the kind they do down there.[2] With us it is good, plain, practical work.["]

Here I broke in to ask him if he practiced to get up in his stage act.

"Hell, no! I'd never seen a stage and my horse had never seen one, too, when we went on at Union Square, New York. They said to me, 'Can it be done?' 'I can do it in a small space on the ground,' I told them, 'and I guess there won't be no trouble here.' There wasn't. 'Teddy' and I went right on that first afternoon and we never gave a better show.

"Who is 'Teddy'? That's my cow pony there. He's the best in our section and he's won many a roping contest, with me and with other boys that I let take him.

"We call everything that's special good down our way 'Teddy.' I'm high on him. He's a fine old bum! I roped for him in the White House and he thinks I'm the greatest in the land and over in Boston young Teddy came to see me."

Will—it's absurd to call him Mister Rogers and be formal with him in the face of that smile, that merry laugh and that infectious boyishness—has been a great traveler. South America knows him well, for he was many months in the Argentine region, where he thinks the great cattle ranges of the world will soon be. There he met the natives who threw bolos and were also quite expert with the lasso. There, too, he took a hand with the bolo himself. And for thirteen months he was in South Africa during the Boer war breaking horses under contract with the British government. Then there was a long stay in Australia, where he learned to cast the boomerang.

Last year he was in England for four months and at the close of his engagement, which took him on the continent as well, he went prowling around and seeing things, "for I always was a fellow to get up and get around," he remarked.

After this year he will go back to ranching, on which his heart is set. It will not be on the extensive scale of a few years ago, when his father's cattle roamed over forty thousand acres. The Cherokee land is too valuable for that. It is underlaid with coal and other minerals, oil and natural gas. So it has been divided up among the members of the nation, each getting about 160 acres. His father and mother, both of whom are quarter-breeds, got the best of their old ranch lands—the finest in the nation—and his father has been adding to it by purchases from less thrifty neighbors. Now they have about a thousand acres.[3] All the money which Will earns in the show business, and it is a little fortune every week, for he is one of the star attractions in vaudeville, goes home to the banker father and is invested in land.

Most of this talk took place in the big, cool stage passageway at the side of the theater, where Will, hot and breathless from his last great feat, which he calls "the crinoleen," hiked himself to get a breath of fresh air the minute the curtain had fallen. But I had come early and I had waited in the wings while he was going through his act. And it was there that I got the truest line on his boyishness.

The other people on the bill were paying him the highest compliment in their power.[4] They were standing watching him. He talked at them in gay asides and they answered back. It was as good as a play to watch him grin and caper about. Just as he was about through pretty Minnie Meredith, one of the Meredith Sisters, came from her dressing-room in the transition stage between the stage makeup and the simplicity of her street appearance.[5] She couldn't wait to finish her toilet. She wanted to see Will in his act again. She, too, joined in the badinage.

Suddenly I heard him call out: "Say, miss, if you keep on joshing me I'll just nacherally have to rope you and drag you out." And the grin that swept over his face was full of the impishness of a kid.[6]

PD. Unidentified clipping, 12 September 1906. Scrapbook A-1, OkClaW.

1. Kemper School in Boonville, Mo., which Rogers attended in 1897–98; he left during the school year (see *PWR*, 1:78–80, 142–44).
2. Vincente Oropeza (see *PWR*, 1:522–23).

3. Rogers's father eventually purchased many of the allotments assigned from his property. Clement Vann Rogers had 79.93 allotted acres from his old ranch; Will Rogers had 78.84 acres. Other individuals holding allotments were Spi (Martin) Trent (69.88 acres); Jane Hicks (10 acres); Rosa Patterson (11.34 acres); Jesse Ross (65.71 acres); Mariah Ross (36.56 acres); Perry Ross and Mariah Ross (30 acres); and Augustus Lowry (21.27 acres). Handwritten notes—written probably by Clement Vann Rogers on letterhead stationery, "The Convention to Form a Constitution For the State of Oklahoma"—reveal that he repurchased practically all of the acreage, giving him and his son a total of 403.47 acres ("List of Taxable Lands Owned by C. V. Rogers" and "Names of the Persons Who Have Allotments in the Home Place," Clement Vann Rogers file, OkClaW).

4. Of special note on the playbill was the appearance of Egbert Van Alstyne and Louise Henry. The following acts were listed on the playbill, in order: Quigg, Mackey and Nickerson (Comedy Musical Offering); Mary Dupont and Co. (In John W. Cope's sketch "Left at the Post"); Bert Marion and Sabel Deane (Singing and Comedy); Egbert Van Alstyne and Louise Henry (Mr. Van Alstyne is known to fame as the author of "Navajo," "Back, Back to Baltimore" and the song hit "In the Shade of the Old Apple Tree," and Miss Henry has made a reputation as "The Sal Skinner Gal." Their combined talents make a neat, pretty and refined specialty); Sisters Meredith (The Maids who made "Hiawatha" famous, Comedy Singing and Dancing); Will Rogers, the Lasso King (The Western boy who has astonished the world with his roping feats); Manhattan Comedy Four (Harmony and Fun. First appearance in the United States after six years' tour of Europe and Great Britain); Four Londons (Europe's Greatest Acrobats) (Keith's Cleveland Theatre playbill, week of 10 September 1906, scrapbook A-1, OkClaW). In addition, two films were shown: *For Sale—An Auto* and *Flora Fiesta, Los Angeles* (Manager's Report by H. A. Daniels, Keith's Cleveland Theatre, week of 10 September 1906, KAC-IaU). The latter film was a kinetograph actuality (a short documentary of "actual" of real-life footage) produced by the Edison Manufacturing Co. and filmed by Robert K. Bonine in Los Angeles on 22 May 1906. According to Charles Musser, *Flora Fiesta, Los Angeles*, was an attempt to give favorable publicity to the week-long festival and to the city. Bonine had just finished filming scenes from the April 1906 San Francisco earthquake, and there was a fear that Los Angeles would have a similar disaster. Many copies of the San Francisco films were sold, but only three copies of the Los Angeles film after nine months of distribution (Musser, *Before the Nickelodeon*, 367–68).

5. The sisters Laura Meredith, Pearle Meredith, and Carrie Meredith were well-known singing and dancing comediennes. According to Joe Laurie, Jr., they were mulattos who were the first to sing the popular song "Hiawatha." To avoid race prejudice against African Americans, they billed themselves as Native Americans in South Africa and England. In 1898 they joined the Black Patti Troubadours and played in the musical skit *At Jolly 'Coon'-ey Island,* by Ernest Hogan; the following year they participated in the troupe's transcontinental tour. During 1905 and 1906 they toured South Africa as the American Indian Squaws and sometimes the Hiawatha Girls. Advertisements called them the "originators of the Indian character in vaudeville and the first to popularize Indian music" (unidentified clipping, 25 December 1905, NN-L-RLC). H. A. Daniels wrote a mixed review of their Cleveland appearance in his manager's report: "These girls sang some character songs in costume. Dutch, Spanish, Chinese, and Indian. They closed with a song in velvet knickerbockers. While they have an excellent act it is not worth the money they are getting. After their last song they went off with very little applause. The audience had tired of them and they had

not give[n] value" (KAC-IaU). The Meredith Sisters also appeared in British music halls and toured in France and Austria. During their world tours they had costumes made, which they used in their eclectic imitations. By 1910 only two sisters, Carrie and Pearle, were in vaudeville, but they were still popular on the Keith and Orpheum circuits. Reviewers praised their ethnic imitations (Dutch girls, Eskimos, Hawaiians); exotic songs (Spanish, Chinese, Indian, and Egyptian themes); and quick changes of many costumes. They performed as late as 1919 (Laurie, *Vaudeville*, 150; Meredith Sisters clippings, Locke env. 1443, NN-L-RLC; Sampson, *Ghost Walks*, 108, 147, 181, 189, 352, 367; *Variety*, 1 April 1911).

6. The Cleveland newspapers praised Rogers's act. The Keith organization was also pleased. H. A. Daniels wrote: "He offers an excellent act that is full of novelty and surprise. His wild western 'patter' took with the audience and every one of his tricks was liberally applauded. From an applause standpoint he was the hit of the show" (Manager's Report, Keith's Cleveland Theatre, week of 10 September 1906, KAC-IaU).

To Tom Morgan
14 September 1906
Cleveland, Ohio

During his visits to Rogers, Ark., Rogers met Tom Morgan, a friend of Betty Blake. Morgan was a columnist and wit known for his humorous local-color stories from the Arkansas region. Rogers and Morgan shared an affinity for southwestern humor, and they would remain friends until Morgan's death in 1928.[1]

Hello   Will just drop you this line to tell you ad.

M. A. Shea 1358 Broadway N.Y.[2]   They switched [me] and I go to Grand Opera House Pittsburgh Pa.[3] Next Week. instead Toledo so address use there I will write to you soon

So long

Will.

APC, rc. TMC-RHM. Postcard hand-addressed to Mr. Tom Morgan, Rogers, Ark. Postmarked Cleveland, 14 September 1906.[4]

1. See Biographical Appendix entry, MORGAN, Tom P.
2. Mort A. Shea, Rogers's agent.
3. During the week of 17 September 1906 Rogers appeared at Harry Davis's Grand Opera House in Pittsburgh. The theater listed prices ranging from 15 cents to a dollar. It consisted of twenty boxes (seating 152); orchestra (seating 860); balcony (seating 686); and gallery (seating 1,100) (*JCOTG*, 181). The playbill was as follows: Mr. and Mrs. W. W. O'Brien (Introducing an Original Sketch); Dale and Rossi (A Duo of Polite Entertainers); James E. Henry and Dorothy D. Young (Eccentric Comedy, Singing and Travesty Entertainers); Eleanor Blanchard (Refined Imitations); Jack Marzelo and Eby Millay (Horizontal Bar Comiques and Burlesque Wrestlers); Willa Holt Wakefield (A Georgia Sunbeam, From the Drawing Rooms of London, New York, and the Southlands; Will Rogers (From the Land of the Cherokees, The

Tom P. Morgan, humorist and friend of Will Rogers, in Rogers, Ark., ca. 1925. *(Tom Morgan Collection, RHM, Neg. N008223)*

Lariat King and His Horse); Katie Rooney (Singing and Dancing Comedienne); Hungarian Huzzar Band (50 Boy Artists In a Varied Program); Clifford and Burke (Black Face Eccentriques in Song, Dance and Story); The Crickets (Joseph Hart's Latest Novelty); Quigley Bros. (The Irish Conversational Comedians); 3 La Maze Bros. (World's Greatest Knockabout Artists) (Grand Opera House playbill, week of 17 September 1906, scrapbook A-1, OkClaW).

4. The postcard featured Rogers in three poses and was titled at the top "The Greatest Catch in Vaudeville." Below was written "Compliments of WILL ROGERS The Larie[a]t Expert."

To Clement Vann Rogers
26 September 1906
Buffalo, N.Y.

BUFFALO, N.Y. <u>Wednesday</u> 190__

Dear Papa

Just got your letter about Spi   Now I think we should give him something even if he did say you could have the land   why I will give him half of what ever you think is right   for if he acts square why I will give him and you ought too.[1]

Here is $100   makes me $1650.00   I left and this is $300.00   makes $1950 in all

I am doing fine[2]   it is getting cool up here   I go to Toronto, Canada. Sunday to play all next week.

Say make that old Mc   whats his name pay rent on that house   if he dont get out of there

Well I will close

write soon   Love to all

Willie.

Next Week

Sheas Theatre

Toronto.

Canada.[3]

ALS, rc. OkClaW. On The Court Inn, 37–39 Court Street ("opposite Shea's Theatre"), Buffalo, N.Y., letterhead. Sherman E. Woolley and James R. Doyle, managers.[4]

1. Trent received $650.91 for 50.07 acres ($13 an acre) on the Rogers ranch ("Lands Bought by C. V. Rogers of Martin Trent with Restrictions Removed" [handwritten notes on "The Convention to Form a Constitution For the State of Oklahoma" letterhead], Clement Vann Rogers file, OkClaW). Another document lists 69.88 acres for Trent ("List of Taxable Lands Owned by C. V. Rogers," Clement Vann Rogers file, OkClaW).

2. Rogers was performing at Mike Shea's Theatre in Buffalo when he wrote this letter. The following performers were listed in order in the playbill: La Vine Cimaron Trio (Refined Acrobatic Comedy and Dancing); Tom Moore (The Only Coon Singer); Marie Wainwright assisted by Frank Sheridan (In a Domestic Difficulty, by Frank Tannehill, entitled *Our Baby*); Fred Ray and Co. (In Roman Travesty); The Crickets (A Ballet of Geisha-Land and the Little Yellow Folk); Sharp Bros. ("The Two Dixie Boys"); Charles F. Semon ("The Narrow Feller"); Will Rogers (Lasso Thrower. A Westerner Who Has Astonished the World with His Roping Feats); The Kinetograph (Kathleen Mavourneen) (program, Shea's Theatre, Buffalo, N.Y., week of 24 September 1906, OkClaW). *Variety* rated Rogers's performance "good" and referred to The Crickets as the headliners (29 September 1906, 13). Mike Shea (1859–1934) was a respected independent theater owner who operated theaters in Buffalo, and also two in North Tonawanda and one in Toronto. He was noted for the quality of his acts and for giving his performers a fair salary (*EV*, 463; Stein, *American Vaudeville As Seen by Its Contemporaries,* 151–54).

3. At Mike Shea's Theatre in Toronto Rogers performed again with La Vine Cimaron Trio, Tom Moore, Fred Ray and Co., and The Crickets. Added to the program were Sam Elton (The Man Who Made the Shah of Persia Laugh) and Walter Jones and Mabel Hite (Presenting a Comedy Musical Sketch) (Shea's Theatre playbill, week of 1 October 1906, scrapbook A-1, OkClaW).

4. The Court Inn was located opposite Shea's Theatre at 37–39 Court Street. It advertised "rooms for men only" but also featured a "Ladies' Restaurant, Rathskeller, Cafe and Bar, and Billiard Room." The inn stressed that the accommodations were fireproof.

To Clement Vann Rogers
30 October 1906
Boston, Mass.

Boston, Mass. Oct. 30. 06

Dear Papa

I intended to send you some money but will wait till next week   I dont hear from May anymore   I am in Boston this week and go to Portland Maine next Week   am back in N.Y. in 3 weeks.   everything in N.Y. is all waiting on the election which is next week   Hughes will be elected Govenar over Hearst.[1]   Tell Godbey to send me exactly what that was and if he has another lot to sell   I might buy them also.

Well I must close.

Write next Week to

Moores Theatre

Portland

Maine.

AL, rc. OkClaW. On B. F. Keith's International Circuit Theatrical Enterprises letterhead.

1. On 6 November 1906 the Republican Charles Evans Hughes (1862–1948) defeated the newspaper magnate William Randolph Hearst (1863–1951) for governor of New York. Hearst ran on the Democratic and Independence League ticket. The morning after the election the *New York Times* reported that Hughes had been elected with a plurality of 63,383 votes (135,817 to 72,434), even though Hearst carried New York City by a 71,644 plurality. Hughes was then a prominent attorney who had gained fame for his investigation of utility and insurance companies. An equally ambitious politician, Hearst was a New York congressman (1903–7) and had been defeated for the 1904 Democratic presidential nomination and twice for New York City mayor (1905, 1909). After his tenure as governor (1907–10), Hughes was appointed associate justice of the Supreme Court and served from 1910 to 1916. As the Republican nominee for president in 1916, he was defeated by Woodrow Wilson. Hughes later served as secretary of state in the Coolidge administration (1921–25) and as chair of the Washington Arms Limitation Conference (1921–22). Rogers often made fun of Hughes on the stage of the *Ziegfeld Follies*. Between 1930 and 1941 he served as chief justice of the Supreme Court (*NYT*, 7 November 1906; *WNBD*, 457, 497).

To Betty Blake
30 October 1906
Boston, Mass.

<u>Boston, Mass.</u> Oct. 30

My Dear old Kid

Say I just got your letter forwarded from N.Y. in reply to my message[1]   I had been here for two days and no letter so tonight after I went home from the Matinee[2]   I sent you a wire asking you if you were sick and could *not* write for it seemed ages since I heard from you   Yes the opearator got mixed for the message said Big success here this time.   You seem to have your trouble with agents   Operators and all those   still they are in your line   perhaps they are just handing you a *lemon*

Listen Kid I dident like your last letter I got just now   you said you wanted to consider me your best friend   Now dont be silly   you know what you are to me and dont say those things   oh one little letter you wrote said "I will be happy if you love me"   Now I sho do keep that letter with me for I like it and if that will constitute your hapiness you are the happy Kid for I sho do love you, old Kid

Say dont say I have been bad for the only reason I did not write was that I waited to hear from you before I wrote   I was as good as could be and not *lushing.*   and not for a minute did I forget you or never shall for you are *mine* and you know I am yours   you just keep on thinking that over for you will find me the most persistent Lover you ever saw.   I just cant help it Dearie you must write me at once Kid   I havent any *plans*   my plans are in your hands   shape them to suit yourself.

Yours   Will

Next Week
Moores Theatre
Portland, Maine[3]

ALS, rc. OkClaW. On B. F. Keith's International Circuit Theatrical Enterprises letterhead. A. Paul Keith, Assistant Manager, E. F. Albee, General Manager and Proprietor of the Keith Theatre, Providence, R.I.[4]

1. During the week of 22 October 1906 Rogers had been appearing at Keith and Proctor's Twenty-third Street Theatre in New York City. The following performers were listed on the playbill: Hendrix and Prescott (Singers and Dancers); Elmer Tenley ("The Manhattan Man"); Julia Redmond and Co. (With Al. Haines and an Excellent Cast in the Merry Farce Comedy, *Too Much Married*); Clarice Vance (The Inimitable Singer of Coon Songs); Will Rogers and his Bronco (Lasso Thrower, First Appearance

Since his Triumphal Tour of Europe); The Allisons (In *Minnie from Minnesota*); Harry Gilfoil (In his Famous Character Creation: "Baron Sands"); The Navajo Girls (In a Musical Oddity); 3 Renards (European Acrobats). Rogers gave two performances daily including Sunday (Keith and Proctor's Twenty-third Street Theatre playbill, week of 22 October 1906, scrapbook A-1, OkClaW).

Before that engagement Rogers had appeared at the Cook Opera House in Rochester, N.Y., the week of 8 October 1906, and at the Grand Theatre in Syracuse, N.Y., the week of 15 October 1906. At the Cook Opera House he performed with the following acts: Charles E. Evans and Co. (First Appearance in Vaudeville, In a One-act Farce by George Arlies entitled *It's Up to You William*); James J. Morton (A Fellow of Infinite Jest); Ed. Reynard (Vaudeville's Greatest Ventriloquist); Will Rogers (The Lasso Expert, First Appearance Here Since His Triumphal Tour of Europe); J. K. Murray and Clara Lane (Operatic Stars, in their Successful One-Act Sketch *A Night at Home*); Marzelo and Millay (Comic Bar Act and Burlesque Wrestling) (Cook Opera House playbill, week of 8 October 1906, scrapbook-A-1, OkClaW). *Variety* reported that Rogers "won well-merited applause for clever exhibition of lasso throwing" (13 October 1906, 14).

The following performers were listed on the Syracuse Grand Theatre playbill: Demonio and Belle (A Unique Blending of Grotesque Comedy Singing, Dancing and Music); J. K. Murray and Miss Clara Lane (The Comic Opera Stars in their Charming Singing Musicale *A Knight at Home*); Will Rogers and Horse (A Study from Life on the Plains, Undeniably the Most Unique Act in Vaudeville); Julian Rose (The Famous and Original Hebrew Comedian); May Duryea and Charles Deland (Presenting the Intensely Funny Domestic Playlet *The Imposter*); The Rialta Four (A Quartette That Can Sing As Well As Comedy); The Four Melvins (The Greatest Troupe of Hand to Hand Gymnasts in the World) (Grand Theatre playbill, week of 15 October 1906, scrapbook A-1, OkClaW).

2. Rogers performed at Keith's Theatre in Boston during the week of 29 October 1906. He played with the following performers: The Mozarts (In the Novel Terpsichorean Skit, *A Cobbler's Dream*); De Chunt (The Equilibrist and his Acrobatic Fox Terriers); The Three Mitchells (Ragtime Diversionists); Cherry and Bates (Comedy Cyclists); Dave Nowlin (The Man With the Flexible Voice); Miss Violet Black (The Clever Ingenue and Her Company, in the Sparkling Comedietta *A West Point Regulation*); Josephine Gassman and Her Pickaninnies (Droll Doings by Darktown Youngsters); The Uessems (The Equilibristic Marvels); Lynn, Fay and Young (Singers and Dancers, A Blithesome Bunch of Beauty and Talent); Will Rogers (His Pard, His Horse and His Lariats in Cowboy Stunts); George Evans (New Bits of Wit and Wisdom by Vaudeville's Greatest Monologuist); Amers and His Famous Military Band (Farewell Week of England's Most Popular Bandmaster) (Keith's Theatre playbill, week of 29 October 1906, scrapbook A-1, OkClaW).

3. James H. Moore also owned the Temple Theatre in Detroit (Leavitt, *Fifty Years in Theatrical Management,* 161, 203). Rogers did not play this theater but was changed to Keith and Proctor's Fifth Avenue Theatre in New York for the week of 5 November 1906. Rogers had obtained a contract from Keith and Proctor Amusement Enterprises on 5 November 1906 to play at this theater and the Harlem Opera House for the week of 12 November 1906 (OkClaW). His salary was $250 a week, and his agent, Mort Shea, received a 5 percent commission for negotiating the contract. Using stationery from New York's Ashland House (located near the theater on Fourth Avenue and Twenty-fourth Street), Rogers wrote his father on 5 November 1906 that his address was the Fifth Avenue Theatre and that "I think I will be here two or three weeks this

time" (Will Rogers to Clement Vann Rogers, 5 November 1906, OkClaW). The play-bill included the following acts: Fifth Avenue Orchestra; The Gagnaux (Presenting their Own Ideas of Juggling and Feats of Equilibrium); Horace Wright (Italian Character Singer); Kitty Stevens (The Popular Comedienne); Mr. and Mrs. W. W. O'Brien (In their Clever Little Comedy: *The Bachelor and the Maid*); Tom Moore (Champion Singer of Coon Songs); O'Brien and Havel (Assisted by Miss Effie Lawrence In their Latest Success: "Tricks and Clicks"); Kelly and Violette (The Ultra Fashion Plates in Song); Will Rogers and Horse (Expert Lariat Thrower); Murphy and Francis (Colored Singers and Dancers); Six Musical Cuttys (Brothers and Sisters Presenting a New Repertoire of Classical and Popular Selections); Mr. Arnold Daly (Presenting a Comediettina in One Act by Bernard Shaw, entitled *How He Lied to Her Husband*); The Elinore Sisters (Sure-Fire Laugh Provokers); Count DeButz and Brother (Comedy Bicyclists). The theater offered continuous vaudeville from 1:00 P.M. until 10:30 P.M. and a Sunday program (Keith and Proctor's Fifth Avenue Theatre playbill, week of 5 November 1906, scrapbook A-1, OkClaW).

4. A. Paul Keith was the son of B. F. Keith. The letterhead also listed the following theaters as part of the Keith chain: Keith's Theatre, Boston; Keith's Bijou Theatre, Boston; Keith's Theatre, Philadelphia; Keith's Bijou Theatre, Philadelphia; Keith's Alvin Theatre, Pittsburgh; Keith's Theatre, New York; Keith's Prospect Theatre, Cleveland; and Keith's Princess's Theatre, London (Keith never presented vaudeville at this last theater).

Certificate of Election of Clement Vann Rogers
14 November 1906
Muskogee, I.T.

CERTIFICATE OF ELECTION

United States of America, Indian Territory, ss:

To <u>Clement V. Rogers</u>

This is to certify, and you are hereby notified, that at the election held in the Indian Territory on the sixth day of November, A.D. 1906, for the election of delegates to the Constitutional Convention for the proposed State of Oklahoma, as provided by the Act of Congress approved June 16, 1906, (Public—No 234), you were duly and legally elected to the office of DELEGATE to said Convention in and for Election District No. <u>64</u> in said Territory, as appears from the canvass of the votes and the determination of the Board of Canvassers of said election now on file in this office.[1]

You are further notified that you must appear at Guthrie, Oklahoma Territory, on Tuesday, the twentieth day of November, 1906, at which time and place you will enter upon the duties of your office after taking the oath of office and qualifying as provided by law.[2]

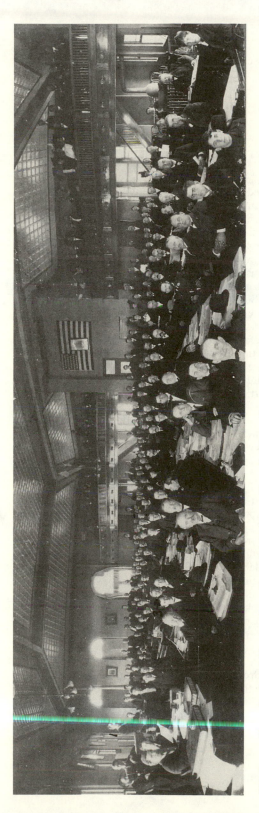

Oklahoma Constitutional Convention, Guthrie, 1906–7. Clement Vann Rogers played a significant role as a delegate in the debate and helped write the constitution. During the proceedings Cooweescoowee District was renamed Rogers County in his honor. *(OkClaW)*

WITNESS our hands and official seal at Muskogee, in said Indian Territory, this 14th day of November, A.D. 1906.

T__ [illegible][3]

Joseph A. Gill[4]

Wm. H. H. Clayton[5]

The Districting and Canvassing Board in Indian Territory.

PDS, with autograph inserts, rc. OkClaW.

1. On 16 June 1906 Congress passed the Oklahoma Enabling Act (the Hamilton Statehood Bill), which stipulated procedures for the creation of a state from Oklahoma Territory and Indian Territory. One hundred twelve delegates were to be elected to a constitutional convention: fifty-five from each of the territories and two from the Osage Nation. The area that encompassed Claremore and Oologah was designated district 64. Given his experience in Cherokee politics, Clement Vann Rogers became the Democratic Party candidate for his district. On 23 June 1906 the *Claremore Progress* suggested that he would be an excellent representative but announced that he would not accept the office. Regardless, on 22 September 1906 the paper announced his candidacy. Like most Downing Party members, Rogers decided to run as a member of the Democratic Party. In the Democratic race he was opposed by T. D. Bard. In early October the convention of Democrats of the sixty-fourth constitutional district unanimously nominated Rogers. In the election he was opposed by the Republican, Dr. Jesse C. Bushyhead, a popular Claremore physician and son of Principal Chief Dennis W. Bushyhead. It was essentially a contest between two friends who were related. Rogers was Bushyhead's uncle by marriage: Bushyhead's mother was the sister of Rogers's wife (see *PWR*, 1:485–86).

In his bid for votes Rogers advocated many reform issues popular among Progressives, but as a former slave owner he also supported racial segregation. The *Claremore Progress* endorsed his candidacy as follows: "A vote for C. V. Rogers is a vote for the initiative and referendum, for separate schools, separate waiting rooms, separate coaches, a railroad commission with power to act and elected by the people and primaries under the control of the law of the state" (13 October 1906). The newspaper felt that Dr. Bushyhead represented a minority of people, while Rogers was the majority's choice: "The wisest way to 'stand up for Claremore' is to vote for Hon. C. V. Rogers, the Democratic nominee" (*CP*, 20 October 1906). By contrast the *Claremore Messenger* appears to have favored Dr. Bushyhead (19 October 1906).

"ROGERS SWEEPS DISTRICT" was the headline in the *Claremore Progress* on 10 November 1906. In the 6 November election Rogers won 815 votes to Bushyhead's 615, and he carried seven of the ten precincts. In his home district of Oologah he won by 100 to 43. He won East Claremore 188 to 144 but lost West Claremore by 5 votes (*CP*, 10 November 1906). Of the 112 elected delegates, 99 were Democrats. In the Official Roster of the Constitutional Convention Rogers was listed as "64 C. V. Rogers, D., Claremore" (OkClaW). Rogers, who was sixty-seven, was the oldest member of the constitutional convention (Clark, "Delegates to the Constitutional Convention").

2. The convention was held in the Brooks Opera House in Guthrie. Formation of the constitution was controlled by the Democrat delegates, who formed a strong farmer-labor bloc. Chaired by its colorful president, the Democrat William H. (Alfalfa Bill) Murray, the convention developed a constitution that reflected early twentieth-

century political progressivism and reformism that was influencing new city and state governments. Besides dividing Oklahoma state government into three branches (executive, legislative, and judicial) with a bicameral legislature, the constitution contained a system of checks and balances, and a bill of rights. It also stipulated certain reform measures, such as the long ballot, election of most public officials, a term limit for the governor, primaries, the initiative and referendum, prohibition of child and convict labor, and a Corporation Commission to control trusts and transportation companies. The constitution also reflected the small-farm economy of the territories by protecting individual ownership of land, prohibiting alien ownership of land, and restricting land ownership by corporations. It also contained a provision for prohibition in the former Indian Territory and Osage Nation for twenty-one years, while a motion to include women's suffrage was defeated. (Opponents feared that women's right to vote would lead to suffrage for African Americans and argued stereotypically that it was not "lady-like" for a woman to vote.)

Although Clement Vann Rogers was not considered one of the ringleaders of the convention, he was very active in the proceedings and chaired the committee on salaries and compensation of public officials. His committee report was adopted by a vote of 74 to 7. Rogers also was a member of the committees on legislation, portraits, homesteads and exemptions, liquor traffic, counties and county boundaries, and impeachment of officers. Charles N. Haskell, the first governor of Oklahoma, recalled Rogers as "one of the soundest, most capable thinkers in our Constitutional Convention. We occupied adjoining seats for four months and nothing of consequence was ever done without conferring with Uncle Clem" (Charles N. Haskell in *Claremore Weekly Progress*, 2 February 1928, quoted in Keith, "Clem Rogers and His Influence on Oklahoma History," 85). During the convention proceedings Rogers was known to have opposed women's suffrage. As a member of the committee on counties and county boundaries, Rogers got into a bitter floor fight over an amendment to remove disputed townships from his home district, Cooweescoowee (Rogers) County, to Nowata County. In a stirring speech Rogers opposed the amendment and stated that he was voicing the wishes of the people: "I claim that when I made this report to the house I was as honest as any man on it. . . . I did it for one purpose, the rights of my people. . . . I came there in 1856 and grew up with those people because I was raised right there, and I am a citizen of the Cherokee Nation and more than that I will say that my interests, that the people I represent, have a life-time interest there" (*Stenographic Report of the Constitutional Convention*, 20 December 1906, quoted in Keith, "Clem Rogers and His Influence on Oklahoma History," 87). The amendment was defeated in a close vote, 41 to 30. Will Rogers once commented about his father's actions: "He laid out the boundaries of our County. (Rogers County.) He had been all over that country. He knew the creeks, the lowlands, the hills, and every square foot of good land. Well, he got a map and a pencil and took in every acre of good soil that was in that whole country. We had to stop him once because he had crossed the line into Missouri. Why, when he got through, our County looked like the antlers of a reindeer" (James M. Cox in Payne and Lyons, eds., *Folks Say of Will Rogers*, 158). In honor of Clement Vann Rogers, the name of Cooweescoowee County was changed to Rogers County by the convention in January 1907 (see Notice from the *Claremore Progress*, 22 December 1906, below).

Despite the opposition of the Republican Party led by President Theodore Roosevelt, the constitution was ratified on 17 September 1907 by a vote of 180,333 to 73,059. The bill was signed by Roosevelt on 16 November 1907. On the same day the duly elected Charles N. Haskell took the oath of office as Oklahoma's first governor.

Oklahoma's constitution was hailed by reformers as an example of Progressive democracy ("Clem and the Constitutional Convention," unpublished ms., OkClaW; Gibson, *Oklahoma,* 328–38; Goble, *Progressive Oklahoma,* 202–27; Keith, "Clem Rogers and His Influence on Oklahoma History," 82–91; Morgan, *Oklahoma,* 82–92).

3. Probably the signature of Tams Bixby (1855–1922), who was head of the Commission to the Five Civilized Tribes. Born in Virginia, Bixby was active in the newspaper business and soon became involved in politics. He became the private secretary to the governor of Minnesota in 1892. In 1897 he was appointed a member of the Commission to the Five Civilized Tribes in the Indian Territory, with the assignment of working with the tribes to divide land among the members and disband their government. Bixby spent the remainder of his career, from 1906 until 1922 (the year of his death), in Oklahoma, as editor and publisher of the newspapers *Daily Phoenix* and *Times Democrat* (*CP,* 27 October 1906; Gibson, *Oklahoma,* 326; Williams, "Tams Bixby," 205–6, 211–12).

4. Joseph Albert Gill (1854–1933) was born in Wheeling, W.Va. He trained for the bar at the University of Illinois and came to Kansas after having lived for seven years in the Northwest. A lifelong interest in politics brought him to the 1896 Republican National Convention as a delegate from Kansas. He was an active supporter of William McKinley's bid for the presidency, and was appointed U.S. judge for the Northern District of Indian Territory in 1899. He was reappointed to the post in 1904 by President Theodore Roosevelt. Roosevelt also appointed Judge Gill, along with Judge Clayton and Tams Bixby, to subdivide the Oklahoma Territory into election precincts after passage of the Enabling Act in 1857 (Gill, Jr., "Judge Joseph Albert Gill," 375–76).

5. William H. H. Clayton served as U.S. district attorney in the late nineteenth century. In 1880 he prosecuted David L. Payne for the land appropriation activities of the "Boomers" who usurped Indian lands. Later Clayton was a senior federal judge in Indian Territory (Clark, "Delegates," 400; Duncan, "Open Letter from Too-Qua-Stee," 307).

To Betty Blake
5 December 1906
Baltimore, Md.

The issue of Rogers seeing other women created considerable tension in his relationship with Betty Blake during their long courtship. With this letter Rogers enclosed a letter from Nina, a vaudeville performer with The Crickets. To prove his faithfulness to Betty, he sent her Nina's letter.

Baltimore, Md.

Dec. 5th. 06.

My Own Dear Betty

Your letter just come and old Kiddie I was just afful glad to hear from you but you kinder waited a while dident you

I kept waiting till I heard from you all this week

I will send you that letter it is from a nice little girl friend of mine whom I met   She was playing in a girl act[1] and I happen to be on the bill with them

3 weeks[2] and lots of times after the show I used to ask her out to hav a little lunch as I always go out after and have a bite to eat and she was such a nice ladylik smart kind of a girl and she got a bit stuck on me and in N.Y.[3] she was at one Theatre and Me at the other and cause I dident come around she wrote me and told me a lot of what she thought of me and I wrote her and just told her exactly how things was and that I liked her fine as a good friend and would do anything for her I could for she was a grand fellow but that she could never recall me having told her that I was stuck on her for I admired her in a different way and that I had a girl that I really loved and this is the letter from her which will go to show you that I am not (as bad as I *have been* and as you think I am[)]

Honest Kid I am trying (and doing it) to be as I think you would like me to be.   I have friends that I jolly along with and go around and have a drink (only beer) with.   but only to kill time and be friendly   Now dont get sore cause I send you this, or dont think I am four flushing trying to show you what a good fellow I am.   I only do it cause I want you to know.   Listen Girlie you are real mean you wont tell me how old you are *not even me*   why I dont care if you are a century plant   you are no "*lemon*" in my estimation   Yes still got that those songs have just neglected sending them.   some are from Mr and Mrs. Van Alstyne   he's the composer of Apple Tree Navajo[4] and all those and some are from Mrs. Josephine Gassman   The Lady with the *Picks* 4 negro Kids.   Oh! yes and a book "Richard the Brazen" wild west and far east.[5]   its pretty good   I have no doubt told you of a dear friend I had in Washington a jewelryman and Wife[6]   Well he come up this eve (you know Baltimore is only 40 miles from Washington) and he is taking me back home after the show tonight with him and I come back tomorrow in time for the show   Hurrah!   got a wire today to play Hammerstein N.Y.   Xmas Week guess I aint glad it is on the opposition circuit but it is absolutely the leading Vaudeville Theatre of the *world* and all performers are tickeled to death to get to play it.   You know its where I made my first hit and played so long and I am a favorite there.   but I cant see how Shea got the Keith people to stand for it as they kick on acts playing for the other side.[7]

Well Kid I go on in a little while   my act is doing great here as Baltimore is one of my best towns[8]   I will write you again in a day or so and send you that stuff also   and you must write me *every day* if you can

for I am certainly loving you a plenty now Kid

Please write me a long good *loving* letter

from your everloving Kid
Will

Next Week.

Keiths Vaudeville.

(I dont know the theatre but that will get it[)]

    Altoona, Pa.[9]

ALS, rc. OkClaW.

1. "Girl acts" were also known as "big acts" or "flash acts"–that is, acts that used up to fifteen people to present a musical comedy or farce with special songs, lighting, scenery, and costume, and thus added variety to the bill. The Crickets (sometimes called The Electric Crickets) was a song-and-dance novelty under the direction of Joseph Hart. The Crickets' act was described as "a Ballet of Geisha-land and Little Yellow Folk. Written by Joseph Hart and Edwin Kendall. Composed and Put on the Stage by Mr. Hart" (Grand Theatre playbill, week of 17 September 1906, OkClaW). It was a popular attraction; an advertisement in *Variety* on 24 November 1906 announced that its time was all booked. Its leads were Norma Seymour, soprano, and W. N. Cripps, tenor. The act consisted of two settings. The first scene was called "The Wisteria Grove" and the second "The Battleship *Maine*." Musical numbers included "The Cricket and the Moon," "Moon Eyes," and "Heroes of U.S.A." Joseph Hart (1858–1921), an actor turned vaudeville writer, manager, and producer, specialized in this type of act. He performed a single wearing blackface and playing the banjo. In 1901–5 Hart became known for his portrayal of "Foxy GrandPa," starring in the play with the same name. Hart became known for his flashy vaudeville productions, including the Eternal Waltz with thirty performers, which was on the Palace's opening bill on 24 March 1913. In 1894 Hart married Carrie De Mar, who performed in several of her husband's sketches. Despite blindness in one eye and deafness, Hart remained active until his death from apoplexy on 3 October 1921 in New York (*EV*, 385; Laurie, *Vaudeville*, 232–37, 487; *VO*, 1:7 October 1921; *WhoStg*, 226).

2. Rogers and The Crickets were on the same playbill for three consecutive weeks: Pittsburgh's Grand Opera House, the week of 17 September 1906; Shea's Theatre, Buffalo, the week of 24 September 1906; and Shea's Theatre, Toronto, the week of 1 October 1906 (playbills, OkClaW).

3. Both Rogers and The Crickets performed at different Keith and Proctor vaudeville theaters in New York City the week of 12 November 1906. Rogers was at the Harlem Opera House and The Crickets performed at the Twenty-third Street Theatre (*NYDM*, 17 November 1906 and 24 November 1906; *NYT*, 11 November 1906).

4. A reference to Louise Henry and Egbert Van Alstyne, who were married at this time. With the lyricist Harry H. Williams, Van Alstyne composed the hit song "In the Shade of the Old Apple Tree" in 1905. Earlier, in 1903, he and Williams had teamed up to write the song "Navajo," considered one of the first Tin Pan Alley tunes to exploit Indian themes. Williams and Van Alstyne continued to compose songs with western themes, including "Cheyenne" (1906) and "San Antonio" (1907). According to Louise Henry, Van Alstyne composed the song "Pony Boy" for Rogers as a result of seeing him perform at the Union Square Theatre in 1905. This work, however, is not listed among Van Alstyne's songs (a song by that title, also called "My Pony Boy," was written by other composers for the musical *Miss Innocence* in 1908) (LHM-LHP; *AmSCAP*, 747; Mantle and Sherwood, eds., *Best Plays of 1899–1909*, 428; *New Grove Dictionary of American Music*, 4:444; Craig, *Sweet and Lowdown*, 79–81).

5. *Richard the Brazen* was a novel by Cyrus Townsend Brady (1861–1920) and Edward Peple, published in 1906 by Moffat, Yard and Co. Brady was a popular novelist and Episcopal clergyman. While working for a railroad, he studied for the ministry and was ordained a deacon in 1889 and a priest in 1890. His first of seventy published novels, most of them historical romances, appeared in 1898. His writings drew on his experiences in the navy and the West, as well as the lore of his family of Indian fighters and his own experiences as a traveling cleric in the Midwest. Among his works were *Recollections of a Missionary in the Great West* (1900), *Border Fights and Fighters* (1902), *The Bishop* (1903), *The Conquest of the Southwest* (1905), and *Arizona* (1914). Many of his stories were made into films and attested to the popularity of his subject matter (*AAB*, 73; *DAB*, 1:582–83; *NYT*, 25 January 1920; *OCAT*, 94).

Richard the Brazen is a romantic adventure story that begins in Texas. The daughter of a wealthy New York financier is saved by a dashing cowboy from certain death in a cattle stampede. As fate would have it, the cowboy and the young woman are the son and daughter of bitter enemies. The young man falls in love with the woman and he goes to her house disguised as a British earl. This plot device creates a situation whereby the young westerner must continually disguise his colloquial expressions and mannerisms in order to "pass" as a refined member of eastern society. The author makes clear that it is the young cowboy who is truly noble and naturally well-bred.

This characterization of a western cowboy among eastern companions probably appealed to Will Rogers who was sojourning among urban vaudevillians. Other similarities between the cowboy of the novel and Will Rogers can be noted. Both are the sons of prominent ranchers, and thus a cut above the average cowboy in class and education, though this does not diminish their ability as riders and ropers. Both sons are rebelling against their fathers—Rogers by becoming a performer rather than a rancher, and the cowboy of the novel pursuing the daughter of his father's enemy. The novel appealed to Rogers for its celebration of the cowboy arts of riding and jumping.

6. In Rogers's scrapbook was the business card of William H. Colmer, professional representative of Castelberg's National Jewelry Co. in Washington, D.C. Listed on the card were Castelberg's other offices or sales representatives in London, Baltimore, and New York (William H. Colmer business card, scrapbook 1902–4, CPpR). With his vaudeville earnings Rogers bought two diamond scarf pins and a large yellow diamond ring from the company on 9 January 1906 (Castelberg's National Jewelry Co. bill of sale, OkClaW). In her biography Betty Rogers wrote that "these were considered important to a rising young man in the theater, and actors believed earnestly that diamonds were a sound investment." Rogers never wore the ring, which was "often in and out of hock." Rogers wanted to buy Liberty Bonds during World War I so he naively gave the ring to a man who said he knew a buyer in the racehorse business, without obtaining a receipt. Many weeks later he finally received $1,000. "He took for granted that every man was honest, until he proved himself otherwise," his wife wrote (Rogers, *Will Rogers*, 99–100).

7. Rogers performed at Oscar Hammerstein's Victoria Theatre of Varieties from 24 to 30 December. Rogers refers to the squabbles between the Keith organization and independent operators. (Morrison, "Oscar Hammerstein I," 14; Spitzer, *Palace*, 12; "'Willie' Hammerstein," *Variety*, 25 December 1913, 17).

8. Rogers was performing at the Maryland Theatre and had performed there earlier from 1 to 7 January 1906. The reviews in Rogers's scrapbook were laudatory, and one particularly commented on his dexterity with the lariat: "He throws two nooses at once, one catching the horse, the other the rider; ties single and double knots in ropes with a twist of his wrist, and on horseback makes a whirling circle of a noose that is

about 100 feet in circumference" (unidentified clipping, scrapbook A-1, OkClaW; see also *Variety,* 8 December 1906, 12). Included on the bill were Coakley and McBride (The Exponents of Black Face Comedy with Some Coon Comicalities That Will Prove Laughable); Mullen and Corelli ("Humorous Peculiarities." These Geniuses of Mirth Who Always Have Good Things Tucked Away); Chester D'Amon (The Great White Mystery in his Wonderful Work of Psychromancy); Miss Sadie Julia Gompers (First Appearance in Baltimore of Talented Daughter of President Samuel Gompers of the American Federation of Labor, with Artistic Vocal Selections); Matthews and Ashley (Boby and Herbert in a Genuine Screamer, *A Smash-up in Chinatown*). Rogers was listed as "G," or number seven, on the playbill and described as "The Man, the Mustang and the Manila, the World's Greatest Lasso Expert Just Returned from a Triumphal European Tour" (Maryland Theatre playbill, week of Monday, 3 December 1906, scrapbook A-1, OkClaW).

9. Rogers performed at the Lyric Theatre in Altoona from 10 to 16 December. The playbill was as follows: Overture by the Lyric Theatre orchestra; Lillian Bender and Alice Earle (Italian Street Musicians); Willie Weston (The Famous Comedian); Katie Rooney (Daughter of Pat Rooney, Singing, Dancing and Impersonating); Matthews and Ashley (presenting Their Latest Laughing Success, *An Upset in Chinatown*); Will Rogers (The Western Cowboy and His Texas Mustang, presenting A Wonderful Exhibition of Lassoing); Mullen and Correlli (In Humorous Peculiarities); Sylvan and Onal (Eccentric Acrobatic Sketch); and American Vitagraph (Lyric Theatre playbill, week of 10 December 1906, scrapbook A-1, OkClaW).

Enclosure:
From Nina
Week of 26 November 1906
New York, N.Y.

<u>New York</u>

Dear friend Will

Am very glad you wrote me as you did as it was just what I needed to restore to me what little common sense I ever had. I hope you will forget that I have been such a fool, as I do not care to loose all your respect and no one apreciates a good, true friend better than I do and they are mighty few. The girl that wins your love may consider herself very fortunate, only wish the average men were more like you. Well be good, trusting every thing is going fine I remain

Sincerely Yours
Nina

We are changed to Harlem[1] next week.

ALS, rc. OkClaW. On The Gerard, 44th Street between Broadway and Sixth Avenue, New York, letterhead.

1. The Crickets performed at Keith and Proctor's Harlem Opera House the week

of 26 November 1906. (See "This Week's Attractions, Keith and Proctor's Opera House," *NYDM,* 1 December 1906, 18; and "Last Week's Bills, Keith and Proctor's Harlem Opera House," 8 December 1906, 16, in which the reviewer commented "The Electric Crickets were a feature of more than ordinary interest." These notices refer to the week before the date of publication.)

Keith and Proctor had leased the theater, refurbished it, and opened it in fall 1906 ("Keith and Proctor Open Harlem House," *NYDM,* 3 November 1906, 18). It would not have been unusual for The Crickets to be suddenly switched to a newly opened theater, such as the Harlem Opera House.

Article from the *Baltimore World*
6 December 1906
Baltimore, Md.

Once again Owen Wister's Virginian *is featured in a newspaper story about Rogers.*[1] *In this article Rogers makes some acute observations about the novel and the popularized image of the West.*

THE VIRGINIAN WAS A MEAN SPIRITED CUSS

No Real Cow Puncher Goes Back on a Pal—
Some Other Queer Yarns Spun in the Green Rooms
By Actors with the Bark On

"Did I ever read 'The Virginian,' by Owen Wister? Well, yes; I reckon I read some of it—say, that book's all wrong; tain't human nature. No man would hang his own pal, no matter what he did."

A real cow-puncher who has punched cattle on a ranch in Indian territory, who has "rode the line" in Mexico, who has "rounded them up" in South America, is at the Maryland[2] this week. His name is "Will" Rogers, I.T., and his personality is a great deal more interesting than his act, which in itself is a clever bit of lasso manipulation such as is often seen in the wild west shows. But when he came off the stage yesterday at the Maryland and sat down on a table "backstage" and drew off the chaps he wears in his act he looked up quizzic[al]ly as the reporter drew near. "I don't know what to talk about," he said, with a frankness that was quite refreshing, when compared to so many other people in the show business. "I just came East because I thought I'd like to see what it was like. I had been very near all over the rest of the world, cattle punching and doing odd things here and there, but when I got here and did this lasso stunt I kinder liked it. I am goin' to stay in it as long as they'll stand for it I reckon, and then I'm going back to the ranch. I like it out West. I was born there."

Sitting on the table with his square-cut, clean-shaven face, he was like the hero of a Western play taken out of it and made to play the part in real life. The red shirt of his act was still on him and seemed a part of him, just as did his boots and soft sombrero.

Then he was asked about "The Virginian."

IT WAS TOO MUCH TO SWALLOW

"Yep, I read it—leastwise, part of it. We wuz all sitting out on the ranch one night in the summer soon after that book came out. There must have been thirty of us there all together and there was men that had rode all over the West a-punching cattle, and we were mightily interested in this yere story until we got to the part where that main guy—that Virginian, with his black hair and brown eyes—catches his pal cattle rustlin' and hangs him. Say, we threw that book away. That wuz too much. We had a mass meeting right then and there and decided that air question without any dissent at all. There wasn't a man in that ranch that night but didn't say that if it had been a pal of his he would have helped him rather than hanged him. Why, if this pal had been a murderer it would have been different, but even that wasn't no hanging affair; but think of stringin' your pal for a few measly calves what wasn't worth hardly anything at all. Another thing, this pal of hisn hadn't been at it long. It was just a streak of luck he had and he went in two or three raids and then skipped.

"Say, let me tell you something"—

Here the cowboy drew his feet up under him on the table as if he was sitting beside a campfire in the West and he tapped his hand significantly on his knee.

EVERY MAN FOR HIMSELF

"There ain't no such West as them fellers what wrote say there are. The law out there is every man for himself. Just so long as you don't bother me then I ain't going to bother you. If you bother somebody else that is their lookout, not mine. Why, there is outlaws out there that come to our ranch and stay all night and we feed 'em and they go their way. It don't make no difference to us. We ain't sheriffs. We ain't the law. Why, sometimes there is bandits that rob trains and come to our ranch to stay all night. We let them stay. What if they did hold up a rich express company for a piece of money and get away with the goods, that ain't our lookout. It's theirs and they have got to ketch em, not us. Just so long as they don't play no tricks with us we treat 'em white."

"Well," interposed the reporter, "is the small town where the cow-puncher goes to blow in his month's wages on wine and women still in existence?"

"Aw, that's all rot," Rogers answered, his face puckering up with a look of disgust settling there. "There's just as many good cow-punchers as there are bank clerks or anybody else in big towns. There's good and bad. Why, some of 'em don't drink at all, and I know a good many of them have thousands of dollars which they have saved from their salary and invested in cattle. There are some that go to church on Sunday and—well, it's just the same as any other job."

"Are there many left—the cow-punchers? Some say they are going out of existence."

"Aw, say." It was plainly evident that all this was news to the cow-puncher who was sitting on the table. "That makes me tired," he said at last. "Of course there are fences, but the cattle has to be worked just the same. You have got to go out and ride on the line just like you used to do, and protect your cattle from thieves. Wherever you have a ranch there is cattle stealers."

Don't Do a Pal Dirt

"Are the women out there scarce?"

"Naw, indeed. There are plenty of them—of course in some places there aren't many ranches. They are a trifle scarce, but not so as you could notice it much. No, say"—and here he laughed. "You have got that book idea of the West. Tain't nothing like you think, and as for that Virginian—well." That seemed to be a thorn in his side. "Say," he added, "you can bank on it, there ain't a man in the West who would do a pal as dirt as that Virginian did. He didn't have no spirit, nor real affection for his bunkie, you can put your last red on that."

It is only at times that Rogers veers into the vernacular of the West, but his talk is very interesting. He claims to have circled the world. His horse used in the act was brought from his ranch, while the brother puncher, whom he carries as an assistant, he got from the Pawnee Bill Show.

PD. Printed in the *Baltimore World,* 6 December 1906. Scrapbook A-1, OkClaW.

1. See article from *Lowell Daily Courier,* 4 December 1905, above.
2. Baltimore's Maryland Theatre was owned and operated by James L. Kernan and was on the Keith Circuit. It had a seating capacity of 1,972, and in 1906 its prices ranged from 15 cents to 75 cents (*JCOGT,* 143).

To Betty Blake
21 December 1906
New York, N.Y.

Returning to New York and with a week off, Rogers attended some Broadway shows. The tone of his letter to Betty Blake expresses considerable enthusiasm about the New York theater.

New York, <u>Friday. Dec. 21</u>

My Own Dear Girl.

Well my pal   heres hoping you have a glorious Xmas and a plum good New Years

I know you will have a good time there at home   I am so sorry I could not come out but I only had the one week and I could not get next week booking set back.[1]   you know I am laying off this week because Wheeling W.Va. house is not open yet   that where I was to of played.   I could collect salary and they told me so themselves but said that if I would release them this week they would see that I was well taken care of and would consider it a personal favor and Shea said if I should hold them and make them pay. that I might loose out in the long run   so I wanted to be in N.Y. this week if I did not go home   so I have had a great time going to all the best shows   you know its the only chance I ever had to go to them for its my first week off   Have been to the Hippodrome[2]   my friend another cowboy works there and we live here togeather   oh its a great show[3]   also went to "The Rose of the Rancho."[4] the new one   its good.   *"The Great Divide"*[5]   oh its fine.   saw it last night. and Montgomery and Stone in the Red Mill.[6]   its great too.   going to see Lew Fields in About Town and a burlesque on The great Decide, tonight.[7] and Madam Butterfly[8] tomorrow and I go to Matinees to all the vaudville theatres.   And oh how I did wish for you here this week to go to all these shows and enjoy them togeather, but we will sometime wont we Dear?

Oh you should have seen me shopping here in these big shops and then is when I did need you   had to fix up a box for home and that would of been your job.   so get ready to perform that next year   you hear me shout?

Kid I sent you a little Xmas remembrance in the shape of a coat.   and a muff.   you should get it as soon as this letter.   Now I dont know if it will fit you and that it is just right.   but I hope it will suit you and prove serviceable for there is such a skin game in buying furs   it may prove to be a *lemon*.   but it is the only thing I could think of that would do you any good and that I thought would please you.

Well Dearie I will jar loose   have a good time and think occasionally of the Kid in the east who loves you best of all else in the world

By-By.   My Darling

Your loving Kid
Will

237 W. 43rd St. N.Y.

ALS, rc. OkClaW. On New York Hippodrome, "largest playhouse in the world, Entire Block, 6th Ave. 43rd to 44th Street," letterhead. Shubert and Anderson, managers.[9]

1. Rogers was listed as a possible performer at a benefit called "A Night with the Vaudeville Comedy Club" on 23 December 1906, a playbill that included top vaudeville performers (OkClaW). Rogers appeared at Hammerstein's Victoria Theatre during Christmas week from 24 to 29 December. The playbill included the following acts: Mlle Chester and Her Statue Dog; Farrell-Taylor Trio (Comedy Musical Act); Miss Ethel Arden, Mr. George Abel and Company of English Artists in *Three of a Kind*; Clarice Vance (Comedienne); Sleede European Pantomime Co. in *Mysterious House*; Smith and Campbell (Comedians); George Felix and Lydia Barry Presenting *The Boy Next Door*; That Quartette (Sylvester, Jones, Pringle, Morrell); Will R. Rogers (Return to America. Expert Lariat Thrower); New Vitagraph Views (Hammerstein's Victoria Theatre playbill, week beginning Monday matinee, 24 December 1906, OkClaW). That Quartette was advertised as the headliner on the bill (*NYT*, 23 December 1906).

2. One of the most famous and certainly the largest New York City theater at this time was the Hippodrome, which stretched for an entire block on Sixth Avenue between Forty-third and Forty-fourth Streets. It was the inspiration of the showmen Frederic Thompson and Elmer S. Dundy and the financier John W. Gates, who had earlier created the amusement center Luna Park. Advertised as the largest playhouse in the world and designed by the architect J. H. Morgan, the Hippodrome seated over 5,200 spectators. Its huge stage (210 feet wide, 110 feet deep, and 60 feet high) was designed for lavish extravaganzas and included movable sections that could be raised by hydraulic lifts. There was space enough for two large circus rings. Its most famous attraction was a water tank with 960,000 gallons of water for aquatic spectacles including waterfalls, fountains, streams, and spillways. The Hippodrome opened on 12 April 1905 with a four-hour double bill, *A Yankee Circus on Mars* and *Andersonville*. But its expensive productions proved too costly. In 1906 Lee and J. J. Shubert leased the theater, and during the next nine years the brothers staged musical spectacles featuring auto races, baseball games, flying dirigibles, and mock earthquakes. Under the management of Charles Dillingham from 1915 to 1923, the theater offered colossal revues and reached its apex with the dazzling 1922 popular revue *Better Times*. In 1923 it was leased to the Keith-Albee chain, and the stage was remodeled for vaudeville. Two years later Radio-Keith-Orpheum (RKO) used the theater as a film venue, and the company eventually sold it. Billy Rose produced the circus musical *Jumbo* there in 1935. In 1939 the theater was razed; the site remained undeveloped until 1952, when a parking garage and skyscraper were erected (Cronican, "Hip, Hip, Hippodrome!"; Fowler, "Hippodromes"; Henderson, *City and the Theatre*, 243; Morgan, "New York Hippodrome"; William Wood Register, Jr., "New York's Gigantic Toy," in Taylor, ed., *Inventing Times Square*, 243–70; van Hoogstraten, *Lost Broadway Theatres*, 95–99; Young, *Documents of American Theater History*, 2.10–12).

3. Rogers's friend was probably playing in *Pioneer Days* at the Hippodrome, a three-act western melodrama that had opened on 28 November 1906 and ran for 288 performances. It was advertised as a dramatic spectacle with a large cast. The production dramatized western life during the gold rush in California. Among its features was a performance of the Sioux war dance by 100 Sioux from the Pine Ridge Agency in South Dakota and a mock battle between mounted cavalry and Indians. Also on the bill was a one-act circus and a spectacle entitled *Neptune's Daughter*. The latter featured twenty-four mermaids mysteriously disappearing in the water tank on stage (Mantle and Sherwood, eds., *Best Plays of 1899–1909,* 527; McNamara, *Shuberts of Broadway,* 43, 45; *NYT,* 25 November and 29 November 1906).

4. *The Rose of the Rancho* was a three-act play by David Belasco and Richard Walton Tully. On 27 November 1906 it opened at the Belasco Theatre, where it ran for 327 performances. It had extended tours for several years and numerous revivals. A typical Belasco production with elaborate staging and melodramatic plot, the play takes place in the late 1850s in Spanish California (Mantle and Sherwood, eds., *Best Plays of 1899–1909,* 527; *OCAT,* 589; *Rose of the Rancho,* program file, NN-L-BRTC).

5. *The Great Divide* was a popular three-act play written by William Vaughn Moody, which opened on 3 October 1906 at the Princess Theatre and ran 238 performances. It reopened at Daly's Theatre on 31 August 1907 for 103 performances. It starred Margaret Anglin (as Ruth Jordan, a New England woman) and Henry Miller (as Stephen Ghent, an Arizona cowboy). Their forced marriage dramatized a clash of cultures between the conservatism of the East and the individualism of the West (Mantle and Sherwood, eds., *Best Plays of 1899–1909,* 242–45; *OCAT,* 305).

6. *The Red Mill* was a two-act musical comedy with book and lyrics by Henry Blossom and music by Victor Herbert. A box-office hit, it opened at the Knickerbocker Theatre on 24 September 1906 and ran for 274 performances. It starred Fred Stone and David Montgomery as two Americans stranded without money in a town in Holland. "The Streets of New York" was the show's most popular tune. The musical went on tour throughout the country and was revived often (*OCAT,* 569; Stone, *Rolling Stone,* 144–46).

Around 1910 Rogers met Fred Stone (1873–1959), and they became close friends. Stone's partner was David Craig Montgomery (1870–1917), who as a young man performed as a contortionist and was billed as "The Human Eel." Then he joined minstrel shows doing blackface comedy acts. Montgomery and Stone first met in St. Joseph, Mo., in 1887, and in 1895 they decided to form their own song-and-dance act, Haverly's Minstrels. At first it was difficult to find work, and at one time they were stranded in New Orleans. They were with Gus Hill's burlesque World of Novelties as the "Eccentric Blackface Comedians." They started in vaudeville performing a two-man blackface act dressed as acrobatic clowns. Soon they were appearing on the roof of the Victoria Theatre and with Hyde's Comedians. By century's end they were headliners, and in 1900 they performed at London's Palace Theatre. Before their role in *The Red Mill,* they had starred on Broadway in *The Girl from Up There* (1901). Their biggest success was the musical *The Wizard of Oz* (1902), in which Stone played the Scarecrow and Montgomery the Tin Woodsman. Two other musical-comedy hits were *The Old Town* (1910) and *The Lady of the Slipper* (1912). Along with other performers, Montgomery and Stone helped found the vaudeville actors' union, the White Rats. Stone appeared with Montgomery until the latter's death on 20 April 1917. Montgomery had become ill while on tour with Stone in the musical *Chin-Chin* (1914). Montgomery was mourned by hundreds at his funeral in New York City. Stone later wrote: "We had in common a whole lifetime of shared experiences, and deep-rooted friendship and trust. We supplemented each other, as is the case with all enduring partnerships. He had a gayety and sparkle and love of life that aroused a response in his audience and his friends" (Stone, *Rolling Stone*, 194, also 85–86, 99–193; *EV*, 479–81; Franklin, *Encyclopedia of Comedians*, 238–39; Golden, *My Lady Vaudeville and Her White Rats*, 72–77; *New York Morning Telegraph*, 13 March 1910; *OCAT*, 643–44).

7. The two-act musical revue *About Town* featured books and lyrics by Joseph Herbert and music by Melville Ellis and Raymond Hubbell. Produced by Lew Fields, it opened at the Herald Square Theatre on 30 August 1906 and ran for 138 performances. *The Great Decide*, a burlesque of *The Great Divide* written by Glen MacDonough, was added to the *About Town* program about 15 November 1906 (Mantle and Sherwood, eds., *Best Plays of 1899–1909*, 517–18).

Lew Fields (1867–1941), born Lewis Maurice Shanfield on New York's Lower East Side, was one of the great stage personalities of his time. With his childhood friend and partner Joe Weber (1867–1942), he performed in many genres, from dime-museum shows (the pair first performed at New York's Chatham Square Museum in 1877) to beer gardens, vaudeville, burlesque, and finally Broadway musical comedy. Weber and Fields became famous for their "Dutch," or German, dialect comedy and their Mike and Meyer knockabout sketches. The tall, thin Fields played Meyer, a city slicker and bully dressed in exaggerated fashion in an overly large checkered suit with a small derby and sporting a small beard and wig. By contrast the rotund, smaller Weber played Mike, a gullible type who was easily fooled, intimidated, and pummeled by Meyer. As the butt of Meyer's dialect jokes and physical assaults, the persecuted Mike evoked both laughter and sympathy from the audience. "Don't poosh me, Meyer," became a famous line in their act. In 1896 they opened Weber and Fields' Musical Hall, where they staged burlesques and satires of plays, comic characterizations, and a full-blown stage show featuring a chorus line. At the time Rogers saw *About Town*, Fields had separated from Weber (1904) and was starring and producing his own shows. Fields staged successful musicals until 1912 when he teamed again with Weber in such productions as *Hokey Pokey* and *Roly-Poly* and in films. In the 1920s he produced musicals written by his son Herbert Fields, Richard Rogers, and Lorenz Hart. *The Vanderbilt Revue* (1930) was his last Broadway production. Fields and Weber performed together at the opening of the Radio City Music Hall on 27 November 1932. Fields spent the remainder of his life in Los Angeles (Distler, "Rise and Fall of the Racial Comics," 73–78, 153–57; *EV*, 539–42; Fields and Fields, *From the Bowery to Broadway;* Gilbert, *American Vaudeville*, 77–79; Isman, *Weber and Fields;* *OCAT*, 253–54).

8. *Madame Butterfly* was a one-act play adapted by David Belasco from a story by John Luther Long. Belasco's production premiered on 5 March 1900 at the Herald Theatre, followed by a long run at Proctor's Fifth Avenue Theatre in 1901; it was revived many times thereafter. The story of a Japanese geisha who falls in love with an American naval officer and commits suicide when he abandons her became the source for Puccini's opera (*Madame Butterfly* clipping file, NN-L-BRTC; Mantle and Sherwood, eds., *Best Plays of 1899–1909*, 359; *OCAT*, 454).

9. In 1906 the producers Lee and J. J. Shubert and Max Anderson obtained a fifteen-year lease on the Hippodrome for $250,000. The Shuberts operated the theater until 1915 and presented extravaganzas such as *The Auto Race* (1907), *Under Many Flags* (1912), and *Wars of the World* (1914). They subsequently gave up the theater, citing unprofitable productions (McNamara, *Shuberts of Broadway*, 43–48).

Notice from the *Claremore Progress*
22 December 1906
Claremore, I.T.

Rogers County was named after Clement Vann Rogers in honor of his contribution to the Constitutional Convention and his long and dedicated service to his region.

The citizens of Cooweescoowee county feel that it would have been a graceful tribute to C. V. Rogers, the oldest member of the constitutional convention, to have the county which he represents named Rogers, and a petition is being circulated to that effect and is being generally signed.[1]

PD. Printed in *CP*, 22 December 1906.

1. At the Constitutional Convention on 11 January 1907 (Clement Vann Rogers's birthday) delegate J. W. Swartz from Chelsea, representing district 61, moved that the name of Cooweescoowee County be changed in honor of Clement Vann Rogers. Swartz stated: "Mr. President, this being the 68th birthday of the patriarch of this assembly, Mr. C. V. Rogers, I move that the house do change the name of this county from Cooweescoowee to Rogers." The motion was seconded by J. K. Hill, who represented district 84; supporting speeches were delivered by W. E. Banks of district 61, C. O. Frye of district 84, and S. W. Hayes of district 85. After the motion passed unanimously, Rogers made the following remarks: "Mr. President and friends of this convention, I feel honored today by your act. When I named this county Cooweescoowee and . . . went home, all my constituents kicked because I gave it that name and . . . petitioned . . . to have the name changed to Rogers, and I thank you gentlemen for naming that county after me" (*Stenographic Report of the Constitutional Convention*, 11 January 1907, quoted from Keith, "Clem Rogers and His Influence on Oklahoma History," 90–91). The renaming was a tribute to Rogers, but reflected disregard for Cherokee history and the area's traditional Native American heritage, since the county's original name commemorated the Indian name of Cherokee leader John Ross. White settlers claimed that the word *Cooweescoowee* was difficult for non-Cherokees and urged anglicization. On 18 January 1907 the *Chelsea Reporter* announced that the county's name had been changed and commented that the "great objection to the name of Cooweescoowee county was the inability of those not familiar with it to spell and pronounce it."

Business Card of The Three Keatons
ca. 1906
New York, N.Y.

When they were in New York the Keatons lived at an actors' boardinghouse, the Carl Ehrich House at 229 West Thirty-eighth Street in New York City, where the food was good and the rooms large, clean, and comfortable. It was operated by a German family named Ehrich. Carl Ehrich (ca. 1861–1926) was the proprietor for twenty-five years.[1] Buster Keaton described this house fondly: "We played so often in New York that we lived in an old fashioned German boarding house on Thirty-eighth Street and I knew that whole neighborhood so I was in ball teams and everything else and I joined the YMCA and got onto the basketball teams and everything else there was."[2] Joe Keaton recommended the Ehrich boardinghouse to Rogers. He gave Rogers the business card of the Three Keatons and wrote the following message on it.[3]

Dear Carl,

3—KEATONS—3[4]

COMEDIANS IN VAUDEVILLE

JOE, MYRA, AND LITTLE BUSTER

HIS BROTHER JINGLES[5] THROWN IN FOR GOOD MEASURE

Permanent Address
Ehrich House
229 West 38th Street
New York

Give this Boy The Room you have—hes my *friend*

Joe.

PDS. OkClaW.[6]

1. The Ehrich House, called in an advertisement a "Professional Boarding House," was a popular theatrical hotel for vaudevillians (Golden, *My Lady Vaudeville and Her White Rats,* n.p.; see also Dimeglio, *Vaudeville U.S.A.,* 135; Laurie, *Vaudeville,* 280). Ehrich died at St. Luke's Hospital in New York on 4 February 1926 (*VO,* 1:10 February 1926).

2. Buster Keaton interview, URL-CLU. One time the Keatons had to evacuate the Ehrich House because of a fire. Buster Keaton recalled: "With the temperature one below zero and the streets outside covered with ice and snow a fire started in the cellar. At two o'clock that morning smoke started billowing up through the floors of the house. We had a large room on the second floor rear, but the smoke was so thick by the time we were awakened that we didn't even have time to dress. 'Where's your father?' asked Mom. I knew he was at the saloon at the corner of Eighth Avenue and 38th Street, but I just shrugged, knowing what she'd say if I told her. There was no time to dress, so I grabbed Jingles and Mom grabbed Sis. We managed to make our way safely to the street with the other boarders. The neighbors took us all of us, wrapped us in blankets, and gave us coffee. As soon as Mom and the kids were taken care of, I tore down to the corner saloon to tell Pop about the fire. He had seen the engines but didn't know the Ehric[h] House was their destination. Shouting to the bartender to wrap me in warm clothing, he rushed out. As it turned out we had lost nothing. Thanks to the firemen the flames never reached above the ground floor. The dining room furniture was destroyed, and Mrs. Ehric[h]'s silverware, stored in the top drawer of the bureau, had melted into one vast lump of metal" (Keaton, *My Wonderful World of Slapstick,* 43).

3. There is no evidence that Rogers stayed there.

4. On The Three Keatons, see Biographical Appendix entry, THE THREE KEATONS.

5. Jingles was Harry Stanton Keaton (1904–66), who was born at the Ehrich House on 25 August 1904. He was named after Harry Houdini and got the nickname Jingles because he made so much noise playing with his toys. Jingles was added to the act as a baby. He would make funny faces at Buster's antics and was part of the closing routine. One time in Portland, Me., Joe Keaton left Jingles alone outside a shop and he was kidnapped. He was found shortly thereafter sitting on a bench at the train depot ("'Jingles' Keaton Kidnapped," *NYDM,* 31 March 1906, 18; Meade, *Buster Keaton,* 40–41). Buster Keaton's sister Louise also joined the act for a time.

6. On the back of the card, in what appears to be Rogers's handwriting, is written: "*Carl Ehrich* 229 W. 38st Ehrich House."

To Clement Vann Rogers
2 January 1907
New York, N.Y.

New York, <u>Wednesday</u>

Dear Papa

I just got a letter from Maud and one from Sallie telling me of your accident and I certainly do feel sorry for you and hope it will heal at once.[1]   I would of wrote but I dident know where to write to you at.   if you dont get better I will come home and stay awhile with you.   I am working in Brooklyn this week and next[2]   I lost one week just before Xmas as the Theatre I was to play in closed up and I lost the week   I am still doing pretty well   Now make them girls write to me and did Joe Hicks[3] get a letter from me to send some blankets to use and tell him to either write or send them

Well I will write soon   hope you are lots better

Love to all
Willie

address for the next 10 days
237 W. 43rd St.
N.Y.

ALS, rc. OkClaW. On New York Hippodrome letterhead.

1. Clement Vann Rogers returned to Claremore for the holidays when the convention recessed on 22 December 1906. Doc Denny congratulated him on successfully debating the county boundary lines and slapped him so hard on the back that he broke one of his ribs. The local newspaper reported that "it was doubtful whether he will be able to attend the meeting of the constitutional convention at Guthrie next week" (*CP,* 29 December 1906; a local rancher named Dock Denny is mentioned in *HRC,* 401).

2. Rogers appeared on the burlesque wheel at theaters managed by Sam Scribner. He performed at many of the same theaters as he had during his 1905 tour. He was at Brooklyn's Star Theatre from 31 December 1906 to 5 January 1907 and at the Brooklyn Gayety Theatre from 7 to 14 January. The program at the Star Theatre was as follows: Annie Goldie (Star Olio. The Original Ginger Girl Singer and Dancing Soubrette); the Nelson-Farnum Acrobatic Troupe (The World's Greatest Acrobats and Pantomimists); Miss Mildred Stoller (A New Idea in Vaudeville. Impersonator of Popular Actresses); Trainor and Dale (In a Laughable Creation); Navajo Girls (The Biggest Act in Vaudeville); and Will Rogers (The Famous Lassoist) (Star Theatre playbill, week commencing Monday matinee 31 December 1906, scrapbook A-1, OkClaW). At Brooklyn's Gayety Theatre Rogers appeared with some of the same acts and, in addition, the Gay Masqueraders and the Watermelon Trust (Gayety Theatre advertisement, scrapbook A-1, OkClaW). At the Gayety Theatre in Baltimore from 14 to 19 January he played again with the Gay Masqueraders. Others on the bill included Charles Farrell (Character Comedian); Coates and Gundry's Original Watermelon Trust; and the one-act comedy *Homeward Bound* by John J. Black. The same program was repeated at Pittsburgh's Gayety from 21 to 26 January (Baltimore Gayety Theatre playbill, week commencing 14 January 1911, scrapbook A-1, OkClaW).

After laying off for a week, Rogers was listed on the 3 February 1907 playbill at New York's Murray Hill Theatre for a special Sunday event. With Rogers were the following acts: Quigley Brothers; Tascott; Martin Brothers; Whitman Sisters and Willie Robinson; Susan Fisher; Nat Carr; and Von Kline and Gibson (Murray Hill Theatre playbill, 3 February [1907], scrapbook A-1, OkClaW).

During the week of 4 to 9 February Rogers appeared at Percy Williams's Brooklyn Orpheum, the flagship theater in his chain and an extremely popular theater in the area. Rogers was described as "the Western Star, America's Best and Cleverest Cowboy in a Series of Wonderful Tricks and Feats with the Lasso." Also on the playbill was the international star from British musicals, Vesta Victoria, described as "the Famous and Clever English Comedienne of 'Waiting at the Church' Fame." Others on the Orpheum program were the Farrell-Taylor Trio (the Popular Fun-Makers); Grace Emmett and Co. (Presenting Her Farce Comedy, in One Act entitled *Mrs. Murphy's Second Husband*); Abdul Kader and His Three Wives (In their Wonderful Exhibition of Rapid-Fire Painting in Oil. Abdul Kabar, by Appointment of the Sultan, is the Royal Portrait Painter of Turkey); The Elinore Sisters (America's Representative Comediennes in a Laugh-Provoking Skit); Eddie Clark and His Winning Widows (Present the Miniature Racing Musical Comedy Sketch *The Tipster*); The Tanakas (Japanese Magicians and Top-Spinners); and Walter Jones and Mabel Hite (Presenting their Latest Eccentric Comedy Skit) (Brooklyn Orpheum playbill, week of 4 February 1907, scrapbook A-1, OkClaW).

3. An individual named Joseph Daniel Hicks (b. 1888) is listed in *OCF*, 1:64. Hicks was distantly related to the Rogers family. He was the son of Edward Daniel Hicks (b. 1866) who married Elizabeth Musgrove, the daughter of Clara Elizabeth Alberty and Francis Marion Musgrove (whose mother was Sally Vann Rogers, whose first marriage was to Robert Rogers, C. V. Rogers's father). Joe Hicks married Francis J. Lindsey, a 1908 graduate of the Cherokee National Female Seminary (*HRC*, 333–34; *WRFT*, 85).

Application
Guion Miller Roll of Eastern Cherokees
8 January 1907

The Eastern Cherokees, who had been removed to the Cherokee Nation West, had sued for reimbursement of unpaid funds due them from the federal government for land, improvements, removal expenses, and items left behind in North Carolina and other states. On 1 July 1902 an act of Congress gave the Court of Claims jurisdiction over claims deriving from treaties the Cherokees had with the United States, and three suits were filed. On 18 May 1905 the court decided in favor of the Eastern Cherokees, and on 30 June 1906 Congress appropriated over $1 million for payment of the claims. The secretary of interior was instructed to identify people who would be eligible for the claims and appointed Guion Miller as a special agent of the Interior Department. Those eligible for funds were all Eastern and Western Cherokees who were living on 28 May 1906 and who could establish that they were members of the Eastern Cherokees in 1851 or descendants of such persons. Claimants had to apply on or before 31 August 1907. As a descendant of Eastern Cherokees, Rogers had to prove his entitlement in the following application. His claim was successful.[1]

Commissioner of Indian Affairs,

Washington, D.C.

Sir:

I hereby make application for such share as may be due me of the fund appropriated by the Act of Congress approved June 30, 1906, in accordance with the decrees of the Court of Claims of May 18, 1905, and May 28, 1906, in favor of the Eastern Cherokees. The evidence of identity is herewith subjoined.

---

1. State full name—
   English name: <u>William P. Rogers</u>
   Indian name: <u>Not known</u>
2. Residence: <u>Claremore,</u>
3. Town and post office: <u>Claremore,</u>
4. County: <u>Cherokee Nation,</u>
5. State: <u>Indian Territory</u>
6. Date and place of birth: <u>Nov. 4, 1879 Cherokee Nation</u>
7. By what right do you claim to share? If you claim through more than one relative living in 1851, set forth each claim separately: <u>For my Mother Mary A. Rogers,[2] My Grandmother, Elizabeth Scrimsher,[3] My Aunt Sarah Catherine Scrimsher,[4] My Great great Aunt Polly Smith, My Cousin Watt Smith.[5]</u>

8. Are you married? ~~Yes~~ No.
9. Name and age of wife or husband: _____
10. Give names of your father and mother, and your mother's name before marriage.
    Father—English name: Clement V. Rogers
        Indian name: Not known
    Mother—English name: Mary A. Rogers
        Indian Name: Not known
        Maiden name: Mary A. Scrimsher
11. Where were they born?
    Father: Cherokee Nation
    Mother: Cherokee Nation
12. Where did they reside in 1851, if living at the time?
    Father: Goingsnake District.
    Mother: Tahlequah District
13. Date of death of your father and mother—
    Father: Living   Mother: ~~Nov.~~ ▲May▲ 28, 1890
14. Were they ever enrolled for annuities, land, or other benefits? If so, state when and where: Mother on the Emigrant pay roll in Tahlequah District in 18[*illegible*]
15. Name all your brothers and sisters, giving ages, and if not living, the date of death:

Name	Born	Died
(1) Sallie C. McSpadden	Dec. 16, 1863	Chelsea, I.T.
(2) Maude Lane	Nov. 28, 1871[6]	Chelsea,I.T.
(3) May Stine	May 31, 1873	Oolagah I.T.

16. State English and Indian names of your grandparents on both father's and mother's side, if possible:
        Father's Side
    Robert and Sallie Rogers Nee Vann
        Mother's Side
    Martin and Elizabeth Scrimsher nee Gunter
17. Where were they born? In Cherokee Nation East[7]
18. Where did they reside in 1851, if living at that time?
    In Cherokee Nation
19. Give names of all their children, and residence, if living; if not living, give dates of deaths:
    (1) English name: John G. Scrimsher Dead
            Elizabeth A. Bushyhead nee Scrimsher Dead[8]

Indian name: <u>Mary A? Rogers my Mother Dead</u>
<u>Sarah Catherine Scrimsher Died without descent</u>
Residence: <u>Martha L. Gulager Eureka, I. T.</u>

20. Have you ever been enrolled for annuities, land, or other benefits?[9] If so, state when and where:
<u>On the Cherokee Authenticated roll of 1880 and am a Cherokee Allottee.</u>

21. To expedite identification, claimants should give the full English and Indian names, if possible, of their paternal and maternal ancestors back to 1835: <u>My Grandfather Mathew Scrimsher lived in the Cherokee Nation East in 1835</u>

REMARKS.

(Under this head the applicant may give any additional information that he believes will assist in proving his claims.)

<u>My Maternal Great Grandmother Catherine Gunter had a sister Polly Smith who with her son Watt Smith were living in the Cherokee Nation in 1851. They are now dead and without descent.</u>

NOTE—Answers should be brief but explicit; the words "Yes," "No," "Unknown," etc., may be used in cases where applicable. Read the questions carefully.

I solemnly swear that the foregoing statements made by me are true to the best of my knowledge and belief.

(Signature) <u>William P. Rogers</u>

Subscribed and sworn to before me this <u>Eighth</u> day of <u>January,</u> 190<s>6</s>7[10]

My commission expires
<u>March 30th,</u> 1908.   <u>[W?]m H. Moyer</u>
Notary Public.

AFFIDAVIT.

(The following affidavit must be sworn to by two or more witnesses who are well acquainted with the applicant.)

Personally appeared before me <u>Nancy Walden</u> and <u>May Wilson,</u> who, being duly sworn, on oath depose and say that they are well acquainted with <u>William P. Rogers,</u> who makes the foregoing application and statements, and have known <u>him</u> for <u>26</u> years and <u>26</u> years, respectively, and know <u>him</u> to be the identical person <u>he</u> represents <u>himself</u> to be, and that the statements made by

[him] are true, to the best of their knowledge and belief, and they have no interest whatever in his claim.

Witnesses to mark.   Signatures of witnesses.

_____   Nancy Walden

_____   May Wilson

   Subscribed and sworn to before me this 3rd day of November, 1906.
My commission expires
Nov. 1st, 1908   John T. Ezzard[11]
                                                           Notary Public.

PDS, rc. OkTahN.

   1. On 28 May 1908 Miller delivered his report stating that 45,847 applications had been filed for 90,000 claimants; of these 30,254 were enrolled as legitimate claimants, 3,203 residing east of the Mississippi River and 27,051 west of the river. The roll of the Eastern Cherokees was approved on 9 June 1909. A supplemental report with additional approved claimants was submitted on 5 January 1910, bringing the total allowed to share in the fund to 30,820. The final roll was approved on 15 March 1910, and payment was made on an equal basis to all people officially approved and enrolled (Clark, *Cherokee Ancestor Research*, 25–28; Wardell, *Political History*, 249–54).
   2. On Will Rogers's mother, Mary America Schrimsher Rogers, see *PWR*, 1:543–48.
   3. Mary A. Rogers's mother was Elizabeth Hunt Gunter Schrimsher (1804–77), who was the daughter of John Gunter (b. ca. 1750–60) and Catherine (Katie), a full-blood Cherokee. Elizabeth was born in Creek Path, Ala., and thus was of Eastern Cherokee descent. She married Martin Matthew Schrimsher (1806–65) in 1831, and sometime after 1835 they moved to the Cherokee Nation West, establishing a plantation in the Eureka community and another home in Fort Gibson (*WRFT*, vi, 110, 120).
   4. Sarah Catherine Schrimsher (1866–92) was the daughter of John Gunter Schrimsher (1835–1905; the brother of Mary A. Rogers) and Juliette Melvina Candy (1841–1930). Sarah married W. E. Sanders (see *PWR*, 1:552–53; Starr, *History of the Cherokee Indians*, 587; *WRFT*, 122).
   5. As Rogers states under "remarks" in the application, Polly Smith was the sister of his great-grandmother on his mother's side, Catherine (Katie) Gunter (d. 1835), who married John Gunter. Watt Smith was Polly's son (*WRFT*, 114).
   6. Maud Lane was born on 28 November 1869. Rogers put information on his sisters' places of residence in the "Died" column. All three of the sisters listed in this section were alive when he filled out this application.
   7. Robert Rogers was probably born in Georgia or Alabama in 1815; Sallie Vann was probably born in Georgia in 1818. Martin Schrimsher was born ca. 1806–7 in Blount County, Tenn. (*WRFT*, vi).
   8. The second marriage of Elizabeth Alabama Schrimsher (Will Rogers's aunt) was to Dennis Wolf Bushyhead, principal chief of the Cherokee Nation (see *PWR*, 1:61, 65n.5, 66, 148, 484–86, *WRFT*, 120, 124).

9. See *PWR*, 1:56–57, 62, 429–31.

10. The document was stamped on the front that it was received 10 January 1907 in the Indian Office Eastern Cherokees. It was assigned no. 9735, which corresponds to Rogers's listing in the roll's general index. A document attached to the application states that Rogers was admitted with the following reason: "Brother of Maud Lane #2379 and is admitted for same reasons."

11. John T. Ezzard was a practicing attorney who had an office in Chelsea, I.T., and apparently was a member of Oklahoma's first legislature (*HRC*, 241, 373).

Review from the *New York Dramatic Mirror*
23 February 1907
New York, N.Y.

COLONIAL.[1]—Harry Bulger[2] and company in Mink's Rink, by John Kendrick Bangs,[3] headed an excellent programme. Mr. Bulger's peculiar comedy methods seemed to meet with favor, and there was a good deal of laughter while he was on the stage. The mechanical appliances used in the act made bigger hits than the performers. Josephine Cohan and company in A Friend of the Family, and Fred Niblo, with his inimitable monologue, it is needless to say, won a very large share of the applause. Sie Hassan Ben Ali's genuine Arabs seemed more reckless than ever, and their tricks were thoroughly appreciated.[4] Snyder and Buckley[5] scored strongly in their new act, and Irene Franklin's[6] latest offering pleased immensely. J. Warren Keane presented a new mystery called Askme: or, The Dial of Eternity. It is a glass dial with figures that are pointed out by some invisible method when people in the audience ask questions. Mr. Keane claims that the dial is capable of giving correct answers to over 300,000 questions, and even if this is an exaggeration the machine certainly was very accurate last week in answering the most puzzling queries. Mr. Keane's other sleight-of-hand work was very cleverly done, and he scored an emphatic success. Will Rogers, the lariat expert, and Eddie Mack,[7] the dancer, completed the programme.

PD. Printed in *NYDM*, 23 February 1907.

1. Rogers appeared at New York's historic Colonial Theatre from 11 to 16 February 1907. Located at 1887 Broadway at Sixty-second Street, the Colonial illustrated the northward expansion of New York's theaters to meet the needs of a growing population in the upper Broadway area. The theater was built by Fred Thompson and Elmer Dundy, who had constructed the New York Hippodrome and Coney Island's Luna Park. Intending to present both musicals and variety, they designed the theater in a Federal style; its interior, embellished with colorful silks, was similar to an English music hall, with balconies close to the stage. The theater seated 647 people in the orchestra, 361 in the balcony, and 257 in the gallery. A few months after the

Colonial opened, Percy G. Williams bought the theater, which he used exclusively for vaudeville. At the time of Rogers's appearance seats ranged from 50 cents to $2. In 1912 B. F. Keith bought Williams's theaters. Five years later Edward F. Albee refurbished the theater and renamed it the New Colonial. During the early 1920s the theater was used for all-black productions, including *Runnin' Wild* (1923), which introduced the Charleston dance; Noble Sissie and Eubie Blake's *Chocolate Dandies* (1924); and *Lucky Sambo* (1925). In 1925 Walter Hampden leased the theater for the presentation of classic plays. RKO used it in the 1930s and 1940s as a neighborhood moviehouse. Later it was made into a television studio used by NBC and subsequently ABC. In 1974 the theater was bought and refurbished by Rebecca Harkness, and it became the home of the Harkness Ballet for a brief period. Facing financial losses from her $11 million investment, Harkness sold the theater. In 1977 its furnishings were sold at auction and the theater demolished for condominiums and a public area, the Harkness Atrium (*JCOTG*, 65; van Hoogstraten, *Lost Broadway Theatres*, 91–94).

2. Harry Bulger (1872–1926) was a well-known comedian and singer from the vaudeville and legitimate stage who was in show business for thirty-five years. In vaudeville and musical comedy he teamed with J. Sherre Matthews in a popular act. As early as September 1891 they performed at Tony Pastor's on Fourteenth Street. In September 1892 they were the stars of the Henry Burlesque Co. at Niblo's Garden Theatre and were featured at the Casino's roof in June 1894. For a time the two formed the Matthews and Bulger Co., which played Harlem's Olympic Theatre in November 1893 and Miner's Eighth Avenue Theatre and Bowery Theatre in January 1894. The two wrote the music and lyrics for, and starred in, two musical farces, including *At Gay Coney Island* (1897). In 1901 Bulger appeared in the musical *The Night of the Fourth*, the two-act burlesque *The King's Carnival*, and the popular extravaganza *The Sleeping Beauty and the Beast*. Just before his performance at the Colonial Bulger had starred in the musical fantasy *The Man from Now* for which he wrote some of the music. Poor health forced Bulger to move into a retirement home for actors. On 15 April 1926 he died of pneumonia at the home of a friend in Freeport, Long Island (*BEWHAT*, 1009; Chapman and Sherwood, eds., *Best Plays of 1894–1899*, 193, 253–54; Mantle and Sherwood, eds., *Best Plays of 1899–1909*, 386, 392, 398–99, 519; *NYTheReI*, 51; Odell, *Annals of the New York Stage*, 15:129, 335, 608, 719, 721, 723; *VO*, 1:21 April 1926).

3. Bangs's *Mink's Rink* was advertised as a travesty on the rollerskating craze. Born in Yonkers, N.Y., John Kendrick Bangs (1862–1922) was a prolific playwright, humorist, editor, and lecturer during his long career. A graduate of Columbia College in 1883, Bangs was on the editorial staff of several magazines, including a stint at *Life* (1884–88) as associate editor. He next operated the humor department of *Harper's Magazine* for eleven years. He subsequently became editor of *Harper's Weekly* (1899–1900), the *New Metropolitan Magazine* (1903), and *Puck* (1904–5). His first book was *The Lorgnette* (1886), and he published over thirty volumes of humor and verse between 1886 and 1910. From the mid-1880s until 1904 he lived in Yonkers, where he ran unsuccessfully for mayor. Bangs was a popular humorous lecturer in his later life and became noted for his talk *Salubrities I Have Met*. Bangs lived in Ogunquit, Me., during his later life. He died in Atlantic City, N.J., on 21 January 1922 at age of fifty-nine (*BEWHAT*, 1000; *DAB*, 1:573–74; Mantle and Sherwood, eds., *Best Plays of 1899–1909*, 478, 519; *WhoStg*, 25).

4. Sie Hassan Ben Ali (d. 1914) and his troupe performed an acrobat act. He was born a Berber in Arabia and was reportedly the chief of thirty desert tribes. Before becoming an entertainer, he was a merchant, a tourist guide and interpreter, a tax col-

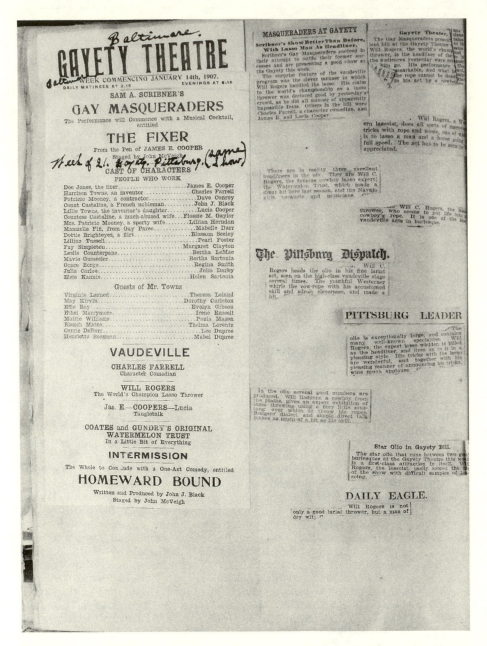

Vaudeville playbills, ca. January—February 1907, from Rogers's scrapbook. *(OkClaW)*

ORPHEUM

BROOKLYN

WEEK OF FEBRUARY 4.
EXTRAORDINARY ENGAGEMENT.

First Appearance in Brooklyn Since her Return to America.

MISS VESTA VICTORIA

The Famous and Clever English Comedienne, of "Waiting at the Church"
Fame, who brings with her Many New and Original Songs, all of which
have been written for her exclusive use. Many of Miss Victoria's Old
Song Hits will be retained, and sung by her during this engagement
as well as the New Ones that she will introduce in her latest offering.

The Popular Fun-Makers,
THE FARRELL-TAYLOR TRIO
In One of the Funniest Acts in Vaudeville.

First Time Here of

Gracie Emmett and Company
Presenting her Farce Comedy, in One Act, entitled
"Mrs. Murphy's Second Husband"

Abdul Kader
—and—
His Three Wives
In their Wonderful Exhibition of Rapid-Fire Painting in Oil.
Abdul Kader, by Appointment of the Sultan, is the
Royal Portrait Painter of Turkey.

The Comedy Stars,
THE ELINORE SISTERS
America's Representative Comediennes, in a Laugh-Provoking Comedy Skit.

Eddie Clark
—and—
His Winning Widows
Present the Miniature Racing Musical Comedy Sketch,
"The Tipster"

The Western Star,
Will Rogers
America's Best and Cleverest Cowboy,
In a Series of Wonderful Tricks and Feats with the Lasso.

THE TANAKAS
Japanese Magicians and Top-Spinners.

The Musical Comedy Favorites,
WALTER JONES and MABEL HI[TE]
Presenting their Latest Eccentric Comedy Skit,
Introducing Many New and Clever Songs and Dances, as well as
Some Exceptionally Funny Eccentric Comedy.
AND A NUMBER OF OTHER VERY GOOD ACTS.

Jack Joyce, the cowboy lassoist who
went to Europe recently with letters of
introduction and the hearty commenda-
tion of Will Rogers, who was the original sensation in his line on the other
side, is playing at the Palace in London
and has won highly favorable notice.

COLONIAL
62ND STREET & BROADWAY

WEEK BEGINNING MONDAY MATINEE, FEBRUARY 11
Matinee Every Day.

EDDIE MACK
In His Novelty Wooden Shoe Dancing.

GEORGE B. SNYDER and HARRY BUCKLEY
Present Their Latest Musical Comedy Skit,
"THE STREET MUSICIAN."
Cast.
William Writers, a writer of popular music..........George B. Snyder
Ludwig Zugposaune, a poor street musician..........Harry Buckley
Concluding with their original novelty, "The Mechanical Musician."

WILL ROGERS
In an Exhibition of Lasso Throwing.

IRENE FRANKLIN
Singing Comedienne

HARRY BULGER and Company
(Late Star of "Man From Now" Company)
In an Original Travesty on The Roller Skating Craze, Entitled
"MINK'S RINK."

J. WARREN KEANE
Presents
His Act of the Cleverest Sleight-of-hand and Magic, Including his
Sensational Mystery,
A S K M E
Or THE DIAL OF ETERNITY.

JOSEPHINE COHAN and Company
Presents a New One-Act Absurdity
"A FRIEND OF THE FAMILY,"
By Will M. Cressy and Fred Niblo.

FRED NIBLO
The American Humorist.

SI HASSAN BEN ALI'S ARABS
In Acrobatic Feats.

MURRAY HILL
Sunday, February 3
QUIGLEY BROS.
TASCOTT | MARTIN BROS.
Whitman Sisters & Willie Robinson
SUSAN FISHER | NAT CARR
VON KLINE AND GIBSON
WILL ROGERS

lector, and a teacher of the Koran. He traveled to London with a troupe of acrobats and eventually joined the Forebaugh Circus. In 1886 Ali arrived in New York with his troupe, and they became a popular acrobatic act. He resided in New York, where he adopted American clothing and manners. He never lost touch with his native country, where he was respected and called Ba, an honorific meaning "faithful." Ali was a life member of the White Rats actors' union and served on its board of directors. He died in Morocco on 20 July 1914 after a short illness and was buried in the United States (*VO*, 1:24 July 1914).

5. George B. Snyder and Harry Buckley were noted for their musical comedy skits. At the Colonial they did a skit called "The Street Musician," in which Snyder played William Writem, a writer of popular music, and Buckley played Ludwig Zugpossaune, a poor street musician. They concluded with an original novelty called "The Mechanical Minstrels." According to Joe Laurie, Jr., Snyder and Buckley "did funny bits between playing their instruments. There was a billy goat head on the wall with a sign on it, 'Buck Beer'. The straight man would go over after finishing a number, pull the horns, and get a glass of beer. The comic would follow him, pull the horns, and get milk! This was carried on all through the act to a real big laugh" (*Vaudeville*, 66; Colonial Theatre playbill, week beginning Monday matinee, 11 February 1907, scrapbook A-1, OkClaW).

6. Irene Franklin (1876–1941) was a popular musical-hall and vaudeville actress and singer who later had a career on screen and radio. Franklin began her stage career at the age of six months in a melodrama called *Hearts of Oak*. She later played many child parts on stage. Accompanied by her mother, an actress, the fifteen-year-old Franklin toured Australia. In June 1892 she performed in Augustus Thomas's *Burglar* and appeared in *The Prodigal Father*. By 1894 she was playing in British music halls, and the following year she began a long career in American vaudeville, with occasional appearances at Tony Pastor's. In vaudeville the red-headed Franklin gained a popular following for her songs and impersonations. She became noted for her mimicry of working women and children, a unique departure since most mimics at this time would impersonate famous people (her routine has been compared to that of Lily Tomlin). Audiences applauded her imitations of waitresses, resentful little girls, chorus girls, salesladies, and dramatic stage actresses. "I get my characters everywhere—on every side," she said. "My waitress had her original in a Childs restaurant where I used to eat in my $60 a week days. The chambermaid really existed in a Philadelphia hotel. I'm always on the alert for a song character" (Franklin, "Making Songs Tell a Story"). She would arrange her waist-length red hair in various styles for her character portrayals. Her repertoire included impersonations of a flirtatious schoolteacher, a hotel maid having a love affair with a traveling salesman, and a waitress. She performed "kid" songs, such as "I'm Nobody's Baby Now" and "Somebody Ought to Put the Old Man Wise," which she sang dressed in rompers. Her song "Expression," in which she imitated numerous facial expressions, was an audience favorite. Her songs also satirized the feminist and prohibition movements. A song called "What Have You Got on Your Hip?" made fun of the hip flask. A contemporary critic wrote that "she combines an almost O. Henry understanding of everyday life with a Eugene Field sense of childhood" (*EV*, 91). After her appearance at the Colonial, Franklin performed a lead part in the musical comedy *The Orchid*, which opened at the Herald Square Theatre on 8 April 1907. From that time on she starred in many stage shows, including *The Summer Widowers* (1910), *Hands Up* (1915, which also included Will Rogers), *The Passing Show of 1917*, *Greenwich Follies of 1921*, and Jerome Kern's *Sweet Adeline* (1929). In 1917 she went abroad with her first husband, the songwriter Burton

Green, to entertain American troops in France. Green, an accomplished pianist, and Franklin toured together in the United States. She popularized Green's song, "Red Head," which became her signature song. After Green's death in 1922, she married the composer and accompanist Jerry Jarnigan (d. 1934) in 1925. They made frequent public appearances together, including a Vitaphone talking picture in 1929. In the 1930s she devoted herself to films, but her screen roles never matched her success in vaudeville. Suffering from acute neuritis, Franklin entered the Actors Fund Home in Englewood, N.J., in 1940. She bemoaned her poverty and decline in popularity, writing to a friend that "another of my Friday the thirteenth birthdays is upon me, but I don't think there are many who will remember me or who care" (*NYT*, 17 June 1941). A few days later, on her birthday, she experienced a cerebral hemorrhage, which led to her death on 16 June 1941 in an Englewood hospital (Chapman and Sherwood, eds., *Best Plays of 1894–1899*, 212; *EV*, 91–93; Franklin, "Back from the Trenches" and "Mike-Wise"; Gilbert, *American Vaudeville*, 347, 349–51; Kinkle, *Complete Encyclopedia of Popular Music and Jazz*, 2:928; Mantle and Sherwood eds., *Best Plays of 1899–1909*, 538–39; Martin and Segrave, *Women in Comedy*, 58–59; *NYT*, 17 June 1941; Odell, *Annals of the New York Stage*, 15:211, 316, 784; *OCAT*, 273; Samuels, *Once upon a Stage*, 75–81; *VO*, 3:18 June 1941; *WhoHol*, 1:564; *WhScrn*, 255; *WhThe*, 879).

7. Eddie Mack (1879–1944), whose real name was Eddie J. Hoffman, was a popular vaudeville dancer. In his early career from 1890 to 1900, Mack was a member of the Manhattan Comedy Four, a song-and-comedy act that consisted of Al Shean (later of the famed Gallagher and Shean), Sam Curtis, and Arthur Williams. Mack, who was short and weighed just over one hundred pounds, often worked as a single and was billed as an Irish tenor and dancer. He was known to describe a baseball game while he danced. At the Colonial he was advertised as performing a novel wooden-shoe dance. For a time he teamed with the Scotsman Roderick Bain MacKenzie, who played the bagpipes while Mack danced, and together they did comedy bits. By 1909 Mack was paired with his wife, Dot Williams, in vaudeville in an act known as Mack and Williams. She sang, played the piano, and did imitations. They apparently introduced the musical staircase dance, which was widely used in the movies and on the stage. A critic described it as consisting of "ten steps connected with electric bells placed at the edge of the step and of different keys. Up and down these steps Mr. Mack danced to the music of the bells and the orchestra, finishing with a very neat dance with Miss Williams" (*New York Mirror*, 16 January 1909, Mack and Williams file, NN-L-BRTC). Their popularity led to their appearance in 16 May 1914 on the cover of the *New York Star*, a show-business trade paper. Later, Mack taught dancing to Hollywood stars. Among his pupils were Betty Grable, Judy Garland, and Mickey Rooney. Mack died of a heart attack in Hollywood on 1 August 1944 (Eddie Mack and Eddie Mack and Dot Williams clipping files, NN-L-BRTC; *EV*, 204; Gilbert, *American Vaudeville*, 181–82; Laurie, *Vaudeville*, 223; *NYT*, 2 August 1941).

Manager's Report, Chase's Washington Theatre
25 February 1907
Washington, D.C.

CHASE'S WASHINGTON

Week Feb. 25th, 1907.

FRED W. MORTON   Plays the harmonica and does a little talking while tearing paper into artistic shapes, the latter being pretty well done. In one.

KINGSLEY AND LEWIS   "After the Honeymoon". Acceptable in this position.[1]

ROGERS AND DEELY   "The Singer and his Valet." We are rather inclined to say that this act pleased. In one.

WILL ROGERS   "Lariat King." Very clever and made a hit. Full stage.

INTERMISSION

THE THREE LIVIERS   Equilibrists on parallel wires. Very difficult work but audience hardly seemed to appreciate the same. Full stage.[2]

CLIFTON CRAWFORD   Songs, character sketches, recitation etc. Duplicated his success of last year. In one.[3]

JULIUS STEGER AND CO.   "The Fifth Commandment". An offering so widely different from anything heretofore seen in vaudeville that it is bound to command the closest attention and most respectful hearing. Well presented and comments will be favorable. Full stage.[4]

THE AMERICAN VITAGRAPH[5]   "The Animation Statue." A pretty good comedy film.

H. Winnifred De Witt.[6]

TD. KAP-IaU.

1. According to the program, Julia Kingsley and Nelson Lewis did a "farcical absurdity" (Chase's Theatre program, week of 25 February 1907, OkClaW).
2. The Three Liviers were described as "European Novelty Acts" (Chase's Theatre program, week of 25 February 1907, OkClaW).
3. A versatile comedian, Clifton Crawford (ca. 1870–1920) performed comic recitations and stories as well as song-and-dance routines. Born in Edinburgh, Scotland, Crawford came to the United States around 1897 and settled in Boston. He began doing amateur shows and eventually, starting about 1902, performed a single act in vaudeville. Noted for his quick change of style on stage, Crawford became well known for his recitation of Rudyard Kipling's "Gunga Din" in vaudeville (an act that he reportedly stole from the monologuist Taylor Holmes). He also had a long stage career that included roles in *My Lady* (1901), *The Jewel of Asia* (1903), *The Three Twins* (1908), and *The Quaker Girl* (1911). Crawford wrote the score for, and starred

in, *My Best Girl,* a three-act musical that opened at the Park Theatre on 12 September 1912. He performed in vaudeville in London from 1914 to 1916, returning to America in 1916 for a starring role in *Her Soldier Boy.* After an appearance in *My Lady Friends* in 1919, Crawford went to London in June 1920 for vaudeville engagements booked by William Morris. Two days after his arrival on 3 June 1920 Crawford fell to his death from his fifth-story London hotel room. A coroner's report stated that his death was accidental, resulting from insomnia. Crawford was buried in Edinburgh beside the grave of his parents (Gilbert, *American Vaudeville,* 294–95; Laurie, *Vaudeville,* 102, 133, 197, 317–18, 294; Mantle and Sherwood, eds., *Best Plays of 1909–1919,* 476; *NYT,* 6 June 1920; *NYTheReI,* 85; *VO,* 1:11 June 1920).

4. The actor and singer Julius Steger (1870–1959) was born in Vienna, Austria, and after singing operatic roles emigrated to the United States as a young man. Steger had a long acting career that began around 1893–94, when he toured with the Marie Tempest Co. In 1896 he joined the Casino Co. and performed a role in *In Gay New-York.* Other early roles included *The Geisha* (1897), *Yankee Doodle Dandy* (1898), *Sally in Our Alley* (1902), *The Music Master* (1905), and *The Dangerous Maid* (1908). Steger gained fame in vaudeville performing musical playlets. *The Fifth Commandment,* written by Willis Steell, became his signature piece. Steger insisted on complete silence when doing *The Fifth Commandment* and as a consequence was nicknamed Shhhhh Steger. In 1915 he made a silent movie with the same title and later appeared in other films. Between 1920 and 1923, he was head of the New York studios of the Fox film corporation and produced silent movies. Steger died in Vienna on 25 February 1959 (*EV,* 478; Laurie, *Vaudeville,* 51; *NYT,* 3 March 1958; *NYTheReI,* 362; Chase's Theatre program, week of 25 February 1907, OkClaW; *VO,* 5:4 March 1959; *WhMuDr,* 291–92; *WhoStg,* 414–15).

5. The American Vitagraph Co. was organized by J. Stuart Blackton and Albert E. Smith in 1897. Their first film featured Blackton doing imitations of Thomas Edison, William McKinley, and other famous personages. The success of these small films for the vaudeville circuit prompted Blackton and Smith to purchase an Edison Projecting Kinetoscope and to form a company, which they called the Edison Vitagraph Co. Presumably, they hoped to capitalize on the Edison name, though Edison had nothing to do with the enterprise beyond selling the machine. Later the company was known as the American Vitagraph Co.

The Vitagraph Co. achieved its first surge of popularity during the Spanish American War by exhibiting a film of a "naval battle" that had been staged with cardboard ships on a kitchen table. This film and others were shown at F. F. Proctor's vaudeville houses. Vitagraph was also successful because its projector gave a steadier image than those of competitors. Additionally, the company made its own films and could offer a unique product. About this time Vitagraph was also buying Edison films, copying them, and selling them at half the Edison rate. When Edison threatened to sue, Blackton and Smith were alarmed, as a suit would bankrupt them. They agreed to become Edison licensees and to produce films for the Edison Manufacturing Co. This gave Edison a percentage of the profit on each film that they sold.

In 1905 Vitagraph was producing newsworthy topical films that became extremely popular. It also produced a range of comedies, chase films, and other fictional subjects. By 1906 Vitagraph had built a studio in Brooklyn at a cost of $25,000 and was becoming the leading producer of American films, thanks to the popularity of their work, which blended comedy with urban sophistication. The company also pioneered animation techniques. By 1907 Vitagraph was six months behind in meeting the demand for prints of its films. During this period, the Vitagraph output was extremely varied, including adaptations of classic literature such as *A Tale of Two Cities* and *Vanity Fair*. By the 1910s the company had expanded to the point of losing the family working atmosphere for which it had been known within industry circles. In 1914 Vitagraph leased its own theater and planned a program consisting entirely of its own films, a business decision that unified production and distribution, and predated the vertical integration that came with the Hollywood studio system. Though the venture was not a success, studio-owned movie theaters showing exclusively their own products were the wave of the future. In 1925 Vitagraph was sold to Warner Brothers (Charles Musser, "American Vitagraph 1897–1901," in Fell, ed., *Film before Griffith*, 23–67; and Musser, *Emergence of Cinema*, 271–72, 277–85, 466–73; Slide, *Big V*, 12, 14, 47, 52, 63, 96, 122).

6. H. Winnifred De Witt was the manager of Chase's Theatre (Chase's Theatre program, week of 25 February 1907, OkClaW).

Excerpt from the Final Rolls of the Five Civilized Tribes
4 March 1907
U.S.A.

In the Curtis Act of 1898 Congress authorized the Dawes Commission (established in 1893) to undertake a census for the purpose of establishing a final roll to be used as a basis for allotment. On 3 March 1905 the Dawes Commission was abolished and its work continued by the Commission to the Five Civilized Tribes. Commission agents traveled across the Indian Territory enrolling people. The task proved long and laborious, with many full-bloods refusing to enroll because they opposed the process. By contrast, many whites claiming to have Native American blood were eager to obtain land. The commission received over 200,000 applications before the rolls closed on 4 March 1907.[1]

No.	Name	Age	Sex	Blood	Census Card
No. 11383	Rogers, Clement V.	63	M	1-4	4747
11384	Rogers, William P.	22	M	1-4	4747

PD. *The Final Rolls of Citizens and Freedmen of the Five Civilized Tribes in Indian Territory.* Prepared by the Commission and Commissioner to the Five Civilized Tribes and Approved by the Secretary of the Interior on or Prior to March 4, 1907. Compiled and Printed Under Authority Conferred by the Act of Congress. Approved June 21, 1906 (34 Stat. L. 325). OkHi.

1. The final rolls contain over 101,526 names organized by Native American heritage. Names are arranged under the following subgroups: citizens by blood, intermarriage, minor children by blood, newborn children by blood, freedmen, minor freedmen, and newborn freedmen. Those on the rolls are listed numerically by subgroup. Among the enrolled were 23,405 freedmen or their descendants, 26,794 full-bloods, and 40,934 who were less than half-blood or who were eligible intermarried citizens. The commission was abolished on 14 August 1914 (Clark, *Cherokee Ancestor Research*, 75–76; Dale and Wardell, *History of Oklahoma*, 288–97; Gibson, *Oklahoma*, 326).

The Cherokees enrolled 40,193 people, the largest number among the five groups. This included 4,924 freedmen, several hundred Delaware and Shawnee Indians, and a large number of white intermarried citizens. Will Rogers and his father, Clement Vann Rogers, were listed under the category of Cherokees by blood. Their age was calculated to 1 September 1902. In a separate published index to the roll, the names are listed alphabetically under Native American heritage. In the index, "Rogers, Clement V." is listed by his roll number (11383) and under his name appears "Rogers, William P.," listed by his roll number (11384) (*Index to Final Rolls of Citizens and Freedmen of the Five Civilized Tribes in Indian Territory*, 374, OkHi).

Notice from the *Claremore Progress*
9 March 1907
Claremore, I.T.

C. V. Rogers, who has been to Washington visiting his son, Willie, returned home the first of the week and left for Guthrie to attend to his duties as delegate from this district.[1]

PD. Printed in *CP*, 9 March 1907. From transcript, OkClaW.

1. By this time Rogers's father had reconciled himself to his son's show-business career. Clement Vann Rogers saw his son perform at Chase's Theatre in Washington, D.C., during the week of 25 February 1907. He seemed to be proud to see his son's name on the theater marquee. In her biography, Betty Rogers wrote that Clement Vann Rogers was accompanied by his daughters Maude and Sallie. On 22 February 1907 the *Chelsea Reporter* published the following notice: "Mrs. Lane and McSpadden left Thursday accompanied by their father for an extended trip to Washington, D.C., and other points." The local newspaper also reported that all three were "spectators during the closing days of the 59th Congress" (*CR*, 8 March 1907). At first Clement Vann Rogers felt his son's salary of $250 was extravagant, but when he saw how large the audience was, he felt the manager should pay his son more. Betty Rogers wrote: "Uncle Clem attended every performance, and after the show he liked to stand around outside to listen to what the people said as they departed the theater. Will was billed as 'the Oklahoma Cowboy' and if Uncle Clem overheard anyone expressing a doubt about Will being a real cowboy, he immediately set him right. 'Sure he's a real cowboy,' he would say, 'and from Oklahoma, too—just like it's printed on the program.' Then, making his identity known, he would add, 'I'll introduce you if you want to know him.' When Will came out of the stage door, his father always had a crowd waiting there to meet him" (Rogers, *Will Rogers*, 120). While in Washington Rogers sent two postcards to Betty Blake. One was a picture of George Washington's home in Mount Vernon, Va., on which he wrote, "Hello Pal. We are right in this place now inside Washingtons old home." The other was a photograph of Washington's four-poster bed, on which he wrote, "Hello Ark. Bed Chat. How are you" (postcards, postmarked 27 February 1907 and 28 February 1907, OkClaW).

To Clement Vann Rogers
18 April 1907
New York, N.Y.

During the month of March Rogers performed in Newark, N.J., New York City, North Adams, Mass., and Gloversville, N.Y.[1] The first two weeks of April were unusual because he was not booked in any theater. In preparation for an upcoming trip to England, he expanded his act to include two other cowboy performers. Rogers wrote the following letter to his father just before leaving for a return engagement at London's Palace Theatre.

April 18.

My Dear Papa

I got the letter and the money all O.K. and am off in the morning for England as I think I can do pretty good over there for a short time[2]   I am taking over two other boys and three horses   I bought two ponies from a boy[3]   they are polo ponies   it makes 4 of us and three ponies   I am going to put on a bigger act[4]   I dont know how I will make out   it will take a lot of money but I think it will pay me in the long run

Dont know how long I will be over there   only going to England   I will write you as soon as I get there

Write me to

Hotel Provence

    Leicester Square

    London.

▲ Lots ▲ Love to all

Willie

ALS, rc. OkClaW. On Hotel Putnam letterhead. Samuel Glantz, proprietor, and N. J. Weiss, manager.

1. Rogers appeared at the Waldmann Theatre in Newark from 4 to 9 March 1907. Among the acts were Bob Manchester's Vanity Fair with Miss Arline (The Big Extravaganza Co. in *On the Fall River Line*); Big Barnold Dog and Monkey Pantomime Co. (Direct from Hammerstein's Theatre); Miss Belle Wilton, Jessie Sharp and Co. (The Only Novelty in Burlesque in *Butterflies* and *Daisies*); Wangdoodle Four (Bob Robinson, Julius Glenn, Harvey Goodall and James White, Presenting their Whimsical Laughing Success *The Darkey Dancing Master*); and Will Rogers (King of the Lariat on Plains and Cattle Trail, assisted by "Buck" McKee, Ex-Sheriff of Pawnee Co., Oklahoma, and favorite bronco, "Teddy," in a Marvelous Exhibition of Skill and Dexterity) (Waldmann Theatre playbill, week commencing Monday Matinee, 4 March 1907, scrapbook A-1, OkClaW).
From 11 to 16 March 1907, Rogers entertained at Percy Williams's Alhambra Theatre, located on Seventh Avenue and 126th Street in New York City. He signed a

contract with Williams on 4 March to give two performances daily at a salary of $250 for the week (B. F. Keith's Booking Offices contract, 4 March 1907, OkClaW). In his scrapbook Rogers added to the playbill in his own hand the name of the famous English comedienne Nellie Wallace (1870–1948). A hilarious comic singer who wore zany outfits and makeup, Wallace was billed in British music halls as "The Essence of Eccentricity" (Busby, *British Music Hall,* 178). Another noteworthy act on the program was Lasky, Rolfe, and Co., "Presenting Ye Colonial Septette in 'An Olde Tyme Halloween'." Jesse Lasky, in partnership with Ben Rolfe, had organized four girls and three boys in an act called the Colonial Septette (see Lasky, *I Blow My Own Horn,* 64). Others listed on the bill, in order, were Robert Recker's Harmonists; the Silverton Trio (European Tight Wire Artists); James F. McDonald (Singing Comedian and Raconteur); Mr. Henri De Vries and His Co. (Europe's Greatest Character Actor in a Remarkable Play of Today, entitled *A Case of Arson*); O'Brien and Havel (Assisted by Miss Effie Lawrence in their Latest Success, "Ticks and Clicks"); and Fields and Ward (Conversation Comedians) (Alhambra Theatre playbill, week beginning Monday matinee, 11 March 1907, scrapbook A-1, OkClaW).

Rogers performed at the Richmond Family Theatre in North Adams, Mass., from 18 to 23 March. Rogers was given star billing as the special attraction, and a review described him as the feature act, a man who "is easily the cleverest performer with the lasso that has ever been seen in this city ("Cowboy Lariat Expert," clipping, scrapbook A-1, OkClaw). On the bill were Miss Sutherole (Comedienne); the Three Perry Sisters (Big Novelty Singing Act); Ray and Taylor (Comedy Musical Act); Warren and Faust (Comedy, Singing and Dancing); and Edison's Latest Motion Pictures (Richmond Family Theatre playbill, week starting Monday matinee, 18 March 1907, scrapbook A-1, OkClaW).

Rogers was in Gloversville, N.Y., from 25 to 30 March, playing at the Family Theatre. Listed on the bill were two acts that had also played in North Adams: Warren and Faust, and The Perry Sisters (Edna, Evelyn and Marguerite in Pajamas). Others were Ned Fitzgibbon (Singer and Violinist); Templer Saxe; Nevada Maynard, Lucile Ashton in "Cured," a Farcical Sketch; and New Motion Pictures (*Difficult Arrest* and *Old Mashers*) (Gloversville Family Theatre playbill, week of 25 March 1907, scrapbook A-1, OkClaW).

2. Rogers sailed on the S.S. *Kaiserin Auguste Victoria,* a mail ship operated by the Hamburg-America Line and captained by H. Ruser. The ship left on 18 April at 9:00 A.M. and was routed to Hamburg via Plymouth, England, and Cherbourg, France (*NYT,* 18 April 1907). Rogers was listed as a first-class cabin passenger under the name of Mr. William Rogers. Another first-class passenger was Mrs. John Jacob Astor, wife of the financier, who was accompanied by a maid and a servant. Buck McKee, two other assistants, and the horses traveled on another ship and did not arrive in time for Rogers's initial performances at the Palace (List of Cabin Passengers of the Twin-Screw Mail S.S. *Kaiserin Auguste Victoria,* OkClaW).

3. Rogers might have bought polo ponies from Jim Minnick, who was raising polo horses in New Jersey. On 14 May 1907 Minnick sent a postcard postmarked from Weehawken, N.J., addressed to Rogers care of the Palace Theatre and forwarded to the Empire Theatre in Coventry, England. On the front was a picture of Minnick on horseback, described as "an expert roper"; the card was signed "to Will Rogers from J. H. Minnick" (OkClaW).

4. Rogers intended to stage a small Wild West show, with Buck McKee and two new cowboys (unidentified), but evidently his plans did not materialize. Not only did the rest of the troupe arrive late, but according to Betty Rogers, the act was "too big"

and "poorly organized." She wrote: "It simply didn't click. Stranded in London, with men and horses to board, Will had to take his regular roping act, just Buck and Teddy, on a tour of the Provinces, to meet expenses and to get his troupe back to the United States" (Rogers, *Will Rogers,* 98).

London Palace Clippings
from Will Rogers's Scrapbook
ca. 30 April 1907
London, England

Arriving in London, Rogers found that his horses and assistants had not arrived, so for a time he was forced to perform alone at the Palace Theatre.[1] The reception of his solo act foretold the success of the vaudeville single he would perform in 1911.

MUSIC HALL.

Will Rogers, the cowboy lassoist, dropped in on London in quite a casual way the other day. His presence was quickly known to Mr. Alfred Butt, who, without losing a moment, introduced Rogers to the Palace programme. Having no horses and no assistants at hand, Rogers was obliged to extemporize an entertainment, which none the less engaged the admiration of the Palace audiences just as completely as ever.

TRIBUNE.
NOVELTIES AT THE PALACE.

Will Rogers, the famous cowboy lassoist, with his rope a hundred yards long, has returned to the Palace this week, and is even more popular than he was a year since. There is an unsophisticated charm about his show which instantly commends it. He gives you an exhibition of skill without any "frills," and the result is quite fascinating.

MILITARY MAIL.
THE PALACE THEATRE.

The latest "turn" in the programme of the Palace Theatre is Will Rogers, the Cowboy Lassoist; he is another Mr. Stubbins, of Cabbage Patch fame. "There is my show," says he in gesture, "What do you think of it?" Owing to the fact that his horses and assistants did not arrive in London from America in time for the opening, Will Rogers elected to "breeze on" (to quote his own expression) and give an exhibition with an array of ropes.

SUNDAY CHRONICLE.

By way of contrast to the tree-felling exhibition at the Hippodrome is the lassoing show of Will Rogers at the Palace. Rogers is no stranger at this house, where he appeared last summer. He is on quite a casual visit to London, but, with a lively recollection of the success he made last year, Mr. Bull [Butt] sought him out and prevailed upon him to put in a little time. The result is a very high trial of Rogers's skill, for he is without the assistants, and the horses, and the other paraphernalia he is wont to employ. He is dependent simply upon his ropes, with which he performs incredible tricks. Rogers never speaks; but his pantomime is delightfully expressive. Personally, he is charming, simple, unaffected, and pleasantly childlike.

PD with autograph inscriptions. Scrapbook A-1, OkClaW.[2]

1. Rogers performed at the Palace Theatre of Varieties from 29 April to 12 May 1907. According to the *Morning Leader,* Rogers lassoed a young Palace attendant as a substitute for his missing pony and made amusing comments (scrapbook A-1, OkClaW). During the week of 29 April the following performers were listed on the program, in order: Madeline Rossiter (Comedienne); Eadie and Ramsden (In a Musical Pot Pourri); Eldra and his Dog "Prince"; Kartelli in a Sensational Wire Act; Audora Castillo (Dans ses Créations Internationales); Malcolm Scott; The Palace Girls (With New Songs and Dances); Alfred Lester (In *A Restaurant Episode* assisted by Miss Lily Mills); Juliette's Sea Lions; Miss Margaret Cooper (At the Piano in Selections from Her Répertoire); Will Rogers (Special Engagement for One Week. The Cowboy Lasso Thrower); Fred Niblo (The American Humourist); Les Trombetta (Grandes Originalites. Dans leurs Oeuvres et Creations); and the Bioscope (Showing the World's Events from Day to Day. Mr. Winan's Horses preparing for the International Show. L'Enfant Prodigue. The Grand National, 1907. Norway's Derby—Ski Racing at Holmenkoln before the King and Queen of Norway and Princess Victoria, March 4th, 1907) (The Palace Theatre of Varieties program, week of 29 April 1907, scrapbook A-1, OkClaW).

During his second week at the Palace Rogers performed with some well-known music-hall stars. Among them was Margaret Cooper (d. 1922), a pianist of considerable dexterity, who sang songs written by her husband and herself ("I Want Someone to Love Me" and "Hello! Tu-Tu"). Horace Goldin (1867–1939) was an illusionist famous for his act of sawing a woman in half with an electric buzz saw and known as "The Royal Illusionist" because of his command performances. Noted for his quick hands and fast pace, Goldwin could do an unusually large number of tricks in his twenty-minute routine. The legendary blackface comedian and singer George H. Chirgwin (1854–1922) wore a white greasepaint diamond around his right eye which contrasted with his blackface make-up. Wearing eccentric clothes (a huge top hat and black tights), he entertained audiences by playing a one-string fiddle and singing his signature songs, *My Fiddle Is My Sweetheart* and *The Blind Boy* in a voice that ranged from baritone to falsetto. He was so popular that he was known to play six music halls in one night (Busby, *British Music Hall,* 35; *EV,* 208–9; Felstead, *Stars Who Made the*

Halls, 38, 62–63, 80, 82, 98, 171, 179; Gilbert, *American Vaudeville,* 308; Mander and Mitchenson, *British Music Halls,* photo nos. 54, 107, 184, 195; Short, *Fifty Years of Vaudeville,* 138; *VO,* 1:5 January 1923; Waller, *Magical Nights at the Theatre,* 194–95).

2. In his scrapbook Rogers wrote in his own hand the name of the London newspaper above each clipping.

To Clement Vann Rogers
ca. 24 May 1907
Coventry, England

May 26.

Dear Papa.

Well I am playing out in a small town this week and go to Liverpool next week[1]   no money to be made here   may be home soon.

Love Willie

address   Palace Theatre
          London

APC, OkClaW. Picture postcard of Kenilworth Castle.[2] Hand-dated 26 May but postmarked 24 May; stamped received in Claremore, I.T., 4 June 1907.

1. Rogers performed at the Empire Theatre in Coventry from 20 May to 25 May.

2. The ruins of Kenilworth Castle are located in the county of Warwickshire in central England. The castle was established by Geoffrey de Clinton around 1120. In the thirteenth century it was owned by Simon de Montfort and in the mid-fourteenth century by John of Gaunt. In the sixteenth century it was given to Robert Dudley, earl of Leicester, by Queen Elizabeth. The castle was made famous by Sir Walter Scott in his 1821 novel *Kenilworth* (*WNGD,* 599).

Review from the *Liverpool Daily Post and Mercury*
28 May 1907
Liverpool, Eng.

Rogers's last stop on his English tour was Liverpool. He was disappointed that his enlarged act did not go well, and he sailed for home on 8 June.[1]

EMPIRE THEATRE.

The programme presented to the patrons of the Empire Theatre,[2] Lime-street, last evening was one composed of excellent and attractive turns, which afforded much delight to both houses and which promise a successful run throughout the week. George Leyton[3] provided high-class enjoyment for both the eye and the ear simultaneously, his naval scene, in which he was assisted by a chorus of local boys, being picturesque so far as costumes and scenic decorations were concerned, while the artiste's powerful yet smooth and cultivated voice, heard along with those of the youthful choristers, was thrilling in the extreme. Will Rogers is billed to perform wonders with an innocent coil of rope, making it an effective weapon of offence or defence. Assisted by a mounted colleague cowboy, he not only lassoes with great dexterity and precision in the ordinary way, but performs such remarkable feats as lassoing both horse and rider simultaneously with different ropes. Still throwing from a distance, he secures the rider's arms, held out together for the purpose, with successive knots. In the Kroney Brothers, lazy coalmen; Herbert Darnley's Dots, in "Helping Mother"[4]; Libby Blondell and her English Johnnies; J. W. Rowley, the well-known Yorkshire comedian[5]; Edith Reynolds and Co., in "The Girl in Grey"; the Trentanovi Sisters, in their gymnastic transformation act; Lady Fauntleroy, in her clever ventriloquism; and the short-sighted cyclist, in his many mishaps, the audience have a grand variety.

PD. Printed in the *Liverpool Daily Post and Mercury*, 28 May 1907.

1. Rogers sailed for home on the S.S. *Philadelphia* and arrived on 15 June.
2. The Empire Theatre was operated by Moss' Empires, Ltd., a large theatrical enterprise much like the Keith organization. It operated many music halls in cities and towns in the United Kingdom. Performances were given twice nightly, and there was also a Wednesday matinee (*Era Dramatic and Musical Annual*, 216–17).
3. The singer George Leyton was born in 1864 in New Orleans. He made his stage debut in London on 3 June 1889 in *True Heart*. On 17 March 1890 he appeared at the Royal Music Hall and from that time on played London's leading variety theaters. He also regularly toured the provinces. His popular songs include "All for a Lady," "All Hands on Deck," "Always Ready," and "Wellington." Leyton died on 5 June 1948 (*BEWHAT*, 1054; *WhThe*, 1485).
4. The songwriter, playwright, and actor Herbert Darnley was born around 1872 in Chatham, England, and died on 7 February 1947. He made his stage debut at the age of four at the Theatre Royal in Plymouth, England, appearing in *The Babes in the Wood*. He formed his own touring company in 1906–7. For a time he also managed the Hippodrome in Mansfield, England. He was known to have written material for the performers Dan Leno and Fred Karno. Darnley wrote many of Leno's successful songs, such as "Mrs. Kelly" and "Buying a House," and authored a play for Leno entitled *Mr. Wix of Wickham*. He was hired as a manager with Fred Karno's enterprises and later produced revues (*BEWHAT*, 1018; Felstead, *Stars Who Made the Halls*, 72, 124; *WhThe*, 602).
5. A music-hall star and comedian, J. W. Rowley was born in 1845 and made his initial stage appearance in November 1867. By 1870 he was performing in London. Rowley was a well-liked music-hall entertainer in England, known for introducing such popular songs as "Patsy Brannigan," "Going to the Derby," and "England Is England Still." Rowley was also a talented dancer. He died on 23 March 1925 (*BEWHAT*, 1079; Felstead, *Stars Who Made the Halls*, 36, 38; *WhThe*, 2083–84).

Article from *Variety*
29 June 1907
Philadelphia, Pa.

In 1907 Marc Klaw and Abraham Erlanger entered vaudeville as competitors to the Keith empire.[1] They were key members of the powerful Theatrical Syndicate, which controlled legitimate theater. In partnership with the Shubert organization (their bitter rivals), they hired William Morris to oversee their booking operation, which they formally called the United States Amusement Co. or Advanced Vaudeville, its more popular name. Their venture premiered at Philadelphia's Chestnut Street Opera House on 6 April 1907. Soon they had approximately fifty theaters under their control and several stars, but their enterprise suddenly ended in late 1907 or early 1908 when they were bought out by the Keith and Proctor interests. Rogers signed a contract with Klaw and Erlanger on 20 June for twenty-five weeks of Advanced Vaudeville engagements at $300 a week, beginning 2 September 1907.[2]

PHILADELPHIA
BY GEORGE M. YOUNG.[3]

CHESTNUT STREET OPERA HOUSE[4] (Klaw & Erlanger, mgrs. Monday rehearsals 9:30).—While this week's bill is featured by several numbers not previously seen in vaudeville in this city, the real honors were carried off by acts familiar here in this line of entertainment. "Looey" is under New Acts and "The Eight Primroses," a "girl act," first time here, barely passed through.[5] Celia Galley, also a recent importation, is here for the first time. Mlle. Galley offered a burlesque of Mme. Otero and her diamonds and an imitation of Mme. Bernhardt.[6] At least this is what the program announced. Mlle. Otero must be given the benefit of the doubt that must have existed after Mlle. Galley finished, while that of Mme. Bernhardt was a burlesque in all that the word implies. In singing a French song, Mlle. Galley for the first time approached her sphere as an entertainer, but showed nothing out of the ordinary. She was accorded a very mild reception. Her failure to create even a mild sensation in New York was attributed to her appearing on a roof, but it certainly could not have been milder than her debut under one. Extracts from "The Man from Now" and "Noah's Ark," two musical comedies in which Harry Bulger recently appeared in here, formed the base for his vaudeville venture, which is called "Mink's Rink".[7] It is a satire on the present skating craze and many bright lines have been introduced. He has an able assistant in Hattie Arnold. The breaking of the wire attached to Miss Arnold introduced some comedy not in the act on Monday, but it prevented the skating scene being given. The sketch was well liked and Bulger was given a warm welcome.

Louise Dresser, last seen here with the Lew Fields company, proved one of the genuine hits of the bill.[8] Miss Dresser changed her repertoire of songs but little from her last vaudeville appearance, but they were received with an enthusiasm which stamps her as one of the most popular entertainers in her line. It was Monday evening before Will Rogers had his act going right, his extra man and horse having missed connections. But Rogers had his lassoo and his wit with him and made a pronounced impression. Delmore and Lee repeated their spectacular ladder act, with showy trappings against a black background.[9] The men are dressed to the best advantage and go through a routine of tricks which are attractive and well executed. Ferroros and his musical dog opened the bill with their familiar offering, followed by Mills and Morris, the "Minstrel Misses," also known here.[10]

PD. Printed in *Variety,* 29 June 1907.

1. Born in Paducah, Ky., Marc Klaw (1858–1936) worked his way through Louisville Law School, earning an LL.B. degree in 1879. For a time Klaw worked as a lawyer in his own practice and also as a reporter for Louisville newspapers. A stint as a drama critic drew him to the theater world, and in 1881 he was employed by the producers Gustave and Daniel Frohman as a lawyer to investigate pirated productions. He next took up theater management and operated touring companies. A major turning point in his career came in 1888, when he joined Abraham L. Erlanger to take over the Taylor Theatrical Exchange, a New York booking agency. By 1895 the Klaw and Erlanger Exchange controlled theatrical bookings in the South and was considered the nation's second-largest agency. On 31 August 1896 the two men formed the Theatrical Syndicate with Charles Frohman, Al Hayman, William Harris, Sr., Samuel F. Nixon, and J. Frederick Zimmerman (in essence it was a merger of three partnerships: Klaw and Erlanger, Hayman and Frohman, and Nixon and Zimmerman). The theater trust eventually controlled the exclusive bookings of over five hundred theaters nationwide. It was a virtual monopoly that brought organizational regulation to the theater industry, reorganized booking routes, and gave exclusive rights to the theater owners and lessees who joined. Klaw and Erlanger were agents for many stars whom they booked only with cooperative theater managers. As producers, they invested heavily in Broadway shows, including editions of the *Ziegfeld Follies,* but their biggest moneymaker was the often revived melodrama *Ben Hur* (1899). Despite opposition from rival producers, managers, and actors, the syndicate reigned over the American theater until about 1910, when the Shubert brothers became serious rivals. Klaw had a talent for booking acts, and he was considered the brains behind the organization. Personal disagreements (including Erlanger firing Klaw's son, Joseph, the firm's auditor) led to the end of the Klaw-Erlanger partnership in 1919 and to court battles between the two over their corporate funds. Klaw formed his own organization in 1920 and built the Klaw Theatre the following year. He retired in 1927 and from 1929 on lived in Hassocks, Sussex, England, where he died on 14 June 1936 (Bernheim, *Business of the Theatre,* 40–74; *DAB,* 11 supp. 2:363–64; "Erlanger Wins Suit against Marc Klaw," *NYT,* 14 July 1923; Klaw and Erlanger clipping file, NN-L-BRTC; Niver, *Klaw and Erlanger Present; NYT,* 15 June 1936; *OCAT,* 407; Peter Davis, "The Syndicate/Shubert War," in Taylor, ed., *Inventing Times Square,* 147–57; *VO,* 2.17 June 1936; *WhoStg,* 270).

Abraham Lincoln Erlanger (1860–1930) was born in Buffalo, N.Y., but grew up in Cleveland, where he worked for various theaters. He became treasurer and then principal manager of Cleveland's Euclid Avenue Opera House. A clever business organizer, he was the dominant figure in the syndicate and the one who, almost singlehanded, made the theater big business. He ruthlessly exploited his competitors, who accused him of stifling competition and attractions that did not cooperate with the syndicate. After Erlanger and Klaw dissolved their partnership, Erlanger continued to produce and finance Broadway productions and to build a series of theaters that carried his name. In 1928–29 his chain of theaters numbered forty-eight. In ill health from paralytic strokes and cancer, Erlanger died in New York City on 7 March 1930. At that time he was still considered the nation's largest owner and operator of legitimate theaters (*NYT,* 8 March 1930; *OCAT,* 235; *VO,* 2:12 March 1930; *WhMuDr,* 110–11).

2. William Morris acted as Rogers's agent in the transaction and received a 5 percent commission. An interesting paragraph typed as a note to the contract stipulated that railroad fares must not average more than $5 per person weekly and that Rogers had to pay his own railroad fare west of Chicago (William Morris Vaudeville Engagement Contract, 20 June 1907, OkClaW; Fields and Fields, *From the Bowery to Broadway,* 229; McNamara, *Shuberts of Broadway,* 42; "Battle Opens," *Variety,* 27 April 1907). See also Biographical Appendix entry, MORRIS, William.

3. George M. Young (ca. 1873–1948) was a theater manager, booking agent, and sports writer. In 1895 Young started as a police reporter with the *Philadelphia Evening Item*; he eventually became a sports writer for the *Philadelphia Times* and *Evening Ledger.* In 1914 he was hired as chief publicity agent for B. F. Keith's Theater in Philadelphia, a position that led to his becoming manager of the theater. Afterward he managed theaters in Philadelphia, Chicago, Atlantic City, and Pittsburgh for the Keith Circuit and the Shuberts. From 1933 to 1943 Young operated a booking agency and publicity office. He died at his home in Philadelphia on 22 April 1948 (*NYT,* 22 April 1948; *VO,* 4:28 April 1948).

4. Another of Philadelphia's lavish theaters, the Chestnut Street Opera House at 1021–29 Chestnut Avenue opened on 17 December 1870 as a legitimate theater. Built on the site of the Academy of the Fine Arts, it had a façade decorated in an ornate Greek Revival style with Corinthian columns and pilasters. The façade featured a projecting cornice and above it a balustrade with a centerpiece adorned with sculptured masks, musical instruments, and floral designs. Inside the auditorium were horseshoe-shaped balconies and two levels of boxes. A crystal chandelier hung from the dome. The theater seated 712 people in the orchestra, 386 in the balcony, and 406 in the gallery. After several years as a male-only variety theater, the Chestnut Street Opera House began to offer vaudeville in April 1907. At that time admission prices ranged from 25 cents to $1.50. It was one of three Philadelphia theaters managed by Samuel F. Nixon and J. Frederick Zimmerman. The Chestnut Street Theater presented legitimate productions until 1940, when it was demolished (Glazer, *Philadelphia Theatres,* 81–82; *Variety,* 30 April 1907).

5. *Looey* was advertised in the playbill as the public premiere of a one-act play by George V. Hobart. It was first performed in New York at the Lambs' Gambol, an event sponsored by an actors' organization. The Eight Primroses were making their first American vaudeville appearance and had performed at the Palace Theatre in London (Chestnut Street Opera House playbill, week beginning Monday, 24 June 1907, OkClaW).

6. Celia Galley was a performer from England who often sang in French and did imitations. This was her first appearance in Philadelphia. She was described in the playbill as a "distinguished Parisian Chanteuse direct from the Jardin de Paris" (Chestnut Street Opera House playbill, week beginning Monday, 24 June 1907, OkClaW; Laurie, *Vaudeville*, 94). Caroline Otero (1868–1965) was a Spanish dancer who performed through 1922. She was known as a courtesan and was the mistress of many exceedingly wealthy men. At her thirtieth birthday party in 1898 she was fêted by royalty from Russia, England, Belgium, and Spain. She was known for appearing on stage wearing more than a million dollars' worth of jewels. At the Folies-Bergères she appeared in a costume consisting almost entirely of diamonds. She retired in her fifties and lost her fortune, estimated at $15 million to $25 million, at the casinos on the Riviera where she lived. An unknown benefactor, however, supported Otero until her death by depositing a modest sum in her bank account each month (*Dance Magazine*, May 1965, 7; Hardy, "Flashes of Flamenco," 21).

The famous stage actress Sarah Bernhardt (1844–1923) was born Rosina Sarah in Paris. The Divine Sarah, as she was called, made her initial appearance in the United States in 1880 and returned to Paris the following year. She next played in America in 1886 and again during the season of 1905–6. Bernhardt appeared frequently on the vaudeville stage. In the winter of 1912 and the spring of 1913 she toured on the Orpheum Circuit and performed single acts from her legitimate theater repertoire (*EV*, 45–48; *WhoStg*, 40).

7. Harry Bulger (1872–1926) was a comedian who also composed music. *The Man from Now* (1906) was written by John Kendrick Bangs and Vincent Bryan, and opened at the New Amsterdam Theatre, New York, on 3 September 1906. Bulger was featured in the show and composed some of the music. The play also traveled to Baltimore and Boston. *Noah's Ark* was written by Percy French and Brenden Stewart, and starred Madge Lessing (Mantle and Sherwood, eds., *Best Plays of 1899–1909*, 519; NN-L-BRTC; *NotNAT*, 1009).

8. The well-known actress Louise Dresser had appeared in Lew Fields's *About Town*, which had run for 138 performances at the Herald Square Theatre beginning 30 August 1906 (Mantle and Sherwood, eds., *Best Plays of 1899–1909*, 517). Dresser and Will Rogers became good friends and performed frequently on the same program (see Biographical Appendix entry, DRESSER, Louise).

9. Delmore and Lee were a vaudeville comedy team that shared circuit programs with performers such as The Three Keatons. In the playbill Delmore and Lee were described as "The Foremost of All American Athletes in their Original Artistic Novelty—a study in Black and White" (Chestnut Street Opera House playbill, week beginning Monday, 24 June 1907, OkClaW; Gilbert, *American Vaudeville*, 18).

10. Playbills refer to a dog act by Ferreros, or Forresto, in which the dogs played toy instruments. Dog acts were the most common animal acts in vaudeville (scrapbook A-2, OkClaW; see also Laurie, *Vaudeville*, 161; and Slide, *EV*, 30). Lillian Mills and Elida Morris were described as the "Original Minstrel Maids" in the playbill (Chestnut Street Opera House playbill, week beginning Monday, 24 June 1907, OkClaW).

Review from *Variety*
6 July 1907
Philadelphia, Pa.

Rogers performed for a second week at Philadelphia's Chestnut Street Opera House. The program was reviewed by a Variety *critic.*

CHESTNUT STREET OPERA HOUSE (Klaw & Erlanger, mgrs.) Three acts were given their first showing here this week—The Goeltz [*Goltz*] Trio,[1] May Ward and her "Dresden Dolls"[2] and Clifford Walker (New Acts).[3] Despite these featured, Will Rogers, the lasso thrower, was given the place of honor on the bill, and held it down in fine style. Rogers closed the show, but everybody waited for him, and his act went with a hurrah. He did not vary his tricks any, but was in good form on Tuesday afternoon. Chevalier De Loris, the marksman, was seen here for the first time in several seasons in vaudeville.[4] His performance is much like those of others of his style of entertainment, but all his tricks are clean-cut and cleverly executed. His best was shooting through a ring held by the woman assistant, using a revolver and lying on his back to make the shot. The undressing and playing the piano tricks were rewarded with liberal applause, as was his patriotic finale. Mme. Sa-Hera [Sa-Heras], also a newcomer here, proved interesting in mind-reading and second sight. The blackboard tricks and calling objects held up in the audience were used, the answers being rapidly given and the signals effectively concealed. A quartet styling themselves "The Country Choir" has adopted the act of "The Village Choir," the dress and general style being taken in almost every detail. Madame Welden, Mary Hutchins, Edward Burns[5] and Walter McPherson are the singers. Their solo singing is not up to those they have copied, but the chorus numbers were well rendered. They are also using the "Annie Laurie" number to open and close, with a grand opera selection. Their best was the rendition of "Cherry," although the alto was husky and sounded strained. They were well liked, and with an original act ought to succeed. Tom Walters, who has been featured in "The Mayor of Laughland," which recently closed a summer run in this city, returned to vaudeville with an act he used some seasons ago as a vaudeville offering.[6] The comedy needs repairing and there is too little of the piano playing, which is the strongest portion. Walters has Major Casper Nowak, a dwarf, who has been with him for some time, the two closing with some well worn material. Forreste [Forresto] and his dog opened the show in good style without anything startling. The act makes a good opening number.

PD. Printed in *Variety*, 6 July 1907. From transcript, OkClaW.

1. The Goltz Trio were European acrobats who were making their first American appearance (Chestnut Street Opera House playbill, week of 1 July 1907, OkClaW).

2. May Ward (1886–1936) was known as the "Dresden China Doll" in vaudeville. At the Chestnut Street Opera House she used eight "Dresden Dolls" in her act. They were costumed to resemble Dresden dolls, and their scenery reflected the same theme. After a long illness Ward died on 5 July 1936 at her home in Far Rockaway, N.Y. (*VO*, 2:15 July 1936).

3. Clifford Walker (1870–1937) was a Broadway actor who was born in England, where he had performed at the London Hippodrome and been well received. He then moved to the United States, where he toured in vaudeville under the aegis of Arthur Hopkins. His act was described as a "pianologue." On stage Walker appeared in the original *Daddy Long-Legs* (1914), a Broadway comedy that ran for 264 performances at the Gaiety Theatre. Other plays included a revival of *School for Scandal* (1925), *L'Aiglon* (1927), *The Wrecker* (1928), and *Peter Ibbetson* (1931). He died of tuberculosis at Liberty, N.Y. (Chestnut Street Opera House playbill, week of 1 July 1907, OkClaW; Clifford Walker clipping file, NN-L-BRTC; *NYT*, 30 April 1937; *OCAT*, 179).

4. Sharpshooters such as De Loris were very popular acts in vaudeville and used bullets that were not injurious. They often relied on optical illusions to give the impression of shooting close to a human figure. De Loris had appeared at the London Hippodrome (Chestnut Street Opera House playbill, week of 1 July 1907, OkClaW; Laurie, *American Vaudeville*, 35).

5. Edward Burns (d. 1970), a dancer, was a member of the dancing team Burns, Twins, and Evelyn. This was The Country Choir's first American engagement (Chestnut Street Opera House playbill, week of 1 July 1907, OkClaW; *VO*, 7:25 November 1970).

6. Tom Waters (ca. 1872–1953) became a successful musical-comedy actor who gained fame as the star of the Broadway musical comedy *The Pink Lady* (1911). In 1890 Waters made his stage debut in *One of the Bravest*, in which he did a piano act. He also appeared in minstrel shows early in his career. In vaudeville he performed an act with his first wife, Lottie Yost, who died in 1900. He was noted for his piano comedy act, "Mayor of Laughland," which toured the United States and abroad. In his later life Waters worked at the State Museum in Harrisburg, Pa., where he died on 10 July 1907 (Laurie, *Vaudeville*, 73, 321; *NYT*, 21 July 1953; *VO*, 4:15 July 1953).

Reviews of *The Girl Rangers*
ca. 2 September 1907
Chicago, Ill.

On 10 August 1907 Variety *announced that Rogers would play in a new production at the famous Chicago Auditorium, an architectural landmark.[1] Around 12 August Rogers traveled to Chicago for rehearsals of his first stage show,* The Girl Rangers, *a three-act musical spectacle.[2] The show opened on the evening of 1 September. Rogers received favorable reviews for his rope act, which he performed as a special attraction between scenes.*

"GIRL RANGERS" OPENS
HUGE LEDERER[3] PRODUCTION AT THE AUDITORIUM PROMISES
ENTERTAINMENT.
FAIR WOMEN, FINE HORSES . . .
BY AMY LESLIE.[4]

In a witty and cleverly delivered speech George Lederer calmly roasted his own show, little as the huge undertaking deserved his satire, at the Auditorium last night, when "The Girl Rangers," a colossal entertainment by Nesbit, Weld, Moody, Lincoln Carter and George Lederer, found its first rush into a whirlwind production.[5]

"The Girl Rangers" is the biggest show to swing I ever encountered in all my varied experience. Nobody less venturesome, inventive and courageous than Mr. Lederer could have brought it into any tangible shape in such short time as that allowed for its manufacture. Especially counting the enormous factor of Lincoln J. Carter with all his gigantic mechanical mysteries crowded into one show. Lincoln J., with all sails set and all hurry music started, is enough for one stage manager to think about, but in "The Girl Rangers" Mr. Carter can be regarded powerful and thrilling as he is, with his realistic machinery, as merely one [*illegible*] element in a stupendous carouse of picture and event.

EVERYTHING IN THE SHOW.

There is in the show lyric opera, vaudeville, melodrama, atmospheric western comedy and not only story, heart interest and tableaux, but a plunge into equestrian spectacle which is almost hippodrome. With an entertainment embracing circus, romance, blazing atmosphere, song and dance, lovely singing and still lovelier women, with apt people to deliver the goods handsomely, "The Girl Rangers" elects to be one of the greatest shows the Auditorium may ever hope to brand with dignified approval.

Naturally plenty of things struck wide of the mark in a first production of this riotously varied sort. The whole second act is built around the wonderful automobile mechanism which so few people saw when Mr. Carter utilized this invention in "Bedford's Hope." Mr. Nesbit is swamped and eliminated mercilessly, but it is almost worth having to sit through one hopelessly bad act in three, for the sake of the thrill the automobile race gives and gives openly and startlingly. . . .

WILL ROGERS' WONDERFUL ROPE ACT.

The one restful, amusing and delightful quarter of an hour in the great big show was the specialty of Will Rogers the "plum good" rope thrower from

Texas. Mr Rogers has a set of teeth which carry him through an Indian massacre without a scratch, so attractive are they in a rakish smile. He is a tanned-up, lean and richly witty cowboy who does not lose his ranch manners in an opry house. His act was considerably lassoed itself by the scenery and Mr. Rogers' impromptu monologue was deliciously witty and acceptable and his rope throwing wonderful.

"GIRL RANGERS" RACE . . .
WILL ROGERS' ROPE WORK . . .

By Amy Leslie.
. . . SHOULD WRITE PART FOR WILL ROGERS.

So much accomplished, the authors of this sizzling show ought to write in a part for Will Rogers. That is, incorporate Will into the story and let him talk. Isn't that the greatest line of ranger conversation ever heard? That plumb good lingo of Texas and the plains. The man has temperament, too, and magnetism and every word he says, every glance of his keen eye, every swift curve of his magic rope comes over the footlights with a flash of power. It would be too bad to spoil a good vaudeville act, but Rogers ought to be in a play. He is a whole show himself. A couple of variety entertainers named Chamberlin[6] are very clever; a man and a woman who throw the rope beautifully and amuse casually with a bright bit of dialogue, but Rogers is a genius and has a kind of shaggy romance about him which is attractive. He is the great big hit with the big show and it does not seem to have interfered with his chest measure.

PD. Unidentified clippings, ca. 2 September 1907. Scrapbook A-2, OkClaW.

1. Designed by well-known architect Louis Sullivan and his partner Dankmar Adler, the Chicago Auditorium became noted for its striking gray stone exterior and impressive interior features. The building is considered to be a foremost example of the Chicago School of architecture, a movement that made important innovations in skyscraper design. The building is located on Michigan Avenue, across from Grant Park, between Congress Street and Van Buren Street. Sullivan and Adler began work on the Auditorium building in 1886 and completed it in 1889. It is believed that Frank Lloyd Wright, who worked for Adler and Sullivan at the time, helped design the building. The exterior expresses Sullivan's belief that a building's form should reflect its function. In addition to a theater auditorium, the building then housed offices and a hotel. The Chicago Auditorium was a huge theater for its time and seated approximately 4,000 spectators in a spacious orchestra, boxes, main balcony, and gallery areas. It was known for its exceptional acoustics and sight lines. The theater opened on 10 December 1889 with a concert by Adelina Patti, and was frequently used for

opera and orchestral concerts. In the early 1900s it was operated by Klaw and Erlanger, who used it for their Advanced Vaudeville programs. During the 1930s the Auditorium was neglected, but it was restored in the 1960s and today is an architectural landmark (Adler, "Chicago Auditorium"; Frick and Gray, eds., *Directory of Historic American Theatres*, 57–58; *JCOTG*, 230; McLanathan, *American Tradition in the Arts*, 374).

2. A reviewer best described the plot: "The Girl Rangers, aside from the girls, proved to be a musical comedy written around the race scene from Lincoln J. Carter's play called *Bedford's Hope*, which raised dust and adjectives in the Great Northern last season. The new piece has a plot, but the Auditorium is such a huge place it is not surprising the plot failed to fill it. . . . The principal item of interest appeared to be that one Brady Bingley, cowboy and high baritone, had been left heaps of money by a deceased relative, and that the money was in the form of Plains City bonds. As the town was what he who uses slang would describe as on the bum, Brad decides to go there and run it until his bonds are called in and cashed. This plan would have worked out all right if it had not been for three pesky chorus men with whiskers who insisted that Brad, besides being a high baritone, was also a cattle rustler. They wanted to hang him before 10 o'clock, and it was the effort of his friends to save him from the chorus that brought about the Lincoln Carter race in the second act. Last night the race did not work as well as it will tonight. The tin wheels of the auto did not run to form, the one attached to the southwest corner ceasing to revolve sometime before the scenery stopped flying by. The train, however, worked beautifully, and the effect is sure to prove excitingly popular. The girl rangers are brought into the plot, and also into the first act, on horseback, from which elevation they sing their first song. They are the daughters of the rattly voiced rancher, whose wife had been so unsympathetic that she continued to present him with girls, when he ordered boys. To get even the rancher brings the girls up to take the place of the requests that were never filled. Aside from furnishing the excuse for the title, the rangerettes have nothing to do with the lost plot" (*Inter-Ocean*, 2 September 1907, Locke env. 2397, NN-L-RLC).

Rogers wrote later that "the chorus girls were all mounted on horses. (That is 12 of them were.) Reine Davis was the star. It was a beautiful show, but too expensive" (*TDW*, 3 February 1935).

3. George W. Lederer (1861–1938) was a well-known producer and manager. Born in Wilkes-Barre, Pa., Lederer joined a semi-amateur comic opera company as a singer. He was next an agent and was employed by the theater manager Michael Leavitt for a time. He also wrote vaudeville sketches and served as a drama critic on the *New York Journal*. He began producing plays in 1878 and in 1893 operated New York's Casino Theatre, which became a popular showplace where he produced hit musicals, including *The Passing Show* (1894) and *The Belle of New York* (1897). Around 1906 he moved to Chicago, where he managed the Colonial Theatre and, in partnership with H. H. Frazee, produced the popular *Madame Sherry* (1910). In his later years Lederer was the general manager for the producer Sam H. Harris. He died on 8 October 1938 in Jackson Heights, N.Y. (*BEWHAT*, 1052; Leavitt, *Fifty Years in Theatrical Management*, 520–22; *OCAT*, 422).

4. Amy Leslie (ca. 1849–1939) was a drama critic for forty years. Born in West Burlington, Iowa, Leslie first pursued an acting career. On stage she was known as Lillie West, and she toured for a time with her first husband, Harry Brown, an opera singer. She began writing for the *Chicago Daily News* using the pen name Amy Leslie. She was appointed drama critic of the paper in 1890, and during her newspaper career

she befriended many famous performers. Leslie retired in 1930 and died in her apartment at Chicago's Parkway Hotel after a long illness (*NYT*, 4 July 1939).

5. Wilbur D. Nesbit co-authored *The Girl Rangers* with Lincoln J. Carter. Nesbit acknowledged that the second act was based on a magazine short story he had published, entitled "When Bingley Owned the Town." Nesbit also wrote the music with Wallace Moody and Arthur Weld.

Arthur Cyril Gordon Weld (1862–1914) was a conductor and composer. Born in Jamaica Plain, Mass., Weld graduated from Harvard College and studied music at the Conservatory of Music in Berlin. While in Europe, he composed classical works, including a string quartet and orchestral suites that were performed in the United States. After his return, Weld settled in Milwaukee, where he was a drama critic and orchestra conductor. He gained popularity as the conductor of the orchestra in the long-running musical *Floradora*, which opened at New York's Casino Theatre on 12 November 1900. Over the years Weld wrote many songs and light operas. He composed many of the songs in *The Girl Rangers*, including the number "Carnations," which accompanied Rogers's act. Later Weld became music director for the producer Henry W. Savage, and in 1914 he served as general manager for James K. Hackett. Weld was the first conductor to introduce the electric light on his baton, so that it would glow in the dark. A commanding figure known to New York audiences, Weld wore a monocle while conducting. He died in an automobile accident as a result of apoplexy (*DAB*, 10:625; *Girl Rangers* program, commencing 1 September 1907, scrapbook A-2, OkClaW; *NYDM*, 14 October 1914; *NYT*, 12 October 1914; *VO*, 1:17 October 1914).

Wallace Moody wrote the book and music for *The Girl Rangers*. He also played the character Upset Higgins, a refined rancher, in the play (*Girl Rangers* program, commencing 1 September 1907, scrapbook A-2, OkClaW).

The prolific playwright Lincoln J. Carter (1865–1926) was co-author, with Wilbur D. Nesbit, of *The Girl Rangers*, and vice president of the Garden City Amusement Co., which presented the show. He was born in Rochester, N.Y., on the day of Lincoln's assassination and was therefore named for the president. Carter moved to Chicago when he was twenty; his first play, *Sidonia*, was produced at the Academy of Music, Chicago, in 1886. A number of melodramas followed, including *The Fast Mail* (1890), *Tornado* (1894), *The Heart of Chicago* (1898), *Under the Dome* (1898), *Remember the Maine* (1898), and *Chattanooga* (1899). It was not unusual to have twenty or thirty road companies performing Carter's plays. Some of Carter's plays were sold to movie studios, and at one time he was a scenario writer for Fox. His last play was *An American Ace* (1919), which ran for only thirty-two performances at New York's Casino Theatre. He died on 13 July 1926 (*Girl Rangers* program, commencing 1 September 1907, scrapbook A-2, OkClaW; Mantle and Sherwood, eds., *Best Plays of 1899–1909*, 508; Mantle and Sherwood, eds., *Best Plays of 1909–1919*, 626; *OCAT*, 128; *VO*, 1:21 July 1926).

6. The Chamberlains did a lasso-and-whip act in vaudeville (Laurie, *Vaudeville*, 36).

Review from the *New York Dramatic Mirror*
14 September 1907
Chicago, Ill.

Rogers played with some well-known stage performers in The Girl Rangers. *The star of the show was Reine Davies,[1] sister of Marion Davies.* The Girl Rangers *played in Chicago until 29 September and then in October traveled to Philadelphia.*

Chicago, Sept. 9.—Chicago's Little Syndicate[2] produced The Girl Rangers at the Auditorium last week, starting a new period of the history of that big theatre under the direction of Klaw and Erlanger. During the week large crowds went and saw and pondered. Some mused on the littleness of the twentieth century dramatic world, where one meets so often the same ideas, scenes, jokes, expressions. Other people in the big audiences at the Auditorium seemed to enjoy the result or sum total of contributions from various sources anyhow. The critics found many kind words to publish about the production, though it was not set forth in any published statement that the entertainment was more than a ticket purchaser could expect for 50 cents. There are three acts in The Girl Rangers. The scene of the first is on the Cherry Blossom Ranch. The three scenes of the second are in a railroad station at Plain City, in a street in front of the station and on the plains near Plain City. The scene of the last act is some place, supposed to be in Plain City, where a "blow-out" is being given. The story, which was not lost sight of, in the first act showed clearly that one Brad Bingley, a young ranchman with a college education, owned Plain City bonds overdue, and that he would have to foreclose his mortgage on the town to get his money. In the second act Mr. Bingley had foreclosed and taken the town on the debt. He was running all the departments of the government so as to get his cash due, refusing to let the fire department go to a fire until the owner of the property ablaze paid his back taxes. In the course of this unique collection Mr. Bingley fell in love with the daughter of the treasurer of the bankrupt town. An unscrupulous rival tried to lure him into a death trap at Bear Creek, some distance from Plain City, after throwing suspicion on him that he was a cattle thief. He was to be lynched on his arrival in Bear Creek, but he started thither to face his accusers, a band of cowpunchers. Just after he left Plain City on a train proofs of Bingley's innocence were secured and the heroine, the daughter of the city treasurer, proposed to overtake the train in an automobile. This gave the opportunity for introducing the thrilling chef d'oeuvre of Lincoln J. Carter, the auto-train race scene of Bedford's Hope. Of course the heroine in the auto, with veil flying and clouds of dust hiding her now and then, won the

Reine Davies (1886–1938) played the lead in *The Girl Rangers* (1907), in which Rogers performed his lariat tricks. *(Photograph by J. Ellsworth Gross, Chicago, NNMuS)*

race. In the last act all the pairs of lovers in the play were assiduously united in betrothal. It is announced that Mr. Bingley collected the sum represented by his Plain City bonds. There were interpolated songs, several original musical numbers, some excellent specialties, and an exhibition of lassooing and other rope throwing which was always skillful and oft in many instances wonderful. The thrower was Will Rogers, and after he had done his novel act opinion was unanimous that he had a right to call himself "the greatest rope thrower in the world." Reine Davies was a pretty heroine. She rode her fine horse at the head of the chorus on horseback, the featured number, handsomely and skillfully. She acted the part gracefully and engagingly, but sang with a voice hardly adequate. Van Rensellaer Wheeler[3] was hearty and genial as a melodrama hero should be, and sang his solos finely. Grace Tyson,[4] whose bright personality is temporarily withdrawn from vaudeville, added much life to the performance, and her topical song was one of the big hits. Lillian Shaw[5] furnished good comedy as the cook, and her Yiddish parodies kept her before the audience until she ran out of encore material. John Bunny[6] as the jolly, old, boasting ranchman with eight pretty daughters, made the part rational and popular. Some of the best real acting was done by Marion Lorne[7] as the deceived Indian maiden, Little Feather. Francis Sullivan's pugilist, in love with the cook, was good. Ogden Wight and Robert Howard as Two-Tooth Thompson and Victim Kelly, ranchmen friends of Bingley's, were a popular pair of stage Westerners. Adolph Jackson[8] as Hipes, the villain, was sufficiently bad in conduct and good in looks. . . .

PD. Printed in *NYDM*, 14 September 1907.

1. Reine Davies later became a Hollywood gossip columnist (see Biographical Appendix entry, DAVIES, Reine).

2. The Little Syndicate was probably a reference to the Garden City Amusement Co., which produced the musical. It was headed by Will J. Davis, president; Lincoln J. Carter, vice president; Harry J. Powers, treasurer; and George W. Lederer, managing director (*Girl Rangers* program, commencing Sunday evening, 1 September 1907, scrapbook A-2, OkClaW).

3. Van Rensellaer Wheeler (ca. 1869–1919) was a concert and opera singer. He played the role of Brad Bingley in *The Girl Rangers*. Born in New York City, Wheeler appeared in many concerts and operas over thirty years. He was best known for his part in *Dolly Vardon* (1902), a two-act comic opera that ran for 154 performances at the Herald Square Theatre. Wheeler played the lead in *Tom Jones* (1907), a comic opera that had sixty-five performances at the Astor Theatre. He died in New York City on 15 February 1919 as a result of acute indigestion (Mantle and Sherwood, eds., *Best Plays of 1899–1909*, 404–5, 550; *Girl Rangers* program, commencing Sunday evening, 1 September 1907, scrapbook A-2, OkClaW; *Theatre Magazine*, December 1907, 319; *VO*, 1:21 February 1919).

4. Born in Saginaw, Mich., Grace Tyson was part of a two-"man" singing-and-dancing act with Arthur McWaters. The two were on the vaudeville stage and "well-known throughout the best circuits" (*Variety*, 9 November 1904). In *The Girl Rangers* she sang several songs, including "The Rah, Rah Girl." She played the part of Constance Fenworthy, described as "a lady, a lawyer and a leader" who chaperoned twelve tourists. Around 1907 Tyson was in *Fun in a Dressing Room* in Chicago, and in 1908 she starred in the burlesque *Mimic World* in Philadelphia. In the latter production she sang "Eyes, Eyes, Eyes," a standard of her vaudeville act. The next year she and McWaters performed on the William Morris Circuit in a piece called "The Thief" from *Mimic World*. Their act was a mixture of songs, travesty, and parody. Tyson performed in the *Ziegfeld Follies* of 1910, and her song "The Mendelssohn Rag" won many

encores. In this show she appeared in a sketch called "In the Music Publisher's Office" with Billie Reeves and Fannie Brice. In 1912 Tyson played in the musical comedy *Mama's Baby Boy*. Tyson and McWaters performed in England and South Africa in 1913–14, then returned to the United States; the two worked together at least until 1916 (Locke env. 2397, NN-L-RLC; *NYDM*, 22 April 1914, 19; *Theatre Magazine*, August 1910, 45; Ziegfeld and Ziegfeld, *Ziegfeld Follies*, 221).

5. The comic singer Lillian Shaw (ca. 1886–1978) appeared in both the *Ziegfeld Follies* and Ziegfeld's nightclub, the *Midnight Frolic*. Irving Berlin wrote two songs for her, "Fiddle on the Yiddle" and "Baby Carriage." In *The Girl Rangers* she played the role of Josephine Burnitt, the cook on the Cherryblossom ranch. In act 1 she sang the song "Down at Coney Isle." Shaw and her partner Francis Sullivan also danced in the production. Shaw performed a popular single act on the vaudeville trail, including the Loew's Circuit. During a New York trip in January 1935, Rogers encountered Lillian Shaw at Leone's Italian restaurant. In his weekly column he wrote that she was "the stage's best character singer. Played in vaudeville with her for years. . . . Lillian looked great. . . . No girl can sing those Jewish character songs like Lillian Shaw" (*TDW*, 3 February 1935). Shaw retired from show business in 1936 and lived in Manhattan, where she died on 3 February 1978 at the age of ninety-two (*Girl Rangers* program, commencing Sunday evening, 1 September 1907, scrapbook A-2, OkClaW; Laurie, *Vaudeville*, 54, 501; *VO*, 8:15 February 1978).

6. Born in New York City, the film star John Bunny (1863–1915) was raised in Brooklyn and began his show-business career in minstrel shows, eventually obtaining parts in Broadway musical comedies. Among them was his appearance with Lew Fields in *Old Dutch* (1909), a two-act musical play in which Helen Hayes made her first New York appearance. In *The Girl Rangers* Bunny played the role of Pete Rossmore, owner of the Cherryblossom ranch. Starting in 1910 Bunny became well known for his comedy roles in silent films. He made over 160 short comedies and several dramatic films from 1910 to 1915. Bunny's large, rotund frame (he weighed nearly 300 pounds) became familiar to audiences, who especially enjoyed his pantomime style. In his films he performed stunts, such as falling from automobiles, racing horses, and flying in airplanes. In many films he played opposite Flora Finch (1869–1940), who portrayed his homely, stubborn wife. Bunny did a series of films in Europe, and his fans followed him wherever he went. In 1914 he starred in his own road show *Bunny in Funnyland*. Bunny died of Bright's disease at his home in Brooklyn, N.Y. (*FilmEnc*, 191; *Girl Rangers* program, commencing Sunday evening, 1 September 1907, scrapbook A-2, OkClaW; Mantle and Sherwood, eds., *Best Plays of 1909–1919*, 405; Laurie, *Vaudeville*, 253; *NYT*, 27 April 1915).

7. Marion Lorne (1888–1968) had a long career as a comic actress that ran from the stage to television. Her real name was Marion Lorne MacDougall. She made her stage debut in 1905 in the three-act farce *Mrs. Temple's Telegram*. Other early plays included *The Devil* (1908), *The Florist Shop* (1909), *The Great Name* (1910), and *Don't Weaken* (1914). Her later stage credits included *Harvey* (1948) and the revue *Dance Me a Song* (1950). Lorne also had a career in films and became well known for her television roles. On television she played the English teacher Mrs. Gurney in *Mr. Peepers* (1952–55), and she had parts in the situation comedy *Sally* (1957–58) and the *Gary Moore Show* (1958). Her last television role was as Aunt Clara in *Bewitched* (1964–68), and in this role she won an Emmy (1967–68) for outstanding performance by an actress in a supporting comedy role. For many years she lived in London with her husband Walter Hackett, an actor and producer. There she acted in plays and managed theaters with her husband. Lorne died of a heart attack in New York on 9 May 1968

(Mantle and Sherwood, eds., *Best Plays of 1899–1909*, 483; McNeil, *Total Television*, 86–87, 266-67, 608, 905; *NYT*, 10 May 1968; *NYTheRei*, 242; *VO*, 4:15 May 1968).

8. The stage actor Adolph Jarchow Jackson performed in many plays in New York before appearing in *The Girl Rangers* as Caesar Hipes, the president of the Plains City Bank. He had parts in *Jack Gordon, Knight Errant* (1890), *The American Minister* (1892), *An Irish Gentleman* (1897), and *Mrs. Wilson, That's All* (1906). He died on 27 November 1907, a few months after appearing in *The Girl Rangers* (NN-L-BRTC; *NYTheRei*, 203).

Vaudeville Notes
ca. 19 September 1907
Chicago, Ill.

During his engagement in The Girl Rangers *Rogers was praised by critics for his running commentary during his performance. The following gags, which he used in vaudeville, were probably written around this time.[1]*

Chicago, _____ 190__

Gags for missing the nose

1) Think I will turn him around and see if I cant throw one on his tail easier.
2) If I dont put one on pretty soon will have to give out rain checks.
3) Ha you Jasper I think I will see if I cant get put one on your nose if its dont make no difference to you mob out there.
4) If I have a ~~lot of~~ whole bunch of good luck I will get this on about the 13th throw if this salary wing or whip dont give out on me.
5) I should of sprinkled a little Mucilage or rosin on his nose this thing might hang on.
6) What did old [*word illegible*] say. "There is hope". Well we are all chuck full of hope—if there was a little better roping and less hoping we would get out of here earlier tonight.
7) Thats one thing I must say for that *ferocious animal* he never was much on sticking his nose into things.
8) Now this is easier to do on a blind horse that dont see the Rope coming.[2]

AMs. OkClaW. Written on The Saratoga European Hotel and Restaurant Co. letterhead.

1. The approximate date of this manuscript has been determined by Rogers's use of the same letterhead in his letter to Betty Blake, 19 September 1907.
2. A reporter quoted two of Rogers's remarks during his performance. One was about a rope trick: "Neauw here's one I call a sort of double back-handed squeegee." Another was about his horse: "Neauw this here horse knows more about this trick than I ever will know" (unidentified clipping, scrapbook A-2, OkClaW).

To Betty Blake
19 September 1907
Chicago, Ill.

Chicago, Sep 19, 1907

My Dearest—

Well have waited two days for that other letter you said in the last one that you would write tomorrow. Why dont you keep your word for I looked for it now for two long days

Well just found out that we do not go to St Louis but to Philadelphia and that I am to remain with the show—aint that good—eru-errr. (growls outside) But I dont think I will be east but a short time and then the first open time I have I will be home and if not till Xmas. Oh, I am coming then show or no show.

Got a dandy letter from Mr. Morgan today[1] I am with Claud every day. Harry Osborne has gone home.

We finish here Sept 29. would stay longer but the house is rented and they have to move.

Now I am only writing this to tell you about that letter so I will stop—Now listen Dear please write often—to the Hotel here.

Yours now Billie

ALS, rc. OkClaW. On The Saratoga European Hotel and Restaurant Co. letterhead.[2]

1. Tom Morgan.
2. The Saratoga Hotel was owned by J. K. Sebres and managed by P. Hicks. It was located at 155–61 Dearborn Street, in the center of the theater district, and catered to performers (*Variety,* 12 December 1908, 109).

To Betty Blake
ca. 7 November 1907
Philadelphia, Pa.

Rogers left The Girl Rangers *in Philadelphia around 19 October 1907 and returned to the vaudeville stage.[1] He rejoined Klaw and Erlanger's Advanced Vaudeville and appeared at the New York Theatre the week of 28 October.[2] The following week he was in Philadelphia, where he celebrated his twenty-eighth birthday on 4 November. Three days later he wrote the following letter to Betty Blake.*

Philadelphia
Peoples Theatre[3]
Thursday Aft.

My Dear Betty.

Well you dont seem to be writing so afful fast after me asking you to forgive me for my long delay   now I thought you would write me a few by now—Now listen Betty that was not my fault and besides I am just supposed to be a bit mad at you for awhile yet for you know you did not just do right when I wrote you from Chicago   But let it go and you get busy with the stationary and lace a few pages out to the old dog for he is just as strong for you as ever.   and always will be.   Well how are things breaking for you in that land and aint it about time to make up your mind to get out and see something

Oh tell Morgan I am *Headlined* over our friends Hyams and McIntyre this week and that Hyams is high on Tom, thinks hes great.[4]

Well I go to Brooklyn Grand Opera House next Week.[5]   I am glad to get back in Vaudeville again   Well I have not got a cent of that $1,275.00 yet and dont think I will.

I am planning on seeing you Xmas if things break right   "G" but I been away a long time aint I.   and I will be so glad to get back again.

Well I will have to stop   I am in my dressing room writing this

Now you write me a nice long letter at once to Grand Opera House Brooklyn.

I will certainly get St. Louis and K.C. this winter soon for they are on this circuit

Well *Idios* my Girl and you be good down there for I know you all are having one big time this winter

Yours as ever.
Billie

ALS, rc. OkClaW.

1. On 26 October *Variety* reported that Will Rogers "left the show last week" and would appear in Klaw and Erlanger's Advanced Vaudeville. *The Girl Rangers* ended its run at Philadelphia's Walnut Street Theatre on 26 October. Located at Ninth and Walnut Streets, this was one of Philadelphia's oldest theaters, built in 1809 and called the New Circus Theatre. It was renamed in 1820 and mostly used as a legitimate theater. The Walnut Street Theatre offered vaudeville in 1900 and burlesque in 1930. It was still in use in the 1970s and 1980s as a performing arts complex and the home of the Drama Guild (Glazer, *Philadelphia Theaters*, 234–36).

2. The New York Theatre was a historic edifice built in 1895, formerly Oscar Hammerstein's Olympia Theatre. Located on Broadway between Forty-fourth and

Forty-fifth Streets, the Olympia with its midtown location marked the beginning of theater in the area. Its huge main auditorium, called the Music Hall, was richly embellished in the style of Louis XIV and consisted of 2,600 seats, including a record 124 boxes (the building's smaller theater was called the Lyric). Three years after its opening, Hammerstein was forced to sell the Olympia at auction because of debt stemming from failed productions. A year later the Olympia Music Hall was renamed the New York Theatre, and it offered a series of musical comedies and drama. In 1907 the theater was managed by Klaw and Erlanger, who staged Advanced Vaudeville here. That same year the building's roof garden, renamed the Jardin de Paris, offered the first *Ziegfeld Follies*; four other *Follies* editions followed. Beginning in 1915 the theater became Loew's New York, featuring vaudeville and films, and in 1935 the structure was demolished (Henderson, *City and the Theatre*, 195–96, 263–64; van Hoogstraten, *Lost Broadway Theatres*, 36–39).

The playbill at the New York Theatre was as follows: Overture ("Advanced Vaudeville" by Cohan); Rawson and June (In Their Unique Performance of Boomerang Throwing); Billy Clifford (The Heavy Swell); Six Brothers Luck (In Their Original Pantomime Absurdity, entitled *The Demon of the Cellar*); Edith Helena (Second Week Here of the Remarkable American Soprano Who Possesses the Greatest Voice Range Ever Known); The Four Bards (Direct from Their Triumph at the Wintergarten, Berlin, America's Greatest Gymnasts); Collins and Hart (The Two "Strong Men"—And the Musical Cat); Klein, Ott Brothers and Nicholson (Introducing Horns, Cornets, Trombones, Saxophones, Xylophones and Organ Chimes); J. Barnold's Dog and Monkey Actors (In the Comedy Uproar, *The Intoxicated Canine*); Miss Hetty King (England's Foremost Male Impersonator); Will Rogers (Return to Vaudeville After a Run in Chicago as the Feature of *The Girl Rangers*, the Cowboy Who Has Astonished the World With His Lasso) (New York Theatre playbill, week beginning Monday matinee, 28 October 1907, scrapbook A-2, OkClaW). Prices for admission ranged from 25 cents to a dollar. Of special note on the playbill was the popular Hetty King (1883–1972), a male impersonator and British music-hall star (on King, see Review from the *Brooklyn Daily Eagle*, ca. 12 November 1907, below).

3. The Peoples Theatre was located at 2649 Kessington Avenue, near Cumberland Street. Constructed in 1890, it was housed in a four-story brick building. Performances were staged twice a day with a matinee at 2 P.M. and the evening performance at 8 P.M. The theater had a seating capacity of 2,336 in orchestra, balcony, and gallery. In the gallery the audience sat on benches. Over the years the People's Theatre was used primarily for stock repertory companies. It was renamed the Desmond in 1924 and then refurbished as the Kent, which opened on 19 January 1928. Eventually it was used as a second-run movie theater, and in the 1960s it specialized in double features. It closed near the end of that decade (Glazer, *Philadelphia Theatres*, 145–46; *JCOTG*, 119, 131).

The playbill was as follows: Overture ("Advanced Vaudeville" by Cohan); Irene Lee and her Kandy Kids (First Appearance Here of the "American Vesta Tilley" In a Repertoire of Songs and Dances); Harry C. Stanley assisted by Sarah L. Cogswell (In the New Musical Comedy Sketch *The German Professor*); Mills and Morris (The Original "Minstrel Misses"); Delmore and Lee (America's Foremost Athletes In Their Original Novelty *A Study in Black and White*); Miss Radie Furman (Character Comedienne); Mr. Johnny Hyams and Miss Leila McIntyre (In Herbert Hall Winslow's Comedy Sketch, entitled *Two Hundred Wives*); Will Rogers (Direct from the New York Theatre in a remarkable exhibition of dexterous lariat throwing and lasso twirling) (Peoples Theatre playbill, scrapbook A-2, OkClaW).

4. John Hyams (1869–1940) and Leila McIntyre (1882–1953) were a popular husband-and-wife team who performed a so-called class act using a photographic studio as a backdrop. Born in Syracuse, N.Y., Hyams was first a song-and-dance man in touring blackface minstrel shows. He became a feature in a male dancing sextet at Hoyt's Theatre, New York. McIntyre was born in New York, played child roles in plays, and first appeared in vaudeville in the act (Harry) Linton and McIntyre. Hyams and McIntyre met as cast members in *Beauty and the Beast,* and they were married shortly thereafter. They teamed in vaudeville in an act that featured witty crossfire gags and specialties. In 1911 they appeared in the Broadway musical *The Girl of My Dreams.* Their first film together was a 1927 short called *All in Fun,* and they also appeared in *The Housekeeper's Daughter* (1939). For many years they appeared in vaudeville and other stage productions. Their daughter, Leila Hymans (1905–77), joined their family act as a youngster. She became a film star in the late 1920s and 1930s (*EV,* 256–57; *FilmEnc,* 667–68; Gilbert, *American Vaudeville,* 362–63; Laurie, *Vaudeville,* 148; Leila McIntyre clippings file, NN-L-BRTC; Mantle and Sherwood, eds., *Best Plays of 1909–1919,* 447).

5. Brooklyn's Grand Opera House was managed by the Hyde and Behman Amusement Co. and directed by Klaw and Erlanger. It had a seating capacity of 2,000 (*JCOTG,* 77, 81).

Article from the *Brooklyn Daily Eagle*
ca. 12 November 1907
Brooklyn, N.Y.

Brooklyn grew dramatically in the late nineteenth century, and in 1906 it had a population of approximately 1.2 million, which included a large middle class.[1] Recognizing its growth, theater owners built many entertainment venues in the area. By 1906 Brooklyn had a thriving cultural life, with nineteen legitimate and variety theaters. Many vaudeville theaters were operated by Percy Williams, and Hyde and Behman. The latter organization operated Brooklyn's Grand Opera House where Rogers performed at this time.[2]

THE GRAND OPERA HOUSE.

That more than the usual degree of interest was aroused by the announcement that the current week at the Grand Opera House was to inaugurate a series of vaudeville festivals arranged by Klaw & Erlanger was shown last evening in the presence of an audience that filled every seat in the playhouse. The programme brought together a number of foreign and native performers and the honors were about equally shared by two of the imported features, and one that was distinctly American.[3] The coming of Hetty King,[4] the English male impersonator, who recently has scored decisively in Manhattan, was, of course, the chief item of interest, but Miss King, who repeated her Manhattan success here, was not the only number upon the bill that met with enthusiastic approval, for it would be difficult indeed to say whether she, Cinquevalli,[5] the wonderful European juggler, who has not for some time been seen here, or Will Rogers, a cowboy, who does amazing things with the lasso, received the larger share of the applause.

PD. Printed in *Brooklyn Daily Eagle,* ca. 12 November 1907. Scrapbook A-2, OkClaW.

1. See Stern et. al, *New York 1900,* 421–25.
2. Early entrepreneurs in the variety field, Richard Hyde (1865–1912) and Louis C. Behman (1885–1902) were schoolmates in Brooklyn. They opened their first theater in Philadelphia and another in Baltimore in 1877. Hyde and Behman's first variety theater in Brooklyn was on Adams Street. Named the Brooklyn Theatre, it was considered, along with Tony Pastor's Fourteenth Street Theatre, the most popular house in the New York area. By 1900 Hyde and Behman had a virtual monopoly of variety houses in Brooklyn through their amusement company (1899). The company organized traveling variety shows and managed performers such as The Four Cohans. In 1906 Hyde and Behman operated the Grand Opera House, the Folly Theatre, and the flagship theater carrying their name. The Grand Opera House had a seating capacity of 2,000 with box seats, orchestra, balcony, and gallery areas. Prices ranged 25 cents in the gallery to $1.50 for a box seat (*JCOTG,* 77, 81). When Behman died in 1902, the organization declined and could not compete with the growing monopoly of the Keith-Albee enterprise (Gilbert, *American Vaudeville,* 13, 14, 181; Laurie, *Vaudeville,* 356, 417–18; *OCAT,* 364).
3. The playbill was as follows: Selection ("Parisian Model" by Hoffman); Zaretsky Troupe (First Appearance in America of the Famous Russian Aggregation, Considered One of the Most Skillful Acrobatic Dancing Troupes in Europe); Miss Radie Furman (First Appearance Here of the Dainty Comedienne, In Her Own Singing Specialty); The Gauts[c]hmidts (A Novelty Imported from Berlin. Comedy Acrobats, with Their Clever Dogs); Miss Hetty King (First American Appearance Outside of New York of England's Foremost Male Impersonator); Romany Operatic Troupe (Second and Last Week of Entire Change of Operatic Selections); Charlie Cartmell and Laura Harris (A Conglomeration of Skirts, Toes, Twists and Kicks); Cinquevalli (The World's Premier Juggler); Charles Kenna (The Street Fakir); Will Rogers (Return to Vaudeville After a Run in Chicago as the Feature of *The Girl Rangers,* the Cowboy Who Has Astonished the World With His Lasso) (Brooklyn Grand Opera House program, week beginning Monday matinee, 11 November 1907, OkClaW).
4. Born in Wimbledon, England, in 1883, Hetty King started show business in 1897 as a clog dancer. After 1905 she gained considerable fame for her impersonation of a sophisticated man-about-town and her portrayals of soldiers and sailors. In her characterizations of debonair gentlemen, she wore men's formal trousers, overcoat, and top hat. At other times she appeared with straw hat and vest, with a cigarette in her mouth. She was well known for her songs "All the Nice Girls Love a Sailor," "Piccadily," and "I'm Going Away." She went to great lengths to declare her femininity offstage and wrote that she disliked women who were masculine. A 1970 film documentary, entitled *Hetty King: Performer,* summarized her career and featured an interview with her. King appeared in variety shows, at summer resorts, and on television until shortly before her death in London on 28 September 1972 (Busby, *British Music Hall,* 92–93; *EV,* 290; Felstead, *Stars Who Made the Halls,* 41–42, 100–1; Laurie, *Vaudeville,* 93, Toll, *On with the Show!* 259–61; *VO,* 2:4 October 1972).

5. Paul Cinquevalli (1859–1918) was a world-famous juggler known for his dexterity in juggling different items. He was born Paul Kestner in Lissa, Poland. For political reasons, his family fled to Germany, and he was educated in Berlin. At age thirteen he became an apprentice to a gymnast and aerialist named Cinquevalli. In 1873 he made his stage debut at Odessa, Russia, billed as "The Little Flying Devil." After injuring himself falling from a trapeze, he turned to juggling and took the name of his mentor. Soon he became a star in British music halls. One of his specialties was playing billiards on his back, and for this stunt he became known as The Human Billiard Table. He concluded his act by hurling a cannonball and catching it on the nape of his neck. Cinquevalli often performed before the royal family, and appeared in the 1912 Royal Command Performance at the Palace Theatre. Beginning in 1888 Cinquevalli was a regular on the American vaudeville stage, and in 1901 he toured on the Keith Circuit. He also performed at theaters around the world, including Australia, India, and South Africa. During World War I he faced prejudice as a German and retired from the stage in 1915. He died of heart disease at Brixton, England, a London suburb, in July 1918 (Busby, *British Music Hall*, 35–36; *EV*, 98–99; Laurie, *Vaudeville*, 21, 23, 133; *VO*, 1:19 July 1918).

To Betty Blake
18 November 1907
New York, N.Y.

NEW YORK Mon- Night

My Dearest Bettie

Well I got your letters last week and of course was glad to hear from you and that you was not sore at me—honest I aint so bad if you only knew me better—oh girl you dont know how I do think of you and if I dont write it or show it—I think it—I think I will be able to get home either Xmas or about Feb 1st as this contract runs out then and I will get to come then sure

Tell Morgan thanks for his letter and will write him.   I cant write you much Bettie for I dont know what to say but hope to get to see you and tell you a lot.

Write me a nice long letter.   This week I am at Shubert Theatre till Saturday. 23.   Newark, N.Y.[1]

Next Week.   Tremont Theatre   Boston. Mass.[2]

Be a good girl and just remember who loves you.

Billie
Goo[d]night.

ALS, rc. On White Rats of America, Inc., 1553 Broadway, New York, letterhead.[3]

1. The following performers appeared with Rogers at the Shubert Theatre: Edna Aug, the Romany Opera Co., Baptiste and Franconi (Balancing act), Billy Van (Comedian), Zaretsky Troupe of Russian Dancers, Willie Zimmerman (Imitations), and the Gaudschmidts (Dog Act) (*Variety*, 23 November 1907).

2. The Tremont Theatre had a seating capacity of 1,405 and contained two horseshoe balconies, the second of which contained wooden pews. It was managed by John B. Schoeffel, and matinee and evening performances were given daily. In the 1930s it was turned into a movie house and later renamed the Astor Theatre (*JCOTG*, 101, 109; King, "From Museum to Multi-Cinema," 10).

Klaw and Erlanger's Advanced Vaudeville was offered at the Tremont. The playbill was as follows: Mlle. Alexandra and Mons Bertie (First Time in America Presenting Their Refined Aerial Act "After the Ball"); Johnny Johns (The Popular Comedian, "The Boy from Dixie"); Eva Mudge ("The Military Girl" in Quick Character Changes. The American Girl Who Captured England); Vasco ("The Mad Musician," the Most Versatile Musician in the World. He Plays Twenty-eight Instruments); Will Rogers (The Cowboy Who Has Astonished the World With His Lasso); Willie Hale and Buster (Fun with the Globe); Mr. Louis Mann and Co. (In a Condensed Version of Leo Ditrichstein's Play, *All on Account of Eliza*); Bob and George Quigley (In a New Conversational Comedy Diversion, "The Congressman At Large"); and The Okabe Family (Unrivalled Japanese Artists, World's Famous Hand-Balancers and Acrobats) (Tremont Theatre playbill, week of 25 November 1907, scrapbook A-2, OkClaW; see also *Variety*, 30 November 1907).

3. No conclusive evidence has been found that Rogers was actually a paying member of the vaudeville actors' union, White Rats of America, Inc., even though his friend Fred Stone and partner David Montgomery were two of its founders. The letterhead listed the following union officers: R. C. Mudge, president; George W. Monroe, vice president; Harry O. Hayes, treasurer; Herman Desco, secretary; and John P. Hill, Colie Lorella, and George E. Delmore, trustees. The office of the White Rats of America was located at Forty-sixth Street and Broadway.

From H. B. Marinelli
25 November 1907
New York, N.Y.

Rogers received from the noted international agent, H. B. Marinelli,[1] the following offer to perform in Europe. The letter illustrates Rogers's growing stature in vaudeville and shows that his name was well recognized abroad.

New York, November 25th, 1907

Rogers, Will
   c/o Tremont Theatre
     Boston, Mass.

Dear Sir:—

Kindly send me your route and mark the time you could accept in Europe. Also state your lowest terms for an engagement at the Wintergarten Berlin.

Advise promptly on this and oblige.[2]

Yours very truly
H. B. Marinelli

TL, rc. OkClaW. On H. B. Marinelli ("The World's Agency") letterhead, Paris, London, Berlin, and New York offices.[3]

1. Born in Thuringe, Germany, in 1864, Marinelli began his stage career as a contortionist known as "The Boneless Wonder." Around 1894 he left the stage because of ill health and became a prominent agent who booked many European stars for the American stage. He helped discover European talent for Willie Hammerstein's Victoria Theatre and for the Keith Circuit. He also brought many American headliners to Europe, including Evelyn Nesbit Thaw. He called his business The World's Agency and had offices in Paris, London, Berlin, and New York. He also booked performers for tours in South America, Africa, and Australia. Marinelli boasted that his agency booked 730 attractions from 1 October 1903 until 30 September 1904. He guaranteed a world tour of three to four years to headliners who signed with his agency. Among his clients were Harry Lauder, Gaby Deslys, Lily Langtry, Sarah Bernhardt, Vesta Tilley, Albert Chevalier, Cinquevalli, Anna Held, Marie Lloyd, and Ruth St. Denis. After the outbreak of war in Europe, Marinelli went to the United States with his family in 1914. The war had halted the international vaudeville business. He was able to secure an exclusive booking contract with the Keith and Orpheum circuits, and his business thrived. Marinelli died in Paterson, N.J., on 7 January 1924 from a cerebral hemorrhage (*EV*, 335; *GHNTD*, 561; Gilbert, *American Vaudeville*, 230, 247–48; Grau, *Business Man in the Amusement World*, 94–95; H. B. Marinelli clippings, Locke env. 1315, NN-L-RLC; Laurie, *Vaudeville*, 37, 133; Leavitt, *Fifty Years in Theatrical Management*, 269–70; *NYT*, 8 January 1924).

2. Rogers did not undertake a European tour at this time.

3. On the back of this letter Rogers wrote his Christmas gift list, which included the names of his nieces and nephews in the families of his three sisters, the McSpaddens, the Lanes, and the Stines.

To Betty Blake
6 December 1907
Baltimore, Md.

Baltimore, Md. <u>Dec. 6</u>

Well My old Pal

I got a letter from you in Boston and it seemed a bit queer   (you said you had written or was going to write three)   I only got one as I have been traveling to fast for my mail lately   I am in Baltimore this Week and go to Washington Next week—Write me there—General Delivery and I will be surer getting it.[1]   Now I am going to ask you something Betty   if I act queer dont *think of it*—I aint treating *you right* and I know *it* but I will later on   I am doing the best I can under the circumstances   *I am in wrong* and will tell you all about it when I see you which might be Xmas and not later than Feb. as my contract goes till then.

When you still refused me last spring—*We both will regret that.*   for we would of been happy and a thousand times more *prosperous*—   Still you was

so *wise* you couldent be showed.   Now you see what it has led too.   I have
not been worth a *dam* since and you are the *direct* ~~cause~~ and unwilling cause
of it.   still I dont blame you   only I wish you had not been so *Bull headed*

Now thets [let's] hope all will come out O.K.   Now you be a good girl and
always remember that I love you more than all   when you know all you will
say I aint such a bad fellow and will always do what is right.

Think lots of me and write to Washington

Yours

Billie.

ALS, rc. On Hotel Raleigh ("in the heart of the city, all modern improvements, every room an outside room—absolutely fire proof European plan"), Baltimore, letterhead. John Tjarks and Co., proprietors.

1. Rogers appeared at the Gaiety Theatre in Baltimore from 2 to 7 December. A
Variety critic reviewed the show: "Charles Robinson and his 'Night Owls' in two good
burlettas, 'Who Stole My Husband?' and 'Solomon the Soldier,' a good-looking chorus and very good olio. Will Rogers is the extra attraction and helps to pack the house.
The others are Mildred Flora, The International Musical Trio, Lawrence Edwards in
a sketch, 'Casey's Finish', Peyser and McDonald, comedians, and Charles Robinson
in his monologue, 'The Tramp and the Hebrew'" (7 December 1907). Rogers performed at the Gaiety Theatre in Washington, D.C., from 9 to 14 December 1907.

Manager's Report, 125th Street Theatre
16 December 1907
New York, N.Y.

CRITICISM

Keith & Proctor's 125th Street Theatre[1]

December 16, 1907.

WOTPERT TRIO   European acrobats. A trio of really remarkable acrobats
and balancers. Some of their work is very cleverly executed. All of their various tricks were applauded and their finish went exceptionally strong. 9
Minutes, Full Stage.

CLARENCE SISTERS[2]   Singers and dancers. This act would be all right in a
continuous house about second or third. Their voices are off color and the
costumes decidedly of a burlesque order. The dancing is fairly good and
seemed to please. 10 Minutes in one.

HARRY CORSON CLARK[E] & CO.[3]   In the comedy "strategy". This is not
a bad act by any means although decidedly overpaid. The comedy is rather
talky and longdrawnout although it is interesting and holds the audience

They secured quite a number of laughs but closed poorly. 21 Minutes Full Stage.

MC CARTE'S MONKEYS   Presume the monkeys were sick today as they worked very badly. The sleigh bells and Barber shop looks like a copy from Calletti. The general pranks of the animals pleased. All the bad features of the act were eliminated when the monkey rode the bicycle to the satisfaction of the crowd which is a remarkable stunt. 9 Minutes full stage.

WILL ROGERS   "The Lasso King". This man's act remains the same as before. He did not go as well as on other occasions. Presume they are getting tired. 11 Minutes Full Stage.[4]

MR. & MRS. GARDNER CRANE[5]   In the well known comedy "Am I your Wife?". Went fully as strong as before. Continual laughter throughout. 22 Minutes Full Stage.

MC MAHON & CHAPPELLE[6] and their PULLMAN PORTER MAIDS   The strongest part of this number is the Mc Mahon & Chappelle Specialty in one which proved to be the strongest laughing number of the bill. Too much sameness between the Watermelon Girls and the Pullman Porter Maids. The audience seemed to like it and gave them some little applause. 24 Minutes.

BILLY S. CLIFFORD[7]   This man held his own here in fairly good shape. Material remains the same as when presented before. 14 Minutes in one.

DELMORE & LEE   "A Study in Black and White". An excellent aerial Ladder act. Novel. All of their work is difficult and well executed. 13 Minutes full stage.

KINETOGRAPH

LITTLE HEROES	Fairly Good
THE TWIN BROTHER'S JOKE	Fair Comedy
THE SHORT SIGHTED SPORTSMAN	Good Comedy
THE PIKER'S DREAM	Fairly Good Comedy

TD. KAP-IaU.

1. Keith and Proctor's 125th Street Theatre, located between Park and Lexington Avenues in Harlem, was originally called the Columbus and next to Miner's 125th Street Theatre. Proctor leased the theater in May 1900 for $25,000 a year. The agreement gave Proctor four theaters in New York City. The 125th Street Theatre had a seating capacity of 3,450 (*JCOTG,* 67; Marston and Feller, *F. F. Proctor,* 63–64, 160).

2. The Clarence Sisters did what was called transformation singing and dancing with quick changes of costumes and scenery. *Variety,* 21 November 1908, described their act at the Hudson Theatre in New Jersey: "They introduce a pony upon the stage after a quick transformation of scenery and costume, appearing as a cowboy and girl

respectively, concluding with a neat skipping rope dance, caused the girls to be the hit of the Hudson bill this week" (NAFR + Series 2, 66:127–28, NN-L-RLC).

3. Actor and comedian Harry Corson Clarke came from a show-business family and was born in New York. As early as 1877 Clarke was engaged in the theater. Legend has it that the fourteen-year-old Clarke opened a theater in his father's barn and was arrested by the police for not having a license. At one time he was associated with the Frawley Theater company and Denver Lyceum Stock company. Clarke suffered from a stomach disorder that interrupted his career. He also formed his own company, which traveled as far as Honolulu. Clarke regularly appeared in Broadway shows, including *Mr. Wix of Wickham* (1904), *The Girl and the Wizard* (1909), *The Red Widow* (1911), and *Tantalizing Tommy* (1912). He died in Los Angeles on 3 March 1923 (*BEWHAT*, 1013; Dobson File, CL; Mantle and Sherwood, eds., *Best Plays of 1899–1909*, 479; Mantle and Sherwood, eds., *Best Plays of 1909–1919*, 457, 479; *OCAT*, 149; *Theatre Magazine*, December 1911, 186, and January 1913, 23).

4. As this criticism of Rogers illustrates, he sometimes received mediocre reviews at this time. By contrast, *Variety* reported on his performance: "Will Rogers always contributes fifteen minutes of real enjoyment. His rope work is well done and liked. The audience took to Mr. Rogers just as quickly as they did to his lassoing" (21 December 1907).

5. Gardner Crane (1874–1939) was an actor and vaudevillian. He appeared in several stage productions, including *Dollars and Sense* (1913), Elmer Rice's *On Trial* (1914), and *The 13th Chair* (1916). His wife, Margaret Crane (b. 1875), was also in vaudeville, and they performed in numerous skits together (Mantle and Sherwood, eds., *Best Plays of 1909–1919*, 202, 587; *NYTheReI*, 84; *VO*, 3:14 June 1939).

6. Tim McMahon and his wife Edythe Chappelle specialized in a cross-talk act with songs and dances. They produced girl acts, including The Watermelon Girls, The Sunflower Girls, and The Pullman Porter Maids. The pair also did skits that featured a thin plot with song and dance. At Proctor's Theatre they performed a sketch called "Why Hubby Missed the Train." In 1908 they joined a vaudeville circuit organized by William Morris. Their two children also may have participated in their act (Laurie, *Vaudeville*, 229, 232–33; McMahon and Chappelle clipping file, NN-L-BRTC).

7. William Clifford Shyrigh (1869–1930), known professionally as Billy (Single) Clifford, was a performer in vaudeville, minstrel shows, musical comedy, and the circus. Born in Urbana, Ill., Clifford joined a circus as a drummer at the age of ten and became a tap dancer. For many years he teamed with his wife, Maud Huth. Clifford and Huth traveled the main vaudeville circuits in the United States and abroad. After their partnership dissolved, Clifford did a popular single act. He owned the Clifford Theatre in Urbana, where he died unexpectedly on 20 November 1920 (Laurie, *Vaudeville*, 198; *VO*, 2:26 November 1930).

Hammerstein's Victoria Theatre Program
23 December 1907
New York, N.Y.

HAMMERSTEIN'S

1   SCOTT AND WHALEY[1]
COLORED SINGERS AND DANCERS

2
THE MURRAY SISTERS[2]
JUST AMERICAN GIRLS WITH AMERICAN SONGS.

3
GRACIE EMMETT AND COMPANY[3]
PRESENTING A COMEDY SKIT, ENTITLED
"MRS. MURPHY'S SECOND HUSBAND."

4
JAMES J. MORTON[4]
MONOLOGUE.

5
WILL R. ROGERS[5]
EXPERT LARIAT THROWER.

6
MEREDITH SISTERS
THE MAIDS WHO MADE "HIAWATHA" FAMOUS.

7
GEORGE FELIX AND LYDIA BARRY[6]
INCLUDING EMILY BARRY, IN
"THE BOY NEXT DOOR."

8
THE AMERICAN COMEDIENNE,
EVA TANGUAY[7]
IN AN ORIGINAL REPERTOIRE OF SONGS.

9
ELLIS NOWLIN TROUPE
COMEDY ACROBATS.

WAIT FOR   WAIT FOR
10   Motion Pictures of the International Boxing Contest,
          between TOMMY BURNS,[8] Champion of America, and
          GUNNER MOIR, Champion of England, held at the
    National Sporting Club, of London, England, by the Vitagraph.

PD. Hammerstein's Victoria Theatre Program. Scrapbook A-2, OkClaW.

1. Harry Scott (1879–1947) and Eddie Whaley (1886–1961) were African Americans who gained fame in England for their cross-talk act. Scott was born in Cleveland, Ohio, Whaley in Montgomery, Ala. At first the two did a vaudeville act in the United States, including a tour of western states in October 1909, but they never achieved popularity in the United States. In 1909 they went to England for an eight-week tour and never returned to the United States. Their first performance in England

was at the Hippodrome in Sheffield on 1 November 1909. In London they made their debut at the Empire Theatre on 8 January 1910. In May of that year they performed at London's Tivoli Theatre. In England they did an act called Pussyfoot (Scott) and Cuthbert (Whaley), a cross-talk routine that derived from the minstrel show. They were also talented musicians and performed a song-and-piano act, with Whaley doing the singing and Scott playing jazz on the piano. For over thirty years they were a success in British music halls, and both became British citizens. In 1933 they turned to radio and did a weekly program called the Kentucky Minstrels. Their partnership ended in 1946. Scott obtained a new partner, Chris Gill. Scott and Whaley had a reunion on 19 May 1947, when they performed together at the Queen's Poplar. Scott died soon after this performance, on 22 June 1947. Whaley retired and operated a hotel in Brighton. He died on 13 November 1961 (Busby, *British Music Hall,* 158; Eddie Whaley, obituary and clipping files, NN-L-BRTC; Harry Scott clipping file, NN-L-BRTC; *NYT,* 15 November 1960; Sampson, *Ghost Walks,* 478, 516).

2. Marion and Victoria Murray (NN-L-BRTC).

3. Gracie Emmett (ca. 1862–1940) was a vaudevillian who became known for her Irish characterizations. Her biggest success was portraying Honora Murphy in the comedy playlet *Mrs. Murphy's Second Husband.* She played the part over 5,000 times, including on a world tour in 1905. She retired in 1928 and died at the age of seventy-eight in Somerville, Mass. (Laurie, *Vaudeville,* 52; *VO,* 3:6 December 1940).

4. Born James Lankton, James J. Morton (1861–1938) was known as the originator of the comic master of ceremonies. Born in Boston, Morton began his show-business career in 1874 singing topical songs with Healey and Biglowe's Hibernian Minstrels for two seasons. During the 1890s Morton teamed with his wife, Maude Revel, in a vaudeville sketch act. By 1906 he was doing a single act. That year he acted as an emcee on the roof of New York's American Music Hall. In vaudeville he became known for his monologue and wry ad-lib patter about other performers on the bill, including revelations about their private life. Sometimes called "The Boy Comic," Morton weighed over 250 pounds (friends referred to him as Big Jim Morton). In his own single he would sing nonsense songs that he composed. Morton wrote his own monologues, songs, and sketches. He also invented so-called "rag time" words–asking and answering his own questions. He was often confused with the vaudevillian James C. Morton. They had a feud because of their similar names, and and James J. spent a lot of money advertising that he was not the other Morton. He appeared in the revue *The Merry-Go-Round,* which opened at Gus Edwards's Music Hall on 25 April 1908. He also appeared on stage in *The Circus Princess, The Field God, Spellbound, Up Pops the Devil,* and *Holka Polka.* Morton was a founder in 1906 of New York's Vaudeville Comedy Club, primarily a social organization, and a member of the White Rats. He lived for ten years at Percy Williams's retirement home for actors at Islip, Long Island, before his death on 10 April 1938 (*EV,* 360, 526; Gilbert, *American Vaudeville,* 168–70, 211, 213, 234; Laurie, *Vaudeville,* 182–83, 199, 242, 268, 294, 311, 488–89; Mantle and Sherwood, eds., *Best Plays of 1899–1909,* 562; *NYT,* 11 April 1938, *OCAT,* 490; *VO,* 2:20 April 1938; *WhMuDr,* 232).

5. The reviewer in *Variety* pointed out that Rogers was now a "comedy talking act." "His incidental remarks are fresh and breezy as can be and the act runs along entertain[ing]ly. Rogers affects not to take himself seriously, and therein lies the novelty of his act" (28 December 1907).

6. George Felix (1866–1949) started his stage career in 1885 at the Boston Museum. Here he performed in *Babes in the Wood* and *Aladdin.* Then he entered vaudeville, doing an act called The India Rubber Man. In vaudeville he appeared with

his wife, Lydia Barry, and her sister Emily. Felix lived at Percy Williams's home for retired actors from 1931 until his death in 1949 (*NYT,* 15 May 1949; *VO,* 4:18 May 1949; *WhMuDr,* 117).

7. Eva Tanguay (1878–1947) was one of the most famous stars in American vaudeville and musical comedy. Although her early life remains obscure, Tanguay began her stage career at an amateur night at Parson's Hall in Holyoke, Mass., her hometown. At age eight she played the character Cedric Errol in *Little Lord Fauntleroy* as a member of the Redding touring company. At age ten she made her New York stage debut in *In Gotham*. During the 1890s Tanguay was a chorus girl in musical comedies. After performances in *My Lady* (1901) and *The Office Boy* (1902), she made a big hit in the musical comedy *The Chaperons* (1903) with her rendition of the popular song "I Don't Care." The latter became her lifelong trademark, and she was often referred to as the "I Don't Care Girl." Tanguay delighted audiences with her frenetic dancing, frivolous manners, shrill voice, sultry and unconventional costumes (one made from coins and dollar bills), tousled blond hair, and whirlwind routines. Beginning in 1908 she performed her sensational Salomé dance in a pearled, thinly veiled costume, a craze at the time. She was among the most highly paid performers in vaudeville, earning from $2,500 to $3,500 a week, and she regularly broke box-office records on the Keith Circuit. A free spirit, Tanguay embodied the independent woman in both her public and private life. Defying the censors and the decorum of standard vaudeville, she sang risqué songs onstage, such as "I Want Someone to Go Wild with Me" and "It's All Been Done Before But Not the Way I Do It." Often temperamental, she left engagements when slighted in any way and once sliced a stage curtain into pieces with a knife because the manager had fined her for missing a matinee. She had a flair for publicity stunts and spent lavishly on advertising her act. Some male critics denounced her controversial image, but her flamboyant, uninhibited personality left audiences cheering. Her two marriages failed, and she lost a fortune in lavish spending, real estate speculations, and the 1929 stock market crash. But when she had money she was known to be very generous and aided charities. Tanguay was still a name in the early 1920s and played the Palace in 1921 and 1924. Ill health eventually caused her stardom to fade. By 1925 she had difficulty seeing because of cataracts and had to be led to the stage. In 1930 and 1931 she attempted a comeback in vaudeville. Later she developed heart problems, Bright's disease, and arthritis, and by 1937 she was confined at home. During her last years in Hollywood she lived alone, destitute and an invalid. Her most frequent visitors were aging vaudevillians. The night before her death on 11 January 1947, her physician visited her Hollywood cottage, where he saw on the walls yellowing photographs of Tanguay at the apex of her career. She left no will, and her personal effects were worth only $500 (Caffin, *Vaudeville,* 35–42; *DAB,* Supplement 4:814–15; *EV,* 450–52, 488–90; Gilbert, *American Vaudeville,* 327–31; James, ed., *Notable American Women,* 3:425–27; Laurie, *Vaudeville,* 58–59; Martin and Segrave, *Women in Comedy,* 68–75; *NYT,* 12 January 1947 and 24 January 1947; *OCAT,* 656; Robinson et al., eds., *Notable Women in the American Theatre,* 855-57; *VO,* 3:15 January 1947; *WhScrn,* 1:83; *WhStg,* 420, 422; *WhThe,* 4:2305).

8. The boxer Tommy Burns (1881–1955) was born in Hanover, Ontario, Canada. His real name was Noah Brusso. He held the heavyweight boxing championship from 1906 to 1908. Burns weighed about 180 pounds and stood 5 feet, 7 inches tall; he was the shortest fighter to win the heavyweight championship. On 23 February 1906 he won the title by defeating Marvin Hart, who had become champion when Jim Jeffries retired. The fight was in Los Angeles, and Burns won in a twenty-round decision. He

lost the title to Jack Johnson on 26 December 1908 in Sydney. Johnson won the fight by a knockout in the fourteenth round. While he was heavyweight champion, Burns defended his title successfully eleven times. During his career from 1900 to 1920 he fought sixty times, winning forty-five fights, thirty-five by knockouts. In 1948 he became an ordained minister in the Northwest. He died as a result of a heart attack on 10 May 1955 in Vancouver, British Columbia (Lardner, *White Hopes and Other Tigers*, 29–30; McCallum, *World Heavyweight Boxing Championship*, 62–63).

To Betty Blake
23 January 1908
Hamilton, Ont.

Hamilton, Ont.
<u>Jan. 23,</u>   19<u>08</u>

My Dearest Betty

Well I got your letter which had been sent on to me from Montreal as it got there after I left[1]   I am playing here in Hamilton, Can[2]—this week and go to Toronto Can.[3]   next week so you can mail me there with a letter.   I did not write you on your trip cause I knew you would be having a good time and not have time to be messing with letters

Well I am up here and just about froze   say Kid but it is some chilly   I havent seen a wheel only on trains   its all *sleds* and snow shoes and skates.   I will get back in the U.S. after next week if I dont freeze.

Well I had my first little sick spell last week in Montreal and it was kinder like a very hard or congestive chill and I went on Matinee then to my hotel and was very bad   called a Dr and he came 4 different times before 12 at night   I missed only the one show as I felt better the next day but I sho got sorter scared and some way I kinder wished for my Betty and would of got well quick.   its all alright away off all the time till you get to feeling bad and then it puts you to thinking and you wish you was home but I feel good now and am all O.K.

Well I hope you did enjoy your trip and wish I could of been home to went around with you in some of the places for I am beginning to get to feel home-sick   Well my present contract will be up in a short time and then I will get home and down to see you the 1st thing

Now I hope you was a good girl on this trip and did not make any new mashes and you are still *heart free*

Now write me a long letter all about your trip and tell me *all*

Well its late at night   just come in from my usual night *feed*   its about 2 A.M. so will be *beating it*   This is a *"lousy"* town   will be glad when Sat comes [4]

Write often and long   your old boy

B—

Gaiety Theatre
    Toronto.
        Can

ALS, rc. OkClaW. On The Waldorf letterhead. R. B. Gardner, proprietor.

1. Before leaving on a vaudeville tour of upstate New York, New England, and eastern Canada, Rogers appeared at New York's Colonial Theatre at Broadway and Sixty-second Street from 30 December 1907 to 4 January 1908. On the bill were Dill and Ward (Singers and Dancers); The Permane Brothers (English Eccentric Clowns, Introducing *The Nightingale's Courtship*); George Felix and Lydia Barry (Assisted by Emily Barry, Present *The Boy Next Door*); Nellie Wallace (First Return Engagement of the English Eccentric Comedienne); Mr. Louis Mann and Co. (In a Condensed Version of Leo Ditrichstein's Play, *All on Account of Eliza*); Friend and Downing (Hebrew Comedians); Horace Goldin (Introducing His Latest Illusions and Magical Novelties); Clifton Crawford (The Author and Comedian); Will Rogers (In An Exhibition of Lariat Throwing); Vitagraph (Colonial Theatre playbill, week beginning Monday matinee, 30 December 1907, scrapbook A-2, OkClaW).

After his Colonial appearance, Rogers performed at Cook's Opera House from 6 to 11 January. The playbill was as follows: The Fadettes of Boston (22 Artists), Willie Pantzer Troupe (Marvelous European Acrobats); Will Rogers (The Cowboy Who Taught the President How to Throw the Lariat); Miss May Tully (The Versatile Character and Emotional Actress and Her Company in Matthew White Jr.'s One-act Play, *Stop, Look, and Listen*); Emma Francis and Arabs (Late of Rogers Bros. Co. with Her Wonderful Arab Boys. Songs and Russian Dances); Nichols Sisters (Kentucky Belles); Dixon and Anger ("The Baron and His Friend," in their new offering *Out West*); Max Duffek (The Musical Contortionist) (Cook Opera House playbill, week of 6 January 1908, scrapbook A-2, OkClaW; see also *Variety*, 11 January 1908; *NYDM*, 18 January 1908). Rogers next performed at Bennett's Theatre in Montreal from 13 to 18 January 1908.

2. Rogers appeared at Bennett's Theatre in Hamilton from 20 to 25 January 1908. The playbill was as follows: Will Rogers (Assisted by Cowboys and a Beautiful Horse, in Expert Lariat Throwing; Murphy and Francis (Colored Entertainers); Goldsmith and Hoppe (Comedy Musical Act); Minnie Kaufman (Expert Cyclist); Le Roy and Woodford (Conversationalists); Countess Rossi Assisted by M. Paula (Novel Singing); Chinko (European Juggler); Bennettograph (Perfect Motion Views); Charles Bradshaw (Presenting *Fix in a Fix*) (Bennett's Theatre playbill, week of 20 January, scrapbook A-2, OkClaW).

3. Rogers appeared at the Gayety Theatre in Toronto from 27 January to 1 February. With Rogers on the playbill were Deeley and Austin (The Dancing Dolls); Nolan and White (The Tramp and the Soubrette); Graham and Randall (In a Novelty Creation *Across the Bridge*); Crawford and Manning (Grotesque Comedians); Moran and Wiser (Sensational Jugglers and Boomerang Hat Throwers) (Gayety Theatre playbill, scrapbook A-2, OkClaW; see also *Variety*, 1 February 1908).

4. Located at the west end of Lake Ontario, Hamilton was settled in 1813. With its harbor and railroad terminus, the city became a transportation and manufacturing center (*WNGD*, 484).

To Betty Blake
6 February 1908
Worcester, Mass.

Worcester, Mass.

Feb 6th.   08.

My Dearest—

Well your letter finally got here it   did not get to Toronto till away after I left and was forwarded on here and reached me today just *now*   it was written on Jan 27.   and get here Feb. 6.   I was just going to send you a wire tonight and tell you where I was at.   I am here this week and go to Brooklyn next week.[1]

Well old pal I was cert[ainly] glad to hear from you and more so to hear you was having such a good time but you always do, do that   you are a pretty lucky girl and a lot of ways   did you ever think it *over* "*Well do you are*"

You have a lot of good times and no worry at all

No that was all right to tell Mary anything and I am glad you did   I wish you could of gotten up to see the home folks and I know they would have loved to had you come for they think you are a fine girl.

Well I will *kinder* know next week about just when I will get home as I have not heard from my agent for several weeks but will see him next week.   I dont hardly think I will get there by the 1st but will perhaps by the last   still I dont know a thing till I get to N.Y.   I am getting kinder homesick and am in a hurry to come and am liable to get in at any time from the 1st on.

Well I was glad to get back to the U.S. after three weeks in Canada and will be glad to be back in old N.Y. again next week as N.Y. and Brooklyn is all *one*

Well I am all well and have not been sick anymore and dont think I will as that was cold more than anything.

Say did you ever see *Howard*   It seems that I cant get west at all   they keep playing me *over* and *over* again around here and never do send me on one of the western Circuits.

So you *snared* you a *promising* lawyer   What all did he promise you.   and you him.

Now you better slack up on that *stuff* for it gets you in bad and I will be getting pretty *sore* some time   you know how jealous I am and what a lot you have to tell me when I see you   all about that what you said was too long to tell one time   I still have all that up my *sleeve* and am still a bit leary on just how you stand and if you dont tell me all these *things,*   Well *I might find out otherwise*

Now you better deal square with me for I have with you as bad as I have been.   You could of prevented it

Well Betty I sho would love to see you and oh what a time we would have talk about staying up late   we never would turn in   we would have so much to tell each other wouldent we.

Well I must stop or I will be getting sentimental and I cant afford to do that you know.

Now write me a nice long letter and just *hope* and *pray* that things turn out all right—

Tell Tom[2] will send his photo soon as I get it

With a lot of love to the best Girl I know ever *knew.*

your old Boy.

B—

Orpheum Theatre
  Brooklyn
    N.Y.

ALS, rc. OkClaW. On New Park Hotel, 57 Park Street, Worcester, Mass., letterhead. John F. Kelleher, manager.

1. Rogers appeared at Sylvester Poli's theater in Worcester, Mass., from 3 to 8 February. A playbill advertisement called him "The Dextrous Fellow from the Golden West Presenting His Latest and Unequalled Series of Cowboy Pastimes." Others on the program were Mr. and Mrs. Sydney Drew, playing in Kenneth Lee's farce *Billy's Tombstones*; the Five Majors (English Entertainers); Tom Moore (The Best Coon Song Singer); Paul Kleist (Presenting a Spectacular Novelty Invested with Odd and Original Surprises and Laughter Getting Ideas); Knight Bros. and Marion Sawtelle (Impersonations and Dances); Frank Bush (The Famous Story Teller With Something To Say That Depicts Funny Humanity); and by Electrograph (The Little Girl Who Didn't Believe in Santa Claus) (playbill advertisement, scrapbook A-2, OkClaW). On Rogers's performance at the Orpheum Theatre in Brooklyn, see Orpheum Theatre Playbill, 10 February 1908, below.

2. Rogers might have meant that he was sending his photograph to Tom Morgan. Morgan received several photographs of Rogers (TMC-RHM). Two were taken by the Otto Sarony Co. studio. One shows a handsome Rogers formally dressed and sitting on a chair with hands in pockets (see frontispiece to this volume), the other shows him in his vaudeville cowboy outfit, standing with a rope in one hand (see illustration on p. 302). The latter was autographed.

Orpheum Theatre Playbill
10 February 1908
Brooklyn, N.Y.

At Percy Williams's popular Orpheum Theatre[1] in Brooklyn Rogers was on the same program as Marie Lloyd.[2] She was considered the foremost comedienne and female singer on the British music-hall stage.

THE ORPHEUM

WEEK BEGINNING MONDAY MATINEE, FEBRUARY 10, 1908
Matinee Every Day.

URBANI AND SON
European Equilibristic Stars

VINIE DALY[3]
In Her Latest Dancing Novelty.

WILLARD SIMMS AND COMPANY[4]
Present the One-Act Comedy, entitled
"FLINDER'S HARLEM FLAT."

Second and Last Week of
ALBERT WHELAN[5]
The Australian Mimic and Comedian

JOSEPHINE COHAN AND COMPANY
Present the New One Act Episode,
"THE GIRL OF THE TIMES."
By Fred Niblo.

CAST.

Harold Square, a "man about town" ....Mr. Hall McAllister

James, his valet ....Mr. John Tremaine

Jane Scribbler, of "The Times" ....Mrs. Cohan

Time and Place—Mr. Square's Apartment at Midnight.

INTERMISSION–TEN MINUTES

"Castles in the Air" ....by Paul Linck

CHARLES LEONARD FLETCHER[6]
Presenting His Latest Novelty, "An Evening With Richard Mansfield"[7]
and Other Stage and Literary Celebrities.

Farewell Appearance Here of
MARIE LLOYD
England's Favorite Comedienne, in Her Latest Song Offering,
Introducing Her Biggest European Song Success,
entitled "The Hag."

FRED NIBLO
The American Humorist.

WILL ROGERS
In An Exhibition of Lariat Throwing.

PD. Scrapbook A-2, OkClaW.

1. The Orpheum was a top-flight theater, considered the best known vaudeville house in Brooklyn. It was built with the financial backing of the Otto Huber Brewing Co. and Thomas J. Adams, Jr., who owned Tutti-Frutti chewing gum. The Orpheum was located at 578 Fulton Street and Rockwell Place, and officially opened on 31 December 1899. It had a large audience capacity: 770 in the orchestra, 371 in the balcony, 316 in the gallery, 20 in the mezzanine, and 326 in the boxes. Tickets were more expensive than the usual vaudeville theater. Williams booked high-class talent, including many European variety stars, such as Marie Lloyd. Williams charged a dollar for the best orchestra seats. The popular theater also offered seats on a subscription basis. Brooklyn families cherished their subscriptions and held them for years. In 1915 the theater was lavishly refurbished by the Keith organization (*EV*, 559–60; *JCOGT*, 85; Laurie, *Vaudeville*, 356–57; Snyder, *Voice of the City*, 93).

2. Marie Lloyd (1870–1922), whose real name was Matilda Alice Victoria Wood, was born in a London district. She began her career at an early age. Several accounts suggest that her first appearance was at the Eagle Music Hall in 1895, under the name Bella Delmere. Soon she changed her name, influenced by the name of a British newspaper, *Lloyd's Weekly News*. By age twenty she was a rage in England, known for her witty and saucy songs. She gained a reputation for singing risqué tunes, such as "She'd Never Had Her Ticket Punched Before." Later she sang character songs such as "One of the Ruins That Cromwell Knocked About a Bit." Her cheeky songs were too much

for the royal family, and she was excluded from two command performances in 1912 and 1919. But the general public adored her, and she frequently broke box-office records while playing the leading London music halls. Lloyd also toured extensively abroad and appeared in South Africa (1896), as well as Australia (1901) where she starred on the opening bill of the Melbourne Opera House. At the time she performed with Rogers she was on a vaudeville tour of the United States. According to his friend Louise Henry, Rogers visited Lloyd's country home outside London during either his 1906 or 1907 trip abroad. Marie Lloyd's life was full of notoriety, mainly through her many lovers, two divorces, and the fact that she lived with a lover while married to another man. She collapsed while performing at Edmonton on 4 October 1922. Three days later she was dead. It was reported that over 100,000 people visited her grave at the time of her burial (Busby, *British Music Hall*, 110; Louise Henry autobiography, LHS-LHP; Mander and Mitchenson, *British Music Halls*, photo nos. 88–91; *NYT*, 8 October 1922; *VO*, 1:13 October 1922, 27 October 1922; Waller, *Magical Nights at the Theatre*, 110).

3. This could have been Vinie Daly, an opera singer, whose picture appeared in the *New York Dramatic Mirror* on 25 June 1913. Her married name was Mrs. J. P. Kohl (Vinie Daly clipping file, NN-L-BRTC).

4. The comedian and actor Willard Simms had an extensive vaudeville and theater career. He appeared on the New York stage in *The Merry World* (1895), *The Lady Slavey* (1898), and *Mother Goose* (1899). His biggest success was as the leading comedian in productions at New York's Casino Theatre. His last stage performance was at the Palace Theatre in his vaudeville skit, "Flinders' Furnished Flat." In 1917 he died in Chicago of pneumonia, aged about fifty (*NYT*, 4 May 1917; *NYTheReI*, 353; *VO*, 1:11 May 1917).

5. Albert Whelan (1875–1961) was a long-time English music-hall and vaudeville comedian. Whelan is considered one of the first high-class comedians; he wore an opera cloak, silk-lined dress coat, top hat and tails, and white gloves on stage. He was also a pioneer in using theme music, and would saunter on stage whistling the waltz "Der Lustige Bruder" (The Jolly Brothers) and would continue singing as he removed his cloak, hat, and gloves. Whelan entered show business in his native Australia, where he was born Albert Waxman in Melbourne. He first gained fame as a musical comedy performer as a member of the team Whelan and Wilson. On 28 October 1901 he made his stage debut as an eccentric dancer at London's Empire Theatre on Leicester Square. He mastered his single act performing a comic monologue, telling funny stories, playing the piano, and singing amusing songs. He toured extensively on the vaudeville stage in the United States before World War I and in the 1920s. In 1912 Whelan appeared with Anna Palova at New York's Palace Theatre. In a Los Angeles vaudeville bill in 1924, at the Orpheum Theatre, he performed songs, stories, and a piano skit. In 1931 Whelan teamed with Billy Bennett in a blackface, cross-talk variety act called Alexander and Mose, which the pair also did on radio. Despite a leg amputation at the age of eighty-two, Whelan was still active professionally during his later years and appeared as late as September 1960 in the British television panel show *Life Begins at Eighty* (Busby, *British Music Hall*, 182–83; Mander and Mitchenson, *British Music Halls*, photo no. 171; *NYT*, 20 February 1907; *VO*, 5:22 February 1961).

6. Charles Fletcher was a dramatic actor. He appeared in such productions as *The Goddess of Liberty*, a musical play that opened at Weber's Theatre in New York on 22 December 1902 (Charles Fletcher clipping file, NN-L-BRTC; *NYTheReI*, 137; Mantle and Sherwood, eds., *Best Plays of 1909–1919*, 406–7).

7. Born in Berlin, Richard Mansfield (1854–1907) was a well-known actor who performed extensively on the British and American stage. His leading roles included *Dr. Jekyll and Mr. Hyde* (1887), *Richard III* (1889), and *Beau Brummell* (1890) (*WNBD*, 648).

To Betty Blake
20 February 1908
Springfield, Mass.

As the following two letters illustrate, Rogers and Betty Blake had finally reached a turning point in their relationship. Each was involved in an affair with someone else, and this caused considerable jealousy on both sides. When he wrote Blake from Springfield, Mass., Rogers was performing on the circuit operated by Sylvester Z. Poli, a prominent theater manager in New England.[1]

Springfield, Mass. Feb 20. 1908

My Dearest Bettie

Well your letter finally reached me   your letters always seem to reach the theatre just after I have left it but they are certainly appreciated when they do come

Well I am on what is called the Poli circuit   he has 7 houses and this is my second one and guess I will play the other five in rotation[2]   I go to Poli's Hartford Conn. next week[3]   it is only a little ways from here.

Well I got a little letter from old Mary   told me about seeing you and you being a fine fellow and all that   I am going to write her and also send her some pictures and some *Music* and you by the way   I will go out and see if I cant dig you up something in the music line and I will send Tom Morgan the pictures   now they are not those large ones but these are all I have but will send him one of each   I only had just yours and Papa's and Sisters of the large ones   the others all the other size   yes he is a good fellow and I certainly would love to see him succeed for he is certainly bright and to see some of these *hams* back here that do get on is a wonder to me for he has all of them tied to a post.

Well I think I will land up there about May the 1st   for I am getting pretty homesick but I better get this while I can.

I look for a bad year next year   I have made no plans at all for them   I may stay home if things are any ways bright out there as I am crazy to get another little bunch of cattle and get back on that old *farm* and tend to what little I have got.   still its hard to give up the money one can make but at the most one more year will let me out   I am still offered that play for next year that is the most likely thing of all   You never do seem to understand me when I ever make any allusion to that which you once wrote and told me was too long a story to tell.   "You know what I mean in regard to your *Dearest friend.* T. H.[4]   you remember what we had our troubles about before I went to Europe.   Now you never did care to tell me what there is or was to it, but me like a big *rummy* I up and told you a lot of stuff (that I had never ought to of told anybody in the world.[)]

Well I am just living life as she comes and havent much confidence in anything   we all make mistakes but as long as we live to the best we know how they cant be considered against one can they?

By the way how are you doing with your *lawer*   Well its *even* for I have fell in love with an *actorine* and *gone plum nutty*   Now you see if you cant get a line or two there on time

Be good and I hope to see you soon   I liked the picture great and it was so thoughtful of you to send it.

Well show time

Lots of Love,

B—

Poli's Theatre

~~c/o~~ Hartford,

Conn

ALS, rc. OkClaW. On The Henking Hotel ("European Plan"), Springfield, letterhead.

1. Poli was a leading vaudeville theater owner and organized his houses into the Poli Circuit in New England. Born in a suburb of Lucca, Italy, Silvestro Zefferino (S. Z.) Poli (ca. 1859–1937) immigrated to the United States in 1881. After building a career as a sculptor, Poli opened a dime museum in 1889 in Toronto with a partner named Robinson. Here they offered a wax museum, curios and freaks, and a variety show. In 1891 Poli leased an abandoned church in Troy, N.Y., where he opened another dime museum with a lecture hall, but within a year the theater was sold. In 1892 he rented a second-floor hall in New Haven, Conn., where he presented variety acts four times a day. Recognizing that New Haven needed a high-class vaudeville theater catering to families, Poli leased a nearby theater and called it the Wonderland. Here he began to offer variety acts in 1893. Expanding his operations in Connecticut, Poli bought and leased theaters in Hartford, Bridgeport, Meriden, and Waterbury. In Massachusetts he opened new vaudeville houses in Springfield and Worcester. He spent lavishly to furnish his new theater (1905) in New Haven, called the Palace, which became his headquarters. Poli also had theaters in Scranton and Wilkes-Barre, Pa. Poli stressed that his theaters offered wholesome family entertainment and were "devoted to progressive and polite vaudeville" (*S. Z. Poli's Theatrical Enterprises*).

Poli was well respected in the vaudeville business and his advice was sought by other managers. He was among the first theater operators to construct a single cantilevered balcony, built in the new Poli Palace (1913) in Springfield, Mass. He

Sylvester Z. Poli (ca. 1859–1937), owner of a leading vaudeville circuit in New England. Rogers frequently performed at the Poli theaters. *(National Vaudeville Artists, 11 May 1924, Eighth Annual Benefit)*

continued to build theaters in New England through the 1920s. Poli believed in improving his theaters and was known to rebuild them as many as three times. He also took over Chase's Theatre in Washington, D.C., in 1912. He was among the first managers to show films in his theaters, in the 1890s. In 1928 Poli sold his theaters to the Fox Theatre Corporation. Four years later Fox went bankrupt, and Poli regained possession of his theaters. In 1934 he merged his theaters with the Loew's corporation. Poli died in 1937 as a result of a heart attack at his palatial home in Connecticut and left an estate estimated at over $30 million (Connors, "American Vaudeville Managers," 48; *EV*, 403; King, "Sylvester Z. Poli Story"; Laurie, *Vaudeville*, 397–400; *S. Z. Poli's Theatrical Enterprises*; *VO*, 2:2 June 1937).

2. Rogers appeared at Poli's Theatre in Springfield, Mass., from 17 to 22 February. The theater was located at 286 Worthington Street. It was renamed the Park Theatre in 1913, and a year later it burned down. Poli built a new theater in Springfield, the Palace (King, "Sylvester Z. Poli Story," 13, 18). The playbill at Poli's Springfield included the following: Overture (Poli's Own Orchestra); Great Scott (The London Fireman in His Marvelous Juggling Act on the Balancing Ladder); Elsie Harvey (Assisted by Field Brothers, Refined Singers and Dancers); Harry and Kate Jackson (In the Laughing Success, *His Day Off*); Tom Moore (The Fellow Who Sings Coon Songs in a Style All His Own); McMahon and Chappelle's Pullman Maids (Presenting As an Interpolation Their Own Success *Why Hubby Missed the Train*); The Italian Trio (Solo Vocalists); and Will Rogers (In Cowboy Pastimes) (Poli's Theatre, Springfield, Mass., playbill, week of 17 February 1908, scrapbook A-2, OkClaW).

3. Rogers played Poli's Theatre in Hartford from 24 February to 1 March. The playbill was as follows: Belle Blanche (Broadway's Favorite Mimic and Entertainers,

in her Artistic Impersonations of Leading Stage Celebrities. Direct from Hammerstein's Where She Was the "Talk of New York"); Cameron and Flanagan (Presenting a Real Novelty, *On and Off*); Willie Hale and Buster (In a Little of Everything Called *Parlor Pastimes*); Rose De Haven Sextette (Presenting the Musical Operetta *The Understudy*); Balzar Brothers (Peerless German Acrobats); Phil and Nettie Peters (In a Laughalogue. With Music Now and Then); and Will Rogers (Notably Special Engagement. World's Champion Lariat Thrower in His Unique Novelty, *Cowboy Pastimes*) (Poli's Theatre playbill, Hartford, Conn., week of 24 February 1908, scrapbook A-2, OkClaW; *NYDM*, 7 March 1908). Poli had acquired his theater in Hartford in 1903. The theater had a capacity of 2,150 people. He introduced high-class vaudeville here beginning 14 September 1903. The theater was demolished in 1919 to make way for the Capitol Theatre. In 1913–14 Poli built the Palace, a more lavish theater (King, "Sylvester Z. Poli Story," 12–13, 15, 18).

4. Thomas W. Harvey (1882–1942), the son of William (Coin) Harvey, the free silver advocate, courted Betty Blake in Monte Ne, Ark. (Coin Harvey's model city) in the early 1900s (see Biographical Appendix entry, HARVEY, Thomas W.).

To Betty Blake
ca. 2 March 1908
New Haven, Conn.

My Dearest (and that goes)

Well Betty I received your crazy letter and honest it knocked me a *twister* You could not of been your same dear old self when you wrote it.

Now I want to not only tell you were wrong in most all you said but I will show you that you were and prove it to you

Now in the first place if you remember *rightly,* this *coolness* of which I fully admit started when you refused to tell me of that T.H. thing Now you know that and I have always treated you coolly since Not because I felt like it but because I just felt that I was *getting back* at you and I done the whole thing purposely and intended to do it in a way till you did tell me, for I honestly felt and do feel that it was *due* me

That last letter remined you of that and you know they all did.

Now *secondly* as to any other girl it is foolish to think of them *ever* in the same breath with you

Now you say about my regretting telling you all of that stuff I did one time. *Yes I* said I felt like a *rummy* to tell you all of my past and then you not tell me one little thing I said it was not fair cause I told you all and you still would not tell me a thing No I am not ashamed of a thing I ever told you and feel *proud* of it I thought it showed *manhood* It only hurt me so bad cause you could not trust me with a *measly* little old *love scrape* cause I know that was all I told you I had always been a *bad boy* and guess I will continue

to be one till you are with me and then its all over   I will put all of this old
life behind and I think I am man enough to do it too.

Yes I got a lot of girls   not one as you say   but several *on* and *off* the
stage.   I dont mean this as *sarcasm* or conceit   its just to put you right.
[*Illegible word deleted*] *several girls* _not_ *sweethearts* or girls that when it comes to
settling down I would consider for a minute   I kinder always thought I knew
about where my love and affection lay.   And I gave you credit for not being
a jealous girl and take a thing that was put in a letter just for a little *sting* the
same as you had put in mine several times   the last in regard to the Lawyer   Now I am the jealous one of the two.   And yet I took it as it was meant
and come back at you with the actor gal one, but no you size it all up wrong
and write that afful letter.

You say I spoke of it as a mistake   yes so they were *lots* of them   I have
done nothing all year but the wrong thing and then you say *thank goodness* it
was discovered in time   You speak as if I had a dark plot to decieve you and
you (*old sleuth*) had discovered it.   Now when I tell you I have made a mistake I mean what I say and I intend to tell you all about them when I get
home.   Not in regard to you or nothing that concerns you   but if its necessary I will explain them to you.   The mistake I spoke of was for telling you
all and then you telling me nothing and if you read your letter properly you
will see it as its meant.   Now if I wanted to break off with you I would do in
a great deal more gentlemanly way than that and one that I think you would
not lose respect for me for it would be to tell you the *plain* facts, whatever they
might be but I hope that will never come to pass on either side   I wouldent
beat about the bush trying to save your feelings but out with the whole
truth   if you think other wise you got me sized up wrong.

Now Betty comes the thing   the whole thing   in your letter that certainly did *hurt,* and I dident think you could accuse me of such.

You say,–("I was idescreet and for that you have never thought well of me.
or at least have never believed me and when I refer to other boys, you invari-
ably grow suspiciously ~~and~~ *sarcastic and _throw_ _unpleasant_ _insinuations._*")

Now Betty plainly, *that's not so* and its the worst thing you could say, for if
all the things I admire and love you for its for you being *good* and *pure* and not
silly and *spooney*   Now I never in all my life insinuated a wrong thing in
regard to other boys   it would be the last thing on earth   why I would fight
any one that would insinuate as much to me as that you acted the least bit
unladylike at any time.   *Why girl* thats why I *love* you.   thats why you are
different from the rest   Why *what we done* I *love you for* if you had not of done
it I would of known you did not *love* me.   I dont think bad of you for that,

cause I knew you was a girl that if you hadent of loved me that wouldent of happened   Why I would trust you every way in the world   you size me up cause I showed you a silly letter once[1]   my good girl   to show you how I knew her to be only fooling   she was *mixed* up with to my own knowledge, with three fellows perhaps writing worse ones to them.   No I know these girls in this business *a little,* and I think there is a little difference between you and them

Now as you have said you would love to tell me that little story why then I know you will when I see you and for the 1st time in a long time I feel that you are dealing as square with me as I am with you.   I came very near closing and coming out there this week but it would of been very foolish for I would of got in bad here as I have this time to play.

Now Betty I want you to cut out all of this foolish talk for when I tell you you are the only girl for me I mean it regardless of how I act sometimes   Now I think I will see you some time soon and oh wont we have a jolly time and wont it be great

Must go do my show now and mail this.   Write at once

your same old boy–

Billy.

This Week.

Poli's Theatre, New Haven, Mass.[2]

ALS, rc. OkClaW. On The Oneco Hotel ("European Plan"), New Haven, Conn., letterhead.

1. See Enclosure: Nina to Will Rogers, week of 26 November 1906, in Will Rogers to Betty Blake, 5 December 1906, above.
2. Poli's Palace Theatre was built in 1905 at a cost of $300,000 and seated 2,800. Here Poli presented vaudeville acts and electrograph films. In 1916 it was gutted for a new Poli's Palace, which opened in 1917 (King, "Sylvester Z. Poli Story," 13, 18).

From Jack Joyce
5 March 1908
Brussels, Belgium

Rogers received the following postcard from Jack Joyce, a friend from his rodeo days. Joyce had been injured in an accident.

March. 5. 1908.

Souvenir of Brussels
Kicked By Bucking Horse operated on same night gave up By Doctors had
2 Bones taken out of Head in Hospital 27 days and the worst of it all I Lost
My Curls and now cant cop any swell Dames.

[*Written on front of card*]:
Dear Billie
    Just a card as a souvenir of what texas Pete done me I hope you are well
I am getting Better as Ever

Old Jack Joyce[1]

APCS, rc. OkClaW. Carte Postale/Postkaart hand-addressed to Will Rogers, Claremore, Indian
Territory, USA; forwarded to Chelsea, I.T. Postmark date 16–17 April.

    1. The message on the front of the card was accompanied by a photograph of Joyce
in suit and tie, and with a bandage patch over his right temple.

Notice from *Variety*
7 March 1908
New Haven, Conn.

*While performing in New Haven, Rogers received the news that his father was ill. He
left his engagement at Poli's Theatre and rushed home.*

ROGERS CALLED HOME

New Haven, Conn., March 5.
    Will Rogers, the lariat thrower, played both performances at Poli's
Monday, and after the night show left suddenly for his home in Idaho. His
departure was occasioned by the receipt of a telegram bringing news that
Rogers' father was dangerously ill.[1] The Five Cliftons were substituted on the
bill.

PD. Printed in *Variety*, 7 March 1908.

    1. The *Claremore Weekly Messenger* reported in its 13 March 1908 issue that Rogers
had arrived on Tuesday, 10 March. Clement Vann Rogers became ill at Chelsea, but
the exact nature of his illness was not reported. Perhaps his age and work at the
Oklahoma Constitutional Convention had taken a toll. He had been ill the year before,
and at that time the *Claremore Messenger* reported that "grave doubts are entertained
as to his recovery" (7 June 1907). Although the *Claremore Progress* of 14 March 1908
reported that he was feeling better, it was not until mid-April that he fully recovered

and was able to return to Claremore: "C. V. Rogers, who has been so dangerously ill for several weeks at the home of his daughter at Chelsea, has so far recovered that he was able to come home the first of the week, and now is to be seen on the street, but looks very thin. He had about as narrow escape from death as ever occurs to man" (*CM*, 17 April 1908). Will Rogers remained home until about 20 April and took the opportunity to visit Betty Blake in Rogers, Ark. (see Will Rogers to Betty Blake, 16 April 1908, below). At that time, as she later wrote, he was thinking of giving up show business: "He was really worried about his father, and on his visits to Rogers I found that his idea of show business had changed. He talked of returning home to stay. He said the same old show afternoon and night was growing monotonous, and that trouping around the country was losing its interest. I felt that at last he was coming around to my way of thinking" (Rogers, *Will Rogers*, 101). This was probably wishful thinking on her part. Indeed, Rogers now found life in Claremore dull compared to New York, London, and Paris. By 27 April his father was better, and Rogers returned to the vaudeville circuit at Poli's Theatre in Bridgeport, Conn.

Last Will and Testament
14 April 1908
Claremore or Chelsea, I.T.

Below is the first existing will that Rogers prepared. His presence at home undoubtedly made him think of his family, his allotment acreage, and the need for such a document.

IN THE NAME OF GOD, AMEN! I, William Penn Rogers being of sound mind and memory, but knowing the uncertainty of human life, do now make and publish this my last will and testament, that is to say:

I do hereby bequeath all that I possess unto my father [*letter crossout illegible*] C. V. Rogers, My Sisters Mrs May Stine Mrs Sallie McSpadden, Mrs Maud Lane each to share equally with the other.

Signed, sealed, published, and declared by the said
William Penn Rogers (SEAL)
William Penn Rogers the testator, as and for his last will and testament; and we, at his request and in his presence, and in the presence of each other, have hereto subscribed our names as witnesses thereto, this ~~April~~ 14 day of April 1908.
W. I. Davis
T. V. Dollius
R[*illegible*]ly
J. B. Baron

PDS, with autograph insertions. OkClaW.

To Betty Blake
16 April 1908
En Route to Claremore

Rogers traveled to McAlester, Okla., to receive a Scottish Rite Masonic degree.[1] On his way home he sent the following postcard to Betty Blake, stating his intention to visit her.[2] The postcard had a picture of the Scottish Rite Masonic Temple.[3]

April 16, 1908

Hello Betty

Well I open in Bridgeport, Conn. the 27, so will see you about Monday or Tuesday as I will be on my way and come by   just finished up and go home tonight   Hope I get a letter at home.[4]

[Written on front of card, over picture]:
The finest ▲ furnished ▲ Temple in the world.
This is where [*words illegible*]
Will write you *tomorrow*

APC, rc. OkClaW. Picture postcard of the Scottish Rite Masonic Temple, McAlester, Okla.

1. Rogers was initiated into the Masons in early 1905 at Claremore, where the fraternal order operated a school (*HRC*, 28). The Masons were a thriving fraternal organization in the Indian Territory. In November 1853 the first Masonic Lodge was located at Flint in the Cherokee Nation, its charter granted by the Grand Lodge of Arkansas. Other lodges were found at the Creek Agency and Doaksville. In 1873 the Grand Lodge of Indian Territory was formed. The Masonic Lodge at Oologah was established in November 1906 and was granted an official charter in August 1907 (Dale, *History of Oklahoma*, 533; *History of Oologah*, 41–42; Workers of WPA, *Oklahoma*, 358).
2. The postcard was postmarked K.C. and Denison R.P.O. 16 April. This was probably a railroad postmark for the train that ran between Texas and Kansas City. Rogers thus wrote the postcard while returning to Claremore.
3. Located on Adams Avenue and Second Street, the temple was described as a "huge, block-long, cream-colored brick and stone building elaborately decorated with algonite and Carthage stone. A great copper sphere, rising fifty feet above the roof, contains multi-colored lenses and when lighted may be seen for several miles" (Workers of WPA, *Oklahoma*, 303).
4. Rogers did not receive a letter when he returned home (see Will Rogers to Betty Blake, 17 April 1908, below).

To Betty Blake
17 April 1908
Claremore, I.T.

GUTHRIE, OKLA.,[1] ____ 190 __

Friday Eve.

My Dearest Betty

Well on my arrival home this morning and did not get a letter from you   I felt affully disapointed—but I guess I expected a little more than I should and after due consideration I know that you are right and if I had of deserved a letter I would of got one so I guess I did not deserve one.

Now I was afful busy at McAlister as we were kept in and did not get a chance to ever get out from the work till late at night and that was not my fault.

Well I go back east in a few days   I think I will get by your house either Monday or Tuesday   I cannot get there Sunday as all of the family are having a dinner at Mauds and all the Family will be there and then I will come by and see you on my way east and do you know I just hate to go some how or nother and I feel kinder blue and I just want you to *cheer me up* for you are the only one that can do it.   you always do have a clear conception of everything and I do so trust you and believe you.   I dont know why but I do   honest I do.

Well I am a *Mason*[2]   Are *you*   and I tell you it is great and it should make me a lot better boy–Well there is plenty of room for improvement.

Well dearie I will have to stop as the train is coming soon and I want you to get this tomorrow

Papa, Maud, Sallie.   Cap, and I are down here spending the day and will stay till the late train and see the *Holy City* played tonight.[3]   I bet its great

Well Betts I will let you know when I come   I think it will be Monday on the *Noon train*

Your old ever loving Kid
Billy.

ALS, rc. OkClaW. On The Convention to Form a Constitution for the State of Oklahoma, Clement V. Rogers, Member Sixty-fourth District, Claremore, I.T., letterhead.

1. Guthrie, originally a desolate station on the Santa Fe railway line, was populated practically overnight during the land rush of 1889, when the Oklahoma Territory was opened to settlers. Thousands of settlers, claiming town lots, arrived on 22 April 1889. Guthrie became the capital of Oklahoma Territory in 1890 and developed into an active commercial center for a large surrounding agricultural area. Rogers undoubtedly stopped at Guthrie because it was considered the center of Masonry in Oklahoma. The city's Scottish Rite Temple was one of the largest Masonic temples in the world

and contained a spacious auditorium that seated 3,500. Guthrie also had a Masonic Home for the Aged and a Masonic Children's Home (Alley, *City Beginnings in Oklahoma Territory*, 13–27; Workers of WPA, *Oklahoma*, 358–60).

2. See Will Rogers to Betty Blake, 4 April 1908, above.

3. The *Holy City* might have been a presentation at the Scottish Rite Temple's auditorium.

To Clement Vann Rogers
29 April 1908
Bridgeport, Conn.

His father having recovered, Rogers returned to the vaudeville stage. His first engagement was at Poli's Theatre in Bridgeport, Conn.[1]

BRIDGEPORT, CONNECTICUT <u>April</u> <u>29</u> 190<u>8</u>

My Dear Papa

Well I got Mauds telegram saying you were just doing fine and I am sure glad   Now you just stay most of the time up at Chelsea and take your Medicine and take good care of yourself and you will soon be all right

I am getting along fine since I opened up here   my act is doing as well as ever.   I will send you some money at the end of the week as I want to start in to pay off that note

Here are a few clippings from todays papers about my act   I think I play Scranton Pennsylvania next week but I am not sure yet.[2]

I seen the Buffalo Bill Show in New York as I came through.[3] I guess I will get that Grip Maud sent about tomorrow.

It is as hot as summer up here and I sho do sweat when I work   my old pony was fatter than ever   he is so fat he can hardly walk

Now I will write you often and will let you know later where to write to me at

Lots of Love to all and you just look after yourself good and when you get able and can I want you to come east and stay a few days with me in each place   you could spare a couple of weeks

your loving son
Willie.

ALS, rc. OkClaW. On Arcade Hotel, Bridgeport, letterhead. S. B. Brewster, proprietor.

1. Rogers appeared at Poli's Theatre during the week of 27 April. His act, described as "Cowboy Pastimes," was advertised as a special added feature. *Variety* reported that Rogers was "greatly applauded" (2 May 1908). Also on the bill were the following acts: author and actor Edward Davis (originator of tragedy in vaudeville presents his new tragic playlet *All Rivers Meet at the Sea*); St. Cecilia Quartet (miss Margaret Hogan with William Tomlinson, Joseph Wieler, Mrs. John M. Fay); Lew

Sully (Words and Music); George W. Barry and Maude Wolford (The Typical Topical Tickle Singers and Talkers); Holden's Original Manikens (The Children's Delight, a Revelation in Mechanical Effects and Comedy); and George W. Diamond and Will C. Smith (Capital Singing Numbers) (Poli's Theatre, Bridgeport, playbill, week of 27 April 1908, OkClaW).

2. Rogers did not travel to Scranton because the theater there had discontinued vaudeville and become a stock theater.

3. Buffalo Bill's Wild West was then playing at Madison Square Garden. Cody presented a program that Rogers must have enjoyed. Besides featuring a re-creation of the Battle of Summit Springs and a great prairie fire, it included cowboys "brought direct from the range"; Indians ("the real red man of the plains in war paint"); Rough Riders "assembled from all nations"; vaqueros ("true types of the Mexican Cowboy"); Wild West girls ("dashing queens of the saddles"); and "a great congress of the world's equestrians" (*NYT,* 26 April 1908).

To Clement Vann Rogers
ca. 11 May 1908
New York, N.Y.

Dear Papa

I just got a nice long letter from Maud and one from Sallie and they both told me how well you were looking and that you was doing fine

Now you must take good care of yourself and take your medicine all the time and you will stay well.

Well things are pretty dull in my line right now as most of the Theatres are closing up for the Summer and I did not work last week and do not work this week but next week I work again and think I can keep busy from then on and I have a good contract offered me for next year and I think I can work the biggest part of the summer

Now write me a few lines when you can and when you feel real well and want to take a trip why just bundle up and come on to me and spend a few weeks.

Love to all the folks

your loving son,
Willie

% White Rats Club.
    47th St. and Broadway
      New york

ALS, rc. OkClaW. On White Rats of America, 1553 Broadway, New York, letterhead (Executive Offices, Telephone 4636 Bryant, Club Room, Telephone 4635 Bryant).

---

5. ON THE WESTERN VAUDEVILLE TRAIL

June 1908–September 1908

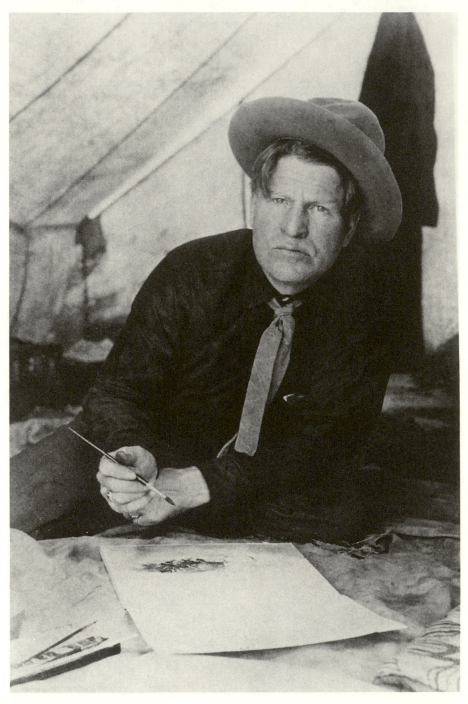

The artist Charles M. Russell (1864–1926) was a good friend of Rogers, who admired and purchased Russell's work. The two men shared a love for the old West. *(OkClaW)*

ROGERS'S FIRST TOUR IN THE WEST DURING THE LATTER HALF OF 1908 WAS A new experience in his vaudeville career. Rogers viewed the trip as a chance to avoid the East Coast with its *"cheap summer houses* and parks all summer where $200 is the best I could of got."[1] Equally important, his western tour gave him an opportunity to perform in new places before different audiences. The worst fear of a vaudevillian was to repeat his or her act too many times in the same town. After three years traveling on the eastern circuits he needed a different audience. "It will put me in a new country that I *never* played and may want too again," he wrote.[2]

Increased immigrant urban population and migration from the farm to the city influenced vaudeville's growth in the West. The expansion of railroads and improved links between cities spurred the development of chains. By the 1890s circuits began to evolve in the Pacific Northwest.

In the 1900s vaudeville in the West became increasingly structured and consolidated. The Western Vaudeville Managers Association, with headquarters in Chicago, played a key role in the consolidation. Its membership included most big-time western circuits and small-time ones as well. The Orpheum Circuit was the most powerful chain in the association, much like the Keith Circuit in the East. In 1906 and 1907 the western and eastern vaudeville managers' associations joined to create the United Booking Offices (UBO). Basically, they agreed to divide the nation into two sections, with the Western Vaudeville Managers Association controlling booking west of Chicago and its eastern counterpart handling booking east of Chicago.

Vaudevillians on the western tour had an exhausting schedule. Distances between cities were large, often many hundreds of miles, and had to be covered by long railroad trips. Trips could last twelve hours or more and sometimes required changing trains. Rogers's train ride from Butte to Spokane, for example, took three days and required several changes. Performers boarded a train on Sunday night after their performance and traveled all night to the next town so that they could appear promptly at rehearsal on Monday morning.[3]

Unlike the eastern tours, vaudevillians on the western circuits generally remained together on the same playbill as they traveled from town to town.

Rogers performed with most of the same vaudevillians at each stop on his tour. Since they were together for several months, the performers formed friendships. Theater owners in the western circuit organized routes both for organizational reasons and to save transportation costs, since they often paid for train tickets (performers paid for housing, meals, agent's commission, and baggage transfer).

Compared to Keith's refined family vaudeville, variety shows in the West were at first less subject to morality codes and stringent regulations. On the western circuits vaudevillians usually could perform on Sundays unless there was a ban in a particular city. Although there were certainly many acts that appealed to families, shows in smaller towns catered to the taste of miners, cowboys, and ranch hands. Urban variety theaters in the West initially had a notorious reputation. In order to increase their audience, organizers of chains gradually developed programs that appealed to the middle class and family values. With the rise of circuits, western vaudeville managers began to have strict rules regarding the acts that played in their theaters—but the regulations were not always easy to enforce. A 1914 study of Portland, Oregon, theaters reported that 80 percent of the acts surveyed were objectionable and contained obscenities, risqué material, and lewd dancing. Given the large number of women and children in the audience, the authors of the report called for increased censorship.[4]

In 1908 Rogers performed on the Sullivan and Considine Circuit. The chain was developed by John W. Considine (1863–1943) and later financed by Timothy (Big Tim) Daniel Sullivan (1863–1913). Sullivan and Considine was one of three major western circuits in 1908 (the Orpheum and Pantages circuits were the other two). Well-known vaudevillians, as well as newcomers such as Charlie Chaplin, performed on the circuit.[5] Considine was the expert in theater management, while Sullivan provided the financial backing.

The man behind the organization was Considine, who was born in Chicago and educated in Catholic schools and at the University of Kansas. An adventurous young man, Considine traveled to the Klondike in search of gold. He wound up opening a cabaret instead—his first experience in show business. Returning to Chicago, he became general manager of the northwest Orpheum Circuit, which had its headquarters in the city. Here Considine opened his first theater, the People's Theatre. In 1889 he settled in Seattle, probably to be closer to the Orpheum's Pacific Northwest operation.

In the 1890s Seattle was an important center of variety theater. Alexander Pantages started his theater chain here. Two other significant theater owners were John Cort[6] and John F. Cordray. A former theater manager in Denver,

Cordray arrived in the Northwest in 1888 and is credited with bringing refined vaudeville to the region. He operated a small chain with theaters in Portland, Tacoma, and Seattle. By 1890 Cort had organized a larger circuit that included theaters in the Pacific Northwest, in the state of Montana, and in San Francisco and other cities. These early Considine theaters were known as box houses, a combination of saloon, variety, and house of prostitution. Considine was once arrested and fined $500 plus costs for violating an ordinance that prohibited the employment of women in curtained boxes in his Spokane establishment. In 1901 he fatally shot the Seattle chief of police but was acquitted on a plea of self-defense.[7] That same year Considine teamed with Tim Sullivan, a powerful New York Tammany Hall politician, who enjoyed the limelight of show business. Sullivan and Considine had mutual interests, and both were strong, egocentric individuals, and had connections with saloons, vice, and gambling.

The life of Big Tim Sullivan (he weighed 220 pounds and stood 6 feet, 1 inch tall) was a rags-to-riches story. He was raised in a crowded tenement in an Irish district in New York. As a youngster, he worked as a newsboy and a bootblack. He was employed on various newspapers until around age twenty-two. With his savings, Sullivan became the owner of several saloons in New York City. The Irish saloon became his entry into Tammany Hall machine politics, and it was where he met neighborhood political bosses. He was selected to run for the second state assembly district in 1886 and won the election. He represented the Bowery, an area densely populated with Eastern European immigrants and the poor. In return for special favors, Sullivan's constituency elected him to the New York state assembly (1886–93), state senate (1893–1902, 1908–12), and Congress (1902–6). For over twenty-five years, Sullivan and his Tammany Hall political machine controlled lower Manhattan below Fourteenth Street.

Before he joined Considine, Sullivan was already involved with show business and had made a fortune investing in the theater. In 1896, in partnership with George J. Krause, owner of concert saloons in the Bowery and the Tenderloin district, Sullivan operated a few New York music halls and burlesque houses. Sullivan invested in seven theaters in New York: the City, Gotham, Circle, Savoy, Olympic, Dewey, and the Family. In local politics, Sullivan supported New York City ordinances that permitted Sunday vaudeville and movies. Additionally, he was a partner with Marcus Loew and William Fox in nickelodeons on the Lower East Side. He invested in Coney Island's Dreamland, professional boxing, and the Jamaica Race Track, and was co-owner of a large thoroughbred horse farm in New Jersey.[8]

With profits from his enterprises, Sullivan bankrolled Considine's theater operations by loaning him considerable funds. With Sullivan's financial help, Considine created a large circuit of vaudeville houses in the West. By 1906 the Sullivan and Considine Circuit operated theaters in Oregon and Washington, and in Victoria and Vancouver, Canada. Other properties included the Family Theatre in Butte, Montana, and the Lyceum Theatre in San Francisco. By 1907 the partners claimed to have nearly forty theaters in their circuit. To expand their operations in the Midwest, they organized the International Theatre Co. in Chicago and began to manage theaters in the region. Most Sullivan and Considine theaters seated more than 1,800 spectators and were elaborately decorated. At one time they had four offices, in Seattle, San Francisco, Chicago, and New York.[9]

The Sullivan and Considine houses were known as 10-cent, 20-cent, and 30-cent theaters because of their low price of admission. The theaters normally offered three performances a day, which included a matinee and two evening shows. In the summer Considine cooled his theaters with blocks of ice in the air shafts. As a result, the chain was called by performers "cold storage vaudeville." The circuit offered vaudevillians a full year's contract and allowed then to borrow money from a bank. It also initiated the "play or pay" contract that guaranteed performers their weekly salary if their act was canceled but specified that if the performers failed to show up, they had to pay the theater manager their salary.[10]

On the Sullivan and Considine Circuit, Rogers traveled from Duluth to San Francisco, stopping at many places to perform week-long engagements. His itinerary included dates in Winnipeg and Vancouver, Canada, and the mining town of Butte, Mont. In the Pacific Northwest he performed in Spokane, Tacoma, Seattle, and Portland. In areas where ranch life and the cowboy were common or of recent memory, audiences were naturally responsive to Rogers's skill with the rope. Everywhere he went, Rogers mostly received rave reviews for his lariat tricks, and in his correspondence he often noted the popularity of his act.

Overall, the western tour strengthened his commitment to show business as a career. His letters during this period rarely mention a desire to return to ranching. Vaudeville, he wrote Betty Blake, "beats that old *farm and ranch* and *Store* thing."[11] On the stage he could make more money, as long as he was able to obtain regular bookings. The life of an entertainer, he wrote Blake, was "very lonesome sometimes but as for hating the work and wanting to give it up, *No* not as long as you can get booked and get a good salary for there is no work in the world as nice and easy as this business when things are coming right."[12]

(From left) Tom Hardin, Texas Air Transport, Inc., pilot; Will Rogers; H. L. Mencken, editor, *American Mercury* magazine; and Amon G. Carter, Fort Worth, Tex., 21 June 1928. Rogers influenced Carter to begin his purchase of Russell's works, which formed the core collection for the Amon Carter Museum in Fort Worth. *(Amon Carter Museum, Fort Worth, Tex.)*

Rogers's trip was not without its travails. At one time he was delayed when a flood damaged railroad lines, and he missed four shows in Butte. Apparently, the flood had done considerable damage to railroad transportation: Rogers had to leave one day earlier to get to Spokane by a roundabout way that took him three days rather than one. The western tour also had its pleasures. Between engagements, he spent several days in Yellowstone National Park. He toured the area by stagecoach and saw spectacular scenery. Rogers stood in awe as he gazed at the Grand Canyon in Yellowstone. "That Canon is great," he wrote Betty Blake. "The most beautiful coloring and the falls are 360 ft and the rocks all different colors."[13]

During his trip west Rogers kept in touch with Betty Blake via postcards and letters. From Butte, he mailed many postcards illustrated by Charles M. Russell. Rogers had met Russell earlier, and over the years they developed a close friendship. The two were kindred spirits who shared a love of the West and the cowboy life. Rogers identified with the subjects of Russell's art, whether Native Americans, cattle drives, or chuckwagons. The postcards he sent Blake illustrated his attraction to Russell's work, and later he would purchase some of his paintings. Years later Rogers urged Amon Carter to buy Russell's work. Carter's large collection became the nucleus for the Amon Carter Museum in Fort Worth, Tex.

During his trip west Rogers's correspondence with Betty Blake reveals that the two had drawn closer. There are fewer references to disagreements over other beaux. "With all my love to the dearest *Girl* I ever knew," Rogers wrote at the end of his letter from Butte. He continued: "(*aint that a pretty little speech*) And I mean it too."[14] He finished the letter with eleven exes.

As he left San Francisco in August Rogers, now nearly twenty-nine years of age, felt confident. His western tour was successful. He knew that vaudeville was thriving in the West and offered opportunities to perform in more theaters. His relationship with Betty Blake had never been better, and he was thinking again of proposing marriage.

1. See Will Rogers to Betty Blake, 4 June 1908, below.
2. Ibid.
3. Singer, "Vaudeville West," 52–57. By 1919 a vaudevillian could buy Herbert Lloyd's guide, *Vaudeville Trails thru the West.* A long-time vaudeville performer, Lloyd listed theaters, hotels, restaurants, railroad rates and schedules, luggage costs, practical suggestions, and city maps showing theater locations.
4. Foster, *Vaudeville and Motion Picture Shows.*
5. In 1910 Chaplin appeared as the lead in Fred Karno's *Wow-wows,* a burlesque sketch about initiation into a secret society. The Karno troupe played the Sullivan and Considine Circuit twice, each tour lasting twenty weeks. Chaplin visited many of the same towns as Rogers and was enthralled with the scenery of the West, what he called "vast stretches of wild land. . . . good for the soul. Such cities as Cleveland, St. Louis, Minneapolis, St. Paul, Kansas City, Denver, Butte, Billings, throbbed with the dynamism of the future, and I was imbued with it." He also wrote: "In those days the Middle West had charm. The tempo was slower, and the atmosphere was romantic; every drugstore and saloon had a dice-throwing desk in the entrance where one gambled for whatever products they sold. . . . Living was cheap. At a small hotel one could get a room and board for seven dollars a week, with three meals a day. Food was remarkably cheap. The saloon free-lunch counter was the mainstay of our troupe. For a nickel one could get a glass of beer and the pick of the whole delicatessen counter" (Chaplin, *My Autobiography,* 124, 128; see also 118, 121, 129, 130, 138).
6. John Cort (ca. 1860–1929) started in vaudeville as a member of the comedy team Cort and Murphy. Later, his Northwest Theatrical Circuit of primarily legitimate theaters was a major chain that eventually expanded eastward. Cort Theatres were in New York and Boston, as well as Chicago, San Francisco, and other western cities, and he publicized the fact that he operated more than two hundred theaters (Elliott, *History of Variety-Vaudeville in Seattle,* 17–23, 27–28, 33, 36–38, 46–47; *OCAT,* 167).

7. Elliott, *History of Variety-Vaudeville in Seattle*, 11–26; Singer, "Vaudeville West," 70–74)

8. Czitrom, "Underworlds and Underdogs," 536–57; *DAB*, 9:198–99; Elliott, *History of Variety-Vaudeville in Seattle*, 34, 53–54; *ENYC*, 1141; Mickols, "Boss of the Bowery"; *NYT*, 15 September 1913.

9. Connors, "American Vaudeville Mangers," 49–50; Elliott, *History of Variety-Vaudeville in Seattle*, 25–26, 33–34, 48, 53–58, 64–65; Grau, *Business Man in the Amusement World*, 140–42; *NYT*, 13 February 1943; *OCAT*, 649; Singer, "Vaudeville West," 74–75; *EV*, 112; *Variety*, 8 June 1907, 30 November 1907, 8 February 1908, and 20 December 1912.

10. Around 1912 the Sullivan-Considine Circuit merged with Marcus Loew's Theatrical Enterprises, a theater chain in the East. This created a transcontinental circuit that also included theaters in Canada. The new organization operated nearly two hundred theaters, which specialized in programs that combined vaudeville and films. After Sullivan died in 1913, Considine was faced with a large mortgage debt. A year later he sold a majority of his holdings to Marcus Loew and his associates for $1.5 million. But Loew's acquisitions were not well managed. Facing a financial loss, Loew rescinded his agreement with Considine in 1915, and the latter regained his theaters. Considine, however, was unable to revive his circuit due to increased competition from the eastern circuits. Eventually, the Orpheum and Pantages organizations bought his theaters. Considine moved to Los Angeles in 1921 and died there on 12 February 1943 from pneumonia (Czitrom, "Underworlds and Underdogs," 558; Green and Laurie, *Show Biz*, 91, 162; Mickols, "Boss of the Bowery"; *NYT*, 15 September 1913; Singer, "Vaudeville West," 75).

11. Will Rogers to Betty Blake, 4 June 1908, below.

12. Ibid.

13. Will Rogers to Betty Blake, 12 June 1908, below.

14. Will Rogers to Betty Blake, 15 June 1908, below.

To Clement Vann Rogers
ca. 4 June 1908
Duluth, Minn.

Duluth, Minn <u>Thursday</u> 1908

My Dear Papa:

I got your letter all right and am so glad that you are doing so well now you must keep up your medicine and take good care of yourself

Well I finish here Sunday night then I dont play next week as it takes most of the time to jump to Butte, Montana. where I play the week after.   I am going to go by the yellowstone Park and stay a couple of days as it is right on my road.[1]

Papa I guess my note there is about due and you better get Godbey[2] to renew it for another 60 days for in a couple of more weeks I will be able to pay a lot of it off.   so you renew it for me for 60 days   Got a letter from Mrs Gibbs[3] but tell her I am out of Canada now and don't know when I will be there again and cant get the Gold coins she spoke of.

Write me for the next 10 days to

Grand Theatre

Butte, Montana

Love to all
Willie.

ALS, rc. OkClaW. On St. Louis Hotel, American and European [plan], Duluth, letterhead. J. T. Michaud, manager.

1. On Rogers's trip to Yellowstone National Park, see Will Rogers to Betty Blake, 12 June 1908, below.
2. C. F. Godbey.
3. Mrs. Ed. H. Gibbs and her husband managed the Lindel Hotel in Claremore where Clement Vann Rogers lived (*PWR*, 1:284, 287n.1).

To Betty Blake
4 June 1908
Duluth, Minn.

To begin his first western tour, Rogers left New York and traveled via Chicago to Winnipeg in Manitoba, Canada. He performed at the Bijou Theatre the last week of May. On 30 May he sent a postcard to Betty Blake with a photograph of cowboys at a roundup camp in the Canadian West and gave his address in Duluth. On 4 June Rogers wrote her again and expressed excitement about his first vaudeville tour in the West.

Duluth, Minn., <u>Thursday</u> 190<u>Eve</u>

My Own Dearest—

Well Sweetheart your letter came yesterday and say you did take your time about writing   I thought you had lost the address.

Well I will try Dearie and tell you a few of the things you asked me about.   Yes it is very lonesome sometimes but as for hating the work and wanting to give it up, *No* not as long as you can get booked and get a good salary for there is no work in the world as nice and easy as this business when things are coming right.   it beats that old *farm and ranch* and *Store* thing.

Now the time to stop is when you have made enough to live without it and when they cant use you any more

Now I am going this summer and next year to make a good little bit of money out of this *bar* misfortune of course and how could I do better at home   I will go there in time enough and have my good place to live and wont have to depend on a business.   thats my *dope* on this thing.

Now you are wrong about this trip.   this is one of the best *paying* trips I ever *took*   for the time.   I will be $1500 or $2,000 ahead of what I was when I left New York.   it will keep me away from those *cheap summer houses* and parks all summer where $200 is the best I could of got.   it will put me in a new country that I *never* played and may want too again.   it is great   my salary as great $275. for the circuit.[1]   it keeps you away from N.Y. during these dull times.   in fact it is lucky all around.   Now I will be able to go back next season new and fresh and at a good salary   you must remember I played 3 years right around those same houses so it does one good to give them a rest.   yes last Sunday I spent all day on the train on this circuit all the acts jump togeather   this same bunch will be togeather till after Seattle.[2]

We finish here Sunday Night as we have to work here on Sunday and then we lose next week jumping to Butte.[3]   I will go by yellowstone and spend a few days   leaving here Monday morning   wont get to see a lot but will get an idea of it.[4]   We open a[t]   Butte on Saturday.   Write to Grand Theatre there for the next 10 days and I will get your first letters on my arrival there

Will leave there on June 20th. for *Spokane*.   then Seattle.   Would like to meet your friend and say its funny you did not let me meet Tom Morgans Sister   I could not *savy* that at all.

No about Tony I only told you that he acted quite a bit different the last time from the first and thats all.   Now please tell me what you mean by him trying to *sting* you.   and why.   and what kind of an understanding did you have with that other fellow.   you know that all seems queer to me but you never tell me.   Say by the way do you know that there is always these lines in all your letters "Cant write you as long letter as had planned too.   the house has been full of company all day." Thats old *stuff* kid and has been done to death   get a new *line* of stuff or either dont plan so big.

Well I will stop the Hotel is full of *Guests*.

Now write me lots and long cause this is a lonesome old trip.

Enclosed find a *picture* cartoon and a Nell Brinkley[5] drawing I just happen to see here on the desk.

Your Boy All the time

Billy.

No I never did try any of TM. stuff yet.[6]

ALS, rc. OkClaW. On St. Louis Hotel, Duluth, letterhead.

1. Rogers was performing on the Sullivan and Considine Circuit.

2. Rogers is referring to his train trip from Winnipeg to Duluth on Sunday, 31 May 1908.

3. Rogers performed at the Bijou Theatre from 1 to 7 June 1908. The booking representative for the Bijou Theatre was located in Winnipeg. No clippings from his Winnipeg or Butte engagement are extant (*JCOTG*, 830; see also postcard, Frank Stine to Rogers, postmarked 2 June 1908, OkClaW).

4. Rogers sent a postcard to Betty Blake, postmarked from Duluth, 8 June 1911, saying that he was leaving that evening and giving his next address, the Grand Theatre, Butte, Mont. (OkClaW). The postcard depicted a ship and the Aerial Bridge in Duluth. Rogers wrote: "Say this bridge is a curiosity its the only one of its kind in America."

5. Nell Brinkley (ca. 1888–1944) was a well-known artist who drew many illustrations of the theater. Largely self-taught, she began at age fifteen drawing boy-and-girl sketches and cartoons for the *Denver Post*. The editor Arthur Brisbane, who worked for the Hearst newspaper chain, hired her, and soon her pen-and-ink drawings were published in the *New York Journal* with added distribution through syndication. She gained fame for creating "The Brinkley Girl," a fashionable female figure who was portrayed in several musicals. She died in New Rochelle, N.Y. (*NYT*, 22 October 1944; *VO*, 3:25 October 1944).

6. Rogers might be implying an interest in using Tom Morgan's folk humor for his stage presentation.

To Betty Blake
12 June 1908
Norris Geyser Basin, Yellowstone National Park

From Butte Rogers traveled to Yellowstone National Park to view its splendid scenery. Established in 1872, Yellowstone National Park was already a famous natural wonder that attracted visitors from all over the world. Because of its pristine beauty, which contrasted sharply with an increasingly urban America, the park drew many writers, painters, and photographers who saw it as one of the last remnants of the untouched wilderness of the West. Visiting the park must have reminded Rogers of his childhood and his love of the West.

Friday. Noon.

My Own Sweetheart

Well old pal I am now at a lunch station for dinner[1]   just drove in from the Grand Canon about 15 miles and will go on back to the *Mammoth*[2]   thats where you start from   its 20 miles from here   will go there   then on out 5 miles to Gardiner   the entrance to the park and where you take the train.[3]   I have been in the park three days counting today   leave tonight at 7:30 from Gardiner to Butte.   and dont know if I will make it or not as I have to open at Matinee tomorrow and I just hear there is a lot of fresh washouts on the line so I may not get there,   but it cant be helped   if I cant I cant   thats all   and will open when I do get there   But I think I can make it allright.

Did you get some cards (Playing Cards) I sent you and a folder postal and some others[4]

Well, this is a great place   wish I had had time to take the regular tour of 5½ days but I only had 2½ so I got me a special rig and they layed out a special trip for me and I have been all alone   only the *driver* since yesterday noon[5]   I was with a bunch the first day and until noon yesterday.   By making this special I seen a lot and most all of it but the big lake[6] and a few Geysers.   I seen the Canon   stayed there last night at the big Canon Hotel.[7]   The first and only Guest.   Oh it did seem funny   A tremendous big hotel.   All the clerks and Waiters and servants and all ready as their first bunch will arrive there tonight   so I had the whole Hotel to myself.   They even had the Orchestra to play while I was in a big dining room that would seat 300.   All alone but them.

Oh I was the *"poplar"* Kid for fair once in my life.

This hotel is away out all alone just up on top of the Canon and last night all kinds of big game were playing around out on a big level place there and some Bears come down at the back hunting up where they throw out all the Garbage.   Oh there was 50 or 75 elk   A lot of young ones and Deer and

Mountain Sheep [and] Antelope. The buffalo are the hardest to see but there is all kinds of game here.[8]

That Canon is great the most beautiful coloring and the falls are 360 ft and the rocks all different colors the Canon is about 1500 or 2000 ft deep, but its the coloring they rave about.[9] not being an artist I dont know it looked fair not as good though as that big rocky ditch down back of your house But they *rave* over it almost as bad as you do ~~that~~ those *trenches* down there.

Where I am now is Norris Basin[10] where a lot of the Geysers are (you know what they are dont you) "I dont" I dont mean "*Geesers*" of course you've seen lots of them *One* in particular[11]

Some of them play every few minutes and shoot up 100 ft and this whole hill where this place is[12] just steaming and smoking and holes blowing off steam in *jerks* just like an Engine and different colored hot pools all with boiling water hot caves and oh Well I wont tell you cause you wouldent enjoy it as much when we come back and see it all and go horseback riding and fishing they limit you to 25 at a time, guess that's poor, eh!

There is a big Military post up at Mammoth and you see the Cavalry drill and the whole park is patroled by Soldiers and also scouts. They carry all the Tourist parties in big 4 and 6 horse Coaches.[13] You go so far eat dinner at a lunch place then on to the 1st hotel and complete a trip of about 150 miles in a big circle in 5½ days[14] of course you can stop over where you please by paying your extra hotel fare and take up the trip the next day with the next bunch or stay a week the Hotel bills are American plan $5.00 a day my little trip of 3 days special rig and all will only cost me about $40 dollars. "G" that would of bought you a swell hat wouldent it and I could of paid 25 cents for a book and read about it. (and perhaps known more) What am I telling you all about the cost and all that I just caught myself doing it. And I dont know it just seems as natural and not improper. does it to you No its alright you should know all I do and all about it.

Well I will have to stop as ~~I~~ my rig is coming (a swell team and buggy by the way)[15] its kinder raining too but I have no more sight seeing and its great to drive through the rain. Hope I get a lot of *mail* from you tomorrow in Butte. it seems a month.

Your only Boy
Aint I.   B—

next Week.   Sullivan and Considine Theatre
    Spokane
        Wash.[16]

ALS, rc. OkClaW. On Yellowstone Park Association letterhead.[17]

1. The Norris Basin lunch station is actually twenty-two miles from Mammoth. In the 1880s it was a dining tent operated by an Irishman named Larry (Bartlett, *Yellowstone,* 61; Haines, *Yellowstone Story,* 2:110, 112).

2. Mammoth Hot Springs, site of about seventy hot springs, served as the administrative headquarters of the park (*WNGD,* 720). The 1908 *Haynes Guide to Yellowstone Park* described the area as follows: "The terrace-building hot springs of Yellowstone Park are the most remarkable development of thermal action to be found, occupying several acres, with many distinct terraces and springs. The present active portion of the hot springs is located on the eastern slope of the Terrace Mountain, from 50 to 300 feet above the plateau, upon which the Mammoth Hotel, Fort Yellowstone, and other buildings are constructed" (Guptill, *Haynes Guide,* 15). Rogers probably stayed at the Mammoth Hot Springs Hotel. Construction on the hotel began in 1882, but was delayed when the Yellowstone National Park Improvement Co. went bankrupt. When finished in 1883 by the Northern Pacific Railroad Co. and other investors, the four-story wooden structure accommodated 800 guests and was furnished at a cost of $60,000. Many wealthy visitors stayed here, and the hotel was considered luxurious for its time. It was torn down in 1936 and replaced by the new and larger Mammoth Springs Hotel (Augspurger, *Yellowstone National Park,* 135–37; Bartlett, *Yellowstone,* 115, 129–31, 150–51).

3. Gardiner, located in Montana, serves as the northern entrance to Yellowstone Park. Gardiner River and Gardiner Canyon are nearby. The Northern Pacific Railroad Co. station, a log structure, was located here. The town also served as a supply point for nearby mining camps, and a hunting and camping expedition point. A large stone arch, dedicated by President Theodore Roosevelt, signaled the entrance to the park (Bartlett, *Yellowstone,* 180; Guptill, *Haynes Guide,* 14; *WNGD,* 428).

4. On a postcard dated 11 June 1908 to Betty Blake, Rogers wrote on the front that he was sending via registered mail a "swell pack of cards (playing) views of the park" (OkClaW).

5. The 11 June postcard to Betty Blake depicted a horse-drawn coaching party in Yellowstone Park. Rogers wrote: "This is one of the coaches that bring you from the Station to the first big hotel where I am now. . . . Wish you was here." He also wrote that he would travel by "special rig" (postcard to Betty Blake, 11 June 1908, OkClaW). The 1908 *Haynes Guide* notes: "Parties desiring special or private conveyances can arrange with the Transportation Co. at Mammoth Hotel" (Guptill, *Haynes Guide,* 139). Rogers probably took advantage of this opportunity.

6. According to the 1908 *Haynes Guide,* Yellowstone Lake was then fifteen miles wide and twenty miles long. It was described as "the largest body of water in North America at this altitude (8,000 feet)" (Guptill, *Haynes Guide,* 9). Its altitude is actually 7,735 feet (*WNGD,* 1361).

7. The Canyon Hotel, completed in 1889, was an early rustic hotel that replaced an 1883 tent camp and an 1886 prefabricated building. Seeking a larger tourist trade, the Northern Pacific Railroad Co. invested $25,000 toward its construction. Located on a hillside 1,000 feet above the Lower Falls, the hotel offered tourists a panoramic view. The three-story hotel originally had 250 rooms; an additional 24 rooms were added in 1901 after its foundations were repaired. At one time it featured a grizzly bear cub chained to a pole and a brass band. The 1908 *Haynes Guide* described the hotel as "modern throughout and equal to any of the excellent stopping places provided for visitors" (Guptill, *Haynes Guide,* 95). In 1910–11, a new Canyon Hotel was built by Harry Child, president of the Yellowstone Park Association. It was a large, sprawling

hotel with oak floors and red birch walls and ceilings. It was torn down in 1960 (Augspurger, *Yellowstone National Park,* 230; Bartlett, *Yellowstone,* 179–81, 184–86; Haines, *Yellowstone Story* 1:274, 277, 2:42, 44, 47, 129, 131).

8. Rogers sent a portfolio of postcards to his sister Sallie that depicted the park's animals, including bears and their cubs, wild buffalo, deer, and elk. The animals were photographed and the cards published by F. Jay Haynes, the official photographer of Yellowstone Park (Will Rogers to Sallie McSpadden, 6 June 1908, OkClaW).

9. Rogers is referring to the Grand Canyon of Yellowstone. Its average actual dimensions are 2,000 feet in width, 1,200 feet in depth, and 10 miles in length. The upper falls measures 109 feet, and the lower falls, 308 feet (*WNGD,* 1361).

10. Norris Geyser Basin was named for its discoverer, Philetus W. Norris (1821–85), the park superintendent and a pioneer explorer, road builder, and historian of Yellowstone. Originally called Gibbon Geyser Basin, it was renamed for Norris in 1881. His reports served to awaken public interest in the park. The basin was discovered in 1872 by E. S. Topping and Dwight Woodruff, but Norris was the first to fully explore and describe it. In 1877 he was appointed park superintendent by President Rutherford B. Hayes, an office he held for approximately five years. The 1908 *Haynes Guide* described the area as follows: "It covers an area of six square miles . . . being one of the highest geyser basins in the Park, and many of its active geysers being of quite recent origin" (Guptill, *Haynes Guide,* 29) (see also Chittenden, *Yellowstone National Park,* 111–12, 181, 156–58).

11. Rogers probably also saw the Old Faithful geyser. He sent a postcard to Betty Blake that depicts an interior scene of the Old Faithful Inn. Constructed in 1904 at a cost of $200,000, the rustic inn had a stone foundation and an exterior of massive logs. The inn's dramatic interior was noted for its large fireplace. He wrote: "Will spend the night there tomorrow night. its 45 miles from here" (Will Rogers to Betty Blake, June 1908, OkClaW; see also Guptill, *Haynes Guide,* 57–59).

12. Rogers ended page 7 of his letter with the word *is* and repeated it at the beginning of page 8; the second instance has been deleted here.

13. Two authorized stagecoach lines, operated by the Yellowstone Park Transportation Co., traveled from the northern and western entrances. The stagecoaches were called Yellowstone Concords and were built by Abbot and Downing of Concord, N.H.. Open at the sides, they were usually painted green and yellow, and had seats upholstered with horsehair (Bartlett, *Yellowstone,* 64; Guptill, *Haynes Guide,* 139).

14. The usual itinerary at this time took about five days. Visitors began at Mammoth and traveled to the Fountain Geyser Basin Hotel for the first night, then on to Old Faithful Inn for the second night, and to the Lake Hotel for the third night. On the fourth night they lodged at the Canyon Hotel. Tourists returned to Mammoth via the Norris Basin (Bartlett, *Yellowstone,* 65).

15. From Mammoth Hot Springs to Gardiner, Rogers probably rode in a horse-drawn Concord coach (Guptill, *Haynes Guide,* 139).

16. Rogers opened at Sullivan and Considine's Washington Theatre in Spokane on 21 June and performed there until 27 June. By 1909 the theater belonged to the Northwest Orpheum Circuit and its name had been changed to the Orpheum, although Considine still managed it (Elliott, *History of Variety-Vaudeville in Seattle,* 56; *Orpheum Circuit of Theatres,* n.p.).

17. The Yellowstone Park Association, incorporated in 1886, was in charge of constructing and operating the park's hotel system. The company, which had a virtual monopoly over the park's accommodations, was an adjunct of the Northern Pacific

Railroad. This association succeeded the Yellowstone Park Improvement Association, which was dissolved in 1885 due to financial problems. The Yellowstone Park Association operated the following hotels: Mammoth Hot Springs, Norris Geyser Basin, Fountain Geyser Basin, Old Faithful Inn, Yellowstone Lake, Thumb of Lake, and the Canyon. These hotels were open from June through September. They were described in 1908 as follows: "In furnishings and table service these hostelries compare favorably with those of other resorts. They are electric-lighted and steam-heated" (Guptill, *Haynes Guide*, 132; see also Chittenden, *Yellowstone National Park*, 119; Haines, *Yellowstone Story* 2:42).

Clipping from Will Rogers's Scrapbook
ca. 15 June 1908
Butte, Mont.

INTELLIGENT PONY.
"TEDDY" LIKES SUGAR, LOVES HIS MASTER
AND IS WISE IN MANY WAYS.

Lovers of horseflesh should not fail to get a glimpse at and, if possible, form the acquaintance of "Teddy," the cayuse employed by Will Rogers, the lasso thrower at the Grand theater, in his rope throwing feats. "Teddy" is an intelligent animal, eats sugar from the mouth of his master, and is fond of carrots, apples and sweetmeats of all kinds. He is devoted to Cowboy McKee, who rides "Teddy" a greater portion of the act. He will follow McKee about the streets like a dog, stand patiently at the curb and wait until he comes out of store, and if the master remains too long will whinny his disapproval. "Teddy" bows his acknowledgement of applause, knows his way to the stable where he is fed, wears rubber shoes and resins his feet in order to keep from slipping. He has had years of experience on the broad prairies, where he was classed as one of the best cow punchers in the country.

PD. Scrapbook A-2, OkClaW.

To Betty Blake
15 June 1908
Butte, Mont.

Butte, Montana _____ 190__

Monday. Eve.

My Betty—

Well say Girl are you sick or have that *bunch* prevailed on you to see differently and you are so occupied with your Banker Boy that you have no time for your Cowboy boy.

Well I am in the great Mining town of Butte. and it is *sho* a hummer. they just throw the *keys* to all the places away and never close up there is some life to this place[1]   Well I got caught in a washout coming from the Yellowstone and was delayed and missed 4 shows   it could not be helped I dont know what they will do about it only take out Salary for the time I missed I guess   but my trip to the Park amply repaid me for all I lost as I enjoyed the trip fine.

Well the old Act is one big hit out here in the vally where people are supposed to know   it is better than the east and think it will be a success all the way out   I go to Spokane next week   Sullivan and Considines Theatre.   then the following week opening June 29.   ~~I dont know the Theatre.~~ oh yes the Coliseum Theatre, Seattle.[2]   would be glad to see your friend while there.

Here is a picture was in todays Butte Paper   good cut don't you think   I like this picture best of all.   it was taken just after receiving a dandy letter from *Ark*

Now say away out here where it takes a year to get a letter you better not be waiting till you get an answer cause it takes too long   you must write every day or so cause I know I write a lot more than you do   why I would of *bet* there would of been a letter here for me when I came but here I have been for three days and not a sign   its been almost 2 Weeks.   look out or you will make a *3 Weeks*[3] out of it.   *Did you ever read it.*   *"Of course not."*

Well I wont write so "afful" ▲ (*Note spelling*) ▲ much now[4] you get busy.

With all my love to the dearest *Girl* I ever knew.   (*aint that a pretty little speech*)   And I mean it too

Your Regular Boy.

Billy.

(▲ These mean ▲ Good wishes x x x x x x x x x x x x)

ALS, rc. OkClaW. On The Butte, European plan, letterhead. H. I. Wilson and F. K. Wilson, proprietors, P. D. Lowell, manager.[5]

1. A mining town founded in 1864, Butte was the site of rich deposits of gold, silver, copper, zinc, and manganese. The town's growth followed on the discovery of the Anaconda copper mine in 1882. By 1900 Butte had a population of about 65,000 people. Many were employed in the mines and lived in boardinghouses. The citizens took pride in their newspapers, schools (including the Montana State School of Mines), churches, railroad system, opera house, and band. Like most western mining towns, Butte had a boisterous night life. The town's support of a vaudeville theater at this time reflected its prosperity (its 13,000 workers in the mines and smelters reportedly earned collectively $1 million a month in 1900). Rogers's opinion of Butte was similar to one recorded in 1900: "It is excessively mild to say that no city in the whole West can boast of such scenes of bustling, crowding humanity as congest the main channels of trade from early morning until far into the night as may be seen in Butte on any day of the week" (Freeman, *Brief History of Butte, Montana*, 20, also 7–19, 21–123; *WNGD*, 196).

Rogers repeated this opinion in a postcard sent to Betty Blake (postmarked 17 June) that depicted a scene of Butte with the Anaconda Hill in the background. Rogers wrote on the top front: "This is the dirtest. *Gamblingese.* corrupt town on earth. *I leave at once.*" On the left side front he wrote: "This Anaconda is one of the worlds richest mines and I am going down in it tomorrow *to get Gold.*" Below on the front he wrote: "Beautiful scenery. there aint a tree in 10 miles!" (OkClaW).

Other vaudevillians commented on Butte's night life. Charlie Chaplin described its redlight district as a place "in which young girls were installed ranging in age from sixteen up—for one dollar." He recalled: "In 1910 Butte, Montana, was still a 'Nick Carter' town, with miners wearing boots and ten-gallon hats and red neckerchiefs. I actually saw gunplay on the street, a fat old sheriff shooting at the heels of an escaped prisoner, who was eventually cornered in a blind alley without harm, fortunately." Harry Richman called the area a "Bull Pen" with over 3,000 prostitutes. On Monday night a special section of the theater was set aside for madams and prostitutes. "With them, you could do nothing wrong," Harpo Marx said (Chaplin, *My Autobiography*, 128; DiMeglio, *Vaudeville U.S.A.*, 189–90).

2. John Considine leased the Coliseum in 1907. It was originally an ice rink, which Considine converted into a large theater. A block-long structure, it was advertised as the largest theater west of Chicago. Rogers did not perform at the Coliseum but at Seattle's Star Theatre (see Will Rogers to Betty Blake, 27 June 1908, above; Elliott, *History of Variety-Vaudeville in Seattle*, 55–56; *Orpheum Circuit of Theatres*, n.p.).

3. *Three Weeks* was a best-selling novel by the prolific British author Elinor Glyn (1864–1943), published in 1907. Glyn became noted for her romantic tales, novels, and short stories. Considered risqué for its time, *Three Weeks* is about the adultery of a beautiful Balkan queen with a young Englishman. Their illicit love affair occurs in Switzerland and Venice, and the novelist's descriptions of their passion offended Victorian sensibilities. An overnight sensation, the author was attacked for her so-called scandalous plot. But Glyn defended her novel as an honest portrayal of an adulterous relationship and noted that her heroine paid for her transgression by dying at the novel's end. In 1909 she wrote a sequel called *One Day.* During her long career she also wrote movie scripts. Her *Three Weeks* and *It* (1927) were made into films. The latter starred Clara Bow as the "It" girl, a role that became synonymous with the liberated flapper of the Jazz Age (Glyn, *Three Weeks*; *NEB*, 5:312–13; *WNBD*, 405).

4. Blake probably made fun of Rogers's spelling, which later became a trademark of his writing.

5. The Butte Hotel was described as a "first-class American and European" hostelry (Freeman, *Brief History of Butte, Montana*, 27).

To Betty Blake
17 June 1908
Butte, Mont.

Butte, Montana _____ 190—

Wednesday. Noon.

My Dearest Sweetheart. ▼ (I have several) ▼

No *hon* I have not   you are the only one and always will be   *the* one and today I just got your letter the only one in 2 Weeks and I aint a bit *sore* and I am writing just as soon as I got it and I have written you every day or so for the last few weeks and just thought of you all the time

But you must not worry about me Girlie cause I am always all right and get by some way cause I have knocked around so much that I just take it as it comes   yes the flood knocked me out of 4 shows and I guess will greatly reduce my salary this week but lord look what it has done to everybody all over the country.

We have to close here one day early to get to Spokane cause ordinarily its one Night run   but we will have to go away around and will be two days and two Nights getting there   some of these lines will not be running for months.

Now listen dear you seem to think I blame you cause I asked you about all that you told me   why I dont   Why I trust you more than I ever did or ever will a soul on earth and I know it was just as you said and you of course were perfectly right in telling me about it.

How was it if you dident like this Harvey Girl and did not trust her that you spent so many nights there supposedly to be her friend   was it only to be near him.[1]   I know you will not like this but honest Betty I am just so rotten jealous that I am *mean* and cant help it.

I just found a lot of great post cards lots of them marked C.M.R. are by a man I know   a cowboy   C. M. Russell (The Cowboy Artist)[2]   he is the greatest artist of this kind in the world   Remington is not in it with him[3]   he lives just above here in Montana but is becoming very noted[4]   had a studio in N.Y last winter and has been at my flat there lots of times[5]

And I just sent you a book *Paid in Full*   I ▲ *have* ▲ seen the show and I think its great   hope you like it if you have not read it

and I have now two books *Lure of the Dim Trail* by *Bowers.*[5]   and will send it later and did I ever send you the Book the *Round Up.*[7]   if I did not will send it also.   Cause you would like it

Not much chance out here to get much late music but if I find any will ship it on.

Are you all living at home now and did you get the house fixed up   I'll bet its dandy   I'll tell you that was lovely of you girls to do that   "G" now look at me with all   make and all   I never yet done a thing for a soul but myself and dont reckon I ever brought any one else a happy time   I sometimes think I am the most selfish boy alive   I spend all of my money but its all on *Willie*.   I could do oh so much if I only knew how or was not so mean. some day I will wake up and have some *sense*.

Well I must keep of[f] that sentimental stuff.

Now see if you cant write longer letters cause 'G' its afful out here and I should get a letter every day.

With all my Love I am
your same old boy.
B—

ALS, rc. OkClaW. On The Butte letterhead.

1. Rogers is referring to Betty Blake's romance with Tom Harvey. His sister was Annette Harvey. Annette and another sister, Hope, were raised by their mother, Anna, in Chicago after Anna left her husband, Coin Harvey, in 1901 (Riley, *Coin Harvey and Monte Ne*, 5; Snelling, "One of the Blake Girls," 39–41).

2. Rogers sent eight postcards depicting Russell's sketches; all were postmarked from Butte on 17 June and addressed to Miss Betty Blake, Rogers, Ark. In addition to the postcard sent on 17 June (see below), Rogers sent the following postcards:

Postcard entitled "Waiting for a Chinook," or "The Last of Five Thousand" (signed CMR). This was one of Russell's best known sketches, depicting a coyote and a starved steer, a victim of the severe winter of 1886, which Russell had experienced as a caretaker on a cattle ranch in Montana. Russell had drawn the sketch in 1887, in reply to Lewis E. Kaufman, co-owner of the herd, who was concerned about the condition of his cattle (Dippie, *Charles M. Russell*, 13). Rogers wrote on the front above and below the starving steer: "Puts me in mind of this winter in Oolagah. The original of this is worth thousands of dollars it is certainly *real*." Above the coyote he wrote: "This is all so true."

Postcard entitled "Sun shine and Shadow" (signed CMR 1907). This card depicts a bear standing above two cowboys eating, the bear looking hungrily at their food. In the distance horses are running away from the scene. The unsuspecting cowboy says: "I wonder what's the matter with them fool Hosses?" The other cowboy, who notices the bear's shadow, says: "I aint wonderin'! from looks them hosses is wise." On the left front Rogers wrote: "This one is a *peach*."

Postcard entitled "All who know me—respect me" (signed CMR 1907). This card depicts a skunk eating the food of three cowboys who stand around watching the animal. Above the skunk Rogers wrote: "Rail Kitty." Above one of the cowboys he wrote: "Let it alone."

Postcard entitled "Where ignorance is bliss" (signed CMR 1907). This card depicts a bear drinking from a bottle; next to the bear is a sleeping cowboy, unaware that his horse is galloping away in the distance. Rogers wrote above the cowboy: "But oh the awakening?"

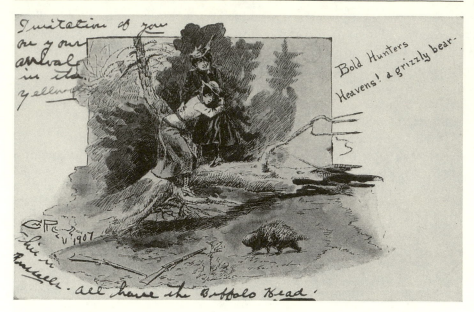

Rogers sent several postcards with illustrations of Russell's work to Betty Blake in June 1908. *(OkClaW)*

"All who know me — respect me."

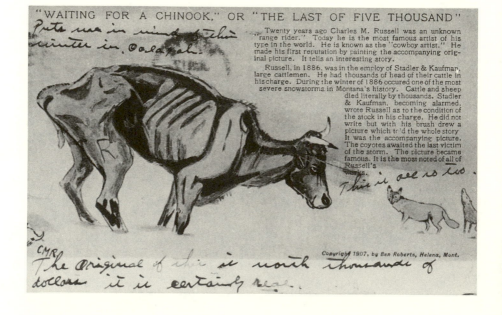

"WAITING FOR A CHINOOK," OR "THE LAST OF FIVE THOUSAND"

Twenty years ago Charles M. Russell was an unknown "range rider." Today he is the most famous artist of his type in the world. He is known as the "cowboy artist." He made his first reputation by painting the accompanying original picture. It tells an interesting story.

Russell, in 1886, was in the employ of Stadler & Kaufman, large cattlemen. He had thousands of head of their cattle in his charge. During the winter of 1886 occured one of the most severe snowstorms in Montana's history. Cattle and sheep died literally by thousands. Stadler & Kaufman, becoming alarmed, wrote Russell as to the condition of the stock in his charge. He did not write but with his brush drew a picture which tr'd the whole story. It was the accompanying picture. The coyotes awaited the last victim of the storm. The picture became famous. It is the most noted of all of Russell's

Copyright 1907, by Ben Roberts, Helena, Mont.

Postcard entitled "White man's skunk wagon no good heap lame." This card depicts two Indians on horseback, a man and a woman; the woman is holding a child. They are looking at a stranded automobile with a flat tire, which the driver and another passenger are attempting to fix. Rogers wrote at the bottom on the front of card: "*Me and my Squaw* giving you and your swell bunch the horse laugh."

Postcard entitled "The Bear in the Park are awfully tame" (signed CMR 1907). This card depicts a man and woman on top of a tree frightened by a bear and two cubs below. One cub says, "Ma snap at that cute one on top"; the other, "That red one aint so worse." Rogers wrote at the bottom front of the card: "come on up *Betty*. the *climate's* fine."

Postcard entitled "Bold Hunters Heavens! a grizzly bear" (signed CMR 1907). This card depicts two women frightened by a grizzly bear and holding each other in desperation. On the left corner, front of card, Rogers wrote: "Imitation of *you* on your arrival in the *yellowstone*." Under the signature with Russell's trademark skeleton buffalo head, Rogers wrote: "This is *Russells*. all have the Buffalo *Head*."

Rogers sent two other postcards postmarked 17 June to Betty Blake. One depicts a mining scene of Butte entitled "Richest Hill in the World, Butte, Mont." The other shows a woman ironing and talking on the phone while another woman sits nearby. It is titled "Are You There? We know Who we Are but know not Who we may Be."

3. That Rogers would relate Russell's work to that of the painter and sculptor Frederic Remington (1861–1909) at this time showed foresight. Today Russell and Remington are often grouped together as artists depicting the landscape, cowboys, and Indian life of the American West.

4. Russell's home and studio was in Great Falls, Mont., located about 110 miles northeast of Butte.

5. Rogers is referring to his room at the Hotel Preston (Putnam) in New York. There is no evidence that Rogers had an apartment.

6. *Lure of the Dim Trail* was a novel by Bertha Muzzy Bower (1871–1940), published in 1907 by G. W. Dillingham Co. Rogers was interested in the novel because it dealt with the West and was illustrated by Charles M. Russell. The story concerns a New York writer, Phil "Bud" Thurston, the son of a cattleman, who goes to Montana to seek material for western adventure stories and discovers the lure of the West. After being held up by robbers on the train, Thurston is hired as a cowpuncher at the Lazy Eight ranch near Billings, Mont. He joins a cattle drive, experiences a stampede, and during a roundup is assaulted by an outlaw gang. Thurston is injured by a bullet in his thigh, while his partner Bob is killed. Thurston wants his own revenge, but the outlaws are apprehended by the sheriff. During his recovery Thurston begins to write and publish magazine stories about his experiences. At the novel's end he rescues the heroine, Mona, from a devastating flood that destroys her home. Earlier in the novel Mona thought Thurston was a coward, but now she views him as a hero, and the two fall in love. Entranced by the cowboy life, Thurston decides to stay in Montana. He had "found himself," writes the novelist and now "loved best to travel the dim trails" (145).

The novel reflects Bower's own attachment to the West. Born in a log cabin near Cleveland, Minn., Bower, whose family name was Muzzy, settled with her parents on a ranch east of Big Sandy, Mont. She was first a schoolteacher in Trout Creek Basin in Montana, where she experienced cowboy life. She married Clayton Bower in 1899, but the marriage ended in divorce. In 1905 she married Bertrand W. Sinclair, but they separated in 1911. Bower was a prolific short-story writer and novelist who wrote romances set in the West. She published sixty-seven novels, many of which featured stereotypes of the cowboy hero and the genteel lady. Her works also conveyed a nostalgia for the natural West, which she felt had been destroyed by the advance of technology and urbanization. Her first novel, *Chip of the Flying U,* was published in *Popular Magazine* in 1904 and in hardcover in 1906. This was the first of fifteen novels dealing with the Flying U, a Montana ranch, and a family with the last name of Happy. The novel's cowboy artist, Chip Happy, may have been modeled on Russell, but the artist refuted this idea, claiming that Chip was based on Bower's husband Bertrand Sinclair, whom Russell nicknamed Fiddle Back. Bower and Sinclair, a cowpuncher born in Edinburgh and later a novelist, became good friends of Russell in Great Falls. Besides *The Lure of the Dim Trail,* Russell illustrated three other Bower novels: *Chip of the Flying U, The Range Dwellers* (1907), and *The Uphill Climb* (1913). *Chip of the Flying U* was made into a film four times. In 1907 Bower and Sinclair moved to California; four years later she divorced him. Bower lived at her mountain home, called the Pocket Ranch, in Quincy, Calif., and perhaps later on a ranch in Albuquerque, N.M. She died in Los Angeles from cancer on 22 July 1940 (Dippie, *Charles M. Russell,* 114–16, 224, 414; Engen, *Writer of the Plains;* Renner, *Charles M. Russell,* 26, 133, 256).

7. *The Round-Up* was a 1908 western novel by John Murray and Mills Miller, published by G. W. Dillingham Co. Set in Arizona, it was a novelized version of Edmund Day's (1866–1923) popular four-act melodrama with the same title, which opened on Broadway on 26 August 1907. The play, starring Maclyn Arbuckle (1863–1931) as a sheriff, concerns Jack Payson, who goes west to meet his old friend Dick Lane (Payson had fallen in love with his wife and he wanted to make amends). The two end up defeating Apaches at their encampment, but Lane is killed and Payson returns home. The novel expands the play into a melodrama in which Lane is a prospector and Payson a ranchman. It describes their conflicts against a desperado coincidentally named Buck McKee and the Apaches who mortally wound Lane. The long description of a roundup in the novel must have brought back memories for Rogers, who had participated in many roundups during his youth (Mantle and Sherwood, eds., *Best Plays of 1899–1909,* 542; *OCAT,* 34, 590).

To Betty Blake
17 June 1908
Butte, Mont.

Rogers met the artist Charles M. Russell in New York between February and April 1908.[1] Sharing a love of the West, the two men became lifelong friends. Rogers would write introductions to Trails Plowed Over *(1927), a collection of Russell's stories, and to* Good Medicine *(1929), a collection of Russell's letters. Rogers also bought some of Russell's paintings and introduced his art to the newspaper publisher Amon G. Carter, Sr. The latter's large collection of Russell's works formed the nucleus of the Amon Carter Museum in Forth Worth. Below is the text of one of the eight postcards Rogers sent Betty Blake from Montana. All were illustrated with Russell's drawings. This one showed Russell with a bottle in one hand, surrounded by cowboys and a Native American.[2]*

[*Written on the front of the card in the margins around the illustration:*]

The one marked x is just an exact reproduction of himself and that is the way he goes all the time in N.Y. with all the swells   he is just the same always kidding and telling stories.

[*In the left margin, Rogers has written:*] These are the characters that he draws   this is him and his friends

[*In the top margin, caption printed in Russell's longhand:*] Here's how to me and my friends   the same to You and Yours

[*In the bottom margin, caption printed in Russell's longhand:*] I savvy these folks [*Rogers has added:*] he always wears a *sash.*

APC, rc. OkClaW. On picture postcard, signed "CR 1907," with Russell's signature symbol of a steer's skull with horns.

1. Other accounts suggest that Rogers and Russell met in Montana or on a train bound for New York (Marquis, "Will and Charlie," 6–7). But Rogers says they met in New York, where Rogers spent considerable time between vaudeville engagements. Although Russell's home was in Great Falls, Mont., he made several trips to New York beginning in early 1904. Rogers could not have met him at this time because he was abroad. More likely their first meeting occurred sometime between February and April 1907, when Russell was again in New York. According to Rogers, Russell visited his "flat" in the city several times during the winter of 1908 (see Will Rogers to Betty Blake, 17 June 1908 [letter], above). On 16 February 1907 Russell's paintings were first exhibited in the East at Plymouth Church in Brooklyn. Rogers performed several times in the city in February and March before sailing to England on April 18. At the time of Russell's death in 1927, Rogers said: "I first met Russell in New York. . . . That was a long time ago. He was there to sell some of his paintings and I was trying to peddle some jokes. The longer we knew each other the better we seemed to hit it off" ("Will Rogers Visits Haunts of Russell after Old Time Western Reception Here," *Great Falls Tribune*, 1 April 1927; see also Dippie, ed., *Charles M. Russell*, 3–4, 63–64, 81–86, 314–15; Renner, *Charles M. Russell*, 27).

2. Dippie, ed., *Charles M. Russell*, vi; see Biographical Appendix entry RUSSELL, Charles M.).

To Betty Blake
21 June 1908
Spokane, Wash.

Spokane, Washington. _____ 190__

Sunday Night.

My Own Betty—

Well listen dear I did think I would get a nice dandy letter or two from you on my arrival here but not a line   in fact I have only had one letter in 3 weeks now

Well *hon* I was the biggest hit here today and tonight I ever was in a long time[1]   Oh I went great   just got in here at 11 today after being 3 days and 3 nights on all kinds of roads   come away down near Salt Lake and then away out towards Portland   just to get a 12 hour run from Butte to Spokane   but thank the lord we had our tickets through and the expenses was on the Northern Pacific railroad[2]   only of course our sleepers and food on the diners   Oh   it was the *affallest* trip I ever had and I have had some trips too.   Well sir in the last town where I missed two days on account of going by the park the Manager on ~~Saturday~~ Friday when I left paid me in full and did not take out a cent   he could of taken out about $75 or 80. dollars. wasent that good of him.[3]

here I go again telling you all my financial troubles.

Here are a bunch of cards from the hotel here where I am at   it is swell but the rooms are *bum*

I am going in the Silver Grill[4] room pretty soon to get my little night lunch and oh but I am tired after that trip and todays work and say it gets you up here in this high Altitude   I find myself almost out of breath when I finish

I sent you a card from Pocatello, Idaho where we "*laid*" ▲ *is that right* ▲ over.   Say did you ever get a deck of cards from yellowstone[5]   tell me cause they were paid for and he was to send them.

We finish here next Saturday Night and then go to Seattle where we open at Coliseum. Theatre.[6] there   so address there please   at once and see if you cant get me a letter there so I will get it on my arrival cause its lonesome there   I hope I can be this big a hit in Seattle and Frisco.[7]

I dident mean only to write you a short note and here is a letter   I'll bet I have wrote you 100 to 1 in the last 5 weeks   I will slow up for a spell now

havent had a hot day on the whole trip yet   only lots of rain.

Be good and write often to your old boy who just loves you to death and does love to get your letters.

Billy.

ALS, rc. On The Spokane, "Ye Sign of Ye Silver Grill," Spokane, Wash., letterhead.

1. Rogers appeared at the Washington Theater in Spokane during the week of 21 June 1908, where he was advertised as the headliner on the program. Among the rave reviews that Rogers kept was the following: "There is a big novelty at the Washington this week in the roping and lasso throwing exhibition of Will Rogers. He acts and looks the typical cowboy and does some of the most remarkable things with a piece of rope, its length seeming to be of no material importance. He handles 100 feet of rope as easily as he does 10 feet. He can make a rope tie a knot in itself while spinning through the air; he can rope a horse and rider both at the same time with two lassos, and in fact

there doesn't seem to be anything that he can not do with a rope. And while he is accomplishing all these and many more not less wonderful things with a rope that seems to be alive he is continually giving vent to a vein of humor that keeps the audience laughing at the same time it is applauding his achievements" ("At the Washington," scrapbook A-2, OkClaW).

Also on the program were the following acts: Burgos and Clara (Novelty Gymnasts); Louise Auber (Singing Comedienne); Al Leonhardt (Juggler); J. C. Nugent, Grace Fertig, and Co. (in *The Absent-Minded Beggar*); Malvene, Thomas and Alfred (Song and Dance Artists); and moving pictures (clipping, scrapbook A-2, OkClaW; *NYDM*, 11 July 1908).

2. The Northern Pacific Railroad was the main carrier in the Northwest. It would be several years before a passenger could travel from Butte to Spokane without going via Salt Lake City and Portland (Davis, "Business Side of Vaudeville," 534).

3. The western circuits, especially the Sullivan and Considine Circuit, had strict rules about missing performances. The Sullivan and Considine organization was known to have started the "play or pay" contract, which was adopted by other circuits. Performers were guaranteed full pay when their act was canceled, but if the performers canceled, they had to pay the theater manager their salary for that week (Connor, "American Vaudeville Managers," 50).

4. The Silver Grille was featured on the Spokane Hotel's letterhead stationery, which Rogers used. Rogers also sent a postcard, postmarked 27 June from Spokane, which featured the main dining room of Davenport's in Spokane. Rogers wrote that he ate at Davenport's "several times" called it "the wonder Restaurant of the West" (OkClaW).

5. See Will Rogers to Betty Blake, 17 June 1908 [letter], above.

6. Rogers opened at the Coliseum Theatre at the Monday matinee on 29 June (Will Rogers to Betty Blake, 27 June 1908, below).

7. Rogers performed at San Francisco's Wigwam Theatre the week of 23 August 1908.

To Betty Blake
23 June 1908
Spokane, Wash.

Spokane, Washington _____ 190__

Tuesday. Eve. 5 P.M.

My Only ▲ (honest) ▲ Sweetheart

Well my Gal I got your first letter written here   also one forwarded on from Butte and say but they did seem good to me and by the way I am *loving* you some at the present time *also*.

I am only writing you this little note as I want to send you these three little clippings from Spokane papers   my act is certainly a success here   if it will only be half as good in Seattle and Frisco.   Yes I would like to meet your friends out there.

today is pretty warm   the only warm day I have seen all year

This place is a beautiful little city   one of the best in the Northwest   a lot better than Butte.

Oh how I do wish I was home this summer and oh what a time we would have and how I would enjoy it   and we would certainly get *good* acquainted wouldent we   But I think I will get there the latter part of August or Sept 1st and will see that you get more than *two Sundays* as the *song* says.

"*Well, you'll get all thats a coming to you and a little bit more.*"

I will stop cause I am so far ahead of you in writing I fear you will never catch up.

Your old ever
loving Kid   Billy.

ALS, rc. OkClaW. On The Spokane letterhead.

To Betty Blake
27 June 1908
Spokane, Wash.

Spokane, Washington _____ 190__
Saturday Eve.

My Sweetheart—

Well my gal I got your two letters today and they are all the candy.   and I just would love to drift into old Rogers now on one of those *almost trains* and not have to dig out at all   just drive out and on and on and tell each other how nice we are with all the *accompanying trimmings.*   oh well when we can it may be nicer so why *rave now.*

Well this is a dandy country up here and a beautiful city and everything nice   I like it cause my act is such a hit   guess I will be a frost in Seattle for unusual success only comes about every other town   I will just about scratch through in Seattle, and to make it worse the nice theatre where I was to play is closing tonight for repairs and they switched to show over to an old bum place and I am afraid your friends will think I am a *kinder shine act*[1]   You see people out of the profession dont know a lot of things about why or what and they think if an act is in a big Theatre it is good and if in a small it is bad   they dont know that the salaries are sometimes just reversed   of course this is the best circuit in the Northwest but some of the houses could be better but it is delightful to work for   they certainly do all they can to make your stay pleasant from the Manager down and you are treated with more respect than on the Eastern circuits.[2]

I dont know where I go from Seattle but I think Vancouver[3]   will let you know or you can write to Seattle and it will be forwarded on without any delay, as Seattle is the headquarters of all this circuit.

Maud is back from Texas and brought *Nell Lane* with her for a months stay and not her mother[4]   dont you know Nell will enjoy it so cause her mother always put at [a] damper on Nells fun.   I wish I was home and we would all have one more time cause Ada, Scrap, Nell and you are all there and still *"single" I hope*[5]   and I really believe you and I could get on better than before and would both enjoy it better.   but the great American public need enlightening on the sports and practices of our great American Cowboy so I guess it *behooves* me to act out a spell for them and postpone the hilarity for an ~~spell~~ endefinite period.

Did you get the book and have you got *Lure of the Dim Trail.* or the *Round Up.*—tell me if not   I will send them cause I have both of them

The weather up here is delightful and not at all hot.

Well my gal I must stop cause this is gettaway Night   we catch a train 30 minutes after I come of[f] the stage and I will have to go some   will perhaps work in my Street clothes, travel all Night from 11. to 3. P.M. tomorrow Sunday to Seattle.   open Monday Matinee and close there the following Sunday Night.

Keep on loving your old boy cause he is a fool about you.

Billy.

Star Theatre.
Seattle.

ALS, rc. OkClaW. On The Spokane letterhead.

1. During the week of 29 June 1908 Rogers performed at the Seattle Star Theatre rather than the Coliseum. In 1908 the Coliseum was leased by Sullivan and Considine to the Orpheum Circuit for its acts. Perhaps the Coliseum, renamed the Orpheum, was undergoing repairs for this transition. Orpheum Advanced Vaudeville opened here on 24 August 1908. The Star was an older Sullivan and Considine theater, where vaudeville was performed as early as 1900 (Elliott, *History of Variety-Vaudeville in Seattle*, 52, 54, 55–56, 67).

2. Rogers was correct that the Sullivan and Considine Circuit was the best in the Northwest. Considine was liked by his performers and had a reputation of never canceling an act. Rogers's remark that performers had more respect on the western circuits reflects the disdain many performers felt for the Keith-Albee chain. Its monopoly over vaudeville engagements through the UBO allowed it to charge performers an extra percentage of their salary (Connors, "American Vaudeville Managers," 49–50).

3. Rogers performed at Vancouver's Orpheum Theatre the week of 6 July.

4. Accompanied by her son Gunter, Maud Lane (Rogers's sister), went to Clarksville, Tex., to visit relatives. Maud's husband, Cap, was born in Clarksville. Nell

was possibly the daughter of Cap's sister or brother (*CR*, 29 May and 10 July 1908; see also *PWR*, 1:498).

5. Ada Foreman and Gazelle (Scrap) Lane were close to Rogers during his youth (see *PWR*, 1:175n.2, 176n.1, 177, 177n.2, 397, 401, 402n.5, 497–98).

To Betty Blake
5 July 1908
Seattle, Wash.

SEATTLE, WASH.
Sunday.—

My Own Girl—

Well *honey* I was out to your friends[1] Miss Randolph and spent from about 11 A.M. to 2:30 and had a dandy lunch and they just treated me fine went out with Mrs. Eaton and family and all had a great day it was the 4th. they have a nice big old country looking place lovely trees and grounds and the girls are great so is Mrs. Eaton they are all jolly and I felt right at home They had all seen my Show one Night[2] 6 ladies in a box and they seemed so to enjoy it and they are allright a little different from what I expected I have promised to call up Mrs. Eaton today and run up to her house a little bit. do you know ~~you~~ she reminds me a lot of *you* and she is just like I imagine you will be when her age and all that (just grand) I promised to come back by if I can and spend next Sunday as I will not be working and will pass through on my way to Tacoma from Vancouver.

They laughed about you saying it was 40 miles out to their place its about 4. right in the edge of the city Well I will stop. One letter all week: leaving here tonight at 12 on the boat for Vancouver.[3] Week 13. Grand, Tacoma.[4] Love Love Love.

Billy.

I sent the 2 books.

ALS, rc. OkClaW. On Palace Hotel, Seattle, Wash., letterhead. Zbinden Brothers, proprietors.

1. Rogers sent a postcard to Betty Blake from Sacramento with a picture on the front taken at a park, showing Rogers with a man named Alexander, who knew Betty's brother, Sandy Blake. Rogers is smiling slightly, with closed lips, and wearing a straw hat. Above the photograph he wrote: "Imitation of a *smile*. almost a *grin*. cute (yes-no.) <u>No.</u>" (Will Rogers to Betty Blake, undated, OkClaW).

2. Rogers was advertised as the headliner. Other performers included Melvene, Thomas and Alfred (Singers and Dancers); Al Leonhardt (Juggler); J. C. Nugent and Co. (in *The Absent-Minded Beggar*); Louise Auber (Singing Comedienne); Burgos and Clara (Gymnasts); and Eddie Rosche (Pictured Melodies). Reviews said there were packed houses every night, with Rogers, called the Lariat King, getting considerable

applause (clippings, scrapbook A-2, OkClaW; *Variety,* 11 July 1908).

3. Rogers wrote his father also from Seattle, stating that he was "leaving in a few minutes for Vancouver B.C." (Will Rogers to Clement Vann Rogers, 5 July 1908, OkClaW).

4. Around 1906 Considine built the Grand Theatre in Tacoma for $100,000 (Elliott, *History of Variety-Vaudeville in Seattle,* 54).

Reviews from Will Rogers's Scrapbook
ca. 7 July 1908
Vancouver, B.C., Canada

With the increase in Vancouver's population after 1900, it was able to support big-time vaudeville. The Orpheum, where Rogers performed, was linked to the Sullivan and Considine Circuit in the Pacific Northwest. In 1905 a new railway, the Vancouver, Yukon, and Westminster, connected the city with the Pacific Northwest and enabled the city to draw variety acts that toured the Sullivan and Considine Circuit. Other circuits operated theaters in Vancouver.[1]

THE STAGE
ORPHEUM.

Out over the amazed and breathless audience a huge ring of rope, swishing and coiling as it circled in ever-increasing circumference, vibrated as if with life, and held the people in wonder and, perhaps, not a little fear. For they wondered what would happen if the eighty-foot lasso could not be controlled by the skilful cowboy, who, from the stage, directed its movements with the ease and grace of one born to rope wild steers on the plains of the West. Suddenly the rope's hiss increased to a whining shriek, it fairly seemed a thing incarnate, inspired with evil, and the timid ones shrank back in horror—then it was over, and the rope, neatly coiled, lay at the performer's feet.

Will Rogers, who at the Orpheum this week held enthralled the audiences with his marvelous feats of skill and strength with the lasso, smiled at the alarm, made a few humorous remarks and bowed to the thunder of applause that swept from the people. Some of Rogers' tricks with his partner, Buck McKee, are extraordinary, particularly his method of roping and tying a man on horseback, and his jumping with the rope.

THE ORPHEUM.

It is very doubtful if Manager Donnellan has ever offered at his Pender Street house a greater novelty, or one that has been more popular with a

Monday night audience than the wonderful exhibition of lariat-throwing and manipulating that Will Rogers introduced for the first time in Vancouver yesterday. Rogers is a Cherokee Indian, a grandson of the famous chief Geronimo,[2] and until a year or two ago, when he first took to the stage, he lived on his father's ranch. He was famed among the cowboys for his deftness and wonderful expertness with the lariat, and his work last night was nothing short of amazing. He was assisted by "Buck" McKee, ex-sheriff of Oklahoma and the clever broncho "Teddy." In half a dozen different and complicated ways he roped man and horse, once throwing the lassoo with his foot, and by way of variation he twisted the loose noose into all sorts of "curlicues" as he himself expresses it. He winds up with what he calls the "crinoleen"[3] in which, mounted on the mustang, he works the loose noose in a circle about his head, gradually enlarging the noose from a diameter of a couple of feet until it is so big that it fills the whole arch and finally catches as the curtain descends. Throughout the turn Rogers keeps up an inimitable run of cowboy talk, illuminated with a smile and show of teeth that are in themselves a whole show. As a matter of fact Rogers is a great big show in himself. There are several other good things at the Orpheum this week.[4]

PD. Unidentified clippings, ca. 7 July 1908, Scrapbook A-2, OkClaW.

1. The Orpheum Theatre, built in 1898, was originally called the Alhambra, and it first presented productions by stock companies. It was located on Pender Street. In 1905 Considine took over the Alhambra and renamed it the People's Theatre. He later changed its name to the Orpheum, which opened in December 1906. Although this theater carried the Orpheum name, it was not formally a part of the Orpheum circuit but a theater managed by Sullivan and Considine. The circuit also operated the Grand, formerly the Savoy, a music hall built in 1898. The Star Circuit offered vaudeville in Vancouver, as well as in Portland, Seattle, Tacoma, and Astoria. The Alexander Pantages Circuit also operated out of Seattle; on 6 January 1908 it opened a vaudeville theater in Vancouver on Hastings Street, and a second one was constructed in 1917. The Orpheum Circuit eventually controlled vaudeville in Vancouver and began operating its own Orpheum Theatre there in 1914 (Elliott, *History of Variety-Vaudeville in Seattle*, 52, 54; Todd, "Organization of Professional Theatre in Vancouver," 3–10, 24).

2. Rogers, of course, was not related to Geronimo, and the statement underscores the hyperbole that was often used to publicize Rogers's Indian heritage.

3. The Crinoline, a big loop also called the Wedding Ring, was the roping trick Rogers used to climax his vaudeville act. The name refers to the material used for a hoop skirt (Dean, *Will Rogers Rope Tricks*, 11).

4. Rogers performed at the Orpheum from 7 to 12 July 1908. The program began with an overture, Herbert's "Serenade," performed by the Orpheum's orchestra, and concluded with the orchestra playing the national anthem. Other performers on the bill were Burgos and Clara (Novelty Gymnasts); Oliver Reece (Beautiful Rendering "Just You and I"); Al Leonhardt (Juggling Eccentrique); J. C. Nugent and Co. (In a Comedy Sketch Entitled *The Absent Minded Beggar*); Louise Auber (Singing

Comedienne); Melvene, Thomas, and Alfred (Character Change Artists in a Melange of Songs and Dances); and Animated Pictures (Latest French Comedy).

Clipping from Will Rogers's Scrapbook
ca. 14 July 1908
Tacoma, Wash.

THESPIANS PLAY ON THE DIAMOND
GRAND AND PANTAGES NINES MEET, THE FORMER WINNING.

The performers at the Grand and Pantages[1] theaters played an exciting game of baseball at Athletic park this morning, the Grand team winning by a score of 15 to 8.

One would never dream that a bunch of comedians could get real serious, but the way those fellows went after Umpire Glenn Matthews whenever the plays became close and exciting showed that they meant business. Once Mr. Matthews came near being mobbed by the Pantages team.

Will Rogers, the lariat thrower, showed that he can do other things besides flinging a rope. He played a good game at first and hit the ball hard. Phil Ott,[2] also of the Grand, is as good a pitcher as he is a comedian and B. B. Vincent played a nice game at first, warbling between plays. Vincent is with the Pantages house and he is some singer.

Dean Worley[3] did a lot of heavyweight rooting for the Grand team and he had a whole lot the best of the little manager from the Pantages, W. J. Timmons.[4] Timmons thinks now that it was Worley's rooting that did the business.

ELECTRO WAS CHARGED.

Electro didn't have much to do in right field, excepting to chase the balls and with a heavy current of "Juice" he was able to skip over the weeds in the outer garden like a jack rabbit. Most of the actors were shy on base running but they made up for this shortage in other ways.

About 500 spectators saw the game. The score by innings and the line-up of the teams follow:

Grand	1	2	2	5	0	3	0	0	2–15
Pantages	0	0	0	0	4	2	0	0	2–8

GRAND.		PANTAGES.
Henry Potter[5]	.s. s.	.Hert. Terry
Phil Ott	.p.	.C. Edwards
Al Stedman[6]	.c. f.	.R. Evans
J. R. Gray	.c.	.Carl Ellis
E. S. Richardson	.r. f.	.Elec[t]ro
Wm. Russell[7]	.3 b.	.Ed. Clark
Will Rogers	.1 b.	.B. B. Vincent
E. Blanchard	.2 b.	.J. Lombard
Fred Morton[8]	.l. f.	.C. Harris

PD. Unidentified clipping, ca. 14 July 1908. Scrapbook A-2, OkClaW.

1. Alexander Pantages (1864–1936) operated a chain of vaudeville theaters that rivaled the Sullivan and Considine Circuit. In Seattle he converted a store into the Crystal Theatre and charged 10 cents' admission for a program of small-time acts and two-reel films. Soon he began to lease or build other theaters. He owned several theaters in San Francisco and in 1909 built the Pantages in Los Angeles. By 1923 he was operating thirty theaters in sixteen states. In 1926 his circuit of forty theaters stretched from the West Coast to Niagara Falls, N.Y., with booking offices in Chicago and New York. His showplace was the 1926 San Francisco Pantages, then the largest theater in the city. Many of his theaters were designed by the architect B. Marcus Priteca (1890–1971) in a style called "Pantages Greek." Like other impresarios, he offered vaudeville that catered to families. In 1929 he lost a lot of money in the stock-market crash and sold most of his theaters to Radio-Keith-Orpheum for a sum reported to be above $3.5 million. That same year he was accused of raping Eunice Pringle, a seventeen-year-old dancer, in an office in his Pantages Theatre in downtown Los Angeles. After a scandalous and much publicized trial, Pantages was convicted and sentenced to fifty years in state prison, but after an appeal leading to a second trial, he was found innocent in 1931. When he died in 1936 from a heart attack, he had only a few theaters, chiefly the Pantages in Hollywood, Calif., which is still in operation (Alfred L. Bernheim, "Facts of Vaudeville," in Stein, ed., *American Vaudeville As Seen by Its Contemporaries*; Connors, "American Vaudeville Managers," 50–51; Crane, "Alexander Pantages," 501–3; DiMeglio, *Vaudeville U.S.A.*, 125–29; Elliott, *History of Variety-Vaudeville in Seattle*, 58–61; *EV*, 387–90; Giesler, *Jerry Giesler Story*, 14–39; Grau, *Stage in the Twentieth Century*, 147–50; Green and Laurie, *Show Biz*, 48; Helgesen, "B. Marcus Priteca," 3–12; Laurie, *Vaudeville*, 401–3; Singer, "Vaudeville West," 75–77).

2. Phil Ott (ca. 1875–1954) was a member of the Four Otts, a musical comedy team comprising his wife, his brother Matt, and Matt's wife. Phil Ott started in vaudeville at age eighteen with his brother Joe's musical comedy troupe. At this time he was performing at the Grand in a skit called "Nearly a Dr." with Nettie Nelson and Al Stedman. He died at the home of his son in Taunton, Mass. (*VO*, 4:7 July 1954).

3. Dean Worley (1873–1927), born in Salt Lake City, was a theater manager at this time with the Sullivan and Considine circuit. Later, he managed Tacoma's Lyceum Theatre and the Empress Theatre in Los Angeles. He was the representative of Thomas Wilkes in 1921–22 and later became Wilkes's general manager (*VO*, 1:9 March 1927).

4. W. J. Timmons (ca. 1872–1917) was a Pantages theater manager for twelve years. He managed Pantages's theater in Tacoma for eight years and when he died was managing the Empress in Kansas City (*VO*, 1:14 December 1917).

5. Henry Potter and May Harris were gymnasts on the same bill with Rogers (Grand Theatre playbill, scrapbook A-2, OkClaW).

6. Al Stedman was in the skit "Nearly a Dr." with Phil Ott and Nettie Nelson. Later he may have teamed with Fanny Stedman in a comedy piano act (Grand Theatre playbill, scrapbook A-2, OkClaW; Laurie, *Vaudeville*, 154, 229).

7. Born in New York City, William Russell (1884–1929) grew up in poor surroundings and as a youngster gave his widowed mother the salary he earned as a messenger and hat checker in a theater. He studied to be a lawyer, but instead decided to become an actor and joined a stock company in Pittsburgh. He was known as Big Bill Russell because of his strength and large physique. Before his film career, he performed on the legitimate stage and in vaudeville. Russell at one time was a semiprofessional boxer and performed in a boxing film serial titled *The Diamond from the Sky* (1915). Beginning in 1911 Russell became a movie actor and made many films. His films were often Westerns that allowed him to display his physical ability and play the role of an adventurous hero (*FilmEnc*, 1189; Grand Theatre playbill, scrapbook A-2, OkClaW; Locke env. 1984, NN-L-RLC).

8. Fred W. Morton was on the same bill with Rogers and was a harmonica player, whistler, and "paper mutilator" (Grand Theatre playbill, scrapbook A-2, OkClaW). Also on the program with Rogers were George F. Keane (Song Illustrator, "Somebody That I Know and You Know Too") and Effie Pearson (Singing Comedienne) (Grand Theatre playbill, scrapbook A-2, OkClaW).

To Clement Vann Rogers
16 July 1908
Tacoma, Wash.

Tacoma.

Thursday.

Dear Papa.

Guess you are home from the convention now and guess you had a big time.[1] I am here this week and go to Portland Ore. next Week then I lay off a week and jump to Sacremento California. so you better write to me there. I play the *Grand Theatre* Portland, Ore. next week.[2] but by the time a letter got there I would be gone so address

"*ACME.*" Theatre

Sacramento. Cal.[3]

Love to all

Willy.

ALS, rc. OkClaW.

1. Clement Vann Rogers left on either 2 or 3 July 1908 to attend the Democratic Party convention. Others who accompanied him were Judge T. J. Brown, George F.

Wyell, and J. F. Flippin. They went on a special train that stopped at William Jennings Bryan's home in Nebraska. Rogers, a Democrat, was a supporter of Bryan. At the convention Bryan was nominated for president and John W. Kern for vice president. On 11 July the *Claremore Progress* reported that the Claremore delegation was "having a great time." In the election, held on 3 November, William H. Taft defeated Bryan by over 1.2 million votes. It was Bryan's third unsuccessful try for the presidency. In the new state of Oklahoma (1907), where citizens voted in their first presidential election, Bryan beat Taft by a vote of 122,363 to 110,474 (*CM*, 3 July 1908; *CP*, 4 July 1908 and 11 July 1908; Gibson, *Oklahoma*, 344; on Rogers's political career, see *PWR*, 1:536–43).

2. Portland's Grand Theatre belonged to the Sullivan and Considine Circuit. Rogers performed here from 20 to 26 July. The bill at the Grand featured some of the same performers as in Tacoma. It included Stine and Evans (in "Wanted, a Divorce"); Parmet, Russell and Co. (in "Around the World in an Airship"); Armstrong and Holly (in "The Expressman"); Potter and Harris (Clever Gymnasts); Effie Pearson (Singing Comedienne); and Frederick Bauer (songs) (*Variety*, 1 August 1908).

A 1914 study of Portland vaudeville and motion-picture theaters found that a large percentage of women and children attended vaudeville shows. As many as 70 percent of Portland's children went to vaudeville theaters and about 24 percent attended the shows once a week or oftener. The investigators who prepared the report complained of morally objectionable features (foul language, suggestive dances, and so forth) in forty-eight out of fifty-eight Portland vaudeville shows. The report recognized the difficulty of regulating national circuit shows and instead called for local censorship (Foster, *Vaudeville and Motion Picture Shows*).

3. Rogers actually performed at Sacramento's Grand Theatre from 3 to 8 August with the same performers as in Portland. In addition to Rogers, the bill was as follows: Potter and Harris (A Gymnastic Display Without an Equal); Miss Effie Pearson (Singing Comedienne); Will H. Armstrong and Magdaline Holly (in "The Expressman"); Latest Set of Motion Pictures; Chas. J. Stine and Olive Evans ("Wanted, a Divorce"); Parmet, Russell and Co. (in "Around the World in an Airship") (Grand Theatre, Sacramento, playbill, week commencing Monday 3 August, scrapbook A-2, OkClaW).

To Sisters and Family
ca. 8 August 1908
Sacramento, Calif.

SACRAMENTO, CAL., _____ 190__[1]

My Dear Gang,

Well I got a few letters from some of you and you seem to be getting on pretty good and all having a time. Well I sho wish I could join you for a short spell but it just looks like I cant cause I am signed for the time out here at a raise of salary   so I will just have to take it   but I will get there a little later on before Xmas   I will perhaps have some open time   you see I am not overlooking any work when I can get it cause I need all I can get and have great prospects of a good year this year   I only lose one week jumping from Frisco to Detroit[2] and then guess I will go along pretty steady for while   but the first time I cant get booked I will jump right home

Well so old Mary[3] is there   well I sho would be there if I had a Ghost of a chance and am glad she is up and going   honest you couldent kill her with a stick   she is too game.   Well I go to Frisco next Week   play one Week then Oakland one Week   then back to Frisco for one week more[4]   then I jump to Detroit Mich. on the old Keith Circuit again.

it is sho hot here   the first hot place have seen all year.   just write for the next two weeks to the National Theatre, San Francisco.[5]   I will get them even if I am in Oakland or at a different theatre there   it is the one I play next Week, opening Monday. 10th.   Would send you post cards from out here but Sallie and her Gang and May know more about this State than I ever will know[6]   I am close to Mays old stomping ground aint I.[7]

Well I will stop   write all of you *lazy Kids* if your Mamas havent time. Love to all

old Uncle E.

Got me a little cheap Kodak[8]
will send you some pictures at once.

ALS, rc. OkClaW. On Hotel Turclu, European Plan, Sacramento, Calif., letterhead. Clunie Block, corner Eleventh and K Streets. Frank Meyer, manager.[9]

1. While playing at the Grand in Sacramento, Buck McKee saw his brother, W. E. McKee, a jeweler in Sacramento. They had not seen each other for seventeen years. Buck McKee and his wife would eventually settle in Sacramento ("After Long Years of Separation, Brothers Meet in This City," *Sacramento Union,* clipping, scrapbook A-2, OkClaW).

2. Rogers left San Francisco around 31 August and opened at Detroit's Temple Theatre on 7 September.

3. Mary Gulager (b. 1880) was a cousin of Rogers. She was the daughter of Frederick William Gulager and Martha Lucretia Schrimsher, the sister of Rogers's mother, Mary America Schrimsher Rogers. She lived in Kansas City, Mo., and was visiting Sallie and Tom McSpadden (Collins, *Roping Will Rogers,* 120, 125; *CR,* 24 July 1908; *PWR,* 200 and n.2).

4. Rogers performed at San Francisco's National Theatre from 10 to 15 August, at Oakland's Bell Theatre from 16 to 22 August, and at San Francisco's Wigwam Theatre from 23 to 29 August (*SFC,* 11 August, 16 August, and 23 August 1908).

5. During the week of 10 August Rogers performed with the following acts at the National Theatre: Parmet and Russell's Singing Travelers ("Around the World in an Airship"); Potter and Harris (Novelty Gymnasts); Stine and Evans ("Wanted, A Divorce"); Armstrong and Holly ("The Expressman"); and Effie Pearson (Singing Soubrette). Part of the Sullivan and Considine Circuit, the National Theatre was managed by Sidney Patrick (Sid) Grauman (1879–1950), who would later become a well-known exhibitor and owner of lavish movie theaters, including the existing Grauman's Chinese Theatre in Hollywood. After making money prospecting in the Yukon, Grauman and his father, David J., operated two theaters in San Francisco, the Lyric

and the Unique. The latter theater, featuring variety acts and early silent films, was destroyed by fire in the April 1906 San Francisco earthquake. As a replacement, Sid Grauman erected the National Theatre, located on Post and Steiner Streets, which opened on 4 June 1906. The theater's seats were pews from a destroyed church, and sawdust covered the floor. Overhead Grauman erected a large canvas tent, which he bought from an itinerant cowboy for $2,000. Grauman recalled: "We built a stage on the Unique's site, hooked up a tent to it, advertised its safety features and called the new house Grauman's National Theater. It was just around the corner from Market Street, so we hired a barker to stand on Market and announce our programs" (quoted from a 1923 interview in Beardsley, *Hollywood's Master Showman*, 29). At the National Grauman presented silent films and six acts of vaudeville. As a reminder of the earthquake, Grauman advertised that in his theater there was "Nothing to Fall on You, Except Canvas." Two years later he erected a new theater on the tent site, and it remained there until 1917. It was in this new National Theatre that Rogers performed two shows a day. At the matinee the audience paid 10 cents or 20 cents; in the evening 15 cents or 25 cents (Beardsley, *Hollywood's Master Showman*, 17–31; Berson, *San Francisco Stage*, 138; *FilmEnc*, 549; Levin, "San Francisco Story," 3, 6, 8; *SFC*, 9 August, 11 August 1908).

6. Tom and Sallie McSpadden and their family made a trip to California in late 1905 and spent several months there. Tom McSpadden went to Los Angeles in January 1907 for health reasons (*CR*, 27 October 1905, 11 January 1907, 8 March 1907).

7. Probably a reference to Clement Mayes McSpadden, the son of Sallie and Tom McSpadden, who worked as a civil engineer on railroads in the West and who died in Los Angeles in 1912. He was probably in California or in another western state at this time. After he visited his family for the holidays, the *Chelsea Reporter* announced that "Clem McSpadden left Wednesday evening for Los Angeles, California, to take up his favorite work, that of railroading" (17 January 1908; see also *PWR*, 1:341–42n.3, 508).

8. George Eastman registered the name Kodak as his trademark in 1888. His first Kodak camera was launched the same year and marketed to the general public, rather than to a specialized class of photographers. The advertising campaign used the slogan: "You push the button, we do the rest" (Collins, *Story of Kodak*, 60). Costing $25, the new Kodak camera stimulated public interest in candid photography, an interest that peaked with the introduction of the Kodak Brownie camera in 1900. The Brownie was a small, simple camera costing only a dollar, and 250,000 were sold in the first year. The advent of this camera expanded the pool of potential photographers. Now anybody, even a child, could take a photograph. For convenience, shutter-bugs could send their film to Kodak for development, or they could have it processed locally at shops. The camera provided the means for a new kind of photograph, the snapshot. These candid shots of life, usually taken outdoors, as the camera required a strong light, were in direct contrast to the arranged portraits that had previously dominated the photographic scene (Collins, *Story of Kodak*, 54–55, 60, 97–103; Mensel, "'Kodakers Lying in Wait'," 28–29).

9. The return address on the envelope advertised the hotel as "strictly first class" with 200 furnished rooms.

To Clement Vann Rogers
18 August 1908
Oakland, Calif.

Oakland Cal.

Aug 18.

Dear Papa.

Well I am playing here in Oakland this week[1] and go back over and play Frisco next week and then that finishes me out here and I have only six days to jump back east to Detroit Mich where I open for my season   but have some weeks open around about Christmas and will be home then.   after you git this *you* all can write to me to Temple Theatre. Detroit Mich, and I will get them when I git there   but I dont open there till Sept 7th.   I am sorry I wont git to come by home but I cant spare the time just now and I am under contract.   I am at the Wigwam Theatre. Frisco. next week.[2]

Lots of Love to all

Willie

ALS, rc. OkClaW. On Will Rogers's letterhead.

1. In Oakland Rogers performed at the Bell Theatre from 16 to 22 August 1908. The same bill as at Sacramento was presented, with Rogers as the headline act. The program included Potter and Harris; Effie Pearson; Parmet, Russell and Co.; Charles J. Stine and Olive Evans; Will H. Armstrong and Magdaline Holly; and two new reels of motion pictures (*SFC*, 16 August 1908).

2. The Wigwam Theatre dated back to approximately 1886, when it was a variety hall featuring opera arias and comedy acts. It was managed by the impresario Gustav Walter, who built the first Orpheum Theatre in San Francisco, which opened in 1887. It was destroyed in the 1906 earthquake and rebuilt. At the Wigwam Theatre from 23 to 29 August 1908 the bill was as follows: Parmet and Russell's Singing Travelers; Armstrong and Holly; Maltese and Co.; the Ferreras; Stine and Evans; other feature acts; and latest motion pictures (Berson, *San Francisco Stage,* 76, 92–93; Gagey, *San Francisco Stage,* 179, 210, 220–21; *SFC,* 23 August 1908).

From Vaudevillians Performing at the Wigwam Theatre
18 August 1908
San Francisco, Calif.

Performers on the western circuit often faced a salary cut when they reached the West Coast after a long tour. The Pantages Circuit, for example, took advantage of vaudevillians and cut their salary 25 percent on their return tour back East.[1] Vaudevillians accepted the cut, knowing that if they refused, they could be stranded out West without work. Rogers usually avoided labor issues, but in this case he sided with his fellow performers who were outraged that their salary had been reduced at San Francisco's Wigwam Theatre. Rogers performed at Oakland's Bell Theatre and appeared at the Wigwam the following week. He was the only performer at the Bell to support the Wigwam artists. For opposing the salary cut at the Wigwam, Rogers received the following letter from vaudevillians performing at the theater.

THE HELL WITH THE BELL
OFFICE OF THE STICKERS

ORGANIZED SINCE THE CUT DAY—
PRESIDENT, WILL ROGERS
VICE-PRESIDENT, WILLIE SELBINI
TREASURE. ALEXANDER & SCOTT
OUTER & INNER GAURD, RIVA-LARSEN
CHAPLAIN
& PREIST APOLLO'S QUARTETTE[2]

AUXILIARY BUNCH.
CHIEF COOK, MISS GROVINI-
BOTTLE WASHER, BRINGHAM
POT "WRASSLER," MISS BERG–
DOG WATCHER, MRS. LOGAN
"BAR" MAIDS, THE LARSON TWINS

SAN FRANCISCO Aug 18th 1908

To the Honorable
    Wm Rogers, Esq.
        our Esteemed Friend & Bro,

Dear Sir—

We feel it our duty to compliment you in behalf of the real "Stickers" of Considenced ▲ Irish ▲-Jew Circuit,[3] to think you as our President, has done such homage to our infant and growing organization.

You are truly worthy of being Captain of this your Show, ▲ first ▲ to think, that you were the only one to refuse your salary, being surrounded as you were by white rats of *professed high* standing, Why the two companies, one at the Wigwam and one at the National[4] could not fine [find] time to confer with the company at the "Louzy Bell" ringing in Oakland as to what they intended doing in regard to "cut day," shows but little brotherly love & Cooperation

No doubt you have learned [*word illegible*] this that the real show of this circuit there an awful *bum* is to the management and that measly cop who shoved our salary at us and we were much disgusted upon arriving at the wigwam to know the show here had accepted the salary "less the cut" and moreso upon learning your show accepted their salarys, except our President.

Please reply and advise what action you are to take.

yours Fraternally

Selbini, Grovini, Riva-Larsen Troupe,

Alex & Scott, Appollo Quartette,

Eckert & Berg & Bringham

ALS, rc. OkClaW. On handwritten letterhead, transcribed above.[5]

1. Laurie, *Vaudeville*, 402; Spitzer, *Palace*, 73–74; Snyder, "American Vaudeville— Theater in a Package," 36–37.
2. The bill advertised in the *San Francisco Chronicle* listed their acts: Selbini and Grovini (Novelty Juggling, Acrobats, etc.); Alexander and Scott ("Two Darkies from Virginia"); Eckert and Berg (High-class Singing Act); Riva-Larsen Troupe (Sensational Trapeze Artists); Apollo Quartet (Bostonian Singers); and Anna Brigham (Whistler) (*SFC*, 9 and 16 August 1908).
3. A reference to the Sullivan and Considine Circuit. Timothy Sullivan was Irish, and John Considine was Jewish.
4. On 9 August many of the same performers from the Wigwam were listed to appear at the National Theatre the week of 10 August. But on 11 August the National advertised Rogers and the acts that had been touring with him on the West Coast. Apparently, there was an earlier conflict between the National management and the Wigwam performers (*SFC*, 11 August).
5. The letter was sent special delivery from San Francisco and postmarked 18 August. It was addressed to "Will Rogers, c/o Bell Theatre, 'Palace of Varieties,' Oakland, Cal, U.S.A."

Biographical Appendix

Name Index

THE FOLLOWING INDIVIDUALS ARE PROFILED IN THE BIOGRAPHICAL APPENDIX.

Acton, Mildred Mulhall Carmichael (1895–1964?)
Albee, Edward Franklin (1857–1930)
Bent, Marion. See ROONEY, Pat, and Marion Bent.
Casey, Georgia Smith (Mulhall) (1872–1955)
Cummins, Frederick T. (1859–1932)
Davies, Reine (1886–1938)
Dresser, Louise (1878–1965)
Hackney, Mabel. See TOMPKINS, Charles and Mabel Hackney.
Hammerstein, William (1874–1914)
Harvey, Thomas W. (d. 1942)
Henry, Louise (ca. 1887–1941)
Houdini, Harry (1874–1926)
McKee, Buck (1871–1944)
McKee, Maud Florence. See McKEE, Buck.
McSpadden, Theodore Raymond (1887–1964)
Minnick, J. H. (Jim) (1881–1947)
Mix, Tom (1880–1940)
Morgan, Tom P. (1864–1928)
Morris, William (1873–1932)
Mulhall, Agnes (Bossie). See WOLFE, Agnes Mulhall.
Mulhall, Charley (1888–1958)
Mulhall, Georgia. See CASEY, Georgia Smith (Mulhall).
Mulhall, Mary Agnes Locke (1859–1931)
Mulhall, Mildred. See ACTON, Mildred Mulhall Carmichael.
Rooney, Pat (1880–1962), and Marion Bent (1879–1940)
Russell, Charles M. (1864–1926)
Shea, Maurice (Mort) A. (1880–1940)
The Three Keatons (Myra Cutler Keaton [1877–1955], Joseph Hollie Keaton
    [1867–1946], and Joseph Francis [Buster] Keaton [1895–1966])
Tompkins, Charles (ca. 1875–1957) and Mabel Hackney (d. 1950)

Williams, Egbert Austin (Bert) (1874–1922), and George Walker (ca. 1873–1911)

Wolfe, Agnes (Bossie) Mulhall (1877–1916)

Biographical Entries

The following alphabetical entries profile individuals mentioned in this volume who were of particular significance to Rogers's family or career. For brief biographies of other persons significant to Rogers's personal life or career who appear in the documents in this volume but are not part of this volume's appendix, see also the appendices in other volumes of The Papers of Will Rogers.

ACTON, Mildred Mulhall Carmichael (1895–1964?). The youngest of the Mulhall family's Wild West performers, Mildred (who was nicknamed Mecca by her father) Mulhall was ten years old when she appeared with Will Rogers in the Mulhall Wild West show at Madison Square Garden. She already knew Rogers well, for he had been a fixture in her family home in Mulhall, Okla., off and on for many years, coming to work at the ranch as a cowboy; to visit the family; to see her sister Lucille; or to train for the Mulhall family show.

The daughter of Zack Mulhall and his young mistress Georgia Smith (who went by the name of Georgia Mulhall), Mildred Mulhall was born in St. Louis. By arrangement within the Mulhall family she was given to Mary Agnes Locke Mulhall to raise soon after her birth, and she grew up believing that Zack Mulhall's wife was her mother. She did not learn the truth of her parentage until she was told by her older brother, Charley Mulhall, when she was sixteen years old (see also CASEY, Georgia Smith [Mulhall]; MULHALL, Charley; and MULHALL, Mary Agnes Locke).

Mildred Mulhall was a petite, pretty, and personable little girl. She dazzled audiences in New York with her ability to drive four-in-hand teams in fancy maneuvers. While she and other family members were performing at Madison Square Garden in 1905, she also gave horseback-riding lessons to society women in Central Park. Like her half-sisters, Lucille and Agnes (Bossie) Mulhall, she was educated part-time at St. Joseph's Convent School in Guthrie, Okla. Her father was arrested for "exhibiting a girl under 14 years of age" when he allowed nine-year-old Mildred to ride a mustang pony in the arena during a Mulhall show at the Delmar Race Track in St. Louis in August 1904 (*StLGD*, 16 August 1904).

Mildred began traveling with the family show in 1905, and when Lucille began a Wild West vaudeville act in 1907, Mildred and Charley joined her on the circuit. In the show Lucille did trick riding on her high-schooled horse, Governor; Charley rode a bucking horse; and Mildred did lariat throwing and trick riding. When Zack Mulhall revived the family Wild West show for a tour in 1910, Mildred was one of the headliners. The Mulhall siblings also appeared together in special rodeos, and horse and livestock shows.

When the Mulhall family show went to Key West, Fla., Mildred met Weller Carmichael, the handsome son of a well-to-do developer. She married Carmichael in 1913, when she was seventeen years old. The couple settled in Ocala, Fla., and they had two daughters, Virginia (Carmichael Pennington) and Martha (Carmichael Swanson Fisch). Will Rogers kept in touch with Mildred Mulhall Carmichael and often came by to visit the Carmichael family when engagements brought him to Florida.

Weller Carmichael was a charming and wealthy man but a philanderer, and Mildred's marriage to him was difficult. In 1931, when the couple's eldest daughter was about to be married, both Zack and Mary Agnes Locke Mulhall died within months of one another, leaving Mildred's half-sister Lucille alone at the family ranch. Mildred returned home to Mulhall, Okla., with her daughter Martha and took up residence with Lucille in the old family house. Charley also joined them. Mildred divorced her husband, and afterward married Owen Acton, a Guthrie oil-lease broker and rancher who was active in Republican Party politics and who had hired Charley to promote a rodeo at his ranch.

After Lucille's death in 1940 Mildred bought the old Mulhall ranch at a sheriff's sale, tore down the old house, and built a new home on the property. Mulhall family memorabilia, including correspondence and mementos from the performing days, were destroyed by a fire that consumed the coachhouse where they were stored. The ranch and farmland were sold in 1946. Mildred Acton taught riding lessons at the convent school she had attended as a girl. She was also very active in community and church affairs, including relief work and the planning of the Guthrie '89er celebrations (oral history interviws with Martha Fisch, WRPP; *Billboard,* 26 August 1911; "Convent Girl the Star of Wild West Show," interview with Mildred Mulhall, 15 May 1910, unidentified clipping, Mulhall scrapbook, MFC; Stansbury, *Lucille Mulhall,* 69, 91, 125, 129, 134–35, 177; see also Biographical Appendix entries for Lucille Mulhall and Zack Mulhall in *PWR,* 1:516–18, 518–21; see also entries for the other members of the Mulhall family in this appendix).

ALBEE, Edward Franklin (1857–1930). Born in Machias, Me., Edward Albee was the son of Amanda Crocker Albee and Nathaniel S. Albee, a prominent shipbuilder. When he was four, his parents moved to Boston, where he attended public schools until the age of twelve. After a series of odd jobs, Albee joined traveling circuses and was employed by P. T. Barnum's circus. At Barnum's he became an outside ticket seller and "fixer," a person known as a trouble-shooter and advance man.

In 1885 he was hired by B. F. Keith to help operate his Gaiety Theatre and Museum in Boston. Noticing that business was bad, Albee redecorated the venue in a Japanese motif and presented attractions, such as a performance of Gilbert and Sullivan's *Mikado* for a 10-cent admission, that drew more patrons. Impressed by Albee's efforts, Keith appointed him general manager of his vaudeville enterprise. In this position Albee played a leading role in the building and refurbishing of Keith theaters in Boston, New York, Philadelphia, and Providence, R.I. For his dedicated service, Keith gave Albee his Providence theater, where during the spring and summer he presented legitimate plays acted by his well-known stock company.

Albee was the driving force behind the power of the Keith Circuit, especially after Keith's semi-retirement in 1909. As general manager of the circuit and its booking agency, the United Booking Offices (UBO), he opposed independent agents and competitive theater owners, blacklisted performers who played in opposition circuits, cut salaries, and increased booking fees. To destroy the White Rats actors' union, he organized a company union in 1916, the National Vaudeville Artists, Inc. (NVA). Performers appearing in his theaters were required to join the NVA.

Albee admired Will Rogers for his generosity and character. Rogers's vaudeville act was just the type Albee liked—respectable, clean, and uplifting. Albee once regretted that he could not attend an Advertising Club luncheon honoring Rogers. He wrote a published letter on 1 December 1922 to the club's president that called Rogers "an entertainer of the rarest quality, a genius, and splendid acquisition to the theatrical profession" ("E. F. Albee Pays High Compliment to Will Rogers," clipping, scrapbook 15, OkClaW). In another letter to Rogers, Albee praised him for helping to raise money at a benefit for the NVA charity fund at five different New York theaters: "You and I who knew vaudeville in its early stages can visualize and appreciate what last night's celebration means to the vaudeville business. . . . You are a source of pride to the entire theatrical business, exalting yourself as you have by your intelligence and your God-given gift of humor bringing laughter as you do to the highest and lowest classes" (E. F. Albee to Will Rogers, 4 May 1925,

OkClaW). In 1927 Albee sent Rogers a telegram upon hearing that he had had a gallbladder operation: "DEAR WILL WE ARE ALL CHEERED BY BULLETINS PREDICTING EARLY RECOVERY IF GOOD WISHES AND PRAYERS OF YOUR LEGION OF FRIENDS AND ADMIRERS CAN BE OF ANY HELP" (telegram, E. F. Albee to Will Rogers, 18 June 1927, OkClaW).

When Andrew Paul Keith, B. F. Keith's son, died in 1918, Albee assumed sole control of the circuit. In 1919 the UBO was reorganized as the B. F. Keith Vaudeville Exchange. During the 1920s Albee extended the Keith-Albee Circuit to include over 300 theaters. The new theaters in the chain offered a mixed bill of vaudeville and photoplays or showed films exclusively. In 1927 Albee merged his holdings with the Orpheum Circuit to form the Keith-Albee-Orpheum Corporation (KAO). Threatened by a corporate takeover, Albee was forced in October 1928 to sell a large share of KAO stock to RCA in a $300 million deal that involved banking firms and Joseph P. Kennedy (father of John F. Kennedy). With Kennedy as the newly appointed chairman of the KAO board, Albee soon lost control, and the Keith-Albee-Orpheum Corporation became Radio-Keith-Orpheum (RKO). Albee retired to Palm Beach, Fla., where he died following a heart attack on 11 March 1930.

Known as the "Viceroy of Vaudeville," Albee left a mixed legacy (*NYDM*, 13 August 1913). He built lavish theaters for the public that made them vicariously feel like royalty. He brought entertainment to the masses through a circuit and its hundreds of theaters. On the other hand many thought him selfish and ruthless. Albee's obituary in *Variety* read: "He was like a bulldog in his advancement. Nothing would stop him and he stopped at nothing" (*VO*, 2:19 March 1930; see also "B. F. Keith's Memorial Theatre," 6–7; Connors, "American Vaudeville Managers," 28–33; Copley, "Story of a Great Vaudeville Manager"; *DAB*, 11, supp. 2:17–18; Eaton, "Wizards of Vaudeville"; *EV*, 5–7; Gilbert, *American Vaudeville*, 197–207; "Heyday of Summer Theater," *Providence Sunday Journal, Sunday Journal Magazine*, 10 April 1983; Jewell, "History of RKO Radio Pictures, Incorporated," 17–33; King, "Keith-Albee et al."; Lasky, *RKO*, 22–29; Laurie, *Vaudeville*, 342–47; *NYT*, 12 March 1930, 32; *Variety*, 10 July 1909).

BENT, Marion. See ROONEY, Pat, and Marion Bent.

CASEY, Georgia Smith (Mulhall) (1872–1955). Georgia Smith was a thirteen-year-old waitress in a roadside boardinghouse frequented by railroad men in Parsons, Kans., when she met Zack Mulhall, a married man with a family who was a livestock agent for the railroad. Mulhall brought the buxom, dark-eyed teenage girl home with him to the Mulhall ranch in Mulhall, Okla., allegedly as a kind of adopted daughter. It soon became apparent to Mulhall's wife that her husband was sexually involved with the young woman. Mary Agnes Locke Mulhall privately confronted her husband about his relationship with the girl, and as a result Georgia Smith, then known as Georgia Mulhall and accepted by the younger Mulhall children as their sister, was ostracized from the family ranch. Zack Mulhall established a separate household for her on Washington Avenue in St. Louis, and for many years he lived a double life, one in Oklahoma with his wife and the other in Missouri with his mistress. Mulhall introduced neighbors in St. Louis to Georgia Mulhall as his wife. Georgia Mulhall and Agnes (Bossie) Mulhall (Zack and Mary Agnes Locke Mulhall's eldest daughter) were close friends, and Bossie spent much of her time as a young woman living at the Mulhall apartment in St. Louis (see WOLFE, Agnes [Bossie] Mulhall).

Meanwhile, Georgia Mulhall was publicly advertised in promotional literature for the Mulhall Wild West show as being Mulhall's daughter, and sister to Bossie, Lucille, Charley, and Mildred. This advertised family reinvented more than just Georgia and Zack Mulhall's relationship. Unknown to everyone but Georgia, Zack, and Mary Agnes Locke Mulhall, Charley and Mildred were actually Georgia's illegitimate children fathered by Zack, and not her siblings (see ACTON, Mildred Mulhall Carmichael, and MULHALL, Charley). It is possible that Zack and Georgia Mulhall also had other children who were raised by foster families.

Georgia Mulhall traveled with the family show for many years. Although she did not ride particularly well, her dark good looks were featured prominently in photographs advertising the show. She participated in the opening ceremonies and lent her beauty to dramatic skits and such acts as the stagecoach robbery, wherein she appeared as a passenger. Her generosity and gregariousness made her a favorite of journalists seeking interviews about the show. She continued to tour with the family when Lucille began her vaudeville act, Lucille Mulhall and Her Ranch Boys, appearing in the publicity for the act but not on stage.

Georgia Mulhall tried repeatedly to break away from Zack Mulhall's influence and establish a separate life for herself. At one time she became engaged to marry another man, but he died suddenly and shockingly after eating the dinner prepared for the wedding party the night before the ceremony. No one else at the table became ill. Zack Mulhall was known to be furious about the impending marriage, and the circumstances of the young man's sudden death were therefore questionable. Many believed that Mulhall had poisoned the man, but no autopsy was done and no proof of the cause of death exists. In 1917 Georgia tried again, this time marrying a young man from Ireland named Casey, who had courted her for some time. This effort, too, turned to tragedy, for she soon discovered (upon intercepting a telegram from Casey's daughter entreating Casey to come home because his wife was critically ill) that her husband, unknown to her, had another wife and family back home in Ireland. The marriage was annulled, but Georgia kept the name of Casey and remained living in Parsons, Kans. Little is known of her life and associations there.

In later years Georgia Casey was severely impoverished. After breaking off with Zack Mulhall in mid-life, she worked at a series of temporary jobs, including one as a child-care provider for a family in Augusta, Ga. As an elderly woman she was reunited with the Mulhalls when her granddaughter, Mildred's daughter Martha Fisch, learned the truth about her, sought her out, and invited her to come live close to her family in Guthrie, Okla. Georgia Casey and her granddaughter shared a strong Catholic faith, and they grew close in Georgia's final years. Martha Fisch continued to care for Georgia until the older woman's death from cancer.

Despite her lack of means and transitory residences, Georgia Casey had carefully maintained through the years a large scrapbook of clippings about the heyday of the Mulhall Rough Riders Congress in 1904–5 and several hundred photographs of the family and the show over more than a decade, including pictures of its appearances in New England and Florida in 1910. These she left for safekeeping with Martha Fisch, who has made them available to historians (oral history interviews with Martha Fisch, WRPP; *Billboard,* 26 August 1911; Mulhall scrapbook, MFC; Stansbury, *Lucille Mulhall,* 22, 51–52, 89–90).

CUMMINS, Frederick T. (1859–1932). Western adventurer turned Wild West show promoter, Frederick T. (Fred, or Colonel) Cummins employed Will Rogers in his Wild West Indian Congress show at the 1904 Louisiana Purchase Exposition in St. Louis.

Cummins's Scotch Irish parents operated a trading post and general store in Council Bluffs, Ia., when he was born. They had been slaveholding farmers in Tennessee, but sold their property at the beginning of the California Gold Rush in 1849 to go west to the gold fields. They traveled as far as St. Louis, where Hiram Cummins was enticed to change plans and spend the winter trapping in the Yellowstone area rather than seeking gold. His wife remained behind in St. Louis. After a successful season, he began a trading post on the

Big Cheyenne River and in 1857 relocated with his wife to Council Bluffs, Ia., an outfitting point for emigrants to California and a major trading point on the Missouri River.

Fred Cummins grew up in daily contact with the Indians who traded at his parents' business—primarily Omahas, Pawnees, Winnebagos, and Sioux. Informally adopted by many of them, he learned several Indian languages as well as hunting skills. At the age of eleven he participated in an initiation rite as a buffalo hunter, accompanying Yellow Smoke, a friend of his father's, on a large hunt in southwestern Nebraska. In a pattern similar to Will Rogers's own youthful experience, combining boarding school with summers on the home ranch, Cummins as a teenager was sent away to school but spent summers on the prairies with Indian friends. As a young adult he briefly participated in his father's business, joining Hiram Cummins in supplying goods by wagon to miners and settlers who swarmed to the gold fields in the Black Hills in 1876. Like Rogers, who was frustrated following in his father's footsteps with the family farm and who left to travel abroad, Cummins in 1877 set out on his own, with some financial help from his father, to travel around the West. He lived in Helena, Mont., for a year and went prospecting in the mountains, returning to Council Bluffs in 1883. He worked convoying stock for the Wadsworth Brothers ranch on the Little Missouri River in Montana and also took a job breaking horses at Beaver Creek. During this period he visited various Indian agencies, including Standing Rock and Pine Ridge, and meeting with Sitting Bull and Red Cloud, Chief Gall, and others. He was formally adopted by Red Cloud, leader of the Oglala Sioux, who gave him the name La-ko-ta in a traditional ceremony.

Cummins's career as a promoter began when he took the title of Colonel and headed the Great Indian Congress at the Trans-Mississippi Exposition in Omaha, Neb., in 1898. Drawing on his network of personal acquaintances and friends of his father, he brought representatives of thirty-one tribes to the exposition, which continued in 1899 under a new name, the Greater American Exposition. His aims at the beginning of his show career were primarily ethnological. As a contemporary observer put it, "the Indian Congress . . . is intended to be a representation of Indian life in all its phases. Indians from every considerable tribe in the United States will be present. They will live precisely as at home on the plains, so far as their domestic life, industries and sports are concerned. . . . their tepees, wickiups and wigwams are scattered in tribal settlements among the cornfields. . . . Dances, religious rites, sports and industries will all be represented. It is not a Wild West show, but a serious ethnological exhibition" (Thanet, "Trans-Mississippi Exposition,"

612). Over time his show began to resemble more and more the model of the Wild West show that had been set by William F. Cody (Buffalo Bill), incorporating elements of the rodeo and the circus, and in its last years it had a Far East element similar to that adopted by the combined Buffalo Bill and Pawnee Bill shows.

The Congress toured New England in 1901 and 1902 and appeared, with Chief Joseph of the Nez Perce, in 1903 at Madison Square Garden, New York City. David Rowland Francis, the president of the Louisiana Purchase Exposition Co., saw the Cummins show at the Pan-American Exposition and invited Cummins to appear at the St. Louis World's Fair. Cummins spent eight months after the Madison Square Garden appearance traveling around midwestern, western, and southwestern states recruiting Indian leaders to come to St. Louis. When the Cummins North American Indian show opened at the Fair, it featured representatives of fifty-one tribes and headlined Geronimo and Chief Joseph, who were both veterans of earlier Cummins shows.

At the St. Louis World's Fair the name of the show was expanded variously to Cummins' Wild West Congress of North American Indians, or Cummins' Spectacular Indian Congress and Life on the Plains, or Wild West Indian Congress and Rough Riders of the World. Cummins served as grand marshal of the huge parade of thousands of performers from all the Pike shows and concessions that heralded the opening day of the Fair. In his shows the Indians, who had been the center of previous shows, were joined by Rough Riders and a roping contingent of cowboys, including Will Rogers. At the beginning of the Fair these new elements were directed by Zack Mulhall, a promoter of roping contests and family Wild West shows. Rifle sharpshooter Nellie Smith and fancy riders Agnes (Bossie) Mulhall and Lucille Mulhall were among the headliners of the cowboy and cowgirl section of the show, as were George Esler (veteran of the Pawnee Bill Wild West show) and Will Rogers's old roping contest buddy Jim Hopkins, who was a Mulhall family friend. Lucille Mulhall was billed as the "Champion Lady Roper of the World" (*WFB* 5, no. 6 [April 1904]: 63). The international and mixed-gender nature of the show was emphasized in its advertising, which announced 850 "Indians, Mexicans, Russians, Cowboys, Japanese, Lady Rifle, Roping and Riding Experts" and promised a "Grand Sham Battle Each Performance" (*StLGD*, 31 July and 16 July 1904). The Custer Massacre show was presented on the Pike "every day and four times daily" by the Cummins company beginning in September 1904, with regular shows at 3 P.M., 5 P.M., 8 P.M., and 10 P.M. (*StLGD*, 2 September and 14 September 1904).

Despite the huge audiences at the Fair and the show's high profile on the Pike, Cummins was plagued by problems: Zack Mulhall was forced to leave the management of the cowboy segment of the show, the Humane Society protested the roping of steers (this led to Cummins's arrest on alleged charges of cruelty to animals), and Cummins found it difficult to meet the payroll for the show's many performers and personnel. A testimonial benefit was held for him "by His Friends, The Pike Showmen," on Sunday, 7 August 1904, with the proceeds of two afternoon and evening shows featuring a conglomeration of the acts from the Pike going to Cummins (*StLR*, 7 August 1904). Despite these efforts on the part of his colleagues, Cummins was forced into receivership by the early fall of 1904. He put the entire show and all its equipment up for sale in September 1904 under Circuit Court order, and also offered to lease out the amphitheater and concession to the close of the Exposition. He ended up entering into a business collaboration with promoters and silent partners Walter L. Main and George C. Satterly. After the Fair closed, they added more melodramatic elements to the Wild West show and also wild animal acts associated with circus entertainment (such as had been seen in Hagenbeck's wild animal exhibit at the St. Louis Fair). Calamity Jane lent celebrity to the new show, and Tom Mix rode in it as a cowboy. Cummins wired Will Rogers at the Putnam House in New York with an offer to join the show at a rate of $25 a week. The telegram stated that a previous message had gone unanswered, and Rogers continued building his career on vaudeville rather than returning to the Wild West business.

The Cummins show traveled cross-country in 1905–6 in a special train with cars outfitted for the promoters, horses and circus animals (including one elephant car), and "four wild west and Indian cars" for the entertainers ("Cummins' Real Wild West Show"). The show did full tours in the United States in 1905 and 1906. After some financial setbacks and an unhappy dissolution of the business partnership with Main, the show traveled in Europe (England, Ireland, Wales, Scotland, Belgium, Germany, Switzerland, France, and Italy) from 1907 through 1911. In England in 1908 the Cummins company appeared with John Calvin Brown's sponsorship in Brighton, Queenstown, Liverpool, and Manchester, billed as the Cummins-Brown Wild West. A Cummins-Brown Wild West amusement park venture in Rome went bankrupt shortly after Cummins sold his interest in it in July 1911.

Upon his return to the United States in 1911, Cummins was as always operating on the edge of financial difficulty. He announced his intention to carry on the show "bigger, better and grander than ever" (*Billboard*, 23 September 1911). He set up offices in the Union Trust Building in Jersey City,

N.J., that were filled with Wild West memorabilia and the photographs of Wild West stars who had begun their careers with his Indian Congress. He met with Pawnee Bill (Gordon W. Lillie; see *PWR*, 1:502–3) to purchase outfitted railroad cars to use for a U.S. tent-show tour and signed Australian whip artists and riders Bill and Marion Waite for the 1912–13 season. Despite his hopes for autonomy, he soon consolidated his show with one owned by Vernon C. Seavers. Seavers was the owner of theaters and an amusement park in Peoria, Ill. He also owned the Young Buffalo Wild West show (previously the Lone Bill Wild West show), which had toured in 1908 and 1909. The Young Buffalo Wild West and Colonel Cummins' Far East show merged with a Circus Emporium and toured for three seasons with Annie Oakley, the famed sharpshooter from earlier Buffalo Bill Wild West shows, as its headliner. Seavers was the show's president and general manager, and Cummins was its director general. Like Cummins's earlier enterprises, this show featured speed contests, stagecoach holdups, exhibitions of fancy riding and high-schooled horses, military drills, trick riding, Indian rituals, Rough Riders, and "a group of wild west girls" (*Billboard*, 3 May 1913). The show was sold at the end of the 1913 season, but Cummins still appeared at the head of the grand entry ceremonies as Chief La-ko-ta, alongside Joe Smith as Young Buffalo, on opening day of the Young Buffalo Shows and Cheyenne Days in Peoria, Ill., in April 1914. In May 1914 Cummins filed for bankruptcy in Queens County, N.Y. In the court action he was freed of $28,102 in debts to creditors by the bankruptcy referee. The *New York Times*, in reporting the ruling, described Cummins as "for years advance agent for Barnum & Bailey's circus" (2 May 1914).

Cummins promoted Wild West vaudeville acts in 1914. He had four acts appearing on the Marcus Loew theater circuit. Fred Gerner and Co. was an animal act that featured two horses, two deer, a monkey, and two women riders, along with Fred Gerner. Cummins also managed Waite's Australian Whip Crackers with the stars from his 1912–13 Cummins–Young Buffalo season, and an act with sharpshooters Billy and Bonita Lee. He starred himself in a patriotic-themed show called The Spirit of '76.

Like Will Rogers's close friend Zack Mulhall, Frederick Cummins was a friendly acquaintance of Theodore Roosevelt and part of the circle of influential men who supported preservation causes and the promotion of the mystique of manliness that infused the popular culture of the West in the early twentieth century. Cummins married Mildred Louise, and the pair made their home in Venice, Calif. Mildred Cummins died there on 3 April 1919. Cummins remained living in the Los Angeles area, and in the 1920s he invested in southern California oil operations. He died on 31 January 1932 at West

End Hospital in Chicago. Still active in show business at the age of seventy-three, at the time of his final illness Cummins was planning to present his Indian Congress and "Massacre of Fort Dearborn" (a regular feature of the Young Buffalo Show years) at the Century of Progress Exposition of 1933 (Cummins' North American Indian Congress program, St. Louis World's Fair, 1904, and related materials, scrapbook A-1, OkClaW; Cummins Wild West to Rogers, ca. 1905, Western Union telegram, OkClaW; "Cummins' Real Wild West Show"; *Billboard*, 29 February, 18 April, 30 May, and 3 October 1908, 9 September, 23 September, 21 October, 16 December, and 23 December 1911, 3 February, 2 March, and 18 May 1912, 3 May 1913, 10 January and 2 May 1914, 20 January 1923, 6 February 1932; Bennitt et al., eds. *History of the Louisiana Purchase Exposition*, 716; Conover, "Sells Brothers Bandchariot," 15; Cooke, "Walter F. Main"; Hill, *Great White Indian Chief; NYT,* 2 May 1914; newspaper advertisement file, St. Louis and the St. Louis World's Fair, 1903, 1904, WBaraC; *New York Clipper*, 3 March, 9 March, and 4 May 1912; Russell, "Golden Age of Wild West Shows"; Russell, *Lives and Legends of Buffalo Bill*, 383–85; Russell, *Wild West: A History of the Wild West Shows*, 64–65, 67–69, 80, 85, 100, 105, 123, 127, 129, 131; *StLGD*, 17 July, 15 August, 14 September, 23 September 1904; Rydell, *All the World's a Fair*, 179; Thanet, "Trans-Mississippi Exposition"; *WFB* 5, no. 6 [April 1904]: 48, and photographs, 51, 63, 72).

DAVIES, Reine (1886–1938). Reine Davies is perhaps best remembered today as the sister of Marion Davies, longtime mistress of William Randolph Hearst. But Reine Davies also had a long career on the stage, and beginning in 1933, she wrote the gossip column "Hollywood Parade" for Hearst's *Los Angeles Examiner.*

Reine Davies, born Irene Douras, was the daughter of Judge Bernard Douras of New York. She was the eldest of four sisters, all of whom went on the stage. She took the stage name Davies, which her other sisters adopted, from a sign on a real estate office operated by a J. Clarence Davies in Long Island. Throughout their lives the family remained close.

During her stage career Reine, a brunette with delicate features, was a headliner on the Keith and Orpheum circuits, and starred in the musical comedy *The Girl Rangers* (1907). Her sister Ethel was among the supporting players, as was Will Rogers. During the week of 25 January 1914 Rogers played the part of a cowboy riding a horse in a motion picture featuring Davies. It was filmed at Rye, N.Y. At the time Rogers was performing at three New York vaudeville houses (see Review and Listings from Three Theater Engagements, ca. 25 January 1914, *PWR*, vol. 3). The *New York Star* reported: "If the reader is around Rye, New York, any of these mornings and sees a cowboy riding along wildly and saving a pretty maiden from an attack by Indians, there is no need for alarm" ("Rogers and Reine Reeling in Rye," clipping, scrapbook A-3, OkClaW). As far as can be ascertained, this was probably Rogers's first movie part.

Reine was also a singer. She appeared in *The Southerners,* a 1904 musical composed by the prominent African American composer Will Marion Cook (1869–1944), and received good reviews in the musical farce *The Blonde in Black* (1903) with Blanche Ring. In 1910 Davies did a single vaudeville act as a singer; she was best known for Will Rossiter's song "Meet Me To-Night in Dreamland," which she sang accompanied by electric bells. She was still in vaudeville in 1913, doing a musical sketch called *Un Peu d'Amour.* In February 1917 Davies performed in the musical farce *Canary Cottage* at New York's Morosco Theatre.

In 1907 Davies married George W. Lederer (1861–1938), a well-known theatrical manager and producer. They had two children: a daughter, Pepi Lederer, who died in 1935, and a son, Charles Lederer, who became the favorite nephew of Marion Davies. Reine gave up her theatrical career to raise her children.

During World War I Reine Davies trained either as an ambulance driver or as a nurse (reports vary), but was unable to serve overseas due to an accident. She was an accomplished horsewoman throughout her life. In 1915 she was thrown by a horse while performing in the silent movie *Sunday;* she suffered internal injuries and two broken ribs in the accident. In the summer of 1922 Davies rented a country bungalow in Freeport, Long Island, an actors' and artists' colony. Here, in June 1922, during a party that Reine threw to honor her sister Marion, Oscar Hirsch, an electrical contractor, was shot; his wife was accused of the crime. In early July Reine Davies sued *Billboard* for $250,000, claiming that the theatrical publication had misrepresented the story. Earlier that year she had been injured in a car accident while riding in an automobile driven by Sime Silverman, the founder of *Variety.* She sued Silverman and the Briarcliffe Lodge Association, the owner of the other car, for $500,000; she was awarded $12,500.

Davies next went to Hollywood, where she became an agent for screenwriters. On 28 August 1933 she joined the *Los Angeles Examiner* and began writing her show-business gossip column, "Hollywood Parade," considered to be among the first of its type.

Davies died unexpectedly in Los Angeles while apparently recovering from spinal meningitis, contracted only two weeks before in Coronado, Calif. William Randolph Hearst and his son George were honorary pallbearers at her funeral at St. Augustine's Church, opposite the Metro studios in Culver City (Mantle and Sherwood, eds., *Best Plays of 1909–1919*, 594; Davies, *Times We Had*, 4–5; Guiles, *Marion Davies*, 22–26, 72–73, 78–79, 108–10, 303; *Los Angeles Examiner*, 3 April 1938; *NYT*, 9 June 1903, 24 May 1904, 26 May 1913, 21 January 1922, 26 June 1922, 6 July 1922; *New York Clipper*, 18 June 1910; *New York Dramatic Mirror*, 19 March 1910, 17 December 1913; *New York Morning Telegraph*, 9 March 1910; *OCAT*, 422; *VO*, 2:6 April 1938).

DRESSER, Louise (1878–1965). Louise Dresser was born Louise Josephine Kerlin in Evansville, Ind., on 5 October 1882. A talented stage and screen actress, she played in five sound films with Will Rogers. Her father, William Kerlin, was a locomotive engineer on a local railway, where he met and befriended young Paul Dresser (1857–1906), who was a songwriter and a brother of novelist Theodore Dreiser. In 1900, some time after Kerlin was killed in a train wreck, eighteen-year-old Louise Kerlin went to Dresser, now established as a songwriter, in hopes that he could help her to launch a stage career. When Dresser learned that she was William Kerlin's daughter, he immediately launched her professionally as "his kid sister," and she adopted his last name as her stage name. She became known for singing two of Paul Dresser's best known songs: "On the Banks of the Wabash" (1899) and "My Gal Sal" (1905), which he wrote especially for her. When Dresser died several years later, the obituary listed her as one of his surviving relatives, and Theodore Dreiser demanded that the newspaper publish a retraction. Louise Dresser was well established by this time, and her career was not affected by the revelation.

After a stint in burlesque and as a singer at a Boston dime museum, Dresser made her vaudeville debut in 1900. She formed a vaudeville team called Louise Dresser and Her Picks, a singing act backed by a chorus of African American children. She was one of several women vaudeville performers who used such a chorus to give their act more variety and a guaranteed high-energy finish. She began to play New York vaudeville stages in 1906. That year she was in the hit musical revue *About Town* with Lew Fields at the Herald Square Theater. At one point in her performances on the Keith Circuit, she was accompanied by a young pianist, George Gershwin, as yet an unknown. Dresser found vaudeville the "hardest branch of the theatrical profession" because the performer "must 'make good' with a vaudeville audience in fifteen or twenty minutes" (*Variety*, 14 December 1907). As her vaudeville career developed, she began to appear in playlets, earning $1,750 a week. She also performed frequently on the legitimate stage, and starred on Broadway for nine years in *A Matinee Idol* (1910), *Broadway to Paris* (1912), *Potash and Perlmutter* (1913), and *Hello Broadway!* (1914, in which she played Patsy Pygmalion).

Dresser was very popular with other players on the theatrical stage, among them Lillian Russell and Pauline Frederick, who urged her to enter silent pictures in 1922. Initially, she had trouble adapting her stage techniques to the screen and was not assigned the starring roles she was accustomed to on Broadway. An opportunity to advance her career came when she was given the title role in *The Goose Woman* (1925). She played Ma Quail in *Mother Knows Best* (1928) and was nominated for an Oscar as best actress. Her character roles of strong middle-aged women were traditionally the type of persona represented by male actors and contrasted sharply with the romantic parts played by many actresses. In this regard, Dresser broadened women's character roles in films.

Dresser's association with Will Rogers dated to their vaudeville years. Rogers was on the same program with her during the week of 24 June 1907 at Philadelphia's Chestnut Street Opera House. A few weeks later, beginning 8 July 1907, they were on the playbill at Pittsburgh's Nixon Theatre. She recalled: "I followed him on the bill, and as I stood in the wings waiting to go on stage, from behind me came the raucous voice, none too suppressed, of the house manager: 'What the so-and-so kind of an act is this the New York office has wished on me?' The gentleman was displeased with Will at the start of his act, but when the audience caught the humor of the man and the act finished with them clamoring for more, we all realized a new star had dawned" (Dresser, "My Friend, Will Rogers," 40).

Dresser's five most memorable sound films were with Will Rogers: *Lightnin'* (1930), *Doctor Bull* (1933), *State Fair* (1933), *David Harum* (1934), and *The County Chairman* (1935). "Since we have both been before the camera, I have played in a number of pictures with him," she wrote. "I have been cast as his sister, his wife, his friend—almost every feminine role; and if the man continues to grow younger instead of older, it is possible I may wake up some day to find myself playing his mother (Dresser, "My Friend, Will Rogers," 72).

In *Lightnin'*, Dresser played Rogers's wife, a woman who worked hard to support her prevaricating, but lovable, husband. In *State Fair*, she played Rogers's wife again, as the farm woman whose champion pickles and mincemeat, once spiked with brandy by her concerned husband, win first prizes at the fair. In *Doctor Bull* Dresser portrayed the wealthy town snob who led an unsuccessful campaign to have Rogers, as Doctor Bull, fired as the town's doctor. Appearing again as Rogers's wife, Dresser played Polly Harum to Rogers's David in the film adaptation of the best-selling novel *David Harum*. In her last film with Rogers, *The County Chairman*, Dresser played the wife of Elias Rigby, political opponent of Jim Hackler (played by Rogers), who many years ago stole Hackler's girlfriend and married her.

In June 1934 Louise Dresser wrote an article for *Screen Book* in which she described the warmth and generosity of Rogers, who had become her good friend. She credited his wife Betty for urging him to make fun of current events and famous personalities along with his rope act on the stage. She wrote: "I only wish it was so that all new-comers to the screen could play their first pictures with Will Rogers, for with him to help them that camera panic from which we have all suffered would be as nothing at all. Kindness and consideration for his cast, for everyone connected with the picture, is a creed with him." Dresser also believed that Rogers's popularity on the screen was due to his appeal to women. "Not that he is any Romeo, but friend Will has more sex appeal than Clark Gable," she wrote (Dresser, "My Friend, Will Rogers," 72). She recalled the time when a cast picture was being taken for a film, and Rogers insisted that the entire cast be included in the photograph, both bit players and stars.

Dresser retired in 1937, after which she volunteered at the Hollywood Motion Picture County House and Hospital. Her retirement resulted from her inability to get new screen roles, which she blamed on rumors that she was deaf.

Dresser was married twice, first to the vaudevillian Jack Norworth, from 1906 to 1908. After their divorce, in 1909 Dresser married Jack Gardner (d. 1950), a singer, Hollywood agent, and casting director. For a time they performed a vaudeville act together. Dresser related how she was warned against marrying Gardner by many of her fellow actresses at a luncheon: they felt that Gardner was too much the ladies' man. Dresser informed them that the warning had come too late, as they were already intending to marry. That afternoon she told Gardner what she had said, whereupon he agreed to marry her.

Dresser spent her last years living alone in a Glendale, Calif., apartment. She died on 24 April 1965 at the Motion Picture Hospital in Woodland Hills, Calif., of an intestinal obstruction, at the age of eighty-six. By the time of her death she had lost most of her fortune in a venture to establish a racing stable. Still, she had kept enough funds to live comfortably in her last years (Dresser, "My Friend, Will Rogers," 40, 72; *FV* 28, 141–43; *FilmEnc*, 389;

LAHE, 25 April 1965; *LAT,* 2 March 1959; Laurie, *Vaudeville,* 56; Louise Dresser Biography file, CLAc; *NYT,* 23 April 1965; Patterson, "I Am Thirty-six and Proud of It," 161–68; Samuels and Samuels, *Once upon a Stage,* 110; Sterling and Sterling, eds., *Will Rogers in Hollywood,* 109, 125, 131, 136, 153; *WhoHol,* 452; *WhScrn,* 1:202; *WhThe,* 2:701).

HACKNEY, Mabel. See TOMPKINS, Charles and Mabel Hackney.

HAMMERSTEIN, William (1874–1914). Willie Hammerstein, as he was best known, was the second oldest son of Oscar Hammerstein. He started in show business as an advance agent for Davis and Keogh melodrama and as a manager of burlesque shows. For a time he owned and managed a vaudeville and amusement resort on 110th Street in New York, called Little Coney Island. He also assisted his father in operating the Olympia Theatre from 1895 to 1898. As business manager of the Victoria Theatre, he turned the theater into a leading vaudeville house by using all types of publicity stunts to publicize the performers. His office in the lobby became an inner circle of vaudevillians, publicists, agents, bookers, and gamblers. Besides engaging novelties and oddities for the Victoria Theatre and its Paradise Roof Garden, he booked vaudeville stars from Europe and America.

In June 1905 he gave Rogers, then a vaudeville novice, an opportunity to perform at the Paradise Roof Garden. This was Rogers's second week in vaudeville. From that time on, he became one of Hammerstein's favorites and performed at the Victoria Theatre numerous times. Indeed, Rogers was on its closing program the week of 26 April 1915, which featured all of Willie Hammerstein's choice acts. Years later in his weekly article Rogers recalled the Victoria: "But it was at the Theatre where they sent me the second week where I made my best hit and stayed at it all summer. That was at the greatest Vaudeville theatre of that and all time. That was Hammerstein's. . . . We have never produced another showman like Willie Hammerstein" (*TDW,* 23 September 1928).

In 1911 Hammerstein resigned from the Victoria over an argument with his father, but he was brought back a few months later when the theater started to lose money. Hammerstein died in 1914 in a sanitarium, where he was being treated for Bright's disease. He was eulogized in *Variety* as a brilliant showman who made the Victoria Theatre into a renowned showplace. Hammerstein was well liked by performers, and many, like Rogers, owed their success to him. His son, the famous lyricist Oscar Hammerstein II (1895–1960), continued the family tradition in the American theater (*EV,* 227–28;

Laurie, *Vaudeville,* 385–95; *NYT,* 11 June 1914; *Variety,* 25 December 1914; *VO,* 1:12 June 1914).

HARVEY, Thomas W. (d. 1942). Thomas (Tom) Harvey was the son of Anna R. Halliday and William Hope (Coin) Harvey (1851–1936). His father was a vocal advocate of the free silver movement and a leading populist in the 1890s. A lawyer, rancher, and former prospector, Coin Harvey was the author of the popular and influential pamphlet *Coin's Financial School* (1894), which sold hundreds of thousands of copies (the pamphlet's central character was Coin, who conducted a series of classes on the benefits of free silver). The treatise argued for monetary inflation through increased coinage of silver. Free silver was Harvey's panacea for the economic problems of 1893, and it was adopted by the Populist Party. In 1900 Coin Harvey moved to Silver Springs, Ark., where Betty Blake was born. A visionary, Harvey turned his large property there into a pleasure and health resort named Monte Ne. The resort featured hotels, an indoor swimming pool, auditorium, casino, dance pavilion, and a lagoon where tourists could ride in a gondola imported from Venice. Its most notable attraction was the Pyramid, constructed in the early 1920s, but never finished. The structure was intended to house books and inventions for future generations—providing a permanent place for what Harvey called the relics of a dying civilization.

As a child, Coin Harvey's son Tom probably suffered from infantile paralysis; he walked with a limp. The Blake family spent the summers in the early 1900s at Monte Ne, five miles from their home in Rogers, Ark. Betty Rogers supposedly met Tom Harvey at a grand ball to celebrate the opening of the Monte Ne Hotel on 4 May 1901. He began to court Betty Blake, and his brother Robert dated Betty's sister Zuleki. The relationship between Harvey and Betty Blake was a point of contention between her and Will Rogers. Rogers's letters to Betty Blake between 1906 and 1908 convey a tone of jealousy. Rogers complains about her dating Harvey. He uses her relationship with Harvey to defend his right to see other women. As it turned out, however, Betty Blake's relationship with Harvey was nothing more than an extended summer romance.

An enterprising young man, Tom Harvey helped erect the theater building at Monte Ne in July 1901. For a time he and his brother lived in a one-story log building at Monte Ne, until it burned down. Harvey reportedly entered the burning house in a vain attempt to save his dog. In 1904 he owned and edited the *Monte Ne Herald* with Tony LeBlanc, a railroad purchasing agent. That same year Harvey was a superintendent of the Monte Ne Railway and a stockholder and charter member of the Club House and Cottage Co. In 1907 he was given the railway by his uncle, Thomas Harvey. Tom Harvey acted as railroad engineer, fireman, brakeman, and conductor.

Tom Harvey eventually became a lawyer and moved to Huntington, W. Va., to be near his mother, who was separated from his father. He practiced law in the town for most of his life. Harvey married Helen Brandebury, and they had three children, Helen, Thomas, Jr., and Ida.

Despite his role in the Rogers-Blake courtship, Harvey remained a friend of the Rogerses after their marriage. He and his wife attended the opening night of the *Ziegfeld Follies* of 1916 as the Rogerses' guests. In May 1926 Rogers visited Harvey in Huntington, where over dinner they talked about old times. Little is known about Harvey's life in the 1920s and 1930s. In March 1942 he committed suicide in Huntington, W. Va. (Faulkner, *Politics, Reform, Expansion,* 187–89; Tom Harvey file, RHM; Riley, *Coin Harvey and Monte Ne;* Rogers, *Will Rogers,* 131; Snelling, "One of the Blake Girls," 89; Yagoda, *Will Rogers,* 80–81, 111, 112, 113n, 118, 146, 223).

HENRY, Louise (ca. 1887–1941). The actress Louise Henry was a close friend of Will Rogers during his early vaudeville years. Born in Winchester, Va., she was the daughter of George Robert Henry, a newspaper publisher who founded the first newspaper in the Shenandoah Valley. Press releases state that Louise Henry's mother was related to General Robert E. Lee. Her parents had a large fruit farm in Virginia, and Louise attended school at the Shenandoah Valley Female Seminary.

Louise Henry's father was a close friend of John Robinson, who operated a circus. He permitted his daughter, then about fourteen, to join Robinson's family and travel with the circus. She became an equestrian with the circus, riding bareback. "I was always fond of horses and the splendid animals in the show fascinated me," she once said. "That's the way I started. . . . There is nothing like it [riding] to give a person grace, perfect poise, and complete mastery of the body" ("Picture Louise Henry Dangling from Rope in a Circus Tent," clipping, LHS-LHP). After leaving the circus, she became a stock performer with the Real Widow Brown Co., which toured the South, and later with the Baldwin-Melville Stock Co. in New Orleans. As an actress in these repertory companies, she gained experience in plays that ranged from the drama *Zaza* to *Uncle Tom's Cabin.* She next spent a season as a leading lady to the actor Louis James (1842–1910), who had his own road company. Later, she was associated with the productions of Charles Edward Blaney, who wrote many melodramas and farces for small-time theaters.

Henry first gained the attention of audiences when she did an act as a singer and character comedienne (The Sal Skinner Gal, a country-bumpkin act) on the vaudeville stage. In a ten- to twenty-minute routine she appeared on stage "with a line of amusing patter, grotesque make-up and ridiculous songs" ("Temple's Bill," clipping, LHS-LHP). "I wore my hair in a pig-tail, I dressed my act as a country girl with a bright gingham dress in front, with a little train, a small straw hat which continually fell off. Wore a child's fur set collar and muff of imitation ermine and held over my head a wee bright striped cotton umbrella (about the size of a dinner plate), with little white mitts on my hands just what my own dear mother called 'half hangers'" (LHM-LHP). Sometimes she told political jokes, which she later claimed gave Rogers the idea for his political gags.

One writer called her performance as The Sal Skinner Gal as "far and away the most popular sketch of its kind on the stage today." The reviewer further commented: "Reared as she was among surroundings that fairly breathed refinement and culture, she transformed herself in to a 'cracker' of the most pronounced type, her language, her gesticulation and her mannerisms making the metamorphism so complete that one is led to wonder why she isn't the real article" ("Louise Henry, 'That Sal Skinner Gal'," *New York Morning Telegraph*, 26 January 1908, clipping, Louise Henry file, NN-L-RLC).

Louise Henry's role as the farm girl Sal Skinner closely resembled the stage character Sis Hopkins, a popular country-bumpkin female figure whose male counterpart on stage was called Toby. The play *Sis Hopkins, the Country Girl* was copyrighted in 1877 by authors Charles H. Boyle and Carrie Graham. Sis Hopkins was made famous by comic actress Rose Melville (1873–1946), who appeared in the part many times, from Broadway musicals in the 1890s to the 1920s. On a vaudeville tour Melville appeared in the sketch *Sis Hopkins' Visit* by Carroll Fleming, who also wrote the play, *Sis Hopkins, A Wise Child*, for her. There were several imitators of Sis Hopkins, and Henry was one of them. Curiously, both Melville and Henry were members of the Baldwin-Melville Stock Co. early in their career. In August 1905 Henry appeared on the cover of *Sis Hopkins Own Book*, a magazine that contained jokes and funny stories. She was pictured dressed in a gingham dress and straw hat and holding an umbrella in the rain. On the cover was written "My name is Sal / An' I'm the Gal / That Knows a Thing you Bet / So When it Pours / An' I'm Outdoors / You See I Dont Git Wet / Sal Skinner."

Known as an eccentric comedienne, Henry had other stage routines as well. She wore amusing outfits and performed imitations, including an Italian woman, Indiana dialect characterizations, and other impersonations, such as the vaudevillian Charlie Case. For her imitations she changed costumes several times during her routine. Henry was especially noted for her impersonation of the popular actress Edna May (1878–1948), known for her role in *The Belle of New York* (1897). As Violet Gray in this musical comedy, May became a star. Henry sang "Canoeing," a song May made famous in *The School Girl* (1904). Henry's act, wrote a critic, "consists of two styles of songs which form a sharp and striking contrast" ("Temple's Bill," clipping, LHS-LHP). One popular song, always greeted with prolonged applause, "I'm Mar-r-ied Now," a spoof on a beau courting a married woman.

Henry's first marriage was to Joe King, and her second to the songwriter Egbert Van Alstyne (1882–1951). A successful composer, Van Alstyne wrote such popular songs as "Navajo," "Back, Back, Back to Baltimore," "In the Shade of the Old Apple Tree," "Good Night, Ladies," and "That Old Girl of Mine," as well as scores for many Broadway musicals. Before teaming up with Henry, Van Alstyne had performed in circuses and vaudeville with Harry Williams, a lyricist who became his songwriting partner. Henry married Van Alstyne on 21 July 1904 in Waukegan, Ill. She was playing at the Cleveland Theatre in Chicago when Van Alstyne proposed. They decided to marry immediately, and Henry was fined for being late for her performance on their wedding day. The two had a very successful husband-and-wife act on the vaudeville stage in which Henry sang many of her husband's songs. Van Alstyne played his songs on the piano and acted as an accompanist for Henry. "Their combined talents make a neat, pleasing, refined specialty that should be in great demand," commented a critic regarding their appearance at New York's Colonial Theatre ("Last Week's Bills," *NYDM,* 27 May 1905, 16). The manager of Keith's Cleveland Theatre wrote that Van Alstyne "offers a little trick piano playing while Miss Henry does some character work. The work of both of them is excellent. Their act was probably the hit of the show from an artistic stand-point. The audience seemed to greatly appreciate Miss Henry's character work" (manager's report, Keith's Cleveland Theatre, week of 10 September 1906, KAC-IaU).

Henry's marriage to Van Alstyne had its problems. On 8 September 1905 the *New York Morning Telegraph* reported that Henry had "not yet recovered from the beating she got at his hands last Friday" ("He's Music Mad, This Navajo, Says His Wife: Mrs Egbert Van Alstyne Explains Why Her Composer Husband Beat Her," clipping, Louise Henry file, NN-L-RLC). In the same article Henry said that her husband had "written so much music that it has made him crazy." Van Alstyne subsequently moved out of their apartment at 195 Second Avenue. Henry filed for divorce, but stopped the proceedings three months later when she and Van Alstyne became reconciled. Nonetheless, two years later their marriage ended in divorce, and Henry then began performing a single act.

In 1908 Henry had ambitions to become a star in light opera, and to this end she studied voice. An article from this time reported that her favorite hobby was collecting diamonds, and that she had purchased in Paris a gold purse studded with diamonds and rubies. In July 1908 she replaced Mabel Hite in *The-Merry-Go-Round,* a musical comedy at the Circle Theatre. While she was at the height of her career, her photograph appeared on the front page of a section in *The New York Morning Telegraph,* dated 23 February 1908 (see illustration, p.135).

Twice Henry made headlines that had nothing to do with her acting career. In 1903 she saved a boy from being run over by a street car in Indianapolis. Another newspaper story related how she cared for a dying man who had been struck by a railway car.

Rogers met Henry during the time he performed on the same program with her at Keith's Union Square Theatre on Fourteenth Street, the week of 12 June 1905. This was Rogers's first appearance in New York vaudeville. Both were on the Keith Circuit and were represented by William Morris. Rogers also played on the same playbill with Henry and Van Alstyne at Keith's Theatre in Cleveland during the week of 10 September 1906.

In an unpublished reminiscence, Henry recalled that Rogers was then "a tall, lean, lanky, shy cowboy with sky-blue eyes and dark-brown straight hair, with his same winning smile which later became so famous. To use his own phrasing, 'he grinned like a possum'" (LHM-LHP). Henry recalled that Rogers's fancy roping and riding performance with Buck McKee and his horse Teddy was a popular novelty act. "Bill would announce his tricks in his slow cowboy lingo that convulsed any audience with laughter," she wrote. "One trick he did when he danced in and out of the huge rope circle I can remember, and when he missed this one he would say, 'Oh shaw' I got all my three through but one'. That remark always got a big laugh. If he made it he would exclaim, 'That was a humdinger'" (LHM-LHP).

Rogers and Henry shared a love of horses. Henry's oldest brother, Robert Monthegue Henry, was a breeder of thoroughbred horses, and Louise enjoyed taking long rides on horseback. It was Teddy, she recalled, who introduced her to Rogers: "Bill laughingly gave Teddy credit for this. He always said Teddy was my horse as I was the only girl Teddy would let ride him with one exception . . . Lucille Mulhall" (LHM-LHP). Together, Henry and Rogers visited Teddy at George Madlines's stable on Forty-second Street near Ninth Avenue.

"He never forgot to dump the contents of the sugar bowl in his pockets for Teddy," Henry wrote. "This animal was so tame that he would take sugar out of our hands. Yes, you could even hold a lump of sugar in your mouth between your teeth and Teddy would take it. He was never known to bite" (LHM-LHP). She and Rogers would go to the old Huttenberg Race Track in Hoboken, N.J., where Jim Minnick trained polo ponies. There she rode Teddy, and she and Rogers became "real friends." During the time they played at the Union Square Theatre Rogers helped Henry buy a cowgirl costume with kid boots, a large sombrero, and a "long whip which Bill taught me to crack" (LHM-LHP). Henry also recalled that Van Alstyne composed the song "Pony Boy" for Rogers, but this tune is not listed among his works.

Henry and Rogers spent considerable time together in New York. He invited her to a dinner, what Rogers called a "feed bag," with his cowboy friends at the Putnam House. There Henry met Jack Joyce, Jim Gabriel, and other of Rogers's intimate friends, whom Rogers called by such names as "Old Hard Luck," "Heknocknee," "Hutahanno," and "Old Dough-belly." The chef at the Putnam, a man named Charlie, was a former cowboy Rogers had met in Argentina. He prepared Rogers's favorite dish (beans), and Henry remembered that Joyce called Rogers "Billy Bean Rogers." Rogers also took Henry to dinner at the Metropole Hotel on Forty-second Street, a favorite vaudevillian spot, and the Roversi, an Italian restaurant on Twenty-ninth Street. They frequented Tony Pearl's spaghetti restaurant and Joel's, where Rogers ordered chili and frijoles. Rogers's close relationship with Henry coincided with his courtship of Betty Blake. Although he never mentioned Henry's name in his correspondence with Betty Blake, Rogers admitted he was seeing other women.

Henry recalled that Rogers's first year in vaudeville was one of constant struggle. She wrote that Rogers told her that "he had to do some tall thinking to keep his head afloat." During lay-off periods Henry and Rogers would do the rounds of booking agents in New York, stopping at the St. James Building on Broadway and Twenty-sixth Street where the Keith office was located and then going on to William Morris's office on Twenty-eighth Street.

Rogers and Henry kept in contact as they traveled to different cities on the vaudeville circuit. Henry often sent Rogers books to read. "I awakened in him a desire to read books," Henry recalled. "Will would write in it several annotations of his own reaction to the passage in the book" (LHM-LHP). In one book he wrote "The Ships That Pass in the Night," a reference to their relationships as traveling vaudevillians who only saw one another either briefly in New York or if they were performing on the same program. On one trip

Rogers sent Henry a photo of himself and two friends, and wrote on it: "We are laughing but we aren't happy—there's somebody *Missing* The 'Hard Luck Gang'. All join me in sending *Love* and all want you to *join*" (LHS-LHP; see illustration, p. 275). Henry pasted the photograph in her scrapbook and next to it placed a story about Rogers's death from the Sunday Rotogravure Section of the *Los Angeles Times* (25 August 1935). Her scrapbook also has a review of Rogers's performance at an Orpheum theater.

Henry's stage career ended when she was suddenly afflicted with tuber-culosis. She recovered in a sanitarium in Saranac Lake, N.Y. Here Henry had an affair with Dr. Jesse S. Heiman who operated the sanitarium. She wrote Will Rogers a letter in February 1909, which she sent via Buck McKee. McKee wrote to his wife about Henry's letter: "She sent it to me to give to Bill. She says she is sick of her bargain. She dont like her '*rich Jew doctor*'. Bill just laughed and tore her letter up. He said 'well poor girl I cant do anything for you now'" (Buck McKee to Maud Florence McKee, 24 February 1909, BMc-C).

By 1911 Henry had married Heiman, and three years later they were liv-ing in Syracuse, N.Y. As the wife of a well-known physician, Henry was the hostess of many social gatherings at their house on East Genesee Street. The Heimans had one daughter, Jessouise (also known as Louise), born around 1911 (a *Variety* clipping dated 25 October 1912 contains a photograph of the baby, identified as the sixteen-month-old daughter of Dr. and Mrs. Jesse S. Heiman of Syracuse, N.Y. [Louise Henry file, NN-L-RLC]). Jessouise stud-ied dance and had her London stage debut at age fourteen. Using her moth-er's name, Louise Henry, as her stage name, she appeared in numerous films between 1935 and 1939, and was under contract to Metro-Goldwyn-Mayer. Like her mother, she had a connection to Will Rogers. She played the charac-ter Arlene Shattuck in *Old Kentucky* (1935), which was Will Rogers's last film. "One of her [my mother's] fondest memories is of Will Rogers," Jessouise said, "who was then in vaudeville, and often appeared on the same bill with her" (Reine Davies Hollywood Parade clipping, LHS-LHP; see also *AmSCAP,* 747; Craig, *Sweet and Lowdown,* 79–81; clippings, LHS-LHP; *EV,* 344; *FYSC,* 1:658; Hitchcock and Sadie, eds., *New Grove Dictionary of American Music,* 4:444; Laurie Weltz to WRPP, 12 May 1994; Louise Henry biographical clip-ping file, Locke env. 683, NN-L-RLC; Mantle and Sherwood, eds., *Best Plays of 1899–1909,* 562; *New York Clipper,* 7 June 1902; *New York Dramatic Mirror,* 8 October 1904; *OCAT,* 69–70, 86, 378, 469, 472; Slout, *Theatre in a Tent,* 72–74, 119n.4; Sterling, *Will Rogers in Hollywood,* 169; Yagoda, *Will Rogers,* 87, 96, 107).

HOUDINI, Harry (1874–1926). Harry Houdini is considered among the greatest magicians and escape artists of all time. He appeared on several vaudeville programs with Rogers, and the two formed an acquaintance built on mutual respect. Houdini was born in Budapest, Hungary, and his name at birth was either Ehrich Weiss or Erik Weisz. Soon after he was born, the family emigrated to Appleton, Wis. He took the name Harry Houdini early in his career as a tribute to Robert Houdin, a famous French magician of the time whose autobiography he had read at age sixteen.

From an early age, Houdini was entranced by show business. His first appearance before the public was in a 5-cent circus in Appleton, Wis. Houdini toured Wisconsin as a contortionist and trapeze artist with the Davenport brothers, the first spiritualists to be seen in the United States. The experience kindled his interest in spiritualism. At the age of seventeen, Houdini appeared on stage as a magician with a friend, Jacob Hyman, in an act called "The Brothers Houdini." In the 1890s he worked often in traveling circuses and dime museums, doing twenty shows a day for $15 a week. He performed magic acts and card tricks, calling himself at one time "The King of Cards." By 1900 Houdini was a recognized vaudeville star known for his tricks involving dramatic escapes from everything from straitjackets to jails. He was billed as "The Undisputed King of Handcuffs," "Monarch of Leg Shackles," and "Champion Jail Breaker."

In 1900 Houdini went to Europe where he felt there were more opportunities for magicians. He staged an escape from Scotland Yard and other sensational exploits, which led to a spot as headliner at the Alhambra Theatre in London. Houdini returned to the United States after a successful four-year tour of European theaters. He was now a celebrated vaudeville headliner, eventually making thousands of dollars a week. Everywhere he went he played to sold-out theaters. In January and February 1925, Houdini established a record for being held over for six weeks at the Hippodrome. His central appeal was as an escape artist. An ingenious mechanic and skilled showman, he devised all types of locked containers, handcuffs, and safes for his act.

Houdini was careful to emphasize that the supernatural played no role in his act whatsoever. He worked to discredit spiritualists as a group at a time when the notion of the supernatural had a particularly strong hold on the public imagination. Ironically, when Houdini died, scores of mediums reported to the public that they had received messages from him. Will Rogers commented: "If Houdini keeps this message stuff up, he's going to put Western Union out of business" (Stewart-Gordon, "Houdini, The Man No Lock Could Hold," 155).

Houdini and Rogers became acquainted on the vaudeville circuit. In January 1906 they were both on the playbill at the Chestnut Street Theatre in Philadelphia. They also appeared together in March 1915 in Louisville, Ky. Houdini was the headliner, but judging from reviews in local papers, Rogers stole the show. In 1925 Rogers recounted a story he had heard from Harry Houdini:

> The worst story I heard today was told to me by Harry Houdini, the great Handcuff King. We were out in Hollywood making movies together, and I was invited to a Party, a wedding party of Harry's. It was his 25th anniversary. I had a speech all prepared, thinking it was his 25th time. I knew he was in Pictures and I naturally thought it was that many times. Harry is a great Character and can come nearer doing a variety of things and doing them well than anyone I know. He told me the following story that happened during his early days knocking around little Theatres before they found out how good he was. A funny looking Rube Guy applied to the Manager of a little Theatre I was playing one time, said he was a Conjurer, and did a freak Act, and wanted a job.
>
> "Who are you?" asked the Manager.
>
> "I am Enoch, the egg man."
>
> "What's your specialty?"
>
> "I eat three dozen hens' eggs, two dozen Ducks' eggs, and one dozen Goose eggs at a sitting, right on the stage."
>
> "Do you realize we give four shows a day in this Theatre?"
>
> "That's all right, I savvy that."
>
> "And you think you can do it?"
>
> "I know I can do it."
>
> "And on Saturdays we give six shows."
>
> "All right."
>
> "And on Holidays we give a show every hour."
>
> "Well if you give shows that fast and often there is just one thing I want to have understood with you, before I go to work. I must have time in between to go out and get my regular meals."
>
> Between you and me, I think it was Houdini himself that did that, I notice he won't look at an egg now. ("Worst Story I Have Ever Heard Today," 23 October 1925, OkClaW)

Houdini's introduction to the movie business was an appearance in a newsreel. He received a tremendous response to this publicity from managers and fans, and became interested in doing films. He began making movies in Hollywood with a sixteen-episode serial called *The Master Mystery* (1917). In 1919 he made *The Grim Game* and *Terror Island* for Adolf Zukor, and he was featured in many more movies. He began his own picture company, Houdini Pictures International, but it was not successful.

At the age of fifty-two Houdini died suddenly due to poisoning caused by an inflamed appendix. He had been telling McGill University students in Montreal that his stomach muscles were hard enough to withstand blows without injury. Tremendous physical strength had always been important in helping maintain the illusion of performing magical escapes and exploits. One student struck Houdini above the appendix without giving him warning. One of these blows burst Houdini's appendix. Houdini refused to cancel the show that was to go on that night. Afterward he was taken to the hospital, where it was found that his appendix was infected. He died after two unsuccessful operations, on Halloween, 1906 (*EV,* 250–52; *DAB,* 5:248–49; NN-L-BRTC; *NYT,* 1 November 1926; Slide, *Vaudevillians,* 74–75; Stewart-Gordon, "Houdini, The Man No Lock Could Hold," 151–55; *VO,* 1:3 November 1926; "When You Coming Back," 82–92; White, "Houdini and his Movies," 46–47).

McKEE, Buck (1871–1944). Buck McKee was Will Rogers's assistant in vaudeville during the time (1905–10) he had a horse-and-roping act on stage. McKee was born on 21 April 1871 in Osage Mission, Kans. He grew up on his father's ranch across the river from the Pawnee Indian reservation, located in Oklahoma Territory. As a boy he participated in range roundups and cattle herding, helping his father drive cattle from Texas and Mississippi to their ranch. Once the cattle were fattened, he and his father herded them to Elgin, Kans., a railroad shipping point. During his youth McKee witnessed the transformation of the open range from unbroken prairie to pastures fenced with barbed wire. For many years he listed as his residence Pawnee, Okla., the county seat of Pawnee County.

McKee once worked as a cowhand on Clement Vann Rogers's ranch, and there he first encountered Will Rogers, who was eight years younger than he. McKee recalled that during a branding he saw young Rogers use his mother's clothesline to rope a calf, which dragged him across the corral, much to the amusement of the other cowhands. Clement Vann Rogers roared: "Willie, get out of that corral. You are not big enough to do anything yourself and you won't let anyone else work." After his father left, Rogers started roping again and remarked to the cowboys: "Poppa don't think much of my calf roping, does he?" (Bagley, "Riding, Roping and Trouping with Will Rogers," 3).

Like many of his fellow cowhands, McKee joined several Wild West shows. He claimed that he was with Pawnee Bill's show for several years. He remembered also being with Frederick Cummins's Indian Congress, the Miller Brothers' 101 Ranch show, and Zack Mulhall's troupe. McKee appeared with

Will Rogers in the Mulhall company of cowboys and cowgirls at the Madison Square Garden Horse Fair in April 1905. In June of that year Rogers went on the vaudeville stage, first using Jim Minnick as his assistant to ride Teddy. Shortly thereafter Rogers hired McKee to care for his show horse.

For five years McKee teamed with Rogers, and during this time he traveled across the United States and made trips to France, Germany, and England. McKee was responsible for caring for the pony, accompanying Teddy on the railroad or ship, and stabling him when they arrived at their next destination. On stage McKee rode Teddy, while Rogers lassoed the horse. "When we first started out," McKee recalled, "our act was just an exhibition of Will's artistry with a rope. Teddy and I were merely props for his spinning riata." To keep from skidding on the smooth stage, Teddy wore felt-bottom boots on his feet. McKee recalled an incident when Teddy slipped on the stage and almost dragged him into the orchestra pit. "Quick as thought Will roped Teddy's head, pulled him up tight with one hand, grabbed me by the shoulder with the other and dragged me from under the horse," McKee said (Bagley, "Riding, Roping and Trouping with Will Rogers," 3).

McKee was more than just an assistant to Rogers. His skill as a horse trainer was critical to the success of the act. Rogers credited McKee with training Teddy: "Buck trained him to do on a slick stage just about what a good turning cowpony can do on the ground." McKee joked with Rogers: "I can get away if anything happens, but the audience can get you" ("Recalling the Days of Teddy, the Cow Pony," 2 June 1935, ms., OkClaW).

Life on the road, however, was not always pleasant. McKee's correspondence with his wife, the vaudeville performer Maud Florence, reveals that he was often unhappy with his salary and living arrangements. He often complained of lack of funds when an engagement was canceled (Rogers had to pay McKee from his weekly salary). McKee almost never stayed in the same hotels where Rogers resided, and his living conditions were inferior to those of his boss. He probably also had to travel second or third class, or in the freight car with Teddy, while Rogers went first class. Indeed, Rogers once said that money became such a problem that McKee rode Teddy to short-distance stops. McKee, of course, never got the billing and publicity Rogers received. Moreover, the rigors of being constantly on the road caused strains in his relationship with his wife, who at the same time was experiencing unemployment in New York and caring for her sick mother.

When Rogers made the transition to using a new horse in the act in the summer of 1910, and then developed a group Wild West act for the stage, McKee stuck with the changes. But when Rogers decided to perform a single vaudeville act in 1911, McKee was left without a job. After five years the horse act was no longer a novelty and had grown rather stale. Rogers therefore decided to change his vaudeville routine to one that depended more on humorous comments mixed with lariat tricks. McKee soon found a position as general manager for a Mr. Myers, a polo-pony dealer on Long Island. Shortly thereafter, he organized his own polo-pony business with Jim Minnick in Meadowbrook, Long Island, N.Y. The successful enterprise included the purchase, training, and resale of polo ponies. During World War I McKee bought and trained horses for the federal government. His business card ("Buck McKee, Pawnee, Oklahoma") describes his work as "Dealer in Polo Ponies" and "Equestrian Trainer" with an address of 323 West Forty-third Street in New York City (BMc-C). A return address on an envelope post-marked 14 March 1914 reveals that he was also once manager of the Monmouth Park Stock Farm in New Jersey (BMC-OkClaW).

In 1908 Buck McKee had married Maud Holmes, a vaudeville actress who used the stage name Maud Florence. Florence performed theater engage-ments while her husband assisted Rogers in vaudeville. According to Rogers, she was a dancer in a vaudeville act that once was on the same program with them. She and McKee met, fell in love, and married. Rarely could they see one another, however, as Rogers traveled the circuits, moving each week from one town to another.

Letters between the McKees reveal that the long separations were often painful for both of them. McKee regularly wrote that he was depressed and lonesome, while Florence missed her husband greatly. She wrote: "I can't stand separating from you anymore, Buck, it just tears my heart out by the roots" (Maud Florence McKee to Buck McKee, 11 May 190[?], BMC-OkClaW). Occasionally, her letters convey a tone of jealousy over other women on the circuit whom her husband might befriend, and she warns him not to flirt with them. Money is a constant problem between them. Florence once had to leave a traveling company in Canada because of a dispute with a person involved with the show. When she was out of work, McKee encouraged her to be aggressive in talking with agents and to take any job offered, not just one similar to the work she had done in the past. Florence resented that Rogers was not paying her husband more. Despite these difficulties the letters show a strong mutual affection (BMc-C; BMC-OkClaW).

Around 1924 McKee and Florence bought the Whipple Ranch in Rose-ville, Calif., near Sacramento. McKee apparently had a brother, W. E. McKee, who lived in the area. The couple opened a riding school that was a success-ful business for many years. According to Rogers, Florence too was an excellent rider. In the spring of 1935 Rogers was in Sacramento where director John Ford was on location filming *Steamboat 'Round the Bend,* with Rogers as the star. He took the opportunity to see his old friends and visit their ranch. In his weekly column, Rogers wrote: "They are excellent teachers and they have learned many young and old people both to ride, and ride correctly, and above all they are so good to their horses, lots of patience, and real love for a horse. He was breaking in some lovely young horses, making gaited horses out of them. He has a fine thoroughbred stallion, and is raising a few young ones himself. It was good to see 'em ("Recalling the Days of Teddy, the Cow Pony," 2 June 1935, ms., OkClaW).

Earlier, in 1922, McKee had appeared in Rogers's film *The Roping Fool,* riding a horse that Rogers used to display his lariat artistry. The Sacramento visit was the last time Rogers saw McKee. McKee invited his old friend to spend three weeks that summer at his ranch. Instead, Rogers went on his ill-fated airplane trip with Wiley Post.

Little is known about the McKees' last years. Buck McKee died in Roseville, Calif., in 1944. Although he and Rogers had had their differences as vaudeville partners, McKee had a lasting fondness for Rogers. He once said: "You know he always had a place in my heart, like a real brother" ("Woman Here Has Photos of Rogers as Vaudevillian," *Sacramento Bee,* 17 August 1935). Rogers wrote about McKee a few months before his plane accident: "Speaking of catching him, I bet he has been roped, (and missed too) more times than any man in the world. He did look great when he come charging in on that stage with that beautiful brown pony" ("Recalling the Days of Teddy, the Cow Pony," 2 June 1935, ms., OkClaW; see also biographical material and correspondence, BMc-C and BMC-OkClaW; *Billboard,* 21 October 1911; Passport Application of Buck McKee, 24 February 1906, above; "Riding and Roping and Trouping with Will Rogers," *Sacramento Bee,* 18 January 1941, magazine section, 3; *WhScrn,* 2:313).

MCKEE, Maud Florence. See MCKEE, Buck.

MCSPADDEN, Theodore Raymond (1887–1964). Theo (also called Ted) Mc-Spadden was the son of Joel Cowan McSpadden and Florence Hoyt McSpadden. He was the nephew of Will Rogers's sister, Sallie McSpadden, through her marriage to Joel Cowan McSpadden's brother Tom. Will Rogers was a close boyhood friend of Theo and his brothers Booth and Forrest. He grew up socializing with all seven children in the family, who lived on the outskirts of Chelsea, I.T. As a teenager Rogers often worked as a cowboy in local cattle roundups, brandings, and drives with Booth, Forrest, and young Theo. All the McSpadden brothers were expert riders and ropers. When Will Rogers participated in southwestern roping-contest circuits at the turn of the century, so did the teenage Theo and his brothers.

After he returned from his travels abroad in April 1904, Will Rogers recommended his seventeen-year-old friend Theo to Zack Mulhall as someone who would make a good cowboy in Mulhall's Wild West show at the St. Louis World's Fair. Mulhall agreed to hire him, and Theo joined the cowboy act at the Fair at the end of May 1904. He lived with Rogers for a time at the Mulhall household on Washington Avenue in St. Louis. When Rogers decided to try his hand doing his roping tricks on the stage, Theo McSpadden came along as sidekick in Rogers's vaudeville debut at the Standard Theater in St. Louis.

Like Rogers, Theo McSpadden stayed loyal to Zack Mulhall after the shooting scandal of July 1904, and he appeared regularly in Saturday afternoon performances of the Mulhall show at the Delmar Race Track. McSpadden left St. Louis after working into August, and he went back to school in Indian Territory in September 1904. Soon thereafter Rogers visited Indian Territory, and he was with Forrest McSpadden when Forrest was tragically killed in a steer-roping accident in October 1904. Rogers rode to get a doctor, but when he returned with help, the young man had already died from the injuries he had received when he was crushed by his falling horse.

The McSpadden family continued to ranch in the Oologah area. Theo McSpadden married Beulah Thomason of Arkansas in 1913, and they raised three girls in Nowata, Okla. (*CR,* 20 May 1904; *HRC,* 299–300, 303–4; memorandum by Paula M. Love, "St. Louis World's Fair Letters," n.d., OkClaW; Tompkins, "My Association with Will Rogers," 10; Will Rogers to Clement Vann Rogers, 4 July [4 August] 1904, OkClaW; see also *PWR,* vol. 1, for biographical histories of the extended McSpadden family).

MINNICK, J. H. (Jim) (1881–1947). Jim Minnick was a rancher, horse trainer and trader, and cowboy performer from Seymour, Tex., who became a good friend of Will Rogers. He competed on the steer-roping circuit and as a young man began to break, train, and sell horses. Like Rogers, he was teenage friends with cowboys Clay McGonigle, Ellison Carroll, and Tom Mix. Two months before the opening of the St. Louis World's Fair Minnick rode in Theodore Roosevelt's inaugural parade (on 4 March 1905) as part of Colonel Seth Bullock's Cowboy Troupe, along with many other westerners, including Rough Riders from the Spanish-American War and Native American leaders.

He came to the Fair with a carload of horses and five cowboys, and offered them to Charles Tompkins for work in Tompkins's Wild West show on the fairgrounds. Tompkins and Minnick had met in 1903, when Tompkins had seen Minnick compete in the bucking competition at the Delmar Race Track in St. Louis; Tompkins was buying horses for the Fourpaugh Wild West shows.

Described as a "medium sized, blond headed boy from Texas," Minnick joined Rogers and the Mulhall family for their appearances in the Mulhall Rough Rider congress at Madison Square Garden in April 1905 (Spring, "Horseman Extraordinary," 14). He and Will Rogers appeared together at the White House on 22 April 1905 in a command performance for Theodore Roosevelt's children. When Rogers made his first appearance on a New York stage at Keith's Union Square Theatre on 11 June 1905, Jim Minnick rode Teddy, the horse that Rogers roped in the act. After the rest of the Mulhall show people had left the East Coast in May 1905, Rogers and Minnick had gone to New Jersey and staked out a plot of flat dirt the size of a stage, where they trained Teddy for the act. Minnick soon returned to his ranch in west Texas and was replaced on stage by Rogers's long-time vaudeville sidekick, Buck McKee.

When he returned to Texas, Minnick went into business with his brother Will, supplying Oklahoma and Texas cow horses to an eastern market for use as polo ponies. The Minnick Bros. Polo Ponies company distributed in the East out of Union Hill, N.J. Minnick introduced Rogers to the game of polo, and when the Rogerses lived on Long Island, Minnick was a regular member of the teams that played polo with Rogers on Sundays in a Massapequa field near the home of fellow vaudevillian Fred Stone. After the Rogerses had moved to California for Rogers to work in film, Minnick visited in the late 1920s to play polo with Rogers in Beverly Hills. The two men had many friends in common, including Buck McKee, Charles Russell, Leo Carrilo, Fred Stone, and Charles Tompkins.

Minnick married a New Yorker, Della Holthausen, who had been educated in Switzerland. They met when she joined a group of people who came out to Minnick's land near Quanah, Tex., in the summer of 1905 as part of a small dude ranch operation he ran for easterners. She was injured in an accident during her visit, stayed behind the others to convalesce, and then married Minnick in a ceremony in New York in 1907. They raised a family of five daughters and one son on a ranch near Crowell, Tex., and in Norman, Okla., where the children could attend school. Della Minnick managed the Minnick ranch when Jim Minnick was on the road with his horse-trading business. Minnick also owned a large horse ranch in the mountains near Cimmaron,

N.Mex., and Rogers loved to visit him there. In addition to raising and selling horses, Minnick frequently served as a judge for horse shows and livestock expositions. One of the founders of the American Quarter Horse Association, Minnick was inducted into the association's Hall of Fame in 1984.

Minnick was one of the last good friends to spend time with Will Rogers before Rogers's death in the summer of 1935. That summer Rogers met Minnick at Charles and Mabel Tompkins's house in El Reno, Okla., and drove with him to Minnick's ranch in the New Mexico mountains, where the two spent time before Rogers proceeded on to see other old friends in Higgins, Tex. Jim Minnick died after suffering a stroke on 30 April 1947 at his home near Crowell, Tex. (Croy, *Our Will Rogers,* 102–3, 159, 243–44, 346, 347, 364; *Fort Worth Star-Telegram,* 21 November 1938 and 1 May 1947; Hartung, "James H. Minnick"; Hendrix, "He Put Will Rogers on the Stage"; Hendrix, "Mis' Minnick and Jim"; Minnick biographical file, TxU-GL; Minnick interview, HCP-MoU; *NYT,* 1 May 1947; Rogers, *Will Rogers,* 89, 158–59; scrapbook A-1, OkClaW; Spring, "Horseman Extraordinary"; Tompkins, "My Association with Will Rogers," 12; Charles Tompkins to Homer Croy, 30 August 1952, HCP-MoU; *Wichita Falls Record News,* 7 March 1977 and 13 March 1984; see also Article from the *Washington Times,* 23 April 1905, above).

MIX, Tom (1880–1940). Thomas Edwin Mix (or Thomas Hezekiah Mix, reports vary) was born on 6 January 1880 at Mix Run in Cameron County, Pa. At the age of eighteen Mix left home to join the army, hoping to see action in Cuba during the Spanish-American War. Despite the many tall tales he told about his wounds and exploits, he never fought in the Spanish-American War. He was assigned to Battery M, Fourth Regiment of the U.S. Artillery. Such artillery units were used to guard the East Coast against attack. Mix was married, for the first time, to Grace I. Allin on 18 July 1902. Several months after the wedding Grace insisted that Mix leave the army as she did not like to live alone. He deserted the army on 20 October 1902, and soon afterward the couple traveled west to live in Oklahoma—probably so that Mix could evade arrest for desertion. Grace Mix continued her work as a schoolteacher, while her husband taught physical education and worked as a wrangler and as a bartender, among other jobs. In 1903 the marriage was annulled by Grace Mix's father, who did not like the idea of his daughter being married to an army deserter.

In 1904 Mix attended the St. Louis World's Fair as a member of the Oklahoma Cavalry Band. At the Fair he met Rogers, and it was here that the latter introduced Mix to fourteen-year-old Olive Stokes, who later became Mix's third wife. Stokes tells the story of how she met Mix. She and Rogers were both from Indian Territory. Rogers introduced her to Mix, who escorted her around the Fair for a day. When her visit to St. Louis ended, Rogers, at Mix's request, feigned an excuse for not being able to see her off at the train station, leaving Mix to accompany her instead. In late 1905 Mix was employed by the Miller Brothers' 101 Ranch show at $15 a month. Soon afterward he married Kitty Jewel Perrine, daughter of the owner of a hotel where Mix often tended bar. The marriage ended a year later. By 1908 Mix had become a top performer with the show. A year later he married Olive Stokes, who was now eighteen.

The Mixes joined the Widerman Wild West show in Amarillo, Tex., in which Mix was a top performer. Soon afterward they quit the show and went to Seattle to organize their own show, but instead they joined Will A. Dickey's Circle D Wild West show. At the time Mix was also employed by Zack Mulhall for his Wild West show. In April 1910 *Billboard* gave a good review of Mix's performance at the St. Louis Coliseum in the Mulhall Wild West show, directed by Jim Gabriel. Rogers also appeared in the show.

Over the next two years Mix went to Mexico with the 101 Ranch show and traveled to Florida to perform in silent films. In early 1912 the Mixes were in Canada on tour with the 101 Ranch Wild West show. In April of that year *Billboard* reported that Mix arrived in Peoria, Ill., to perform with Young Buffalo Bill's Wild West and Colonel Cummins's Far East. Olive Mix returned home to Dewey, Okla., for the birth of a baby, Ruth, born on 13 July 1912. Mix returned also to Dewey and was appointed the town's night marshal.

In 1912 the Selig company was filming movies in Oklahoma, and Mix was offered a job playing supporting roles. In 1914 he was made a director of his own unit under Selig. In 1915 Mix was assigned by Selig to make films in Arizona. Here his leading lady was Eugenie Forde, with whom Mix had an affair. Mix also met Forde's daughter Victoria, who became his leading lady and eventually his fourth wife. In 1916 Selig's company sent an efficiency expert to Mix's unit to recommend methods of cutting costs. Annoyed by the interference, Mix left Selig and joined the Fox film company. The Fox films had significantly higher production values, including outstanding photography, and a markedly better release system. Mix began making features for Fox that were box-office hits. Like the Selig pictures, the Fox films centered on daring exploits and riding tricks. Mix churned out one formula-style popular Western after another. By 1926 his salary at Fox was $17,000 a week. However, by 1928, Fox terminated Mix's contract. His pictures had become very expensive to produce, and Fox was more interested in putting money into sound film.

Mix went from Fox to the Film Booking Office of America (FBO), a low-budget film distribution and production company. Mix made five rather unsuccessful films from 1928 to 1929. In May 1929 he started a tour with the Sells-Floto Circus at a starting salary of $10,000 a week. These years were not kind to Mix; the stock market crashed, and he lost a substantial amount of money. He was sued by the U.S. government for tax evasion and by Zack Miller for breach of contract (Mix lost). The Sells-Floto Circus closed because of the Depression. Mix underwent surgery to correct a badly healed shattered shoulder, and was also hospitalized with a case of peritonitis, from which he almost died. While Mix was in the hospital he received a get-well telegram from Betty Rogers: "Will is on his way to China he will be glad to know you are better we are all holding a good thought for you and know you will soon be well again" (Exhibit Script, Betty Rogers telegram, Tom Mix Collection, OkHi).

Suddenly Mix's luck changed when he received a lucrative offer from Universal to make six talkie Westerns at $30,000 per picture. In 1932 he married his fifth wife, Mabel Ward. Together they toured the country with a Wild West show called the Tom Mix Roundup in 1932 and 1933. The show consisted of Mix and his horse Tony, two other horses, rope tricks, and the Ward sisters' aerial act. In 1933 the Tom Mix radio show, sponsored by Ralston, was launched, a program that continued for seventeen years. In 1934 Tom joined up with the Sam B. Dill Circus, which he bought in 1935 and renamed the Tom Mix Wild West Show and Circus Combined. It was a large circus that had to be transported in thirty-four semi trucks, sixteen smaller trucks, and twenty-six house trailers. The years from 1935 to 1937 were successful for the Mix circus, considered to be one of the largest, most popular circuses on the road. In 1938 circus business in general was at an all-time low. The Mix circus, as well as many others, did not survive this season and disbanded. Mix next did a European vaudeville tour but was forced to return to the United States in 1939 when war broke out. In 1940 he died alone in his car while driving fast on an Arizona road.

Over the years, Rogers and Mix had many encounters. Zack Miller told how one day Mix was regaling an audience of dude vacationers at the Mulhall ranch about his experience in the Boer War. Rogers didn't believe a word of the story and said to him: "Tom Mix, you egotistical SOB, anyone listening to you would think there isn't a bit of difference between you and Jesus Christ, anyway, he admitted to being born in a manger and you won't" (Zack Miller,

Jr., to Homer Croy, 22 September 1952, HCP-MoU). Rogers told a story about visiting Mix on the movie set during an incident when Mix was shot by a villain: "I went out with him to Edendale, the other day. They were pulling some awful stunts. Tom Mix got in a stage coach, and stayed until they spilled him out over a bank. Then somebody took a shot at him with a rifle. Real shot. Why he had William Tell's son shipwrecked. A bullet hit him on the Sheriff's badge and glanced off. I said: 'None of that for mine. I'll stick to my . . . two-a-day. There I haven't got anything to look out for but my audience, and I'm awful good at dodging!'" (clipping, scrapbook 1914, CPpR).

Another story deals with the time Rogers and Mix appeared together with the Zack Mulhall troupe at the Madison Square Garden Horse Fair in late April 1905. They were living in rooms at the Putnam House and found themselves without their salaries. They concocted a plan to confront Mulhall in the bar as he would be paying for drinks, largely as a publicity gesture. When the time came for Mulhall to pay, he gave a twenty-dollar bill to the bartender. When the bartender handed back the change, Mix and Rogers grabbed it and ran out of the room.

Mix and Rogers were both presented to the public as icon cowboys and emblems of the American West. Still, their personas differed. Rogers articulated the values of American commonality, plain talk, and common sense, while Mix personified American individualism, bravura, and the adventurous frontier spirit. At times Mix seemed to imitate Rogers by writing for publications in the hope of gaining more public recognition. Mix wrote commentary for *Variety, Photoplay, Cosmopolitan,* and *Liberty,* and a syndicated column for the Hearst papers. However, his writing, often acerbic, did not attract a following. His various employers in publishing hoped he would become another Will Rogers, but Mix lacked a coherent philosophy to impart, and the experiment failed.

Although Tom Mix never achieved the broad-based popularity enjoyed by Will Rogers, his standing among young boys was unequaled, both at home and abroad. The Boy Scout troops of Europe chose Mix as their official idol, mounting photos of him in all Scout tents. When Mix arrived in Europe on his 1925 tour, he was greeted at one stop by a crowd of 20,000 Boy Scouts. One article, which touted Mix as "The Highest Salaried Man in Hollywood," exclaimed: "Every boy believes in him. He is the daily model. Each tries to emulate Tom in feats of strength and daring. That is why Mix is responsible for the sturdy right arm of many an ambitious youth" (Douglas, "The King of the Western Heroes," clipping, Tom Mix biographical file, CLAc). One English writer recalled nostalgically his movie-going days as a boy, and wrote that Mix's films offered "the good-hearted American democratic idealism which at one time established a model for the rest of the world. . . . Mix speaks up for the rights of the individual, for the institutions and apparatus of democracy and how it makes plain sense to treat people like human beings, not brutes" (Moorcock, "Songs of Innocence," 36). Mix himself stated, ten years before his death: "In some little way I can convince the boyhood of America that neither smoking, drinking, nor gambling are essential and that physical fitness always wins out over dissipation. That is why I try to make my characters those of men of high ideals" (Tom Mix, "How I Broke into the Movies," in Herman, ed., *How I Broke into the Movies,* 115; see also *Billboard,* 16 April 1910 and 27 April 1912; Birchard, *King Cowboy,* 3, 5, 8–23, 115–32, 215, 218–19, 229–32, 265–67; Bradbury, "Tom Mix Circus 1936 Coast to Coast Tour," 5–8; Cary, "From the Old Frontier to Film," 43; Mitchell and Everson, "Tom Mix," 387–97; Mix, *Fabulous Tom Mix,* 4–7; Mix, *Life and Legend of Tom Mix,* 40, 45–50, 105–6; Moorcock, "Songs of Innocence," 36; Norris, *Tom Mix Book,* 13, 37, 52, 59, 115; *NYT,* 12 April 1925; Thayer, "Tom Mix Circus and Wild West, Part One—Season of 1934 and 1935," 19, 21–22; Thayer, "Tom Mix Circus and Wild West, Part Two—Seasons of 1936, 1937 and 1938," 11).

MORGAN, Tom P. (1864–1928). Author and humorist Tom Perkins Morgan was a friend of both Betty and Will Rogers. Morgan spent his adult life in Rogers, Ark., where he pursued a career as a full-time writer. He also operated a newsstand and bookstore for twenty years. In Rogers, he met local girl Betty Blake. He met Will Rogers while Rogers was courting Betty, and the two men became lifelong friends. Apparently Morgan, who had performed in the theater, promoted Rogers's career to Betty, and this helped advance their romance. Rogers called him his "booster." "I believe he really helped me out with my wife, for when he would see some little mention in the Theatrical papers about me, (and it would be mighty little too) why he would send or take them up to Betty" ("Politics and Jackie and a Certain Humorist," weekly article ms., published, 28 and 29 July 1928, OkClaW).

Morgan was a regional humorist who made wry observations about the life and customs of country folk in rural Arkansas. Rogers called him "one of the greatest humorists in America" (Rogers, "Worst Story I Heard Today," *TDW,* 3 August 1925). Morgan was intimately connected to his subject matter, never straying from Arkansas despite invitations from the Rogerses to visit New York and California. Rogers once told the following story: "The Curtis people brought him to Philadelphia to do some work for them; he saw their *Saturday*

Evening Post building, got scared, and went home without going to see them" (Rogers, "Worst Story I Heard Today," *TDW,* 3 August 1925).

Before settling in Arkansas, Morgan resided in other parts of the United States. He lived in Connecticut until age ten and in Kansas until age twenty-six. He once traveled with a dramatic company called the Payton Comedy Co. and a circus. His performances were remembered in a newspaper article of 1915: "He did funny parts on the stage, had a good Uncle Hiram kind of monologue, a song and a dance, and doubled on base drum in the band. It was good to meet up with Mr. Morgan, for he is an entertainer of rare potency, and can tell stories in the Arkansas language which are funnier'n a bushel of monkeys but which must be heard to be appreciated" ("Meeting Old Friends," TMC-RHM).

At the time of his death Rogers wrote a tribute to Morgan in his weekly column: "It was always original, it was nobody's idea. An old Batchelor, he lived to himself. If he had gotten out and mixed with people and had a chance to see all that was going on with his queer way of describing things, he would have raised quite a rumpus as a writer." Rogers was greatly impressed by Morgan's fluency with local slang, idioms, and expressions, which gave his razor-sharp observations a particular bite. In his tribute, Rogers wrote: "Somebody is always yapping about being a Humorist. Well this man WAS a Humorist. One of the best ones in America. I venture to say he has written stuff that has made more people laugh than any man in America" ("Politics and Jackie and a Certain Humorist," weekly article ms., published, 28 and 29 July 1928, OkClaW).

Through a charming veneer of rustic language, Morgan's poignant insights into human nature quietly enter the reader's mind. Morgan kept with him a small notebook in which he continually wrote down stories and expressions told to him by the local people. Morgan once wrote: "The folk who live in the Ozark Mountains have a viewpoint that is different from that of the rest of the world, and the fund is inexhaustible. All a writer has to do is keep his ears and his eyes peeled" ("Tom P. Morgan," TMC-RHM).

The audience for Morgan's work went well beyond Arkansas. His stories were published in *Puck, Judge, Country Gentleman, Saturday Night, Youth's Companion, Golden Days Magazine, Frank Leslie's Illustrated Newspaper,* and many other magazines. Morgan joked that his contributions ruined the publications that ran them: "It took me fifteen years of solid contributions to kill *Puck*" (Billie Jines, "Mystery of Tom P. Morgan Is Resolved," *Northwest Arkansas Morning News,* 3 May 1987, clipping, TMC-RHM). Between 1912 and 1928 he wrote a daily column for the *Kansas City Star* under the name

Tennyson J. Daft. A local paper commented about Morgan in 1917: "Mr. Morgan is living a dual life. To his friends he is known as the proprietor of a flourishing book store. In the store he is a dignified business man, but at home he is Tennyson J. Daft, writer of the worst rhymes ever penned by man" ("As Jay Sees Tom P.," TMC-RHM).

Morgan lived in a nine-room house, but only furnished two of the rooms–his bedroom and his office. He usually ate at a restaurant half a block away. His meal, three times a day, was coffee, french fries, steak, and pie. Five years before his death he had a severe stroke, and his doctor prescribed a more balanced diet. His meals were brought to him by nurse Vera Key, whom he came to regard as a daughter.

Vera Key was also assigned to live with Morgan during his recuperation. She wrote, in the preface to *The Short Stories and Wit of Tom P. Morgan,* of the great, and sometimes humorous, lengths to which she went to avoid disturbing the writer who had lived for so many years alone. When Morgan recuperated, he began to take his meals at the house of Vera Key's mother. While ill, Morgan received a telegram from Will Rogers that read: "I just got home and heard you was sick. You must have been listening to the convention speeches on the radio. It like to have got me, too. When you get better you got to come out to see me. Nothing to bother you but climate. If there is anything you need, why just holler" (Jines, "Mystery of Tom P. Morgan Is Resolved").

When Morgan had a second stroke, Vera Key quit nursing school and returned to Rogers to take care of him, as he would not allow anyone else in the house. Morgan died a week later. He willed his house and his entire collection of writings to Vera Key in return for her friendship.

Though Morgan's tongue-in-cheek humor has the sunny ease of leisurely conversation on a comfortable front porch somewhere down South, his own words about the process of writing suggest that the work did not come easily. Morgan wrote: "We do not get out material by inspiration, but by theft, assault and battery, and otherwise. A solemn, honest, peace-loving commonality is grabbed, thrown down, turned inside out, and reconstructed into an absurdity. A feeble, hoary-headed idea is ruthlessly set upon, crippled, torn to pieces, put together backwards with a new head or tail on it; the King's English is deliberately murdered–all for a joke! . . . The ability to manufacture the common or domestic variety of humor does not come by inspiration—it is a disease!" (Hancock, "Some Humor of Some Humorists," 22).

Morgan wrote works of all lengths, but a suggestion of the type of plain humor that he was known for is strikingly evident in his very short pieces. One such piece, called "The Reason," is spiked with acute observations: "One half of the world does not know how the other half lives! Well, it is gratifying to think that one half of the world attends to its own business" (Black, *Short Stories and Wit of Tom P. Morgan,* 55). Insights about human nature are scattered throughout other stories. From "Slightly Different": "'Papa, what does a United States Senator earn?' 'The average Senator does not *earn* my son; he amasses'" (ibid., 74). From "A Sufficient Reason": "'But, tell me, why are you citizens so bitter against Senator Smugg?' 'Why, confound him, he keeps telling that he was born here!'" (ibid.).

As these examples suggest, the wry wit of Morgan, especially regarding politics, sounds much like Will Rogers's humor. Although the influence of Morgan's humor on Rogers is impossible to prove, some interesting comparisons can be made. Certainly, the skeptical perspective on politicians is reminiscent of of Rogers. So is the constant implication attesting to the absurdity of everyday life. Morgan and Rogers shared a real affection for the common-sense observations of average country folk and a suspicion of the wealthy and pompous city slicker. While Morgan wrote in the voice of country characters, Rogers impersonated that voice, whether by uttering laconic one-liners on the vaudeville stage or later in writing his own daily and weekly newspaper columns. Finally, coming from neighboring states, Arkansas and Oklahoma, the two men shared that region's tradition of rural tall-tale humor that elevates the country yokel to wise sage.

A hint of Morgan's possible influence came in a letter Will Rogers wrote Betty Blake: "No I never did try any of TM. [Tom Morgan's] stuff yet" (to Betty Blake, 4 June 1908, above). Perhaps Betty had sent Rogers some of Morgan's "stuff." If so it at least reinforced Rogers's interest in and later use of folk humor.

Morgan was sixty-four at the time of his death. In his tribute Rogers wrote what would have been a fitting epitaph: "He died as I think he would have like to. He saw all he wanted to see. He did what he wanted to do. He had his Life, he had his laughs, he was satisfied, and when you are satisfied you are successful. For thats all there is to success is satisfaction. Now you kids all know Jackie Coogan. But you old time readers will always remember the name Tom P. Morgan. We've lost A Humorist" ("Politics and Jackie and a Certain Humorist," weekly article ms., published, 28 and 29 July 1928, OkClaW; see also clippings, TMC-RHM; Black, *Short Stories and Wit of Tom P. Morgan,* 55, 74, 77; Rogers, "Worst Story I Heard Today," *TDW,* 3 August 1925.)

MORRIS, William (1873–1932). William Morris gained fame in American show business as a prominent agent. His career spanned the shift from vaudeville to films, and his clients included the stars. He was Will Rogers's first vaudeville agent and managed his fledgling stage career in 1905. He was well known for stating that the sign "William Morris" would never be taken down over his office. He was correct: the agency he founded in 1898 still bears his name.

Little is known about Morris's youth. He was born Zelman Moses in Schwarzenau, located in Silesia. His father, a dry-goods merchant, had once been wealthy but had lost his fortune by lending bond money to his brother, who was convicted for smuggling vodka from Poland. Seeking to make a new start, the elder Morris went alone to the United States. In Schwarzenau, the young Morris and his sister peddled needles, thread, and other small items from a wheelbarrow. Their mother sold all the family's possessions, and they traveled to America in steerage class on the S.S. *Ems* from Bremen to New York. Morris was nine years old at the time. After a rough voyage, the family found the elder Morris living in a crowded tenement on the Lower East Side.

The young Morris grew up in the Jewish area. He attended public school, where his classmates called him "Sheeny Moses," which prompted him to change his name to William Morris. The family were very poor, and Morris worked delivering bags of coal and ice in a horse-drawn cart at dawn. He left school to clerk in a grocery store and sold newspapers in the morning. In his teens, Morris obtained a job as an office boy for a firm that published cloak-and-suit trade papers for the garment industry. Ambitious, he moved up quickly from subscription clerk to bookkeeper and then became advertising manager. A natural-born salesman, Morris at twenty years of age was averaging $10,000 yearly by selling advertising space. In the economic downturn in 1893, however, the firm went bankrupt and he had to find another job.

Morris turned to show business. He found a job as office boy with Michael Bennett Leavitt (1843–1935), a show producer, and next with George Liman, a leading agent. He helped Liman get a large number of clients, booked Liman's acts in vaudeville theaters, and was eventually promoted to general manager. After Liman's death, his widow refused to continue the partnership. Morris consequently left to form his own business in 1898 in an office on Union Square. Above the door he inserted four exes (representing a *W* over an *M*), a trademark that became permanently associated with his agency. Morris was soon booking acts for some of the most prominent vaudeville managers in the country. He boasted that his clients could play twelve weeks in New York without repeating at a theater. At this time he was supposedly earning over $100,000 a year, and he had become a power in the vaudeville world.

Morris played a pivotal part in launching Will Rogers's vaudeville career in 1905. He was responsible for booking Rogers's initial appearances at

Hammerstein's Paradise Roof Garden (19–25 June and 17 July–13 August). At the time Morris was the Victoria's main booking agent and a good friend of Willie Hammerstein, the theater's manager. That same year he also secured contracts for Rogers at Proctor's Twenty-Third Street Theatre (10–16 July) and Proctor's Newark Theatre (28 August–3 September), as well as engagements at Morrison's Rockaway Beach (N.Y.) Theatre (14–20 August) and Percy Williams's Manhattan Beach (N.Y.) Theatre (21–27 August) (vaudeville contracts 14 June 1905, 1 July 1905, 21 July 1905, and 28 July 1905, OkClaW).

Rogers's business relationship with Morris ended sometime in the fall of 1905, most likely due to the growing conflict between B. F. Keith and Morris over booking policy. Morris sent Rogers a tentative schedule of vaudeville appearances from 4 September 1905 to 19 February 1906 (William Morris vaudeville schedule, OkClaW). The schedule included theaters owned by Poli and Proctor but none owned by Keith. Rogers did not accept the schedule and never played these engagements. Morris, however, orchestrated the deal for Rogers to perform at the Victoria Theatre the week of 6 November. On 9 November 1905 Morris wrote Rogers asking that Rogers inform him of "your lowest salary for a season's work next season with a dramatic production"— an engagement that never materialized (William Morris to Will Rogers, OkClaW). Morris was listed as the agent on Rogers's contract to play at the Victoria Theatre the week of 5 March 1906, but Rogers did perform there at that time (vaudeville contract, 3 February 1906, OkClaW). Instead, he was back home preparing for a European tour and had a new agent, Mort Shea (see SHEA, Maurice [Mort] A.).

A primary reason for Rogers's change of agents was that Morris's business and power had dramatically declined due to upheavals in the vaudeville industry. By May 1906 most theater owners and managers whom he worked with, including Proctor and Poli, had left Morris to link their theaters with the Keith organization through the United Booking Offices (UBO). In 1907 Percy Williams and Oscar Hammerstein also allied with the UBO. The result was that the theater owners who allied themselves with Keith could no longer book acts through Morris. Performers who signed with Morris were blacklisted by the UBO. Morris, an iconoclast, fought the Keith-Albee organization and vehemently opposed the UBO's policy of charging a booking commission. Morris consequently lost the bookings of over forty vaudeville theaters and many other performers as well as Rogers. Stressed and exhausted over these developments, Morris became ill with tuberculosis and spent considerable time recuperating at Saranac Lake in the New York Adirondacks.

The indefatigable Morris soon began to regain his prominence in the vaudeville business. In 1907 he became the exclusive booking agent for the United States Amusement Co., informally called Advanced Vaudeville, a new circuit operated by Marc Klaw and Abraham Erlanger and the brothers Lee and Jacob J. Shubert. Advanced Vaudeville was formed to challenge the vaudeville monopoly of Keith-Albee and the UBO. The organizers promoted Advanced Vaudeville as a new, more lavish and sensational form of entertainment with low admission prices in large theaters. Without the special talents of William Morris, Advanced Vaudeville would probably never have become a reality. Morris inspired the confidence of artists and took a personal interest in the enterprise. He was reputed to have obtained $1.5 million worth of vaudeville contracts. Advanced Vaudeville premiered on 26 August 1907 at the New York Theatre with much fanfare. Many other theaters across the country offered Advanced Vaudeville shows with headliners including Joe Welch, W. C. Fields, and The Three Keatons.

Rogers was soon back with Morris. On 20 June 1907 Rogers signed a contract with Klaw & Erlanger to appear in Advanced Vaudeville for twenty-five consecutive weeks starting on 2 September 1907 at a salary of $300 weekly. After *The Girl Rangers* closed in late October 1907, Rogers played several Advanced Vaudeville dates, beginning with the New York Theatre on 28 October 1907. Through November he played Advanced Vaudeville performances at Philadelphia's People's Theatre, Brooklyn's Grand Opera House, Newark's Schubert Theatre, and Boston's Tremont Theatre. But Advanced Vaudeville failed to make a profit. On 9 November 1907 Klaw, Erlanger, and the Shuberts struck an agreement with the UBO. Acts under contract were turned over to the UBO, reportedly for up to $1.5 million. Klaw, Erlanger, and the Shuberts agreed to disband their vaudeville circuit by February 1908 and to leave vaudeville for a period of ten years. In essence, Morris was once again a victim in the vaudeville wars, and he was out of a job.

Although most show people believed Morris to be finished, he once again made a comeback. On 1 May 1908 he announced the formation of his own amusement company, a vaudeville opposition circuit. He launched a secret booking trip to Europe in late January to sign international attractions and visited London and the Continent's major capitals. His most famous client was the Scotch comic star and singer Harry Lauder, whom Morris signed for a cross-country tour at $3,000 or more per week. With Lauder and other vaudeville headliners signed, Morris announced that his burgeoning circuit would consist of thirteen houses for the coming season. His flagship theater was New York's American Music Hall, located on the southeast corner of Eighth

Avenue and Forty-second Street. "With this one house I can fight and whip the combined interests of vaudeville," Morris said (Grau, *Business Man in the Amusement World*, 12). Refurbished at a cost of $50,000, it opened on 4 May 1908. The American Music Hall featured two-a-day vaudeville with stars from the legitimate stage and big-name variety headliners such as Lauder. On 19 July 1909 Morris also reopened the American Roof Garden, a two-story theater complex where he offered summer performances twice a day.

The Morris Circuit became popular with audiences. Morris controlled and operated a string of American Music Hall theaters across the country. At one time he had offices in New York, Chicago, Boston, and New Orleans, as well as London, Paris, and Berlin. Fearing his success, the UBO threatened to bar any Morris acts from their theaters for two years. Morris challenged the Keith-Albee syndicate by offering UBO acts up to forty weeks of performance time on his own circuit. Many vaudeville artists preferred Morris and in defiance of the UBO blackball signed with him. In 1910 Morris came up with his "big bill" policy, a program of up to twenty-two quality acts without the usual headliner and with a low admission fee. "Though his bills ran to twenty and even twenty-two acts," recalled Sophie Tucker, "he was careful to have only one singer, one mimic, one wire walker or trapeze performer on each bill" (Tucker, *Some of These Days*, 89). Tucker was one of his rising stars, and he got her to give up her blackface "coon shouter" act. Morris also booked Fred Karno's comedy company, featuring the young Charlie Chaplin, into the New York American Music Hall. He guaranteed his feature acts twenty-two consecutive weeks without return dates, and he offered large weekly salaries to attract stars. By September 1910 the Morris Circuit had theaters across the country, a good talent list, and a strong capital base.

Once again, however, financial trouble plagued Morris, largely due to the sudden death of a major backer, his attorney George M. Leventritt, who had handled financial matters for the Morris Circuit. In need of capital, Morris began to search for new underwriters. In February and March 1911 Marcus Loew purchased a large interest in the Morris company, and Morris agreed to turn his theaters into venues operated by Loew. The Loew and Morris Consolidated Booking Office had its headquarters in New York's American Music Hall Building on West Forty-second Street. But by the end of 1911 Morris had lost control of his theaters, and he ended his business partnership with Loew.

Morris began a new chapter in his career. "Show business is a see-saw at best," he once wrote. "It can take you way up and way down: I've been both places several times" (*Variety*, 27 October 1926). He turned to organizing vaudeville road shows and booked special acts. Morris soon regained his prominence in the agency business. Although his performers were blacklisted by the UBO, he continued to have many headliners as his clients, including Sophie Tucker, Harry Lauder, Nora Bayes, the Dolly sisters, and Walter C. Kelly. He obtained dates for them at major theaters in New York and other cities. He opened the Wonderland in 1913, a roof-garden amusement park in the New York Theatre building with carnival acts, freak shows, and a merry-go-round. He transformed the roof garden into a cabaret with an exotic floor show and dancing, called the Jardin de Danse. By 1917 Morris had made a truce with Albee, and he was finally able to book UBO-affiliated performers. His list of clients grew in the 1920s, as did his staff. In 1927 he opened an office in Hollywood to serve the growing movie industry. Two years later he merged his agency with Paramount and was granted exclusive booking rights with the film company. In 1929 he started a radio department and handled radio shows starring Dinah Shore, Fred Allen, Fanny Brice, and Burns and Allen. He also established a music division; among his clients was Duke Ellington. By the late 1920s most of his clients were in movies, including such stars as Rudolph Valentino, James Cagney, and Joan Blondell. Around 1929 Morris unsuccessfully attempted to promote a television receiver invented by Ulysses Sanabria.

By this time Morris had been afflicted with heart disease for several years. After suffering a stroke in 1930, he retired to his large home on Lake Colby in the Adirondacks. His son William, Jr., and personal secretary Abe Lastfogel became the agency's chief executives, with Lastfogel managing the New York office and the young Morris, the Los Angeles office. William, Jr., had begun working for Morris in 1916. Lastfogel began as an office boy for Morris in 1912 and then became his secretary and treasurer.

William Morris, Jr., and Lastfogel developed the company into one of the best known talent agencies in the world. With offices in New York City, Beverly Hills, and Nashville, and international offices in London, Rome, Munich, and Sydney, the William Morris Agency today includes divisions and departments in motion pictures, music, television, theater, literature, and finance. It produces many projects in the media, ranging from Oscar-winning films and television syndication packages to country-music albums and "infomericals" ("William Morris Agency," press release, 22 July 1994).

On 1 November 1932 Morris suffered a fatal heart attack at age fifty-nine while engaged in his favorite pastime, a game of pinochle in the card room at the Friars Club in New York City. Some say vaudeville died with Morris. By 1932 radio and sound movies had displaced vaudeville as the nation's most popular forms of entertainment. A few weeks after Morris died, the Palace Theatre, the country's foremost vaudeville showplace, added films to its programming. Morris was eulogized by his show-business colleagues as a superb showman who through his independence and creativity had launched and developed the careers of many performers, among them Will Rogers.

The death of William Morris marked the end of a generation of entrepreneurs who had built the entertainment industry in the early twentieth century. Moguls such as Marcus Loew (d. 1927), Edward Albee (d. 1930), and Florenz Ziegfeld (d. 1930) were already dead. On 27 October 1926 *Variety* published a William Morris number that contained tributes from a variety of people. Among the contributors was Will Rogers, who wrote: "I wanted to be in the Bill Morris number, and I couldn't think of anything to say about him (that hasn't been said). If Bill Morris dies poor (which he perhaps will because he is on the level)—but if he does die poor, he will die the richest theatrical personage—he will have a friend to match every rich man's dollar" (Allen, *Vaudeville and Film*, 235–45; Bernheim, *Business of the Theatre*, 68–69; Connors, "American Vaudeville Managers," 70–74; *EV,* 464–65, 515–16; Fields and Fields, *From the Bowery to Broadway,* 229; Frick, *New York's First Theatrical Center,* 124; Gilbert, *American Vaudeville,* 226–28, 238–39, 338, 372–78; Goldman, *Jolson,* 40–41; Grau, *Business Man in the Amusement World,* 12, 84, 194–98, 320–22; Grau, *Forty Years Observation of Music and the Drama,* 34; Grau, "Napoleon of the Vaudeville World," 117, x; Herrick, ed., *Who's Who in Vaudeville,* 6; Laurie, *Vaudeville,* 370–74; Johnson, *Roof Gardens of Broadway Theatres,* 84, 95–100; Knapp, "Historical Study of the Legitimate Playhouses on West Forty-Second Street between Seventh and Eighth Avenues," 181–82, 193–94, 206–7, 214; Lauder, *Roamin' in the Gloamin',* 166–71; Leavitt, *Fifty Years in Theatrical Management,* 190, 198–200, 206, 213, 305, 596, 690–92, 713; Lewis Erenberg, "Impresarios of Broadway Night Life," in Taylor, ed., *Inventing Times Square,* 164; Malvern, *Valiant Minstrel,* 150–53; McNamara, *Shuberts of Broadway,* 42; *OCAT,* 421, 490; "Profiles: The Quiet Guy in Lindy's," parts 1 and 2, *New Yorker,* 20 April and 27 April; Rose, *The Agency,* 13–51; Sobel, *A Pictorial History of Burlesque,* 42–49; Spitzer, *The Palace,* 14–15; Stoddart, *Lord Broadway,* 122–24; Tucker, *Some of These Days,* 86–89, 229; van Hoogstraten, "American Theatre," in *Lost Broadway Theatres,* 28–31; William Morris file, NNMus; *Variety,* 26 April 1905, 19 May 1906, 23 February, 9 March, 10 May, 29 June, 31 August, 18 October, 16 November, and 28 December 1907, 11 January, 7 March, and 14 December 1908, 13 February, 1 May, 17 July, and 31 July 1909, 23 July, 17 September, and 10 December 1910, 27 October 1926 (William Morris number); *VO*, 2:8 November 1932; Zeidman, *American Burlesque Show*, 33–34).

MULHALL, Agnes (Bossie). See WOLFE, Agnes Mulhall.

MULHALL, Charley (1888–1958). Charley Mulhall was the son of Zack Mulhall and his mistress Georgia Smith (Mulhall) Casey. He was born in St. Louis, but little is known about his early life. As a young boy he was brought to the Mulhall ranch, where he was raised by Mary Agnes Locke Mulhall, who was already caring for his three-year-old sister Mildred as if the girl were her own child.

Charley matured into a handsome, blond, curly-headed and debonair young man. He specialized in bronco and trick riding in the family act and also drove the stagecoach in robbery skits and participated in the relay races and Pony Express rides. He appeared with the family throughout the Wild West show period (1890s–1905, 1910) and on into the vaudeville years. He turned seventeen on the opening night of the Mulhalls' appearance at Madison Square Garden in 1905 and was not yet twenty when he joined his half-sister Lucille Mulhall on the Orpheum and Keith circuits riding bucking horses on stage.

In July 1913 Charley was appearing with his father, his mother Georgia, and his half-sister Lucille in Arlington and Beckman's Oklahoma Ranch Wild West show in Winnipeg. He had a short-lived marriage to a Mulhall show cowgirl named Lulu: the couple were married in 1913, and Lulu sued for divorce in November 1914 on the grounds that Charley had deserted her three days after the wedding. In 1915 he married Iva Park, the daughter of Montana ranchers. They lived for a time in Montana, established a family (two sons and a daughter), and by World War I had moved to California, where Charley worked as a stunt rider in the film industry and tried to make a career as an actor in Westerns.

At the time of Mary Agnes Locke Mulhall's and Zack Mulhall's death in 1931 he had proven unsuccessful in Hollywood and was divorced from Iva Park Mulhall, who retained custody of their children. Helped financially by someone in Los Angeles (probably Will Rogers), Charley returned to live in Oklahoma. His half-sister Lucille, to whom he had always been very close, was also twice divorced and retired from active show business. She had been living at the old family ranch and caring for their ailing parents. His sister Mildred Mulhall Carmichael came west from Florida, and the three siblings were reunited at the Mulhall ranch.

Charley Mulhall became an arena director for the state fair in Oklahoma City and other organizations, and mounted specialty acts with Lucille Mulhall for occasional rodeos that he promoted. In 1933 he married Esther Childers of Guthrie. He worked as a security guard at a golf and country club, where he entertained members with stories of his Wild West days. He remained very close to Lucille Mulhall and was her primary confidante during the unhappy final years of her life. After Lucille died in 1940, Charley and Esther Mulhall moved to Yukon, Okla., where they both worked at the nearby Cimarron Flying School. Charley became very ill and was confined to a nursing home in Oklahoma City, where he took his own life (Mulhall scrapbook, MFC; Mulhall small collections file, WBaraC; oral history interviews with Martha Fisch, WRPP; *Billboard*, [26 August 1911], 18; [5 July 1913], 32; [5 December 1914], 22; [9 December 1933], 53; *Daily Oklahoman*, 9 February 1941; Stansbury, *Lucille Mulhall*, 9, 39, 49, 50, 86, 89, 91, 114, 165, 175, 177).

MULHALL, Georgia. See CASEY, Georgia Smith (Mulhall).

MULHALL, Mary Agnes Locke (1859–1931). The matriarch of the Mulhall clan, Mary Agnes Locke Mulhall raised her own children and several members of the extended Mulhall family, and managed the Mulhall ranch. A native of St. Louis, she was orphaned as a girl and taken in and raised by an aunt and uncle, who also informally adopted Zack (Vandeveer) Mulhall, an orphaned nephew. Mary Agnes was well educated in St. Louis schools and at St. Mary's Academy at Notre Dame, from which she graduated with honors. She married Zack Mulhall in 1875, and their first three children, Agnes, Logan, and Lucille, were born in St. Louis. Logan died of typhoid fever in 1895, and two more children, twin girls, died in infancy.

With the opening of Oklahoma Territory in 1889, the Mulhalls pioneered what became the town of Mulhall. Like Will Rogers's mother, Mary America Schrimsher Rogers, "Mother" Mulhall was well known and loved in her community for her hospitality and generosity in times of sickness and need. She took in whoever might need shelter and came to her door, including at one point a wounded Jesse James, whom she secretly nursed and hid from authorities. When Will Rogers visited the Mulhalls, he found in Mary Agnes Locke Mulhall a woman who treated him much as his own mother had. She was witty and kind, and enjoyed the antics he performed for her amusement at the piano while she was cooking meals. Like Mary Rogers, Mary Agnes Locke Mulhall was also very devout and a great lover of flowers. The Mulhall ranch was a scene very much like the one Rogers knew in his childhood on the

Rogers ranch before his mother's death. Cowboys and hired hands participated in the family life, and big Sunday dinners were held. Members of the community would come to visit and socialize after church services. Mary Agnes Locke Mulhall was very fond of Will Rogers, but Zack Mulhall disapproved of the relationship that was obviously developing between Rogers and Lucille Mulhall, for whom Zack had professional plans.

When Zack Mulhall traveled on business as a livestock agent for the railroads or was living in his second home in St. Louis, or when the family was away appearing at rodeos, on the vaudeville circuit, or in the Mulhall Rough Riders Congress shows, Mary Agnes Locke Mulhall stayed behind and maintained the ranch and farm. She also raised two of Zack Mulhall's children by Georgia Smith (Mulhall) Casey, as well as her daughter Agnes's son William and Lucille's illegitimate daughter Margaret. She was active in various clubs and community organizations in the Mulhall and Guthrie area. She lived her whole life in Mulhall and died there in January 1931 after a long struggle with cancer. In a eulogy written upon the death of Zack Mulhall in September 1931, Will Rogers wrote that "his wife, Mrs. Mulhall, will always be remembered by me as just about as fine a character as I have ever known. She was a grand old lady. She had many trials and hardships, but she stood up under them like a Saint" (syndicated column, "Rogers Mourns an Old Friend," *Atlanta Journal,* 18 October 1931, MFC; see also "Tiny Times" editorial on Mary Agnes Mulhall, ca. 1930, unidentified clipping, MFC; *Cedar Rapids Evening Gazette,* 14 April 1914, Mulhall file, OkClaW; oral history interviews with Martha Fisch, WRPP; Koch, "Zack Mulhall"; *Guthrie Daily Leader,* 20 January 1931; *ME,* 18 January, 8 February, 1 March 1901, 3 January 1902, 6 January 1905).

MULHALL, Mildred. See ACTON, Mildred Mulhall Carmichael.

ROONEY, Pat (1880–1962), and Marion Bent (1879–1940). Pat Rooney and Marion Bent were among the most popular husband-and-wife acts in vaudeville. Rooney and Bent often played on the same bill with Will Rogers, which led to a lifelong friendship. Pat Rooney II was born in New York City on the Fourth of July. He was the only boy in a family of five sisters, and his parents were professional vaudevillians. His mother was the actress Josie Granger; his father Pat was an immigrant Irishman who began his career as a boxer and then became a song-and-dance man. Part of his success was his appeal to immigrant Irish audiences. Pat II wrote of his father: "There was no green-whiskered burlesque of the Irishman in his rough makeup, but his humor was born of the real shamrock. . . . His dancing clinched his success. It was as true to Ireland as a come-all-ye" (*Variety,* 20 December 1912).

Pat Rooney II's best known dance routine, a clog dance called "The Daughter of Rosie O'Grady," was often erroneously remembered as having been performed by his father, although he had died fourteen years before the 1919 debut of that particular piece. As a dancer Pat II was described as "a sort of electrified hairpin" (Slide, *The Vaudevillians,* 128). Rooney began dancing in vaudeville at age ten with his parents and continued until the demise of that entertainment form. Thus he was among the small number of performers to see the beginning and end of vaudeville's golden era.

Rooney married Marion Bent on 10 April 1904. They had met on the set of *Mother Goose,* a musical that opened at the New Amsterdam Theatre in December of 1903. Bent was also from a performing family, being the daughter of cornet soloist Arthur Bent and the dancer Alice Lawless.

The team of Rooney and Bent was well liked by audiences, and at one time they commanded fees of $4,000 weekly. They were regularly booked solid for weeks at a time. Their act consisted of song, dance, and comic dialogue with a slightly absurdist edge. Their signature song was "She's the Daughter of Rosie O'Grady." In the 1920s their New York apartment was a center of night life, a place where theater people gathered after hours. In 1921 they appeared together in the musical *Love Birds.* In 1925 they starred in another musical, *The Daughter of Rosie O'Grady,* which was developed around Rooney's classic dance of the same name. Bent retired from the stage in 1932 due to arthritis. The two had performed together as a dance-and-comedy team for about thirty years.

Rooney and Bent had one son, Pat Rooney III. He was born while his father was playing in Providence, R.I., in a show called *Simple Simon.* Upon receiving news of the birth, the new father held a celebration at a local hotel, traveled to New York by train to see the baby, and returned in time to perform in the next show. As a boy, Pat III was often cared for by his grandmother, Josie Granger, while his parents were traveling, just as Pat II had been cared for by his grandmother years before.

Pat III performed occasionally with his parents, but never made a real career in the theater, although the three of them appeared together in a page advertising their act in the *National Vaudeville Artists Yearbook* for 1927. The copy read: "Watch for 1928–29 Rooneyisms." Pat III performed an extraordinary dance with his father, in which the two men would mirror each other, working back to back. One season Pat II's sister Kate impersonated Pat Rooney I, and she, Pat II, and Pat III were billed as the "Three Generations: Pat the First, Pat the Second, and Pat the Third."

The first time Rooney and Bent were on the same vaudeville program with Will Rogers was at Percy Williams's Manhattan Beach Theatre, the week of 21 August 1905. At that time Rogers had been on the vaudeville trail for only a little over two months, while Rooney and Bent were experienced vaudevillians. The three seem to have become good friends rather quickly because in November 1906 Rogers was invited to their Manhattan home for a party. Rooney and Bent were noted for their hospitality to fellow vaudevillians (see Pat Rooney and Marion Bent to Will Rogers, 17 November 1906, OkClaW). Later, Rooney told Rogers to eliminate the horse from his roping act and to concentrate instead on the lasso stunts and the humorous chatter.

By 1914 Rogers and the team of Rooney and Bent often interacted on stage during a program. They performed on the same program at Keith's Chestnut Street Theatre, the week of 9 February 1914 (see Manager's Report, Keith's Chestnut Street Theatre, 9 February 1914, *PWR,* vol. 3). There they appeared in each other's act, poking fun at one another. Rogers was on the same playbill with them again at Toledo's Arcade Theatre, the week of 8 October 1905 (see Article from the *Toledo Times,* 11 October 1905, above). At Chicago's Majestic Theater in December 1914 Rooney and Bent were crowned "King and Queen" of comedy. As part of the fun, Rooney was presented on stage with an iron cross by Will Rogers. A review from that time recounts how Rogers poked fun at Rooney during his act and pretended to lasso Rooney as he stood in the wings. When Rooney came on during his own act, he brought a coil of rope and gave an imitation of Rogers. Whereupon Rogers, as he stood in the wings, roped Rooney and tried to pull him off the stage. However, Rooney succeeded in pulling Rogers to center stage instead, where they performed for a short time together, to the delight of the crowd. As a finale, Rooney gave an amusing imitation of Rogers (*Chicago Herald* clipping, scrapbook 1914, CPpR). Their last vaudeville appearance on the same playbill was at the Palace Theatre, the week of 7 February 1915 (see Reviews from the Palace Theatre, ca. 8 February 1915, *PWR,* vol. 3). The three continued to be good friends, and Rogers invited Rooney and Bent to his ranch for a vacation during the summer of 1935.

That same year Rooney and Bent and their son performed at New York's Capitol Theater in celebration of the couple's thirty-second wedding anniversary. At that time they were honored by the Friars Club at a dinner. The 1940s was a time of difficulty for Rooney. His wife died in 1940. The costs of his wife's long illness and real estate losses led Rooney to declare bankruptcy a year later. His debts totaled $8,000, and his assets were listed at about $200, including his clothes. In 1942 Rooney married the dancer Helen Ruon (whose stage name was Janet Reade and who was the divorced wife of his son). Shortly after her death in 1943 he married Carmen Schaffer and remained with her the rest of his life.

In 1949 Rooney celebrated his sixtieth year in show business by appearing at the Orpheum Theatre in San Francisco. He performed renditions of his dances from vaudeville's golden era. That same year he performed at New York's Palace Theatre in a variety show that featured old-time vaudeville head-liners. In 1950 Rooney played Arvide Abernathy in the original stage version of *Guys and Dolls*. He received nightly accolades for singing "More I Cannot Wish You." In addition, he appeared often on television, frequently on the Ed Sullivan show. In 1952 Rooney looked back at his career and commented that he had been one of the first to write dance steps down on paper, a common practice today. He maintained his youthful weight of 130 pounds until his death at age eighty-two. He gave up drinking for the sake of his health at age sixty-seven, and two months before his death gave up his habit of fourteen cigars a day. In September 1962 he died of a heart attack at his Manhattan apartment in the Sherman Square Hotel at Broadway and Seventy-first Street (Pat Rooney biographical file, CLAc; Pat Rooney biographical file, NNMus; Pat Rooney Collection, PR-TxU, file J7: 2, 6, 16, 36, 42, 61; "Pat Rooney on Orpheum Vaudeville," *Oakland Tribune*, vaudeville clipping file, CSf-PALM; *Variety*, 20 December 1912; *VO* 5:12 September 1962).

RUSSELL, Charles M. (1864–1926). The great western artist Charles Marion Russell was a lifelong friend of Will Rogers, the two sharing a love of the West and the cowboy life. Russell was born on 19 March 1864 in Oak Hill, Mo., a suburb of St. Louis. Like Will Rogers, the young Russell was not particularly interested in education and left a military boarding school in New Jersey after one term. As a boy, he much preferred reading dime novels about the West. He frequently visited the St. Louis waterfront, where he watched the river-boatmen, trappers, and fur traders travel up the Missouri River. A self-trained artist, Russell developed an early interest in art. He sketched scenes around him on the margins of schoolbooks, on sidewalks, and on the front steps. He also began modeling small animals and horses using clay.

Russell was an adventuresome youth known as Kid Russell to his friends. In 1880, shortly before his sixteenth birthday, he and a family friend, Pike Miller, left for Montana Territory, where Russell worked as a shepherd on Miller's ranch. Russell next became a trapper and hunter, and in 1882 he worked as a cowhand, night herder, and horse wrangler. He worked for about ten years as a cowboy with outfits in central and northern Montana. He participated in cattle drives and experienced many events that he later portrayed in his work.

In his spare time Russell drew watercolor sketches of the cowboy life around him. Around 1885 he ordered canvas and oil paint from the East and started painting in that medium. During roundups he drew on whatever he could find and once used the ends of beer kegs and a silk lining from a Stetson. In early 1887 he drew a watercolor sketch on a postcard called "Waiting for a Chinook," a picture of a starving steer about to perish in the cold Montana winter and be devoured by wolves. The work symbolized the death of thousands of cattle during that harsh winter. The sketch became extremely popular, and its reproduction began Russell's reputation.

In 1888 Russell lived among the Blood Indians in Canada, where he learned their language and participated in their hunting expeditions and ceremonies. This experience inspired his depictions of Native American life. Russell began to receive commissions, and he sold some illustrations to magazines and book publishers. In 1893 he decided to devote himself entirely to painting.

In 1896 Russell married Nancy Cooper (1868–1940); she managed his artistic career, arranged exhibitions, and publicized his work. A year after their marriage they moved to Great Falls, Mont., and in 1900 they built a home in the town, to which they added a log cabin studio in 1903. In his studio Russell painted in the mornings, while in the afternoon he met with his cronies at local saloons such as the Mint (its owner, Sid Willis, built a major collection of Russell's work). Now a museum, the Great Falls home became Russell's permanent residence. In 1903 the Russells went to New York where Russell exhibited his work, sold a painting for $500, and signed contracts with publishers to do book illustrations. At the 1904 St. Louis World's Fair, Russell displayed his paintings at the Palace of Fine Arts. Rogers was then appearing at Wild West shows on the Pike, but the two men did not meet at this time.

Russell occasionally traveled to New York to attend exhibitions of his work. During a visit to the city in the winter of 1908 he met Rogers. Rogers recalled: "I first met Russell in New York. That was a long time ago. He was there to sell some of his paintings and I was trying to peddle some jokes. The longer we knew each other the better we seemed to hit it off" ("Will Rogers Visits Haunts of Russell after Old Time Reception Here," *Great Falls Tribune,* 1 April 1927, microfilm reel 2, CMR-MHS). The artist visited Rogers at the Putnam House (later called Hotel Preston), where Rogers usually stayed in New York. Perhaps Rogers visited Russell's studio near Fortieth Street and Broadway. At this time Russell, Rogers, and several others (Fred Stone, Ed Borein, and Leo Carillo) formed a coterie of westerners in Manhattan.

Rogers and Russell had much in common. Not only were they artists in their own realms, but also they shared a passion for the West, the outdoor life, and horses, and an understanding of Native American culture. They had experienced the rugged life of the frontier, roundups, cattle drives, and horse wrangling. Russell and Rogers enjoyed spinning folksy yarns and telling tall tales, evident both in Rogers's writings and in Russell's published stories, which he wrote under the pseudonym Rawhide Rawlins. In their writing both shared a penchant for western vernacular, a tendency toward misspelling, and a indifference for the rules of syntax, grammar, and punctuation.

Over the years their paths crossed in New York, London, and southern California. When Rogers saw Russell's work exhibited in Manhattan, he immediately liked his art. During a vaudeville date in Butte, Mont., in June 1908, Rogers sent Betty Blake many postcards illustrated by Russell. He also gave her a book, Bower's *The Lure of the Dim Trail,* illustrated by Russell. In 1925 Russell saw Rogers perform in the *Ziegfeld Follies,* and he and his wife were frequently invited to visit the Rogerses.

In 1917 Russell wrote Rogers informing him that he and his wife could not visit him in New York because they needed to care for their new adopted baby, Jack. "Wev got a six months old boy at our camp and we think hes a little young for trail work so we are going to class herd him a while." Russell also wrote: "My wife got a letter from your best half asking us to come and camp with you all we both thank you verry much but we wont worke your range this year." Above the letter Russell drew "the long promised sketch" he had promised (Russell, called a "word painter," often drew sketches on his letters to friends). The drawing showed a cowboy on a bronco roping a steer. "It represents an old time cow dog mounted on a bronk," wrote Russell (Russell, *Good Medicine,* 27).

In the 1920s Russell and Rogers often saw one another in southern California. Beginning in 1920 Russell spent extended winters in Los Angeles where his paintings attracted the interest of film stars, such as William S. Hart (a longtime friend), Douglas Fairbanks, and Harry Carey. Russell was a frequent guest at Rogers's home in Beverly Hills. They also met at Hart's ranch in Newhall, Calif. In 1923 Rogers and Russell attended a large gathering of friends at the actor Harry Carey's large ranch in Saugus. During the picnic Russell entertained the guests by telling tall tales. Rogers felt Russell was a great storyteller. He wrote: "Why you never heard me open my mouth when you was around, and you never knew any of our friends that would let me open it as long as there was a chance to get you to tell another one. I always did say that you could tell a story better than any man that ever lived" (introduction to Russell, *Trails Plowed Under,* xiv).

In the 1920s Russell was at the height of his fame as a western artist, noted for his paintings and sculptures that depicted the passing of the old West. Rugged cowboys, courageous Indians, wild animals, and the untamed wilderness dominated his compositions. Exhibitions of his work were held in European and American cities. In southern California, Russell was part of a cadre of western painters that included the artist Joe De Yong, a disciple of Russell, and the Santa Barbara painter Ed Borein. The latter two also befriended Rogers, and together they formed a coterie of friends who liked to ride, reminisce, tell stories by the campfire, and spend time together (Rogers collected De Yong's and Borein's art).

Russell and Rogers also frequented the salon of Charles Fletcher Lummis (1859–1928), a writer, historian, archaeologist, and bibliophile who celebrated the Southwest and its Spanish, Mexican, and Indian roots in his work. Accompanied by their wives, Rogers and Russell joined other luminaries at Lummis's famous parties, called "noises," held at his rustic stone house, El Alisal, located by the Arroyo Seco, a few miles from downtown Los Angeles. Those invited were asked to sign the guest books, which read like a Who's Who of Los Angeles in the 1920s. The Russells and Rogerses signed Lummis's guest book on 21 February and 7 March 1920 (CLC-SWM). The 21 February event was in honor of the writer and naturalist John Burroughs (1837–1921). On warm summer nights a Mexican barbecue was served on the patio. At the soirées Russell told stories, and Rogers sometimes sang and performed rope tricks.

In 1921 Russell visited Rogers at the Goldwyn studio where he was filming *A Poor Relation.* The two were photographed together sitting on a step in front of Stage One. In a letter to Rogers, dated 21 May 1921, Russell asked Rogers to show his friend Jim Hobbins the Goldwyn studio. (Russell wrote similar letters to Douglas Fairbanks and William Hart.) The salutation was misspelled as "Rodgers," and Russell addressed Rogers as "Friend Bill." Rogers's meeting with Hobbins never took place (Dippie, ed., *Charles M. Russell,* 315).

Over the years Rogers collected Russell's paintings and sculpture. In his weekly article at the time of Russell's death he called Russell the "Cowpunchers' Painter." He wrote: "I loved his paintings; could sit by the hour and look at one and marvel at the exact detail, every piece of rope, every saddle string, every hair on the horse laying just the way it should, and every painting had a touch of humor in them" (*TDW,* 21 November 1926). Rogers bought the 1897 watercolor *Squaws with Travois,* depicting a camp movement of the Plains Indians. He also purchased *The Buffalo Hunt No. 39* (1919), a dramatic scene showing three Indians on horseback pursuing a herd. Russell had intended to display the painting at the Minneapolis Institute of the Arts, but when Rogers bought it the artist had to paint another buffalo hunt scene (No. 40) for the show. Russell made a bronze sculpture (undated; height 11 1/4 inches, base 5 x 9 7/8 inches) of Rogers riding on horseback, a symbol of their shared love of the West and their friendship. Several Russell bronzes sit atop the sideboard in the dining room at Rogers's Pacific Palisades house. There are also watercolors and etchings by Russell on the walls (as well as works by Ed Borein).

Suffering from rheumatism and a goiter, Russell was in failing health by the mid-1920s. On 24 October 1926 he died as a result of a heart attack at his home in Great Falls. The Rogerses telegraphed their condolences to his widow and for the funeral ordered a floral arrangement resembling a saddle. In his weekly article Rogers called Russell "the greatest Artist the west has ever produced. . . . To have known Charley and just sit down and listen to him was the greatest remembrance of anyone's life who had that pleasure" (*TDW,* 21 November 1926).

Rogers's relationship with Russell was far from over. A year after Russell's death, Rogers wrote the introduction to *Trails Plowed Under: Stories of the Old West* (1927), a collection of Russell's tales. Rogers lamented the loss of his friend: "Hello Charley old hand, How are you? I just thought I would drop you a line and tell you how things are a working on the old range since you left. Old Timer you don't know how we miss you, Gee but its been lonesome since you left, even to us away down here in California, where we didnent get to see near as much of you as we wanted to anyhow" (xiii). In 1929 Russell's wife asked Rogers to write the introduction to *Good Medicine,* a publication of Russell's letters that were embellished with his drawings. In the introduction Rogers celebrated his friend as a great artist, storyteller, letter writer, humorist, and humanitarian.

In the spring of 1927, Rogers returned to Great Falls, where he visited Russell's studio, saw exhibits of his work, and performed at the Grand Theater. While in Great Falls Rogers bought a Russell oil, *Moving Camp* (1894), for $2,500 as a gift for his daughter Mary. He also purchased three watercolors: *Wild Horse Hunters* (1905) for $800, *Indians in Camp* (1896) for $500, and *Quiet Day in Chinook* (1895) for $500. In addition, he contributed $500 to the Chamber of Commerce for a Russell memorial.

Rogers is credited with introducing Amon G. Carter, Sr., the Fort Worth, Tex., newspaper owner, oilman, and philanthropist, to Russell's art. "It was Rogers who brought Russell's work to the attention of his friend Amon G. Carter, Sr.," wrote Jan Keene Muhlert, director of the Amon Carter Museum in Forth Worth (foreword to Dippie, ed., *Charles M. Russell,* vi). Carter started collecting Russell's art in 1935. By the end of the 1940s Carter had bought many more Russell paintings from Russell's widow. In 1952 Carter bought the large Russell art collection from Sid Willis, owner of the Mint Saloon in Great Falls, for over $200,000. Carter's collection forms the nucleus for Russell's exhibited work at the Amon Carter Museum, which opened in 1961.

Rogers's admiration for Russell is best expressed in his final words in the introduction to *Good Medicine:* "He not only left us great living Pictures of what our West was, but he left us an example of how to live in friendship with all mankind. A Real Downright, Honest to God, Human Being" (introduction to Russell, *Good Medicine,* 16; see also CMR-MoSHi, research and microfilm material; Dippie, ed., *Charles M. Russell; NYT,* 13 April 1924; Renner, *Charles M. Russell,* 26, 29, 78, 126, 226, 236–39, 239; Renner, *Paper Talk,* 7–12, 98; Russell, *Good Medicine;* Russell, *Trails Plowed Under; TDW,* 21 November 1926; Yagoda, *Will Rogers,* 171–74).

SHEA, Maurice (Mort) A. (1880–1940). Mort Shea, theater owner and talent agent, managed Will Rogers in his early vaudeville career. He also managed such notables as Vernon and Irene Castle and Elsie Janis. Shea was the founder of the Felber and Shea Circuit, which eventually became the Shea Theatre Corporation operating primarily motion picture theaters in New England, New York, Ohio, and Pennsylvania. During the 1930s Shea was also a partner in a group of Paramount theaters.

Shea became Rogers's booking agent in late 1905, probably after his appearance at Hammerstein's Victoria Theatre, the week of 6–12 November. At this time Rogers was thinking about leaving vaudeville and returning home. "'Going back home with the boys,' was his expression," said Shea. "He told me he was disgusted with the East and had his ticket to go back Wednesday night. I insisted that he stay here. I delivered the contracts" (Mort Shea interview, HCP-MoU). On 1 December 1905 Shea wired Rogers at the Park Theatre to say that he had obtained a special Sunday night engagement for him on 3 December at New York's Casino Theatre (From Mort A. Shea, 1 December 1905, above).

Shea remembered that Rogers told jokes right from his start in vaudeville. "He used to do a monologue between a rope and a horse. One of his best wisecracks he ever made—made his rope go 'way out, about two thirds out, then he'd muff it, just to kill time. Then he used to turn to the audience, and then he used to jump in and out of it. He used to muff it purposely and he would say, 'I got all my feet through but one'. That never failed to get a laugh" (Mort Shea interview, HCP-MoU).

Shea, who had good European connections, was instrumental in arranging Rogers's appearance at Berlin's Wintergarten Theatre in April 1906 (vaudeville contract, 28 March 1906, OkClaW). A notice in *Variety* on 17 February 1906, which Rogers kept in his scrapbook, was headlined "Will Rogers for Germany" and announced that Mort Shea had handled the booking and Alex Steiner had made the arrangements (scrapbook A-1, OkClaW). On 28 April Shea bought a large advertisement in *Variety* that featured three photographs of Will Rogers roping, with the headline: "Opened at Wintergarten, Berlin April 1st . . . Created a Sensation." According to Shea, Rogers's success at the Wintergarten led to his engagement at London's Palace Theatre in May. "The manager of the Wintergarten got in touch with Alfred Butt of the Palace Theatre in London—and after many conferences Mr. Butt decided to let Rogers open" (Mort Shea interview, HCP-MoU).

Under Shea, Rogers's salary jumped to $250 a week, from which he had to pay his agent a 5 percent commission. "Never had a scratch of the pen between us," Shea recalled. "He would owe me sometimes six months and he would come in and pay me all at once" (Mort Shea interview, HCP-MoU). In a letter to Betty Blake, Rogers wrote that he had wired Shea $150—"I got it from the Manager last night" (28 April 1909, OkClaW). Shea found Rogers to be an "ordinary fellow" both on and off stage. "Never used any make-up," he said. "Just pulled on a pair of chaps on the stage and walked on. Tied a handkerchief around his neck and walked on" (Mort Shea interview, HCP-MoU).

Shea obtained vaudeville bookings for Rogers until at least December 1908, including a contract on the Keith Circuit for sixteen weeks, beginning 3 September 1906, at a salary of $250 per week (vaudeville contract, 24 March 1906, OkClaW). "The reason that I stopped booking him was that I took on a number of theaters and gave up the agency business," recalled Shea (Mort Shea interview, HCP-MoU). Vaudeville contract records dated 14 December 1908 indicate that the agent, Pat Casey, booked Rogers on his Western Vaudeville Association Circuit tour in early 1909.

Shea was known as an amiable person and was well liked in the show-business profession. He and his wife, Margaret L. Brooks, were the parents of three sons and one daughter. Shea died on 19 October 1940 after having been ill for several years (*NYT,* 20 October 1940; *VO,* 3:23 October 1940).

THE THREE KEATONS. The Three Keatons were a knockabout vaudeville act consisting of Myra Cutler Keaton (1877–1955), her husband Joseph Hollie Keaton (1867–1946), and their son, Joseph Francis (Buster) Keaton (1895–1966), who later became famous in his own right. Joe Keaton was born in Prairie Creek Township, Ind., some seventeen miles from Terre Haute. By the time he was twelve, it was clear that his interests lay in playing pool rather than attending school, in fighting with the local boys, and in entertaining the local farmers. As a young man, he became a drifter who roamed across the West, traveling from town to town on freight trains. There are many stories about his adventures, many either false or exaggerated. According to Buster Keaton, his father went to Oklahoma Territory in 1889 and that year participated in the Land Run. With a stake of $100 he claimed some federal government land, which he soon sold for $1,000; he then went to California to become an entertainer. Another story is that Joe staked a homestead claim for his father in the Cherokee Outlet or Strip. Legend has it that Joe Keaton met Will Rogers in either the Indian Territory or Oklahoma Territory. None of these accounts has ever been proven. More than likely, it was their common experiences out west that drew Joe Keaton and Rogers together. They played the vaudeville circuits together on several occasions during their years in show business.

While in Oklahoma Territory, at the age of twenty-six, Joe Keaton joined the Cutler Comedy Company, a traveling medicine show. He was hired for $3 a week plus board and transportation. He was expected to be a circus performer, handyman, and bouncer. Wearing blackface, Keaton did a comic monologue, sang songs, and danced a jig. Soon he fell in love with Myra Cutler, the daughter of the circus owner, F. L. Cutler. As a young girl, Myra played the piano, bull fiddle, and cornet on stage, and later the saxophone. Keaton and Cutler eloped in 1894. They performed as a team in several traveling medicine shows. Myra played the cornet, while Joe performed a knockabout dance act and a blackface routine. During their years on the road Buster Keaton was born, in Piqua, Kans., a railroad town.

The Keatons began in vaudeville around 1899. They got several bookings in New York, including an engagement at Tony Pastor's variety theater. They had a novel knockabout act called "The Man With the Table." One of Joe Keaton's specialties was to jump from the floor onto the seat of a chair as it stood on a table. He performed this stunt at six shows a day. The jump was easy to miss and crowds knew this, clamoring to see if he would do it or take a tumble. The climax of the act came when Myra would sit in the chair on the table and hold out a cigar box. Joe would then kick high into the air and shatter the cigar box.

Practically from birth, Buster Keaton accompanied his parents on their tours. He slept in a stage trunk in the evening while his parents worked. As a toddler, he would suddenly appear on stage while his parents were performing. Once he fell down a flight of stairs, but fortunately was unhurt. Learning of the incident, an actor friend called him Buster, and the name stuck. He joined the act at the age of five and appeared on stage for the first time in October 1900. Buster soon became the centerpiece of his parents' act. He first did imitations and dancing, which drew praise from reviewers. One critic wrote: "Mr. Keaton, Sr., is an acrobat of no mean accomplishments, but his young son, about five years of age, not only executes the stunts set for him but he gives his sire a few points better" (Myra Keaton Scrapbook, CBevA, 41). Buster Keaton remembered his role more modestly: "Well we just did a rough, knock about act. I'd just simply get in my father's way all the time and get kicked all over the stage" (Buster Keaton interview, oral history collection, URL-CLU).

Buster was known on the vaudeville stage as "The Human Mop" and billed as "The Little Boy Who Can't Be Damaged." His stage costume featured a suitcase handle mounted between the shoulders by which he would be pulled and pushed around. One time Buster was used as a human cannonball to silence a group of hecklers. The impact of Buster broke the nose of a heckler and smashed the ribs of another. On a different occasion, Buster was unconscious for eighteen hours as the result of a kick from Joe. Once while they were playing the Palace in London, Alfred Butt asked Joe Keaton if Buster was his own son or adopted. When Joe told him that Buster was his own son, Butt said: "My word . . . I imagined he was an adopted boy and you didn't give a dam what you did to him" (*Variety*, 11 December 1909). An x-ray of Keaton in 1935 showed cracked vertebrae that had calcified.

Urban-reform organizations thought the Keatons were exploiting child labor. New York's Gerry Society (the Society for the Prevention of Cruelty to Children) had the act banned from New York theaters for two years, as part of its effort to regulate child labor in show business. In many cases, Buster Keaton recalled, they could evade the law successfully "because the law read, no child under the age of sixteen shall do acrobatics, walk wire, play musical instruments, trapeze, . . . but none of them said you couldn't kick him in the face" (Buster Keaton interview, URL-CLU). For some time Buster was billed as a midget in an effort to evade regulation as well as to add interest to the act. By the time Buster was twelve it was no longer possible to pretend he was a midget. When he was thirteen, his father announced in the trade papers: "BUSTER IS SIXTEEN BUSTER IS SIXTEEN BUSTER IS SIXTEEN" (Dardis, *Keaton*,

19). After Buster's baby brother Harry (Jingles) was born around 1904, he was no longer advertised as a midget. Instead, the act was presented as "Joe, Myra, Buster and Jingles Keaton: Joe Keaton, the Man with the Wife, Two Kids and a Table and Two Chairs and Some Rosin" (*NYDM*, 2 June 1906).

When in New York the Keatons lived at the Ehrich House on West Thirty-Eighth Street, where the food was good and the rooms were clean, roomy, and comfortable. It was operated by a German family; Carl Ehrich (ca. 1861–1926) was its proprietor for twenty-five years. Joe Keaton once recommended the Ehrich boardinghouse to Will Rogers on his Three Keatons business card (see Business Card of The Three Keatons, ca. 1906, above). In 1927 Joe sent a telegram to Rogers when he was in the hospital recovering from a gallbladder operation. It stated: "What ever Cal [President Coolidge] wired you is my sentiments exactly" (telegram, OkClaW). Rogers performed several times on the same vaudeville program as The Three Keatons. One occasion was at Hammerstein's Victoria Theatre, the week of 25 January 1914 (see Review from *Variety*, 30 January 1914, *PWR*, vol. 3).

The Three Keatons' vaudeville act ended when Buster Keaton reached twenty-one and when his father's alcoholism made him an increasingly unreliable performer. When the act ended, Myra Keaton encouraged her son to perform on his own, and he soon went on to great success as a silent-movie comedian. One day in 1917 he watched Fatty Arbuckle shoot a movie, and he became entranced with the camera and the possibilities of film. His most famous film work appeared between 1923 and 1927 and included *Our Hospitality* (1923), *Sherlock Jr.* (1924), *The Navigator* (1924), and *The General* (1927).

Joe Keaton sometimes performed in his son's early films and played in five of the nineteen short silent comedies. In the early shorts, Buster Keaton makes use of the high-energy antics that he learned on the vaudeville stage. In one film, *The Playhouse* (1922), he consciously recalls images from his vaudeville past. The film depicts a typical nine-act vaudeville program, including orchestra, an animal act, novelties, dancers, and minstrels. The entire film is acted by Keaton himself; he plays the parts of all the vaudevillians as well as members of the audience. Several shorts resemble the knockabout antics and acrobatics of Keaton's vaudeville days. In *Neighbours* (1919) Joe and Buster Keaton perform a vaudeville-like comic sequence: Pa K (Joe Keaton) is beating a rug on a clothesline in the background. As he looks away, Buster is substituted for the carpet and Joe beats him instead. As Buster is pegged to the rope by his shoes, he pivots on the line and swings down, smacking Joe to the ground. Joe removes the clothespins, and Buster drops down into a pail of water. In many films, Buster Keaton is pursued by the police, just as the Keatons spent many years evading the Gerry Society. Thus Buster's experience in vaudeville as one of The Three Keatons shaped the art of one of the great screen comedians (Blesh, *Keaton,* 41; Buster Keaton, interview, Arthur Friedman Turning Point Series, oral history collection, URL-CLU; Buster Keaton interview, oral history collection, NNC, 1; *DAB,* suppl. 8:313–16; Dardis, *Keaton: The Man Who Wouldn't Lie Down,* 12–19, 23–24; Dimeglio, *Vaudeville USA,* 99–100; *EV,* 498–99; Keaton, *My Wonderful World of Slapstick,* 15–19, 43; Meade, *Buster Keaton;* Myra Keaton Scrapbook, CBevA; *NYDM,* 2 June 1906; *NYT,* 21 May 1903; Oldham, *Keaton's Silent Shorts; Variety,* 11 December 1909).

TOMPKINS, Charles (ca. 1875–1957), and Mabel Hackney (d. 1950). Champion cowboy performer and Wild West promoter Charles Tompkins was a friend and colleague of Will Rogers. He was born in Round Rock, Tex., in 1873 or 1875 and began working as a cattle-ranch hand when he was twelve years old. He drove cattle on the Abilene, Tex., to Dodge City, Kans., trail in 1886–87 and became a hand at the XIT Ranch outside Darhart, Tex., participating in the last of the XIT Ranch's huge cattle drives to Montana. Like Will Rogers, he began his career in entertainment in the 1890s, when he entered roping contests as a competitor. He was an outstanding rodeo performer in both riding and roping. In the late 1890s he began working in Wild West shows, and in the early 1900s he served as an arena director for various productions. In 1904 he directed a Congress of Champion Ropers and Riders at the St. Louis World's Fair.

Rogers had known Tompkins since roping-contest days. They met during a roping event in San Antonio, Tex., in the fall of 1901, not long before Rogers left for his travels in South America and beyond. Tompkins remembered that Rogers approached him to praise him for his performance in that day's steer-roping session. He recalled that he was sitting in front of the Southern Hotel when Rogers "came along and sit down in this chair facing me with his legs over the chair and his face to the back of the chair. He was small and a wirey looking little fellow, dark hair and I knew at once that he had some Indian blood in him, as I knew Indian Territory folks very well" (Tompkins to Homer Croy, 1 August 1952, HCP-MoU). While Rogers was in Argentina and South Africa in 1902, Tompkins worked as the arena director with the Buckskin Bill Wild West show at Paducah, Ky. He directed the great Fourpaugh Wild West shows in St. Louis in 1903, and developed his own show for the St. Louis World's Fair in 1904. Rogers worked briefly for Tompkins's Congress of

Champion Ropers and Riders in St. Louis, following Zack Mulhall's banishment from the fairground in June 1904. He and Tompkins saw each other again in New York in 1905, when Rogers was appearing in vaudeville and living at the Putnam Hotel. Tompkins later joined Rogers as a bronco rider in Rogers's short-lived 1911 group act, Will Rogers and Company.

Tompkins married Mabel Hackney in 1904, and for the next several years they collaborated in the Wild West business. Hackney was an expert professional rider who had won dozens of awards in horse shows and was particularly famed for her show jumping. She was a veteran of the Wild West scene, having worked with the Buffalo Bill Wild West show before riding with Tompkins's Congress of Champion Ropers and Riders and the Mulhall shows during the St. Louis World's Fair. After appearing in St. Louis in 1904, she and Tompkins joined McCaddon's Great International Circus for a tour of Europe in 1905 (Charles Tompkins served as assistant arena director). The tour was a financial disaster, and the Tompkinses lost the money they had invested in it. They returned to the United States and kept an apartment in New York City. Rogers was a frequent guest there as he started out in his career in vaudeville in 1905. Charles Tompkins worked for the Interborough Rapid Transit Co. in the subway division during that time. One of the attractions of the Tompkins household for Rogers was Mabel's good home cooking, and she often sent care packages with a pot of navy beans to Rogers to eat for supper at the theaters where he was performing. Tompkins recalled Rogers's generosity during this period, stating that Rogers gave so much of his money away to others that he had little left over for himself or Buck McKee. One of the people Rogers helped out was a circus performer, a friend of the Tompkinses, who suffered from tuberculosis and found herself too ill to continue work in New York, with no funds to return home to her husband in St. Louis (Rogers paid for her travel). He was also generous with the stagehands who handled Teddy for his act.

The Tompkinses played fairs in the United States with their own troupe, Tompkins Real Wild West show, from 1906 to 1912. Charles Tompkins also performed with the Klaw and Erlanger *Round Up* act at the Grand Opera House on 23rd Street in New York. The Tompkinses were working with Tompkins's Wild West show when Rogers came to visit them in the off season in New Hope, Pa., to look at their horses and discuss their joining with him in his Will Rogers and Co. stage act. The Tompkinses helped him develop the act; they stabled the horses and helped train them, and worked with the initial members of the act, including Florence LaDue and her husband Guy Weadick, Wyoming bronco rider Goldie St. Clair, and Tillie

Baldwin. The group stage act proved unwieldy and unprofitable because of its size, and after a few performances it disbanded. The Tompkinses appeared in a stripped-down version with just four riders that Rogers used in the spring of 1911.

From 1913 to 1917 the Tompkinses operated Tompkins's Real Wild West and Frontier Exhibition in combination with the Cooper-Whitby Circus and in collaboration with Dr. Henry Wilson Turner and Mary A. Turner of New Hope, Pa. The Turners both had experience in the circus, and the horses used in the show were wintered at their Pennsylvania farm. The new Wild West show was designed to tour eastern Pennsylvania, New Jersey, and New York in the spring and summer, and Maryland and Virginia in the fall. Featured performers in the show included the Tompkinses, Dixie DeVere (a "great cowgirl rider"), Milt Hinkle (the "South American Kid"), Chief Running Deer, Owasso, Doc Dill, Augie Ontevares Gomez (who worked as an extra in Tom Mix's films), bulldogger Lafe Lewman, African American trick rider Hank Drake, Mal Bates, and Chick Varnell, who had a Roman rings slack wire act (Bradbury, "Tompkins Wild West Show," 26). Varnell remembered that of all the many Wild West shows and circuses he worked with, Tompkins's productions had a special quality and excellence to them that inspired strong loyalty among his performers. The show included aerial wire and acrobatic acts, trick bicycle riding and contortion, and trained animal acts, mixing Wild West acts with elements from the European circus. It worked in an open-air arena with plank seating and a canvas cover, and moved from town to town, usually relocating some ten to fifteen miles per night. The show closed with the onset of World War I.

Charles and Mabel Tompkins left show business and moved to El Reno, Okla., where Charles opened an automobile agency, which he operated until the mid-1930s. He also served as the mayor of El Reno. The Tompkinses last saw Will Rogers in 1935, when he came by to visit them in El Reno shortly before leaving on his fatal airplane tour. Jim Minnick was also visiting the Tompkinses when Rogers arrived.

Mabel Tompkins died 29 March 1950. Charles Tompkins became a director of the Old Trail Drivers Association of Texas, based in San Antonio. He died on 29 May 1957 in Meridan or Glen Rose, Tex., following a heart attack. Rogers preserved a clipping in his personal scrapbook from 1902–4 depicting Tompkins whirling a lasso aboard a galloping horse, part of an advertisement for Tompkins Famous Riders in Cincinnati, Ohio (*Billboard,* 10 May 1913; Bradbury, "Tompkins Wild West Show"; Croy, *Our Will Rogers,* 74–76, 125–27, 346; memorandum by Paula M. Love, "St. Louis World's Fair

Letters," n.d., OkClaW; scrapbook, 1902–4, CPpR; Russell, "Golden Age of Wild West Shows"; Russell, *Wild West: A History of the Wild West Shows;* Spring, "Horseman Extraordinary"; Tompkins, "My Association with Will Rogers"; Tompkins Wild West small collections file, WBaraC; Charles Tompkins to Homer Croy, 1 August and 11 August 1952, 16 October 1953, and Mary A. Turner to Homer Croy, 10 September 1952, HCP-MoU; *VO,* 5 June 1957).

WILLIAMS, Egbert Austin (Bert) (1874–1922), and George Walker (ca. 1873–1911). As a vaudevillian and featured performer in the *Ziegfeld Follies* during its World War I–era "golden age," Bert Williams was lauded by theater reviewers and co-stars as a brilliant and versatile comic performer (Wertheim, ed., *Will Rogers at the Ziegfeld Follies,* 12). His long stage career bridged the transition from minstrelsy to vaudeville and variety. He was also a recording artist, and he translated some of his skits from the stage into parts in early films. Williams pioneered as a black comic breaking into a show-business world dominated by white theater and circuit operators, studio heads, agents, performers, audiences, and critics. He worked in vaudeville and on Broadway for many years with a partner, George Walker, as part of the team Williams and Walker, and he was a star of the *Ziegfeld Follies* for several seasons between 1910 and 1918. At the *Follies* he was the colleague of Will Rogers, Eddie Cantor, and W. C. Fields. The four appeared together, along with Fanny Brice, as the comic line-up in the *Follies* of 1917.

Williams protected some of the details of his family's private life from public knowledge, and as a result there is some dispute among biographers over his birthplace and family history. His parents, Frederick Williams, Jr., and Julia Monceur Williams, named him Egbert Austin Williams. It is most often said that he was born in the city of Nassau on New Providence, one of the islands of the Bahamas and part of the British West Indies. Others give his birthplace as Antigua, one of the Leeward Islands of the West Indies. Through his paternal grandparents he was of mixed Danish, Spanish, and African heritage. His grandfather, Frederick K. or Svend Eric Williams, was Danish. A former diplomat, he was a landowner in the Caribbean. He married Emiline Arymbrister, a woman of Spanish and African descent, who was from the West Indies, and they had a son, Frederick Williams, Jr. Frederick married Julia Monceur.

When Bert Williams was a young boy, Frederick and Julia Williams moved to the United States. They may have lived first in Harlem, relocating there when Bert was a toddler, so that Frederick Williams could work in the scenic design trade in the theater district. If so, they moved back to the West Indies for a time before moving again, when Williams was still a young boy, first to

Florida and then to San Pedro, Calif. Bert Williams spent much of his teenage years in Riverside, Calif., where his father was employed on the railroad and in the citrus fruit industry, and his mother worked as a laundress. He graduated from Riverside High School, and by some accounts attended classes at Stanford University or took correspondence courses in civil engineering. While still a teenager he turned to show business, touring the Monterey Bay and East Bay regions of northern California with a wagon of young people who clowned, sang, and played banjos for rural audiences.

In the early 1890s he entertained at lumber camps on the northern California coast and worked in saloons and restaurants in San Francisco while seeking gigs as a singer in music halls. He joined Martin and Seig's Mastodon Minstrels, a minstrel group made up of five white and five African American performers. When he was twenty years old Williams met George Walker, who was nineteen. Walker, like Williams, was eager for a life on the stage. The two formed a duo and performed with the Mastodon Minstrels. Williams played banjo, and Walker, the end man, sang. They found work in San Francisco variety houses and cabarets as the team of Walker and Williams (later known as Williams and Walker). Between 1893 and 1895 the pair performed at Halahan Horman's Midway Plaisance variety hall on Market Street in San Francisco. Wearing blackface and dressed in tattered clothes or ridiculous-looking formal attire, Williams played the straight man and banjo player, and Walker was the comedian. In 1895 they signed onto a traveling medicine show as entertainers. The medicine-show circuit took them through Texas and on up through western states to Chicago. They experienced overt racial hostility from white crowds in the Texas part of the tour, which caused both men to vow never again to perform in the southern sections of the United States.

Once in Chicago they joined John Isham's *Octoroons,* a variety show with an all-black company that had first been produced in New York by John Williams Isham. The show abandoned the traditional minstrel format, with semi-circle and interlocutor, and presented instead a series of acts featuring comics, singers, and chorus girls. Williams and Walker did not stay long with the show. They soon reorganized their old act with "coon songs," rhythmic dancing, banjo playing, and the cakewalk, and presented themselves as The Two Real Coons. They made a study in contrasts. Walker, who was short and stocky, played the dandy in flashy street clothes, while Williams, who was tall and thin, played a clownish character who was down and out, with ill-fitting jacket and huge shoes. In September 1896 they traveled to New York City and appeared as a specialty act in *The Gold Bug,* a musical farce by Glen McDonough and Victor Herbert that played at the Casino Theater.

At that time New York vaudeville theaters were dominated by such teams as McIntyre and Heath, Lew Dockstader, and other white men doing black-face acts. Williams and Walker competed with this trend as black men doing coon song, cakewalk, and dance routines in blackface. In real life a light-skinned West Indian who had spent most of his life in cities, Williams played the stage persona of a very black-skinned rural southerner who spoke in dialect. At the beginning of their vaudeville years Williams and Walker played music halls in Boston and New York, featuring Williams singing "Oh, I Don't Know, You Ain't So Warm." Wearing a bright jacket or checkered suit and bell-bottom trousers on stage, Walker personified the conceited and scheming wiseguy who talked fast and walked with a strut. Walker made fun of his part-ner, who impersonated the downtrodden sadsack who walked with a shuffle. They ended their program with the cakewalk. Much of their repartee and characterizations derived from the minstrel show (the burned-cork makeup, contrasting stereotypes of the lazy, ragged plantation slave versus the urban dandy, and the comic dialogue between the interlocutor and end man). They soon added two women to the act, making their team in effect a small com-pany. They were offered an extended contract at Koster and Bial's Music Hall after receiving rave reviews in early November 1896, and found themselves in demand at the best variety theaters. They were billed at Tony Pastor's Music Hall, Oscar Hammerstein's Olympia Roof Garden, and Keith's Theatre in Boston. From October 1897 to May 1898 they toured with McIntrye and Heath, going from New York to the Orpheum Theater in San Francisco. The success of their act was part of the cakewalk craze of the late 1890s.

When not on tour, the pair shared an apartment on 53rd Street in New York. Their home became a gathering place for vaudevillians, including mem-bers of Sissieretta Jones's Black Patti Co., another all-black company that also did a big cakewalk number at the end of their performances. Aida (Ada) Overton (1880–1914) of New York was one of the dancers with the Black Patti Co. She met Williams and Walker during a photo shoot for a cigarette adver-tisement and soon became the choreographer and main dancer with the Williams and Walker act. In September 1898 Williams and Walker took over Ernest Hogan's part in *Clorindy,* a comic operetta with a cakewalk finale set on a southern plantation. It was written by Will Marion Cook and the poet Paul Laurence Dunbar, both of whom were frequent guests in the Williams and Walker apartment.

Williams and Walker toured in over sixty performances of *Clorindy* before joining the cast of *A Lucky Coon.* In the next few years they did *Senegambian Carnival* (1898), *The Policy Players* (1900), and *The Sons of Ham* (1900). On

22 June 1899 George Walker married Aida Overton, and a year later, during the 1900 run of *Sons of Ham,* Bert Williams married Lottie Cole Thompson. She, like Overton, was a dancer with the Williams and Walker company. Lottie Cole was born in Chicago, where Williams met her during his cross-country tour in 1897, and she had formerly been married to Sam Thompson. She danced in all of the Williams and Walker acts until Williams entered the *Ziegfeld Follies,* whereupon she retired from the stage. Although they had no children of their own, the Williamses raised Lottie's three orphaned nieces as if they were their own daughters.

Success in vaudeville led to Williams and Walker's appearance in path-breaking black musical comedies that introduced African themes. The second tour of Williams and Walker in *Sons of Ham* was followed by *In Dahomey* (1903–5), *In Abyssinia* (1906), and *Bandanna Land* (1908). *In Dahomey* was the first all-black musical staged at a leading Broadway theater. It was very successful and went on tour in England between Williams and Walker's 1903 and 1904 Broadway bookings.

Following the highly popular run of *In Dahomey,* Williams and Walker joined Ernest Hogan, Abbie Mitchell Cook, and other black vaudevillians in forming the Colored Actors Beneficial Association. In July 1908 they collaborated in a similar professional group called the Frogs, which was a men's club that included physicians and lawyers as well as actors.

George Walker was elected the first president of the Frogs. Although Williams is the better known of the two partners because of his longer career, Walker also made important contributions to the development of black musical theater and productions. He helped produce many of the Williams and Walker musicals. He was also a successful songwriter and recording artist. Offstage, he was an outspoken critic of segregation and fought for equal rights for African American performers. Early in 1909 Walker became acutely ill while performing in Chicago in *Bandanna Land.* He was rushed from the stage to the hospital, where he was diagnosed with syphilis. Not long after learning of his illness, he was forced to stop working and receive care in a nursing home. Meanwhile, Aida Overton Walker, dressed as a man, took over his role playing with Williams in *Bandanna Land.* Marriage had done little to curb Walker's active social life, and he was involved in a series of well-known affairs with members of chorus lines and vaudeville actresses, including headliner Eva Tanguay, who appeared with Williams and Walker at the Colonial Theater in the summer of 1908. Walker died of paresis, the advanced stages of syphilis, on 6 January 1911, in Islip, N.Y. Bert Williams helped support his friend financially when Walker was no longer able to perform. He paid for

Walker's medical treatment during his long critical illness and provided burial expenses at his death.

Williams appeared in vaudeville as a single act in the summer of 1909, perfecting his storytelling technique, in which he used aspects of African American folktales and fables to create stories with a punch line and a moral twist, and increasing the amount of time in the act devoted to pantomime. Meanwhile, the Williams and Walker company produced a new show, *Mr. Lode of Koal,* appearing for the first time without George Walker or Aida Overton Walker. The show toured from October 1909 to March 1910.

After Aida Overton Walker stopped performing with Williams and the company, she played leading roles in *The Red Moon* and *His Honor the Barber* (1910–11) and performed as a single in vaudeville until 1914, when a kidney ailment forced her to retire. She died two months after she stopped working, on 11 October 1914, in New York.

Meanwhile, Williams continued to supplement tours with the company with work as a single performer. He joined Florenz Ziegfeld's *Follies* for the May 1910–May 1911 season. The *New York Age* review of the show stated that the "work of the colored comedian stands boldly out, from an artistic standpoint, above everybody and everything" (23 June 1910). Williams returned for the *Follies* of 1911 and 1912, working in skits with the British comic Leon Errol. He was also president of the Frogs organization, and in 1913 he headlined a Frogs ragtime variety show that toured down the East Coast from Manhattan to Richmond, Va.

During this period Williams remained one of the few African American performers who could play first-class theaters on the Keith vaudeville circuit; the majority of black vaudeville performers were booked in second-rate segregated theaters. African Americans were also typically excluded from black roles on Broadway and in musical theater productions, where black parts were played by whites in blackface. Williams returned to the *Follies* in 1914, and was a veteran with the show when Will Rogers joined it in 1916. Williams appeared with the *Follies* in the New Amsterdam Theater through 1917 and in the *Midnight Frolic* in 1918. Williams felt hampered in working with *Follies* writers. Unlike Alexander Rogers (who wrote much of the material used in the Williams and Walker shows), the *Follies* writers were not interested in Williams's desire to create full characterizations or to use African American stories and jokes in his skits, and they gave him little opportunity to dance. Williams's performances gave ideas to other players, however, including Will Rogers, who in 1918 proposed to Ziegfeld that he impersonate Bert Williams in blackface in a *Follies* skit about a man who brings a mule decorated like an automobile to be serviced at a gas station. Williams appeared in his last *Follies* show in 1919, along with Gus Van, Ray Dooley, and his good friend Eddie Cantor. In some ways the show took his career full circle, for he appeared in an act with Cantor that cast the two blackface comedians in traditional roles as Tambo and Bones in a minstrel show. Reviewers noted that in Williams's *Follies* years he was given little material and material of poor quality, and that "he was in the *Follies,* but not allowed to be part of the *Follies*" (Smith, *Bert Williams,* 202).

Songs Williams introduced on stage included "You Got the Right Church But the Wrong Pew" and his trademark tune, "Nobody," written by Alexander Rogers ("When life seems full of clouds and rain / and I am full of nothin' but pain / Who soothes my thumpin', bumpin' brain / (*pause*) Nobody!") (Samuels and Samuels, *Once upon a Stage,* 187). Williams briefly acted in one-reel films for the American Biograph Co. in the summer of 1916. His moving pictures included *A Natural Born Gambler,* distributed by the General Film Co. in July 1916, which featured Williams in a role based on his poker-game stage skit. In the film, Williams's game is raided by authorities and his gambler ends up dealing hands to imaginary players in prison. Williams also made musical recordings from October 1901 to February 1922, including seventeen songs recorded under contract with Columbia Records during the *Follies* years from 1914 to 1918. Other Columbia recordings included a version of "Nobody" (recorded between 1906 and 1911) and the anti-Prohibition tune "Bring Back Those Wonderful Days" (1919).

In an age when black intellectual W. E. B. DuBois wrote of the doubleness of black identity, and poet Paul Laurence Dunbar wrote of African Americans having to "wear the mask" in white society, outwardly playing roles of subservience to meet white expectations while protecting hidden inner self-respect and rage, Williams perfected blackface performance in which he presented a stage persona—a bumbling clown or often in *Follies* skits a railroad porter—that was completely unlike his own reticent, dignified demeanor. "It was not until I was able to see myself as another person that my sense of humor developed," he observed, consciously describing the doubleness of his own personal and professional lives (Williams "Comic Side of Trouble," 35). His comedy and self-mockery on stage was always presented with an edge of pathos. *Follies* co-star W. C. Fields commented that "Bert Williams is the funniest man I ever saw and the saddest man I ever met" (Samuels and Samuels, *Once upon a Stage,* 190).

Williams, whose health had been shaky since 1918, became ill with pneumonia and collapsed on stage during an evening performance of *Under the*

Bamboo Tree in Detroit on 25 February 1922. He was brought to his home at 2309 Seventh Avenue in New York, where he lapsed into a coma and died on 7 March 1922 (*New York World,* 7 March 1922; *NYT,* 17 July 1918; *Richmond Planet,* 11 March 1922; *VO,* 1:10 March 1922; Berson, *San Francisco Stage,* 86–89; Cantor, "Bert Williams"; Cantor, *Take My Life;* Chapman and Sherwood, eds., *Best Plays of 1894–1899,* 177, 181; Charters, *Nobody;* Cook, "Clorindy, the Origin of the Cakewalk"; *EV,* 556–59; Fausett, "Symbolism of Bert Williams"; Ferguson, "Black Skin, Black Mask"; *OCAT,* 716–17; Rowland, ed., *Bert Williams;* Sampson, *Blacks in Blackface,* 76–91; Samuels and Samuels, *Once upon a Stage;* Slide, *Vaudevillians,* 168–70; Smith, *Bert Williams;* Toll, *On with the Show!* 121–27; Washington, "Interesting People: Bert Williams"; Wertheim, ed. *Will Rogers at the Ziegfeld Follies,* 207; Williams, "Comic Side of Trouble"; Woll, *Black Musical Theatre,* 32–49).

WOLFE, Agnes (Bossie) Mulhall (1877–1916). The eldest child of Mary Agnes Locke Mulhall and Zack Mulhall, Agnes Mulhall was known throughout her life as Bossie. Born in St. Louis, and raised there and on the Mulhall ranch in Mulhall, O.T., Bossie Mulhall combined the horseback-riding skills of the rest of her family with high-society tastes and habits.

Educated in St. Louis, she spent much of her time in that city at the home of Georgia Mulhall, and she became part of the St. Louis socialite scene. Her social status was reflected in the invitation she received to attend President McKinley's inaugural ball in 1901, when her father's Mulhall Cowboy Band was in Washington, D.C., to march in the inaugural parade. She drove her team of horses in the grand parade for Oklahoma Territory governor Jenkins in May 1901, and caught Theodore Roosevelt's eye at the Rough Riders' Reunion in Oklahoma City. She played the piano and possessed an excellent singing voice, appearing as a soloist at many public events. She performed with the Frisco Cowboy Band at the Grand Opera House in San Antonio and other venues in 1902–3, and sporadically appeared as a rider in the family Wild West and roping-contest exhibitions, including the Rough Riders Congress at Del Mar Gardens, St. Louis, in 1902. In 1905 she joined the family show in its appearances with Will Rogers in Madison Square Garden in spring and in the Miller Brothers' 101 Ranch show in June.

Agnes Mulhall was periodically in very poor health and suffered from respiratory illness. She married Dr. W. C. Wolfe, a Mulhall, Okla., dentist, and they settled in the town of Marshall, Okla. They had one son, William (Billy) Wolfe, born in 1913. Billy Wolfe was a toddler when his mother died of pneumonia. Dr. Wolfe was unable to care for the child, and the boy was taken in and raised by Mary Agnes Locke Mulhall at the Mulhall family ranch. Dr. Wolfe suffered a fatal heart attack when Billy was still very young. As a young man Billy became well known in the Guthrie, Okla., area as an excellent regional baseball player (oral history interviews with Martha Fisch, WRPP; Mulhall scrapbook, MFC; *ME,* 1 March, 17 May, 8 November 1901, 18 April 1902, 30 January, 13 March, 12 June, 18 September 1903, 14 April and 16 June 1905, 9 February, 9 March, 18 May 1906; Koch, "Zack Mulhall," 15, 17–18; Stansbury, *Lucille Mulhall,* 7, 9, 15, 23, 33, 37, 51, 67, 77, 149).

Bibliography

THE SOURCES USED IN THIS VOLUME ARE LISTED IN THREE CATEGORIES: BOOKS, articles and chapters in anthologies, and unpublished and miscellaneous sources. Titles given in quotation marks in the document endnotes and in the Biographical Appendix entries may be found either in the "articles and chapters" section or among the "unpublished and miscellaneous sources." See also the list of symbols and abbreviations in the front matter of the volume.

BOOKS

Allen, Robert C. *Horrible Prettiness: Burlesque and American Culture*. Chapel Hill: University of North Carolina Press, 1991.

_____. *Vaudeville and Film, 1895–1915: A Study in Media Interaction*. New York: Arno Press, 1980.

Alley, John. *City Beginnings in Oklahoma Territory*. Norman: University of Oklahoma Press, 1939.

Allwood, John. *The Great Exhibitions*. London: Studio Vista, 1977.

Anderson, Donald F. *William Howard Taft: A Conservative's Conception of the Presidency*. Ithaca, N.Y.: Cornell University Press, 1973.

Anderson, Judith Icke. *William Howard Taft: An Intimate History*. New York: W. W. Norton, 1981.

Arpad, Joseph J., and Kenneth R. Lincoln. *Buffalo Bill's Wild West*. Palmer Lake, Colo.: Filter Press, 1971.

Ashby, LeRoy. *William Jennings Bryan: Champion of Democracy*. Boston: Twayne Publishers, 1987.

As I Recollect. Claremore, Okla.: Pocahontas Club, 1949.

Augspurger, Marie M. *Yellowstone National Park: Historical and Descriptive*. Middletown, Ohio: Naegele-Auer Printing, 1948.

Baedeker, Karl. *London and Its Environs: Handbook for Travellers*. 10th rev. ed. Leipzig: Karl Baedeker, Publisher, 1896. 20th rev. ed. Leipzig: Karl Baedeker, Publisher, 1906.

_____. *Paris and Environs, With Routes from London to Paris: Handbook for Travellers*. 16th ed. Leipzig: Karl Baedeker, 1907.

Baker, Paul R. *Richard Morris Hunt*. Cambridge, Mass.: MIT Press, 1980.

Balio, Tino, ed. *The American Film Industry*. Madison: University of Wisconsin Press, 1985.

Baral, Robert. *Revue: The Great Broadway Period*. New York: Fleet Press, 1962.

Barrett, C. J. *The History of Barn Elms and the Kit Kat Club Now the Ranelagh Club*. 2d. ed. London: Stationers' Hall, 1889.

Barrett, Stephen M. *Geronimo's Story of His Life*. New York: Duffield, 1906.

Barrie, James Matthew. *What Every Woman Knows: A Comedy*. London: Hodder and Stoughton, 1918.

Bartlett, Richard A. *Yellowstone: A Wilderness Besieged*. Tucson: University of Arizona Press, 1985.

Beal, Merrill. *"I Will Fight No More Forever": Chief Joseph and the Nez Perce War*. Seattle: University of Washington Press, 1963.

Beardsley, Charles. *Hollywood's Master Showman: The Legendary Sid Grauman*. New York: Cornwall Books, 1983.

Bennitt, Mark, et al., eds. *History of the Louisiana Purchase Exposition*. 1905. Reprint. New York: Arno Press, 1976.

Berg, A. Scott. *Goldwyn: A Biography*. New York: Alfred A. Knopf, 1989.

Bergan, Ronald. *The Great Theatres of London: An Illustrated Companion*. London: Admiral, 1987.

Bernheim, Alfred L. *The Business of the Theatre*. New York: Actors' Equity Association, 1932.

Berson, Misha. *The San Francisco Stage: From Golden Spike to Great Earthquake, 1869–1906*. San Francisco: San Francisco Performing Arts Library and Museum Series 4, February 1992.

Birchard, Robert S. *King Cowboy: Tom Mix and the Movies*. Burbank: Riverwood Press, 1993.

Birk, Dorothy Daniels. *The World Came to St. Louis: A Visit to the 1904 World's Fair*. St. Louis: Bethany Press, 1979.

Birkby, Carel. *The Pagel Story*. London: Hodder and Stoughton, 1948.

Birkmire, John H. *The Planning and Construction of American Theatres*. New York: John Wiley and Sons, 1906.

Bishop, Joseph Bucklin. *Theodore Roosevelt's Letters to His Children*. New York: Charles Scribner's, 1919.

Black, J. Dickson. *The Short Stories and Wit of Tom P. Morgan*. Bentonville, Ark.: J. D. Black, 1988.

Blackstone, Sarah J. *Buckskins, Bullets, and Business: A History of Buffalo Bill's Wild West*. Westport, Conn.: Greenwood Press, 1986.

Blesh, Rudi. *Keaton*. New York: Macmillan, 1966.

Blumenthal, George, with Arthur H. Menkin. *My Sixty Years in Show Business*. New York: Olympia Publishing, 1936.

Boatright, Mody Coggin. *The Morality Play on Horseback: Tom Mix*. Austin, Tex.: Encino Press, 1968.

Bordman, Gerald. *American Musical Theatre: A Chronicle*. New York: Oxford University Press, 1992.

———. *Jerome Kern: His Life and Music*. New York: Oxford University Press, 1980.

Bowser, Eileen. *The Transformation of Cinema 1907–1915*. New York: Charles Scribner's Sons, 1990.

Brooks, Tim, and Earle Marsh. *The Complete Directory to Prime Time Network TV Shows: 1946–Present*. New York: Ballantine Books, 1979.

Brown, Carole, and Leo Knuth. *The Tenor and the Vehicle: A Study of the John McCormack/James Joyce Connection*. Colchester, England: Wake Newlitter, 1982.

Brown, T. Allston. *A History of the New York Stage: From the First Performance in 1732 to 1901*. 3 vols. New York: Dodd, Mead, 1903.

Bryan, William Jennings, with Mary Baird Bryan. *The Memoirs of William Jennings Bryan*. Philadelphia: John C. Winston Co., 1925.

Bryan, William Jennings, with Mary Baird Bryan. *Speeches of William Jennings Bryan*. New York: Funk and Wagnalls, 1909.

Buel, James William, ed. *Louisiana and the Fair: An Exposition of the World, Its People and Their Achievements*. St. Louis: World's Progress Publishing, 1906.

Buhle, Paul. *Popular Culture in America*. Minneapolis: University of Minnesota Press, 1987.

Burrill, Bob. *Who's Who in Boxing*. New Rochelle, N.Y.: Arlington House, 1974.

Busby, Roy. *British Music Hall: An Illustrated Who's Who From 1850 to the Present Day*. London: Paul Elek, 1976.

Byers, Chester. *Roping: Trick and Fancy Rope Spinning*. New York: G. P. Putnam's Sons, 1928.

Caffin, Caroline. *Vaudeville*. New York: M. Kennerley, 1914.

Cantor, Eddie. *As I Remember Them*. New York: Duell, Sloan and Pearce, 1963.

_____. *My Life Is in Your Hands*. New York: Blue Ribbon Books, 1932.

Cantor, Eddie, with Jane Kesner Ardmore. *Take My Life*. Garden City, N.Y.: Doubleday, 1957.

Carter, A. Cecil, ed. *The Kingdom of Siam Ministry of Agriculture, Louisiana Purchase Exposition, St. Louis, U.S.A., 1904*. New York: G. P. Putnam's Sons, 1904.

Castle, Irene. *Castles in the Air*. Garden City, New York: Doubleday, 1958.

Ceram, C. W. *Archaeology of the Cinema*. London: Thames and Hudson, 1965.

Chambers, John Whiteclay. *The Tyranny of Change: America in the Progressive Era, 1890–1920*. New York: St. Martin's Press, 1992.

Chaplin, Charles. *My Autobiography*. New York: Simon and Schuster, 1964.

Chapman, John, and Garrison P. Sherwood, eds. *The Best Plays of 1894–1899*. New York: Dodd, Mead, 1955.

Charters, Ann. *Nobody: The Story of Bert Williams*. London: Macmillan, 1970.

Chittenden, Hiram Martin. *The Yellowstone National Park*. Norman: University of Oklahoma Press, 1964.

Claghorn, Charles Eugene. *Biographical Dictionary of American Music*. West Nyack, N.Y.: Parker Publishing, 1973.

Clancy, Foghorn. *My Fifty Years in Rodeo: Living with Cowboys, Horses and Danger*. San Antonio, Tex.: Naylor, 1952.

Clark, Dick. *Cherokee Ancestor Research*. Modesto, Calif.: Holland Printing, 1979.

Cockfield, Jamie H., ed. *Dollars and Diplomacy: Ambassador David Rowland Francis and the Fall of Tsarism, 1916–1917*. Durham, N.C.: Duke University Press, 1981.

Cohan, George M. *Twenty Years on Broadway and the Years It Took to Get There: The True Story of a Trouper's Life from the Cradle to the "Closed Shop."* New York: Harper and Brothers, 1924.

Cohen-Stratyner, Barbara, ed. *Popular Music, 1900–1919*. Detroit, Mich.: Gale Research, 1988.

Collings, Ellsworth. *The Old Home Ranch: Birthplace of Will Rogers*. 2d ed. Claremore, Okla.: Will Rogers Memorial, 1982.

Collins, Douglas. *The Story of Kodak*. New York: Harry N. Abrams, 1990.

Collins, Reba. *Will Rogers: Courtship and Correspondence, 1900–1915*. Oklahoma City: Neighbors and Quaid, 1992.

Collins, Reba, ed. *Roping Will Rogers Family Tree*. Claremore, Okla.: Will Rogers Heritage Press, 1982.

The Complete Portfolio of Photographs of the World's Fair, St. Louis, 1904: The Sights, Scenes and Wonders of the Fair Photographed. Chicago: Educational, 1904.

Comtois, M. E., and Lynn F. Miller. *Contemporary American Theater Critics*. Metuchen, N.J.: Scarecrow Press, 1977.

Connecticut, Commission of. *Catalogue of the Furniture and Works of Art in the Connecticut State Building at the Louisiana Purchase Exposition*. Hartford, Conn.: Magazine, 1904.

Craig, Warren. *Sweet and Lowdown: America's Popular Song Writers*. Metuchen, N.J.: Scarecrow Press, 1978.

Cressy, Will M. *Continuous Vaudeville*. Boston: Richard G. Badger, 1914.

Croy, Homer. *Our Will Rogers*. New York: Duell, Sloan and Pearce. Boston: Little, Brown, 1953.

Dale, Edward Everett, and Morris L. Wardell. *History of Oklahoma*. New York: Prentice-Hall, 1948.

Dardis, Tom. *Keaton, the Man Who Wouldn't Lie Down*. New York: Scribner, 1979.

Davies, Acton. *Maude Adams*. New York: F. A. Stokes, 1901.

Davies, Marion, Pamela Pfau, and Kenneth S. Marx, eds. *The Times We Had*. Indianapolis: Bobbs-Merrill, 1975.

Davis, Britton. *The Truth about Geronimo*. New Haven: Yale University Press, 1929.

Day, Donald. *Will Rogers: A Biography*. New York: David McKay, 1962.

Dean, Frank. *Will Rogers Rope Tricks*. Colorado Spring, Colo.: Western Horseman, 1969.

Debo, Angie. *Geronimo: The Man, His Time, His Place*. Norman: University of Oklahoma Press, 1976.

————. *Tulsa: From Creek Town to Oil Capital*. Norman: University of Oklahoma Press, 1943.

DeGregorio, William A. *The Complete Book of U.S. Presidents*. 2d ed. New York: Dembner Books, 1989.

Delehanty, Randolph. *Walks and Tours in the Golden Gate City San Francisco*. New York: Dial Press, 1980.

DiMeglio, John E. *Vaudeville U.S.A.* Bowling Green, Ohio: Bowling Green University Popular Press, 1973.

Dippie, Brian W., ed. *Charles M. Russell, Word Painter: Letters 1887–1926*. Fort Worth, Tex.: Amon Carter Museum, 1993.

Downing, Antoinette F., and Vincent J. Scully, Jr. *The Architectural Heritage of Newport, Rhode Island, 1640–1915*. 2d rev. ed. New York: Clarkson N. Potter, 1967.

Dunning, John. *Tune In Yesterday: The Ultimate Encyclopedia of Old-Time Radio*. Englewood Cliffs, N.J.: 1976.

DuPriest, Maude Ward, Jennie May Bard, and Anna Foreman Graham. *Cherokee Recollections: The Story of the Indian Women's Pocahontas Club and Its Members in the*

Cherokee Nation and Oklahoma Beginning in 1899. Stillwater, Okla.: Thales Microuniversity Press, 1976.

Elliott, Eugene Clinton. *A History of Variety-Vaudeville in Seattle: From the Beginning to 1914*. Edited by Glenn Hughes. University of Washington Publications in Drama 1. Seattle: University of Washington Press, 1944.

Engen, Orrin A. *Writer of the Plains: A Biography of B. M. Bower*. Culver City, Calif.: Pontine Press, 1973.

Erenberg, Lewis A. *Steppin' Out*. Westport, Conn.: Greenwood Press, 1981.

Everett, Marshall. *The Book of the Fair: The Greatest Exposition the World Has Ever Seen Photographed and Explained: A Panorama of the St. Louis Exposition*. St. Louis: Henry Neil, 1904.

Ewen, David. *American Songwriters*. New York: H. W. Wilson, 1987.

Ewen, David, ed. *American Popular Composers: From Revolutionary Times to the Present*. New York: H. W. Wilson, 1962.

Fall, Thomas. *Jim Thorpe*. New York: Crowell, 1970.

Faulkner, Harold. *Politics, Reform, Expansion, 1890–1900*. New York: Harper and Brothers, 1959; Harper Torchbook, 1963.

Fell, John, ed. *Film before Griffith*. Berkeley: University of California Press, 1983.

Fellows, Dexter. *This Way to the Big Show: The Life of Dexter Fellows*. New York: Viking Press, 1936.

Felstead, Theodore S. *Stars Who Made the Halls: A Hundred Years of English Humour, Harmony and Hilarity*. London: T. Werner Laurie, 1946.

Fields, Armond, and L. Marc Fields. *From the Bowery to Broadway: Lew Fields and the Roots of American Popular Theater*. New York: Oxford University Press, 1993.

50 Jahre Wintergarten. Hildesheim, Germany: Olms Presse, 1975.

Fisher, James. *Al Jolson: A Bio-Bibliography*. Westport, Conn.: Greenwood Press, 1994.

Foster, William Trufant. *Vaudeville and Motion Picture Shows: A Study of Theaters in Portland, Oregon*. Portland: Reed College, 1914.

Fox, Charles Donald. *Famous Film Folk: A Gallery of Life Portraits and Biographies*. New York: George H. Doran, 1925.

Francis, David Rowland. *Russia from the American Embassy, April 1916–November 1918*. New York: Charles Scribner's Sons, 1921.

_____. *A Tour of Europe in Nineteen Days: Report to the Board of Directors of the Louisiana Purchase Exposition of European Tour, Made in the Interest of the St. Louis World's Fair*. St. Louis: n.p., n.d. [ca. 1903].

_____. *The Universal Exposition of 1904*. 2 vols. St. Louis: Louisiana Purchase Exposition Co., 1913.

Franklin, Joe. *Joe Franklin's Encyclopedia of Comedians*. Secaucus, N.J.: Citadel Press, 1979.

Freeman, Harry C. *A Brief History of Butte, Montana: The World's Greatest Mining Camp*. Chicago: Henry O. Shepard, 1900.

Frick, John W. *New York's First Theatrical Center: The Rialto at Union Square*. Ann Arbor, Mich.: UMI Research Press, 1985.

Frick, John Ward, and Carlton Gray, eds. *Directory of Historic American Theatres*. New York: Greenwood Press, 1987.

Friedland, Michael. *Jolson.* New York: Stein and Day, 1972.

Frohman, Charles. *The Maude Adams Book.* New York: C. Frohman, 1909.

Gagey, Edmond M. *The San Francisco Stage: A History.* New York: Columbia University Press, 1950.

Gammond, Peter. *The Oxford Companion to Popular Music.* Oxford: Oxford University Press, 1991.

Gibson, Arrell M. *Oklahoma: A History of Five Centuries.* Norman, Okla.: Harlow Publishing, 1965.

Giesler, Jerry. *The Jerry Giesler Story* (as told to Pete Martin). New York: Simon and Schuster, 1960.

Gilbert, Douglas. *American Vaudeville: Its Life and Times.* New York: Whittlesly House, 1940.

Glad, Paul W. *The Trumpet Soundeth: William Jennings Bryan and His Democracy, 1896–1912.* Lincoln: University of Nebraska Press, 1960.

Glazer, Irvin R. *Philadelphia Theaters: A Pictorial Architectural History.* Philadelphia: The Athenaeum of Philadelphia and Dover Publications, 1994.

———. *Philadelphia Theatres, A–Z: A Comprehensive, Descriptive Record of 813 Theatres Constructed since 1724.* Westport, Conn.: Greenwood Press, 1986.

Glyn, Elinor. *Three Weeks.* 1907. Reprint. London: Duckworth, 1974.

Goble, Danney. *Progressive Oklahoma.* Norman: University of Oklahoma Press, 1980.

Golden, George Fuller. *My Lady Vaudeville and Her White Rats.* New York: Broadway Publishing, 1909.

Goldman, Herbert G. *Fanny Brice: The Original Funny Girl.* New York: Oxford University Press, 1992.

———. *Jolson: The Legend Comes to Life.* New York: Oxford University Press, 1988.

Gomery, Douglas. *Shared Pleasures: A History of Movie Presentation in the United States.* Madison: University of Wisconsin Press, 1992.

Goodwin, Doris Kearns. *The Fitzgeralds and the Kennedys.* New York: St. Martin's Press, 1987.

Grandeur of the Universal Exposition at St. Louis: An Official Book of Beautiful Engravings Illustrating the World's Fair of 1904. St. Louis: Louisiana Purchase Exposition Co. and Samuel Myerson Printing, 1904.

Grau, Robert. *The Business Man in the Amusement World: A Volume of Progress in the Field of the Theatre.* New York: Broadway Publishing, 1910.

———. *Forty Years Observation of Music and the Drama.* New York: Broadway Publishing, 1909.

———. *The Stage in the Twentieth Century.* 1912. Reprint. New York: Benjamin Blom, 1969.

Gray, James H. *A Brand of Its Own: The 100 Year History of the Calgary Exhibition and Stampede.* Saskatoon, Saskatchewan: Western Producer Prairie Books, 1985.

Green, Abel, and Joe Laurie, Jr. *Show Biz: From Vaude to Video.* New York: Henry Holt, 1951.

Green, Stanley. *Encyclopaedia of the Musical Theatre.* New York: Dodd, Mead, 1976.

Grossman, Barbara. *Funny Woman: The Life and Times of Fanny Brice.* Bloomington: Indiana University Press, 1991; Midland Book, 1992.

Günter, Ernst. *Geschichte des Variétés.* Berlin: Henschelverlag, 1981.

Guernsey, Otis L., Jr., ed. *Best Plays of 1967–68.* New York: Dodd Mead, 1968.

Guiles, Fred Lawrence. *Marion Davies.* New York: Bantam Books, 1972.

Guptill, Albert B. *Haynes Guide to Yellowstone Park: A Practical Handbook.* St. Paul, Minn.: F. J. Haynes, 1908.

Gurock, Jeffrey S. *When Harlem Was Jewish: 1870–1930.* New York: Columbia University Press, 1979.

Haines, Aubrey L. *The Yellowstone Story: A History of Our First National Park.* 2 vols. Yellowstone National Park, Wyo.: Yellowstone Library and Museum Association, 1977.

Halliwell, Leslie. *Leslie Halliwell's Film Guide.* 7th ed. New York: Harper and Row, 1989.

Hampton, Benjamin B. *History of the American Film Industry.* New York: Dover, 1970.

Hanes, Col. Bailey C. *Bill Pickett, Bulldogger.* Norman: University of Oklahoma Press, 1977.

Hanson, John Wesley. *The Official History of the Fair, St. Louis, 1904: The Signs and Scenes of the Louisiana Purchase Exposition.* St. Louis: J. W. Hanson, n.d. [ca. 1904].

Harding, Alfred. *The Revolt of the Actors.* New York: William Morrow, 1929.

Hart, James D. *The Oxford Companion to American Literature.* 4th ed. New York: Oxford University Press, 1965.

Hartnoll, Phyllis, ed. *The Oxford Companion to the Theatre.* 3d ed. London: Oxford University Press, 1967.

Henderson, Mary C. *The City and the Theatre: New York Playhouses from Bowling Green to Times Square.* Clifton, N.J.: James T. White, 1973.

Herbert, Ian, ed. *Who's Who in the Theatre.* 17th ed. Detroit: Gale Research, 1977.

Herman, Hal C., ed. *How I Broke into the Movies: Signed Autobiographies by Sixty Famous Screen Stars.* Hollywood, Calif.: H. C. Herman, 1929.

Herrick, Howard, ed. *Who's Who in Vaudeville 1911.* New York: Dupree and Pope, 1911.

Herrick, Robert. *Together.* New York: Macmillan, 1908.

Hickok, Ralph. *A Who's Who of Sports Champions: Their Stories and Records.* Boston: Houghton Mifflin, 1995.

Hill, Richmond C. *A Great White Indian Chief: Thrilling and Romantic Story of the Remarkable Career, Extraordinary Experiences, Hunting, Scouting and Indian Adventures of Col. Fred Cummins. . .* Ossining, N.Y.: Rand, McNally, n.d. [ca. 1912].

Hinsley, Curtis M. *Savages and Scientists: The Smithsonian Institution and the Development of American Anthropology, 1846–1910.* Washington, D.C.: Smithsonian Institution, 1981.

A History of Oologah: Our First One Hundred Years, 1890–1990. Oologah, Okla.: Privately printed, 1990.

Hitchcock, H. Wiley, and Stanley Sadie, eds. *The New Grove Dictionary of American Music.* 4 vols. London: Macmillan Press, 1986.

Honduras, Dirección General de Estadística y Censos. *La República de Honduras: Breve reseña para la exposición de San Luis, Missouri, Estados Unidos de America.* Tegucigalpa: Tep. Nacional, 1903.

Hoshi, Hajime. *Handbook of Japan and Japanese Exhibits at World's Fair, St. Louis, 1904.* N.p.: N.p., 1904.

Houdini, Harry. *A Magician among the Spirits.* New York: Harper and Brothers, 1924.

Howard, Diana. *London Theatres and Music Halls, 1850–1950.* London: Library Associates, 1970.

Howe, Irving. *World of Our Fathers.* New York: Harcourt Brace and Jovanovich, 1976.

Hyde, George E. *Red Cloud's Folk: A History of the Oglala Sioux Indians.* Norman: University of Oklahoma Press, 1937.

———. *Spotted Tail's Folk: A History of the Brulé Sioux.* 2d ed. Norman: University of Oklahoma Press, 1974.

International Exposition, St. Louis, 1904: Official Catalogue of the Exhibition of the German Empire. Berlin: G. Stilke, 1904.

Irwin, Will, ed. *Letters to Kermit from Theodore Roosevelt, 1902–1908.* New York: Charles Scribner's Sons, 1946.

Isenberg, Michael T. *War on Film: The American Cinema and World War I, 1914–1941.* London: Associated University Presses, 1981.

Isman, Felix. *Weber and Fields: Their Tribulations, Triumphs and Their Associates.* New York: Boni and Liveright, 1924.

James, Edward T., ed. *Notable American Women, 1607–1950.* 3 vols. Cambridge, Mass.: Belknap Press, Harvard University Press, 1971.

Jelavich, Peter. *Berlin Cabaret.* Cambridge, Mass.: Harvard University Press, 1993.

Jenkins, Henry. *What Made Pistachio Nuts?: Early Sound Film and the Vaudeville Aesthetic.* New York: Columbia University Press, 1992.

Jessel, George. *Elegy in Manhattan.* New York: Holt, Rinehart and Winston, 1961.

———. *So Help Me: The Autobiography of George Jessel.* New York: Random House, 1943.

Jessel, George, with John Austin. *The World I Lived In.* Chicago: Henry Regnery, 1975.

John McCormack, His Own Life Story. Boston: Small, Maynard, 1918.

Johnson, Stephen Burge. *The Roof Gardens of Broadway Theatres, 1883–1942.* Ann Arbor: University of Michigan Press, 1985.

Jordan, Teresa. *Cowgirls: Women of the American West.* Garden City, N.Y.: Anchor Press, 1982.

Katchmer, George A. *Eighty Silent Film Stars: Biographies and Filmographies of the Obscure to the Well Known.* Jefferson, N.C.: McFarland, 1991.

Keaton, Buster. *My Wonderful World of Slapstick.* Garden City, N.Y.: Doubleday, 1960.

Kennedy, Fred. *The Calgary Stampede Story.* Canada: T. Edwards Thonger, 1952.

Ketchum, Richard M. *Will Rogers: The Man and His Times.* New York: American Heritage and Simon and Schuster, 1973.

Kinkle, Roger D. *The Complete Encyclopedia of Popular Music and Jazz, 1900–1950.* 4 vols. New Rochelle, N.Y.: Arlington House, 1974.

Kirk, John Foster. *A Supplement to Allibone's Critical Dictionary of English Literature and British and American Authors.* Vol. 1. Philadelphia: J. B. Lippincott, 1897.

Lardner, John. *White Hopes and Other Tigers.* Philadelphia: J. B. Lippincott, 1951.

Lasky, Betty. *RKO: The Biggest Little Major of Them All.* Santa Monica, Calif.: Roundtable Publishing, 1989.

Lasky, Jesse L., with Don Weldon. *I Blow My Own Horn.* London: Victor Gollancz, 1957.

Lauder, Sir Harry. *Between You and Me.* New York: James A. McCann, 1919.

_____. *Roamin' in the Gloamin'.* Philadelphia: J. B. Lippincott, 1928.

Laurie, Joseph, Jr. *Vaudeville: From Honky-tonks to the Palace.* New York: Henry Holt, 1953.

Lax, Roger, and Frederick Smith. *The Great Song Thesaurus.* 2d ed. New York: Oxford University Press, 1989.

Leavitt, Michael Bennett. *Fifty Years in Theatrical Management.* New York: Broadway Publishing, 1912.

LeCompte, Mary Lou. *Cowgirls of the Rodeo: Pioneer Professional Athletes.* Urbana: University of Illinois Press, 1993.

Ledbetter, Gordon. *The Great Irish Tenor.* London: Duckworth, 1977.

Lester, Robert, ed. *Russia in Transition: The Diplomatic Papers of David R. Francis, U.S. Ambassador to Russia, 1916–1918.* U.S. Department of State. Frederick, Md.: University Publications of America, n.d. [ca. 1985]. [Microfilm with guide.]

Lloyd, Herbert. *Vaudeville Trails thru the West: "By One Who Knows."* San Francisco: San Franciso Publishing and Advertising, 1919.

Lockwood, Charles. *Manhattan Moves Uptown: An Illustrated History.* Boston: Houghton Mifflin, 1976.

Lost Theatres of London. East Kilbride, Scotland: Thomson Litho, 1976.

Louisiana Purchase Exposition Board of Lady Managers. *Report to the Louisiana Purchase Exposition Commission.* Cambridge, Mass.: Riverside Press, 1905.

Louisiana Purchase Exposition [Commission]. *Daily Official Program: World's Fair Louisiana Purchase Exposition, St. Louis, U.S.A., 1904.* St. Louis: World's Fair Program Co., 1904.

_____. *Sights, Scenes and Wonders at the World's Fair: Official Book of Views of the Louisiana Purchase Exposition.* St. Louis: Official Photographic, n.d. [ca. 1904].

_____. *Universal Exposition, St. Louis, U.S.A., 1904: Commemorating the Acquisition of Louisiana Territory: Its Story and Purpose.* St. Louis: The Exposition, n.d. [ca. 1904].

Louisiana Purchase Exposition Company. *Manual of the Louisiana Purchase Exposition, World's Fair, Saint Louis, 1904: Containing Lists of Officers and Committees of the Company and of the Commission.* St. Louis: Woodward and Jiernan Printing, 1904.

Mallen, Bernardo. *Mexico Yesterday and Today, 1876–1904.* English ed. Mexico: Muller House, 1904.

Malvern, Gladys. *Valiant Minstrel: The Story of Sir Harry Lauder.* New York: Julian Messner, 1943.

Mander, Raymond, and Joe Mitchenson. *British Music Halls.* Rev. ed. London: Gentry Books, 1974.

Mantle, Burns, and Garrison Sherwood, eds. *The Best Plays of 1899–1909 and the Year Book of the Drama in America.* Reprint, New York: Dodd, Mead, 1944.

Mantle, Burns, and Garrison Sherwood, eds. *The Best Plays of 1909–1919 and the Year Book of the Drama in America.* New York: Dodd, Mead, 1933.

Marquis, Arnold. *A Guide to America's Indians: Ceremonials, Reservations, and Museums.* Norman: University of Oklahoma Press, 1974.

Marston, William Moulton, and John Henry Feller. *F. F. Proctor: Vaudeville Pioneer.* New York: Richard R. Smith, 1943.

Martin, Linda, and Kerry Segrave. *Women in Comedy.* Secaucus, N.J.: Citadel Press, 1986.

Mast, Gerald. *Can't Help Singin': The American Musical on Stage and Screen.* Woodstock, N.Y.: Overlook Press, 1987.

Mates, Julian. *America's Musical Stage: Two Hundred Years of Musical Stage.* Westport, Conn.: Greenwood Press, 1985.

May, Lary. *Screening Out the Past: The Birth of Mass Culture and the Motion Picture Industry.* New York: Oxford University Press, 1980.

McArthur, Benjamin. *Actors and American Culture, 1880–1920.* Philadelphia: Temple University Press, 1984.

McCabe, John. *George M. Cohan: The Man Who Owned Broadway.* Garden City, N.Y.: Doubleday, 1973.

McCallum, John D. *The World Heavyweight Boxing Championship.* Radnor, Pa.: Chilton Book, 1974.

McCormack, Lily. *I Hear You Calling Me.* Milwaukee: Bruce Publishing, 1949.

McCullough, David. *Mornings on Horseback.* New York: Simon and Schuster, 1981.

McKelvey, Blake. *Rochester, The Quest for Quality: 1890–1925.* Cambridge, Mass.: Harvard University Press, 1956.

McLanathan, Richard. *The American Tradition in the Arts.* New York: Harcourt, Brace and World, 1968.

McLean, Albert F., Jr. *American Vaudeville as Ritual.* Lexington: University of Kentucky Press, 1965.

McNamara, Brooks. *The Shuberts of Broadway: A History Drawn from the Collections of the Shubert Archive.* New York: Oxford University Press, 1990.

McNeil, Alex. *Total Television: A Comprehensive Guide to Programming from 1948 to 1980.* New York: Penguin Books, 1980.

Meade, Marion. *Buster Keaton: Cut to the Chase.* New York: Harper Collins, 1995.

Menke, Frank G. *The Encyclopedia of Sports.* 5th rev. ed. Revisions by Suzanne Treat. South Brunswick, N.J.: A. S. Barnes, 1975.

Mix, Olive Stokes, with Eric Heath. *The Fabulous Tom Mix.* Englewood Cliffs, N.J.: Prentice-Hall, 1957.

Mix, Paul E. *The Life and Legend of Tom Mix.* London: Thomas Yoseloff; South Brunswick, N.J.: A. S. Barnes, 1972.

Mix, Tom. *West of Yesterday.* Los Angeles: Times-Mirror Press, 1923.

Montana, World Fair Commission of. *Montana: Its Progress and Prosperity, Resources and Industries . . ..* St. Louis: C. P. Curran Printing, 1904.

Moquin, Wayne, and Charles Van Doren, eds. *Great Documents in American Indian History.* New York: Praeger, 1973.

Mordden, Ethan. *Broadway Babies: The People Who Made the American Musical.* New York: Oxford University Press, 1983.

Morehouse, Ward. *George M. Cohan: Prince of the American Theater.* New York: J. B. Lippincott, 1943.

Morgan, H. Wayne, and Anne Hodges Morgan. *Oklahoma: A Bicentennial History.* New York: Norton, 1977.

Morris, Juddi. *The Harvey Girls: The Women Who Civilized the West.* New York: Walker, 1994.

Moses, L. G. *Wild West Shows and the Images of American Indians, 1883–1933.* Albuquerque: University of New Mexico Press, 1996.

Mould, David H. *American Newsfilm 1914–1919: The Underexposed War.* New York: Garland Publishing, 1983.

Muscatine, Doris. *Old San Francisco: The Biography of a City from Early Days to the Earthquake.* New York: G. P. Putnam's Sons, 1975.

Musser, Charles. *Before the Nickelodeon: Edwin S. Porter and the Edison Manufacturing Company.* Berkeley: University of California Press, 1991.

_____. *The Emergence of Cinema: The American Screen to 1907.* New York: Charles Scribner's Sons, 1990.

Musser, Charles, with Carol Nelson. *High-class Moving Pictures.* Princeton, N.J.: Princeton University Press, 1991.

Niver, Kemp R. *Biograph Bulletins 1896–1908.* Edited by Bebe Bergsten. Los Angeles: Locare Research Group, 1971.

_____. *D. W. Griffith, His Biograph Films in Perspective.* Edited by Bebe Bergsten. Los Angeles: John D. Roche, 1974.

_____. *Early Motion Pictures.* Edited by Bebe Bergsten. Washington, D.C.: Library of Congress, 1985.

_____. *Klaw and Erlanger Present Famous Plays in Pictures.* Edited by Bebe Bergsten. Los Angeles: Local Research Group, 1976.

Norris, M. G. "Bud." *The Tom Mix Book.* Waynesville, N.C.: World of Yesterday, 1984.

Nye, Russell. *The Unembarrassed Muse: The Popular Arts in America.* New York: Dial Press, 1971.

Oberfirst, Robert. *Al Jolson: You Ain't Heard Nothing Yet.* San Diego, Calif.: A. S. Barnes, 1980.

Odell, George C. D. *Annals of the New York Stage.* 15 vols. New York: Columbia University Press, 1927–49.

Official Handbook of the Ceylon Court: Louisiana Purchase Exposition, St. Louis, 1904. Colombo: G. J. A. Skeen, 1904.

Oldham, Gabriella. *Keaton's Silent Shorts: Beyond the Laughter.* Carbondale: Southern Illinois University Press, 1996.

Orpheum Circuit of Theatres. New York: Orpheum Theatre and Realty, 1909.

Page, Brett. *Writing for Vaudeville.* Springfield, Mass.: Home Correspondence School, 1915.

Patterson, Joseph Medill. *A Little Brother of the Rich.* Chicago: Reilly and Britton, 1908.

Payne, William Howard, and Jake G. Lyons, eds. *Folks Say of Will Rogers: A Memorial Anecdotage.* New York: G. P. Putnam's Sons, 1936.

Peiss, Kathy. *Cheap Amusements.* Philadelphia: Temple University Press, 1986.

Pickard, Roy. *A Companion to the Movies.* London: Lutterworth Press, 1972.

Poling-Kempes, Lesley. *The Harvey Girls.* New York: Paragon House, 1989.

Porter, Willard H. *Who's Who in Rodeo.* Oklahoma City: Powder River Book, n.d. [ca. 1982–83].

Purdy, Helen Throop. *San Francisco As It Was, As It Is and How to See It.* San Francisco: Paul Elder, 1912.

Read, Jack. *Empires, Hippodromes and Palaces.* London: Alderman Press, 1985.

Reed, Langford, and Hetty Spiers. *Who's Who in Filmland.* 3d ed. London: Chapman and Hall, 1931.

Reid, Robert Allan. *The World's Fair Souvenir Book of Views*. St. Louis: R. A. Reid, n.d. [ca. 1904].

Renner, Frederic G.. *Charles M. Russell: Paintings, Drawings and Sculpture in the Amon Carter Museum*. New York: Harry N. Abrams, 1974.

_____. *Paper Talk: Illustrated Letters of Charles M. Russell*. Fort Worth, Tex.: Amon Carter Museum of Western Art, 1962.

Report of the State Recreational Inquiry Committee. California State Printing Office, 28 September 1914.

Riske, Milt. *Those Magnificent Cowgirls: A History of the Rodeo Cowgirl*. Cheyenne: Wyoming Publishing, 1983.

Ritter, Lawrence. *Lost Ballparks*. New York: Penguin Books, 1994.

Roach, Joyce Gibson. *The Cowgirls*. Denton: University of North Texas Press, 1990.

Robbins, Phyllis. *Maude Adams, An Intimate Portrait*. New York: Putnam, 1956.

Roberts, David. *Once They Moved like the Wind: Cocise, Geronimo, and the Apache Wars*. New York: Simon and Schuster, 1993.

Robinson, Alice M., Vera Mowry Roberts, and Milly S. Barranger. *Notable Women in the American Theatre*. Westport, Conn.: Greenwood Press, 1989.

Robinson, David. *Buster Keaton*. London: Secker and Warburg with the British Film Institute, 1969.

_____. *From Peep Show to Palace: The Birth of American Film*. New York: Columbia University Press, 1996.

Rogal, Samuel J. *A Chronological Outline of American Literature*. New York: Greenwood Press, 1987.

Rogers, Betty. *Will Rogers: His Wife's Story*. 1941. New ed. Norman: University of Oklahoma Press, 1989.

Rollins, Peter C. *Will Rogers: A Bio-Bibliography*. Westport, Conn.: Greenwood Press, 1984.

Rose, Al, and Edmond Souchon. *New Orleans Jazz Family Album*. Baton Rouge: Louisiana State University Press, 1967.

Rose, Frank. *The Agency: William Morris and the Hidden History of Show Business*. New York: Harper Business, 1995.

Rosenthal, Harold, and John Warrack. *Concise Oxford Dictionary of Opera*. 2d ed. New York: Oxford University Press, 1979.

Rosenzweig, Roy. *Eight Hours for What We Will: Workers and Leisure in an Industrial City, 1870-1920*. New York: Cambridge University Press, 1983.

Rowland, Mabel, ed. *Bert Williams: Son of Laughter*. New York: English Crafters, 1923.

Russell, Charles M. *Good Medicine: The Illustrated Letters of Charles M. Russell*. Garden City, N.Y.: Doubleday, 1929.

_____. *Trails Plowed Under*. Garden City, N.Y: Doubleday, Doran, 1944.

Russell, Don. *Lives and Legends of Buffalo Bill*. Norman: University of Oklahoma Press, 1960.

_____. *The Wild West: A History of the Wild West Shows*. Fort Worth, Tex.: Amon Carter Museum of Western Art, 1970.

Rydell, Robert M. *All the World's a Fair: Visions of Empire at American International Expositions, 1876-1916*. Chicago: University of Chicago Press, 1980.

Sampson, Henry T. *Blacks in Blackface: A Source Book on Early Black Musical Shows.* Metuchen, N.J.: Scarecrow Press, 1980.

———. *The Ghost Walks: A Chronological History of Blacks in Show Business, 1865–1910.* Metuchen, N.J.: Scarecrow Press, 1988.

Samuels, Charles, and Louise Samuels. *Once upon a Stage.* New York: Dodd Mead, 1974.

Schezen, Roberto. *Newport Houses.* New York: Rizzoli, 1989.

Schoor, Gene, and Henry Gilfond. *The Jim Thorpe Story: America's Greatest Athlete.* New York: Messner, 1951.

Schuster, Mel. *Motion Picture Performers.* Suppl. 1. Metuchen, N.J.: Scarecrow Press, 1976.

Seiverling, Richard P. *Tom Mix: Portrait of a Superstar, A Pictorial and Documentary Anthology.* Hershey, Pa: Keystone Enterprises, 1991.

Sell, Henry Blackman, and Victor Weybright. *Buffalo Bill and the Wild West.* New York: Oxford University Press, 1955.

Sheean, Vincent. *Oscar Hammerstein I: The Life and Exploits of an Impresario.* New York: Simon and Schuster, 1956.

Shirk, George H. *Oklahoma Place Names.* Norman: University of Oklahoma Press, 1965.

Short, Ernest. *Fifty Years of Vaudeville.* London: Eyre and Spottiswoode, 1946.

Simon, Louis M. *A History of the Actors' Fund of America.* New York: Theatre Arts Books, 1972.

Sklar, Robert. *Movie-made America.* New York: Random House, 1975.

Slide, Anthony. *The Big V: A History of the Vitagraph Company.* Metuchen, N.J.: Scarecrow Press, 1976.

———. *The Vaudevillians: A Dictionary of Vaudeville Performers.* Westport, Conn.: Arlington House, 1981.

Slide, Anthony, ed. *Selected Vaudeville Criticism.* Metuchen, N.J.: Scarecrow Press, 1988.

Slout, William L. *Theatre in a Tent.* Bowling Green, Ohio: Bowling Green University Popular Press, 1972.

Slout, William L., ed. *Broadway below the Sidewalk: Concert Saloons of Old New York.* San Bernardino, Calif.: Borgo Press, 1994.

Smallwood, James M., and Steven K. Gragert, eds. *The Coolidge Years: 1925–27, vol. 2 of Will Rogers' Weekly Articles.* The Writings of Will Rogers, 3d ser. Stillwater: Oklahoma State University Press, 1980.

Smith, Bill. *The Vaudevillians.* New York: Macmillan, 1976.

Smith, Eric Ledell. *Bert Williams: A Biography of the Pioneer Black Comedian.* New York: McFarland, 1992.

Snyder, K. Alan. *Defining Noah Webster: Mind and Morals in the Early Republic.* Lanham, Md.: University Press of America, 1990.

Snyder, Robert W. *The Voice of the City: Vaudeville and Popular Culture in New York.* New York: Oxford University Press, 1989.

Sobel, Bernard. *A Pictorial History of Burlesque.* New York: Putnam, 1956.

Spitzer, Marian. *The Palace.* New York: Atheneum, 1969.

Springer, John, and Jack Hamilton. *They Had Faces Then.* Secaucus, N.J.: Citadel Press, 1974.

Stange, G. Robert, ed. *The Poetical Works of Tennyson.* Boston: Houghton Mifflin, 1974.

Stansbury, Kathryn. *Lucille Mulhall: Her Family, Her Life, Her Times.* 1985. 2d rev. ed. Mulhall, Okla.: Homestead Heirlooms Publishing, 1992.

Staples, Shirley. *Male-Female Comedy Teams in American Vaudeville, 1865-1932.* Ann Arbor, Mich.: UMI Research Press, 1984.

Starr, Emmet. *History of the Cherokee Indians and Their Legends and Folk Lore.* 1921. Reprint. New York: Kraus Reprint, 1969.

Steckbeck, John S. *Fabulous Redmen: The Carlisle Indians and Their Famous Football Teams.* Harrisburg, Pa.: J. Horace McFarland, 1951.

Stein, Charles W., ed. *American Vaudeville As Seen by Its Contemporaries.* New York: Da Capo Press, 1984.

Sterling, Bryan, and Frances N. Sterling, eds. *Will Rogers in Hollywood.* New York: Crown, 1984.

Stern, Robert A. M., Gregory Gilmartin, and John Montague Massengale. *New York 1900: Metropolitan Architecture and Urbanism, 1890–1915.* New York: Rizzoli International Publications, 1983.

Stoddart, Dayton. *Lord Broadway: Variety's Sime.* New York: Wilfred Funk, 1941.

Stone, Fred. *Rolling Stone.* New York: McGraw-Hill, 1945.

Sturtevant, William C., gen. ed. *Handbook of North American Indians.* Vol. 10: *Southwest.* Edited by Alfonso Ortiz. Washington, D.C.: Smithsonian Institution, 1983.

Sunday, William E., Marcel M. DuPriest, Marilee Brenhardt, and Quannah Archer Chu-lee-wah. *Gah Dah Gwa Stee.* Pryor, Okla.: Byron Smith, 1953.

S. Z. Poli's Theatrical Enterprises. [Booklet, ca. 1908.] Reprint. Notre Dame, Ind.: Theatre Historical Society, 1978.

Taylor, William R., ed. *Inventing Times Square: Commerce and Culture at the Crossroads of the World.* New York: Russell Sage Foundation, 1991.

Toll, Robert C. *Blacking Up: The Minstrel Show in Nineteenth-century America.* New York: Oxford University Press, 1974.

———. *The Entertainment Machine: American Show Business in the Twentieth Century.* New York: Oxford University Press, 1982.

———. *On with the Show!: The First Century of Show Business in America.* New York: Oxford University Press, 1976.

Toole-Stott, R. *The Circus and Allied Arts.* 4 vols. Derby, England: Harpurt, 1962.

Traub, Hamilton, ed. *The American Literary Yearbook.* Vol. 1: 1919. Henning, Minn.: Paul Traub Publishers, 1919. Reprint. Detroit: Gale Research, 1968.

Tuchman, Barbara W. *The Proud Tower: A Portrait of the World before the War: 1890–1914.* New York: Macmillan, 1966; Bantam Books, 1967.

Tucker, Sophie, with Dorothy Giles. *Some of These Days: The Autobiography of Sophie Tucker.* Garden City, N.Y.: Doubleday, Doran, 1945.

U.S. Department of State. *A Catalogue of the Exhibit of the Department of State at the Louisiana Purchase Exposition, St. Louis, 1904.* Washington, D.C.: GPO, 1904.

The Universal Exposition: A Portfolio of Official Photographic Views of the Louisiana Purchase Exposition, St. Louis, 1904. St. Louis: Portfolio Publishing, 1904.

Van Hoogstraten, Nicholas. *Lost Broadway Theatres.* Princeton, N.J.: Princeton Architectural Press, 1991.

Vaudeville Managers' Protective Association, 1912 Yearbook. Chicago: General Publicity Service, 1912.

Vaudeville Year Book, 1913. Chicago: Western Vaudeville Managers' Association, 1913.

Visscher, William Lightfoot. *Snapshots of the Saint Louis Exposition, 1904.* Chicago: White City Art, 1904.

Wallace, W. Stewart. *A Dictionary of North American Authors Deceased before 1950.* Toronto: Ryerson Press, 1951.

Waller, Charles. *Magical Nights at the Theatre: A Chronicle.* Melbourne: Gerald Taylor, 1980.

Wandell, Harry B. *Wandell's Annual: Louisiana Purchase Exposition in a Nutshell: 1,000 Facts about the World's Fair.* St. Louis: n.p., n.d. [ca. 1903].

Ward, Larry Wayne. *The Motion Picture Goes to War: The U.S. Government Film Effort during World War I.* Ann Arbor, Mich.: UMI Research Press, 1985.

Wardell, Morris L. *A Political History of the Cherokee Nation, 1838–1902.* Norman: University of Oklahoma Press, 1938.

Waterhouse, Richard. *From Minstrel Show to Vaudeville.* New South Wales: New South Wales University Press, 1990.

Waters, T. A. *The Encyclopedia of Magic and Magicians.* New York and Oxford: Facts on File Publications, 1988.

Wearing, J. P. *American and British Theatrical Biography.* Metuchen, N.J.: Scarecrow Press, 1979.

Weeks, Philip. *Farewell, My Nation: The American Indian and the United States, 1820–1890.* Washington Heights, Ill.: Harlan Davidson, 1990.

Wertheim, Arthur Frank, ed. *Will Rogers at the Ziegfeld Follies.* Norman: University of Oklahoma Press, 1992.

Wesser, Robert F. *A Response to Progressivism: The Democratic Party and New York Politics: 1902-18.* New York: New York University Press, 1986.

Westermeier, Clifford P. *Man, Beast, Dust: The Story of Rodeo.* N.p.: World Press, 1947.

Wheeler, Robert W. *Jim Thorpe, World's Greatest Athlete.* Rev. ed. Norman: University of Oklahoma Press, 1979.

White, G. Edward. *The Eastern Establishment and the Western Experience: The West of Frederic Remington, Theodore Roosevelt, and Owen Wister.* New Haven: Yale University Press, 1968.

Wilmeth, Don B. *Variety Entertainment and Outdoor Amusements.* Westport, Conn.: Greenwood Press, 1982.

Wilmut, Roger. *Kindly Leave the Stage!: The Story of Variety, 1919–1960.* London: Methuen, 1989.

Wister, Owen. *The Virginian: A Horseman of the Plains.* New York: Macmillan, 1902.

Witherspoon, Margaret Johanson. *Remembering the St. Louis World's Fair.* 1973. 7th printing. St. Louis: Comfort Printing, 1992.

Woll, Allen. *Black Musical Theatre: From Coontown to Dreamgirls.* Baton Rouge: Louisiana State University Press, 1989.

_____. *Dictionary of the Black Theatre: Broadway, Off- Broadway, and Selected Harlem Theatre.* Westport, Conn.: Greenwood Press, 1983.

Workers of the Writers' Program of the Works Projects Administration in the State of Oklahoma, comp. *Oklahoma: A Guide to the Sooner State.* Norman: University of Oklahoma Press, 1941.

Worth, Paul, and Jim Cartwright. *John McCormack: A Comprehensive Discography.* New York: Greenwood Press, 1986.

Wrenn, Walter Scott. *The Rand-McNally Economizer: A Guide to the World's Fair, St. Louis, 1904: Locating and Describing the Buildings, Statuary, Principal Exhibits, Amusements on the Pike, and Interesting Features of the Louisiana Purchase Exposition.* Chicago: Rand, McNally, 1904.

Yagoda, Ben. *Will Rogers: A Biography.* New York: Alfred A. Knopf, 1993.

Young, William C. *Documents of American Theater History.* 2 vols. Chicago: American Library Association, 1973.

_____. *Famous Actors and Actresses on the American Stage.* New York: R. R. Bowker, 1975.

Zeidman, Irving. *The American Burlesque Show.* New York: Hawthorn, 1967.

Zellers, Parker. *Tony Pastor: Dean of the Vaudeville Stage.* Ypsilanti, Mich.: Eastern Michigan University Press, 1971.

Ziegfeld, Richard, and Paulette Ziegfeld. *The Ziegfeld Touch: The Life and Times of Florenz Ziegfeld, Jr.* New York: Harry N. Abrams, 1993.

ARTICLES AND CHAPTERS IN ANTHOLOGIES

Acton, Mildred Mulhall. "The Original Cowgirl." *Ranchman,* February 1942, 6–7.

Adler, Dankmar. "Chicago Auditorium." *Architectural Record* 1 (July 1891–92): 415–34.

Albert, Dora. "The Rogers 'Carry On'." *Rexall Magazine,* June 1943, 3, 10.

Allen, Jeanne Thomas. "Copyright and Early Theater, Vaudeville, and Film Competition." In *Film before Griffth,* edited by John Fell, 176–87. Berkeley: University of California Press, 1983.

Allen, Robert C. "B. F. Keith and the Origins of American Vaudeville." *Theatre Survey* 21 (November 1980): 105.

_____. "Contra the Chaser Theory." In *Film before Griffth,* edited by John Fell, 105–15. Berkeley: University of California Press, 1983.

American Horse et al. "The Massacre at Wounded Knee on December 19, 1890." In *Great Documents in American Indian History,* edited by Wayne Moquin and Charles Van Doren, 267–71. New York: Praeger, 1973.

Armstrong, Jerry. "The Guy Who Started the Stampede." *Western Horseman* 24 (August 1959): 6–7, 62–65.

Bagley, Harry B. "Riding, Roping and Trouping with Will Rogers: Buck McKee Was Boyhood Pal and Vaudeville Partner of Famous Humorist." *Sacramento Bee,* magazine section, 18 January 1941, 3.

Bayes, Nora. "After the Play." *New Republic,* 4 June 1918, 297.

_____. "Why People Enjoy Crying in a Theater." *American Magazine,* April 1918, 33–35.

Berkery, Denny. "Tompkins Wild West Show 1913–17: A Supplement." *Bandwagon,* May–June 1971, 30–31.

"B. F. Keith's Memorial Theatre." *Marquee,* Spring 1983, 1–31.

Bird, Carol. "May Vokes." *Theatre Magazine* 36 (October 1922): 241.

Blathwayt, Raymond. "The Control of a Great Music-Hall: Mr. Alfred Butt and the Palace Theatre." *World's Work* (London) 17 (February 1911): 248–53.

Botkin, Sam L. "Indian Missions of the Episcopal Church in Oklahoma." *Chronicles of Oklahoma* 36 (Spring 1958): 40–47.

Bradbury, Joseph T. "Tom Mix Circus 1936 Coast to Coast Tour." *Bandwagon,* April–May 1952, 5–8.

_____. "Tompkins Wild West Show, 1913–1917." *Bandwagon,* March–April 1971, 4–15.

_____. "Tompkins Wild West Show 1913-17, Supplement." *Bandwagon,* May–June 1971, 30–31.

_____. "Tompkins Wild West Show, Supplement 2." *Bandwagon,* November–December 1971, 26–28.

Brenneman, Lyman. "A Look Backstage at the Hippodrome." *Marquee,* Spring 1973, 8–9.

Brown, A. Ten Eyck. "The Forsyth Theater and Office Building, Atlanta, Ga." *American Architect* 96 (18 August 1909): 63– 66.

Cantor, Eddie. "Bert Williams—The Best Teacher I Ever Had." *Ebony,* June 1958, 103–6.

Carney, Peter P. "President Coolidge Applauds Topperwein's Skill at Pemberton Shoot." *Winchester Record,* August 1925, 4.

Cary, P. "From the Old Frontier to Film." *Wild West* 7 (October 1994) 42–48.

Castle, Irene. "My Memories of Vernon Castle." *Everybody's Magazine,* December 1918, 36–41; January 1919, 38–42; February 1919, 50–55; March 1919, 39–42.

Chang, Reynolds. "Miller Brothers 101 Ranch Real Wild West Show, Part One: 1925 and 1926." *Bandwagon,* March–April 1975, 3–17.

_____. "Miller Brothers 101 Ranch, Part Two: 1927–1931." *Bandwagon,* May–June 1975, 3–14.

Chavanne, Paul J. "The Boston Orpheum." *Marquee,* Fall 1972, 19– 21.

Clancy, Foghorn. "Memory Trail." *Hoofs and Horns,* May 1942, n.p.

Clark, Blue. "Delegates to the Constitutional Convention, 1898." *Chronicles of Oklahoma* 48 (Winter 1970–71): 400–414.

Clark, Neil M. "They Said He'd Never Dance Again." *American Magazine,* May 1931, 50.

Clinton, Fred S. "The Indian Territory Medical Association." *Chronicles of Oklahoma* 26 (1948): 23–55.

Coburn, Walt. "Tom Mix's Last Sundown." *Frontier Times,* August– September 1968, 6–11, 48.

Collins, Reba. "A Fond Farewell: 'Love, Reba.'" *Will Rogers Roundup,* October 1993, 2.

_____. "Will Rogers' Daughter Mary: A Storied Life." *Oologah Lake Leader,* 4 January 1990, 10.

"Colonial Theatre Sixty-Fifth Street Blvd." *Architecture and Building* 30 (1890): n.p.

Conover, Richard E. "The Sells Brothers Bandchariot and Their 50-Cage Menagerie." *Bandwagon,* May–June 1966, 14–15.

Cook, Will Marion. "Clorindy, the Origin of the Cakewalk." In *Anthology of the American Negro in the Theatre,* edited and compiled by Lindsay Patterson, 50–55. New York: Publishers Co., Association for the Study of Negro Life and History, 1967.

Cooke, Louis E. "Walter F. Main: America's Best Railroad Shows." *Bandwagon,* July–August 1967, 3–8.

Copley, Frank B. "The Story of a Great Vaudeville Manager." *American Magazine,* December 1922, 46–47, 152–55.

Cox, James A. "Fred Harvey, the Righteous Restaurateur." *Smithsonian,* September 1987, 130–39.

Crane, Warren Eugene. "Alexander Pantages." *System: The Magazine of Business* 37 (March 1920): 501–3.

Cronican, Frank. "Hip, Hip, Hippodrome!" *Marquee,* Fall 1972, 3–5.

Cross, Wellington. "Why Are Actors Conceited?" *Theatre Magazine* 43 (March 1926): 24.

"Cummins' Real Wild West Show." *Banner Line,* 15 April 1954, 5.

"Cummins' Wild West Show." *Bandwagon,* July–August 1962, 4.

Czitrom, Daniel. "Underworlds and Underdogs: Big Tim Sullivan and Metropolitan Politics in New York, 1889–1913." *Journal of American History* 78 (September 1991): 536–58.

Davis, Hartley. "The Business Side of Vaudeville." *Everybody's Magazine,* October 1907, 527–37.

Davis, Norris N. "Al Latell Leads a Dog's Life–But He Likes It." *American Magazine,* April 1924, 68–69.

DeFoe, L. V. "Fred Stone, Expert Clown." *Green Book Magazine,* June 1915, 1003-11.

Deloria, Vine, Jr. "The Indians." In *Buffalo Bill and the Wild West,* 45–56. New York: Brooklyn Museum; Museum of Art, Carnegie Institute; and Buffalo Bill Historical Center, 1981.

Dresser, Louise. "My Friend, Will Rogers." *Screen Book,* June 1934, 40, 72.

Duncan, DeWitt Clinton. "Open Letter from Too-Qua-Stee." *Chronicles of Oklahoma* 47 (Autumn 1969): 307.

Eaton, Walter Prichard. "The Wizards of Vaudeville." *McClure's Magazine,* September 1923, 43–49.

Eltinge, Julian. "How I Portray a Woman on the Stage." *Theatre Magazine* 150 (August 1913): ix, 56, 58.

Everson, William K. "Songs of Innocence." *Sight and Sound* 2 (December 1992): 63.

Fausett, Jessie. "The Symbolism of Bert Williams." *Crisis,* 24 May 1922, 12–15.

Ferguson, Blanche. "Black Skin, Black Mask: The Inconvenient Grace of Bert Williams." *American Visions* 7 (June–July 1992): 14–16, 18.

Fiedler, Leslie. "The Legend." In *Buffalo Bill and the Wild West,* 84–95. New York: Brooklyn Museum; Museum of Art, Carnegie Institute; and Buffalo Bill Historical Center, 1981.

Fogarty, Frank. "Frank Fogarty Talks on the Grin as an Asset." *New York Dramatic Mirror,* 27 May 1914, 20.

"A Foot in Each World." *True West,* May–June 1979, 26–27, 46.

Fowler, Andrew C. "Hippodromes." *Marquee,* Fall 1993, 4–28.

Franklin, Irene. "Back from the Trenches." *Theatre Magazine,* December 1918, 336.
_____. "Making Songs Tell a Story." *New York Dramatic Mirror,* 16 December 1914, 19.
_____. "Mike-Wise." *Theatre Magazine,* July 1929, 26.
Fulton, A. R. "The Machine." In *The American Film Industry,* edited by Tino Balio, 27–42. Madison: University of Wisconsin Press, 1985.
Gabriel, Jim. "Frontier Celebration Events." *Billboard,* 10 September 1910, 20.
Geronimo. "Reasons for Leaving the Reservation" (statement to General Crook). In *Great Documents in American Indian History,* edited by Wayne Moquin and Charles Van Doren, 259–61. New York: Praeger, 1973.
Gill, Joseph A., Jr. "Judge Joseph Albert Gill." *Chronicles of Oklahoma* 12 (September 1934): 375–76.
Glazer, Irvin R. "The Atlantic City Story." *Marquee,* Winter and Spring 1980, 4–12.
_____. "The Metropolitan Opera House—Philadelphia." *Marquee,* Summer 1979, 3–15.
Gossard, Wayne H., Jr. "Three Ring Circus: The Zack Miller–Tom Mix Lawsuits 1929–1934." *Chronicles of Oklahoma* 58 (Spring 1980): 3–16.
Grau, Robert. "A Napoleon of the Vaudeville World." *Theatre Magazine* 116 (October 1910): 117.
Gray, Christopher. "The Ghost behind a Huge Sign." *New York Times,* 29 January 1989.
"Guy Weadick Travelled Rocky Trail before Hitting Pay Dirt in 1912." *Calgary Herald,* 9 July 1949, 24, 31.
Hancock, La Touche. "Some Humor of Some Humorists." *Bookman* 16 (September 1902): 15–22.
Hardy, Camille. "Flashes of Flamenco: The American Debuts of Carmencita and Otero." *Arabesque: A Magazine of International Dance* 9 (May–June 1983): 16–23.
Hartung, A. N. "James H. Minnick." *Back in the Saddle,* May 1948, 13, 30.
Havig, Alan. "The Commercial Amusement Audience in Early 20th-century American Cities." *Journal of American Culture* 5 (Spring 1982): 1–19.
Headley, Robert K., Jr. "Source Records for Theater History." *Marquee,* Winter 1969, 9–12.
_____. "The Theatres of Milwaukee . . . A Brief Theater Reconnaissance of Milwaukee." *Marquee,* Winter 1971, 3–12.
Helgesen, Terry. "B. Marcus Priteca, 1890–1971: The Last of the Giants." *Marquee,* Spring 1972, 3–12.
Henderson, Sam. "Show Biz Western Style." *Wild West,* October 1994, 34–40, 72.
Hendricks, Gordon. "The History of the Kinetescope." In *The American Film Industry,* edited by Tino Balio, 43–56. Madison: University of Wisconsin Press, 1985.
Hendrix, John M. "He Put Will Rogers on the Stage." *West Texas Today,* March 1936, 14, 28.
_____. "Mis' Minnick and Jim." *Hoof and Horns* 5 (February 1936): 12, 26.
Hinkle, Milt. "Memoirs of My Rodeo Days." *Real West,* September 1968, 35–37.
_____. "The Way a Wild West Show Operated." *Frontier Times,* February–March 1969, 20–23, 50–52.

"How to Put 'Em Across." *Green Book Magazine* 9 (July 1912): 45- 49.

"Ideas about Husbands." *Green Book Magazine* 10 (August 1913): 210–14.

Joseph, Chief. "The Fate of the Nez Perces Tribe." *In Great Documents in American Indian History,* edited by Wayne Moquin and Charles Van Doren, 237–51. New York: Praeger, 1973.

Judson, William. "The Movies." In *Buffalo Bill and the Wild West,* 68–83. New York: Brooklyn Museum; Museum of Art, Carnegie Institute; and Buffalo Bill Historical Center, 1981.

Kahn, Ely J. "Ziegfeld Theatre." *Architectural Record* 61 (May 1927): 385–93.

Kajiyama, Tameo. "Personality and Its Use in Vaudeville." *New York Dramatic Mirror,* 31 December 1921, 1058.

"Keith Palace Theater, Cleveland, Ohio." *Architecture and Building* (May 1923): 110–11.

King, Donald C. "From Museum to Multi-Cinema." *Marquee,* Summer 1974, 5–10, 15.

———. "Keith-Albee et al. . . ." *Marquee,* Summer 1975, 3–10.

———. "New York's Oldest Existing Theatre—The Union Square." *Marquee,* Spring 1974, 48.

———. "Sylvester Z. Poli Story: From Wax to Riches." *Marquee,* Spring 1979, 11–18.

Koger, Alicia Kae. "Harrigan's Theatre." *Marquee,* Winter 1983, 16–18.

LaLanne, Bruce. "Hippodrome Memories." *Marquee,* Summer 1983, 14–16.

Lamar, Howard R. "The Cowboys." In *Buffalo Bill and the Wild West,* 57–67. New York: Brooklyn Museum; Museum of Art, Carnegie Institute; and Buffalo Bill Historical Center, 1981.

Lansburgh, G. Albert. "Some Novel Features of a Strictly Fireproof Theater Building." *Architect and Engineer of California, Pacific Coast States* 17 (June 1909): 37–41.

LaRue, Grace. "Just the Singing of a Song." *New York Dramatic Mirror,* 16 December 1914, 18.

Lasser, Michael. "The Glorifier: Florenz Ziegfeld and the Creation of the American Showgirl." *American Scholar* (Summer 1994): 441–48.

Laurie, Joe, Jr. "Vaudeville Dead? It's Never Been." *New York Times Magazine,* 14 October 1951, 25, 67, 70–71.

———. "Vaudeville's Ideal Bill." *New York Times Magazine,* 15 May 1949, 24–25.

Lazzara, Robert L. "Orpheum Theatre, San Francisco California." *Marquee,* Fall 1983, 16–17.

Levin, Steven. "San Francisco Story: From the Fire to the Fair." *Marquee,* Winter 1975, 3–9.

Liebenguth, Jane Anne. "Music at the Louisiana Purchase Exposition." *Missouri Historical Society Bulletin,* October 1979, 27–34.

Loney, Glenn. "Denishawn in Vaudeville and Beyond." In *Musical Theatre in America: Papers and Proceedings of the Conference on the Musical Theatre in America,* edited by Glenn Loney, 179–85. Westport, Conn.: Greenwood Press, 1984.

———. "Theatres of 42nd Street." *Marquee,* Fall 1977, 15–16.

MacMechen, Thomas R. "The True and Complete Story of the Pike and Its Attractions." *World's Fair Bulletin* 5 (April 1904): 4–36.

"Madison Square Garden: An Account of the Passing of One of New York City's Architectural Landmarks." *American Architect* 128 (20 December 1925): 513–18.

Manning, Fowler. "The Part Our Field Representatives Are Playing." *Winchester Record* 1 (22 November 1918): 1–4.

Marquis, Arnold. "Will and Charlie." *Frontier Times* 41 (June–July 1967): 6–9, 47–49.

_____. "Will Rogers and His Horses." Part 1. *Western Horseman* 28 (February 1963): 28–30, 71–73.

Martin, George. "The Wit of Will Rogers: The Story of a Cowboy Who Has Become a Famous Comedian." *American Magazine,* November 1919, 34–35, 106–10.

McCabe, Lida Rose. "Carmencita and Her Painters." *New York Times Book Review and Magazine,* 8 July 1923, 4, 23.

McCall, John Clark, Jr. "Loew's Grand, Atlanta, Georgia." *Marquee,* Summer 1977, 11–13.

McGee, W. J. "Anthropology." *World's Fair Bulletin* 5 (February 1904): 4–9.

_____. "The Anthropology Exhibit." *Harper's Weekly,* April 1904, 683.

McLean, Albert F. "Genesis of Vaudeville: Two Letters from B. F. Keith." *Theatre Survey* 1 (1960): 82–95.

_____. "U.S. Vaudeville and the Urban Comics." *Theatre Quarterly* 1 (October–December 1971): 47–52.

McSpadden, Herb. "Horses and Horse Collars." *Ranchman,* November 1942, 11–12.

Meacham, Jon. "What Will Rogers Could Teach Rush Limbaugh." *Washington Monthly,* January–February 1994, 16–22.

Mensel, Robert E. "'Kodakers Lying in Wait': Amateur Photography and the Right of Privacy in New York, 1885–1915." *American Quarterly* 43 (March 1991): 24–30.

Meserve, John Barlett. "Trinity Episcopal Church, Tulsa." *Chronicles of Oklahoma* 17 (September 1939): 269–73.

Miller, Lee. "Tom Mix, Old Time Sheriff." *Real West,* November 1958, 30–31, 61.

Miller, Michael. "Proctor's Fifty-eighth Street Theatre." *Marquee,* Summer 1973, 7–15.

Mitchell, George, and William K. Everson. "Tom Mix." *Films in Review* 8 (October 1957): 387–97.

Moorcock, Michael. "Songs of Innocence." *Sight and Sound* 2 (October 1992): 36–37.

Morgan, J. H. "New York Hippodrome." *Architects and Builders Magazine* 37 (August 1905): 490–99.

Morrison, William. "Oscar Hammerstein I: The Man Who Invented Times Square." *Marquee,* Winter 1983, 3–15.

_____. "Oscar Hammerstein I, Part II: Impresario in Excelsis." *Marquee,* Summer 1984, 17–23.

Mould, David H., and Charles M. Berg. "Fact and Fantasy in the Films of World War One." *Film and History* 14 (September 1984): 50–60.

"Movie Theatre History in Wisconsin." *Marquee,* Fall 1980, 3, 6, 7.

Mullett, Mary B. "Climbing a Greased Pole Was Fred Stone's First Triumph." *American Magazine,* December 1926, 19, 132–39.

Parkinson, Tom. "Horse King of the World." *Bandwagon,* May–June 1974, 18–22.

Parson, Chauncy L. "Ralph C Herz, An Introspective Comedian." *New York Dramatic Mirror,* 26 April 1911, 11.

Patterson, Ada. "I Am Thirty-six and Proud of It." *Green Book Magazine* 13 (January 1916): 161–68.

———. "When Blanche Ring Smiles." *Theatre Magazine* 19 (April 1914): 198.

"Personal." *New York Dramatic Mirror*, 7 May 1913, 7.

"Personals." [Caroline Otero obituary.] *Dance Magazine*, May 1965, 7.

"Photo Record of the Poli Empire." *Marquee*, Spring 1979, 19–28.

Red Cloud. "Speech at Cooper Union, New York, July 16, 1870" and "Reasons for the Trouble between the Indians and the Government during the Ghost Dance Excitement of 1890." In *Great Documents in American Indian History*, edited by Wayne Moquin and Charles Van Doren, 211–13, 263–66. New York: Praeger, 1973.

Reynolds, Chang. "101 Ranch Wild West Show." *Bandwagon*, January–February 1969, 4–21.

"Riding, Roping and Trouping with Will Rogers." *Sacramento Bee*, magazine section, 18 January 1941, 3.

Ring, Blanche. "The Great American Husband." *Green Book Magazine* 10 (August 1913): 210–14.

Robinson, C. O. "Tom Mix Was My Boss." *Frontier Times* 43 (1969): 18–20, 42–43.

Robinson, Jack. "Brooklyn's Magnificent Ruin: The Bushwick." *Marquee*, Winter 1986, 22–23.

———. "8 Big Acts—A Glance Backwards." *Marquee*, Winter 1977, 3–10.

———. "Fourteenth Street, Cradle of American Vaudeville." *Marquee*, Winter 1983, 19–20.

———. "A Stroll through Harlem." *Marquee*, Summer 1981, 10–12.

Rodgers, John J. "Pursued by Songs." *Green Book Magazine* 13 (June 1916): 1102–6.

"Roof Gardens Open the Summer Season." *Theatre Magazine* 53 (July 1905): 158–59.

Roth, Barbara Williams. "101 Ranch Wild West Show." *Chronicles of Oklahoma* 43 (Winter 1965–66): 416–31.

Russell, Don. "The Golden Age of Wild West Shows." *Bandwagon*, September–October 1971, 21–27.

Safer, Karen J. "The Functions of Decoration in the American Movie Palace." *Marquee*, Spring 1982, 3–7.

Schallert, Elza. "Louise Dresser: Tribute on Birthday." *Los Angeles Times*, 2 March 1959, 1, 30.

Singer, Ben. "Early Home Cinema and the Edison Home Projecting Kinetoscope." *Film History: An International Journal* 2 (1988): 37–70.

Slotkin, Richard. "The Wild West." In *Buffalo Bill and the Wild West*, 27–44. New York: Brooklyn Museum; Museum of Art, Carnegie Institute; and Buffalo Bill Historical Center, 1981.

"Special Anniversary Issue: The Roxy Theatre." *Marquee*, Winter 1979, 1–28.

Sprague, Stuart Seely. "Meet Me in St. Louis on the Ten-Million-Dollar Pike." *Missouri Historical Society Bulletin* 32 (October 1975): 26–32.

Spring, Agnes Wright. "Horseman Extraordinary." *Western Horseman*, November 1949, 14–15, 32, 34, 36–37.

Stainton, Walter H. "Irene Castle." *Films in Review* 16 (1965): 347–55.

Stewart-Gordon, James. "Houdini, The Man No Lock Could Hold." *Reader's Digest,* February 1976, 151–55.

Stone, Fred. "A Clown Who Built a Skyscraper with Laughs." *American Magazine,* October 1917, 32–34, 88–95.

Sturtevant, C. G. "A Famous Circus Fan." *The Whitetops,* November 1936, 3–4.

Sugrue, Thomas. "The Newsreels." *Scribner's Magazine,* April 1937, 9–32.

"Texas, Houston." *Marquee,* Winter 1978, 12.

Thanet, Octave. "The Trans-Mississippi Exposition." *Cosmopolitan,* October 1898, 599–614.

Thayer, Stuart. "Tom Mix Circus and Wild West, Part One—Season of 1934 and 1935." *Bandwagon,* March–April 1971, 18–23. "Part Two—Seasons of 1936, 1937 and 1938." *Bandwagon,* May–June 1971, 4–11.

"A Thirty-Five Year Test of Materials: A Non-technical Report of an Investigation Conducted upon the Razing of Madison Square Garden." *American Architect* 128 (20 December 1925): 519–24.

Todd, Robert B. "The Organization of Professional Theatre in Vancouver, 1886–1914." *BC Studies* 44 (Winter 1979–80): 3–24.

Tompkins, Charles H. "Gabriel Brothers Wild West." *Westerners Brand Book 13* (October 1956): 64.

_____. "My Association with Will Rogers." *Old Trail Drivers Convention,* October 1953 (Will Rogers Memorial Edition), 7–12.

Ver Halen, Charles J. "Young Buffalo Wild West." *Billboard,* 6 May 1911, 5.

Walton, Florence. "The Most Striking Episode in My Life." *Theatre Magazine* 29 (January 1919): 14.

Washington, Booker T. "Interesting People: Bert Williams." *American Magazine,* September 1910, 600–601, 603–4.

Weadick, Guy. "Here and There." *Billboard,* 18 February 1911, 20; 25 February 1911, 24; 8 April 1911, 31; 13 January 1912, 23.

West, Magda Frances. "The Manns and Their Mountains." *Green Book Magazine* 10 (February 1913): 321–28.

"When You Coming Back." *Los Angeles Magazine,* October 1979, 82–92.

White, Jack R. "Houdini and His Movies." *Classic Film Collector* 2 (Winter 1970): 46–47.

Williams, Bert. "The Comic Side of Trouble." *American Magazine,* January 1918, 33–34, 58.

Williams, Percy G. "Vaudeville and Vaudevillians." In *The Saturday Evening Post Reflections of a Decade, 1901–1910,* 45–47. Indianapolis: Curtis Publishing, 1980.

Williams, Robert L. "Tams Bixby (1855–1922)." *Chronicles of Oklahoma* 39 (September 1941): 205–12.

Wolf, Rennold. "The Greatest Comedian on the American Stage." *Green Book Magazine* 9 (June 1912): 1173–84.

_____. "Nora Bayes, an Expert in Songs and Matrimony." *Green Book Magazine* 11 (April 1914): 571–80.

Woodward, R. T. "The Continuous Performance." *Illustrated American,* 4 November 1898, 358–59.

Woolf, S. J. "Gus Edwards's Academy." *New York Times Magazine,* 23 March 1941, 12, 19.

Zellers, Parker. "The Cradle of Variety: The Concert Saloon." *Educational Theatre Journal* 20 (December 1968): 578–85.

UNPUBLISHED AND MISCELLANEOUS SOURCES

America and the Holocaust: Deceit and Destruction. Public Broadcasting System, 1993. Videocassette.

Boone, M. Elizabeth. "Torpedo in Dance Shoes?: The Portraits of Carmencita by John Singer Sargent and William Merritt Chase in the Context of Nineteenth-Century Spanish-American Conflict." Paper presented at the American Studies Association Annual Conference, Nashville, Tenn., October 1994.

Connors, Timothy D. "American Vaudeville Managers: Their Organization and Influence." Ph.D. diss., University of Kansas, 1981.

Cook, Susan C. "Irene Castle Watches Her Step: Dance, Music, and Dangerous Pleasures." Paper presented at the American Studies Association Annual Conference, Nashville, Tenn., October 1994.

De Young, Charles Daniel. "David Rowland Francis, American in Russia." Ph.D. diss., University of Wisconsin, 1949.

Distler, Paul. "The Rise and Fall of the Racial Comics in American Vaudeville." Ph.D. diss., Tulane University, 1963.

Dunn, Jonathan Alexander. "A History of the Will Rogers Ranch and State Historic Park in California." Master's thesis, University of Southern California, 1986.

Fisch, Martha. Oral history sessions on the Mulhall family history. Conducted with Barbara Bair of the Will Rogers Papers Project. Guthrie, Okla., January 1994. WRPP.

Francis, David Rowland. David R. Francis Collection, Missouri Historical Society, St. Louis.

Gustafson, Antoinette McCloskey. "The Image of the West in American Popular Performance." Ph.D. diss., New York University, 1988.

"Historical Data—Will Rogers Ranch." Unpublished ms., ca. 1940. CPpR.

Jewell, Richard Brownell. "A History of RKO Radio Pictures, Incorporated, 1928–1942." Ph.D. diss., University of Southern California, 1978.

Keith, Harold. "Clem Rogers and His Influence on Oklahoma History." Master's thesis, University of Oklahoma, 1938.

Knapp, Margaret May. "A Historical Study of the Legitimate Playhouses on West Forty-second Street between Seventh and Eighth Avenues in New York City." Ph.D. diss., City University of New York, 1982.

Koch, Iris. "Zack Mulhall, His Family, and the Mulhall Wild West Show." Master's thesis, Oklahoma Agricultural and Mechanical College, 1940.

Louisiana Purchase Exposition Collection, Missouri Historical Society, St. Louis.

Mickols, Robert Anthony. "The Boss of the Bowery: The Life and Times of Big Tim Sullivan." Master's thesis, University of California, Santa Barbara, 1957.

Mudd, A. I. "History of Polite Vaudeville in Washington, D.C." Copy, NN-L-BRTC.

[Mulhall], Georgia Smith Casey. Scrapbook of newspaper clippings and photographic albums of the Mulhall Wild West Show and Mulhall Family [ca. 1904–1910]. Original, MFC; microfilm, OkHi.

Orpheum Circuit 1925. Pamphlet. Copy, Illinois State University, Special Collections, Milner Library.

Riley, Robert. *Coin Harvey and Monte Ne.* N.p.: n.p., n.d. Booklet, RHM.

Sandmeier, Emil. "To the Docents [of] Will Rogers State Historical Park." Unpublished ms., Emil Sandmeier private papers, Pacific Palisades, Calif.; copy, WRPP.

Singer, Stanford P. "Vaudeville West: To Los Angeles and the Final Stages of Vaudeville." Ph.D. diss., University of California, Los Angeles, 1987.

Snelling, Lois. "One of the Blake Girls: The Story of Betty Blake (Mrs. Will Rogers) and Her Benton County Family." Ca. 1977. TMS. OkClaW.

Snyder, Frederick Edward. "American Vaudeville–Theatre in a Package: The Origins of Mass Entertainment." Ph.D. diss., Yale University, 1970.

Souvenir and Opening Program of the Orpheum Circuit's New Orpheum Theatre. Sioux City, Iowa, 19 December 1927.

Summer Days and Nights in New York. Pamphlet. N.p.: n.p., n.d. [1898]. Copy, New York Public Library.

Wakefield, John A., Norris B. Gregg, and Norton F. White. "The Division of Concessions and Admissions." In *Louisiana Purchase Centennial: Dedication Ceremonies, St. Louis, U.S.A., April 30th and May 1st–2d, 1903,* 36. N.p.: n.p., n.d. Box 8, Exhibitions and Fairs, University Research Library, UCLA.

Wyche, Sue Martin. "History of Chelsea: Research Report." Northeastern State College, Okla., 1974. Copy, Chelsea Public Library, Chelsea, Okla.

Index of Performers and Acts

This index lists performers and acts (including those from vaudeville, burlesque, music hall, musical comedy, and variety) mentioned or referenced in this volume in connection with Will Rogers's stage career.

Stage performers who were personal friends of Rogers are listed in the General Index (and indicated herein by cross-references). For Wild West performers and shows, Broadway and Off-Broadway productions, musicals, and various vaudeville-variety plays, sketches, and stock companies, see the General Index.

References to notes that provide primary biographical information about an individual are preceded by an asterisk (*). References to illustrations are printed in **boldface** type.

General Index

References to illustrations are printed in **boldface** type.

References to notes that provide primary biographical information about an individual or historical background about a theater are preceded by an asterisk (*).

For page numbers of correspondence between given individuals and Will Rogers, see Documents list in the preliminary matter of the volume (*ix–xiii*).

For Will Rogers's vaudeville itinerary for the time period covered by this volume, including the particular theaters and cities where he appeared in his act, consult the Chronology in the preliminary matter of the volume (entries from 12 June 1905 to 29 August 1908) (13–21). The Chronology and Documents lists may also be used as guides to help locate particular documents of interest within the volume by date or time period.